AMERICAN GOVERNMENT

Essentials & Perspectives

SECOND EDITION

Jack E. Holmes
Hope College

Michael J. Engelhardt
Luther College

Robert E. Elder, Jr.
Hope College

McGraw-Hill, Inc.

New York   St. Louis   San Francisco   Auckland   Bogotá   Caracas
Lisbon   London   Madrid   Mexico City   Milan   Montreal   New Delhi
San Juan   Singapore   Sydney   Tokyo   Toronto

This book was set in Palatino by Better Graphics, Inc.
The editors were Peter Labella and Fred H. Burns;
the production supervisor was Friederich W. Schulte.
The cover was designed by Wanda Lubelska.
R. R. Donnelley & Sons Company was printer and binder.

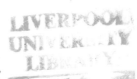

AMERICAN GOVERNMENT

Essentials & Perspectives

This book is printed on recycled, acid-free paper containing
10% postconsumer waste.

2 3 4 5 6 7 8 9 0 DOHDOH 9 0 9 8 7 6 5 4

ISBN 0-07-029769-X

Library of Congress Cataloging-in-Publication Data

Holmes, Jack E.
    American government: essentials & perspectives / Jack E. Holmes.
    Michael J. Engelhardt, Robert E. Elder, Jr. — 2nd ed.
        p.   cm.
    Includes bibliographical references and index.
    ISBN 0-07-029769-X
    1. United States—Politics and government.   I. Engelhardt,
Michael J.   II. Elder, Robert E., (date).   III. Title.
JK274.H652   1994
320.473—dc20   93-38965

ABOUT THE AUTHORS

JACK E. HOLMES is professor and chair of political science at Hope College, Holland, Michigan. Professor Holmes received his Ph.D. from the University of Denver Graduate School of International Studies. He previously served in the politico-military section of the Army General Staff and as a district assistant to Congressman Don Brotzman. He has made several contributions to professional journals and is the author of *The Mood/Interest Theory of American Foreign Policy* published by the University Press of Kentucky.

At Hope College, Professor Holmes initiated model United Nations and campaign management programs as well as a number of new courses. He has led several of the college's Washington Honors Semester programs. He has been an active participant in the Republican party and in the wilderness preservation movement. Most of his writing is done at his summer home near Red Cliff, Colorado.

MICHAEL J. ENGELHARDT is assistant professor of political science at Luther College in Decorah, Iowa. He was born in Lansing, Michigan, and attended Hope College where he met and studied under the two coauthors of the text, Jack Holmes and Bob Elder. Professor Engelhardt received his Ph.D. from the University of Wisconsin at Madison in 1984 and taught at the University of Illinois at Champaign-Urbana, Hope College, and Vanderbilt University before moving to Luther in 1988. He has published several articles on United States foreign and military policy regarding low-intensity conflicts.

Professor Engelhardt has initiated the use of Mock Senate simulations at Luther College. He is active in the Iowa Republican party and is a member of Habitat for Humanity.

ROBERT E. ELDER, JR. is professor of political science at Hope College, Holland, Michigan. He received his Ph.D. from Duke University in 1971. Political philosophy and political psychology are two areas of special interest to him. He is the author and coauthor of many journal publications in the United States and abroad. At Hope College, Professor Elder has been instrumental in encouraging the Student Internship Program and in developing the Washington Honors Semester, for which he has led student groups in Washington intermittently over the past two decades. Professor Elder has most recently been honored with a Fulbright Exchange Fellowship, under which he traveled and gave lectures in several countries in South Asia, while serving as a visiting professor at the University of Colombo in Sri Lanka. Most election years, Professor Elder disagrees with his two coauthors.

CONTENTS

PREFACE

Why this text on American government? Those who select such texts certainly have a myriad of choices representing a variety of approaches. Our reason for writing this text is that none of the others treat controversy as a integral part of the American system and examine the nature of conflicting perspectives in American politics. In this book, we treat alternative perspectives throughout the text and end each chapter with a section devoted to four major perspectives (conservatism, liberalism, libertarianism, and populism) and two other perspectives (Marxism and feminism). The validity of this reasoning was affirmed by the positive response to our first edition.

Other special features include:

profiles that look at persons and issues in greater depth than is possible in the main text

incorporation of insights gained from governmental as well as academic experience

viewpoints of authors who grew up and completed their graduate work in three different regions of the country and who represent two different generations

active student involvement in every phase of the development of both editions of the book.

The average student using this textbook will do so to meet a college core requirement. We see our challenge as showing why government is important to this student now and in the future. We hope the student will learn many of the skills needed to participate in government; we want college graduates to be aware of how the system works and how to influence it. Our goal is that our readers remain or become interested citizens.

To accomplish our objective, we believe that alternative viewpoints must be an integral part of the subject. Some textbooks champion one viewpoint throughout; others present alternative viewpoints but do not reflect current political realities. Our goal is to present alternative perspectives in terms of current political realities. We look at the Congress, the presidency, the judiciary, and the bureaucracy with recent examples and pay special attention to how the institutions are viewed differently by those who hold each of the six alternative viewpoints. In doing so, we try not to ascribe particular wisdom to any one side but rather to encourage the student to come to his or her own conclusions. Our study of parties, elections, interest groups, and media recognizes that coalitions must be formed to succeed in the American political system. Foreign and economic policy are viewed as the products of compromise and negotiation among perspectives and groups, not as the result of the operation of laws or outside forces.

In deciding which categories to use for classifying participants in the American political system, we were impressed by the scheme William S. Maddox and Stuart A. Lilie present in *Beyond Liberal and Conservative: Reassessing the Political Spectrum*, published in 1984 by the Cato Institute, a libertarian think tank. In addition to the standard conservative and liberal political perspectives, they identify libertarian and populist perspectives. The populist perspective seems to us to encompass left leaners and right leaners who, we think, are not necessarily comfortable with one another, but we included the perspective because populists have done well in American politics and because we wanted our readers to understand populism. To these perspectives we added Marxism, as it provides the primary critique of capitalism and the basis for political and economic systems important throughout most of the twentieth century. Although Marxism seems today to have failed, it remains useful in promoting critical thinking. It is also important to note that supporters of Marxism maintain that what failed in the former Soviet Union and Eastern Europe was not true Marxism. Democratic socialism has enjoyed more success, but as it has never been a major force in the United States, we treat it only as a combination of the liberal and Marxist perspectives, which are covered in every chapter.

In this edition we have also included a feminist perspective, as we believe it is a force worthy of attention in the study of American government. The decision to include it as a perspective outside the mainstream was made with the recognition that parts of it are attractive to the mainstream. In fact, since some of the major perspectives have adopted some ideas raised by feminism, it is not likely that it will become a separate, mainstream perspective. Utilization of ideas raised outside the mainstream is normal in American politics when the ideas are not as foreign as they are in the case of Marxism. Our treatment of both Marxism and feminism emphasizes the unique criticisms they raise of the American political system.

Since we believe that the American system works in the largest sense, we are more conservative than many of our colleagues and than all other major texts considering alternative viewpoints. But we do not present ourselves as spokespersons for the conservative community. Indeed, we hope that readers on both sides of the left-right political spectrum will be happy with parts of this book. Those on the left, however, probably will want us to cover more of the structural problems that result in unfair outcomes, while those on the far right probably will want us to be more supportive of their interpretations. As conservative pragmatists we agree with Winston Churchill, who thought democracy was the worst form of government except for all the others. We support participation and promote awareness of disagreement to encourage compromise. At the same time, we note possibilities for reform.

Each of us has taught at a small liberal arts college for a collective average of eighteen years, and our experience has given us a good sense of just what students retain—and it is often not what professors hope they retain. We wanted to produce a textbook that would do everything possible to promote student retention and learning. In doing so, it has been our firm resolve not to permit the complexity, which properly is the subject of analysis in advanced courses, to interfere with learning the basics for intelligent citizenship. We hope the profiles and case studies we provide suggest the complexity without the burden of too much detail.

We also undertook this project because each of us has had some Washington and internship experience that we wanted to bring to bear on a text which we hope bridges the gap between the academic world and the real world. We want to interest students in practical politics by explaining the nature of disagreements and by showing how disagreements have both theoretical and practical aspects.

This text has been developed over the course of a decade and a half and has been tested on dozens of classes with different instructors and evaluated by anonymous surveys of students. We are confident in saying that it will promote student interest and prepare students for a variety of classroom approaches. We have had several reviews by colleagues, but we have made a determined effort to retain "user-friendliness" while at the same time addressing the quite legitimate points raised in these reviews.

In a related vein, it has been our experience that professors want an understandable and accurate text that frees them to use their creative abilities in lecture, discussion, and simulation settings. Accordingly, we have made an instructor's manual an integral part of our effort and are particularly appreciative of the work of Professor James Zoetewey in preparing it. Our resolve has been to have our supporting materials ready from the beginning and to make using our text enjoyable for our colleagues as well as their students.

The American political system has become even more difficult for the average student and citizen to grasp in the three years since our first edition. It seems as if a wider variety of perspectives and interests have learned how to make their point within the system. To cope with fragmentation, we need a clearer sense of what is good for the whole, not just individual parts. Before the needs of the whole can be understood, however, the effective citizen must understand the basic perspectives and how they differ; problems cannot be solved until the bases of disagreements are recognized.

The election of 1992 brought twelve years of Republican control of the White House to an end and gave the Democrats control of the presidency as well as Congress. There is now potential for movement away from the deadlock under which the national debt has risen to new heights. However, since voters are used to government spending at a level that is beyond current revenue, it is a difficult time for any political leader. We have worked to reflect these difficulties in our analysis while at the same time affirming that leaders are charged with making difficult decisions of the type that can resolve a crisis.

Reviewers and users of the first edition have made valuable suggestions for this edition. The chapter on the judiciary has been split in two—one chapter on the judicial process and one on civil rights and liberties. World events have altered the foreign policy landscape, and that chapter has been revised accordingly. We also adopted suggestions for improving the internal integration of chapters, especially Chapter 5.

The liberal, conservative, libertarian, and populist perspectives have remained strong in both the electorate and the government, and we have tried to be fair to each. The truth of the matter is that in our conservatism we are more representative of the American body politic than of the political science profession. We are also more supportive of the system than are many colleagues, who have been trained to recognize and analyze problems. However, we believe that our outlook can stimulate thinking by both students and faculty. And that, in the end, is more important to our objective than writing a text bland enough to be accepted as fair by a profession of astute observers with different perspectives.

Our readers will rightfully be the judges of whether we did what we set out to do, and how well we did it.

NOTE TO STUDENTS

We have endeavored to make this a "user-friendly" textbook. To be certain we promote student interest, we have involved our own students in every step of manuscript preparation. Summaries for each chapter are extensive enough to highlight major points and give you some idea of how well you understand a chapter. Key terms are boldfaced and defined in each chapter. The Glossary also contains definitions of the key terms and expands on them where we think expansion is useful. The Constitution and all amendments are included, along with the Declaration of Independence, in Appendix A. Key legislation and landmark U.S. Supreme Court cases are identified in the text as well as in separate chronological listings in Appendix B and Appendix D, which also include entries not covered in the text. The presidents of the United States and their parties are listed in Appendix C. Your instructors have been helpful in giving us suggestions, and we would be glad to receive suggestions from you as well.

ACKNOWLEDGMENTS

We want to thank all those who made direct and indirect contributions to this book.

We are appreciative of the work done by Hope College students for the first edition. Don Hones put many of our ideas in rough draft form. Karin S. Wiechmann used her excellent abilities to coordinate our efforts in the final stages of the book. Paul Bolt played this role in earlier versions. Elizabeth Pechta was most helpful with editing and permissions. Erik Davies, Joe Kuiper, Todd K. Lanting, Kristin J. Long, Kristin Michel, Ben Vonk, and Dirk Weeldreyer applied their fine writing and research skills to improve many of the chapters. Scott DeWitt, Heidi Elder, Drew Mogridge, and Joe Murray played major roles in improving parts of the book. Jon Christinidis, Elizabeth Cross, Jeff Fraser, Keith Hopkins, Kevin Kossen, Mark McDowell, David Rhem, Dan Stid, Thomas TerMaat, Jeff Welch, and John Wyma were most helpful with our early reference work, writing, and proofreading. Christine Brink, Subhash Chandra, Jeff Clark, Becky Collins, Hayley Froysland, Dan Goeman, Stephanie Grier, Brian Haight, Scott Kaukonen, Brian Keisling, David Kraska, Alan Keip, Chad Latsch, Holly Moore, Kurt Oosterhouse, Scott Patton, Tom Roodvoets, Craig Sharp, Lance Smith, Kurt Stegenga, Joel Toppen, Michael Van Huis, Yvette Van Riper, Seth Weeldreyer, Laura Whitwam, and Ron Weigerink provided excellent assistance as we completed our reference work, writing, and proofreading. Jack Holmes's 1990 and 1993 American foreign policy classes were most helpful in checking galleys. Beth Adams and Cindy Cox of Luther College helped Mike Engelhardt with material for the instructor's manual and galleys. All these students stimulated the endeavor with their enthusiasm.

Several Hope College students provided important assistance in producing our second edition. Dan Brady, Amy Ferris, Amy Grasman, Phumla Mazamisa, Sarah McClure, Jennie Mroz, James Oonk, Adam D. Schwartz, Kgothatso Semela, Sharla Utz, Brett Vander Slik,

Sarah VanHarken, and Jeff Vetters assisted in draft preparation and coordination. Reynolds Brissenden, David Charnin, Craig Ikens, Steven Johnson, and Scott Sawicki each spent at least a summer working on important aspects of manuscript preparation; their assistance was particularly helpful as the manuscript was completed.

Hope College's several encouragements of this project, including aid from the Frost Social Science Center and sabbatical leaves for Jack Holmes and Robert E. Elder, have been essential to its completion. Barb Kilbry, Sally Smith, Sandy Tasma, and Kate Ten Haken were our most patient typists through several drafts and editions. Richard Burtt, Faye Christenberry, Elaine Cline, Helen Einberger, Kelly Gordon-Jacobsman, David Jensen, Carol Juth, and David O'Brien of the Van Wylen Library provided valuable reference assistance on short notice. Professors Annie Dandavati, Pilkyu Kim, and Steve Samson were most helpful in field-testing the book on their classes.

McGraw-Hill Senior Editor Jim Anker, Political Science Editors Bert Lummus and Peter Labella, and Senior Editing Supervisors Jeannine Ciliotta and Fred Burns guided us through major improvements. Developmental editor Ann Hofstra Grogg gave us many excellent suggestions and attacked our wordiness with great efficiency. Professor James Zoetewey provided many useful suggestions as he prepared the instructor's manual. Professor Charles Huttar read the galleys and identified important areas for improvement.

We are grateful to the following reviewers provided by our publisher: James P. Dahlberg, Morehead State University; Joyce G. Denning, University of Lowell; Larry Elowitz, Georgia College; Herbert M. Levine; Rex C. Peebles, Austin Community College; David H. Ray, University of Oklahoma; Martin P. Sutton, Bucks County Community College; Conrad P. Waligorski, University of Arkansas; and Marilyn A. Yale, Morehead State University. In addition, Professors Sally Friedman, State University of New York at Albany; Allen Hertzke, University of Oklahoma; Robin Klay, Hope College; Michael Nelson, Vanderbilt University; Timothy G. O'Rourke, University of Virginia; and Dr. Marvin Kosters of the American Enterprise Institute provided helpful reviews on individual chapters.

Responsibility for all matters of fact and opinion is, of course, solely our own.

Jack E. Holmes
Michael J. Engelhardt
Robert E. Elder, Jr.

1

PERSPECTIVES ON AMERICAN GOVERNMENT

Between 1977 and 1986, a debate took place in South Carolina: should Terry Roach live or die? One October night in 1977, Roach and two friends had been out "cruising" when they came across teenagers Tommy Taylor and Carlotta Hartness parked in the Taylor family car. Roach shot Taylor three times in the head and, with the help of his friends, dragged Hartness out of the car, where they proceeded to rape her. When they were finished, Roach and his friends fired five bullets into the head of the fourteen-year-old girl.

Roach was found guilty and sentenced to death. But there were some complications. Terry Roach was mildly retarded, leading some to wonder whether he should be held fully responsible for his actions. Moreover, he was suffering from a degenerative brain condition that further diminished his judgmental capabilities. But the real concern for opponents of the sentence was Roach's age. Terry Roach was seventeen years old.

Over the next nine years, lawyers, judges, and politicians wrestled with Roach's fate. Those who advocated the death penalty pointed out that any leniency Roach could expect on account of his age and ambiguous mental awareness was outweighed by the heinous nature of the act. Others, including former President Jimmy Carter and Mother Teresa, pleaded with South Carolina's Governor Richard Riley to stay the execution, arguing that to execute Roach for a crime he committed while he was still a juvenile possessing limited intelligence would in itself be a barbarous act.

*In January 1986 the debate stopped; Terry Roach was put to death in the electric chair (**Newsweek**, 13 January 1986, 74; **Time**, 20 January 1986, 22–23).*

Should government have the power and authority to take the life a citizen? Most liberals would vehemently oppose such absolute power over any individual, arguing that execution is too severe a punishment to be acceptable in a civilized country. Most conservatives would argue that execution is a punishment necessary for criminals who have committed extremely violent crimes. Many conservatives claim that capital punishment will protect society from hardened criminals and serve as a deterrent, making potential criminals reconsider before actually committing the crime. Liberals disagree, arguing that capital punishment is no more of a deterrent than life imprisonment and that if a criminal is in prison at least there is a chance for reform.

OUR APPROACH

This debate and most other debates involving politics divide individuals and align them in opinion groups. Although one example cannot illustrate the liberal or conservative position, it can suggest differences in political thought. These different systems of thought, or **perspectives**, often determine people's attitudes toward the role of government and politics in society. *American Government: Essentials and Perspectives* focuses on American government in terms of these differing viewpoints. Although the six perspectives that frame the approach of this book will be explained in greater depth later in this chapter, you should be introduced now to the basic principles each embodies. Generally speaking, conservatives view the government as important in maintaining order and ensuring national security. Liberals see the government as important in promoting human welfare, and they strongly advocate individual rights. Libertarians seek to limit government and believe the individual should be free from government regulations. Populists place their emphasis on majority rule and support the role of government in upholding moral and religious values. Marxists want a restructuring of government and the economy to ensure that all people benefit from the fruits of their labor. Feminists view male dominance as pervasive, and they want government to initiate changes to improve women's

status. These perspectives represent views current in the American populace, but it is important to remember that one individual may adhere to aspects of several perspectives simultaneously. There are no absolutes in political science or, for that matter, in individual thought.

Debates in **politics** (the science or art of government), like the debate over the death penalty, are different from those in the physical sciences. **Political science** is an attempt to study politics systematically, but political scientists cannot test their hypotheses in a laboratory. They cannot experiment with the death penalty as a chemist experiments with chemicals. In government there are no universally right or wrong answers, no frameworks of universally accepted laws that shape inquiries and conclusions. Those who study **government** (the authoritative allocator of resources for a society) have not been able to agree on how government either does or should work. Yet elected officials must make decisions on critical questions like the death penalty.

There are several different ways to settle debates about politics. One person or a small group of people may have the power to decide who is right. A government in which one person makes all the major decisions and has no responsibility to the people he or she governs is a **dictatorship.** A government in which a small group of people make most of the decisions is an **oligarchy.** Both these types of governments are examples of **authoritarianism,** governments in which control is in the hands of an individual or group of individuals. The People's Republic of China, controlled by a single political party, is an oligarchy. Until the 1990s, the majority of countries in the world were oligarchies or dictatorships. The United States has been one of the smaller number of countries governed by elected representatives who make decisions by majority rule while guaranteeing certain fundamental rights to those holding minority opinions. This form of government is called **representative democracy.** Because the United States permits a high degree of freedom of expression, American students must be able to understand and evaluate the differing perspectives that they will inevitably encounter as they attempt to arrive at their own position on issues and conclusions about government policy. We have sought to incorporate these different points of view in our textbook.

One of the most difficult tasks in writing a textbook that incorporates alternative viewpoints is to be objective and yet meaningful. Since people often hold strong viewpoints, the only way to avoid offending anyone is to be exceedingly general, but being general can, in turn, make the reader wonder what the argument is all about. Thus, although we have tried to be objective, it is likely that our textbook reflects our own political values to some degree. We want to acknowledge them: Jack Holmes is a conservative with libertarian tendencies; Michael Engelhardt is a libertarian with conservative tendencies; and Robert Elder is a liberal with some populist tendencies.

Our textbook is somewhat more conservative and libertarian than other viewpoint textbooks. It also asks whether the American system of government works, and we believe that it does. We do not defend the system as the best possible in every sense, and we often suggest improvements. But we do not condemn the system; nor do we complicate our presentation with unnecessary analysis. We want those who use our textbook to understand how the system works, why people disagree and need to compromise, and just what can be accomplished through the action of government.

THE ORIGINS OF AMERICAN POLITICAL PERSPECTIVES

Although Americans have a distinctive style of politics, American political perspectives were not developed in a vacuum. The nation's Western heritage, including Greek, Roman, Judeo-Christian, and, in particular, English political and social ideas, has been a major influence on its political thought.

Early English Liberalism

A foreshadowing of the political perspective known as **liberalism,** which believes in changing society through government intervention to promote fairness and protect individual rights, can be seen in ancient Greece and Rome. In those early civilizations middle- and lower-class groups struggled to escape the dominance of ruling aristocracies and in some cities, such as Athens, created democratic institutions to safeguard their rights. Some liberal principles are also embodied in the teachings of Christianity, particularly in the emphasis on human dignity and the equality of all before God.

Liberalism as a political doctrine owes its origins to a struggle between the English monarchy and nobility and a rising new group of merchants and landowners outside the nobility. By the seventeenth century, these new property owners dominated the House of Commons, the lower house of Parliament, and wanted property laws to reflect their interests. During this struggle between the Crown and the Commons, the contending sides developed different political philosophies. The king's supporters were called conservatives because they stressed order, tradition, and authority. The supporters of Parliament moved toward a position known as liberalism (originally called Whiggism), which emphasized greater freedom in the area of individual rights. The major focus of this struggle was property rights, although religion was also at issue. In 1688 Parliament finally triumphed in the so-called Glorious Revolution, in which King James II was overthrown.

Many writers defended the parliamentary cause in the revolution, but the most influential on the development of liberalism was John Locke (1632–1704), whose *Two Treatises of Government* was published in 1689. Locke's work was an uneasy balancing of potentially incompatible ideas that are important to understanding current American political debate. The reasons for this incompatibility, which ultimately caused a split in liberalism, will be apparent from discussion of the major elements in Locke's theory of government. These can be summarized as follows:

Human rationality   Locke's view of human nature is a mixture of rationalist and Christian insights. He recognized that human beings have many selfish instincts which bring them into conflict with one another. Locke also believed, however, that people are endowed with a divine spark which makes them rational creatures, able to understand nature's laws.

Natural rights   Locke held that people were by nature free and had equal rights. By this he meant the "equal Right that every Man hath, *to his Natural Freedom*, without being subjected to the Will or Authority of any other Man" (Locke 1967, 322). No one was born without natural rights. The rights Locke defined as natural to man were life (physical security), liberty (personal control), and property (the fruits of one's labor). No person should be arbitrarily deprived of these rights.

Equality   For Locke, equality was not so sweeping as to include political equality. Fewer than 200,000 males in Locke's England (out of about 2 million adults, one-half of them males) were permitted to vote, yet nowhere in Locke's letters or writing is there a proposal for electoral reform (Durant and Durant 1965, 90; Hill 1975, 213). Equality of opportunity as expressed in public education or modern voting requirements would have been beyond his understanding. Locke did not believe that human beings were the same in ability or intelligence, but that all men were equal in the eyes of God and were capable, with effort, of understanding the laws of nature and of God. He also believed that the rights of life, liberty, and property should apply equally to all men.

Again, the struggles between Crown and Parliament made it clear that courts needed to become neutral interpreters of a common law giving preference to neither Crown nor wealth.

Limited government   Locke's **social contract theory** of government explains the origin of society and government and outlines the respective authority and responsibility of government and individuals under their contractual obligation. Locke stated that prior to the creation of a well-ordered society humankind lived in a state of nature, subject to the struggle of individual needs and passions (Pangle 1988, 244–51). Realizing that all would benefit if settled rules for conduct were established and enforced, men had come together in a social contract, agreeing to choose a government to protect each other's lives, liberty, and property. If a man's property was taken without just cause or he was denied the right to worship God in the manner he chose, government should act to ensure restitution. The power given to government was never arbitrary or uncontrolled, however; it was limited by the law of nature. Rulers were to exercise power only for the purpose of safeguarding natural rights, not for their personal gain.

Majority rule   Locke was committed to rule by a majority within Parliament; he also believed that Parliament should be elected by the majority of those permitted to vote. For early liberals, majority rule meant rule by only the small percentage of Englishmen who had enough property to vote, but as suffrage expanded, Locke's theory was interpreted to justify **democracy,** or rule by a majority of those adults who decide to vote.

Minority rights   Locke was also committed, with some qualifications, to the protection of minority groups in society. In *A Letter Concerning Toleration* (1689), he argued that the government should grant religious freedom to members of all faiths except Catholics, who, he believed, were subversive because they were loyal to the pope rather than the country they lived in, and atheists, who, he believed, were untrustworthy (Locke 1937, 208–13). For Locke's time, proposing this amount of religious freedom was revolutionary.

The right of revolution According to Locke, the ruler who violated the people's right to life, liberty, or property lost the right to rule and was no better than a common robber. The people had the right and the duty to unseat such a ruler, by force if necessary, and to establish a new government to protect their rights. In response to the question of who should judge when the government had abused its power, Locke replied, *"The people shall be Judge"* (Locke 1967, 445). Of course Locke assumed that even after a revolution the new government would be dominated by the educated, property-owning classes.

The idea of progress During the generation following Locke's death in 1704, one additional idea became important to the liberal tradition: the idea of progress. Both Jewish and Christian traditions have treated history as a meaningful progression. The Old Testament decreed that events had meaning because God governed the universe, and the view of history as meaningful continued into the New Testament. During the century after Locke, however, English and French intellectuals became highly critical of organized religion and full of optimism about the power of human intelligence (Becker 1932). Man and his reason became the measure of all things. During this period, advances in science and technology occurred much more rapidly than before, and human progress seemed as inevitable as stability had seemed in the Middle Ages. A more secularized view of progress, which defined history in terms of human progress rather than of divine governance became part of the liberal creed.

The English Conservative Reaction

Modern political conservatism also has its roots in the struggle between the Crown and Parliament. It came to full flower in Europe in reaction to the French Revolution of 1789. Locke's liberalism had gained widespread support in France, where the monarchy was more corrupt and repressive than it had been in England. Reform in French society was so long overdue that it produced a revolution more thorough and violent than those in England and the United States. European aristocrats, perceiving their dominance threatened by the liberal ideas that had sparked the revolution, mounted an intense counterattack, both militarily and intellectually. Their ideas are the basis of **conservatism**, which believes that people need the direction and structure of religion and tradition.

In England the intellectual leader of the conservative movement was the politician Edmund Burke (1729–97), whose *Reflections on the Revolution in France* (1790) was a vigorous response to the French variant of liberalism. Burke's critique of liberalism was based upon a more pessimistic view of human nature than that held by Locke or the French liberals. Burke viewed human beings as irrational, capable of goodness but frequently ruled by blind passions and evil and selfish desires. The main checks on these destructive impulses were religion and the stabilizing influence of custom and tradition. Burke did not favor trying to force religion on people, but he was convinced that a strong church was essential to maintain morality and civil order, and he was horrified by the antireligious tendencies of the French revolutionaries (Harbour 1982, 11–31; see also Burke 1955, 102–20). Stressing the importance of tradition, Burke was naturally less optimistic than the liberals about the possibility of human progress. "We are afraid," he wrote of himself and his followers, "to put men to live and trade each on his own private stock of reason, because we suspect that this stock in each man is small, and that the individuals would do better to avail themselves of the general bank and capital of [knowledge accumulated by] nations and ages." Challenging the liberal claim to have discovered new political principles that could shape a more just society, Burke argued, "We knew that *we* have made no discoveries and we think that no discoveries are to be made, in morality, nor many in the great principles of government, nor in the ideas of liberty, which were understood long before we were born" (Burke 1955, 97, 99).

Burke also challenged the liberal concept of majority rule. He did not believe that the masses of the people had any natural right to rule. People were inherently unequal in ability and talent, so majority rule would leave public affairs in the hands of those least qualified to conduct them. "There is no qualification for [participation in] government but virtue and wisdom" (Burke 1955, 57), Burke wrote, and he felt that these qualities resided mostly in the property-owning and educated classes that dominated English politics. It was necessary for these groups to conduct the government for the good of all. Though not opposed to individual freedom, Burke and his supporters saw the need for a strong state that would keep order, not promote change. Burke did support the economist Adam Smith's ideas for freeing the economy from unnecessary regulations, as well as some other reforms in the English system of government, but he opposed any revolutionary attempts to abolish class distinctions and equalize rights in society.

The Split in English Liberalism

The concepts underlying Locke's philosophy, although logically consistent as he expressed them, rest in an uneasy balance. If one alters or expands upon the definition of these concepts, the balance can give way to opposition. Three examples will illustrate these inconsistencies.

First, freedom and equality can coexist only so long as they focus on property rights or equal protection in courts of law. When the notion of equality expands to encompass equality of opportunity or social equality or economic equality, the tension with a property-rights–based concept of freedom begins to increase. Should government tax property in order to ensure equality of educational opportunity? Should government enforce equality in the workplace for women and minorities, or should property owners have the freedom to use their property (money, land, business) as they see fit?

A similar problem exists with reference to the role of government. According to Locke, government is supposed to sustain individual rights; it is also supposed to keep a low profile. If rights are defined broadly enough, however, a low profile for government becomes virtually impossible. Should government protect the right to life by guaranteeing the safety of food and drugs or extend property rights by subsidizing home ownership? The tension between a government that must be limited and a government that must protect rights is obvious.

Finally, majority rule inevitably clashes with minority rights. Suppose the majority believes, as Locke did, that Catholics are dangerous. If laws prevent Catholics from holding public office or assembling to worship (there were such laws in England and in some of the American colonies before the Revolution), the natural right to liberty is clearly violated. On the other hand, if the majority is forbidden to pass anti-Catholic laws or laws that may injure any other religious, racial, ethnic, or political minority, the majority is no longer ruling in the sense of being able to do whatever it wants in government. Moreover, some minorities may indeed be dangerous and threaten the legitimate interests of the majority. It is clear that unrestricted majority rule is incompatible with unlimited minority rights.

During the late eighteenth and nineteenth centuries, these potential incompatibilities in Lockean principles split the liberal response to the vast changes in English society caused by the industrial revolution. Large numbers of people were moving from country to city because factory work was increasingly available, just as landowners were experimenting with new agricultural methods that reduced the need for farm labor. Historians disagree over whether, if you were poor, life in the city was better or worse than life in the country had been (von Hayek 1944; Ashton 1961, 201–35; Floud and McCloskey 1981, 177). In both places, conditions were grim. For example, workdays in coal mines of twelve to sixteen hours at low wages were not uncommon for both women and men (Ashton 1961, 22). At the same time, however, the growth of industry was creating a larger and more prosperous business class. The divergence of views between business and its supporters and those seeking to restrain business eroded the Lockean consensus.

Libertarianism Businessmen were among the most enthusiastic supporters of early liberalism. Frequently burdened with heavy taxes and restrictions by royal governments, they were attracted to liberal ideas concerning the sanctity of private property and limits on the power of government. As a result, liberalism became closely identified with **capitalism**, an economic system with free markets that features private ownership of the means of production and minimal government intervention. A major segment of liberal opinion still identifies strongly with capitalism. This strain of thought, which also stresses individualism, may be termed **libertarianism**.

A major contribution to the development of libertarianism (though he did not use the term himself) was made by Adam Smith (1723–90), a Scottish economist whose *Wealth of Nations* (1776) is the classic statement of **laissez-faire** economy (a French term that means "hands off," or limited government control of the economy). Smith believed that an **invisible hand** of self-interest guided economic activity so as to promote the good of society. Left to themselves, manufacturers would have to produce the goods consumers wanted (otherwise,

they would not be able to stay in business) and thus benefit both themselves and society. "It is not from the benevolence of the butcher, the brewer, or the baker that we expect our dinner," wrote Smith, "but from their regard to their self-interest. We address ourselves, not to their humanity, but to their self-love, and never talk to them of our necessities, but of their advantages." Restrictions on trade were not only inefficient but oppressive since they violated property rights and infringed on individual liberty. Smith did believe the state should play a role in limited areas, such as defense, education, and the building of roads and canals, but he hoped that fees and tolls would make government education and road building self-supporting (Smith 1981, 1:26–27, 2:723, 758–68; see also Smith 1948, 425–48). Smith himself was no particular friend of businessmen, whom he accused of often seeking government benefits for their industries at public expense. In fact, Smith at times saw benefits in certain types of goverment activities, such as encouraging the arts through the use of public subsidies, that contemporary libertarians like Milton Friedman might oppose. As time went on, however, the majority of those in commerce and industry came to believe that Smith's notion of a **free market economy** (one with minimal government controls on the behavior of individuals and businesses) was the best route to prosperity and individual freedom.

Reform liberalism By the early nineteenth century other liberals found much to criticize in capitalist society. Once it became accepted that people had rights, child labor and slum housing, which had existed before the industrial revolution and the rise of capitalism, were perceived as injustices. When the free market did not appear able to correct these abuses, some liberals began to search for another engine of human progress.

The English political philosopher John Stuart Mill (1806–73) and later the "Oxford Idealist" Thomas Hill Green (1836–82) first asserted a more activist role for government in society. Rejecting the notion that government should confine itself to passive protection of rights, Mill argued that the state could and should act as an agent of progress, improving the lot of humankind. Without abandoning belief in individual freedom, he contended that government should move to restrain abuses by business and undertake functions, like education and the protection of women and children in the labor force, that the private sector was incapable of performing adequately (Mill 1965, vols. 2–3). Inspired by Mill, some liberals in Parliament, called "radicals" by their colleagues at the time, began to push government to take a larger role in the economy to ease the condition of the working classes.

By the end of the nineteenth century, the early liberal consensus had been shattered for good. One group of liberals, the libertarians, continued to emphasize freedom, property rights, and limited government as the paramount values, although paying some attention to the rights of minorities. The other group emphasized equity and the need for active government to protect rights. This group, though referred to as radical at the time, is the forerunner of the perspective known as liberalism in the United States today.

THE EVOLUTION OF AMERICAN POLITICAL PERSPECTIVES

American politics is dominated by four major political perspectives. Three of these—conservatism, liberalism, and libertarianism—have roots in the English political heritage. The fourth—populism—is distinctly American, though parallels may be found in other societies. The United States differs from many other countries in that all four of its major political perspectives share early liberal assumptions to some degree. However, only the libertarian perspective preserves Locke's ideas

in something close to their original form; the other three perspectives have modified, integrated, or discarded elements of the early liberal tradition (Maddox and Lilie 1984, 1–21; see also Medcalf and Dolbeare 1985; Hartz 1955). The following discussions consider each perspective as it has emerged in the United States and affects American politics today.

Conservatism

Conservatism in its English form was never fully transplanted to the United States. The country has never had a nobility or an established state church for conservatives to defend; nor have notions of rule by a talented elite been very popular. Yet some conservative principles have found support. Religious faith has been widespread among the people, as has the sense that government needs to be involved in upholding moral values. American history, like that of most other countries, provides abundant reasons for skepticism about human nature, and at various times Americans have felt a need for strong government to control the destructive impulses of citizens. The distinctive American conservatism that evolved has borrowed from elements of Burke's conservatism and early liberalism.

American conservatives place somewhat more emphasis than Burke did on the benefits of the free market system. In this respect their views are also little distinguished from those of moderate libertarians. What conservatives cannot accept about libertarians is their optimism about human nature, their highly negative views on government, and their arguments for unchecked individual choice in the realm of morality. Human nature is too flawed to permit unrestricted choice in life-styles, say conservatives; destructive "private" behavior does, in the end, hurt society. The state cannot take the place of the family or the church, but it has a duty to support the morality taught there, even if certain markets must be restrained. As a group of Catholic conservatives put it, "We object to those base forms of commerce—in abortion, pornography, prostitu-tion, and drugs—which make direct war upon the necessary moral strength of any free re-public" (Lay Commission, 1984, 56). Unlike libertarians, conservatives do not see legisla-tion against such "base commerce" as an in-fringement on individual rights.

Conservatives also value strong govern-ment to promote the nation's internal and external security. Domestically, they favor stronger measures against crime and are skep-tical of the possibility of rehabilitating crimi-nals. Sharing Burke's abhorrence of violent revolution, they have seen a serious threat to the United States and the other Western de-mocracies from communism and the Soviet Union, and they strongly backed President Ronald Reagan's drive to increase American defense spending in the early 1980s. In con-trast, libertarians recognize national defense as a legitimate role for government but tend to view the military as another wasteful govern-ment bureaucracy and believe that the United States is overcommitted to alliances with other countries (Ravenal and Van Cleve 1985, 19–50).

Conservatism's most important influence on American history came with the framing of the Constitution (see Table 1.1). The framers, though greatly indebted to liberal thought, were strongly influenced by the skeptical, con-servative view of human nature. After the new government was established, conservative principles were embodied by the Federalist party of Alexander Hamilton and John Adams, which favored strong central government, elite rule, established churches at the state level, and some government efforts to promote in-dustrial development (Fischer 1969). The Fed-eralists went down to defeat at the hands of the Jeffersonian Republicans, an early liberal-populist coalition, but the Whig party of the pre–Civil War era and then the Republican party adopted some of their ideas while dis-carding open advocacy of elitism and state churches. Since the Civil War, the Republican party has best represented the conservative view in the United States, generally support-ing free market economics (with some govern-ment intervention, more to aid than to regulate business) along with moral legislation that on occasion limits freedom in the economic realm. Today's Republicans are a coalition of conser-vatives (see Profile of Orrin Hatch), liber-tarians, and right populists, though a few conservatives and many populists can be

TABLE 1.1 POLITICAL PERSPECTIVES IN U.S. HISTORY

	1789–1824	1824–1900	1900–1950	1950–1994
Conservative	Some framers, Federalists	Whigs (1830–54), some Repub-licans	Many Republicans, some southern Democrats	Many Republicans, some southern Democrats
Liberal	Some framers, some Jeffer-sonian Re-publicans	Some Jacksonian Democrats	Progressives (1900–20), New Dealers (1930s)	Many northern Democrats, some southern Democrats, civil rights and environ-mental groups
Libertarian		Some Repub-licans	Many Republicans	Libertarians, many Repub-licans, some Democrats
Populist	Some Jeffer-sonian Re-publicans	Many Jackso-nian Democrats, populists (1890s)	Labor, some racist and antiforeign groups	Labor, some Democrats, George Wallace supporters (1968), New Christian Right, Jesse Jackson sup-porters (1984–88), many Ross Perot supporters (1992)

PROFILE
Orrin Hatch: A Conservative's Conservative

Orrin Hatch (Courtesy Senator Orrin Hatch)

During a lengthy filibuster against a prounion labor law reform bill, liberal senators took to calling him "Borin' Orrin." Orrin Hatch, the junior senator from Utah, may indeed lack Ronald Reagan's personal magnetism, but he yields to no one in his fierce devotion to the conservative cause.

Orrin Hatch was born March 22, 1934, in Pittsburgh, Pennsylvania, the son of a Mormon lathe operator. To put himself through Brigham Young University and then through the University of Pittsburgh Law School, he worked beside his father as an apprentice lather and still carries his union card. Hatch entered private law practice in Utah but stayed out of politics until 1976, when Ernest Wilkerson, the president of Brigham Young University and a staunch conservative, convinced him to run for the Senate. Endorsed by Ronald Reagan, the neophyte politician defeated an experienced Republican rival in the primary, then went on to challenge incumbent Democrat Senator Frank Moss. The Hatch-Moss race was a classic confrontation between liberal and conservative. Moss stressed the benefits of federal aid programs he had brought to the state, while Hatch argued that limiting government and taxes was a better approach. Utah's voters, a conservative lot (two-thirds are Mormons), preferred Hatch's message.

During his first four years in the Senate, Hatch gained a reputation as a fierce opponent of the liberal Democratic majority. Serving on the Labor Committee and Judiciary Committee, he tangled with Ted Kennedy, whom he said he respected as an "honest liberal," on issues ranging from labor law to abortion. Like Kennedy, he was not afraid to challenge strong opponents on issues he considered matters of principle. Believing labor leaders had lost touch with ordinary workers, Hatch

found in the Democratic party as well, particularly in the South.

Liberalism

Modern liberalism made its first strong appearance in the United States with the **progressive movement** of the early twentieth century. Backed by urban middle-class professionals and small businessmen, the progressives supported tighter regulation of big business and some limited social welfare programs like workmen's compensation. Progressives were active in both political parties and ran third-party campaigns in 1912 and 1924, but since Franklin Roosevelt's New Deal liberalism has been based mostly in the Democratic party. For most of the past half-century the Democratic party has been the majority party among those who vote in the United States, so the

opposed the labor movement on virtually every issue. Once, at a Washington reception, he ran into George Meany, then head of the AFL-CIO federation of unions. When Meany warned him that the AFL-CIO would spend $4 million to defeat him in the 1982 election, Hatch responded coolly that "that would be wonderful" for Utah's economy. Hatch won reelection easily.

When the Republicans won control of the Senate in 1980, Hatch became chair of the Labor Committee. Given the opportunity to pass legislation instead of just reviewing it, he became a bit more flexible, cooperating with Kennedy and other Democrats to pass health care bills. But on the Judiciary Committee, which deals more with social issues, Hatch was his old conservative self. A devout Mormon, he believes passionately that abortion is murder and has worked for years, so far fruitlessly, for a constitutional amendment giving Congress and state legislatures the power to ban the practice.

The Democratic victory in the 1986 elections sent Hatch back into the minority in the Senate but may have made him even more ideologically conservative. During the remainder of Reagan's second term, Hatch defended Oliver North's activities in support of the Nicaraguan rebels (see Controversy in Chapter 11) and led the fight for Robert Bork's confirmation to the Supreme Court (see Controversy in Chapter 8). Hatch continued his defense of conservatism in the Bush administration, supporting a constitutional amendment against flag desecration, limits on the rights of criminal defendants, and the nomination of Clarence Thomas to the Supreme Court (see Controversy in Chapter 8). Hatch is willing to cooperate with the Democratic majority to achieve ends in which he believes. In the 101st Congress, Hatch led support for a bill in an area he has long favored: child care. Even though his position angered many of his Republican allies, he remained firm. Like that of Congressman Henry Hyde, whose support of food stamps (see Profile in Chapter 6) has angered some conservatives, Hatch's approach of "Let us get with the real world and let us try to solve these problems" demonstrates family-oriented conservatism.

As a member of the Foreign Relations Committee, Hatch has been active in foreign policy and national defense. He opposed reduction of funding for the Strategic Defense Initiative, opposed halting production of the B-2 bomber, and supported President Bush in the 1991 vote authorizing the use of force against Iraq.

Despite a lack of personal charisma, Hatch seems to appeal to Utah's religious conservative electorate and will undoubtedly remain a leading warrior for conservative causes during the next decade. His position as ranking minority member of the Senate Judiciary Committee allows him to have a major say about the judicial system.

Source: Politics in America 1987, 1523–26; Vetterli 1982, 115; Cohen and Mitchell 1988, 180; *National Journal,* 19 August 1989, 2088–92; *Politics in America* 1991, 1497.

---

liberal reformers whose historic role has been to question and criticize established institutions have in a sense become the "establishment" themselves.

What distinguishes the perspective we now call liberalism from early liberalism is this changed view of the proper role of government. Modern liberals continue to see concentrated power as a threat to individual freedom, but they see the threat coming as much from big business as from big government. According to many liberals, Adam Smith's "invisible hand" is dead. Major industries are now controlled by giant corporations, which often do not compete but cooperate to fix prices and divide up markets. Often they transfer manufacturing to overseas facilities, leaving government to take care of the unemployment and related social problems their departure creates. Liberals complain that libertarian and conser-

PROFILE
Edward Kennedy: A Liberal's Liberal

Edward Kennedy (Reuters/Bettmann)

Senator Edward Kennedy is an excellent example of the liberal approach to both domestic and foreign policy. Kennedy has followed a consistent liberal path ever since entering politics. For over thirty years he has been an articulate defender of liberal causes in the Senate. If Orrin Hatch is a conservative's conservative, Kennedy is a liberal's liberal.

Born February 22, 1932, the fourth son and ninth child in the wealthy and politically active Kennedy family, "Ted" Kennedy first entered politics in 1962 when he ran for the Senate seat from Massachusetts that his brother John had vacated after being elected president. Kennedy won his first race by a wide margin. As a senator, he soon showed himself a strong supporter of civil rights legislation, antipoverty programs, and, after John Kennedy's assassination in 1963, gun control legislation.

In 1968 Kennedy campaigned for his brother Robert until Robert was assassinated after winning the California primary. Crushed by the tragedy, Kennedy rejected moves to nominate him for president or vice-president in 1968 but was widely believed to have the inside track for the 1972 nomination. However, on June 18, 1969, Kennedy's car swerved off a bridge after a party on Martha's Vineyard, an island off the coast of Massachusetts. A companion, Mary Jo Kopechne, drowned. Kennedy did not report the incident for several hours. An incident like this, which raised many questions, makes it difficult for a person of any perspective to advance to the presidency.

The incident possibly kept Kennedy out of the 1972 and 1976 presidential races, but he continued to appeal to liberals across the nation through his support of social programs, particularly national health insurance. Unlike some politicians, he held

vative policies of shying away from economic regulation help the rich at the expense of lower- and middle-class Americans. Without government supervision, liberals argue, business is likely to abuse its powers and victimize both workers and consumers. A substantial government presence is seen by liberals as essential in the marketplace (Thurow 1985; Galbraith 1984; Galbraith 1987). Furthermore, as the United States now competes in international trade with many countries that foster private industry, the American free market economy is at a disadvantage. Liberals argue that a political system with few linkages between government and business is simply obsolete in the modern world.

Besides being suspicious of business power, liberals are anxious to have the government actively promote human welfare in areas untouched or inadequately served by the private

to his views even when they were unpopular. For example, he risked the wrath of his hitherto loyal Boston Irish constituents when he supported school integration there. Kennedy has been less active on foreign policy, but he supported withdrawal from Vietnam and pressure on governments, like that in South Africa, that violated human rights.

By 1980 Kennedy was discontented with the conservative trend apparent in President Jimmy Carter's policies. Convinced by Carter's low popularity ratings that Carter could be beaten, Kennedy decided to challenge him in the Democratic primaries. He ran on a platform calling for government wage-price controls to halt inflation and more social and less military spending. Although he gained the support of the labor movement and many Democrats in the industrial Northeast, Kennedy was not popular in the South, and the Iran hostage crisis triggered a surge in Carter's support. Ironically, Kennedy's failed candidacy probably contributed to Ronald Reagan's election by delaying the consolidation of Democratic efforts until after the Democratic convention, even though Kennedy supported Carter in the general election.

Kennedy has not been a candidate for president since 1980. In the Senate, he remains one of the most consistent supporters of liberal positions. He spearheaded the efforts to impose sanctions on the white supremacist government of South Africa. He fought Reagan's efforts to support the contras in Nicaragua. He is against capital punishment because of its history of racial bias (more blacks charged with murder receive capital punishment than whites). He has also fought conservative nominations to the Supreme Court including those of Robert Bork, David Souter, and Clarence Thomas. His reasons for opposing the Souter nomination are revealing: "There is little in his [Souter's] record that demonstrates real solicitude for the rights of those who are the weakest and most powerless in our society. . . . We [the Senate] must vote our fears [of Souter], not our hopes [for Souter]."

Kennedy's main policy interest is health care, and he has vowed to concentrate the remainder of his senatorial career on achieving comprehensive health care for all Americans. Yet his goal of national health insurance remains only marginally closer to fulfillment today than when he first talked about it twenty-five years ago. He still pushes the program but no longer calls for it to be fully sponsored by the government. Instead, he favors something a bit closer to President Bill Clinton's plan, a hybrid system requiring private employers to insure workers while government covers the poor or unemployed. Still in his early sixties and a popular figure in his home state, Kennedy will most likely be returned to his Senate seat when he runs for reelection in 1994 and remain an important figure in the Democratic-dominated Senate for some time to come.

Source: Burns 1976; David 1972; Sherrill 1976; Hersh 1972; Burns 1984, 80–89; *Politics in America* 1991, 673–74; *Congressional Quarterly Almanac 1991*, 263.

---

market. They support increased spending for public services like education and health care (see Profile of Edward Kennedy). Emphasizing equality as much as libertarians stress freedom, liberals are concerned about what they see as an unfair distribution of income in the United States. Many favor taxing the rich to pay for social welfare programs that improve the quality of life for the poor. These liberal concerns were represented in the 1992 campaign of Bill Clinton, who called for increased expenditures on education, government cooperation and planning in research and development in industry, and a 1.5 percent tax on businesses that have fifty or more employees and do not have job-retraining programs for their workers. Clinton's plan also included increasing taxes on persons earning more than $200,000 and imposing a surcharge on millionaires (*Washington Post National Weekly Edi-*

Steve Benson. Reprinted by permission: Tribune Media Services.

tion, 17–22 September 1992, 20). Proposals Clinton made in his first few months as president placed most of the burden on the wealthy and aimed at the benefits of new spending stimulating the economy in areas that would help the middle and lower classes. Liberal concerns had been highlighted even more in the 1988 campaign of Michael Dukakis, who called for an increase in spending in several social service areas in addition to education.

In spite of their reliance on government to solve an increasing number of problems, liberals have not abandoned belief in individual freedom. Generally they agree with libertarians that government should not intervene in matters of personal conduct. For example, abuses of personal freedom, such as stepping on the American flag, unlike abuses of economic freedom, are not something the govern-

ment should solve. Liberals have energetically defended freedom of speech and other civil liberties from government incursions. One point of disagreement between liberals and libertarians concerns government action to protect minority groups from discrimination. Liberals have championed such legislation for many years, while libertarians opposed it on the grounds that discrimination by private individuals or businesses is not a matter in which government should become involved. In this instance liberals can be viewed as putting natural rights as embodied in the Bill of Rights above both majority rule and individual autonomy. Liberals have also placed an increasing emphasis on the tendency of wealth to create inequities between rich and poor citizens. These inequities, they believe, give unfair political advantage to the wealthy. Thus liberals emphasize "leveling the playing field" so that all participants may begin the economic and social competition on an approximately equal basis.

Libertarianism

Contemporary libertarians are the closest of the four major political perspectives to Locke's early liberalism. Libertarians retain the belief in rationality, progress, natural rights, limited government, majority rule, and the right of revolution. It is Smith's doctrine of limited government and free markets, however, that they are most often heard defending. The libertarian views with alarm the trend toward increasing government power in the United States and other Western democracies. Libertarians stress the link between economic and political freedom. Limiting the amount of money an individual can contribute to a campaign, libertarians point out, restricts freedom of expression. They contend that freedom can exist only in a society with private ownership and free markets. Under a system of government ownership (socialism), where many individuals are dependent on the state for their source of income, independent thought will be stifled and tyranny will grow (Friedman 1962; von Hayek 1944; Nozick 1974). Libertarians differ on how severely the scope of government must be limited to preserve freedom. Some would allow limited state assistance to "deserving" poor people (Murray 1984, 219–39), while others believe all such assistance should be left entirely to private charities (Nozick 1974). All look to the private business sector rather than the government to promote freedom and progress.

Libertarians also believe it is important for the individual to remain as free in the realm of personal conduct as in the economic marketplace. Laws against abortion, drug use, pornography, gambling, and unorthodox sexual practices are oppressive, say libertarians, and deny the individual's independence and moral autonomy (Maddox and Lilie 1984, 15). Like others, libertarians may regard some individual choices as immoral, but they do not accept the state's right to intervene unless the people concerned are directly harming others.

From the end of the Civil War in 1865 to the 1930s, libertarian principles were often articulated in connection with the making of economic policy in the United States, though not policy on moral issues, because both major political parties were heavily influenced by business interests that wanted to keep government regulation of the economy to a minimum. When businessmen could benefit from government intervention they were less likely to make libertarian arguments. One example of business turning its back on libertarian principles was its acceptance of substantial government subsidies in the form of land grants for rail and road rights-of-way in the nineteenth century. In the 1930s libertarian policies were abandoned following the economy's failure to recover on its own from the Great Depression and following the election of Franklin Roosevelt as president in 1932. Since then, people promoting libertarian views on the role of government have been in the position of fighting a holding action against the growth of government; perhaps this is why they are sometimes called "conservatives" even though their perspective is far from that of Burke. Another reason is that libertarians now tend to be concentrated in the Republican party, which also has more conservatives within its ranks than the Democratic party.

Although libertarianism is a minority view in the United States today, it seems to have experienced a resurgence in the last decade, attracting those dissatisfied with taxes and "big government" (see Profile of David Stockman). Some of the most ardent libertarians formed a Libertarian party in 1971, which, in 1992, ran Andre Marrou as its candidate. Most libertarians, however, have remained within

PROFILE

David Stockman: A Libertarian's Frustration

David Stockman (Donald L. Miller)

In his late forties, David Stockman is one of the richest, and certainly one of the most controversial, ex-budget directors in American history. The $2.5 million he received as an advance on *The Triumph of Politics* (1986) and the book's uncomplimentary picture of policy-making in the Reagan administration caused some Reaganites to brand Stockman as disloyal. Loyalty aside, Stockman's career illustrates the obstacles facing anyone attempting to promote the libertarian philosophy of limited government in practical politics.

Born in Fort Hood, Texas, in 1946, Stockman grew up on a farm near Scottdale, Michigan. His devout Methodist family believed, as he later put it, that "God voted Republican." Influenced by liberal professors at Michigan State University, he became an antiwar activist and a "soft-core Marxist." After graduation, Stockman enrolled in Harvard Divinity School, partly, he admits, to extend his draft deferment but partly because "I believed revolution was God's work." Growing bored with

theology, he began to take courses in political science. Slowly his political views changed. He became convinced that government was not the servant of the underprivileged but the tool of greedy special interest groups. By the time he left Harvard to take a job as an aide to Republican Congressman John Anderson of Illinois, Stockman was a dedicated libertarian.

Stockman left Anderson in 1976 to make a successful run for the House in his old home district in southwest Michigan. During his two terms, he opposed government spending and interference with the free market. His reputation for consistency and for being well informed helped earn him an invitation from President Reagan to direct the Office of Management and Budget (OMB). Stockman accepted eagerly, even though he disagreed with Reagan's stand on social issues—"I didn't want economic regulation," he said, "and I didn't want moral regulation"—because he believed the Reagan administration offered the best chance to effect a "revolution" that would decisively reverse the growth of government.

Within weeks of taking office, the young revolutionary found himself at odds with many of his colleagues. Stockman wanted Reagan to cut both taxes and spending, but the president was listening to the view of Congressman Jack Kemp of New York, who argued that cutting taxes but not government services would stimulate the economy enough to increase income from taxes. Secretary of Defense Caspar Weinberger called for massive increases in defense spending; Stockman supported some increases but thought Weinberger was giving a "blank check" to a military bureaucracy. In the end, Stockman got many of the budget cuts he wanted, but the president gave the others what they wanted, too—tax cuts and defense spending increases far beyond what the budget cuts could pay for.

Although distressed by what he saw as Reagan's capitulation to the kind of special interest politics that had made government grow in the

BOOM!

STOCKMAN

SUPPLY SIDE ECONOMICS

Frank Evers. Courtesy New York *Daily News*.

first place, Stockman tried to be a team player. During 1981 his office produced estimates of future deficits that he now admits he knew were too small. At the same time, he was airing his doubts to William Greider, assistant editor of the *Washington Post*. In the December 1981 *Atlantic*, Greider detailed Stockman's disagreements with administration policies. Stockman later said he was "taken to the woodshed" by the president, but he kept his job.

Stockman served as OMB director until August 1985, but grew increasingly discouraged by Reagan's failure to cut back government more deeply. In his book, released after his resignation, Stockman concludes gloomily that a libertarian revolution is impossible because libertarians are not strong enough politically. In his introduction, Stockman repeats his dreams and regrets lost chances:

It was minimalist government—a spare and stingy creature, which offered even-handed public justice, but no more. Its vision of the good society rested on the strength and productive potential of free men in free markets. It sought to encourage the unfettered production of capitalist wealth and the expansion of private welfare that automatically attends it. It envisioned a land the opposite of the coast-to-coast patchwork of dependencies, shelters, protections and redistributions that the nation's politicians had brokered over the decades. The true Reagan Revolution never had a chance. . . . He [Reagan] was a consensus politician, not an ideologue. He had no business trying to make a revolution because it wasn't in his bones.

Following his career in federal government, Stockman entered the private sector as a "Wall Street banker" affiliated with the Blackstone group. His position has not kept him from advising his former associates through interviews with the media. In 1992 Stockman warned both Congress and the president against trying to get government to fix the economy. In the wake of what Stockman described as the "ruble rubble" (the disintegration of the former Soviet empire), he also argued for cutting defense's share of the gross national product in half.

True to his libertarian convictions, Stockman sees the nation's current problems as stemming from unintelligent decisions made in the marketplace during the 1980s:

I think they [large consumer debts] are going to have an impact on consumer savings, which have been at historically minimal levels

over the last four or five years. They are also going to affect consumer spending which has actually exceeded available cash flow since the early 1980s. After consumers pay their taxes, which are rising, and pay the interest on the huge debt balance that accumulated in the '80s and after you account for sources of income that we never really see, such as mandatory employer contributions for pensions and other fringe benefits, the available share of current income that ends up being spent is going to fall significantly. This represents a key weakness [in economic recovery].

Whether Stockman will ever return to politics is not clear, but the ideas he expresses are pointed and vigorous critiques of American government from the economic side of the libertarian perspective.

Source: Stockman 1986, 8–9; Greider 1981, 27–54; *National Journal*, 3 May 1986, 1082; Greenya and Urban 1986; *U.S. News and World Report*, 6 May 1991, 62; Stockman 1992, A21.

---

the Republican fold (MacBride 1976; see also Whitaker 1982; *The Libertarian Party Represents You!* 1992, 1; *National Review*, 21 October 1991, 32–33).

Populism

Populism is an indigenous American perspective that emphasizes the majority rule aspects of early liberalism. Power in the hands of the "little person" is emphasized in an effort to counterbalance significant concentrations of power, either public or private. In England the majority of the people did not get the vote until long after the Glorious Revolution, but in the United States nearly all white males had voting rights within a few decades after the

American Revolution. Ordinary farmers and workers began to demand the same rights to participate in government and share in its benefits as the upper and middle classes enjoyed.

Populism appeared early in American history; the Jeffersonian Republicans used populist arguments to good effect against the Federalists, though their party was in fact led by wealthy southern slaveholders. Andrew Jackson, elected president in 1828, also reflected populist values. Though well-off himself, Jackson opened federal jobs to those outside the elite and eliminated monopoly privileges previously granted to some businesses. At the same time, he pursued very harsh policies against Native Americans, whom most white Americans hated (Schlesinger Jr. 1946; Remini 1981; see also Hofstadter 1974, 56–85).

The origins of the modern populist movement are in the late nineteenth century, when the first political party calling itself populist was formed by southern and western farmers who felt they were mistreated by banks and railroad companies and were powerless in the face of the major economic forces of their day. From its beginning, populism has emphasized empowerment as a way in which the "little person" can assert his or her rights over and against large concentrations of economic power. The Populist party tried to bring all middle- and lower-class people together against the "big interests" by supporting labor unions and economic (but not social) equality for blacks (Hofstadter 1955, 60–130; see also Pollack 1962; Goodwyn 1976; Boyte and Riessman 1986).

The movement's "darker side" expresses itself in the victim's stereotypical perceived need for scapegoats, and, for populists, scapegoats have often been minorities.

Disagreement about the nature of historic populism has led to continuing disputes about whether traditionalists (right) or progressives (left) have the stronger right to inherit the populist mantle. Our conviction is that both sides are justified in staking a claim, for populism was and is concerned about empowerment both for the purpose of restoring or maintaining traditional values and for breaking up large concentrations of economic power (Hertzke 1993).

The historic populist movement failed, partly because many farmers did not agree with its relatively progressive stance on social issues, and the populists merged with the Democrats. In the wake of defeat, some populists turned to racist and anti-Catholic crusades (Woodward 1938), while others joined new farm protest movements like the Nonpartisan League of North Dakota and the Farmer-Labor party of Minnesota. The economic side of populism was also preserved in the labor union movement.

During the Great Depression of the 1930s, economic issues predominated, and Americans with populist inclinations turned to the Democratic party and Franklin Roosevelt's New Deal. Time has faded the memory of the New Deal, and populists are once again being pulled in two directions. Liberal anti-discrimination laws passed in the 1960s alienated some populists, particularly in the South, from the Democrats. Others, concerned about rising crime and moral decay, were attracted to the New Christian Right, a movement allied with conservatives to push for government enforcement of some aspects of Christian morality (Zwier 1982). This style of populism, which is most concerned with social issues, is termed **right populism** or right-wing populism (see Profile of Pat Buchanan).

Historic populism placed greatest emphasis on economic inequities caused by concentrated economic power. From the beginnings of the populist movement in the 1890s, there have been populists who have called upon their followers to ignore racial and ethnic divisions and unite in common opposition to the rich. Early in his career Tom Watson, a leading southern populist of the 1890s, called on black and white farmers to bury their differences: "You are kept apart that you may be separately fleeced of your earnings. You are made to hate each other because upon that hatred is rested the keystone of the arch of financial despotism which enslaves you both. You are deceived and blinded that you may not see how this race antagonism perpetuates a monetary system which beggars both" (Watson 1967b, 371–72).

This strand of the populist tradition, which we call **left populism** or left-wing populism, is being revived today by populists like Jesse Jackson (see Profile) and Senator Tom Harkin of Iowa. It focuses on economic issues and accuses right-wing populists of dividing the ordinary people and, intentionally or unintentionally, helping the privileged (Boyte, Booth, and Max 1986, ix–x, 6–26). Right-wing populists counter that the United States is engaged in a moral war over alternative life-styles and

PROFILE

Pat Buchanan: Right Populist

Pat Buchanan (UPI/Bettmann)

He has been called a "pit bull of American politics" and himself acknowledges that some of his writing has been "rough as a cob." Patrick Buchanan may never be elected president, but his 1992 campaign for the Republican nomination made him a leading spokesperson for right populism in the United States. Like previous right populist leaders, such as George Wallace, Buchanan stirred strong emotions: his friends saw him as a stand-up guy who told it like it was; his enemies saw him as an anti-Semite, a racist, and a fascist. To George Bush and other traditional Republicans, his candidacy was a troubling sign of discontent among the populists attracted to the GOP by Ronald Reagan.

Patrick J. Buchanan was born in 1938 into a middle-class Washington, D.C., Catholic family. His father, a combative Scots-Irishman, made each of his seven sons hit a punching bag in the basement four hundred times each day or risk a whipping. Young Pat learned his lessons well: he was suspended from Georgetown University for a year for punching two policemen who stopped him for speeding—"I was ahead on points until they pulled out their nightsticks," he recalls. Later, at Columbia Journalism School, he belted a liberal fellow student in the mouth. After graduation from Columbia, Buchanan began to fight with words instead of fists, becoming an editorial writer for the conservative *St. Louis Globe-Democrat*.

While he was writing for the *Globe-Democrat*, a friend, Don Hesse, introduced Buchanan to Richard Nixon. When Nixon became president, Buchanan was hired as a speechwriter. Whenever Nixon wanted hard-hitting attacks on his opponents, he turned to Buchanan, whom a colleague describes as "a damn good, slug-em-right-between-the-eyes speechwriter." After Nixon's fall, Buchanan became a newspaper commentator and television journalist. On such programs as PBS's "McLaughlin Group" and CNN's "Crossfire," he transformed the formerly sedate and dull format of the political talk show into a setting for lively and heated debates that sometimes turned into shouting matches.

While serving as White House communications director in the Reagan administration, Buchanan found himself shut out of policy influence by more moderate advisers, including the president's wife, Nancy, who distrusted him. Buchanan eventually concluded that the Republican party was dominated by elitists, a conclusion reinforced when

Reagan was succeeded by George Bush. A militant anticommunist during the cold war, Buchanan called for a return to pre–World War II isolationist policies, arguing, "now that communism has been defeated, America should come home." Buchanan opposed the Persian Gulf War, which most conservatives supported, as a needless foreign entanglement, and he called for halting all foreign aid. By late 1991, Buchanan was so dissatisfied with Bush's performance that he announced his own candidacy for the presidency.

Throughout his campaign, Buchanan emphasized populist themes that distinguished him from the conservative and libertarian traditions. Like conservatives, he favored lower taxes, but unlike them he wanted to cut the military and reduce the U.S. international role and thus the defense spending burden on the taxpayer. Like libertarians, he wanted a free market economy, but unlike them, he wanted government involvement in promoting traditional morality. "The Republican party," he said in his autobiography *Right from the Beginning*, "should stand for traditional values even if that means standing against laissez-faire." He called himself a "trade hawk" and promised to protect workers' jobs from "unfair" Japanese competition, opposing the libertarian free trade philosophy.

Buchanan generated the most controversy when he talked about race and ethnicity. Unlike right populists of the past, he did not advocate racial segregation, but he made it clear that he aimed to represent "the Euro-Americans, who founded the United States." He opposed statehood for Spanish-speaking Puerto Rico and called for restricting non-European immigration to keep American culture from becoming "some landfill called multiculturalism." "Why are we more shocked when a dozen people are killed in Vilnius [Lithuania] than by a massacre in Burundi [Africa]?" he asked an English interviewer. "Because

they are white people. That's who we are. That's what America comes from." The loudest uproar came when Buchanan accused American Jews of being an "amen corner" for Israel and of wanting war in the Persian Gulf for the sake of Israeli and not American interests. Mainstream conservatives like William F. Buckley, Jr., called this statement anti-Semitic.

After his 1992 bid failed, Buchanan eventually supported Bush's reelection campaign, but he remained controversial within the Republican party. In a speech to the Republican convention he blasted the Democratic party as a haven of homosexuals and radical feminists and attacked Bill Clinton's wife, Hillary Rodham Clinton, for allegedly supporting the idea that "12-year-olds should have the right to sue their parents." The speech created so much dissension in the party that some Republicans accused Buchanan of contributing to the party's defeat in November.

Although a wealthy man (like many populist leaders in the past), Buchanan saw himself as speaking for the common person's values. In his autobiography, he proposed a number of populist constitutional amendments, including the initiative and referendum (see Chapter 3) at the national level and giving Congress power to set aside Supreme Court decisions. Most Americans, he was sure, shared his views because they had been brought up to believe as he did. "Country, faith and flag," he wrote, "these are the things worth dying for; these are the things worth fighting for; these are the things worth living for." Everything about Pat Buchanan's past suggested that, despite the failed 1992 campaign, he would continue to fight for populist causes.

Source: Buchanan 1988; *Newsweek*, 27 January 1992, 22–24; *New York Times*, 1 March 1991, 1; *Christian Science Monitor*, 13 April 1992, 9; *Congressional Quarterly Weekly Report*, 22 August 1992, 2543.

Jesse Jackson: Left Populist

Jesse Jackson (Reuters/Bettmann)

Jesse Jackson and his followers might be offended at seeing him paired here with Pat Buchanan. Yet both reflect the majoritarian values embodied in historic American populism. Like Buchanan, Jackson has run for president without ever receiving a party's nomination. But both remain forces to be reckoned with in American politics.

Jesse Louis Jackson was born October 8, 1941, in Greenville, South Carolina, the illegitimate son of a sixteen-year-old girl. A star athlete in high school, he won a football scholarship to the University of Illinois in 1959. Denied the chance to play quarterback because he was black, he transferred to all-black North Carolina Agricultural and Technical College, where he helped organize black students for civil rights protests. After graduating in 1962, he attended seminary, then joined the staff of Dr. Martin Luther King's Southern Christian Leadership Conference (SCLC). In 1966 King made Jackson head of Operation Breadbasket, a SCLC project in Chicago.

Reverend Jackson first gained national attention after King's assassination on April 4, 1968. As rioting swept black neighborhoods across the country, Jackson appeared on television and called on young blacks to "put your rocks down, put your bottles down," and follow the slain leader's creed of nonviolence. His effort to halt the violence made him a national black leader. By 1971 he had left the SCLC and had his own independent organization, People United to Serve Humanity (PUSH).

Jackson's activities as head of Operation Breadbasket and, later, PUSH reflected a populist orientation. Denouncing Chicago business leaders for discrimination against blacks, he led boycotts against one store chain after another until owners agreed to hire more black workers. He also strongly advocated increased spending on social programs, more government regulation of business, and affirmative action programs to make up for past discrimination against blacks. At the same time, the Baptist preacher appealed to the social conservatism of his black constituents. Unlike traditional liberals, Jackson in his 1984 run for the presidency condemned abortion, supported tougher measures against the crime that plagued black communities, and blamed some black problems on eroding morality rather than white racism. Urging young blacks to shun "hustling" in favor of school and work, he told them, "Nobody can save us from us but us."

When Jackson announced his candidacy, he was opposed by black leaders, who were backing former Vice-President Walter Mondale. Despite some resistance from the black political establishment, Jackson's dynamic style and slashing attacks on President Reagan's conservative economic policies won him the support of the black churches and, through them, the black masses. Jackson received more than 80 percent of the black vote in the Democratic primaries, and many new black voters registered as a result of his candidacy. His credentials as an opponent of racism came into question when he made a derogatory reference to Jews and accepted support from Louis Farrakhan, leader of the racist Black Muslim religious sect. Jackson also visited Cuba and praised Fidel Castro. These incidents hindered Jackson's hope to build the "Rainbow Coalition," which he had long

Don Wright. Courtesy *The Palm Beach Post*.

advocated, composed of blacks and poor whites against the rich.

In his 1988 campaign, Jackson deemphasized strictly black concerns in favor of economic populism. He even tempered his stand on abortion to broaden his appeal to Democratic constituencies. He continued to call for economic reforms that went well beyond conventional liberalism, including controls on the closing of plants by corporations. Yet, excluding the issues of race, abortion, the Equal Rights Amendment, affirmative action, and foreign policy, Jackson, even in 1988, sounded like earlier southern populists, including George Wallace.

Jackson emerged from the twenty-state primary in March 1988 (Super Tuesday) as the major opponent of Michael Dukakis. At the Democratic National Convention his "virtual lock" on the black vote gave him enough leverage to affect the party platform but not enough to secure the nomination. Following Dukakis's defeat in the 1988 election, there was much speculation about Jackson's future political intentions. During the primary campaign, criticism had been directed at his lack of experience in elected office.

When Jackson's name was mentioned as a possible candidate for mayor of the District of Columbia, he declined to run. Ceding the mayor's office to Sharon Pratt Kelly, Jackson ran for and won the post of "shadow senator" instead. This position as District of Columbia spokesperson in the Senate has some visibility but no political power. Jackson turned increasingly to work in the mass media, sponsoring his own television program and appearing on many talk shows.

In the 1992 presidential election, Jackson was angered by what he felt were Clinton's blatant efforts to recapture right populists (Reagan Democrats). He argued that minority issues were being ignored, or at least downplayed, in the Clinton campaign. While he worked on voter registration drives and for black candidates throughout the nation, he rarely spoke with warmth about Clinton. Because the African-American vote is so crucial to any national and many state-level Democrat's chances of election, Jesse Jackson is likely to play a role in the politics of his party for years to come. Whether he will ever again choose to become a candidate for national or state office, however, remains a question.

Source: Landess and Quinn 1985; Reed Jr. 1986; Faw and Skelton 1986; *Congressional Quarterly Weekly Report*, 23 July 1988, 2011; *New York Times*, 19 June 1992, A1, A24; *New York Times*, 14 June 1992, A30; *New York Times*, 28 February 1990, A20.

TABLE 1.2   THE FOUR MAJOR POLITICAL PERSPECTIVES COMPARED

DISTINCTIVE EMPHASIS	FAVOR	CANNOT ACCEPT	AGREE WITH
	Conservatism		
Traditional economics and social frameworks	• Free market system • Strong measures against crime • Strong government role in promoting national security • Strong government role in upholding moral values	• Liberal and libertarian optimism about human nature • Libertarian negative views on government • Libertarian opposition to government regulations of morality	• Libertarian laissez-faire views • Populist emphasis on traditional values
	Liberalism		
Equality and minority rights	• Tighter government regulations on business • Strong government role in providing public services (education, health care) • Strong government role in promoting equal economic opportunity • Progressive taxes to support social welfare programs • Strong government role in protecting minority groups from discrimination	• Libertarian negative views on government • Libertarian opposition to government planning and regulating of the economy • Conservative and libertarian reliance on the free market system	• Populist support for strong government role in assisting common people • Libertarian tolerance on social issues

the nature and role of families and that moral issues take precedence over economic issues (*Congressional Quarterly Weekly Report*, 22 August 1992, 2526–27; Youngdale 1975, 117–49).

The two strands of populism have been important in recent elections because they constitute voting blocks that tend to be Republican if right populism is emphasized and Democratic if left populism is emphasized. Ross Perot, in his campaign for the presidency in 1992, used elements of both strands of populism as well as libertarianism (see Profile in Chapter 4). Table 1.2 outlines ways in which the major perspectives relate to one another.

PUBLIC OPINION AND PRACTICAL POLITICS

Most Americans do not spend a great deal of time thinking about political issues, and their beliefs are difficult to label. Public opinion surveys reveal, however, that 92 percent of Americans have political beliefs that roughly fit one of the four major perspectives identified in this textbook (see Table 1.3). The remaining 8 percent are either wholly inattentive to politics or divided among two or more of the perspectives. Of these perspectives, the libertarian has grown the most in the last decade, while the number of Americans described as inattentive

TABLE 1.2   *(Continued)*

DISTINCTIVE EMPHASIS	FAVOR	CANNOT ACCEPT	AGREE WITH
		Libertarianism	
Individual freedom	• Free market system • Limited government role in all areas • National defense as a legitimate government role but must be efficient and nonentangling	• Conservative support for regulating morality • Liberal support for regulating the economy, especially to protect minority groups from discrimination	• Conservative laissez-faire views • Liberal tolerance on social issues
		Populism	
Majority rule and empowerment of the common people	• Strong government role in empowering the "little person"	• Liberal and libertarian view that morality should not be regulated	• Liberal support for strong government role in assisting common people • Conservative emphasis on traditional values
		Right Populism	
Traditional morality	• Government enforcement of majoritarian views		
		Left Populism	
Economic equality	• Government action to break up concentrations of power		

declined. In terms of percentages, liberals and populists are in the middle, behind libertarians but ahead of conservatives. In the largest sense, all four groups are well represented in almost all age, regional, racial, income, educational, and religious categories.

A few trends are worth noting. Liberals have the highest education levels, but libertarians have the highest income level by a slight margin. Nonwhite and lower income Americans are more apt than other Americans to be populist, but white populists are most likely to be hostile to nonwhites, making it hard for populists to work together. Conservative and populist perspectives are strongest in the West and South, where income is usually lower than in the Northeast and Midwest. Populists have the youngest average age, while libertarians have the oldest average. Conservatives as a whole have a higher percentage of members of Christian churches than the other perspectives.

Figure 1.1 suggests a way to conceptualize the differences among the perspectives on government regulation. Conservatives and libertarians agree on the need to keep government regulation of the economy to a minimum but disagree on government enforcement of morality. Liberals want more regulation of the economy and less regulation of personal be-

TABLE 1.3   SELECTED CHARACTERISTICS OF THE MAJOR POLITICAL PERSPECTIVES, 1991

	PERCENT OF POPULATION	AVERAGE AGE	NORTHEAST/ MIDWEST v. SOUTH/WEST (IN PERCENTS)	PERCENT WHITE	PERCENT WITH HOUSEHOLD INCOME OVER $30,000	PERCENT WITH AT LEAST SOME COLLEGE	PROTESTANT/ CATHOLIC (IN PERCENTS)
Conservative	18.4	46	41.4/58.6	86	38.7	37.9	60.9/35.6
Liberal	23.5	44	51.4/48.6	90	48.1	55.8	60.4/25.2
Libertarian	27.8	50	45.8/54.2	93	49.6	48.5	63.9/26.9
Populist	22.2	41	41.0/59.0	70	38.0	44.8	65.7/20.0

Note: The percentages add up to less than 92 percent because the remaining people in the survey (8.1 percent) were wholly inattentive or divided among two or more perspectives. Because of the split-form sampling system employed by the General Social Surveys, construction of the scale resulted in 472 eligible respondents, one-third of the total possible sample. Because of this system and the fact that these four classifications expand upon the normal categories of political analysis (liberal/conservative, Democrat/Republican), this table should be interpreted with care.

Source: General Social Surveys. National Opinion Research Center at the University of Chicago. Compiled by Marc Maynard, Roper Center Survey, Storrs, Conn.

Figure 1.1   How the Perspectives Differ on Government Regulation

		The Economy	
		Regulate	Do Not Regulate
Morality	Regulate	Populist	Conservative
	Do Not Regulate	Liberal	Libertarian

Source: Maddox and Lilie 1984, 5.

havior. Populists believe that the majority has the right to regulate the behavior of minorities with regard to both economics and morality. For them there is no purely private sphere of life immune from government regulation, unless the majority chooses to recognize the need for change.

As the Perspectives section at the end of the following chapters in this textbook will demonstrate, the root beliefs of the four major perspectives permit evaluation of institutions and issues at the level of their observers and practitioners. One perspective's concern about an issue, however, does not preclude another perspective's concern for the same issue.

While we acknowledge overlaps among perspectives and differences of opinion, even subgroups, within them, our purpose is to introduce the general differences among American political perspectives.

Diverging views among the four major political perspectives make compromise necessary for the American system of government to work. Yet compromise may take a long time to emerge because beliefs are deeply felt. Politicians can be reluctant to take strong stands on issues because at least some of the people they represent are likely to hold strong opposing views. Almost all political leaders must and do compromise, but it is important to remember that those who participate in the system are compromisers who start out from different perspectives. As the course of U.S. history indicates, crises and strong presidents often reframe American political alignments (see Table 1.1). The Great Depression and the Democrat Franklin Roosevelt provide one example.

Roosevelt was a liberal with an elite New York background and family ties to a number of American presidents. He took advantage of the unpopularity of the Republican President Herbert Hoover to get elected on a mild reform

Duane Powell. Copyright 1992, *Raleigh News & Observer*. Distributed by Los Angeles Times Syndicate. Reprinted with permission.

plank in 1932. Once in office, Roosevelt took an activist stance, working toward new programs that solidified a new coalition of liberals, both varieties of populists, and the conservative South. Libertarian principles were discredited by the force of the Great Depression, which had thrown one-fourth of American workers out of work. Republicans were reduced to saying no or maybe to a very popular president. While Republicans preached about the national debt, Roosevelt and the Democrats were winning elections through appeals to the common people that were reinforced through government spending.

One of Roosevelt's supporters was a young broadcaster-turned-actor named Ronald Reagan. Gradually this Democrat became a Republican, partly out of concern that Democratic foreign policies might have been too "soft" on the adversaries of the United States. When Reagan ran for president in 1980, he modified the Republican message to emphasize a tax cut instead of just a balanced budget. In essence, Reagan was making promises in the hope of attracting new converts. By also supporting conservative social stands attractive to populists, he initiated a "creeping realignment" that helped Republicans. Support for liberal policies was reduced, although New Deal programs were not phased out. Democratic liberals argued that the poor were being neglected, but at least at the presidential level of politics Reagan managed to gain a working majority (Leuchtenburg 1983, 209–35).

Both Roosevelt and Reagan understood that elections are won by appealing, through promises, to a diverse group of voters. From the perspective of long-range national interest, the problem with promises is that they often involve benefit programs and tax reductions that can increase the federal debt.

In their attempt to win elections, politicians combine parts of different perspectives, trying to find the combination that will give them victories on election day. Politicians represent-

ing small and relatively homogeneous constituencies may find victories easy to achieve. They may even be able to hold to one perspective. Ted Kennedy, the liberal's liberal, for example, and Orrin Hatch, the conservative's conservative, can probably win Senate elections in their respective states again and again. Those who run for president, however, or for senator or governor in a large state with a diverse population, must trade some ideological purity for the skills of communication and compromise. Once in the presidency, Roosevelt used skills honed as governor of New York to emphasize the plight of the "little person" and the need for government intervention. Likewise Ronald Reagan, former governor of the populous and even more diverse state of California, used communication skills to build his volatile coalition of conservatives, populists, libertarians, and even liberals, attending to the imperatives of pragmatism rather than the absolutism of ideology. President Bill Clinton has worked hard to be "a new kind of Democrat" who reaches beyond his party's liberal base.

As Roosevelt's and Reagan's success demonstrates, the perspectives people adopt are one important factor in American politics, but not the only factor. For several reasons, what happens in the political world may not conform to what any of the major perspectives envisions as the ideal society. First, many people combine at least some beliefs from different perspectives to form individual views on how the government should affect individual lives. Few politicians and few voters are ideologically pure, and it is important to keep this in mind as you read the profiles in this textbook. We have labeled people as belonging to a perspective, but perspective rarely serves as an accurate predictor of position on every issue. For example, although Jesse Jackson best fits the label of a left populist, his position on affirmative action reflects a liberal rather than populist stance.

Safe Again This Election

The Family

Apple Pie

The Flag

The Deficit

WHY DOESN'T SOME CANDIDATE HAVE THE COURAGE TO TELL ME THE TRUTH THAT WILL COST HIM MY VOTE?

Toles. Courtesy *Buffalo News*.

Second, not all supporters of a perspective apply it with equal consistency. All libertarians want limited government and all populists emphasize majority rule, but there are differences among them on just what government activities are permissible and what rights the minority should be allowed. Jack Kemp, who looks at this writing to be a leading conservative candidate for president in 1996, represented a working-class district in Congress prior to his appointment as secretary of housing and urban development by President George Bush. Kemp also believes that government should legislate morality. On this basis he should be a populist. His support for market-oriented programs to achieve economic development in depressed areas suggests libertarianism. This somewhat contradictory combination of right populism and libertarianism makes Kemp appear, to many observers, to be a conservative.

Third, pressures of immediate self-interest can lead people to act inconsistently. If, for example, a libertarian member of Congress represents a steel-producing area hard hit by foreign imports, he or she may be pressured by constituents into voting for import restrictions that intrude on the free market. Likewise, a liberal member of Congress may be compelled to vote against civil rights legislation by populist constituents, as Arkansas's Senator J. William Fulbright did in the 1960s.

Finally, the American political process demands compromise. Although most politicians sincerely believe in one perspective more than the others and work to advance it, perfect consistency can be purchased only at the price of political ineffectiveness.

MARXISM: A ROAD NOT TAKEN

A number of different perspectives, from radical ecology to facism, stand outside the American consensus. While they do not have the popular support of mainstream perspectives, they provide important insights into the American political system. We have selected to examine two for the critiques they offer. The first is Marxism.

Despite its failure to thrive in the United States and the recent collapse of communist governments in the Soviet Union and Eastern Europe, the Marxist perspective remains important for American students for several reasons. First, Marxist forms of socialism represent a markedly different strain of ideology from American perspectives in terms of the organization of the economy and the definition of government's role. Moreover, the Marxist emphasis on economic causation and class conflict has had a major impact on all the social sciences because of the insights it provides. And, until recently, Marxist-Leninist governments have been the major rivals of the United States in the international arena. Between World War II and 1990, the military forces of the former Soviet Union and Eastern Europe were the greatest single threat to American security and interests.

Marxist ideological thought is still among the most influential in the world. Many in formerly communist nations continue to distrust what they see as the excessive individualism and resultant economic inequalities in countries like the United States. Marxist ideas are still part of the European scene, although with different emphases than previously. China, with the largest population in the world, still calls itself Marxist. Third World nations like India, industrial giants like Japan, and some nations in Western Europe such as Italy still have active Marxist political parties. Hostilities in Europe and Asia have drawn the United States into conflicts in the past and could do so again; Americans should understand the possible ideological roots of such conflicts.

In other European nations elements of Marxism's economic critiques of capitalism and the political concepts of liberalism have combined in an approach known as **democratic socialism**. Believing that Marxists are unduly authoritarian and liberals unduly naive about the inequities of capitalism, social democrats support democracy at the same time that they advocate various types of socialism, some of which include government ownership of industry. Orthodox Marxists believe that democratic socialism is weak and will lead to a restoration of capitalism. In the United States, however, democratic socialism has had more appeal than Marxism because it combines the strongest aspect of Marxism—its critique—with liberalism, a major American perspective. Yet neither democratic socialism nor Marxism ever approached the status of a major perspective. Under these circumstances, we include the Marxist perspective as a critique and leave it to you to consider the possibilities for democratic socialism in the United States, based on an understanding of its components.

Today, the nations of Eastern Europe are attempting transitions from Marxism-Leninism to democracy and some private ownership. These evolving governmental systems will not necessarily become democratic; perhaps they will combine authoritarianism and democracy in systems that will challenge conventional thinking (Pye 1990, 3–19). They might also combine socialism and capitalism in dynamic new forms. But, with much dependent on the political skills and survival of charismatic leaders like Boris Yeltsin, we hesitate to predict the future of these nations.

In any case, an understanding of Marxism is essential to students of politics, and the Marxist perspective will be included in the Perspectives sections at the end of the following chapters in this textbook.

Marxist Theory

Marxism arose in response to the same capitalist abuses that gave rise to Mill's liberalism. Instead of emphasizing reform, however, Marxism rejects capitalism and private property and calls for revolutionary change in the economic system. The blueprint for revolution is laid out by Karl Marx (1818–83) and Friedrich Engels (1820–95) in *The Communist Manifesto* (1848).

Influenced by French and German revolutionary thought, Marx and Engels had a much greater commitment to economic equality than did the Anglo-American political philosophers. Marx and Engels argued that human history was a story of class struggles. Conflict was inevitable between the ruling class (the group controlling the economy) and the oppressed class (the group that did all the labor). Marxists thought that the most recent historical form of this struggle would soon end in victory by the working class. This victory would actually eliminate the need for government, which Marx and Engels saw as a product of class oppression. The idea of freedom, so essential to Anglo-American political thought, to Marx meant understanding proper social and economic relationships, not the right to do as one chooses. More important than political equality (the right to vote) was the redistribution of wealth to ensure social and economic equality (Marx and Engels 1967, 57–78).

Marx and Engels argued that the majority of people were not "free," morally or psychologically, to accept or even understand their view of history as class struggle. For this reason, they suggested that only a small minority of workers who understood history would be in charge of a Marxist society. When they spoke of government, they called it a dictatorship "by" rather than "over" the working class (Raddatz 1978, 195, 198, 209, 217; see also Padover 1978, 222–50; Harding 1981, 2:84–86).

Vladimir Lenin (1870–1924), leader of the first successful communist revolution, later argued that the working class in Russia was not large enough to have developed a strong sense of class consciousness and the need for revolution. While the state modernized, a dictatorship "over" the majority by the Communist party would be necessary (Harding 1981, 2:100–108). The new Soviet Union established after the Bolshevik Revolution in 1917 and most of the regimes in Eastern Europe established after World War II claimed to be practitioners of Marxism-Leninism.

In later life Marx and, particularly, Engels seemed to soften their position on the need for a violent revolt by the working class to overthrow the ruling class. This change came in reaction to the electoral successes of German socialism as a democratic political force. In the preface to the 1895 edition of Marx's *Class Struggles in France (1848–1850)* (1850), Engels stated that the growth of social democracy

> proceeds as spontaneously, as steadily, as irresistibly, and at the same time as tranquilly as a natural process. We can count even today on two and a half million voters. If it continues in this fashion, by the end of the century we shall conquer the greater part of the middle section of society and grow into the decisive power in the land (Engels 1964, 27).

In Marxist theory, **socialism** refers to the stage of society between capitalism and communism. During this stage, the people are ruled by the dictatorship of the proletariat, under which the base of communism is built. In a socialist society, both the political power and the means of production are centralized. Non-Marxist definitions of socialism stress government ownership of the means of production. **Communism,** which is the end goal of Marxist theory, refers to a classless society with common ownership of the means of production. The term **Marxism** encompasses the political, economic, and social theories expressed by Karl Marx and Friedrich Engels. These theories maintain that history progresses through class struggles and that society will move from capitalism to socialism and eventually to a worldwide communist society. Finally, **Marxism-Leninism** refers to Lenin's qualifications and implementation of Marx, including the idea of a dictatorship "over" rather than "by" the proletariat.

Marxism-Leninism is the idea of government that operated in the former Soviet Union and Eastern Europe, and, prior to recent efforts at political and economic reform, anticommunists often cited those governments as demonstrating the negative results that can occur in applications of Marxist-Leninist ideology to the real world. Yet identifying all Marxists with the former Soviet Union or Eastern European communists is a mistake, for the Marxist position has always been diverse. Currently Russia, most other members of the Commonwealth of Independent States, Poland, and the Czech Republic have joined governments in Hungary and the former Yugoslavia in moving away from a centralized economy and toward more decentralized market-related systems. Russian President Boris Yeltsin has worked hard to move Russia toward a market economy. Even so, these reforms and the attempts at rapprochement with the West have been triggered by severe domestic difficulties, with the real potential for political instability if the changes do not satisfy the people of these countries.

Marxism in the United States

Marxist ideas have been available in the United States from the 1850s on. In fact, Karl Marx wrote a popular column in the *New York Daily Tribune* for ten years during the 1850s and 1860s (Payne 1968, 268–70). The first Marxist political group founded by Marx's friend Joseph Weydemeyer in 1853 was short-lived. But by 1870 the First Communist International,

founded by Marx in London in 1864, had established several "sections" in the United States under a central committee composed largely of German immigrants. It was peripheral as a political force and by 1872 had ceased to function (Freymond and Molnar 1966, 21).

The first Marxist party in the United States was the Socialist Labor party, founded in 1877 and patterned on the German Socialist Labor party (Rosenstone, Behr, and Lazarus 1984, 89). It, too, had only limited success. After 1890 its foremost spokesperson was Daniel De Leon, a great communicator who successfully attracted many non-German Americans to the Marxist standard. But by refusing to cooperate with non-Marxist trade unions, he split and mortally wounded the party. His action led to an "anti–De Leon" faction that merged with the social democratic Socialist party of Eugene V. Debs (Quint 1953, 332–40). De Leon attempted to compete with Debs for working-class votes through his leadership in the more radical Industrial Workers of the World (IWW), but he was barred from IWW membership in 1908 over his reluctance to commit himself to revolutionary terrorism and various forms of industrial sabotage (Herreshoff 1967, 153–58).

Although the appeal of Marxist socialism declined in the 1920s following Lenin's death and the struggle between Josef Stalin and Leon Trotsky, Marxism experienced a brief resurgence during the Great Depression of the 1930s (Cantor 1968, 231–36). The Communist Party of the United States of America (CPUSA), under Earl Browder, grew to include approximately eighty thousand members (Foster 1952, 420–21). Browder argued for peaceful forms of coexistence between capitalism and communism, but soon after World War II he was expelled from the party, which thereafter connected itself much more closely to Soviet foreign policy (Foster 1952, 469). The growing cold war between the Soviet Union and the United States and the anticommunist witch hunts led by Wisconsin's Senator Joseph Mc-

Carthy in the early 1950s ensured that communism would no longer be marketable in the United States under that name and tainted those who called themselves socialists as well (Baritz 1971, 331–33).

The revived student movement of the 1960s and 1970s was attracted to the humanistic aspects of Marx's critique of capitalism, such as his explanation of worker alienation, but it rejected the Marxist societies that dominated Eastern Europe as failures and much of Marx's theory as obsolete. The revisionist Marxism of C. Wright Mills and Herbert Marcuse served as the basis for the New Left critique. Although the Students for a Democratic Society (SDS) attempted to create an alliance with the working class, its success was minimal and its impact outside the university community limited (Adelson 1972, 208, 249–64). With the end of the Vietnam War, it vanished as a force in American political life. Although Marxist parties frequently run candidates for office in presidential elections (see Profile of Angela Davis), they usually garner considerably less than 1 percent of the vote.

What are the reasons for Marxist socialism's lack of success in the United States? The sociologist Daniel Bell has suggested that American socialism was simply too dogmatic to operate effectively in the American political landscape (Bell 1967, 5–12). The political theorist David McLellan points out that the United States lacks a feudal past and has less entrenched class privilege to overcome. He emphasizes that the frontier may have provided a safety valve for unrest by attracting skilled labor and keeping unemployment low. Finally, he suggests that the waves of immigration and the consequent diverse ethnic identity of the American working class may have prevented the labor movement from developing a cohesive class consciousness (McLellan 1979, 321).

Perhaps the main reasons for the failure of Marxism in the United States are to be found in the prosperity of its working classes. Throughout most of American history, wages, living standards, and working conditions have improved more rapidly than in other industrial countries. As one disappointed early twentieth-century socialist put it, socialism has "foundered on shoals of roast beef and apple pie" (Sombart quoted in McLellan 1979, 321).

FEMINISM: ADVOCACY OF WOMEN'S RIGHTS AND INTERESTS

We have chosen feminism as the second of two perspectives that critique the American system for three reasons. First, while a majority of women do not subscribe to this viewpoint in its entirety or to the exclusion of major viewpoints, some of the major perspectives have embraced certain parts of its agenda. Thus feminism has had a major impact on the lives of American women and regularly interacts with the political system.* Second, an emerging feminist scholarship suggests that men and women, due to both biology and culture, relate to the world in different manners and that these differences, in turn, lead men and women to give priority to different public policy issues. It is certainly the case that as more women have become elected officials, issues relating to the physical and mental health of the family have been given higher priority (Gilligan 1982, 24–63; see also Fricke, Holden, and Elder 1992, 1–63). Finally, feminism differs in fairly distinctive ways from each of the other perspectives discussed in this book, and the

---

* While feminism clearly is growing in strength among educated women, it is not embraced by a majority of women. In 1989, 58 percent of all women did not consider themselves feminists, while only 33 percent of female college students did not consider themselves feminists. However, only 14 percent of all women considered themselves strong feminists in a 1990 survey (*American Enterprise*, November/December 1991, 92–93).

PROFILE
Angela Davis: American Marxist

Angela Davis (UPI/Bettmann)

Though she has run for vice-president and been the defendant in a celebrated trial, Angela Davis is no longer a household name in the United States. When she ran as Gus Hall's running mate on the Communist party ticket in 1984, she was decisively repudiated by the electorate, as all previous communist candidates had been before her. Nonetheless, this articulate professor of philosophy continues to work for what Marx would have wanted, a socialist society that does not make its profits by exploiting its poorest members.

Angela Davis was born in Birmingham, Alabama, in 1944, the daughter of a service station owner and a teacher. Though her parents were part of Birmingham's black middle class, Davis began to experience the effects of white racism at four, when her family moved to a house on the edge of a white neighborhood. "What made them [whites] different," she says, "was the frown on their faces, the way they stood a hundred feet away and glared at us, their refusal to speak when we said 'Good afternoon.' " When other black families moved across the street into the white area, their homes were often bombed, and Birmingham's white police never investigated. So many bombings took place that the neighborhood became known as "Dynamite Hill."

When Davis was fourteen, her parents, who had both been active in the civil rights movement, took her out of the segregated, inferior black school system in Birmingham and sent her to a progressive high school in New York. There her teachers, many of whom were schooled in Marxist analysis, introduced her to *The Communist Manifesto*, which "hit me like a bolt of lightning." Davis became persuaded that capitalism, not just racist whites, was responsible for the oppression of blacks. Marxism "could be an ideal socio-economic arrangement; every person could give to the society according to his ability and his talents, and in turn he could receive material and spiritual aid in accordance with his needs." Before she finished high school in 1961, Davis was a convinced Marxist.

After attending Brandeis University and the University of Frankfurt in Germany, Davis went to the University of California, San Diego, in 1967 to study for a Ph.D. in philosophy under Herbert Marcuse, a noted Marxist philosopher. While

contrasts it suggests aid in the understanding of other perspectives. The Profile of Molly Yard provides an example of the feminist political perspective in the American political system.

It is important to define **feminism** at the outset because, as with Marxism, ideological enemies have succeeded in attaching negative connotations to the word "feminist." Just who is a feminist? To say that a feminist is someone

there, she joined various black power groups like the Black Panther party and the Student Nonviolent Coordinating Committee (SNCC). By 1968, disillusioned with the infighting among these groups and the sexism of many of the male members, Davis was looking for a disciplined Marxist party with a consistent ideology. She became a member of the Communist Party of the United States of America (CPUSA) in July 1968.

Davis first came to public notice in 1969, when she was teaching at the University of California at Los Angeles. First, Governor Ronald Reagan tried to get her fired under an old law that prohibited communists from teaching at state universities. Then she became involved in a defense committee for George Jackson, a black convict in California's Soledad Prison, with whom she fell in love. On August 7, 1970, Jackson's brother Jonathan entered the Marin County Courthouse with three guns belonging to Davis. In an apparent attempt to free his brother, he freed three black prisoners and took Judge Harold Haley and four others hostage. In the ensuing gun battle, Jonathan, Judge Haley, and two of the prisoners were killed. Charged as an accomplice to murder, kidnapping, and conspiracy, Davis fled California but was arrested in New York on October 13, 1970.

Davis's trial became "an international theatrical event." The Soviet government, the CPUSA, and numerous liberal groups, including some mainline religious denominations, mounted an energetic defense campaign, alleging that Davis was innocent and once again being persecuted by Governor Reagan and the capitalist system for her political views. Her defense counsel showed that Davis had bought the guns openly and argued that such a brilliant scholar would never be foolish enough to provide weapons for a jailbreak that could be traced to her. Members of the jury evidently agreed that Jonathan Jackson had taken Davis's

guns and acted alone. On June 4, 1972, they declared her not guilty on all counts. While the trial was going on, George Jackson was killed in an apparent escape attempt.

Since regaining her freedom, Davis has worked to "preserve and build upon the movement" to free "all the others who [remain] draped in chains." Her vice-presidential race was not a serious bid for the office. Rather, she intended to use her celebrity status to draw public attention to Marxism and the Communist party and to attract converts from among the nation's discontented. In her autobiography Davis admits that most of the ordinary American workers whom she wants to liberate still see communism as "not only the enemy, but something immoral, something dirty."

The breakup of the former Soviet Union has sent ripples through communist parties throughout both the First and Third World. Angela Davis and a number of her supporters were "expelled" from the CPUSA in 1992 for wanting to be able to nominate and elect their party officials. She is still convinced that race makes too much of a difference in American life and in her own words is working in "my political practice right now. . . to find ways of coming together in a different way. I'm not suggesting that we do not anchor ourselves in our communities. But I think, to use a metaphor, the rope attached to that anchor should be large enough to allow us to move into other communities. I think it's a really exciting moment." Davis continues to teach political philosophy at the University of California, Santa Cruz, and works to achieve a society where there will be no "Dynamite Hill."

Source: Davis 1974; Lader 1979; *Fortune*, 20 April 1992, 189; Davis 1992, E11.

---

who wishes to advance the rights of women is deceptively simple. Phyllis Schlafly, the conservative Republican president of the Eagle Forum, has little that is good to say about feminism but espouses what she considers to be the traditional interests and welfare of women at every opportunity. She would reject the title "feminist" and yet claims to know more about the true interests of women than feminists. There are a variety of self-declared

PROFILE
Molly Yard: One American Feminist

Molly Yard (UPI/Bettmann)

Molly Yard, at age eighty, looks more like a doting grandmother (which she is) than a retired president of the National Organization for Women. But this grandmother goes mountain hiking with her grandchildren and gives them female dolls that wear construction clothes. This grandmother organized a demonstration outside the White House and said that Ronald Reagan should be impeached. Looks can be deceiving.

Yard was born at a Methodist mission station in Chengdu, the capital of Szechuan Province,

China, in 1912. Her parents had strong social consciences and an understanding of what it costs to pursue ideals. Twice her father lost his job for speaking out on behalf of the poor and oppressed —once his position as a missionary and once the chaplaincy of a major American university.

If Yard's instinct for reform was instilled by her parents and their experiences, her sensitivity to the oppression of women was gained from her earliest period in China and reinforced during most of her working life. "I can still hear," she recalls, the terrified, pained cries of young girls whose feet were bound and unbound. On returning from China she remembers having a naively idealistic view of what it would be like for herself as a girl in the United States, then realizing that even in this nation both athletic and academic preferences were still being given to men. During the Depression years of the 1930s while Yard attended Swathmore, it was her mother's in-home business that kept the family going. Yard remembers her mother's strength during this period and her concern that all her daughters would get the college education she did not have.

Yard's adult life reads like an outline of political reform in the United States. During college she campaigned successfully for the abolition of campus fraternity and sorority systems after a Jewish friend was refused admittance. Her Swarthmore yearbook wrote of her: "Molly . . . with the help of smiling blue eyes . . . manages to escape even the slightest hint of disheveled radicalism. But by

advocates for women, and to distinguish those who are really going to improve the status of women from those who are not inevitably requires some judgments about what is in women's best interest, thus making the definition ideological. For purposes of this book feminists are defined as those who advocate women's rights and interests in all aspects of society, but not those who are expressly anti-

feminist (leaving out Schlafly); a feminist values women and their contributions to society as well as recognizes the historic oppression of women. Feminist demands are the definitions of issues and the policy proposals made by avowed feminists.

As with all the perspectives we examine, the feminist perspective has subdivisions. Social feminists consider women to be funda-

temperament she is an authentic agitator. No abuse is too well established, no precedent too accepted, no majority too overwhelming to silence her." Following graduation, Yard served as the first chair of the National Student Union. In this capacity she met and was befriended by Eleanor Roosevelt, whose husband's New Deal she was criticizing. In the 1940s, Yard was actively involved in national Democratic politics, an interest that continued into the early 1960s. She worked in the successful Senate campaigns of Joseph Clark and with the 1960 Citizens for Kennedy presidential campaign. In 1963, she was a Pennsylvania organizer for Martin Luther King's famous march on Washington. In 1964, she led a massive march in Pittsburgh that culminated in delivering thousands of letters to Pennsylvania's representatives and senators in Congress demanding passage of the 1964 Civil Rights Act.

Yard's consciousness of society's discrimination against women has deepened during the years. Her decision to keep her own name after marrying brought ridicule and difficulties. When she tried to open a bank account in her name and that of her husband, she was told initially that an account with two names on it was possible only if the individuals were not married: she could open the account as her husband's mistress, but not as his wife. Later, as a senior staff member in the VISTA program, Yard discovered that she and the one other woman on the staff were not invited to senior staff meetings. They decided to walk into a staff meeting, uninvited: "They couldn't throw us out," she recalls. Even on the Pennsylvania Democratic Committee women were vastly outnumbered. It was the blatant sexism of American society that finally drove Yard into feminist politics. She became active in the Pennsylvania chapter of the National Organization for Women in the early 1970s and joined the NOW Strike Force, which aimed at getting ERA ratified between 1972 and 1985. When her friend Eleanor Smeal retired as national president of NOW and she was asked to run, she was nearly seventy-five. "I thought if I were 10 years younger, I would love to do it. . . . Then I remembered Elizabeth Cady Stanton and Susan B. Anthony never stopped, even in their 80s."

It was during Yard's term as NOW president, 1987–91, that NOW cooperated in the campaigns to oppose Robert Bork's nomination to the Supreme Court, to support Patricia Schroeder's short-lived drive for the presidency, and to battle Operation Rescue antiabortion activists, suing them under statutes first created to catch racketeers. Abortion opponents were "instructing their children to bite our people on the legs and forming flying wedges," stated Yard, who also said, "they have no right to close down a legitimate business." Five decades as a political reformer have taught Yard some patience, although they have not smoothed the sharpness of her tongue or quenched her incurable optimism. "You have to watch change over a long period," she says. One biographer noted that few have seen more than Molly Yard, "who can remember when women were not welcome at Presidential conventions as delegates, let alone as candidates."

Source: People Weekly, 12 October 1987, 38; Current Biography Yearbook, 1988, 631–33; Public Interest Profiles, 1992–1993, 1992, 171–72.

mentally different from men and to require special legislation that meets their needs. Egalitarian feminists downplay biology and sexual differences and want men and women to be treated identically by the law. Radical feminists focus on sexual differences and perceive Western patriarchy (including that of Western religions) as explaining male dominance. Liberal or reform feminists focus on the similarities of women and men as human beings and citizens and seek to dismantle stereotypes and remove inequalities in economic and personal opportunity. All feminists agree that laws should be changed to improve women's lives. Feminists also split along race, ethnic group, class, and age lines. The priorities of black feminists like Angela Davis are affected by the heritage of slavery and the experience of discrimination. The priorities of Third World feminists are influenced by the heritage of colonialism and the experience of poverty.

Although such differences are considerable, most differences among feminists are no stronger than those between liberals such as Senator Ted Kennedy and President Bill Clinton. Both believe that government should be activist, but Kennedy places more emphasis on government solutions to social problems than does Clinton. Despite differences among feminists, however, the vast majority share agendas for women's rights in political institutions and the policy arena (Stetson 1991, 6–9). This text emphasizes such common ground.

Feminism in American History

Anglo-Saxon law and culture have traditionally treated women as inferiors, subjugating them or "protecting" them "in their best interest." For centuries, women did not have the right to decide whom they would marry, the right to hold property once they married, the right to make contracts, or the right to participate in political decisions. Women could not attend schools of higher education or practice any of the learned professions. Only thirty-five years ago women basketball players played by rules that prevented them from running on the court because they were deemed too frail for strenuous exercise.

Some women have been concerned about such political and social inequality since the beginning of the Republic. The oft-quoted letter of Abigail Adams to John Adams at the time of the Declaration of Independence offers an insight. After expressing a desire for American independence and noting the need for a legal system, Abigail Adams asked that "you would Remember the Ladies, and be more generous and favourable to them than your ancestors. Do not put such unlimited power into the hands of Husbands. Remember all Men would be tyrants if they could" (Adams 1975, 121).

These are strong words, even in revolutionary times, for a future first lady. They proclaim concerns that occupied some women throughout the course of American history: a desire for equal treatment in the social and economic spheres and for the same political rights as men. Our text will focus on political rights, specifically the right to vote and to hold office, as well as the growing numbers of women in elective and appointed governmental positions, and progress in legislative policy areas of importance to women.

Some women, in a few places and times, did vote before the general enfranchisement of women that came with passage of the **Nineteenth Amendment** to the Constitution in 1920. Since 1920 the proportion of women to men as well as the absolute number of women in American society has continued to grow (*Historical Statistics of the United States* 1975, 9). The result is that women are now a majority of the electorate and are increasing their numbers and percentages at all levels and in the vast majority of the institutions of American government. Even so, the overall numbers of women holding elective and appointed office in government still lag far behind their actual numbers in the population and behind percentages in similar categories of political or governmental office in other industrialized countries. For example, despite the depiction of 1992 as the year of the woman, there were in 1993 only forty-eight women in the House of Representatives, 11 percent of the total number of representatives. Even if the United States had this percentage in 1989–90, it would have been tenth if ranked along with the thirteen countries in the European Parliament in 1989 and thirteenth if ranked with the eighteen countries of Western Europe in terms of women in the lower house of parliament in 1990 (Janova and Sineau 1992, 117, 120). In the percentage of women in cabinet-level positions, the United States was in the middle range among developed nations during the same period.

The three hundred women and a few men who answered Elizabeth Cady Stanton's call for a women's rights convention in Seneca Falls, New York, in July 1848, discussed not only the social, civil, and religious condition and rights of women but also women's political rights and especially the right to vote. The Declaration of Sentiments passed by the convention echoed the Declaration of Independence asserting "that all men and women are created equal; that they are endowed by their creator with certain inalienable rights: that among these are life, liberty and the pursuit of happiness" (quoted in Wellman 1991, 9, see also 9–37; see also Rossi 1982, 1–43).

After leaving Seneca Falls, this band of reformers promoted egalitarian ideals at the local, state, and national levels. Three major reform movements linked these signers together: the legal reform movement that sought to change the law so women could own property; the moderate abolitionists; and the radical abolitionists led by William Lloyd Garrison. Many of the latter were Quakers, the first religious organization in modern times that allowed women to preach.

After the Civil War and the abolition of slavery, many women hoped that the **Fourteenth Amendment**, passed in 1868 to confer citizenship on former slaves, might advance the cause of women's rights as well. Specifically, they hoped that the amendment's **Equal Protection Clause**, asserting that no state could "deny to any person within its jurisdiction the equal protection of the laws," might be applied to women. One test was presented to the Supreme Court. When Myra Coby Bradwell was denied admission to the Illinois Bar on the ground that she was a married woman and therefore not a fully free agent, she appealed to the Supreme Court. In 1873, in *Bradwell v. Illinois*, the Court rejected her appeal, stating in a concurring opinion that the "natural and proper timidity and delicacy which belong to the female sex evidently unfits it for many of the occupations of civil life" (quoted in Ker-

ber and De Hart-Mathews 1987, 477, see also 476–78). While Bradwell's case was being considered, the U.S. Supreme Court also ruled that the Fourteenth Amendment's range could be strictly limited and the Equal Protection Clause would apply only to state actions involving race. The only discriminatory laws that courts would strike down after Bradwell were those that were totally capricious and where no plausible reason based on the inherent distinctions between the sexes could be found (Stetson 1991, 18–20).

Until the 1960s, few feminists argued that the Equal Protection Clause was applicable to women. Instead, some supported a separate amendment to the Constitution explicitly guaranteeing that "equality of rights under the law shall not be denied or abridged . . . on account of sex." This **Equal Rights Amendment** (ERA), first drafted by Alice Paul and the National Woman's Party and introduced in Congress in 1923, had long generated controversy. Initially, it had been opposed by the League of Women Voters and many former suffragists for its potential to undermine special protections granted to women in the workplace—maximum hours legislation, for example, and restrictions on night work and "heavy" work (Kerber and De Hart-Mathews 1987, 488–89). The attempt to resurrect and pass the ERA continued on and off into the early 1980s against the backdrop of a series of court cases that began to expand the protection of the Fourteenth Amendment to other than racially based groupings. In *Reed v. Reed* (1971), for example, the Court undercut the Bradwell case by stating that states that gave preference to males as executors of wills were in violation of the Equal Protection Clause of the Constitution. The Court's reversal was no doubt affected by the civil rights movement of the 1950s and 1960s, the enactment of civil rights legislation in 1964, and the passage of the ERA by the Senate and the House and its referral to the states for ratification in 1972 (Kerber and De Hart-Mathews 1987, 488–89). Taking notice of the efforts of the women's movement to amend the Constitution, the Court began to extend the interpretation of the Equal Protection Clause to reflect the changing role of women in society. Although insulated from politics, justices are aware of changes and relevant events outside the courts and generally find ways of accommodating them (Stetson 1991, 21–24).

The feminist agenda today includes social legislation to assure parity in educational and job opportunities and equal benefits and treatment of women relative to men in occupational benefits and in the eyes of the law. Most feminists realize that women in the United States have come a long way from the time when Elizabeth Cady Stanton addressed the crowd of three hundred in Seneca Falls. In the Perspectives section of each chapter we will explore further how far American women have come and the distance that remains to be traveled before they achieve full parity with men.

Feminism and Other Perspectives

Feminism, although acknowledging some contributions by the four major perspectives, takes issue with points of each.

Lockean liberalism aimed at freeing males from the oppression of certain traditional institutions, including the monarchy and, in its more extreme forms, the church. By suggesting that all men held certain rights over and above those that were granted them by government and in later years arguing that the suffrage for males should be expanded, liberalism set the stage for women and persons of color to justify their rights on the same basis (universal inalienable rights not limited by legislation). Wherever discrimination existed in the public sphere, feminists have often allied themselves with liberals in acting "affirmatively" to put an end to such practices. But many feminists argue that liberals' concern to protect the private spheres of individual lives, although working to women's benefits in issues like abortion (a liberal would argue for the

right of each woman to determine her future), actually ignores deeply ingrained patterns of male domination within the home that have prevented women from making use of the political rights gained by liberal reforms. Thus in the minds of such feminists, although liberals may be natural allies in public sector reforms, their reluctance to enforce changes in male lifestyles impedes the transition to gender parity. Most feminists understand the dangers inherent in government regulation of the private realm but wish liberal males would be more vocal in advocating equality within the family, which they feel is necessary for women's liberation to be complete (Pateman 1991, 116–37).

Feminists have found less to agree about with conservatives than with liberals, although the conservative worldview does emphasize the importance of the role of the woman in society and particularly in the family. Early liberalism, reflecting the male-dominated society from which it sprung, was late in addressing women's concerns. Conservatives, because they revere the stability and continuity of society, have always conceded women an important place as protector and promoter of the family and values related to the family. The problem that feminism has with conservatism is that the conservative position has only slowly and with great reluctance conceded women the right to an equal position in the public sphere, whether it be jobs or political rights. In the private sphere, too, conservatives generally reflect the patriarchal notion that the woman should subordinate herself to the man in decisions affecting the family.

Feminism has difficulty aligning with libertarianism, too. Although many libertarians have supported a woman's right to choose abortion, some have argued that the fetus also has rights. Libertarians most often cross swords with feminists on issues relating to affirmative action in the marketplace. Feminists argue and most liberals agree that government needs to facilitate the development of day care centers and promote policies in the private sector that permit a woman to take

2

THE CONSTITUTION

Americans do not hesitate to express dissatisfaction, sometimes even disgust, with the performance of their government. Yet the **Constitution**, the written document that is the fundamental law of the United States, is rarely subject to such criticism. The American public seems to regard the Constitution with a respect bordering on idolatry. A survey published in 1980, which asked citizens to state their views on the Constitution, elicited responses like these from 76 percent of those polled:

> The Constitution is a masterpiece. It applies to today as well as 200 years ago. To me it expresses all of the hopes and dreams that our forefathers, the beginners of the country, had in mind. The Constitution stands between order and chaos, between organized government and anarchy, between ruthless power and helplessness. Without it man defends his rights by strength alone. If the Constitution is tampered with we will be sealing our own fate, for it is the one true guardian of our rights and freedoms (Baas 1980, 244–45, 252).

Yet this overwhelmingly positive image of the Constitution is not based upon any clear or detailed understanding of what the document says. Surveys prompted by the two-hundredth anniversary of the 1787 Constitutional Convention in Philadelphia show considerable public ignorance concerning the basic provisions of the Constitution. According to one such poll by the Hearst Corporation, only 54 percent of Americans know that the purpose of the Constitution was to create a national government, while 26 percent confused it with the Declaration of Independence from England in 1776. Only 41 percent could identify the Bill of Rights, and nearly 49 percent believed that the president could suspend the Constitution during a war or national emergency. (No such power exists, though some presidents have violated some parts of the Constitution, citing national emergency as a justification.) Fifty percent thought a moment

Two giant steps for mankind!

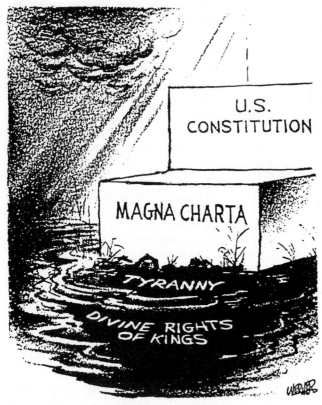

Charles Werner. Courtesy *Indianapolis Star*.

of silence for prayer in public schools was constitutional (organized prayer was banned by a 1962 Supreme Court decision as an establishment of religion), and 64 percent believed that the Constitution makes English the official language of the United States. (Although there is a movement for a constitutional amendment making English the official language, no language is now designated as official and some government programs actually require the use of another language.) Nearly half thought that the Constitution contains the Marxist declaration, "From each according to his ability, to each according to his need" (*Lansing State Journal*, 15 February 1987, A8; *Washington Post*, 15 February 1987, A13; Kammen 1986).

It appears that Americans know that the Constitution is important and want to believe in it but know very little about its origins, basic principles, or effect on the workings of government today. Before considering alternative perspectives, it is therefore worth exploring how the United States came to base its government upon this document.

FRAMING THE CONSTITUTION

Ten of the thirteen British colonies that came to make up the United States were granted written charters by the English Crown, spelling out the relationship between the colony and the mother country. Three were under the control of private companies, which also granted charters to their colonists. The Revolution made new governments necessary for the newly independent states. Accustomed to conducting their affairs under a written document, the states adopted constitutions between 1776 and 1780. These constitutions closely paralleled the old colonial charters in form, with a governor and usually a **bicameral** (two-house) **legislature**, but there were some significant changes. Influenced by John Locke's ideas on natural rights, most of the states specified the basic rights of the people. The various state constitutions provided a model for many important features of the later national Constitution.

The **Continental Congress**, composed of delegates appointed at first by provincial revolutionary conventions and later by state legislatures, assumed responsibility for conducting the war against the British. After the American colonies proclaimed their independence from Great Britain with the **Declaration of Independence**, which created the original confederation of thirteen states in 1776, Congress moved to give itself legal authority to carry out those functions, mostly connected with war making, that obviously had to be handled at the national level. The result was the **Articles of Confederation**, written in 1776–77 and ratified by all the state legislatures by 1781.

The Articles of Confederation gave formal structure to what already existed—an alliance of free and independent states. The **Confederation Congress** was given a seemingly impressive list of powers: to declare war and make peace, to conduct foreign relations, to coin and borrow money, to handle Indian affairs, and to establish a post office. The Articles made clear, however, that final authority rested with the states. Congress was given no power to tax people directly; instead it was forced to depend on voluntary state contributions for funds. There was no national executive or judicial branch, and each state retained the right to regulate trade with other states and with foreign nations. The structure of the Confederation government also emphasized state **sovereignty**, or final authority to decide a political question. Each state, regardless of population, had one vote in Congress, and a two-thirds majority was required for any legislation. Amendments to the Articles required unanimous consent of the states.

Under the Articles of Confederation, Congress settled some important problems. The peace treaty with England was successfully negotiated, and the mechanism by which new western territories would be created was outlined in the Northwest Ordinance of 1787. It soon became apparent, however, that the Articles had several glaring weaknesses that prevented the Confederation government from carrying out even the modest functions assigned to it. The lack of a power to tax was one major weakness. Even during the war, the states did not always provide enough funds on time, as George Washington's ragged and hungry soldiers could attest. Once peace was restored, state contributions ceased almost entirely. Without money, Congress could not maintain a navy to protect American ships in the Mediterranean from North African pirates or raise an army to aid frontier settlers against hostile Indians. Soon the British and other European powers were taking advantage of a weak United States. Debts incurred during the Revolution remained unpaid, undermining confidence in the government and angering those who had lent it money. The absence of a power to regulate trade among the states, another major weakness, led to destructive interstate trade wars, with states taxing each other's goods as they crossed state lines. Efforts to give Congress more power were frustrated by the requirement for unanimous consent to amendments. The vote of one state, Rhode Island, blocked attempts to give the confederation power to lay tariffs on imports (Collier and Collier 1986, 3–17).

The weakness of the Articles affected the lives of all Americans, but the wealthy and powerful were especially frustrated. George Washington, for example, owned extensive western lands that would be worthless unless the Indians were pacified. Merchants were irked by state trade restrictions, and lenders were distressed by the inability of the government to pay its debts. In 1786 delegates from five states met in Annapolis, Maryland, to discuss some of these problems. Those attending the **Annapolis Convention** decided that nothing could be accomplished without basic revisions to the Articles, and the delegates went back to their states to work for a new convention that would make the needed reforms.

The appeal for a convention might have gone unheeded had it not been for **Shays' Rebellion**, a populist small farmers' uprising in Massachusetts in 1786–87. Burdened by unfair taxes imposed by a merchant-dominated state legislature, several thousand farmers rose in revolt under Captain Daniel Shays, a Revolutionary War veteran. Although the rebellion was easily suppressed by the state militia, exaggerated accounts of it reached the other states and convinced many property owners of the need for a strong central government that could deal with internal as well as external threats (Szatmary 1980, 120–34). All the state legislatures, except that of Rhode Island, agreed to appoint delegates, and in May 1787 the **Constitutional Convention** met in Philadelphia. It was this convention that, over the next five months, produced the present United States Constitution.

Where They Agreed: The Nationalist Consensus

Thomas Jefferson may have been exaggerating when he called the Constitutional Convention "an assembly of demi-gods" (quoted in Dye and Ziegler 1987, 25). Nevertheless, the fifty-five delegates were, almost without exception,

among the new nation's most prominent and respected citizens. Eight were signers of the Declaration of Independence. Thirty had served in the Revolution, forty-two had been in the Confederation Congress, and nearly all had held office at the state level. Twenty-six had attended college at a time when only a tiny fraction of the population had a higher education. Among the delegates were wealthy businessmen such as Robert Morris and Elbridge Gerry, great planters such as George Mason, eminent lawyers such as Alexander Hamilton, and political thinkers such as James Madison (see Profile). Though not especially active in the deliberations, George Washington lent his prestige to the convention. The delegates epitomized wealth, power, and success and together had hundreds of years of combined political experience (Rossiter 1966, 79–156; Mead 1987, 33–39).

The views of the delegates are difficult to classify according to the scheme presented in Chapter 1. Clearly they were heavily indebted to the ideas of John Locke and other early liberals. None of them questioned that people had natural rights, that the people had the right to choose their own government, and that government had to be limited to prevent oppression. At the same time, the record of the convention shows a strong conservative tendency among most delegates and a skeptical, Hobbesian view of human nature. Historians disagree about the political views of the framers, some suggesting the framers were elitist conservatives (Wood 1969, 494–518) and others saying they were democratic liberals (Diamond 1981, 61–105; Morgan 1988, 263–87). Throughout the convention, hardly a favorable mention was made of democracy as a form of government. Popular government as practiced in some of the states (Rhode Island was often cited as a horrible example) seemed to the framers to be leading to mob rule and threatening property rights. Still, the framers also hesitated to trust the upper classes, whom they often described as greedy and avaricious, with supreme power. Benjamin Franklin, responding to another delegate's proposal for high property qualifications for federal office-holders, remarked that "some of the greatest rogues [I] was ever acquainted with, were the richest rogues" (quoted in McDonald 1985, 239). Apparently, the convention agreed—no property qualification was set. In fact, due to the controversy and different characteristics of individual colonies, the framers left the setting of election qualifications to each state. Most states at first excluded large numbers of people from voting eligibility but later expanded their electorates.

To most of the framers, the solution to reconciling tensions among their values was **republicanism**, or government run by delegates elected by the people. Government should represent all groups, but no one group should be allowed to predominate and oppress the others. The importance of such balanced government to the framers can readily be seen in methods ultimately chosen for selecting national officials. While the House of Representatives, elected directly by the people, was expected to represent the masses, the indirect selecting of the Senate (by state legislatures), the president (by an electoral college), and the Supreme Court (by the president with the ad-

vice and consent of the Senate) gave the rest of the national government the ability to check the "democratic" House (Eidelberg 1986; see also McDonald 1985, 57–96).

Closely allied to the desire for balanced government was a belief in **separation of powers** among the branches of government and a system of **checks and balances** whereby the powers of each branch are constrained by the powers of the others. With their conservative distrust of human nature and their liberal suspicion of concentrated power, the framers believed that liberty could only survive if the law-making, law-enforcing, and law-interpreting functions were entrusted to different people. Concentrating all these powers in the hands of one person or group, even if popularly elected, would lead to **tyranny**, or oppressive use of absolute power. All the framers agreed that there had to be separate **legislative** (law-making), **executive** (law-enforcing), and **judicial** (law-interpreting) **branches** with distinct duties and the power to check and balance one another. The legislative branch generally makes the laws, the executive branch generally administers governmental programs, and the judicial branch is generally responsible for the administration of justice. The specific responsibilities of the branches are listed later in this chapter and elaborated in Chapters 6, 7, 8, and 10.

Bob Thaves. Frank & Ernest reprinted by permission of NEA, Inc.

PROFILE

James Madison: Father of the Constitution

James Madison (Library of Congress)

James Madison, the most influential of the fifty-five delegates to the Constitutional Convention, was born in Orange County, Virginia, on March 16, 1751, the son of a wealthy planter. After graduating from Princeton College in New Jersey, where he was noted for writing humorous poems at the expense of fellow students, Madison plunged into revolutionary politics at the ripe age of twenty-five, being elected to the 1776 convention to draw up Virginia's new constitution. From that time on, he became one of America's first full-time politicians, engaging in public service until his retirement from the presidency in 1817. (His only defeat in a popular election came in 1777, when he temporarily lost his seat in the Virginia legislature because he refused to treat the voters to free liquor, as was then the custom, and was labeled "undemocratic" by his opponent.)

In Virginia politics, Madison was best known as a champion of religious freedom and church-state separation; together with Thomas Jefferson he succeeded in 1786 in pushing through the legislature, over Governor Patrick Henry's opposition, the Statute for Religious Freedom. Both during the Confederation period and at the Constitutional Convention, Madison was a firm nationalist. At the convention he took copious notes, and many of the positions for which he argued became part of the Constitution. His original Virginia Plan would have given Congress the power "to legislate in all cases to which the separate States are incompetent"—more like today's national govern-

---

The system developed at Philadelphia clearly shows the framers' belief in the need for checks and balances (see Figure 2.1). The legislative power of Congress, already divided between the House and the Senate, could be checked by a presidential veto. Congress could check the president, however, by its power to override vetoes by a two-thirds majority of both houses and to **impeach** (arraign with the possibility of removal from office) a president who has abused his power. In addition, Congress was given a check upon the executive branch with the requirement that the Senate consent to treaties and confirm appointments and upon the judicial branch with the requirement that the Senate confirm the appointment of justices. Congress was also given the power to organize the federal court system and propose amendments to the Constitution. The president could exercise some control over the judicial branch with his power to appoint federal judges, but they were to be appointed for life and the Supreme Court was at least implicitly given the power to declare laws uncon-

ment than the Articles of Confederation. He also favored allowing Congress the right to veto state laws. Madison was forced to give in on these points, but the system adopted by the convention reflected his thinking more than that of any other delegate.

During the ratification struggle, Madison collaborated with Alexander Hamilton and John Jay of New York to write a series of essays explaining and defending the Constitution. Known today as *The Federalist Papers*, these essays are a classic statement of political theory and still studied as a guide to the intent of the framers. Though Madison argued strongly that a Bill of Rights was not needed, he eventually concluded that only such a bill could solidify public support for the new government. Winning election to the First Congress, Madison took charge of writing a Bill of Rights based on states' bills of rights. Ten of the amendments he framed were accepted by Congress and the states.

With the battle for the Constitution won, Madison joined with his old friend Thomas Jefferson in opposing Treasury Secretary Alexander Hamilton's economic policies, which favored northern commercial interests over the agricultural South. Since Hamilton and his supporters, who had appropriated the name Federalist, controlled the national government, Madison and Jefferson formed the Democratic-Republican party, which was more states' rights–oriented than Madison had been in

the past and included many former Anti-Federalists. During Jefferson's presidency, Madison served as secretary of state, then was elected president in 1808.

Unfortunately, Madison took office at a time when relations with Great Britain were deteriorating. A faction of Democratic-Republicans called War Hawks pressured the president to take a hard line with the British, and war broke out in 1812. Madison probably should have tried harder than he did to avoid war, for the United States was poorly prepared and suffered many defeats, including the burning of Washington, D.C., in 1814. Though the nation emerged from the War of 1812 with its territory intact, Madison is ranked by most historians as no better than an average president.

After leaving office in 1817, Madison served as rector of the University of Virginia, which he and Jefferson had founded, and in one last constitutional convention, held in Virginia in 1829 to revise the state constitution he had helped to write in 1776. Revered as the Father of the U.S. Constitution, he died on June 28, 1836.

Source: Brant 1941–61, vols. 1–6; Koch 1966; *New York Times Magazine*, 29 July 1962, 12–13; Rakove 1986, 77–86; Riemer 1986; Pritchett 1968, 22.

---

stitutional. Most of the state constitutions had already followed this model in one way or another, but the new national Constitution embodied separation of powers and checks and balances to an even greater extent.

Even with broad agreement on basic political principles, the Constitutional Convention probably would not have been successful had its members not shared a commitment to **nationalism**, or a bond they felt that made them want a strong national government to succeed. A number of ardent **states' rights** advocates,

who believed that state governments should retain a degree of autonomy in relation to the national government, had been elected to the convention but had declined to serve, not wanting anything to do with an effort to strengthen central authority. The delegates who did attend were, with a few exceptions, proponents of a strong central government with broad powers. Once in Philadelphia, they further removed themselves from scrutiny by the states' rights forces by voting to close their meetings to the public. While a few of the

Figure 2.1   Checks and Balances

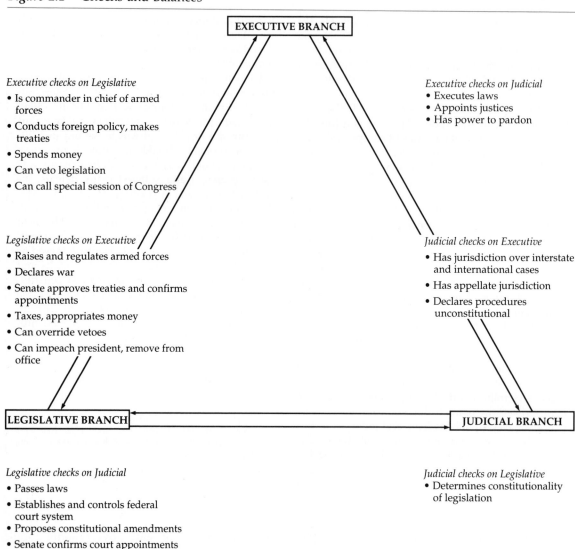

EXECUTIVE BRANCH

Executive checks on Legislative
- Is commander in chief of armed forces
- Conducts foreign policy, makes treaties
- Spends money
- Can veto legislation
- Can call special session of Congress

Executive checks on Judicial
- Executes laws
- Appoints justices
- Has power to pardon

Legislative checks on Executive
- Raises and regulates armed forces
- Declares war
- Senate approves treaties and confirms appointments
- Taxes, appropriates money
- Can override vetoes
- Can impeach president, remove from office

Judicial checks on Executive
- Has jurisdiction over interstate and international cases
- Has appellate jurisdiction
- Declares procedures unconstitutional

LEGISLATIVE BRANCH   **JUDICIAL BRANCH**

Legislative checks on Judicial
- Passes laws
- Establishes and controls federal court system
- Proposes constitutional amendments
- Senate confirms court appointments
- Can impeach justices, remove from office

Judicial checks on Legislative
- Determines constitutionality of legislation

delegates objected to such secrecy, most agreed that closed sessions would prevent the general public from misinterpreting any information about the convention that otherwise might leak out (Mitchell and Mitchell 1975, 51–52). Then the convention passed a resolution "that a national government ought to be established consisting of a supreme Legislative, Executive, and Judiciary." Thus, the delegates decided early on that the Confederation was not worth saving and began to construct an entirely new system, in violation of instructions authorizing them only to amend the Articles (Kelly and Harbison 1963, 124).

Coexisting with nationalism, however, was a respect for **federalism**, or a division of power between the states and the central government. At one point Alexander Hamilton proposed abolishing the states and creating a completely centralized government, but few in the convention were willing to go that far. Rather than abolishing the states, the convention sought to combine federalism and nationalism in a new way (Zuckert 1987, 132–50).

Where They Disagreed: A Bundle of Compromises

According to one writer, the triumph of the framers was the establishment of three fundamental principles that have since sustained the United States. "They are," he writes, "compromise, compromise, compromise" (Cooke 1973, 144). The fact that the framers shared so many views in common did not make the work of the Constitutional Convention easy. If there were broad areas of agreement, there were also sharp disagreements and conflicts of interest. That those conflicts could be resolved is a tribute to the framers' political skill.

The most serious of the conflicts concerned the composition of the legislative branch. Early in the convention, the Virginia delegation presented a plan devised by James Madison and afterward known as the **Virginia Plan**. It provided for a national legislature consisting of a House and a Senate, the House to be elected by the people and the Senate to be elected by the House. In both houses, representation was to be apportioned by population; each state would have one representative for every thirty thousand inhabitants. This plan, of course,

Ed Stein. Reprinted with permission of the *Rocky Mountain News*.

worked to the advantage of large states like Virginia, since they would have a larger vote in Congress than states with smaller populations, instead of an equal vote as under the Confederation.

After the Virginia Plan had been under discussion for some time, William Paterson of New Jersey, a small state, presented a plan of his own. Paterson's proposal, known as the **New Jersey Plan**, called for modifying the Articles by giving Congress the power to tax and to regulate trade and by creating an executive and a judicial branch. The basic structure of Congress, however, would remain unchanged. There would be a single house with members elected by the state legislatures and one vote for each state. Paterson and his colleagues believed this was the only way to ensure that the small states would not be overwhelmed by the larger states.

The debate was long and bitter. The Virginia Plan had the support of all the southern states, which, at that time, were expected to grow faster than the North, plus Massachusetts and Pennsylvania, the two largest northern states. The New Jersey delegates held fast to their position, however, and they were joined by those of Delaware and Connecticut. New York, a large state with a majority of states' rights supporters in its delegation, also backed the small state position. These delegates vowed never to accept a legislature with representation based purely on population. Faced with the possibility of the convention's dissolving, the Connecticut delegation suggested appointing a committee to search for a compromise. The committee ultimately arrived at the system we know today—a two-house Congress with proportioned representation in the lower house and state equality in the upper house (see Figure 2.2). This plan, often called the **Great Compromise** or Connecticut Compromise, contributed more than anything else to the success of the convention. It operates to this day, although the **Seventeenth Amendment** in 1913 replaced the election of senators by their state legislatures with direct popular election.

Three other important compromises made during the convention revolved around the relationship between the northern and southern states. The North, which hoped to develop its new manufacturing industries, wanted Congress to have power to tax **imports**, goods coming into the country from foreign countries. The South, which exported agricultural products and had little desire to become involved in manufacturing, was opposed to any federal tax on either imports or **exports**, goods going out of the country to foreign countries. The South finally agreed to support giving Congress power to tax imports on the condition that no export taxes be levied. This arrangement is known as the **Commerce Compromise**.

Another conflict between the two sections occurred over the question of including black slaves in counting the population for purposes of representation and taxation. The South insisted that slaves be counted as people for purposes of representation, which would have given southern whites much more representation in the House than if only whites were counted. The northern delegates insisted that since slaves were treated as property under the law, they should be counted only for purposes of taxation, giving the North control of the House and the South the lion's share of any further tax burden. The solution finally agreed upon called for counting each slave as three-fifths of a free white person for both representation and taxation. This ingenious expedient, known as the **Three-fifths Compromise**, remained part of the Constitution until the Civil War. In yet another compromise, the North agreed to allow the African slave trade, regarded as immoral even by many southerners, to continue for twenty more years, on the condition that it could then be prohibited by Congress (Wiecek 1987, 167–84).

Other issues divided the convention on the basis of political principles rather than section-

Figure 2.2   The Great Compromise

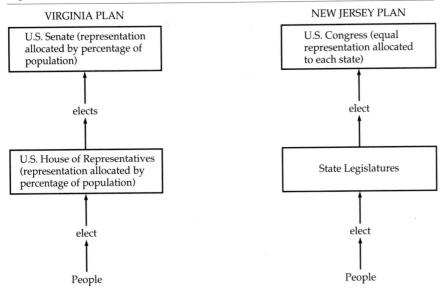

VIRGINIA PLAN

U.S. Senate (representation allocated by percentage of population)

↑ elects

U.S. House of Representatives (representation allocated by percentage of population)

↑ elect

People

NEW JERSEY PLAN

U.S. Congress (equal representation allocated to each state)

↑ elect

State Legislatures

↑ elect

People

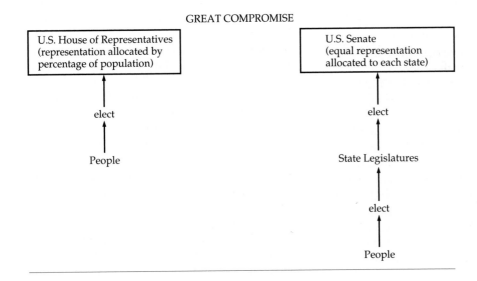

GREAT COMPROMISE

U.S. House of Representatives (representation allocated by percentage of population)

↑ elect

People

U.S. Senate (equal representation allocated to each state)

↑ elect

State Legislatures

↑ elect

People

al interests. Election of the president was a controversial point, with some delegates favoring popular election, some election by both houses of Congress, and some by the House or the Senate only. In the end, an **electoral college** was given the power to choose the presi-dent, with electors to be chosen by each state in any manner it saw fit (see Chapter 4). Some delegates objected strenuously to proposals that allowed a standing army, which they saw as a threat to liberty. The convention accepted a standing army, but with control divided between the president (made commander in chief) and Congress (given the power to raise armies and declare war). The powers of Congress were also a subject of sharp debate, with the most nationalistic delegates favoring unlimited powers and others arguing for strictly limited legislative powers. This question was resolved by enumerating specific powers while reserving for Congress the right to pass other legislation deemed "necessary and proper" for carrying out the enumerated powers (see Chapter 6; Collier and Collier 1986, 3–17).

THE RATIFICATION STRUGGLE AND THE BILL OF RIGHTS

The new Constitution was entangled in controversy as soon as its contents became known. Supporters of the existing system saw it as a revolutionary change and resolved to fight it with all their strength. The struggle of the **Federalists** (who supported the ratification of the Constitution) to overcome this opposition led to yet another compromise that would change the constitutional order.

Much of the opposition to the Constitution came from those expressing populist ideas. They believed that the rich men of the Constitutional Convention had created an "aristocratic" document designed to subvert the principles of the Revolution and perhaps even to restore an English-style monarchy. The secrecy surrounding the convention added to the distrust with which populists regarded the wealthy framers. Amos Singletary, a Massachusetts farmer and supporter of Shays' Rebellion, revealed these suspicions when he warned:

> These lawyers, and men of learning and moneyed men, that talk so finely, and gloss over matters so smoothly, to make us poor illiterate people swallow down the pill, expect to get into Congress themselves; they expect to be managers of this Constitution, and get all the

power and all the money into their own hands, and then they will swallow all us little folks like the great *Leviathan*; yes, just as the whale swallowed up Jonah! (quoted in Kenyon 1966, 1).

Although exaggerated, Singletary's fears were partially justified. The convention had not been an aristocratic conspiracy, but the indirect election of senators and the president and the life tenure for justices of the Supreme Court were indeed intended to limit the power of the poor majority. The **Anti-Federalists**, who opposed ratification of the Constitution, had proposed many amendments that had a populist flavor, including more frequent elections, more power for juries in the federal court system, and a ban on monopolies (Ketcham 1986, 217–26; Lienesch 1988, 138–56). Despite such proposals, the lower classes were divided on the issue, with most city dwellers and farmers well enough off to raise crops for sale supporting the Constitution and most subsistence farmers, who produced only enough to meet family needs and were not dependent on trade, supporting the Anti-Federalists (Main 1961, 187–286).

Other Anti-Federalists, like Patrick Henry (see Profile) and George Mason of Virginia, Luther Martin of Maryland, and George Clinton of New York, were as wealthy and well educated as the leading Federalists but opposed to the Constitution for a variety of reasons. Some did not think any truly national government could work in a country as large and diverse as the United States. Some were state officials who feared losing power and sources of revenue. For many, the decisive objection was the absence of a bill of rights. Shortly before the convention adjourned, George Mason had proposed the addition of such a bill. Without much discussion, the idea was voted down on the grounds that Article I of the Constitution already enumerated the powers given to Congress and no power to deny rights had been conferred. Whatever the

Patrick Henry: Anti-Federalist Firebrand

Patrick Henry (Library of Congress)

Patrick Henry, the greatest orator of the Revolutionary era and leader of the Virginia Anti-Federalists, was born May 29, 1736, the son of a substantial planter. At the age of fifteen, Henry left home to open a general store but went bankrupt. After two more business ventures failed, he turned to the law in 1760. Henry first came to public notice in 1763, when he defended Virginia taxpayers against a suit by clergy of the established Church of England who wanted payment of church taxes in tobacco despite a drought that had ruined the crop. In 1765 he was elected to the Virginia legislature, just as the English Parliament was passing the Stamp Act. Henry became celebrated for his fiery and eloquent denunciations of English policy, culminating in the famous "Give me liberty or give me death" speech delivered in the Virginia revolutionary convention in 1775.

Henry's leadership of the revolutionary cause made him the most popular leader in the state. He was elected governor five times during and after the Revolution (for one-year terms), but he never served in the Confederation Congress as most of the Federalists did, which may help to explain his lack of concern about the weaknesses of that body. His only political defeat during this time was the passage of Jefferson's and Madison's Statute for Religious Freedom separating church and state in Virginia. (Henry believed in religious freedom as much as they did and opposed a single established church, but he wanted the state to give financial support to all Christian churches.)

Henry was elected to the Constitutional Convention but refused to attend, reputedly saying later that he "smelt a rat." His motives for opposing the Constitution were complex. He correctly noted that the opening phrase of the Preamble, "We the people," indicated a shift from a confederacy of equal states to a national government, and he genuinely believed that such a government would inevitably be remote from the people, corrupt, and tyrannical. Again, he correctly predicted that the new Congress would have a northern majority that might disregard southern interests. At the same time, he was clearly bitter toward Madison over the religious issue and other political disagreements and not inclined to support a Constitution backed by his rivals. During the Virginia convention considering ratification of the Constitution, Henry was at his oratorical best, exhorting the delegates to hold fast to state sovereignty: "This government is not a Virginian but an American government. Is it not, therefore, a consolidated government? The genius of Virginia called us for liberty [during the Revolution] . . . the genius of Virginia did and will again, lead us to happiness."

After ratification, Henry became reconciled to the Constitution but not to his old foes Jefferson and Madison. After leaving public life for several years to devote himself to law practice and land speculation, he then returned to politics as, of all things, a member of archnationalist Alexander Hamilton's Federalist party. Apparently he was seeking revenge on Jefferson and Madison, who were not supporting states' rights as Democratic-Republicans. Henry had just been elected once again to the Virginia legislature when he died on June 6, 1799.

Source: Beeman 1974; Kenyon 1966, 238–64; Campbell 1969.

merits of the argument, the failure to include a bill of rights was a serious political error that caused many who probably otherwise would have been Federalists and supporters (including George Mason) to oppose ratification of the Constitution.

The eventual victory of the Federalists owed much to the fact that they made the rules under which the ratification process was conducted. Although the Articles of Confederation required unanimous consent for any amendments, the convention included in the Constitution a provision that the new government would begin to operate as soon as it was approved by nine states—a two-thirds majority—although the other four would not be compelled to join. Moreover, ratification was placed in the hands of special state conventions elected for the purpose rather than in the hands of state legislatures, which might have been reluctant to cede part of their power to the national government.

Despite these advantages, it is doubtful whether the Constitution could have been ratified by the requisite number of states had the Federalists not made concessions on the issue of a bill of rights. In several states, key Anti-Federalist delegates changed sides after being assured that the Federalists would join in supporting amendments to the new Constitution guaranteeing the people's and the states' rights. New York and Virginia, two large states vital to the Constitution's success, were reluctant to ratify. The eventual margins of victory in these states were narrow: in New York, the vote was 30–27; in Virginia, it was 89–79 (McDonald 1958, 259, 287).

With the nine necessary ratifications by June 1788, the new national government was set up by 1789. Rhode Island became the last state to ratify in 1790, and then only to avoid being treated as a foreign country by the United States and subjected to tariff barriers on its goods. James Madison wrote a variety of amendments, twelve of which were approved by the First Congress and ten of which were

ratified by the states in 1791. It is these ten amendments that today are known collectively as the **Bill of Rights** (see Appendix A).

The first nine amendments in the Bill of Rights were designed to protect individual rights from infringement by the national government. Madison tried to get the First Congress to make some of the rights in the Bill of Rights binding on the states, but his effort was rejected. Not until the 1920s did the Supreme Court begin to apply the Bill of Rights to state governments (see Chapter 9). The **First Amendment** guarantees freedom of religion, freedom of speech and the press, and the rights of assembly and petition for redress of grievances and prohibits an established church. The **Fifth Amendment** guarantees that no one can be deprived of life, liberty, or property without the due process of the law. Other rights listed in the Bill of Rights include the right to keep and bear arms, freedom from "unreasonable" search and seizure, the right to a public trial by jury, and protection from "cruel and unusual punishments," along with many other protections for those accused of crimes. The **Ninth Amendment** says that the Constitution's not naming other rights does not mean they are denied to the people.

The **Tenth Amendment**, the one the Anti-Federalists wanted most, reserves to the states or to the people all powers not specifically granted to the national government. It solidified the division of power between the states and federal government (see Figure 2.3). Clearly, the words of the Bill of Rights are ambiguous and admit to a number of different interpretations. The changing interpretation of the protections they embody is a major topic of Chapter 9.

THE LIVING CONSTITUTION

In a democratic republic, a constitution is not chiseled in stone. While the basic structure established by the framers of the U.S. Consti-

Figure 2.3   Constitutional Division of Powers

Legislative (enacts laws)	Executive (enforces the laws)	Judicial (interprets the laws)
• Raises and regulates armed forces • Declares war • Approves treaties, confirms appointments (Senate) • Taxes, appropriates money • Borrows and coins money • Regulates interstate commerce • Overrides presidential veto • Can impeach officials and remove them from office • Sets up and controls federal court system • Proposes constitutional amendments • Makes all laws "necessary and proper" to carry out these powers	• Serves as commander in chief • Makes foreign policy, negotiates treaties • Prepares federal budget • Can veto legislation • Can call special sessions of Congress • Executes the laws • Appoints justices • Can pardon individuals	• Has original jurisdiction over interstate and international cases • Has appellate jurisdiction as fixed by Congress • Can review and rule on the constitutionality of legislation • Can declare procedures unconstitutional

Powers Reserved to the States
• Can tax • Regulate education • Administer police power, criminal justice • Fix family and inheritance law • Regulate intrastate commerce • Regulate zoning and public health • Assume all powers not expressly given to the federal government

Note: The Constitution grants limited taxing power to the Congress in order to "pay the Debts and provide for the common Defence and general Welfare of the United States" (Article I, Section 8). One of the limits placed on such taxing power is the prohibition of direct taxes unless apportioned according to the population. The courts have usually given the Congress considerable leeway concerning the definition of a direct tax. The Supreme Court did, however, in *Pollock v. Farmers' Loan and Trust Co.* (1895) declare the federal income tax a direct tax and therefore unconstitutional. This decision was reversed by the Sixteenth Amendment.

tution has endured, this eighteenth-century document has been adapted to meet changing demands, often in ways that have altered its fundamental character. The journey from 1787 to the present has not been easy.

Responses to Change

The Civil War was the most serious crisis for the Constitution, involving not only the question of whether a state had the right to secede from the Union but also the controversial issue of slavery. When these issues could not be resolved under the Constitution, war broke out between the citizens of the nation. Arguing the importance of a strong central govern-

ment, President Abraham Lincoln contended that states did not have the right to secede. He declared a state of "insurrection" in April 1861 (he could not declare war, since this power belongs to Congress) and in some cases suspended the granting of **writs of habeas corpus** (court orders requiring that police officials explain why an individual has been arrested and jailed). The Union and the Constitution, amended after the war to prohibit slavery and enfranchise black men, endured.

The framers did not anticipate a modern economy, yet the power they gave to Congress to regulate foreign and interstate commerce— the **Commerce Clause**—has allowed the federal government to regulate unfair business practices while still permitting a somewhat laissez-faire market system. The Constitution has also proved flexible enough to respond to social change. When other branches seemed indecisive on the controversial issue of segregation, for example, the judicial branch became an important actor (see Chapter 9). With increasing federal responsibilities, the president's power to appoint federal officials with the advice and consent of the Senate has created a growing number of governmental agencies, often referred to as the bureaucracy (see Chapter 10). Other, less noticeable adaptations have come about through the evolution of customs and usages not specified in the Constitu-

tion. The initiation of appropriation bills in the House of Representatives is an example.

Avenues of Change

The most direct way of changing the Constitution is through a **constitutional amendment** (see Figure 2.4). Amendments can be proposed by a national convention called by Congress when it is petitioned to do so by two-thirds (thirty-four) of the state legislatures, but all the amendments later added to the Constitution have actually been proposed by congressional vote. After an amendment has been passed by a two-thirds vote in both houses of

Figure 2.4   Course of a Constitutional Amendment

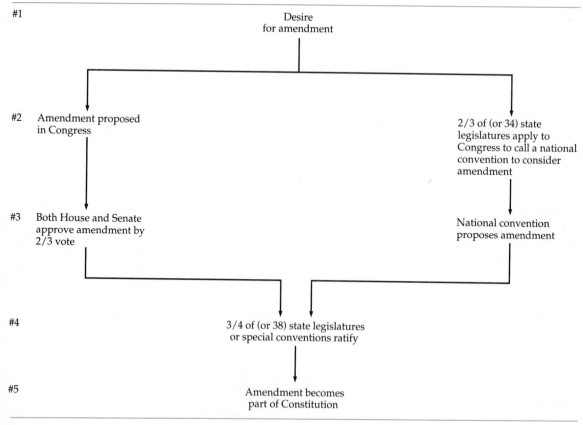

#1   Desire
for amendment

#2   Amendment proposed
in Congress

2/3 of (or 34) state
legislatures apply to
Congress to call a national
convention to consider
amendment

#3   Both House and Senate
approve amendment by
2/3 vote

National convention
proposes amendment

#4   3/4 of (or 38) state legislatures
or special conventions ratify

#5   Amendment becomes
part of Constitution

Congress or by the national convention, it must be ratified by three-fourths (thirty-eight) of the states, either by the state legislatures or special state conventions. Only the **Twenty-first Amendment**, which repealed the **Eighteenth Amendment** banning "the manufacture, sale, or transportation of intoxicating liquors," was ratified by state conventions. The amendment process compels supporters of an amendment to obtain majorities in a larger proportion of the states than the framers themselves needed to secure ratification of the Constitution. It is not hard to see why only twenty-seven amendments, including the first ten, have been adopted since 1791.

In recent years, one old amendment has passed while several new ideas for constitutional change have gone down to defeat. The Equal Rights Amendment (ERA), favored by most liberals, failed to be ratified by the congressionally set deadline of June 1982. An amendment to give the District of Columbia representation in the House and Senate also failed to achieve ratification. However, in 1992

Michigan became the thirty-eighth state to ratify an amendment first introduced by James Madison in 1789, providing that congressional pay raises take effect only after the election of a new Congress, an arrangement that would give the voters an opportunity to vote for or against members who had raised their own salaries. Because Congress did not set a time limit in 1789, this amendment did not have to meet a deadline as the ERA did. Still, some constitutional experts question its validity, and the issue may be resolved in court (*Congressional Quarterly Weekly Report*, 9 May 1992, 1230–31). At the same time, a proposal for an amendment requiring a balanced budget has enjoyed substantial support in Congress but has yet to gain the required two-thirds vote (*Congressional Quarterly Weekly Report*, 9 May 1992, 1233–37). Conservative amendments to restore prayer in public schools, prohibit flag desecration, and halt busing to achieve school integration have failed to attract enough support to pass Congress and be submitted to the states.

William Costello. Courtesy artist.

Another avenue for constitutional change is **judicial reinterpretation**, a restrictive interpretation of a constitutional provision that in effect minimizes the provision. For example, the Tenth Amendment reads as though the states have much more power than they actually have based on court interpretation. Since the case of *Marbury v. Madison* in 1803 (see Chapter 8), the Supreme Court has claimed the right to declare acts of Congress and the state legislatures unconstitutional. Since there is often disagreement on the proper way of interpreting the Constitution, judges are able, in effect, to rewrite the document through interpretations that have authority over acts of the legislative branch. Some reinterpretations, such as the court's reversal of the legality of "separate but equal," have changed the meaning of the Constitution as much as any constitutional amendment.

The process of amending the Constitution is very formal and often quite difficult. Likewise, judicial reinterpretation is encumbered in court rules and procedures. Consequently, legislative actions, executive acts, actions by government agencies, and changes in custom and usage have maintained the "living" Constitution. Its flexibility has kept the document intact for more than two hundred years and revered as the protector of American freedoms.

PERSPECTIVES

Conservative

Alexander Hamilton, one of the most conservative members of the Constitutional Convention, signed the Constitution reluctantly, feeling it was far too democratic. Today's conservatives look far more favorably on the Constitution but fear that its basic principles, which have sustained the Republic for so long, have been seriously undermined.

Conservatives believe that much of the success of the framers stems from the fact that they were an elite, set apart from their fellow citizens by wealth, experience, and education. Their healthy antimajoritarianism led them to establish a government of checks and balances instead of one that allowed an impassioned majority to rule unrestrained. The framers were, however, a public-interested elite, equipped by training and inclination to serve the nation. Hence they limited the rulers as well as the ruled by making officials responsible, directly or indirectly, to the people. The Anti-Federalists forced a further limiting of government by securing the addition of the Bill of Rights. To today's conservatives, one of the most important parts of the Bill of Rights is the Tenth Amendment, which was meant to restrict the national government's control to those functions affecting all thirteen states, thus allowing the widest degree of local self-determination consistent with American nationhood (Rossiter 1966, 38–56; Evans 1975; Berns 1987).

Unfortunately, say conservatives, the constitutional framework has not been able to withstand the persistent and determined assaults of liberals. Liberals do not really believe in limited, constitutional government (except for limiting government's power to uphold moral values) because limited government conflicts with their "utopian" schemes for transforming society. Over the past fifty years, say conservatives, liberals have succeeded in changing some parts of the Constitution beyond the recognition of the framers, not through amendments but through reinterpretations that violate the framers' intent. The clearest case is the liberal reversal of the Tenth Amend-

Eugene Payne. Courtesy *Charlotte Observer*, WSOC-TV, Charlotte.

ment to allow the national government to intervene in any problem it thinks is not being handled properly by states and localities. In this area conservatives feel the nation has departed so far from the path marked by the framers that federalism is in danger of disappearing altogether (Evans 1975, 44–49).

Within the national government, the three branches still check and balance each other, but there are disturbing signs. One is the delegation of enormous powers by Congress to the federal bureaucracy, which is not only unelected but has become so vast and intricate as to be uncontrollable by the president or Congress. Conservatives believe that the people, including government officials, are no wiser or more capable of being trusted with power now than they were in 1787. Centralization of power, first at the national level and then in bureaucracy and the judiciary, has already led to a serious loss of freedom, particularly in the economic realm. If the framers could view the United States today, conservatives suggest that they would be shocked and dismayed at how liberals have treated their Constitution.

From the conservative perspective, the United States must return to limited government and federalism. One means is to elect conservative presidents who will appoint conservative judges, who will consider the rights of the states at least as important as the rights of individuals. In the meantime, conservatives support constitutional amendments to allow states to regulate abortion and voluntary prayer in public schools and to prevent the desecration of the American flag. Conservatives also support reform proposals that will allow Congress to reclaim much of the power it has delegated to the bureaucracy (see Chapters 3, 8, 9, and 10.)

Liberal

While conservatives trace many of the nation's problems to its departure from the principles of the Constitution, liberals are more likely to see problems with the Constitution itself as a framework for government in the nation's third century. While liberals usually share the conservative admiration for the framers as individuals, they question how relevant a two-hundred-year-old Constitution can be to today's challenges.

Liberal criticisms focus on the same aspects of the Constitution that conservatives praise: its anti-majoritarianism and its requirement of limited and divided government. The framers' fears of the masses and unrestrained democracy, liberals say, created a system that makes action much more difficult than inaction. Opponents of change have one opportunity after another to halt a reform—in the House, in the Senate, with a presidential veto, or with a Supreme Court decision. Except on rare occasions when there is widespread agreement that change is needed, as in the early years of Franklin Roosevelt's New Deal, the Constitution has become, in the words of one liberal observer, "a structure that almost guarantees stalemate today" (Cutler 1980, 127).

If private markets were adequate to produce a

John Branch. Courtesy *San Antonio Express and News.*

just society, as conservatives and libertarians think, liberals would not be disturbed by the limits the Constitution puts on government action. But with so many social and economic injustices in need of correction, liberals believe that limited and divided government more often works to protect the privileged and powerful, whose interest it is to prevent or postpone change, rather than to protect the people against tyranny.

Although liberals have always favored constitutional reform, the exact type of reform has varied. In 1885 the liberal political scientist Woodrow Wilson, who later became president, advocated moving away from separation of powers and toward an English parliamentary democracy in which the majority party chooses the executive and dominates government (Wilson 1885). From the 1930s through the 1950s, liberals tended to favor the delegation of more power to the president and executive branch agencies. But their enthusiasm for presidential power began to wane with President Lyndon Johnson's Vietnam policies and President Richard Nixon's abuses of office. For most liberals, assigning more and more power to the executive is no longer seen as the best cure for deadlock (Schlesinger Jr. 1973). Liberals also worry that the conservative court of recent years is too prone to legislate morality.

Recent liberal proposals for constitutional change focus on reducing the separation between the executive and legislative branches and thus the potential for stalemate. To guarantee that the executive and legislative branches would be controlled by the same party, Lloyd Cutler, counsel to the president during the administration of Jimmy Carter, has proposed extending the terms of the president and House members to six years, electing the entire Senate at the same time, and requiring voters to vote for a "team ticket" of president, vice-president, senator, and representative of the same party (Cutler 1980, 141–42). Henry Reuss, a liberal former House member, advocates bringing members of Congress into the president's cabinet, a practice now forbidden by the Constitution's prohibition against a member's holding civil office, to improve coordination of policy between the branches. Reuss and James MacGregor Burns, a liberal political scientist, suggest that allowing Congress to vote "no confidence" in the president and force a new presidential election while also allowing the president to dissolve an uncooperative Congress would increase the likelihood of one party's controlling both branches (Burns 1984, 190–211, 234–37). Although not endorsed by all liberals, these proposals illustrate the widespread liberal desire for reforms that would enable government to act more quickly and effectively (Schlesinger Jr. 1985, 50–54).

At the same time, liberals often applaud national protection of minority rights. Liberals want the First Amendment rights and the rights of the accused applied to the states and broadly interpreted to prevent state and local governments from infringing on the rights of unpopular groups. Liberals are especially wary of the conservative emphasis on property rights and conservative attempts to return powers to the states. They point out that federalism has often been used to justify the oppression of minorities, particularly blacks in the South.

Libertarian

Libertarian views on the Constitution appear to resemble those of conservatives, particularly in their celebration of the framers' ideal of limited and divided government. Milton Friedman, the libertarian economist, points out that the framers, like libertarians today, "regarded concentration of power, especially in the hands of government, as the great danger to freedom." Hence they produced a Constitution "intended to limit government power, to keep power decentralized, to reserve to individuals control over their lives" (Friedman and Friedman 1980, 286). Libertarians believe that by making it hard for government to "get things done," the framers freed the people to build the world's most dynamic economy.

Unfortunately, say libertarians, the Constitution has been "reinterpreted and given new meaning" by liberal jurists who have rendered the barriers to government action "ineffective." Pernicious effects have followed. One is the concentration of power in Washington, which has steadily made government more remote from the majority of the people. Another is the proliferation of greedy special interest groups, which now feel "entitled" to claim privileges and subsidies from the government simply because government is big enough to deliver them. While pursuit of individual self-interest in the market promotes the good of society, pursuit of group interests through an overgrown government unrestrained by effective constitutional limits leads to conflicting and chaotic policies aimed at "helping" everybody at everybody else's expense. For example, one government program encourages people to stop smoking, while another subsidizes well-connected tobacco farmers. Some agencies struggle to slow inflation, while others implement minimum wage laws, farm price supports, and regulations that raise prices (Friedman and Friedman 1980, 287,

291–92). Specific programs may cancel each other out, but the overall effect has been the steady erosion of liberty and the emergence of an overtaxed, overregulated, overgoverned society—the opposite of what the framers labored to build.

Like conservatives, libertarians want to restore what they see as the original intent of the Constitution. To this end, some have joined conservatives in supporting a constitutional amendment requiring a balanced federal budget, which, they hope, will pressure Congress to restrain spending and the growth of government. (Some liberal politicians have also endorsed this amendment because of its widespread public support, while noting that the Reagan and Bush administrations, filled with conservatives and libertarians, nonetheless ran up record deficits.) Other libertarian proposals for constitutional reform include denying Congress the power to impose wage-price controls, protective tariffs on imports, or a progressive income tax or to spend more than a fixed percentage of the gross national product (Friedman and Friedman 1980, 298–310).

Populist

Revolutionary-era populists opposed the Constitution, believing it to be stacked in favor of its authors. As time went on, populists accepted the Constitution, partly because it was so flexible. The presidential election, intended by the framers to insulate the president from popular control, gradually became a popular election in all but name (see Chapter 4). The election of senators by their state legislatures, another device to limit majority rule, was replaced by direct popular election under the Seventeenth Amendment in 1913.

Some of the original populist arguments against the Constitution are no longer relevant today. But right populists still object to the powers of federal judges appointed for life. In the past half-century, the courts have been increasingly aggressive in protecting minority rights, particularly rights against racial discrimination and the rights of criminal suspects. Since some of these decisions have been unpopular, right populists argue that the Constitution allows judges to trample upon majority rule. For example, polls consistently

showed a vast majority of the public opposed to court-ordered busing to achieve school integration, yet the people had no recourse, as the federal judges who ordered busing could not be removed by the voters (Lichter, Lichter, and Rothman 1986, 222–24). On the other hand, left populists disapprove of court decisions earlier in the century that gave corporations the same rights as individuals (Manley and Dolbeare 1987). Both types of populists see the judiciary as an elite that can threaten democracy. As one member of a Boston antibusing group put it:

> The dictatorship our ancestors fought to defeat has been reestablished here. Garrity [the federal judge who ordered busing in Boston] is the same as King George. He is appointed for life. Nobody can say nothing to him. His decisions are like laws. They are as unjust as taxation without representation. And the people have no choice but to revolt (quoted in Lukas 1985, 317).

Marxist

The Constitution is the most secure pillar of the established order in the United States, so it is hardly surprising that Marxists, who advocate radical change in that established order, take a critical view of it. To a large extent their view is based on the work of Charles A. Beard, an early twentieth-century historian whose *Economic Interpretation of the Constitution of the United States* (1913) challenged many long-held assumptions about the framers and the government they created. Although Beard himself was not a Marxist—he rejected Marxist socialism but was a strong advocate of government economic planning (Beale 1976)—his view of the Constitution accords closely with the Marxist perspective.

Beard saw the Constitution as "essentially an economic document" written by representatives of the upper classes whose financial interests were not well served by the Confederation. He pointed out that the delegates had some very personal reasons for wanting a strong central government. Forty of the fifty-five delegates owned government bonds that could not be paid off unless the central government had taxing power. Fourteen owned western lands that could not be sold unless Indian resistance could be ended, and eleven were merchants suffering from the state trade restrictions. Beard asserted that "the overwhelming majority" of these men stood to become even more wealthy if the Constitution they were writing was adopted. He also pointed out that the actual provisions of the Constitution invariably favored the interests of the rich, especially the limiting of popular election to the House of Representatives (Beard 1913, 73–151). There has been considerable disagreement among experts as to Beard's claims (McDonald 1958; Brown 1956; Manley and Dolbeare 1987).

Marxists today accept Beard's economic interpretation of the Constitution and add that the class interests of the framers were inevitably reflected in their decisions (Parenti 1987, 63, 66–68). Marxists acknowledge that today's Constitution is better than the original one, because the masses have struggled for changes like the abolition of slavery and the extension of the vote to non-property owners, blacks, and women. But they see the Constitution as still grossly deficient in not providing for social justice or guaranteeing vital economic rights like decent housing or education. Even political rights, say Marxists, have little meaning for the majority. For example, the press may be free from government controls, but its ownership by wealthy capitalists and dependence on corporate advertising make it unlikely to criticize the economic system.

From the Marxist perspective, the trouble with the Constitution is basic: it puts property rights above human rights. This radical defect cannot be cured by piecemeal reforms but only by a fundamental reordering of the economy in the interest of American workers.

Feminist

Feminists see the Constitution and its interpretation by male judges as a product of the patriarchal domination that has always characterized Western culture. This document, written by and for males, did not acknowledge women as individuals with equal rights and privileges. The post–Civil War amendments regarding the status of blacks provided a basis for change, and feminists at first hoped that the Equal Protection Clause of the Fourteenth Amendment would become a vehicle for according women the same rights men enjoyed in political, social, and economic arenas. But in *Bradwell v. Illinois* (1873) (see Chapters 1 and 9) the Court held for the first time that women and men operated in separate spheres and that the protections embodied in the Fourteenth Amendment did not apply to women. Courts did hold, however, that women could not be discriminated against in frivolous ways.

Following *Bradwell*, feminist energies concentrated primarily in the suffrage movement, but after the right to vote had been guaranteed in the

Nineteenth Amendment, feminists divided over whether women needed the specific protections the courts had allocated to them in the workplace or whether there was need for another constitutional amendment outlawing sex as a basis for distinctive treatment in the law. Social feminists argued that women deserved special protections in their workplace because of their roles as wives and mothers. Radical feminists argued for an Equal Rights Amendment (ERA) and gender neutrality in the courts although they recognized the inherent dangers gender neutrality posed for women in a patriarchal society in which a largely masculine body of law would continue to be interpreted primarily by male justices (McGlen and O'Connor 1983, 366–87).

Beginning in the 1960s, feminists began a two-pronged assault on the Constitution. The movement for an Equal Rights Amendment first introduced in the 1920s continued, but feminists also began to argue that the Equal Protection Clause of the Fourteenth Amendment *did* apply to women. In a series of decisions, the Court agreed. Ironically, ability to use the Equal Protection Clause to redress discrimination, coupled with civil rights legislation protecting women, undercut efforts to pass the ERA, which had been resubmitted to the states in 1972 but failed to be ratified by the required thirty-eight States before time ran out in 1982. Some social feminists continue to argue that women are sufficiently distinct from men to preserve the special status that the law has traditionally provided. These feminists prefer a case-by-case approach that allows for the preservation of special privileges they fear an Equal Rights Amendment might actually take away. Radical feminists continue to believe that only a constitutional amendment will ensure the legal rights of women.

Since the lapse of the ERA in 1982, the split in the feminist perspective on the Constitution has continued. All feminists, however, recognize the power of law for changing society. They continue to promote legislation that will benefit women and to seek explicit constitutional protections for the rights women have won. Laws and rulings regarding abortion, rape, and the rights and responsibilities of parents and offspring are of keen interest. The body of law is, after all, a male creation, and it needs to be changed to incorporate the female point of view. As the feminist Ava Baron has stated, "To use the law as an effective strategy in the feminist struggle for gender equality requires changing the male perspective embedded in law" (Baron 1987, 493). To change the male perspective is not simply a matter of increasing the number of women in the judiciary; there must be more women appointees connected to broader feminist struggles for social change. Feminists concede that the Constitution as now interpreted is superior to that created in the summer of 1787. But further reinterpretation is necessary if the freedom and equality advocated so strongly by Jefferson in the Declaration of Independence is to become the experience rather than merely the dream of a majority of American women (Stetson 1991, 14–41; McGlen and O'Connor 1983, 366–87; Baron 1987, 474–563).

DOES THE CONSTITUTION WORK?

Most Americans today would not want to live under the Constitution of 1787. The Constitution did not create slavery or the inferior status of women, but it left those injustices intact. It also limited direct popular participation in the national government to the election of one house of Congress. Why, then, do Americans today so revere the Constitution?

We believe that the answer lies in the flexibility built into the document by its framers. Some of the adjustments, like the end of slavery and the direct election of senators, have come through constitutional amendments. Others, like enhanced status for women, have come primarily through court decisions and legislative action. The existence of different routes to change has kept the Constitution vital. And although Americans should be cautious about altering the Constitution, further changes are likely to be needed in the future.

SUMMARY AND REVIEW

The United States Constitution is one of the most revered, albeit misunderstood, documents in history. Drawing heavily on the models of the original thirteen state constitutions, the national Constitution arose out of a tide of dissatisfaction with the Articles of Confederation. All but one of the state legislatures sent delegates to Philadelphia in 1787 to the convention that would eventually produce the U.S. Constitution.

Almost without exception, the delegates were men of wealth and power who shared a firm commitment to the Lockean concepts of natural rights and limited government as well as a conservative mistrust of a democracy that would threaten property rights. Their solution was republicanism, or representative government. They believed that the separation of powers and a system of checks and balances were the best guarantees of liberty. Their strong commitment to nationalism was tempered by a healthy respect for federalism, or power sharing between the states and the central government.

Despite these areas of agreement, sharp disagreements remained—chief among them the composition of the legislative branch. Again compromise prevailed, with the two-house legislative structure we know today satisfying both the large states, which wanted propor-

tional representation, and the small states, which wanted equal representation. Regional differences were overcome by the Commerce Compromise, which allowed import taxes but forbade export taxes, and the Three-Fifths Compromise, which counted each slave as three-fifths of a free white person for purposes of both representation and taxation.

Yet the new Constitution, sent to the states in September 1787, was extremely controversial. Opponents, called Anti-Federalists, included common people, who feared an aristocratic conspiracy, as well as wealthy intellectuals, who objected to the absence of a Bill of Rights. The Federalists' willingness to include such a bill proved decisive, and the new government was set up by 1789. The Bill of Rights—the first ten amendments to the Constitution—was ratified in 1791.

The U.S. Constitution, the oldest in the world, has changed over the past two hundred years through changes in custom and usage, the amendment process, and judicial reinterpretation. Although judicial reinterpretation has often been controversial, as in the area of women's rights, the most important ingredient in constitutional change will always be public opinion. The basic flexibility of the Constitution and its responsiveness to public consensus best explain its endurance and success.

IMPORTANT TERMS

Annapolis Convention
Anti-Federalists
Articles of Confederation
bicameral legislature
Bill of Rights
checks and balances
Commerce Clause
Commerce Compromise
Confederation Congress
Constitution

constitutional amendment
Constitutional Convention
Continental Congress
Declaration of Independence
Eighteenth Amendment
electoral college
executive branch
exports
federalism
Federalists

Fifth Amendment
First Amendment
Great Compromise
habeus corpus
impeach(ment)
imports
judicial branch
judicial reinterpretation
legislative branch
nationalism
New Jersey Plan
Ninth Amendment

republicanism
separation of powers
Seventeenth Amendment
Shays' Rebellion
sovereignty
states' rights
Tenth Amendment
Three-fifths Compromise
Twenty-first Amendment
tyranny
Virginia Plan

3

THE FEDERAL SYSTEM

It is August 2002 and the people of the West have had enough. For years they have chafed under federal environmental and land-use restrictions that some felt retarded their economic development. Others feared that the national government would permit the West to be torn up in the name of energy production to fill the furnaces and gas tanks of the East. Then the national government required states receiving aid for highway construction to raise their legal drinking age to twenty-one. In Washington the measure was seen as a reasonable way to cut down on teenage drunk driving; in the West, as another federal intrusion on states' rights. Then nuclear waste from the entire country was forced on Nevada. Finally, when an eastern Democrat won the presidency in 2000 and used his power to challenge state control over water rights dissident western Democrats and Republicans formed a "Freedom" party. Wearing the ten-gallon hats that have become their trademark, Freedom party delegates met in Cheyenne, Wyoming, and endorsed a platform calling for state "nullification" of unconstitutional national policies. Some radicals favor forming a "Republic of the West." The president, vowing to preserve the Union at all costs, has suddenly moved one hundred thousand troops from overseas to military bases in four western states. Outside the bases, protesters gather. The Freedom party vows that the protests will be peaceful, but worried soldiers see rifles in some protesters' pickup trucks.

A fantasy? Certainly. No one seriously believes that conflict between the national government and the states is likely to lead to another civil war. Yet conflict is an ever-present reality in the American federal system. Western states have indeed rebelled against land-use regulations on the national government's land in their states. A Colorado state senator once characterized Congress' efforts to impose a national speed limit and drinking age as "blackmail tactics" that violated "the basic principles of federalism as designed by our founding fathers" (Hopper 1987, 7). At the same time, the states and the national government cooperate in a host of areas to solve national problems; without such cooperation, the United States would have collapsed long ago. This intriguing mix of cooperation and conflict between nation and states is the subject of this chapter.

THE CONSTITUTIONAL EVOLUTION, 1789–1994

When they met in Philadelphia, the framers were part of a minority who thought of themselves as Americans first. Most people, even if they supported a stronger national government, thought of themselves as Virginians, Pennsylvanians, or natives of another state first and as Americans second. Their allegiance to individual states did not end with the ratification of the Constitution; many years later, one-quarter of a million Americans died and more than a million took up arms to defend *states' rights*—state powers within the federal system—against what they felt to be encroachment by the national government.

That few Americans today would put loyalty to their state above loyalty to the nation is both a cause and a result of the growth of the power and responsibilities of the federal government since 1789. Even the most nationalistic of the framers would be amazed at the extent to which the national government has become involved in activities defined in their time as exclusively state or local responsibilities. This does not mean, however, that state and local governments no longer have important powers; the American states and localities continue to enjoy a degree of **autonomy**—independence from central control—matched in few other democratic societies. It is the continuing importance of the states, as much as the fact of increasing national power, that makes the federal system important to

serious study of American national government.

Federalism in the Constitution

The Constitution represents a compromise between the nationalism of most of its framers and their need to gain support from the locally oriented majority. James Madison's Virginia Plan proposed giving Congress power "to legislate in all cases to which the separate States are incompetent" (quoted in Pritchett 1968, 22), a sweeping grant of power indeed. Those who favored power residing in the individual states feared that a strong national government would undermine their hope for a truly representative government, which they believed could function only in a relatively small area. Madison, however, made a strong argument for a centralized government, and, after some debate, a compromise was reached (Diamond 1993, 42–47). It was decided that the new Constitution would follow the example of the state constitutions and give the new national government specific **enumerated powers.**

These powers, sometimes referred to as delegated powers, were contained within Article I of the new Constitution. The first three articles of the Constitution list the powers of the legislative, executive, and judicial branches of government, respectively, implying that all powers not listed would remain in the hands of the states.

Still, the **Elastic Clause**—Article I, Section 8—gave Congress the power to make all laws "necessary and proper" for carrying out the enumerated powers. In *McCulloch v. Maryland* (1819), the Supreme Court interpreted the clause broadly by approving the establishment of a national bank, a power not specifically delegated to the national government in the Constitution. The Court determined that the Elastic Clause gave Congress the right to choose its means for carrying out the enumerated powers. The national government thus gained **implied powers**, which are considered

Calhoun had developed a theory justifying state nullification of national laws. An extreme conservative even for his time, he believed that only the propertied classes should have a voice in government. The problem was that property owners in the United States were divided by sectional interests. Northern manufacturers and merchants were coming to dominate the national government, and with increased power they could impose their will upon the outnumbered southern planters, as they had in 1828 by enacting a high tariff on the foreign-manufactured goods the South needed. Southerners called this the "Tariff of Abominations." According to Calhoun, the system of checks and balances could not prevent this tyranny by the majority, for the North had both more population and more states than the South and could control both houses of Congress and the election of the president. Someday the North might even move to abolish slavery, an act Calhoun feared would lead to a general lower-class revolution throughout the country.

Fortunately, said Calhoun, the Constitution provided an answer. Since the states had entered voluntarily into the Union, they retained their sovereignty and thus the right to refuse obedience to any national law that infringed on their rights. Congress could legislate for the whole country only by obtaining the consent of the majority in each and every state.

Andrew Jackson, a southerner and a slaveholder, opposed the Tariff of Abominations as much as Calhoun did, but he was horrified by the South Carolinian's theory of nullification. To Jackson, a populist, the Constitution was not a contract between the states but an act of the people, who alone had the right to alter or dissolve it. Therefore no state could ever nullify a law, even a bad one, passed by the majority of the people through their elected representatives in Congress. Besides, argued Jackson, if minority rights were to be placed above majority rule, what about the minority of South Carolinians who opposed nullification? Allowing all minorities a veto would ultimately bring government to a standstill.

Jackson's proclamation, given on December 10, 1932, asked South Carolina to stop resisting national authority. In January, he asked Congress to pass a force bill giving him authority to use force against South Carolina. At the same time, however, he called upon Congress to reduce the tariff rates to keep the rest of the South from rallying behind nullification. By March, a new tariff bill had been approved by Congress, and South Carolina—deserted by the rest of the South—withdrew its nullification law. Jackson had outmaneuvered Calhoun, but the theory of nullification remained alive and helped to inspire the secessionists of 1861. If Jackson had used force against South Carolina in 1833, would the Civil War have been averted—or broken out thirty years earlier?

Source: Current 1966; Freehling 1966; Remini 1984; von Holst 1980.

---

came under the liberal Presidents John Kennedy and Lyndon Johnson in the 1960s. Under their New Frontier and Great Society programs, more federal funds became available to the states and localities for a wider range of programs than ever before. Between 1960 and 1968 the number of different grant programs tripled (from 132 to 379), and federal aid dollars more than tripled (from $7 billion to $24 billion). States and localities were now dependent on the national government for 22 per-

cent of their funds (Conlan 1988, 6; Howitt 1984, 8).

Another major change instituted during the Kennedy-Johnson years was an increased trend toward federal-local partnerships. Prior to 1960 most federal aid went to states, where rural-dominated legislatures frequently administered federally funded programs in a more conservative manner than their liberal designers intended. Southern states, for example, often made it hard for people to qualify for welfare assistance in rural areas during the summer so farm workers would be compelled to work for low pay during the harvest (Bensel and Sanders 1986, 53–59). Under Kennedy and especially under Johnson, much federal aid bypassed state legislatures and was channeled directly to city governments and even to private social action groups run by liberal activists. The Johnson administration also increased the number of **project grants**, which are given at the discretion of federal administrators and are useful for experimental projects; **formula grants** had usually been given automatically to states that met statutory requirements for programs such as building highways (Palmer 1984, 15–17). Project grants further increased the national government's ability to influence state and local decisions by holding fiscal strings.

Conservative Reforms

Conservatives and libertarians viewed the liberal-sponsored growth of grants with alarm. They thought equalizing government services less important than local self-determination, which seemed to be slipping away. At the same time, it was clear that sufficient political support did not exist for a total dismantling of the federal aid networks, even when the country elected more conservative presidents like Richard Nixon and Ronald Reagan. Conservatives, therefore, sought to reform the system in order to minimize state and local dependence on the national treasury and to decrease national influence over state and local policy-making.

President Nixon's formula for pruning back growth of the grant system called for the national government to make some funds available to the states and localities without putting strict controls on their use. Known as **revenue sharing**, this program was intended to allow the lower levels of government to benefit from the national government's revenue-collecting ability while returning control to the state and local level. Initially hailed by many conservatives and some liberals who thought it might be a way to channel more funds to states and localities in need (Reuss 1970), revenue sharing was also popular with state and local governments. Still, the program was not without its critics. Liberals complained that aid to local community action groups was cut back or terminated as revenue sharing increased. On the other hand, federal aid continued to increase as the Democratic Congress ensured that the major Johnson era grant programs were maintained, even as revenue sharing increased. By 1977 federal aid to the states and localities was up to $68.4 billion, more than triple the 1969 total (Palmer 1984, 32). Many conservatives felt that Nixon had accomplished little in returning power to the states and localities: they seemed to be growing even more dependent on federal money.

Under President Jimmy Carter, the number of grant programs began to increase again, reaching 539 by the end of his administration (Howitt 1984, 14). President Ronald Reagan made it one of his highest priorities to cut back both the number and dollar amounts of federal aid programs. His approach was more conservative than Nixon's because he sought to remove federal money, not just the federal strings attached to it. Between 1980 and 1988 federal funding for state and local governments dropped from more than 18 percent to 13.3 percent of their revenue, a smaller percentage than at any time since 1959. Local governments often complained that states did not act to replace enough of the local revenue lost from the national government (Howitt 1984, 14; *Statistical Abstract, 1992*, 284; *National Journal*, 26 November 1988, 3001–05; see also Nathan et al. 1987). And although the drive for economy forced many cuts, including the elimination of revenue sharing, conservatives did not achieve the kind of far-reaching changes in the federal aid system they hoped for. President George Bush did not change the pattern initiated by the Reagan administration. A tight

"STEP RIGHT UP—EVERYBODY GETS ONE STAR AND PART OF A STRIPE"

Herbert Block. From *Herblock Through the Looking Glass* (W. W. Norton, 1984).

governmental Relations 1985, 139–43). Grant trends can be explained in part by the party and ideology of a president in office. The Democrats, who were mainly liberals, stressed national goals when allocating these funds and preferred to stipulate how the money should be spent. They also sought to concentrate on urban areas. Republicans, on the other hand, who were mainly conservatives, advocated a decrease in the stipulations and regulations attached to federal grants and attempted to spread the allocated funds more widely. The economic situation also plays a major role in shaping grant trends (Palmer 1984, 51–53).

The trend during the last few decades of allowing local governments leeway in the spending of federal grants has given these governments increased authority to determine which local groups and projects will receive the funds. Local groups must now work closely with local governments to ensure that their goals are reached. In such cases local governments gain more responsibility for decision making and are actually strengthened by federal grants. An example of the process is the Community Development Block Grant (CDBG), which gives money to cities to use for a wide variety of building projects. President

federal budget will make it difficult for President Bill Clinton to increase federal funding to state and local governments in a dramatic way, but he did propose increasing community development block grants as part of his failed 1993 economic stimulus program (*National Journal*, 13 March 1993, 611–14; *National Journal*, 1 May 1993, 1061).

INTERDEPENDENCE AND INDEPENDENCE

Grant programs have led to a certain amount of fiscal interdependence in American government (U.S. Advisory Commission on Inter-

Robert Dornfried. © Dornfried/Rothco.

Clinton sought to expand this program to stimulate the economy in 1993 but failed partly because critics focused on cities that wanted to use the money for projects like swimming pools and golf courses (*Congressional Quarterly Weekly Report*, 10 April 1993, 907–9).

Where the States Still Count

When one compares the activities of the national government today with those of the national government created in 1789, it may seem as if all the meaningful functions of the states have been swallowed up. But that is not so. While few functions of government today may be reserved to the states in the absolute sense that the authors of the Tenth Amendment intended, public policy regarding many issues is still set by state and local governments. On other issues, power is shared among federal, state, and local authorities. Some scholars have compared today's federal system to a marble cake, in which the colors are swirled together. **Marble-cake federalism**, in which state and federal powers mix and penetrate each other in constantly changing patterns, is very different from the structure of **layer-cake federalism**, in which federal and state powers are strictly separated (Grodzins 1966, 37–49; see also Elazar, 1987).

Two of the most important functions controlled by states today are general police powers and public services like education. While the national government is involved in some funding and interstate aspects in these areas, the basic powers belong to the states and their designated local government units.

Among the powers reserved to the states by the Constitution are general **police powers** over law enforcement and criminal justice. These powers, which enable state and local governments to make and enforce public safety laws, are an important means of ensuring division of power; they prevent the national government from making uniform rules about public safety matters unless they are interstate in nature. Perhaps the most dramatic indication that the states retain their importance is that they are allowed to put criminals to death. Though the Supreme Court has set limits on this power (the death penalty cannot be mandatory for a whole category of crime like murder, and judges must have discretion in sentencing), the final decision on whether to have and use a death penalty rests with the states. Fourteen states have no death penalty, and three others have a capital punishment statute but have imposed no death sentences since 1980. The other thirty-three all have prisoners under death sentences. The South takes a conservative attitude toward crime; since 1980, about two-thirds of all executions have occurred in Florida, Georgia, Louisiana, and Texas (*Statistical Abstract, 1992,* 200; *World Almanac, 1993,* 949–50). Penalties for lesser offenses also vary dramatically from one state to another because of mandates by state legislatures and the practices of local judges. Civil laws regulating marriage and divorce are likewise under state control, as are regulations pertaining to insurance and professional licensing.

Another area in which states maintain their importance concerns **public services**. Since the national government contributes only part, and for some services a very small part, of the money in this area, states can and do spend dramatically unequal amounts for public services. Public education, for which only 6 percent of the funds come from the national level, is the most important example.

The wealth of a state plays a major role in disparities in the amount of money allocated to education (see Table 3.1). In 1990 the average household income in the top five education-funding states was $34,443, while the average in the bottom five was $24,355 (*Statistical Abstract, 1992,* 448). Economic differences are not the only variable, however. Pennsylvania is below the national average in income but taxes its citizens to support a high level of spending in education. Other states with higher incomes have taken another path; California is ninth in

**TABLE 3.1   PER PUPIL SPENDING ON ELEMENTARY
AND SECONDARY EDUCATION, 1990**

TOP FIVE STATES*		BOTTOM FIVE STATES	
1. New Jersey	$8,439	46. South Dakota	$3,312
2. New York	8,094	47. Arkansas	3,272
3. Connecticut	7,934	48. Mississippi	3,151
4. Rhode Island	6,523	49. Idaho	3,037
5. Massachusetts	6,170	50. Utah	2,730

* Alaska is excluded because its high living costs exaggerate the difference in spending between states. Figures for all states include state and
local spending plus federal aid.

Source: Statistical Abstract, 1992, 154, 448.

average household income but thirtieth in educational spending (*Statistical Abstract, 1992,*
154, 448). Similar disparities exist in funding
levels for many other government services
provided by states, with northeastern and
midwestern states usually spending more than
southern and western states, even after income disparities are accounted for.

One reason for these interstate differences
is that the different states and regions have
different **political cultures**—different perspectives on politics and government. The Northeast was settled largely by English Puritans
with a moralistic orientation to politics that
stressed government's responsibility for the
moral life of the community. While this impulse once had conservative consequences
(support for religious teaching in public
schools, for example), it is now associated with
the liberal emphasis on equal opportunity and
social justice. One way of pursuing these liberal goals has been to educate the masses—
hence the greater willingness to spend on
schools. The South, in contrast, has a traditionalist orientation—a conservative political
culture that tolerates a high degree of elite
control of politics. Southern populism has only
rarely been able to overcome southern elitism.
Thus even a fairly rich southern state like
Texas spends little on education. The Midwest
and West are divided between the liberal mor-

alism brought by Yankee settlers from New
England and an individualist or libertarian
view, favored by many non-English immigrants, that stresses the right and responsibility of the individual to get ahead on his or
her own. Some of these states are high spending, and some are low spending (Elazar 1966,
79–116). Political culture relates strongly,
though not perfectly, to current education
spending levels.

Other variables explain differences among
states. One theory maintains that party competition and voter participation within a state
greatly influence public policy. For example, in
a state with a high level of party competition
and voter participation, public policy would
presumably move toward an increase in
spending to gain support for the political party
in power and satisfy the demands of the voting
public. Another explanation for interstate differences emphasizes economic factors as the
primary determinant in state policy. In essence, this theory asserts that the more funds
available to a state, the more money the state
will spend (Dye 1987, 310–12).

States have wide discretion in many other
aspects of education policy. Although the national government mandates certain programs
providing services to disadvantaged, handicapped, and non-English-speaking students,
states are generally allowed to set their school

curricula, academic standards, and disciplinary procedures or to delegate such decisions to local school districts. Some states, for example, require schools to select textbooks from a list approved by a state textbook commission; others allow local school boards to make their own rules for textbook selection. States also set student requirements. Texas has imposed a statewide "no pass, no play" rule requiring students to pass all their courses in order to participate in extracurricular activities; in some schools, the rule wiped out whole football teams and choirs ("No-Pass No-Play" 1986, 50–52, 56). In most other states, such decisions are made locally.

States are allowed to set their own policies in other public service areas as well. While a large part of the funds for welfare programs comes from the national government, the states set the level of benefits for each recipient, and these vary even more than education spending levels. In 1990 average monthly payments to families in Aid to Families with Dependent Children (AFDC) ranged from $640 in California to $121 in Alabama (*Statistical Abstract, 1992*, 371). Some welfare programs are entirely state funded, and these may be terminated by the state at will. In 1991 Michigan's conservative Governor John Engler persuaded the legislature to eliminate welfare for able-bodied individuals with no children, throwing more than ninety thousand people off the rolls and, in some cases, onto the streets. Engler stressed the obligation of adults to provide for themselves and the need to balance the state budget during a severe recession (Kaza 1991, 74–77; *Economist*, 18 January 1992, 13).

The people have also gained increased power at the state level. Reforms by populists and liberals during the progressive era early in this century (see Chapter 10) made state governments more responsible to a majority of the voters. Such reforms included the **recall**, a special vote called by petition that may remove a legislative, executive, or judicial official before the end of the term; the **initiative**, which allows voters to propose a law or constitutional amendment by obtaining a certain number of signatures on a petition; and the **referendum**, which is a yes-no vote by qualified voters on certain public policy issues (Simmons and Dvorin 1977, 138).

John Crawford. Courtesy *Alabama Journal*.

Where Local Governments Count

All local governments are units of state governments, and states often delegate their powers to them. One power exercised primarily by local governments is **zoning**, the power to decide what can or cannot be done with a particular piece of property. It is in the area of zoning that local governments most often come into conflict with one another. Persons working on private projects will often try to play one local government against another to get the most favorable zoning decision. In these cases, negotiations among local governments are common.

States come into conflict with local governments over property use, too. It is not unusual for state governments to differ with local units over specific projects, such as the placement of an airport or freeway. The state might think the facility needed, while local government might want it placed elsewhere—or compete with other local governments to have it. On the other hand, local communities might want convention centers or industrial parks while the state is reluctant to provide funds. On projects with a major public purpose, all governments exercise **eminent domain**, the power to take over private property provided it is taken for a public purpose and just compensation is awarded.

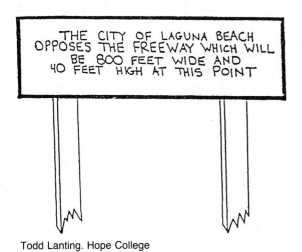

THE CITY OF LAGUNA BEACH OPPOSES THE FREEWAY WHICH WILL BE 800 FEET WIDE AND 40 FEET HIGH AT THIS POINT

Todd Lanting. Hope College

In disagreements with state governments, local governments are at a disadvantage because they are the creatures of state governments and could, theoretically at least, be abolished at the will of the state. A legal principle known as **Dillon's Rule** states that a municipal corporation can exercise only those powers granted to it by state law, those implied from the granted powers, and those essential for the purpose of the organization. If there is any doubt about where the power resides, it belongs to the state (Nice 1987, 137–38). In an example of state-local government conflict, Arlington County, Virginia, a close suburb of Washington, D.C., has been frustrated by its lack of authority to pass ordinances and taxes due to Virginia's adherence to the rule (*Arlington Courier*, 23 December 1992, 3).

Local governments are also much more dependent on state funds than states are on the national government, and funding gives the states additional leverage (Nice 1987, 146–47). Often, however, compromises are reached. For example, a freeway desired by the state might be built, but at a location acceptable to the local government. A convention center desired by the local government might get state funding, but of a limited nature.

Special districts also call for cooperation among different levels and units of government. These are districts created under state supervision for special purposes. One of the most common types is school districts. Sometimes their boundaries are the same as those of local government units, sometimes not. A school district, for example, might cover an entire county, whereas an emergency services district might cover one or two towns. Some transporation districts cover an entire metropolitan area. Thus a family in one area might be under the jurisdiction of several different districts, while a family in another area will have all public services provided by a single local government unit. In the end various district administrations must work together, but coordination is not always easy to achieve.

Again, the states set the rules, deciding how local governments and special districts are set up, but local residents have some influence over the matter.

RESOLVING CONFLICTS IN A FEDERAL SYSTEM

Regionalism—a consciousness of regionally based interest, aims, or political beliefs— occurs when regions with distinct social, political, and economic interests compete for position within a federal government. Thus the United States, as a federal system, has long suffered the friction of regionalism. Early in the Republic the competition between North and South threatened the nation's very existence. Today changes in the economy have created a new set of regions. Competition between states in the **frostbelt** (Northeast and Midwest) and **sunbelt** (South and West) over federal funds hampers the national effort to relieve the budget crisis. The competing interests of rural, urban, and suburban areas and national-state-local conflicts over federal lands in the West also demonstrate the complexities of American federalism and the need for cooperation among all levels of government.

Regional Conflicts

The Northeast and the Midwest were long the center of American industry. Their factories and cities attracted workers from southern and border states devastated by the Civil War and characterized by poverty. Times have changed for both the North and the South. Population growth in recent decades has been much greater in the South and West than in the frostbelt states of the Northeast and Midwest, and the sunbelt also contains the fastest growing metropolitan areas. The rapidly growing states of the West and South gained a number of additional seats in Congress as a result of the 1990 census and are likely to continue to gain seats in the 2000 census (*Statistical Abstract, 1992*, 255).

In the 1960s and 1970s, people were attracted to the sunbelt because of its milder climate, greater recreational opportunities, and lower living costs. Industries were attracted by lower taxes and lower labor costs. Many companies took advantage of the sunbelt's greater possibilities for energy development. As a consequence, sunbelt states experienced major economic growth while, in general, the frostbelt region bore the brunt of tough economic times. Some frostbelt states recovered a bit in the 1980s, but the general trend has not been reversed. The massive expenditures required to modernize aging frostbelt machinery placed additional strains on industries already suffering from high energy and labor costs. As people and industries moved out of northern cities, taxes had to be increased to replace lost funds. In a "snowball" effect, the higher taxes drove out even more people and industries. The result was an eroding economic base and increased unemployment.

In recent years the sunbelt has had problems as well. Population growth combined with a laissez-faire orientation toward urban planning has created problems for cities like Phoenix and necessitated tax increases (Caraley 1977; Stone and Sanders 1987). Declining energy costs have hurt the economies of states like Louisiana and Texas and made the advantage perceived by businesses moving south in the 1970s seem less certain. Labor costs, though still cheaper in the South than in the North, have been rising in the South as northern costs for labor have been restrained. During the last few years, sunny California has been suffering "frostbelt" problems. Despite these changes, the general movement south and west continues. It is estimated that 20 million of the 23-million-person population growth in the United States during the 1980s was in the southern and western states (*Chicago Tribune*, 1 April 1990, 1, 9).

The battle between the frostbelt and sunbelt regions focuses on the distribution of federal tax dollars among the states. Earlier in the century, when the North's economy was expanding, that region received fewer dollars in federal funds than it contributed in taxes, and funds were directed to the poverty-stricken South and the developing West. Today, despite lack of growth in the frostbelt states and expansion in the sunbelt, the northern states still receive fewer federal funds in relation to tax dollars than the states of the South and West (*National Journal*, 2 July 1977, 1034). For example, in 1976 fourteen states in the Northeast and East North Central regions sent $32.7 billion more to Washington in taxes than they received in federal funds. Meanwhile, southern and western states enjoyed a $23.1 billion surplus in their **federal balance of payments** (*National Journal*, 26 June 1976, 878–91), which is the difference between taxes collected in a state and the budgetary appropriation spent by the federal government in that state. While a growing awareness of the discrepancy in federal allocations has resulted in some correcting shifts, these have been slow, and the imbalance continues (*National Journal*, 7 February 1981, 234). As of 1988, for every $1 of taxes sent to the national government, the South and West received $1.13, while the Northeast and East North Central received only $.84 (*Statistical Abstract, 1992*, 22; *Vital Statistics on American Politics* 1992, 319–20).

In an effort to stem the flow of federal funds away from their region, legislators in the Northeast-Midwest Congressional Coalition (NMCC), along with the Northeast-Midwest Senate Coalition and the Northeast-Midwest Institute, have sought ways to change government funding laws so that the North might receive more benefits. The NMCC has secured a closer connection between the level of federal aid, economic decay, and unemployment problems. For example, prior to 1977 funds for the Community Development Block Grant (CDBG) program, which promotes urban redevelopment, were allocated according to a formula based primarily on the percentage of poor people in a community and so clearly favoring the sunbelt states with their lower incomes. In 1977 northerners succeeded in changing the formula to take into consideration the percentage of housing units in a community built prior to 1940, so as to favor older northern cities (Weinstein and Wigley 1987, 18–19). In essence, activists in the NMCC convinced their regional colleagues that assertive action was needed to protect regional interests. The result was a greater concern for fairness in the allocation of federal funds and an improved position for the frostbelt states, which continue to press for revision of the formula to include population growth and out-migration, employment growth, income growth, unemployment, rate of capital investment, and rate of deterioration of existing facilities (Dilger 1981, 197–206).

The frostbelters also want cost of living factored into estimates of **per capita income** (total personal income earned in an area divided by the total population to determine the average personal income per individual in the area) because the income advantage in the North is partially canceled by higher prices and taxes (Northeast-Midwest Congressional Coalition et al. 1979; Dilger 1981, 197–206; Northeast-Midwest Congressional Coalition et al. 1988).

The sunbelt has responded with its own interest groups: the Southern Growth Policies Board (SGPB), the Western Governors' Policy Office (WESTPO), the Western Congressional Coalition, and the Sunbelt Institute, which does research in support of the southern and western points of view. Sunbelt members of Congress currently argue for federal funding formulas based on considerations like poverty levels or per capita income, which remains higher in the frostbelt.

Both sides have stressed that some imbalance in federal expenditures in the states is good. They agree that the national government exists in part to even out the distribution of funds and thereby help those states or areas whose people need help the most. The discussions between the regional coalitions center on who is, in fact, the neediest. Although neither side claims to be promoting regionalism, the battle for funds has divided the Congress along frostbelt-sunbelt lines. This conflict among the states is not likely to tear the country apart as did the Civil War; and, indeed, the imbalance in funding has narrowed. But regional rivalry does complicate the cooperation among local, state, and national levels of government that is necessary in a federal system.

Rural-Urban-Suburban Conflicts

Political struggles among urban, rural, and suburban areas have an even longer history than frostbelt-sunbelt conflicts. At its beginning, the United States was a rural society. Alexander Hamilton's attempt to implement pro-urban policies of industrialization was defeated by the more popular agrarianism of Thomas Jefferson. Cities and industry grew throughout the nineteenth century, but political power remained with the rural areas.

The 1920 census showed that, for the first time, more Americans lived in urban areas than in rural areas. But states standing to lose representation delayed the reapportionment of seats in the House of Representatives until after the 1930 census. In the meantime, the first federal programs to aid farmers were passed. Such programs have continued despite the rapid decline in rural population and representation in the House, in part because less populous rural states have disproportionate power in the Senate. In 1964 the Supreme Court ruled in *Westberry v. Sanders* that congressional districts had to be nearly equal in population, and the resulting reallocations increased representation for urban areas. These

new representatives, in turn, supported President Lyndon Johnson's Great Society programs with their expanded federal grants to cities (Farkas 1971).

Just as cities became dependent on federal aid, an increasing number of Americans were moving to the suburbs. As before, this population shift led to a gradual shift in representation in the U.S. House. Suburbanites, who tend to be more affluent, have been reluctant to support large federal expenditures for the cities, and they supported President Ronald Reagan's reduction of grant programs. Now some older suburbs are beginning to experience "urban" problems, like crime, and suburban support for federal aid programs may be on the rise.

Local governments and political leaders have formed interest groups, like the National League of Cities (NLC) and the United States Conference of Mayors (USCM), to increase federal aid, preferably with few regulations attached. Occasionally these groups work together to achieve a specific goal, as the NLC and USCM did in helping Congress draft clean air and water programs. They often follow up on such programs to ensure that adequate federal aid is granted. At the same time, some national agencies view such groups as a threat to their control over such programs (Haider 1993, 124–31). For example, late in 1989, the Department of Health and Human Services (HHS) and liberals on the House Health and the Environment Subcommittee expressed frustration at efforts by the National Governors Association to prevent further increases in Medicaid benefits that would raise state health budgets because of matching funds. States acknowledge that health care for the poor is a problem, but they are not willing to support policy changes that will increase their costs (*National Journal*, 16 December 1989, 3044–47). By 1992, funding of health care in general had become a major crisis that presidential candidate Clinton pledged to address if elected. In this policy area, as in others, government interest groups are likely to play an important role in future grant allocations.

National-State-Local Conflicts: An Example

One of the most controversial issues in the western United States, the ownership of **federal lands** by the federal government, shows in detail the intertwined nature of the American federal system. The West, settled relatively late in American history, long served as a reserve of mineral and natural resources. Even after western territories attained statehood, large, semiarid areas never passed into private hands, and population remained sparse. Today the federal government continues to own 54.5 percent of the total acreage in the Rocky Mountain and Pacific Coast states (*Statistical Abstract, 1992,* 207), as Figure 3.1 shows.

The operation of federal land within these states can be complicated. Reorganizational

"Boy, We Could Develop That Into Some Fine Stumps"
Herbert Block. From *Herblock's Here and Now* (Simon & Schuster, 1955).

Figure 3.1 Percentage of Federal Land by Region and State

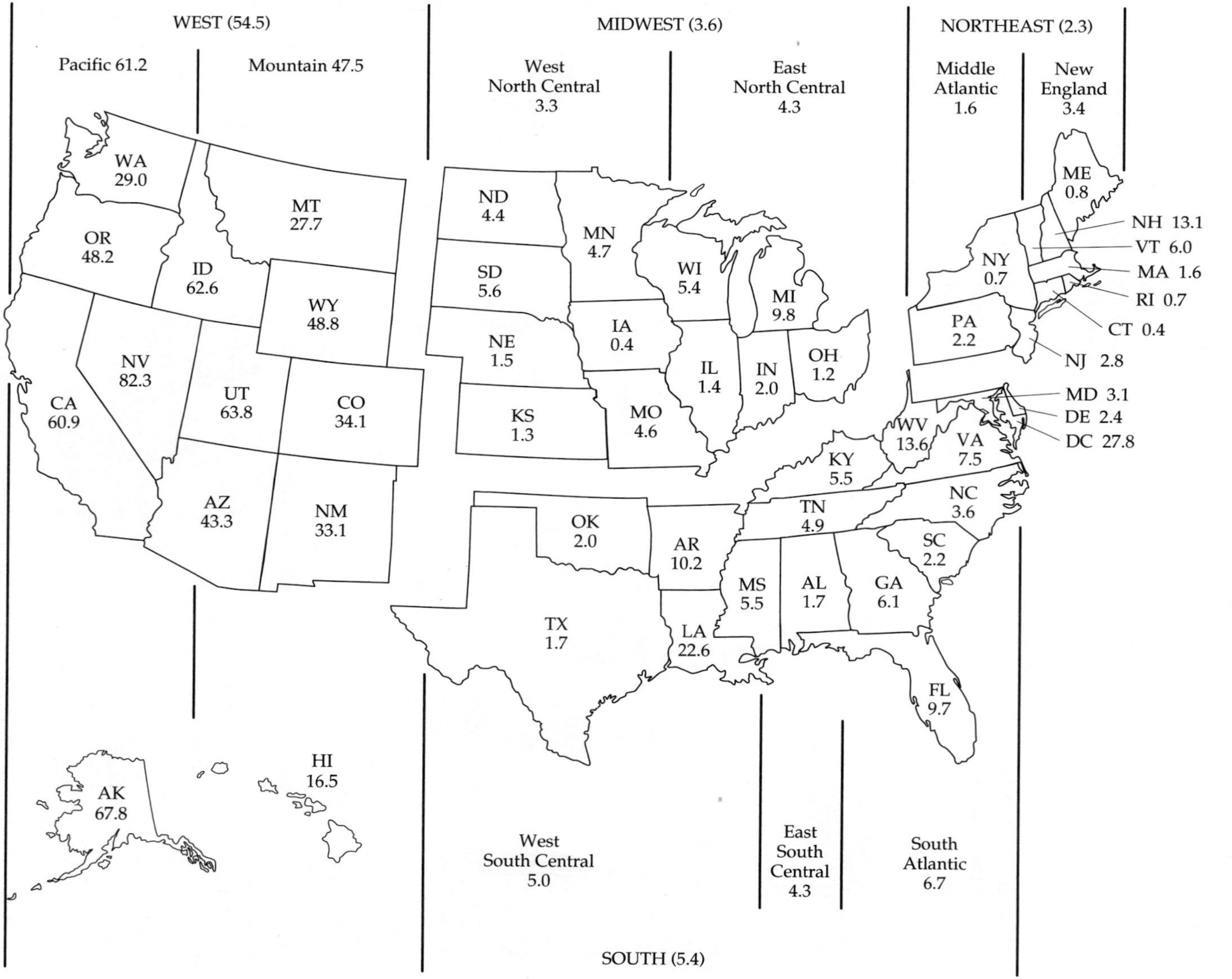

NORTHEAST (2.3)

New England 3.4
- ME 0.8
- NH 13.1
- VT 6.0
- MA 1.6
- RI 0.7
- CT 0.4

Middle Atlantic 1.6
- NY 0.7
- NJ 2.8
- PA 2.2

SOUTH (5.4)

South Atlantic 6.7
- MD 3.1
- DE 2.4
- DC 27.8
- WV 13.6
- VA 7.5
- NC 3.6
- SC 2.2
- GA 6.1
- FL 9.7

East South Central 4.3
- KY 5.5
- TN 4.9
- AL 1.7
- MS 5.5

West South Central 5.0
- AR 10.2
- LA 22.6
- OK 2.0
- TX 1.7

MIDWEST (3.6)

East North Central 4.3
- OH 1.2
- MI 9.8
- IN 2.0
- IL 1.4
- WI 5.4

West North Central 3.3
- MN 4.7
- IA 0.4
- MO 4.6
- ND 4.4
- SD 5.6
- NE 1.5
- KS 1.3

WEST (54.5)

Mountain 47.5
- MT 27.7
- WY 48.8
- CO 34.1
- NM 33.1
- ID 62.6
- UT 63.8
- AZ 43.3
- NV 82.3

Pacific 61.2
- WA 29.0
- OR 48.2
- CA 60.9
- HI 16.5
- AK 67.8

Source: Statistical Abstract, 1992, p. 207.

moves after the 1980 Alaska Lands Bill reduced the number of agencies, departments, and bureaus having control over federally owned land from fifty-six to forty-six. Most of the land, however, is administered by one of four agencies in two federal departments: the National Park Service, Fish and Wildlife Service, and Bureau of Land Management in the Interior Department and the Forest Service in the Agriculture Department (Culhane 1981, 44; see also Clawson 1983). The federal land-use policy operating in a given area influences the development of nearby private lands, and the U.S. government must take private lands into account when considering a change in land-use designation. Wilderness or recreation use encourages business on nearby private land aimed at visitors and tourists. When federal land is administered as **multiple-use land**— that is, for a variety of economic and recreational uses—economic activity intensifies (Shanklin 1962, 1). The people who move in expect federal, state, and local services.

Thus, while zoning on most of the private land in the West is designated by local governments, it depends greatly on the status of nearby federal lands. Individual states also have the power to control water use, regulate fishing and hunting, and administer police services in state and private lands as well as most federally owned lands. This complex, entangled jurisdictional structure creates great potential for problems.

Many westerners are very angry with the federal government's policies for federal multiple-use lands, which have been subjected to increasingly restrictive regulations. Ranchers, miners, water developers, and loggers must meet a multitude of federal requirements to operate on federal lands. In addition, these interests are prohibited from using most federal lands that are designated or under consideration as possible wilderness areas (see Controversy). Today environmentalists are strong supporters of wilderness preservation, and the Endangered Species Act (1973) can prohibit commercial use of large tracts of land to protect habitats, as lumber interests discovered in 1990 when the northern spotted owl was put on the Endangered Species List.

Responding to the growing discontent over federal land policies, the Nevada state legislature in June 1979 claimed for itself all federal land administered by the Bureau of Land Management within Nevada's boundaries— meaning most of the 87 percent of Nevada then owned by the national government (*National Journal*, 21 March 1981, 476–81, *National Journal*, 26 November 1988, 2997–3000). Some other western states with large areas of federally owned land joined the **Sagebrush Rebellion** with similar actions (Webb 1980, 18–21, 32). President Reagan supported the idea of land transfer, and his first appointments included administrators sympathetic to the western perspective, notably Interior Secretary James Watt. While the most drastic demands for land transfers subsided, tensions over federal land policies continue, as evidenced by the uproar over restrained fire suppression in national parks and wilderness areas during the summer of 1988. Although designed to promote natural processes, these policies also have the potential to reduce or expand tourism and hurt or help local economies.

Political perspectives on federal lands are complex. Libertarians are strongest in those parts of the country where there are the most federal lands, possibly because federal lands mean a large federal presence that is often resented. Marxists theoretically favor government ownership and yet find themselves least popular in the parts of the country with the most government land ownership. Populists cheer because the federal government keeps large companies from controlling so much land, but they are also distressed over the national government's becoming so powerful. Liberals and conservatives tend to favor national government control over the lands whenever the national government acts in a manner favorable to their viewpoint. Thus lib-

CONTROVERSY
The Complexity of Federalism

Jack Holmes in Holy Cross Wilderness Area (Tom Phillips)

When someone buys a summer home to get away from it all, he or she does not want the threat of a water project intruding on peace and privacy. But that is what happened to Jack Holmes, one of this textbook's authors. In setting out to discover who would dare inundate his property, he received a firsthand lesson in marble-cake federalism.

During the first two years of his explorations, Jack discovered that the water project was intended to protect water-rich, people-poor western Colorado from people-rich, water-poor eastern Colorado. Indeed, he found that numerous water projects were planned for several parts of his county, which includes the ski resort of Vail, by several different local government entities with competing goals. The most threatening project, however, was not the one that would inundate his home but the one that would divert water from the middle of Holy Cross Wilderness, a western Colorado wilderness area, to eastern Colorado.

Jack's initial hope was that the Forest Service, as land manager and owner of 85 percent of the county in which the wilderness was located,

would protect it in the name of the people of the United States. Not true. Water law is a state matter mostly left alone by the Forest Service, and 80 percent of the people of Colorado live in eastern Colorado. Colorado has a complex, first in time, first in right water law system that gives employment to 70 percent of the nation's water lawyers and benefits projects backed by big money. Thus some federal lands, including the Holy Cross Wilderness, can have up to 90 percent of the water flowing through them removed. Land and water ownership are separate issues in Colorado.

The proposed project in the wilderness caused Jack and several friends to form the Holy Cross Wilderness Defense Fund. Studies for the project were done by federal, state, and local agencies as required by federal, state, and local regulations. Jack started teaching an annual summer course on wilderness research skills. Students did important preliminary environmental research, proposed alternatives, and even produced a videotape. Their work helped the agencies involved and gave the defense fund an idea of the areas in which to seek independent expertise.

To opponents it seemed as if the motions were being gone through with outcomes already determined in favor of the projects. To proponents, it seemed like unending paper requirements. It was not long before the issue was in both the state and federal courts. There is talk of a compromise that might be acceptable to environmentalists.

Regardless of the ultimate outcome, Jack believes that at least the public interest has been served by the formation of the fund and by the active involvement of students. Jack and the students also learned the complex operations of American federalism. They prepared this list of the major agencies involved in the decision to remove water for municipal use from the Holy Cross Wilderness:

FEDERAL AGENCIES

Forest Service, Department of Agriculture, Homestake Phase II Lead Agency: prepared Environmental Impact Statement. Project would be in wilderness land under its jurisdiction.

Bureau of Land Management (BLM), Department of Interior: provided original easement for the project since land was once under its jurisdiction.

Corps of Engineers, U.S. Army: divides regions according to river drainage, complex in Colorado because the state includes several basins. San Francisco Region provided Dredge and Fill Permit for project; Omaha Region prepared Metro Denver Systemwide Water Environmental Impact Statement.

Fish and Wildlife Service, Department of Interior: comments on stream flow and endangered species (such as peregrine falcon).

U.S. Courts: decided that the Forest Service and Corps of Engineers followed the law when issuing project permits.

U.S. Congress: added clause to legislation creating Holy Cross Wilderness in 1980 stating that wilderness did not preclude a water project. A state delegation makes decisions for most intents and purposes.

U.S. President: can allow a water project in the wilderness. A proposed water project in a neighboring wilderness was not allowed after former President Gerald Ford, who has a home in the Vail area, phoned President Reagan.

STATE AGENCIES

More responsive to East Slope of Rocky Mountains, where the majority of the population lives. Water used primarily for agriculture.

State Legislature: makes water laws under guidelines in state constitution. (Former President Carter got into trouble for questioning state authority.)

Governor: recent Colorado governors have considered water diversion but have not actively endorsed or opposed it.

State Courts: interpret water rights and state land-use authority.

Water Roundtable: forum where Eastern and Western Slopes have talked about water issues.

Water Conservation Board: sets minimum streamflows.

State Engineer: responsible for seeing that water law and minimum streamflows are followed.

Division of Wildlife: comments on game and fish matters, which are mostly under state jurisdiction.

LOCAL AGENCIES

Do they cooperate or not? Why? State water law gives advantage to water developers who have money (e.g., cities).

Denver Water Board: large system; all suburbs have a part of future projects.

Aurora: suburb of Denver, which wants some independent water regardless of cost. Suburban Denver is growing faster than Denver itself.

Colorado Springs: city sixty miles south of Denver. Could get existing available water from the already completed Homestake Phase I if Aurora and Denver Water Board systems were integrated.

Eagle County: county where project is proposed refused to issue permit for the project. But state legislature could change the law, or courts may overrule.

INTERSTATE COMPACTS

Agreement between states usually divide water. Colorado must let so much water downstream. Its extra water is on the Western Slope in the drainage of the Colorado River basin, which is usually dry before it reaches the ocean because California and Arizona have overused the water. Colorado's Colorado River water is needed most on the Eastern Slope, which means it must be diverted underneath the continental divide; Colorado can do this with its water.

PRIMARY OPPOSITION GROUP

Holy Cross Wilderness Defense Fund.

FOREIGN GOVERNMENT

The government of Mexico is guaranteed a set amount of Colorado River water of fixed quality. The federal government must pay if too much high-quality water is removed in Colorado.

erals are more likely to support environmental protection and conservatives economic development, although some conservatives would still rather have the land controlled by the individual states. Perhaps this very complexity of perspectives serves to keep the central government's role strong in the area of federal lands.

The 1970s uncovered another arena of potential conflict between western governments and the national government. A series of energy shortages, due in part to American dependence on foreign sources of energy, led to a push for the development and use of domestic energy. The federal government encouraged bringing in more Alaskan oil, converting oil-burning industries to "clean" western coal, developing greater production of other western energy sources such as oil shale, and deregulating domestic oil prices. The result was an energy boom in which the federal government had to help state and local governments by providing proper zoning, police protection, and educational services to new residents attracted by increased employment activity. Nevertheless, state and local governments bear ultimate responsibility in these areas.

Should another energy boom occur, new federal water projects might be required to supplement the scarce supply, much of which is now used for agriculture. The federal government can surely influence western interests by promoting new water projects to meet the needs of an expanding population. The federal government might also find its land-use

designations causing problems if state and local governments in the West became uncooperative. As the energy issue illustrates, the question of land-use control has often strained relations between western state and local governments and the federal government. From a western perspective, a state can hardly be expected to cooperate with a federal government that can oscillate between promoting energy development one moment and wilderness protection the next. From a national perspective, the western states simultaneously decry the meddling of the federal government and demand maximum federal subsidy with minimum restriction (Wright 1985, 64–65).

The various governments are dependent upon each other for projects such as water, that serve mutual interests. But their relationship is especially complicated when projects serve national interests to the detriment of localities. In a recent example the federal government pushed for a nuclear waste disposal site at Yucca Mountain in Nevada. The site was opposed by state and local officials, who employed zoning power to prolong issuance of permits in the hope that the national government would lose resolve. The disposal site was specifically in the national interest: it would benefit mostly "outsiders" and have limited advantages for Nevada. Control of federal lands in the West demonstrates not only the complexity of American federalism, but the need for cooperation.

PERSPECTIVES

Conservative

In the early days of the Republic, the conservative Federalists were accused by their Jeffersonian opponents of wanting to scrap the federal system and establish a "consolidated" national government. Except for a few like Alexander Hamilton, this accusation was not really true. Early American conservatives favored a stronger central government to defend the country and to break down state trade barriers that hindered the growth of the capitalist economy, but most did not want national involvement in matters like education or law enforcement that each colony had always handled for itself under Britain.

Since then, conservatives have moved gradually but decisively toward a states' rights interpretation of the Constitution that would limit federal assumption of implied powers and expand the reserved powers of the states. Dividing government powers between national and state levels fits with the pessimistic, conservative view of human nature. Centralizing power in the hands of a small group of flawed humans in the national government appears to conservatives to carry with it a serious danger of abuse of power. At the same time, conservatives want to use government to uphold community morals. Since moral standards vary across the country, each state and community must have the power to determine and enforce its own moral standards. A less creditable reason for conservative support of states' rights was southern support for slavery and later for racial segregation. These issues have split conservatives, and many northern conservatives voted for civil rights legislation in the 1960s (Whalen and Whalen 1985, 29–70).

In arguing for states' rights against national power, conservatives stress the diversity that still prevails in American society. While admitting that the United States is one nation with common interests that the national government must serve, they stress the differences among the various states and regions. Differences in economic inter-

ests, political and moral values, and even the style of spoken English are apparent to a casual traveler. Conservatives argue that in such a diverse society nationally mandated standards and programs are bound to prove unsuitable somewhere. More important, centralization denies the people any direct control over government decisions.

From the conservative perspective, the system of federal aid for states and localities has been a disaster. Despite enormous expenditures, most federally funded programs, such as welfare, have not produced the intended results (Murray 1982, 15). Without repealing the Tenth Amendment, the national government has made it ineffective by "giving" funds to state and local governments (funds taken in the first place from the people in the several states through the income tax) and then using the threat of withholding such "aid" to dictate how the states and localities are supposed to carry out the functions reserved to them under the Constitution. While stripping the states and localities of power, the system strips them of responsibility as well as allowing them to spend money without raising it. Governors, mayors, and county officials have become beggars, constantly seeking ways to convince Washington to make "someone else" (who?) pay their community's bills. As one conservative cynically puts it:

> What [a mayor] means when he says that his city *must* have state or federal aid to finance some improvements is (1) the taxpayers of the city (or some important group of them) would rather go without the improvement than pay for it themselves; or (2) although they would pay for it themselves if they had to, they would much prefer to have some other taxpayers pay for it. In short, the [state and local] "revenue crisis" mainly reflects the fact that people hate to pay taxes and that they think that by crying poverty they can shift some of the bill to someone else (Banfield 1974, 7–8; see also Murray 1988, 232–92).

Herbert Block. From *Herblock on All Fronts* (New American Library, 1980).

Conservatives have backed different strategies for returning power to the states and localities. President Nixon's revenue-sharing program, for example, kept the flow of federal funds to the states going but let state and local officials determine how the money would be spent. President Reagan, believing that the states and localities should take responsibility for raising as well as spending their own money, pushed to cut federal aid and force the states to decide which programs were worth keeping (Bender and Stever 1986). Recently the Supreme Court, led by conservative Chief Justice William Rehnquist, has moved to hand power back to the states in areas as diverse as the death penalty and pesticide regulation (*National Journal*, 8 October 1991, 1980–83). Conservatives continue to hope that returning power to the states will decrease spending, lower taxes, and increase accountability. Admittedly, a return to true federalism would be difficult for those states and cities most addicted to federal "aid." However, conservatives believe that, as with any other addiction, the way to stop is simply to stop.

Liberal

While conservatives value order and libertarians freedom, liberals value equality. Their emphasis brings them inevitably into conflict with federalism, for a federal system almost always produces inequalities among states. In the view of many liberals, these inequalities have been and remain a barrier to the achievement of true democracy and social justice in the United States.

The most dangerous inequality produced by federalism, say liberals, has been the inequality in rights from one state to another. For most of the nation's history, states' rights conservatives advocated what was, in effect, the right of some states to do wrong by ignoring or infringing upon basic freedoms. The most apparent examples are in race relations, where majorities oppressed minorities for generations in the name of federalism. Before the federal courts intervened, South Carolina exercised the "right" to spend ten times as much on the education of each white child as on each black child in its segregated school system, a greater disparity than exists in South Africa today. Mississippi spent nine times as much on each white as on each black, and Alabama, Florida, Georgia, and Louisiana more than three times as much. Mississippi actually had a law that barred illegitimate children, who were mostly black, from attending public schools at all, in effect imposing ignorance by statute (Wolters 1984, 67; Williams 1987, 210–11).

Minorities were not the only victims of states' rights, liberals say. At one time some states denied poor defendants the right to a court-appointed attorney, tried people twice for the same offense, and allowed police to conduct searches without warrants. A number of states had laws permitting the involuntary sterilization of the "feebleminded," convicted criminals (on the theory that crime was hereditary), and even children who presented discipline problems (Tribe 1985, 1–35, esp. 12–14). Special interests are usually able to function more successfully in small, local areas than would be the case if their efforts were concentrated at the national level. This is

why problems such as racism are able to gain a foothold more easily within a federal framework (Riker 1964, 155).

In recent years state invasions of personal liberty have been curtailed by the vigorous action of the federal courts, but liberals fear a return to the discriminatory practices of the past if conservatives have their way and return control over the liberties of their citizens to the states.

Inequalities in resources among the states remain a serious problem. From a liberal perspective, there is little excuse for maintaining a system in which some states spend half as much on education and provide one-fourth as much in welfare benefits as others. While liberals may concede some merit in the conservative argument that local control is valuable, for them this benefit is outweighed by the injustice done to poor people in states and communities that cannot or do not provide adequate services to their citizens.

While states could do more to correct such inequalities, it is unlikely that they will because they compete to attract business investment with low taxes. Not every public function needs to be financed by the national government, but low-income states and communities need much more assistance from Washington, and higher-income areas must pay for this assistance if anything like a just society is to be achieved (Peterson, Rabe, and Wong 1986, 231–36). Deciding which states are most in need is a tricky business, as the discussion of regionalism indicates.

Besides being inequitable, liberals argue, federalism is often inefficient. State boundaries drawn long ago no longer conform to concentrations of population; the New York metropolitan area, for example, extends across northern New Jersey and western Connecticut. At the local level, government is even more inefficiently organized. The Los Angeles metropolitan area extends over five counties, 157 city governments, and innumerable special districts for everything from schools to mosquito control (Lockwood and Leinberger 1988, 54). This maze of overlapping jurisdictions leads to a waste and duplication of effort that prevents government from performing even some of the things conservatives and libertarians agree are essential. Law enforcement, for instance, is left primarily to local police, with some involvement by the states, but drug traffickers and other organized groups of criminals stubbornly refuse to limit their activities to a single city or county. Jurisdictional limitations have so hindered law enforcement that it has been necessary to create a Federal Bureau of Investigation to handle some types of interstate crime. Yet, as federal agencies are small relative to state and local police forces operating in the same area and themselves have limited jurisdiction, jurisdictional confusion remains a major problem for law enforcement.

With all their criticisms of the states, one might think that liberals would call for the abolition of federalism and the establishment of a unitary government, with all power concentrated at the national level. A few have, but for the most part, liberals have stopped short of calling for the dismantling of federalism. They recognize that such a proposal would not be politically viable; loyalty to the states is still too strong among most Americans. They also recognize that federalism can benefit liberals as well as conservatives by allowing states to adopt liberal social programs before the whole nation is prepared to do so. An example of such liberal experimentation at the state level is Oregon's recent decision to provide health insurance coverage to all citizens not presently covered. The plan is to be paid for by excluding from coverage high-cost treatments such as organ transplants, in effect rationing health care by the state's ability to pay (*Modern Healthcare*, 27 January 1991, 26–28). Liberals see such state efforts as possible models for a future national health insurance system. Finally, liberals share some of the conservative and libertarian fear of big government and recognize that too much centralized control could be both inefficient and oppressive.

Despite these reservations, liberals continue to favor expansion of the national government's role in solving problems. They believe that federal aid to the states and cities should be increased, not cut as President Reagan did, and targeted to those areas most in need, like the large cities. Liberals would like to see the national government take over programs like welfare completely and step up its involvement in other areas, like education, health care, and drug enforcement, where the states and localities have clearly failed to solve critical problems (Moynihan 1986, 105–94; See also Beer 1993, 256–59). There is, of course, no guarantee that the national statement will succeed either, but liberals maintain that it must not shirk its responsibilities in the name of federalism.

Libertarian

At first glance, leading libertarians seem to hold the same view of federalism as conservatives. "If government is to exercise power," says the libertarian economist Milton Friedman, "better in the county than in the state, better in the state than in Washington" (Friedman 1962, 3). Like conservatives, libertarians deplore the growth of the national government and applauded President Reagan's efforts to prune it back. Both conservatives and libertarians agree on the pernicious effects of the federal grant system, and neither are very concerned about unequal levels of government service under the federal system.

Despite this surface similarity, libertarians actually support federalism for reasons quite different from those of conservatives. Libertarians have little concern for the rights of states as political communities; states' rights are important only as they contribute to individual freedom and independence. "If I do not like what my local community does," says Friedman, "I can move to another local community. If I do not like what my state does, I can move to another. If I do not like what Washington imposes, I have few alternatives in this world of jealous nations" (Friedman 1962, 3). From this perspective, federalism is valued not because it permits government to express diverse local interests and values, but because it allows the individual to escape government more easily. To libertarians, government at all levels is, at best, a necessary evil; state and local governments, being smaller, simply have less potential for evil than the national government.

Having little of the conservative attachment to the states, libertarians do not hesitate to criticize them as sharply as they do the national government when they interfere with economic freedom. One example of such interference is state laws licensing various trades and professions, an area largely untouched by the national government. Hundreds of different occupations, ranging from pharmacists to well diggers to piano tuners, require a license in one state or another, and most of the state licensing boards are controlled by members of the profession being licensed. Such boards have a clear interest in limiting the number of new competitors they license, thus limiting competition. Libertarians view the present state licensing systems as a serious infringement on consumer choice and on the right of the individual to choose his or her own occupation. Therefore they favor federal action to restrict or even eliminate licensing restrictions (Friedman 1962, 137–60). A conservative might oppose some state licensing laws but probably would not want to see states lose the right to license.

Another change libertarians would like to see in the federal system is the implementation of so-called school choice plans, which would allow parents to select any school they wanted for their children (including, in some versions, private schools) and still allow states to get federal funding for education. Although some liberals support school choice as a way of opening suburban schools to the urban poor, the idea appeals to libertarians because it would shift power in education away from the state and local governments, not to the national government, but to individual parents. The Bush administration tried without success to get the idea adopted on a national scale. If school choice is ever adopted at this level, it will initiate a major change in American federalism (*National Journal*, 26 January 1991, 205; *New York Times Magazine*, 24 November 1991, 52–59).

While they place the most emphasis on economic freedom, libertarians value other freedoms as well. Hence they are closer to liberals than to conservatives regarding the importance of national protection for individual rights. Conservatives are correct, libertarians say, in believing that the national government has gone too far in extending its powers over the individual, but wrong when they assert that states and localities should do the same thing by censoring books or films they deem objectionable, banning abortions, or outlawing homosexuality. After the Civil War, the Fourteenth Amendment gave the national government the responsibility of protecting individual rights against the states (for the libertarian point of view, see Macedo 1986, 17). This responsibility, along with the other functions explicitly granted in the Constitution, should be enough for a limited government to fulfill.

Populist

To populists, the good of the majority is the primary purpose of government, and this view shapes their attitude toward federalism. When the majority needs government assistance and state or local governments are not equipped to provide it, populists do not want the Tenth Amendment or some abstract concept of states' rights to get in the way of national action. The populist platform of 1892 strongly demanded national action. Citing rampant corruption at the ballot box and asserting that the colossal fortunes of a few had been built off the fruits of the toiling of millions, it called for a graduated income tax and expanded government power. Even Franklin Roosevelt's liberal New Deal programs were criticized by populist leaders like Huey Long of Louisiana for not going far enough. Long proposed a national Share the Wealth plan to guarantee every family a minimum income financed by heavy taxes on the wealthy, as well as federal financing of education, public health, major public works, and nationalization of the railroads. Had Long's dream been implemented (he planned to run for president in 1936 but was assassinated in 1935), it would have made the national government even more powerful than it is today (*Guide to U.S. Elections* 1985, 54–55; Williams 1969, esp. 676–706, 843–47).

While most populists are quite comfortable with the use of national power to aid the underprivileged, other effects of the growth of the national government trouble them. Congress and the federal bureaucracy frequently feel compelled, for the sake of national goals, to impose regulations and standards that either irritate local majorities (like the fifty-five-mile-per-hour speed limit) or compel them to grant additional rights to minorities (as with the civil rights laws). At this point, the right-wing populist is likely to begin seeing the national government as dominated by an elite that does not understand the needs and feelings of "little people." George Wallace's 1968 presidential campaign was filled with attacks on

the national government, many of them racially based but also appealing to populist resentment of remote Washington rule makers. Pat Buchanan's 1992 presidential candidacy sounded similar themes. Black populists and more left-wing, white populists, of course, opposed Wallace and generally still favor expansion of the national government. Populist elements can be seen in other states' rights efforts like the western Sagebrush Rebellion.

With these qualifications, populists are still probably closer to liberals than to conservatives or libertarians in their view of federalism; while they may oppose specific uses of national authority, they do not advocate a return to the limited national government of fifty or one hundred years ago.

Marxist

To Marxists, federalism is definitely a secondary issue. Since economic structures dominate and determine the workings of political systems, it is relatively unimportant whether the United States has a federal structure of government so long as the capitalist economic system holds sway. Marxists have produced, however, some interesting analyses that challenge both the conservative and libertarian view that local control leads to diversity and freedom and the liberal view that greater national control leads to equality.

According to Marxists, the main difference between the American national government and the state and local governments is that, while national politics often reflects clashes between different capitalist interests, state and local politics are usually dominated by a monolithic, corporate business elite. In some cases, a city or state may be dominated by a business firm, like the Du Pont Corporation in Delaware. More often, the heads of the major banks, manufacturing companies, and retail stores in the area dominate. Internal conflicts in these "community power structures" are rare, because all members basically seek the same goals: low business taxes, good public services (financed by regressive taxes on middle- and lower-income residents), strong law enforcement

to protect property rights, and a well-trained but docile labor force. Elected state and local government officials cannot oppose these business demands even if they want to because business can move out of an uncooperative state or community, leaving the government with an unemployed work force and an eroding tax base (Domhoff 1983, 157–97; for an earlier analysis of community power structures, see Hunter 1953).

From this perspective, the conservative celebration of local autonomy is a transparent fraud; "local control" is only for members of the local power structure. The average citizen pays the bulk of the costs of the system, and any benefits he or she gets (for example, jobs for workers created by a good business climate in a state) are purely accidental. On the other hand, liberal programs of aid to states and cities have proved largely futile because the local power structure can usually control the implementation of federal programs for its own benefit. For instance, federally financed urban renewal programs, advertised as the answer to slum housing, are turned into programs to clear low-income people from valuable inner-city land coveted by local business. In Atlanta, for example, one-seventh of the city's population, mostly poor blacks, was displaced to make room for business expansion and highways; almost no new public housing was built (Domhoff 1983, 183; see also an early critique by the libertarian Anderson 1964). Nationwide, the number of poor people injured by this one probusiness policy alone runs into the millions.

Most Marxist-Leninist governments have been highly centralized with little opportunity for local autonomy. Centralization is not the path American Marxists wish to follow, however. Believing that overcentralization and overbureaucratization have prevented the Chinese, and formerly the Soviets, from realizing the goals of socialism,

American Marxists argue that a socialist revolution could initiate radical decentralization. Workers could manage their own enterprises instead of taking orders from a selfish management in a distant city, and residents of neighborhoods and small towns could make local decisions directly instead of deferring to orders from the state or national government. This kind of control at the local level would be real democracy and self-government, with people participating in the decisions that affect their lives instead of having those decisions made for them by an exploitative elite at the state or national level.

Feminist

Feminists share with liberals an ambivalence about the federal nature of the U.S. political system. A feminist from a conservative state like Louisiana might wish for a stronger central government to protect choice in regard to abortion. A feminist coming from a liberal state like Maryland may wish for less restrictive federal guidelines on abortion applied nationwide. Feminists who supported the Equal Rights Amendment and believe it was defeated by a handful of male legislators in two or three "backward states" are naturally critical of the continuing power of states. Further, national legislation in regard to child day care and civil rights in 1991 gave women redress for sexual harassment and provided more and safer day care.

Federalism does make possible, however, levels of political participation by women that would be less likely in a completely centralized system. Despite President Clinton's efforts to appoint women to positions of power in his administration, there are still more women in significant positions at the state and local levels than in the federal government. States and localities remain the major training ground for both male and female national officials. Although few women are governors (three in 1992), most women elected to federal office first cut their political teeth in state or local government positions. For example, Mayor Dianne Feinstein of San Francisco became Senator Feinstein from California. In August 1992, women held 18 percent of state legislative seats, almost twice the percentage that they held at the national

level, even after the 1992 election (more than 10 percent) (Jones 1992, 110, 111). Despite fears that economic cutbacks and recent court decisions protecting seniority would take away gains that women and minorities have made in the state and local bureaucracy, the good news for feminists is that these governments seem to have held the line and preserved the great proportion of all jobs secured under affirmative action provisions during the previous decade (Wilson 1992, 14–15).

Still, feminists argue that policy development supportive of women's rights has been slowest in areas constitutionally reserved to the states, like law and order and education. Only ten states have a policy requiring the arrest of a spouse in domestic violence cases. Such violence killed more American women during the Vietnam War than combat killed the American men who fought in it, and domestic violence still remained the leading cause of injury to women in the 1980s. Three hundred fifty thousand battered women are without emergency shelter annually. Half of all homeless women are domestic violence victims. In thirty states, it is still legal for men to rape their wives. U.S. women have less access to education and fewer options regarding birth control than their European counterparts. Three-fourths of all high schools still violate federal laws banning sex discrimination in education. College women still only receive 70 percent of the aid that undergraduate males get in grants and work-study jobs. Women's college sports programs have never equaled men's in funding despite Title IX requirements. Only seven states have passed antidiscrimination regulations that cover all levels of education (Jones 1992, 111). On the other hand, some states have tried new laws and ways of thinking before the country at large was ready.

Most feminists see arguments for states' rights as ignoring issues important to women. At the same time, local politics is an excellent training ground for future political power at the state and even national level. Thus for feminists federalism remains a mix of good and evil. While some states have pioneered in addressing women's issues, national programs that address marital and educational rights may need to be enacted and enforced before the federal system can work to the benefit of women.

DOES THE FEDERAL SYSTEM WORK?

Balancing local, state, and national interests is not easy. Too much decentralization can, as liberals point out, lead to serious inequalities. Overcentralization, as conservatives and libertarians note, can be oppressive. Either extreme can cause a nation to break apart.

We believe that the American federal system works better than it once did in balancing state and national interests. All three of us support extension of equal civil rights to citizens of all states; here centralization has been a positive development. One of us would like to see greater equality in government services across the nation; the other two tend to fear centralization and applaud efforts to return power to the states. The federal system is flexible enough to accommodate both views at different times and on different issues.

The federal system has addressed the frost-belt-sunbelt disagreement over federal funding in a manner that pleases neither side completely but has considered both arguments as well as a number of other ideas. The same is true with several conflicting ideas involving federal lands and rural-urban-suburban struggles.

Some would prefer to see the complexity of the American federal system replaced with a centralized system; this would be easier said than done. A vast number of decisions are made at the state and local level. Citizens are involved in these decisions, and their involvement is democracy at work.

SUMMARY AND REVIEW

The American federal system is a paradoxical blend of conflict and cooperation among the national, state, and local governments that pervades almost every area of government concern. While it is true that the framers would be amazed at the extent to which national power has grown, the continuing importance of the states makes an understanding of American federalism essential.

Despite the Constitution's Elastic Clause, the enumeration of powers of the national government and further constriction of national power under the Tenth Amendment seemed to guarantee a clear, unambiguous set of distinctions between national and state authority. Such a sharp division of powers was quickly put to the test, however, notably with the Louisiana Purchase. Gradually, the lines began to

4

PARTIES AND ELECTIONS

Suppose you wanted to run for Congress. What would it take for you to win? A lot more than you might think (Maisel 1982). Once you decide to run, you will have to recruit campaign workers, develop an organization, produce radio and television ads, and travel your district to become better known. You will also have to consider negative campaigning. Should you use ads attacking your opponent, since it might be the most visible way of getting your message across? Likewise, how will you defend yourself if your opponent decides to use negative ads against you? All this will take money, lots of money. By the time you have won or lost, you may have accumulated a debt of several hundred thousand dollars.

Will your political party help? Yes, particularly if you are a Republican, but neither party has the resources to fully support a candidate's campaign. You will have to raise most of your money yourself. Before you can expect significant party support, you must win the nomination in a primary, and in this endeavor you will be mostly on your own. The candidate-centered politics of the United States puts a heavy burden on those who seek public office (for a practical guide on campaigning techniques, see Guzzetta 1993).

At first glance, the life of a candidate can seem quite glamorous; you are, after all, at the center of attention. If elected, you will be making a lot of important decisions. People of all kinds will be most friendly to you and happy when you decide an issue their way.

The first glance, however, does not last too long. As a candidate, you will have little or no time for your family. Your spouse will have almost the entire responsibility for children and the home. While being the center of attention is rewarding at times, it is not something you can simply turn off when you desire privacy. Those important decisions you make will indeed please some people, but often an equal number will be angry with you. You'll need to have thick skin. In addition, *people will always think they have to see you to get their point across. Should you lose, even if only by a small margin, you risk being viewed as a failure. It is also true that most candidates take a pay cut when elected to a higher office.*

This chapter is devoted to the role of parties, which are vital in a mass democracy to narrow the choices of candidates for the electorate, and to elections in American national government. Understanding elections is essential to understanding the kinds of people who are elected to office.

POLITICAL PARTIES

Political parties are groups organized to gain elective office. The United States has had parties almost from the beginning of its existence, but unlike many other systems, it has usually

Malcolm Hancock. © 1993 MalEnt., Inc.

had only two major parties. Here we will look at the history and functions of parties in the United States, with a concentration on their role in government.

The Role of the Parties

The framers of the Constitution held **factions** —James Madison's term for interest groups— in low esteem. Madison argued in Number 10 of *The Federalist Papers* that factions represented selfish interests that the new Constitution would check and control (*Federalist Papers* 1961, 129–36). Today, however, parties function as broad-based coalitions, not the narrow factions Madison feared, and most observers believe that they are essential to a democratic form of government (Epstein 1986, 30–39).

What makes parties so important in a democracy? One of their most vital functions is simply to select candidates and narrow the choices voters must make. Few voters know much about individual candidates, but most have some impression of the two major political parties and some idea of what they stand for. Party labels thus make it easier to decide how to vote. They explain why fewer people vote in nonpartisan elections and primaries, in which no labels appear on the ballot, and why independent voters vote less often than those who identify with a party.

Parties perform other vital functions as well. Party organizations encourage people to participate in politics by working in campaigns, giving money, or even running for office themselves. Parties in government attempt to develop programs to solve problems, and voters can judge the parties by how well their programs work. Some scholars even reverse Madison's position and argue that strong parties are necessary to control the influence of **interest groups**, organizations of individuals who join together voluntarily to influence public policy on the basis of a shared interest or objective. Since a party must be large to have any hope of winning elections, it has to include a broad range of people and groups. Democrats may label Republicans as selfish exploiters and Republicans may attack Democrats as irresponsible spenders, yet both parties come closer to representing the views and interests of most Americans than do interest groups like the National Rifle Association, the Chamber of Commerce, or the Americans for Democratic Action, which represent only a single segment of society (Schattschneider 1942).

The State of the Parties

While political scientists may consider political parties essential to a democracy, many American citizens do not. The number of Americans who were temporarily willing to support Ross Perot's independent candidacy for president in 1992 shows clearly that many Americans have weak or no loyalties to the two major parties. While American parties have always been weaker than those in other countries, the recent decline in support for the parties has both politicians and scholars worried.

The decline of party in the electorate has many causes. Civil service reforms have reduced the number of jobs and other favors parties can use to reward their supporters. Since voters' incomes and living standards are generally much higher than they were in the nineteenth century, such favors are less needed anyway. Another cause of party decline is the growing importance of the mass media, particularly television, in politics. Candidates have found that they can "sell" themselves to the public through commercials and news events without relying on party organizations to campaign for them. As a result, campaigns now tend to focus on candidate personalities rather than party positions on issues, further eroding the importance of parties and encouraging voters to be **ticket-splitters**, crossing party lines to vote for candidates of both parties (*American Enterprise*, July/August 1991, 28–37). Reforms in the nomination system have further weakened parties by allowing primary voters, many of whom have weak

ties to the party, to choose candidates (explained below).

While many observers are concerned that parties are becoming too weak to implement policy and make democracy work, there are also signs of party renewal. National and state organizations are now stronger than they have ever been before, and party unity is growing in Congress (Crotty 1984, 280–83; Ferguson and Rogers 1986, 40–77; Kayden and Mahe Jr. 1985, 59–122; Epstein 1986, 158–62). Still there is little indication that the American public wants the kind of centralized, highly disciplined parties that exist in other democracies. In most democracies, it would have been impossible for a maverick like Ross Perot to challenge established political parties, even temporarily. Most Americans probably prefer a relatively weak party system that allows such a challenge (*American Enterprise*, July/August 1991, 28–37).

The History of the Parties

Political candidates and factions in the United States have been organized into several different party systems since the making of the Constitution. Following the Civil War, the two-party system as it exists today took form. As Abraham Lincoln's **Republican party** sought to impose Reconstruction on the defeated South, the **Democratic party,** which traces its roots to Thomas Jefferson, increasingly came to control politics in that region. In the South blacks were denied voting privileges and faced segregation and discrimination through a variety of **Jim Crow laws**. In the North and Midwest urban **political machines**—strong party organizations ruled by a boss or a small group of autocratic leaders—increasingly supported the Democratic party, as did new immigrants in these regions. The dominant Republican party became identified more and more with small town, Protestant viewpoints and large business interests, which still support the Republicans today.

During the late nineteenth century the United States became increasingly urban and industrial. Americans reacted in varied ways to the growth of corporate power. Populists viewed large corporations as undiluted evils that should either be broken up or, if they were indispensable like the railroads, nationalized and brought under government control (Watson 1967a, 23–26; Davis 1967, 169–203). But populists were largely rural people, accustomed to small-scale enterprise. Many urban Americans saw the modern corporation as potentially beneficial, provided its abuses were brought under control. The idea that strong government might play a benevolent role in controlling the abuses of private enterprise became popular in the early twentieth century, giving rise to the **progressive movement**, which emphasized reform in both political parties (Hofstadter 1974, 266–367). The progressive ideology, supporting a capitalist economic system tempered by extensive state regulation, became the basis for modern liberalism.

To others, the system seemed to be working well. The newly rich class of businessmen who ran the large corporations might not have been paragons of morality, but Adam Smith's "invisible hand" of the market seemed to be leading the economy forward. Having become accustomed to minimal government, many Americans feared that regulation would destroy both freedom and prosperity. Libertarianism, an ideology opposing extensive government intervention in the economy, became increasingly popular.

Twentieth-century Republicans have been mostly libertarians and conservatives. They have consistently been strongest in small towns and suburbs and among the upper and middle classes. Until the Great Depression, the Republicans enjoyed majority status. A similarity of beliefs on economics, if not on social issues, has allowed the libertarian-conservative coalition to stay together.

In opposition to libertarians and conservatives, who were strong in the business sector,

agrarian populists and urban liberals combined with southern farmers and urban immigrant workers to form the early twentieth-century Democratic party. The Democrats also continued to maintain regional dominance in the South, which, although socially conservative, had never forgiven Republicans for Reconstruction. The Great Depression, beginning with the stock market crash during the presidency of the libertarian Republican president Herbert Hoover, gave the Democrats national dominance. In 1932 the liberal Democratic candidate Franklin Roosevelt was able to convince even small town Americans that substantial government involvement in the private sector was the only way to restore the nation's economic health.

Somewhat reluctantly, the Democrats began to support civil rights for blacks and other minorities after World War II. By the late 1960s, however, civil rights issues had caused southern whites to split away from the Democratic party. And when civil rights progress was followed by urban riots and rising crime in the black community, a more general "white backlash" developed, involving conservative and populist Democrats throughout the country. This backlash was intensified by affirmative action policies that gave some minorities preferential treatment in hiring and in education, treatment that to many whites looked like "reverse discrimination." Republican politicians capitalized on the turmoil caused by these civil rights issues. Their calls for "law and order" began to cut into the Democrats' working-class support (Edsall and Edsall 1991, 137–53; Brown 1991, 77–104). Two more trends favoring the Republicans were a growing upper middle class resentful of taxes and continued migration from the frostbelt to the more conservative sunbelt (see Chapter 3).

From 1968 to 1988 the Republicans won all but one of six presidential elections. Had it not been for the Watergate scandal (see Chapter 7) of 1973–74 and President Gerald Ford's unpopular pardon of Richard Nixon, Republicans might well have won all six. Particularly striking is the Republican showing in the South, where Republicans used to be almost nonexistent. In 1980 every southern state except President Jimmy Carter's home state of Georgia went for Ronald Reagan. In 1984 and 1988 the entire South gave its electoral votes to the Republicans (Lamis 1984, 39–43, 210–16; Pomper 1989, 130–31).

While the Republicans triumphed at the presidential level, Democrats continued to do well in congressional, state, and local elections. Democratic dominance at these levels reflected continuing support for liberal-populist economic and social welfare policies. Some opinion polls, in fact, showed that Americans

shifted a little to the left during the Reagan administration, after a turn toward the right in the 1970s (Schwab 1991, 17–32; Mayer 1992, 3–17). With Republicans in the White House and Democrats controlling Congress, it became harder for either party to get its way, and Americans grew increasingly frustrated with both parties.

The combination of frustration with congressional gridlock and difficult economic conditions led to a Democratic victory in the 1992 presidential election. The independent candidate Ross Perot capitalized on Americans' frustration with the political system in general by calling for major changes. Candidate Bill Clinton claimed to be "a new kind of Democrat"

Chuck Asay. Courtesy *The Gazette Telegraph*, Colorado Springs.

who would improve the economy. In the face of Perot's call for a new way of doing things and Clinton's focus on the economy, President George Bush was unable to win a second term. Most Democrats lower down on the ticket were not helped by Clinton's victory, and a number of Republican congressional candidates did better than their presidential candidate in a reversal of normal trends. Of sixteen southern states, Clinton carried eight while doing even better in most of the rest of the country and retaining the Democratic base vote. In addition, his appeal as a "new Democrat" had some success. His performance in office will have a major bearing on the future of both political parties as well as the Perot movement.

Organization and Functions of the Parties

Although each of the two major political parties is usually spoken of as a single unit (as when the press reports that "the Republicans" oppose President Clinton's budget), it is more useful to think of each party as having three major components. First, there is the **party in the electorate**, the ordinary citizens who identify with and support a party. Second, the **party organization** is the structure created to set party policies and assist candidates in getting elected. Finally, the **party in government** consists of members of a party who have been elected to public office and seek to cooperate to accomplish party goals. Although the three components of the parties work together, they serve different functions and can be analyzed separately.

Parties in the electorate   Political scientists use the term **party identification** to describe people's loyalty to a particular political party. Since the Civil War, most Americans have identified with either the Republican or the Democratic party. Often the reasons for being a Republican or a Democrat have to do more

with family tradition, social pressure, or place of residence than with political beliefs. There are significant differences between Democratic and Republican party voters, however, and party identification makes it easier for an individual to choose a candidate to support.

Libertarians and conservatives who *strongly* support the free market economy and limited government regulation have most often adhered to the Republican party. Liberals and populists advocating extensive government involvement on behalf of the underprivileged are inclined to support the Democrats. These generalizations do not, of course, hold in every instance. Social issues like abortion or school prayer, for example, may cause a voter to vote for a party with which he or she disagrees on other issues. Regional differences on party affiliation are also still important. But since the breakup of the "solid Democratic South," party allegiance is determined more by national than by regional concerns (Ladd Jr. and Hadley 1975, 129–77).

Party identification was extremely fluid in the 1980s, reflecting the weak ties most Americans felt with either political party. In 1980, before Reagan took office, 46 percent of those surveyed called themselves Democrats and 24 percent Republicans—a ratio of almost 2:1. By 1985, however, the gap had narrowed to 38 percent Democrats and 33 percent Republicans (*Perspectives on the Reagan Presidency* 1988, 28). While the Republican and Democratic percentages changed significantly, the percentage of **independent voters**—those who vote on a candidate's qualifications and position on particular issues rather than on party affiliation—changed by only 1 percent, from 30 percent in 1980 to 29 percent in 1985.

By February 1990 a Gallup poll showed Democrats, Republicans, and independents each with 33 percent (*New York Times*, 21 January 1990, 15; *National Journal*, 17 March 1990, 620; *People, the Press and Politics*, September 1990, 2). However, the sagging economy in the early 1990s brought an upturn in Democratic identification and some decline in Republican identification. If independents who leaned toward one side or the other were counted as party identifiers, the Democratic party had slightly over 50 percent support in November 1991, and the Republican party slightly over 40 percent (*American Enterprise*, January/February 1992, 95). Election day voters in 1992 described themselves as 39 percent Democrat, 34 percent Republican, and 27 percent independent (*National Journal*, 7 November 1992, 2543). Collectively, these polls indicate that the Democrats are the majority party, but the Republicans are competitive.

The performance of President Clinton and the Democratic Congress will have an important impact on these figures in the future. The strongest Democratic identifiers today are blacks, attracted by Democratic support for social welfare and civil rights legislation: around 80–90 percent of blacks usually support the Democratic party. Republicans have no comparable support group but have pockets of strength among business and professional people as well as white Protestants. Hispanics, unionized workers, low-income people, and intellectuals are more likely to support the Democratic party than the Republican party. Jews, a high-income group, are strongly Democratic due in part to their history of overcoming discrimination and their sympathy for other oppressed groups like blacks. Republicans are strongest among the one-quarter of Americans with family incomes over $50,000 a year (these make up one-third of the voters) but also receive crucial support from white fundamentalist Christians, historically a lower-income group. Catholics have been historically Democratic but now tend to swing between parties. During the Reagan years Republicans gained a slight lead among young voters, but this lead was lost by President Bush in 1992 (*American Enterprise*, May/June 1992, 108; *American Enterprise*, January/February 1993, 90–93).

The percentage of independent voters has generally increased since the 1960s, as white southerners have left the Democratic party and younger voters have failed to form party attachments as their parents did. There has also been a sharp increase in the number of **ticket-splitters**, voters who vote for two or more candidates from different parties. One effect of ticket-splitting is **divided government**, with one party in the presidency and another controlling Congress. In 1988 the majority of voters in more than one-third of the congressional districts voted for one party for president (usually Republican) and the other for the House of Representatives (usually Democratic). In 1900, only 3.4 percent of districts had such split results (*Vital Statistics on Congress, 1991–1992*, 64–65). In 1992, however, Republican candidates for the U.S. House ran 8 percentage points ahead of Bush, while Democratic candidates ran 10 percentage points ahead of Clinton (*American Enterprise*, January/February 1993, 93). Many experts believe that the increase in the number of ticket-splitters and independents is caused by television coverage, which tends to stress a candidate's personality over party affiliation or stand on the issues. Both major parties aim to win independent voters, for this group now makes the difference in many elections. Reagan was notably successful in attracting independents, receiving 55 percent of their votes in 1980 and 63 percent in 1984 (Petrocik 1981, 78–79; see also Hill and Luttbeg 1983, 32–35; Ladd Jr. 1978, 35–36). President Bush also did well among independents in 1988 (Pomper 1989, 67), receiving 55 percent of their vote, but he dropped to 31 percent in the three-way race of 1992. Republican congressional and state candidates, however, have yet to enjoy the same degree of success. For an analysis of the 1992 election, see Table 4.1.

Party organization Compared to political parties in other countries, American parties are weak and decentralized, although more centralization has been introduced in recent years. In the United States party members can participate in or change from one party to another as they please. Most pay no contributions to parties and are not very active in them, although

TABLE 4.1   WHO VOTED FOR WHOM, 1992

	CLINTON	BUSH	PEROT
All (100%)	44%	37%	19%
Men (46)	41	37	21
Women (54)	47	36	17
Whites (87)	40	39	21
Blacks (8)	83	11	7
Hispanics (3)	62	24	14
Didn't complete high school (6)	56	27	18
High school grad (25)	44	36	21
Some college (29)	43	36	21
College grad (24)	41	39	20
Postgrad (16)	50	35	15
Age 18–24 (11)	47	31	22
25–29 (11)	41	35	24
30–39 (25)	42	38	21
40–49 (24)	44	37	19
50–59 (13)	42	39	19
60 + (16)	50	37	12
Family income*			
Less than $15,000 (14)	59	22	19
$15,000–29,999 (24)	46	34	20
$30,000–49,999 (30)	42	37	21
$50,000–74,999 (20)	41	41	18
$75,000 or more (13)	38	46	16
Protestants (56)	34	45	21
Catholics (27)	42	37	21
Jews (4)	78	10	11
Family financial situation compared with 1988			
Better (25)	25	60	15
Worse (34)	62	13	25
About the same (41)	42	41	18
Democrats (39)	78	10	13
Republicans (34)	11	72	18
Independents (28)	39	31	30
Liberals (22)	69	13	18
Moderates (50)	49	30	21
Conservatives (29)	18	64	17
Vote in 1988			
Bush (53)	22	58	20
Dukakis (27)	83	5	12
Didn't vote (15)	50	24	26
Union households (19)	56	23	22
Nonunion households (81)	42	39	19

* Comparable income categories were used in 1988.

Source: Voter Research and Surveys exit polls for 1992 and CNN-Los Angeles Times exit polls for 1988 cited, in National Journal, *7 November 1992, 2543. Copyright 1992 by National Journal, Inc. All rights reserved. Reprinted by permission. Such polls can have minor variations within overall results. In the 1992 presidential election the actual results were Clinton (43), Bush (37), and Perot (19).*

activity increases at election time. Many party supporters are active only when they see a candidate they personally want to support (Schlesinger 1965, 764–801). Parties are organized at national, state, and local levels, but only recently have national and most state party organizations become very effective.

At the apex of the party organization is the **national committee**, which consists of representatives from each state and is headed by a national chair (see Figure 4.1). The Democratic National Committee also includes representatives from support groups like organized labor.

In the early 1960s the Democratic and Republican national committees were described as practicing "politics without power" because of their limited responsibilities. Their main role was to organize and prepare for the presiden-

tial nominating conventions every four years; activity between conventions was limited. Since then, however, the national committees have become much more active. The Republicans led the way under national chairs Ray Bliss in the mid-1960s and Bill Brock from 1976 to 1981. They developed a sophisticated operation that raised $4.6 million for the Reagan campaign in 1980, $19.2 million for Republican House and Senate candidates in 1982, and additional funds for state legislative races. The Republican National Committee also started a Campaign Management College to train Republican campaign managers, conducted extensive voter registration and get-out-the-vote drives, and launched a major effort to recruit candidates at all levels. Although the Democrats at first lagged far behind the Republicans in improving their national party organization, by 1990 they were spending about $10 million for House and Senate candidates, up from $1.9 million twelve years earlier. The Republican National Committee, in the meantime, leveled off in the amount of money spent on candidates and then saw it decline. Still, with their congressional candidate support totals at $13.6 million, the Republicans remained ahead of their Democratic opponents (Cotter and Hennessy 1964; Adamany 1984, 78–85; *Vital Statistics on Congress, 1991–1992*, 94–95; see also Herrnson 1988). National party organizations are probably stronger and more effective today than at any time in the nation's history.

State party organizations have also become more important. Until the late 1960s, party organizations in most states consisted of a state party committee that, like the national committee, was usually active only during election campaigns. Since then, many state party leaders have employed full-time paid staffs that engage in fund-raising, voter education, and candidate recruitment. The Republicans have the most effective state parties due to their extraordinary success in fund-raising and organization, but Democratic state parties are copying Republican techniques (Cotter et al. 1984, 13–36).

Figure 4.1   American Political Party Organization

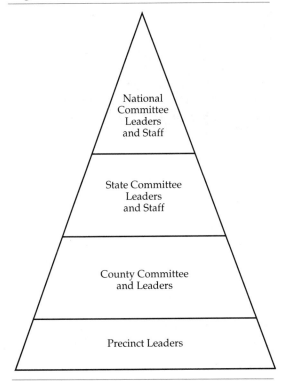

National Committee Leaders and Staff

State Committee Leaders and Staff

County Committee and Leaders

Precinct Leaders

Local parties usually are organized around the **precinct**, a unit of about two hundred to a thousand voters. Precinct party organizations are headed by precinct leaders or captains, who are elected by party members or appointed by higher-level party leaders, depending on the state. Most are volunteers serving without pay. The main duties of precinct organizations are registering voters believed to be supporters of the party, making sure the voters get to the polls during elections, and working for party candidates by distributing leaflets, placing lawn signs, and similar activities. Between the precinct and the state levels, most counties have Democratic and Republican party committees to coordinate the activities of the precinct-level organizations.

Unlike national and state organizations, local party organizations are probably weaker than they used to be in most parts of the country, due largely to the elimination of **patronage**, the placing of party supporters in government jobs. The populist president Andrew Jackson was the first to endorse the "spoils system" ("to the victors belong the spoils"), and patronage was long a fixture of government service at all levels (see Chapter 10). Patronage ensured each party a loyal corps of party workers eager to help in campaigns in return for the prospect of getting or keeping a government job (Mayhew 1986). However, most liberals and some politicians adhering to other perspectives considered the patronage system corrupt and worked for civil service laws to protect government workers from politically motivated dismissals. Some patronage jobs still exist, but their number has been greatly reduced, thus undermining support for local party organizations. The increasing use of mass media (see Chapter 5) has also reduced the need for grass-roots organizations in close touch with the people. Each level of party organization does help, however, to inform voters of the issues and to get the electorate involved and interested in the election process.

Specific party procedures and organizations vary by state and party. In general, committees and delegates to higher-level conventions are selected by delegates from lower levels. Conventions sometimes defer to the wishes of officeholders. Convention delegates usually represent geographic units in national, state, and county conventions. Staff persons for the national committees are usually selected by party leaders. The resources national and state committees can make available to help candidates are the source of their power.

Parties in government   Parties cannot affect government policy unless their candidates get elected to office and those candidates, once elected, work together to achieve the party's goals. In the British **parliamentary system**, which has been copied in most democratic countries, a strict system of party discipline prevails. A candidate who is put on the ballot under the party's label agrees to vote in Parliament the way party leadership directs. Failure to observe this pledge is likely to lead to expulsion from the party and probable defeat at the polls in the next election. The party is organized with a view toward national issues and with the national party leadership controlling the actions of the party's elected officials. Legislative and executive power are concentrated in a prime minister who remains in office for a set period of time or until he or she loses a vote in the lower house of Parliament or is ousted by the party leadership.

The American system stands in marked contrast to the British system. Although both houses of Congress and all state legislatures except Nebraska's are organized along party lines, few mechanisms for enforcing party discipline exist. Candidates for Congress and state legislatures are nominated locally, with little participation by the national party, and once elected are not subject to significant penalties if they vote in opposition to their party leaders. Congressional and state legislative party leaders generally rely on persuasion and appeals to party loyalty to rally legislators behind the party programs, although preference in committee assignments and access to party offices and privileges encourage some to "toe the party line."

Despite lack of formal party discipline, studies of legislative voting show substantial differences in policy outlooks between Democrats and Republicans and a significant degree of party solidarity and **party-unity voting**—a majority of one party's members of Congress opposing a majority of the other party on a vote. Most studies of roll call votes in Congress show that party is the best predictor of voting. Party is not equally important on all legislative issues, however. It is less decisive on farm subsidy issues or western water projects, on which constituency pressures often override party loyalty, and also on issues like civil rights and labor-management relations, on which southern Democrats have tended to vote with Republicans. Party-unity voting in Congress began to decline in the early 1960s, reaching a low of 34 percent in 1969. Since 1983 it has returned to higher levels (*Vital Statistics on Congress, 1991–1992*, 198). The average party-unity voting of both houses of Congress in 1992, during the second year of the 102d Congress, was 58.5 percent. Such relatively high party unity reflects the bitterness of divided government in the later part of the Reagan-Bush years (*Congressional Quarterly Weekly Report*, 19 December 1992, 3849–51).

Parties do not exist in all government units. The state of Nebraska and many cities and towns hold **nonpartisan elections**, in which people vote for candidates as individuals; party labels do not appear on the ballot. In these communities party in government is relatively unimportant, though officials may privately have party affiliations. Many states require that judges be elected on a nonpartisan basis in order to promote judicial impartiality, but candidates may still be known as members of one or the other major party.

Minor Parties

A unique aspect of the American party system is two-party dominance. Rarely has a **minor party**, or third party, organized on the basis of ideas or interests inadequately represented by the two major parties been a serious contender for national power. Part of the difficulty for minor parties arises from the widespread acceptance of early liberal ideas. Because most Americans accept Locke's early "liberalism" (which can be defined so as to also include libertarianism and elements of populism and conservatism; see Chapter 1) as the guiding political principle, parties espousing radical ideas tend to be met with skepticism, if not hostility (Hartz 1955). Marxism is a "hard sell" in a country that has long accepted the early liberal idea of private property as a fundamental right. Likewise, American notions of individualism, progress, and equality work against the establishment of an extremely conservative party dedicated to order, tradition, and elite rule.

In addition to the liberal consensus, the **single-member district system** of electing members to Congress and state legislatures also discriminates against minor parties. In the United States, each House and most state legislative districts elect a single representative. It is a "winner-take-all" situation: the candidate who gets the most votes is elected. Some democracies use a **proportional representation system**, in which the parties run slates of candidates and their representation in the legislature is determined by the percentage of the vote the slate receives. In these countries no one or two parties are dominant, but numerous small parties vie for power. To see how these different systems produce different results, examine Table 4.2. The effect of the single-member district system is to discourage people from voting for minor party candidates in the first place, since their votes will be wasted on candidates who have little chance of being elected.

In practice, the political strength of the two major American parties varies by single-member district. In almost all cases, either the Democrats or the Republicans, and usually both, are stronger than any minor party. This situation reinforces the American two-party system, since the two parties win almost all of the seats. The stronger of the two major parties usually wins a number of seats greater than its percentage support by the electorate. For example, in the sixteen congressional elections from 1960 to 1990, 53 percent of the American electorate voted for Democratic candidates, but the Democrats won 61.2 percent of the seats in the House. Republican candidates got 45.1 percent of the vote but only 39 percent of the seats (*Vital Statistics on Congress, 1991–1992*, 49–50). In 1992, Republicans received 46 percent of the votes and 40.6 percent of the seats (*American Enterprise*, January/February 1993, 92, 105).

It is the minor parties, however, that are most hurt by single-member districts. Even if a minor party received 10 percent of the vote in a state, as Party C did in Table 4.2, it would probably win no House seats because it did not get the highest number of votes in any single district. Even if a party received 10 percent of the vote nationwide (more than 9 million votes), it would probably win very few seats.

The all-time high popular vote for a minor party candidate was the 27.4 percent achieved by Theodore Roosevelt when he ran on the Progressive party ticket in 1912. He had been defeated for the Republican party nomination by incumbent William Howard Taft, who went on to get fewer votes than Roosevelt in the general election. The Democratic candidate, Woodrow Wilson, won the election as a result, the only time since the Civil War that one of the major parties was so openly split (*Presidential Elections since 1789* 1975). Ross Perot's 1992 campaign for president as an independent garnered 19 percent of the vote.

Minor parties and independent candidates usually find it difficult even to get on election ballots. Ballot qualifications are determined by the states. Often a certain number of signatures from various parts of a state are required. Some states require minor parties to have received a certain percentage of the popular vote in the last election. Given all these obstacles, why do significant minor parties arise from time to time? And why would anyone vote for such a party? One reason is that the two major parties, in their attempt to unite people from different perspectives, fail to clearly represent any one perspective consistently. Suppose, for example, that a voter is a libertarian who supports free markets (favored by the Republicans) but also abortion and gay rights (backed by the Democrats)—how does he or she decide which party to support? A similar prob-

TABLE 4.2   HOW THE SINGLE-MEMBER DISTRICT SYSTEM HELPS THE MAJORITY PARTY

SINGLE-MEMBER DISTRICT SYSTEM*		
	Percentage of Vote	Seats Won
Party A	50%	10
Party B	40%	0
Party C	10%	0

PROPORTIONAL REPRESENTATION SYSTEM		
	Percentage of Vote	Seats Won
Party A	50%	5
Party B	40%	4
Party C	10%	1

* Assumes strength is spread evenly across districts.

lem confronts a populist who wants labor union rights (a Democratic priority) but opposes strong government support of racial integration (another Democratic priority). Voters like this, who are dissatisfied with much of their own party's position, may be attracted to a minor party candidate. Minor party and independent efforts are often advanced during periods of economic instability, which can cause voters to blame both major parties for their problems. The economic climate of 1992 may account for Ross Perot's being able to attract substantial popular support without spelling out clear positions on the issues.

When a minor party does show signs of gaining strength, one of the two major parties usually takes up some of its issues, thus checking the growth of the minor party. A clear case of this kind of preemption occurred in 1968, when the right populist George Wallace campaigned for president on the ticket of the American Independent party. Wallace appealed to conservatives and populists, most of them former Democrats, who opposed racial integration, wanted tougher measures against crime, and did not understand why the United States did not go all-out to win the Vietnam War. Responding to Wallace's strength in the polls, the Republican Richard Nixon adopted a "southern strategy," which addressed some of the right populist concerns expressed by Wallace. As a result, Wallace did not do as well as expected in the election and soon after abandoned his party, which shrank to insignificance without him (Rosenstone, Behr, and Lazarus 1984, 110–15). The ability of the major parties to steal their issues is yet another reason minor parties have been unsuccessful. In 1992, independent candidate Ross Perot captured the support of many Americans by calling for budget discipline (see Profile). It will be more difficult than usual for the major political parties to steal this issue since it will require unpopular tax increases, spending cuts, or both.

A large number of minor parties and candidates aspire to public office in the United States, but they are rarely successful in winning even lower-level offices. Why do they run in presidential elections when their chances of victory are so slim? In fact their intentions may not be so much to win the presidency as to use the campaign to educate the public about their positions and to recruit members (see Profile of Angela Davis in Chapter 1). David McReynolds, the 1980 presidential candidate for the Socialist party, realized that his party had "long-range views" and little chance of obtaining enough support to win in the near future. He felt, however, that success was measured not by votes but by the communication of ideas. Other minority party candidates want to press the major parties to deal with certain issues and to establish a foundation for victory in future elections. Some minor party and independent candidates do, however, run to win (Smallwood 1983, 78, 283–84), and occasionally one does. Bernard Sanders, a Socialist running as an independent from Vermont, was elected to the U.S. House of Representatives in 1990.

Despite the alternatives minor parties offer, Americans rarely turn to them. Voters who are dissatisfied with the major parties are likely to vote for the one that seems the lesser of the two evils. Long-standing party loyalties reinforce this tendency. In addition, large numbers choose not to vote at all. Unless traditional party loyalties weaken dramatically, or the American electoral system is changed, two-party dominance will continue (Sabato 1988, 37–40).

ELECTIONS

In the United States, elections determine who holds office and makes public policy. Thus election campaigns are the primary arena of competition between political parties. The fol-

Ross Perot: A Populist Billionaire Runs for President

Ross Perot (Reuters/Bettmann)

ROSS FOR BOSS read the bumper stickers that suddenly sprouted on cars all over the country. Veteran political observers who at first spoke dismissively of "Perotnoia" came to acknowledge the first serious independent candidacy for president in a quarter-century. H. Ross Perot was not elected president in 1992, but his candidacy showed deep populist discontent with the dominant liberal and conservative perspectives in American politics.

Although Perot frequently portrays himself as a man risen from poverty who has "lived the American dream," he was actually born the son of a prosperous cotton broker in Texarkana, Texas, in 1930. He grew into a straight-laced youth who neither smoked nor drank and was focused on success from an early age. After graduating from high school, he won an appointment to the Naval Academy, graduating in 1953. Four years later, he left the Navy (partly, he said later, because many other officers had low moral standards), married

Margaret Birmingham, and went to work as a salesman for IBM. By 1961, he was the company's top salesman.

While working for IBM, Perot discovered that many customers wanted to buy data-processing services rather than computers. When the company refused to take his advice and enter this market, he quit and founded his own company, Electronic Data Systems (EDS) in 1962. Within five years, Perot was one of the richest men in the United States. He drove his employees hard, requiring sixty- to eighty-hour weeks without extra pay and ruthlessly firing homosexuals and adulterers. In return, he gave his employees his unqualified support, frequently paying for surgery and helping in other emergencies. In 1979, he even financed a jailbreak to free two employees imprisoned by the Ayatollah Khomeini's government in Iran. He was not above seeking political influence to gain government contracts: by 1974 Perot was the country's largest individual political contributor.

Perot first came to public notice in the late 1960s when he attempted to buy the release of American prisoners of war (POWs) held in North Vietnam. Although this effort failed, Perot became known as a friend of the Vietnam veterans. After the war, Perot was increasingly in demand for public duties: he led a commission that pushed through major reforms in the Texas school system, was active in antidrug abuse campaigns, and contributed more than $100 million to charitable causes. At the same time, he became increasingly involved in secret operations of various kinds. He helped finance Oliver North's Iran-*contra* activities (see Chapters 7 and 11) and has spent millions of dollars in so far unsuccessful attempts to rescue American prisoners he believes are still being held in Southeast Asia.

Although friends and associates had long urged him to run for office, Perot resisted all invitations to enter politics until February 1992.

"After They've Chewed Up A Few, You Get Your Pick Of What's Left"

Herbert Block. From *Herblock on All Fronts* (New American Library, 1980).

ends up dropping out. This phenomenon of "momentum" has led to some strange outcomes. The incumbent President Lyndon Johnson, for example, was forced to withdraw from the race in 1968 even though he won the New Hampshire primary because challenger Eugene McCarthy did better than expected. On the other hand, momentum did little to help the Democrat Richard Gephardt and the Republican Robert Dole, candidates in the pri-

maries of 1988. Each won the Iowa caucuses, but neither survived Super Tuesday, twenty primaries on the same day, most of them in southern states, held six weeks later (Aldrich 1980, 100–36).

Another effect of the primary system is to eliminate most candidates early and narrow the race to two or three. In 1992 George Bush found himself without a serious Republican opponent from mid-April on, as Pat Buchanan faded. On the Democratic side, Jerry Brown hung on until the convention, but Bill Clinton's nomination was assured by late May.

The national convention itself, once an important political event, has lost significance in the past thirty years. The convention used to select the nominee from a field of candidates, often after considerable maneuvering and many roll call votes. Now the votes of delegates are largely bound by primary and caucus results, and following state campaigns the nominee is a foregone conclusion. Since 1956 all nominations have taken place on the first ballot, and conventions have been largely media events. They have been structured to give the candidate free public exposure, provide a forum for attacks on the other party by speakers (usually conveniently timed for maximum television coverage), bury ill feelings created by the nomination struggle, and unite the party behind the victor. The national convention is also in charge of drafting a nonbinding **party platform**, which states the goals and ideals of the party and is used to gain voter support (Wayne 1992, 137–68; see also Gilligan 1988, 45–54).

Who Votes and How?

One noted political scientist said, "Americans like elections, but we don't like to vote" (Weissberg 1985, 58). This ironic statement appears justified in view of what has happened to **voter turnout**—the number of eligible voters who actually vote—in the United States over the last quarter century. In the 1960 presidential election 62.8 percent of the eligible voters cast ballots; in 1992 the figure was 55 percent, up from a low of 50 percent in 1988. Still, an overall general decline persists despite major efforts by both political parties to register new voters. Turnout for congressional races in recent **midterm elections** (those general elections in the off years between presidential elections) has averaged 13 percentage points lower than in the presidential race. In the 1990

elections turnout was only 33 percent (*Vital Statistics on Congress, 1990–1991*, 48). Many analysts attribute low turnout in elections since 1984 to an increasing use of negative advertising by candidates, which seemingly convinced many voters that no candidates were worthy of support. In 1992, when voters were worried about the economy and wanted substantial change, and when a strong independent candidate stimulated interest, turnout was still only 55 percent. Whether this slight upswing was indicative of a new trend is yet to be determined.

Explanations for low and declining voter turnout fall into two basic categories. One sees voting and nonvoting as an individual decision and looks for individual characteristics that might explain why some people vote and others do not. Scholars pursuing this approach have found that education is the variable most likely to promote voting. Factors like income, occupation, and race, which had been previously thought to affect voting, were found to be unimportant once education was taken into account. Older people were found to be more likely to vote than younger people, and men slightly more likely to vote than women, but age and sex were secondary factors (Wolfinger and Rosenstone 1980, 13–60). Education most likely affects voting because it is more difficult for the poorly educated to gather information on the candidates and issues; for them, nonvoting can be a rational alternative to uninformed voting.

The second approach looks at institutions in general and election laws in particular to explain voter turnout. Before 1890, voter turnout in the United States was as high as it is now in European democracies, although today most European democracies far exceed the United States in voter turnout. Then the populist revolt threatened the power of many leaders of major political parties. To prevent vote fraud, most states instituted laws requiring voters to register in advance and report any change in residence. Many states also required a minimum period of residence. Slight as they may

CAMPAIGN '86

Scott Willis. © 1986 Willis—San Jose *Mercury News*.

seem, these requirements evidently discourage voting. Minnesota and Wisconsin now allow registration up to election day; turnout has increased, but not fraud. It is estimated that if all states adopted registration reforms, turnouts would increase by 9 percentage points, with most of the increase among the less educated (Kleppner 1982, 26, 50–61; Wolfinger and Rosenstone 1980, 61–88). In 1993 President Clinton signed a "motor-voter" registration bill that requires states to give people a chance to register to vote when they obtain or renew a driver's license.

If voting did increase, would the outcomes of elections change? Many in both parties have assumed that higher turnout would help the Democrats, since more people from the less-educated and lower-income groups would be voting. However, recent studies have found

that no presidential election since 1952 would have been swayed even by 100 percent voter turnout. In fact, if everyone had voted in 1984 and 1988, Ronald Reagan and George Bush would have won by greater margins (*American Enterprise*, July/August 1992, 58). Voters and nonvoters appear to share similar political beliefs (Bennet and Resnick 1990, 771–802). Even if nonvoters held beliefs substantially different from those of voters, election outcomes are less likely to be affected by getting them to vote than by convincing existing voters to switch parties, since each voter converted subtracts one from the opposition's total as well as adding one to one's own (*American Enterprise*, July/August 1992, 55).

Neither explanation of voter turnout answers all the questions. If more education tends to promote turnout, why has turnout fallen over the last twenty-five years when ed-ucational levels have been continually rising? If removing barriers to registration tends to promote turnout, why did the large-scale reg-istration drives conducted in 1984, 1988, and 1992 not produce more voters? Some scholars answer these questions by pointing to a larger institutional cause—the political system it-self—as a cause of nonvoting. They contend that the two major political parties are too weak to formulate and enforce opposing pro-grams of government for the voters to choose between and, at the same time, too strongly entrenched to be dislodged by a minor party. Thus some voters see little difference between the parties and their candidates for office. Fur-thermore, many of the most important deci-sions are made not by elected officials but by unelected judges, bureaucrats, and leaders of private interest groups. Seeing no way to make a real impact on the system, many people ra-tionally choose not to vote even though they are dissatisfied with government (Zipp 1985, 50–61). If this argument is valid, American de-mocracy may be in serious trouble.

Locke's idea of popular sovereignty pre-sumed a small, highly educated male elector-ate that would choose representatives in a rational, self-interested manner. Voters would protect themselves against oppression by vot-ing for candidates whose views on public is-sues coincided with their own. Once elected, officials might, from time to time, exercise in-dependent judgment by resisting a popular policy they considered unwise, but if they could not justify their decisions to the people, they would ultimately be removed from office.

Early studies of voting, conducted in the 1950s, were very depressing to those who ac-cepted the traditional image of the voter as a rational decision maker. Polls conducted by the Survey Research Center at the University of Michigan revealed that party affiliation was far more important than any other factor in determining voting, including stands on the issues. Even more surprising was the weak re-lationship between party affiliation and voter preference on the issues. Voters identified with the Republicans or Democrats out of habit and tradition rather than because they agreed with party policies. Party identification was so strong that voters often failed to recognize when the opposing party held a position with which they agreed: a Republican who agreed with the Democratic candidate on foreign pol-icy or civil rights was likely to misperceive the candidate's position as being in opposition (Campbell et al. 1960). It was difficult to see how such uninformed voters could hold their representatives accountable, as liberal theory requires.

However, the importance of party as a fac-tor in voting has declined since the 1960s. More and more voters are independents and ticket-splitters. Some studies contend that vot-ing on the basis of rational choice on issues, instead of on personality or party affiliation, has increased, but other studies dispute this (Nie, Verba, and Petrocik 1976, 156–173). Party identification remains strongest among Repub-licans, whose party became sharply more con-servative and libertarian in recent decades.

While issue voting has increased and party voting continues to be important, many voters also cast their ballots based on the personal qualities they perceived in a candidate, what is often referred to as the candidate's **image**. Most voters react negatively to a candidate who is seen, justly or not, as shifting positions, taking a disagreeable stand, being uncon-cerned about the welfare of ordinary people, or being generally untrustworthy. Gary Hart's marital infidelity ultimately destroyed his bid for the presidency in 1988, but Bill Clinton was skillful enough to overcome similar image problems in 1992. Conversely, projecting an image of strength, competence, honesty, and compassion can help a candidate win the sup-port of voters who take a different position on the issues. In 1984, for example, 40 percent of those who classified themselves as "very lib-eral" voted for Reagan, citing "qualities of leadership" as more important than stand on issues (*National Journal*, 10 November 1984,

2131; *Washington Post*, 8 November 1984, A45). Political campaigns sometimes work to achieve such results by emphasizing the negative aspects of the opposition candidate.

Such evidence raises questions about the knowledge that voters have and the viability of democratic popular sovereignty. If image and party often matter much more than issues, how are elected representatives to be held accountable for what they do? Yet voters do seem to hold politicians accountable for some of the results of their policies. In 1992, voters who felt they were "better off than they were four years ago" voted for President Bush, while those who saw themselves as worse off voted for Bill Clinton. In addition to their personal fortunes, voters seem to judge elected officials by how well the country fares under their leadership. Election results show that the party in power during an economic recession tends to suffer losses in the next election, while an administration that presides over prosperity is likely to be reelected (*National Journal*, 10 November 1984, 2132; Tufte 1978, 3–64). All this seems to indicate that over the long term, voters may be more rational than they appear (Page and Shapiro 1992). This correlation does not imply that voters hold government accountable for every mistake—Ronald Reagan, for example, suffered little long-term loss in popularity from recurrent scandals in his administration—but it does show that certain types of failure are likely to bring electoral retribution, and persistent inattention to public needs will likely return an elected official to private life sooner rather than later. Many observers felt that George Bush invited this fate in 1992 with his consistent emphasis on foreign over domestic issues (see Controversy).

Presidential Elections

The presidential election is the only national election held in the United States. The general election campaign begins in August after the national conventions, but, to win the party nomination, many candidates start campaigning years before the election. Jimmy Carter, for example, began his race for president in 1973, three years before the election, although he did not attract significant public notice until after the January 1976 Iowa caucuses.

One difficulty faced by presidential candidates is that the electoral strategies needed to win the nomination differ from those needed to win the general election. Because voters in Republican primaries are more conservative and libertarian, and voters in Democratic primaries more liberal and left populist than the voters in the general election, positions necessary to win primaries may be too extreme to win the general election. After the convention, candidates often try to move back toward the center of the **political spectrum**—the range of political perspectives among the public—to appeal to general election voters, but they are not always successful. The Republican Barry Goldwater in 1964 and the Democrat George McGovern in 1972 overpowered their opponents in the nominating contests but ended up being tagged as "extremists" and losing badly in the general elections. On the other hand, Reagan's experience shows that it is possible to take strong positions and at the same time build wide popular appeal.

Following the national conventions and the final wording of party platforms, presidential candidates seek to appeal to voters through both image and issues. One element in this appeal has been, in recent years, televised presidential debates. These are becoming increasingly well-managed media events. The first televised presidential debates were held in 1960 between the Democrat John F. Kennedy and the Republican Richard Nixon. Polls taken afterward showed that those who had listened to the debate on radio thought that Nixon had won, but television viewers, who constituted the majority, thought Kennedy was the winner. The youthful and attractive Kennedy impressed viewers, while Nixon, who wore a gray suit and appeared unshaven, clearly

CONTROVERSY

The Incredible Election of 1992

Ross Perot, Bill Clinton, and George Bush (AP/Wide World Photos)

Had the events of the 1992 election campaign been written as the plot of a political novel, it would have been dismissed as grossly improbable. Eighteen months before the election, the incumbent president enjoyed a 90 percent approval rating. On election day, he received only 37 percent of the vote, the lowest for any incumbent since 1912. An eccentric billionaire with a history of involvement in secret operations mounted a $69-million campaign and gained nearly one-fifth of the vote, despite dropping out of the race temporarily. The governor of a small southern state captured the Democratic party's nomination with a moderate platform and survived allegations of adultery and

draft dodging to win the White House. Surely the author of such a tale would have to have been a fantasist the equal of Jules Verne.

It was the American economy, above all, that made the fantasy come true. While some economists proclaimed the end of the recession, few voters noticed. The surge of popularity President George Bush received after the victory in Operation Desert Storm faded quickly as more Americans joined unemployment lines and the White House took no action. An old-style conservative, Bush was convinced that the economy would right itself and that hasty government action would do more harm than good. He may have been correct, but Americans expected the kind of leadership from the president they had seen during the war. Bush was further weakened when Patrick J. Buchanan, a right populist television commentator (see Profile in Chapter 1), entered the race for the Republican nomination.

Nevertheless, most Americans expected Bush's reelection, chiefly because the Democratic candidate initially appeared so vulnerable. Bill Clinton, the governor of Arkansas (see Profile in Chapter 7), ran a shrewd campaign, taking advantage of the southern Super Tuesday primaries to build up a lead over Democratic rivals Bob Kerrey, Jerry Brown, Paul Tsongas, and Tom Harkin. Yet Clinton appeared to be "damaged goods." Reports of adultery and evasion of military service in Vietnam appeared to back up opponents' characterizations of him as "Slick Willie." Many Democrats lamented that stronger candidates like New York Governor Mario Cuomo and New Jersey Senator Bill Bradley had decided against entering the race.

Minor party and independent efforts usually start when many voters are dissatisfied with both major party candidates. As the likelihood of a Bush-Clinton contest increased, more and more Americans turned to H. Ross Perot (see Profile in this chapter), a Texan who had made $3 billion in the computer business. In February, on the "Larry King Live" talk show, Perot issued a challenge to his followers: collect petition signatures to put me on the ballot in all fifty states and I will run for president. Although Perot avoided specific issues, his past success and folksy, caustic attacks on Washington politicians rallied the disillusioned of both parties. By June 1992, he was actually leading in the polls, with Bush second and Clinton a distant third.

Slowly, Clinton started to make a comeback. Though Jerry Brown stayed in the race until the end, the other Democrats dropped out and endorsed Clinton. Meanwhile, Perot began to drop in the polls. On July 19, during the Democratic national convention, he abruptly announced that he would not run after all. Shocked supporters rallied behind Clinton, who suddenly enjoyed a 20-point lead in the polls.

Through all this, George Bush seemed strangely passive. He made little effort to campaign once the Buchanan challenge had faded in the spring, preferring to appear presidential and save his energy for the general election campaign. At the Republican convention in August, Bush tried to mend fences with the right wing of his party by allowing Buchanan and Pat Robertson to deliver major speeches that sounded harsh and negative, accusing Democrats of lacking "family values" and supporting abortion, homosexuality, and obscene art. Vice-President Dan Quayle had already made himself a target of ridicule when he attacked the television series "Murphy Brown" for favorably depicting unwed motherhood.

Bill Clinton's electoral strategy, which had raised doubt among traditional Democrats in the primaries, played better in the general election campaign. Instead of focusing on the problems of the poor and minorities as past Democratic candidates had, Clinton stressed the concerns of the middle class. He promised them a tax cut, paid for by higher taxes on the wealthy, and aid for sending their children to college. At the same time, he disdained "tax-and-spend" economics and promised to move toward a balanced budget. His choice of Senator Albert Gore of Tennessee, another southern moderate, as his vice presidential candidate also won praise. Although Clinton seemed to be promising everything to everyone, his strategy was working: at the end of September he was still leading by nearly 20 points.

Suddenly, the entire picture changed as Perot, claiming to be responding to pleas from his supporters (many of whom were now paid workers for his campaign), reentered the race. Initially, his erratic behavior won him little support, but his stock rose after he was invited to participate in the presidential debates. He effectively ridiculed Bush and Clinton for blaming each other for all the nation's problems, suggesting that both parties "should be put in a blender." Financing his campaign with his own money was also popular in a year when voters were angry about a congressional pay raise and check bouncing.

In the end, Clinton won, though by a lesser margin in popular votes (43 percent to 37 percent) than predicted in most polls. Ross Perot did not win a single electoral vote, but 19 percent of the 100 million Americans who voted for president voted for him. Considering all the reasons Perot gave Americans to distrust him, his showing was a clear indication of how much they distrusted traditional politicians. Perot's presence seemed likely to be felt in American politics in years to come.

As for George Bush, he was partly a victim of the Republican party's past success and an inability to communicate a vision of what he wanted to see the United States become. Republican victories drove the Democrats to select a nominee with a moderate image who could not be labeled a spendthrift liberal as Bush had labeled Michael Dukakis in 1988. The collapse of communism for which American leaders of both parties had worked for so long hurt the Republicans in two ways: it fueled the recession on the East and West coasts, where defense industries were concentrated, and it removed anticommunism as a force unifying conservatives, libertarians, and right populists in the Republican party. Had the Soviet Union still existed, Buchanan's disruptive candidacy would have been unlikely. Bush's own passivity contributed to the outcome, but so did events beyond his control.

Source: Des Moines Register, 5 November 1992, 8A; *Time*, 2 November 1992, 29–43; *National Journal*, 7 November 1992, 2537–44; *Congressional Quarterly Almanac 1992*, 3A–7A.

showed a lack of familiarity with the medium (Jamieson 1984, 122–68).

Television debates were revived in 1976 and have been held in every presidential campaign since. In the second of three debates between President Gerald Ford and challenger Jimmy Carter in 1976, Ford made an incorrect statement about the situation in Poland which some say cost him that year's close election. In 1980 Ronald Reagan's practiced television manner helped him negate President Carter's attempts to portray his opponent as an extreme conservative. When the debate was held the race appeared close, but the next week Reagan opened up a decisive lead. In 1984, President Reagan was not so fortunate—most observers thought he lost both debates with Walter Mondale. Nevertheless Reagan came back to win a crushing victory. The 1988 debates between Michael Dukakis and George

Bush were a draw (Asher 1988, 178–79; Kessel 1984, 192, 214–15; *Newsweek*, 21 November 1988, 124; *New York Times*, 15 October 1988, A8). The 1992 debates helped strengthen Ross Perot and saw George Bush hold his ground and recover support from traditional Republicans but they probably were won by Bill Clinton, who convinced enough voters he was presidential material.

Today debating has become a science in which a candidate's main job seems to be to stay out of trouble by saying nothing that will hurt his or her campaign. Candidates often raise only those issues in which a clear and favorable distinction can be drawn with the opposition. As an example of what can go wrong, a newspaper reporter on the 1988 presidential debate panel asked Dukakis how a person who had brutalized Dukakis's wife should be punished. The hypothetical case

GREAT MOMENTS IN AMERICAN HISTORY -By El Dani

AND ON THE SIXTH DAY OF NOVEMBER, 1984 A.D. (ALARMED DEMOCRATS), THE PROPHETS SURVEYED THE VAST REPUBLIC AND SAW THAT IT WAS GOOD . . .

AND THE SAGELY, AGELESS GREAT COMMUNICATOR SAW THE SELF-SAME GOODNESS AND CAST HIS OWN VOTE, THEN RETREATED TO REST . . .

AND AT THE APPOINTED HOURS, GREAT WERE THE MULTITUDES THAT ALSO CAST THEIR VOTES, AND GREATER YET WAS THE TILT OF THE LAND . . .

AND WHEN THE TILT WAS COMPLETE, THE LAND TOOK THE FORM OF A VISAGE, VICTORIOUS, AND SPOKE: "FOUR MORE YEARS . . ."

Dani D'Umuk Aguila. © 1984. Courtesy of New York *Filipino Reporter*.

forced Dukakis to address an issue he would otherwise have avoided. His response, focusing on his stand against capital punishment and betraying no emotion about the thought of an attack on his wife, impacted negatively on many viewers. Coverage of the debate reinforced Dukakis's image as personally cold, analytical, and soft on crime (*New York Times*, 14 October 1988, A14). The incident also serves as an example of how candidates may find it impossible to keep campaigns focused on issues instead of image.

One way a candidate can control his or her image is to buy time on television separate from the debates. While all the candidates in 1992 used campaign advertisements, Ross Perot broke new ground by presenting program-length "infomercials" detailing his views on economic questions and his plans to solve the federal budget deficit. A surprising number of Americans watched these programs, confounding predictions that no one would watch half-hour discussions on politics. Another new form of campaigning in 1992 was the talk show appearance, in which the candidates responded to direct or phoned-in questions from ordinary citizens.

While Democrats remain the majority party with their coalition built on liberal and left populist voters, Republicans have done well in most recent presidential elections. From 1952 through 1992, Republican presidential candidates have received a total of 432.8 million votes, compared to 389.4 million for Democratic candidates. Republicans have won five of the last seven presidential elections, four of them by comfortable margins of more than 10 percent. Republicans clearly benefit from bases they have developed in the West and South. Many conservative or populist Democrats in these areas vote against the national Democratic ticket, which is usually headed by a liberal, while remaining good Democrats locally. In 1988 Bush carried every southern state and all the western states except Hawaii, Oregon, and Washington. In addition he carried large eastern and midwestern states like Illinois, Michigan, New Jersey, Ohio, and Pennsyl-

Jimmy Margulies. Courtesy *The Record*.

vania, but even if Dukakis had won those five states, he still would have lost the election.

In 1992, Clinton made enough inroads in the South and especially the West that he won. Several factors help explain the Democratic victory. The Democrats benefited from competition among factions within the Republican party. Moreover, the Republican national organization could not compensate for Bush's lack of a clear domestic program. Still, the Democratic victory was not accompanied by gains in the Senate, and there actually was a loss of eight Democratic House seats, mostly due to redistricting following the 1990 census. The Democrats did retain control of Congress, however. President Clinton clearly has an opportunity to redefine the Democratic party and increase its popularity.

Ross Perot's independent candidacy had a number of interesting effects. His summer

Figure 4.2   The Presidential Election, 1992.

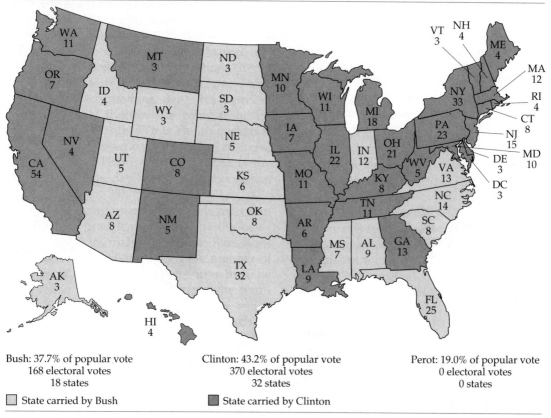

Bush: 37.7% of popular vote
168 electoral votes
18 states

Clinton: 43.2% of popular vote
370 electoral votes
32 states

Perot: 19.0% of popular vote
0 electoral votes
0 states

☐ State carried by Bush   ■ State carried by Clinton

Note: Despite the all-Southern Democratic ticket, Bush carried eight southern states with 116 electoral votes to eight southern states with 65 votes for Clinton. Clinton swept the Northeast and West Coast, however, where the recession had been most severe, for more than 200 electoral votes. Bush's fate was sealed when Clinton won all the industrial midwestern states except Indiana, Dan Quayle's home. Bush held onto a belt of plains states from Kansas to North Dakota and to the mountain states of Idaho, Utah, Wyoming, and Arizona, as well as Alaska. But Clinton penetrated even this Republican heartland, winning Montana, Colorado, Nevada, and New Mexico, states that had not voted for a Democrat for president since 1964. As James Carville, a Clinton strategist, put it, Clinton "picked" the electoral lock that the Republicans had put on the South and West (quoted in *Congressional Quarterly Almanac* 1992, 5A).

Source: Congressional Quarterly Weekly Report, *7 November 1992, 3549.*

withdrawal resulted in a major rise in the polls for Clinton. During the debates after Perot re-entered the race, his candidacy helped focus attention on problems. By election day most polls indicated Perot voters would have split evenly between Bush and Clinton had Perot not been on the ballot.

Clinton, however, with 43 percent of the popular vote, did not win by a majority, a reminder that the **popular vote**—the actual number of votes cast for each candidate—does not elect the president. Rather the vote that counts is the tally in the **electoral college**, which was established by the framers as a check on the power of the majority and a compromise between those at the Constitutional Convention who wanted direct popular election and those who wanted election by Congress or the state legislatures (see Chapter 2). In the electoral college, each state is accorded electoral votes that equal the number of that state's United States senators and representatives; the **Twenty-third Amendment**, adopted in 1961, also gave the District of Columbia representation in the electoral college. Thus Alaska, with two senators and one representative, has 3 electoral votes; Michigan, with two senators and sixteen representatives, has 18 electoral votes. A total of 538 electoral votes are at stake, and a candidate must receive a majority (270) to become president. Votes for president are actually cast by electors selected by the two political parties and pledged to support the party's candidate. A few electors have violated their pledge, but never enough to affect the outcome of a presidential election. If no candidate receives a majority, the House of Representatives is given the responsibility of choosing the president, with each state, not each representative, having one vote, and a majority of twenty-six delegations required to win.

The electoral vote can produce a result different from the popular vote because, traditionally, all of a state's electoral votes are awarded to the candidate who wins the state's popular vote. Only Maine, with 4 electoral votes, does not follow this practice. Thus a candidate who wins the popular vote in California, even if by only a few votes, is entitled to all California's 54 electoral votes. It is theoretically possible for a candidate to become president by winning just eleven large states—California, Florida, Illinois, Michigan, New Jersey, New York, North Carolina, Ohio, Pennsylvania, Texas, and Virginia. The other candidate could receive every single popular vote in the remaining states—more than half the national total—and still be defeated. Of course, this example is extreme and unrealistic, but it is obvious that the winner of the popular vote can be defeated by an opponent who wins the right combination of states. This situation actually occurred in the presidential elections of 1876 and 1888, and it has come close to happening in several elections since. In 1976 a change of a few thousand votes in the states of Hawaii and Ohio would have given Gerald Ford another term as president, although Jimmy Carter won the popular vote by more than 1.5 million votes. (For the distribution of electoral votes, see Figure 4.3).

Even when a minority president is not elected, the existence of the electoral college has several important effects on the election campaign. One is that candidates tend to neglect states they are fairly sure they will win or lose and concentrate on the states where the race is close. In 1992, for example, Bush did not attempt to campaign in California, New York, or Illinois because it was generally recognized that their electoral votes would go to Clinton and that votes for the Republican candidate would be wasted. Under direct popular election, all votes would count, so candidates would have an increased incentive to campaign everywhere, even in states where the opposing party had a majority.

Another effect of the electoral college is to give more power to the states with large numbers of electoral votes, especially California, Florida, Illinois, New York, Ohio, Pennsylvania, and Texas. Candidates campaign harder in these states than they would under direct

Figure 4.3   State Size according to Population: The 1992, 1996, and 2000 Electoral Votes

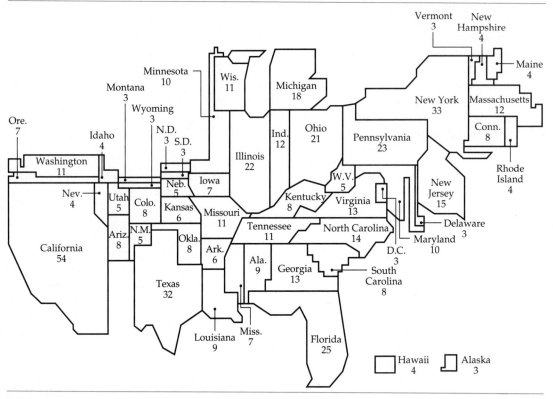

Note: Each state has a vote in the electoral college equal to the number of its representatives and senators.
Source: New York Times, *27 December 1990, B6.*

popular election and often take care not to alienate groups disproportionately concentrated in them. Among the groups benefiting from the system are the Jewish community (only 2.5 percent of the national population, but heavily concentrated in New York), city dwellers, and blacks in the North. On the other hand, residents of rural areas, the Great Plains, the Rocky Mountains, and the Deep South, where votes are not typically close, do not often see presidential contenders (Wayne 1992, 18–22).

The electoral college also affects the fortunes of minor parties, encouraging some and discouraging others. In order to get any electoral votes, a minor party candidate must win a **plurality**—more votes than any other candidate but not necessarily a majority—in at least one state, so a candidate with supporters scat-

tered across the country has little chance of affecting the outcome. In the 1992 election Ross Perot, with 19 percent of the popular vote but no regional base, did not carry a single state. However, if a minor party has its supporters concentrated in a few states, it has a remote chance of keeping either major party from obtaining a majority and then bargaining to throw its electoral votes behind whichever major party candidate is willing to make concessions to avoid an election in the House. George Wallace hoped to pull off such a coup in his 1968 presidential bid, but he failed to win enough of the southern states to deny Richard Nixon a majority.

The electoral college appears difficult to justify in a modern democracy; it not only carries the potential of defeating the will of the people but seems to benefit some groups while harming others. Reforms proposed range from direct popular election to modified electoral college systems that would reduce or eliminate the possibility of a minority president. One proposal gives a "bonus" of 102 additional electoral votes to the candidate who wins the national popular vote. This plan would ensure that the popular vote winner would always win the electoral vote while preserving the importance of the states. Another plan divides each state into districts, with one elector from each district, thus eliminating the "winner-take-all" system and the advantage for large states. The simplest plan, of course, would be to abolish the electoral college altogether and move to direct popular election, with a runoff election if no one candidate reached a certain percentage (most plans suggest 40 percent) of the vote (Wayne 1992, 290–97).

Congressional Elections

While party, issues, and image seem to determine voting in presidential elections, a fourth consideration plays a critical role in congressional races. That consideration is the advantage conferred upon **incumbents**—those currently in office—when they run for reelection. The record of the past forty-five years shows how reluctant voters are to unseat House members especially. In the twenty-three congressional elections from 1946 to 1990, an average of 91.7 percent of all the House incumbents who sought reelection were successful (*Vital Statistics on Congress, 1991–1992*, 58). In the 1992 elections, 88.3 percent of House incumbents won, though many others had chosen not to seek reelection, largely on account of their role in the House bank scandal (see Chapter 6). Incumbents who lose are often implicated in scandals or questionable activities. Redistricting following the 1990 census also caused several House members to retire (*National Journal*, 7 November 1992, 2558–59). President Bush may have helped some incumbents by taking much of the blame for the weak economy. Apparently, a House incumbent can lose, but it takes effort.

Brian Duffy. Courtesy *Des Moines Register*.

For senators, the incumbent advantage is real but not as overwhelming. The reelection rate for senators averaged 80.6 percent from 1946 to 1990, but fluctuated from a low of 55.2 percent in 1980 to a high of 96.9 percent in 1990 (Davidson and Oleszek 1985, 62; *Statistical Abstract, 1992*, 264). In the 1992 elections, 81.5 percent of Senate incumbents seeking reelection won (*National Journal*, 7 November 1992, 2555, 2558–59; *Congressional Quarterly Weekly Report*, 28 November 1992, 3719). Incumbent advantage, as well as the realities of campaign finance, sometimes scares off good challengers before they start. Of course members of Congress frequently leave office voluntarily through resignation or retirement, so turnover is higher than the figures imply, but an incumbent who chooses to stay has an excellent chance of holding his or her seat for a long time.

Members of Congress would probably like to believe that the high reelection rate is due to their own job performance; perhaps the public is so satisfied with the way Congress is working that no one sees any reason for change. Yet opinion polls show that most people have little regard for Congress as an institution. Why, then, are legislators reelected at such a high rate? One reason is that incumbent members of the House have almost twice as much name recognition as their challengers in preelection polls (Hinkley 1981, 43–50; *Vital Statistics on Congress, 1989–1990*, 56). Incumbents are better known because they have campaigned before, because the media report what they say and do as news, and because they work so hard at being recognized. Most members visit their districts regularly to keep "in touch" with constituents. They also send literature to constituents free of charge, within prescribed limits, through the **franking privilege**, which permits members of Congress to send mail by using their signatures instead of stamps. The frank is useful for presenting the member's views to the people, for obtaining their opinions through questionnaires and polls, and most of all, for reminding them of their "man or woman in Washington."

A challenger could overcome the name recognition problem through campaign advertising designed to make his or her name as well known as the incumbent's, but few challengers have money to mount such a campaign. Campaign contributors typically give to incumbents, whose views are better known and who are more likely to win in any case. It is not the incumbent's spending, but the challenger's lack of resources, that makes the difference. For example, House incumbents who spend little on their campaigns usually win anyway, but the few challengers who win are nearly always those who have been able to raise substantial war chests. Usually it takes at least $1 million for a challenger to make up for the inherent advantages enjoyed by the incumbent (*Vital Statistics on Congress, 1989–1990*, 57).

Of course incumbents also have the advantage of being in Congress, where they can deliver what a challenger can only promise.

Most members of Congress devote considerable time and effort to helping citizens who have problems of one kind or another with the government. Although only a small proportion of the constituents can be helped in this way, those who do receive assistance are likely to become loyal supporters and may influence friends and relatives to become supporters as well. Most members also work tirelessly to bring government projects, ranging from dams to post offices to military bases, to their districts, or to prevent existing facilities from being closed in budget-cutting efforts. The longer a member serves in Congress, the more seniority he or she acquires and the more power to bring such **"pork barrel" projects** to constituents (see Chapter 6; Fiorina 1977). Early in his administration, President Clinton was criticized for channeling such pork-barrel projects to Democratic Congressional districts in his unsuccessful economic stimulus plan (*Congressional Quarterly Weekly Report*, 10 April 1993, 907–9).

Despite all these advantages, incumbents do lose, particularly in the Senate. Senate incumbents may not fare as well as House incumbents because the Senate, regarded as a more prestigious body, attracts better challengers. In addition, senators must please the diverse population of a state, whereas House members' districts are usually more homogeneous. Not only do popular governors and House members often seek to graduate to the Senate, but well-known sports figures (Bill Bradley of New Jersey), military heroes (Jeremiah Denton of Alabama), and astronauts (John Glenn of Ohio and Harrison Schmitt of New Mexico) have made successful Senate challenges. In fact Senate challengers have nearly as much name recognition—85 percent—as Senate incumbents, while House challengers have only 45 percent (Hinckley 1981, 113; see also *Vital Statistics on Congress, 1991–1992*, 45). Finally, the one disadvantage of any incumbent—a voting record on thousands of issues with which voters may disagree—is easier to communicate to a state than to a congressional district because people are not as aware of congressional district boundaries and senators are generally better known.

Although incumbency seems to be the overriding factor in explaining the outcome of congressional elections, party is important, too. Many congressional districts have been dominated by one party for decades, some for a century or more. In such areas the incumbent advantage is less important than party allegiance in explaining the vote. In more evenly balanced districts, incumbents do not do as well when their party does poorly nationally. In 1980, for example, a number of previously secure Democratic incumbents lost their seats, and so did some Republicans in 1982. Given Bush's defeat in 1992, Republican incumbents were lucky to do as well as they did.

Throughout the twentieth century, the president's party has lost seats in Congress in every midterm election but one. The political scientist Barbara Hinckley calls this "the curious case of the midterm election" (Hinckley 1981, 50–53; see also *Vital Statistics on Congress, 1991–1992*, 53), and the reasons for it are not clearly understood. At one time the midterm loss was attributed to the absence of the **coattail effect**—the tendency for a winning presidential candidate to carry his party's House and Senate candidates to victory. But the coattail effect has greatly diminished in recent presidential elections, so it can no longer fully explain the midterm slump.

Another theory is that presidents, who are usually very popular after their election, invariably offend some groups of voters while in office, and that these dissatisfied people tend to vote for the opposition party in the midterm election. Still another theory holds that a self-fulfilling prophecy is at work: stronger candidates from the opposition party may run in the midterm election because they expect to win, while the president's party has a hard time getting good candidates (Hinckley 1981, 114–17; Jacobson and Kernell 1981, 60–71).

Funding

Adequate funding is essential for any candidate for a major office. It takes a lot of money to retain the people who can determine the best way to phrase the candidate's message. Polling helps the experts avoid mistakes, and it, too, is expensive. Once the message is formulated, it must get to the voters, most often through expensive television commercials but also through direct mail or another medium if television does not suit a district. Congressional candidates can easily spend hundreds of thousands of dollars, senatorial candidates into the millions, and presidential candidates into the tens of millions. Contributions come from individual contributors, political parties, and **political action committees** (PACs), organizations that are independent of candidates or political parties but give money to candidates who support their position (see Chapter 5; Sabato 1984, 7).

A candidate's need for campaign money can be viewed in many different ways, but one distinction is especially important. The need to raise money might be helpful to the public interest if it sorts those who have public support from those who do not. The process could provide the public with a smaller number of candidates who can be viewed in greater detail. On the other hand, fund-raising might be so time consuming that it gives a special advantage to those who have their own money or cater to monied interests. Viewpoints regarding this distinction have a considerable impact on opinions of campaign finance issues.

Elections today are a regulated industry on the theory that limits on and reporting of contributions will prevent the kinds of abuses practiced by Richard Nixon and others (see Controversy on the Watergate scandal in Chapter 7). In 1971 the Federal Election Campaign Act (FECA) placed tighter requirements on campaign disclosures. Amendments to FECA in 1974 provided public funding for major party presidential candidates, established a limit of $1,000 per candidate per election on contributions individuals could make in federal elections, and allowed PACs set up by labor unions, corporations, or interest groups to give a maximum of $5,000 per election to any number of candidates (Sabato 1984, 8; see also Sorauf 1988, 34–39).

Presidential candidates are eligible for public funding if they meet certain thresholds of financing before a convention or receive a nomination from a major party or minor party with strong support (defined as 5 percent of the general election vote). Major presidential candidates have accepted this money even though it limits their total spending. Ross Perot, however, did not take public funds in 1992; he paid for his campaign with his own money. Proposals to provide public funding for congressional candidates have run into opposition. Many Republicans point to the already large federal deficit and worry that spending limits will make it hard to defeat incumbents. Incumbents are reluctant to vote for legislation that will fund their opponents and to face public criticism for voting money to their own campaigns. But public funding would even out differences in campaign resources between candidates, reduce the impact of special interests, and greatly lessen the time a candidate must devote to raising money (*Congressional Quarterly Weekly Report*, 17 December 1988, 3526–27).

The effects of election reforms are many. With individual giving limited, candidates have come to rely more and more on PAC money, thus giving PACs more power. Some observers argue that the greater influence of PACs has diminished the influence of political parties. Others argue that political party influence was on the decline before FECA. PACs are now especially powerful in congressional campaigns. In the 1990 congressional elections, 4,172 PACs gave $159.1 million to the candidates (see Table 5.2; *Vital Statistics on American Politics 1992*, 175, 182–83). This was more than one-third of the funds given to House candidates (see Table 5.3; *Vital Statistics on Congress, 1991–1992*, 91–92). In most cases, the money was given primarily to incumbents.

During the ten years from 1983 to 1993, members of the U.S. House received more than $285 million from PACs (*Washington Post*, 15 March 1993, A17).

In 1976 the Supreme Court, in *Buckley v. Valeo*, ruled that the $1,000 limit on independent expenditures was a violation of the constitutionally guaranteed right of citizens to participate in political activity. One consequence is that individuals and PACs now spend money on **independent expenditures**, money spent without the knowledge or concurrence of the candidate—$14.1 million in 1988—in presidential elections, where public financing reduces the need for direct contributions to the candidates. Another effect of *Buckley v. Valeo* is that wealthy individuals may spend as much as they want of their own money when they run for office. This provision made Ross Perot's 1992 independent candidacy possible. Yet another loophole in the campaign finance laws is **soft money**—donations by national-level party organizations to state and local political parties that are not subject to contribution limits but can be used by the parties to assist candidates to national office (Sorauf 1984b, 5–6; *Vital Statistics on Congress, 1989–1990*, 110; *National Journal*, 8 November 1988, 2516–19; see also Sorauf 1988, 209). The soft money loophole, designed to assist parties by allowing party-building activities, grew from $19.6 million in the 1984 presidential election to $66 million in the 1992 presidential election (*Congressional Quarterly Weekly Report*, 15 May 1993, 1191). As soft money expenditures have gone up, independent expenditures for major party presidential candidates have gone down.

PACs have been accused of corrupting the political process by reinforcing informal private-public interconnections. One observer states flatly that "congressmen now owe their first loyalty to PAC interests rather than to party or public interests" and that "money can buy individual congressmen's votes." He cites as evidence the fact that members who receive money from a PAC are more likely to vote in

Steve Sack. Courtesy *Minneapolis Star Tribune*.

accordance with the PAC's interest than are members who received no contribution (Easterbrook 1984, 70–72).

This reasoning is simplistic, however, because money may follow votes rather than the other way around. For instance, a libertarian member of Congress who votes his or her conscience on the issues is likely to please business PACs, while a liberal who votes in accordance with his or her convictions will favor labor PACs. Both will then receive contributions from the groups they have helped, though neither has been bought. The impact of PACs is thus a difficult "chicken-egg" question that has been the subject of numerous statistical studies. The results of these studies vary, but the weight of the evidence seems to be that PAC contributions have less of an effect on voting by members of Congress than party affiliation and constituent interests. Members seem to vote the way one would expect them to vote if there were no PACs rather than switching positions to obtain PAC gifts (Sabato 1984, 126–40; see also Sorauf 1984b, 307–17).

PACs continue to be important in political campaigns because of the funding they provide, yet concerned politicians have supported legislation restricting campaign spending. At first Democrats led proposals to limit PAC spending, and Republicans, dependent on money from business PACs, opposed them. Recently, PAC money has shifted to favoring incumbent Democrats, and an increasing num-

ber of Republicans have become interested in limiting PACs (*Congressional Quarterly Weekly Report*, 17 December 1988, 3525). The problems of this system became especially apparent during the savings and loan crisis of the 1980s. The industry had contributed money to candidates in each party, and the access gained caused some members of Congress to urge federal regulators to act cautiously in investigating suspected dishonesty by officers of these associations. Some of these associations later failed, costing the federal government billions of dollars in payments to depositors who had federally insured accounts.

Soft-money strategies have also been criticized. Even in the publicly funded 1988 presidential election, nearly half the funds were spent as soft money. Such money allows considerable room for corruption, the very thing public financing was established to eliminate. Reform solutions on soft money, including more stringent controls on and the disclosure of campaign funds and activities, are not polarized around party lines (*Congressional Quarterly Weekly Report*, 17 December 1988, 3526–27).

President Clinton's 1992 presidential election campaign platform included promises of campaign finance reform. Limitations on PACs, voluntary spending limits, public funding to those who abide by the limits, and restrictions on the soft money loophole are under active consideration. Since President Bush had vetoed campaign reform legislation in 1992, it is likely that some kind of legislation will pass given Democratic control of both houses of Congress and the presidency in 1993–94. However, Congress appears less enthusiastic about major reform than the president.

In 1992 an increasing number of states enacted term limits on their members of Congress. Fifteen states now have such limits. While the constitutionality of term limits enacted by states for federal elections has not been tested in court, such limits clearly reveal voters' concerns about incumbency advantage.

PERSPECTIVES

Although presidential candidates are not bound by their party platforms once elected to office, platforms are probably the best method of determining a party's overall political stance. Written by representatives from the various wings, platforms put forth the party's final conclusions on a broad range of issues. The documents, often quite long, are hammered out during the national conventions every four years and coincide with the nomination of a presidential ticket. The party's nominees are thus given a manifesto to campaign on and, if elected, to implement.

While the Republican platform of 1992 represented contemporary conservatism, and the

Democratic platform liberalism, there is some difficulty using examples from political party platforms to represent the remaining four perspectives. The views of minor parties tend to be uncompromising and ideologically pure, and you should bear in mind that moderates within the libertarian and Marxist perspectives might not endorse every position in the party platforms that follow. No explicitly feminist party exists, but the possibility of one has been raised by feminists dissatisfied with all the parties. The positions of right and left populists are represented by candidates within the two major parties.

Conservative: The Republican Platform of 1992

The 1992 Republican platform was clearly conservative, even more so than the party's nominee. While expounding libertarian ideas about the proper role of government in the economy, the platform took strongly conservative stands on almost every other issue, illustrating the strength of the conservative perspective within the party (all details and quotations from *New York Times*, 16 August 1992, 19).

While the Democrats criticized the economic record of the Reagan and Bush administrations, the Republicans called the 1980s "an era of growth and prosperity such as the world had never seen." They pointed out that "inflation has fallen to its lowest level in 30 years" while "interest rates dropped 15 percentage points." Acknowledging the pain of the recession of the early 1990s, the Republicans urged voters not to turn back to government for solutions: "We believe government has a legitimate role to play in our national life, but government must never dominate that life. . . . The Democrats argue that government must constantly override the market. Republicans regard the worst market failure as the failure to have a market."

Mocking Democratic calls for "public investment" to revive the economy, the Republicans

charged that "the latest Democratic scam is to raise taxes for 'investment'—a code word for more government spending." Pledging to oppose taxes, the Republican platform called on voters to elect "a Republican Congress [which] will foster investment where it does the most good, by individuals within the private sector." A similar antigovernment approach was revealed in the rejection of national health insurance, a keystone of the Democratic platform: "Republicans believe government control of health care is irresponsible and ineffective. We believe health care choices should remain in the hands of the people, not the government bureaucrats." Recognizing the difficulty many middle-class Americans have in paying for health care, the platform advocated tax credits for health care expenses.

The issue of abortion was a contentious one at the Republican convention, with the party's strong libertarian wing pressing for a softening of the party's antiabortion stance. Conservative views prevailed, however. The platform proclaimed, "We believe the unborn child has a fundamental right to life which cannot be infringed. We therefore reaffirm our support for a human life amendment to the Constitution." The Republicans also stated their opposition to "efforts by the Democratic Party to include sexual preference [i.e., homosexuals] as a protected minority receiving preferential status under civil rights statutes at the Federal, state, and local level." They also opposed gun controls, reminding voters that "those who seek to disarm citizens in their homes are the same liberals who tried to disarm our nation during the cold war." "Immoral" art was also attacked: "We condemn the use of public funds to subsidize obscenity and blasphemy masquerading as art."

In the realm of foreign policy, the Republicans tried to take credit for the demise of the Soviet Union. "Never in this century," they asserted, "has the United States enjoyed such security from foreign enemies. With President Bush leading the free world, the Soviet empire has collapsed . . . Eastern Europe is liberated. Germany is peacefully united. Nuclear arsenals are being cut to fractions of their former size. A democratically elected Russian president sits in the Kremlin." The Republicans recommended no major changes in foreign policy, endorsing Bush administration initiatives in Arab-Israeli peace negotiations and free trade with Mexico. At the same time, they warned against accepting the Democratic position that large additional defense cuts could be made, pointing to continued instability in many parts of the world and the existence of aggressive regimes such as Saddam Hussein's in Iraq.

On other issues, the Republicans sounded less ideological but still showed an unmistakable conservative tilt. Environmental protection, they agreed, is important, but "private ownership and economic freedom are the best security against environmental degradation." Proposals to cut fossil fuel consumption to halt the greenhouse effect (see Chapter 13) were condemned as unjustified and extremist. One of the few new government programs advocated in the platform was private school tuition subsidies to "give lower and middle income families the same choice of schools—public, private or religious—that families with more resources already have." Throughout the 1992 platform, the Republicans emphasized private initiative, limited government, and moral traditionalism.

Liberal: The Democratic Platform of 1992

Attempting to win back populist and conservative voters lost to the Republicans in the 1970s and 1980s as well as to exploit libertarian disagreements with Republican stands on social issues, the Democrats tried to write a platform less liberal than that in recent presidential elections (all details and quotations from "Guide to the 1992 Democratic National Convention" 1992, 59–67). Still, the Democratic platform of 1992 remained closer to liberalism than to any of the other perspectives.

It was on economic issues that the Democrats sounded a new note. Responding to nominee Bill Clinton's belief that past platforms had been too big-government oriented, the Democrats stated, "We reject both the do-nothing government of the last 12 years and the big government theory that says we can hamstring business and spend our way to prosperity." Sounding almost like Republicans at times, the Democrats affirmed, "We believe in free enterprise and the power of market forces." They also argued, however, that a "national economic strategy" was needed to overcome the economic slowdown. Citing the need for "both private and public investment," they called for major increases in spending for road and bridge repairs to create jobs and for investment tax credits to encourage business to build more factories. With an eye on middle-class voters, the Democrats advocated extending tuition aid to all college students regardless of income, with a repayment requirement after graduation.

As if to make up for their moderate economic stance, the Democrats took firmly liberal positions on social and moral issues. They asserted, "All Americans should have universal access to quality, affordable health care—not as a privilege but as a right," and they called for a national health insurance system. They promised to "end the inequalities that create educational ghettos among school districts and provide equal education opportunity for all "through increased funding for education, as well as for Head Start and job-training programs. On civil rights, the Democrats affirmed "support [for] ratification of the Equal Rights Amendment, affirmative action, stronger protection of voting rights for racial and ethnic minorities, including language access to voting, and continued resistance to discriminatory English-only pressure groups" (referring to efforts to make English the official U.S. language). In fact, antidiscrimination as a national policy was mentioned more often in the Democratic platform than any other issue, reflecting the values of this liberal and multiethnic party.

Abortion marked a clear divide between the parties, with the Democrats asserting, "It is a fundamental constitutional liberty that individual Americans—not government—can best take responsibility for making the most difficult and intensely personal decisions regarding reproduction. The goal of our nation must be to make abortion less necessary, not more difficult or more dangerous." The party took an equally uncompromising stand for gay and lesbian rights, inviting a gay man with AIDS to speak at the convention and calling for "an end to Defense Department discrimination" barring gays and lesbians from the military. President Clinton's talk about reform made this a major issue shortly after he took office. On the other hand, the platform made a bow in the direction of moral traditionalism by calling for a crackdown on parents who fail to pay child support and declaring that "welfare should be a second chance, not a way of life." On the issue of crime, stricter gun controls and more police on the streets were advocated, but this time the Democrats made clear that they "do not support efforts to restrict weapons used for legitimate hunting and sporting purposes."

The foreign-policy segment of the platform was probably the most traditionally liberal, stressing the promotion of democracy abroad through nonmilitary means (see Chapter 11). The Democrats supported aid to "the fragile democracies in Eastern Europe and the former Soviet Union" while calling for reimposing sanctions on South Africa until black majority rule is achieved. They asserted that while "America is the world's strongest military power, and we must remain so," its position could be maintained with substantial cuts in the defense budget beyond those proposed by the president. On global environmental issues, the Democrats accused the Bush administration of being "an obstacle to progress" and called for binding international treaties to combat global warming, ozone depletion, species extinction, and other environmental threats. On trade, they called for tougher negotiations with trading partners to ensure that "the conduct of world trade is fair," but they stopped short of endorsing protectionist policies advocated by some elements of the party.

While the 1992 platform was less recognizably liberal than Democratic platforms of the past and paid more attention to the role of private enterprise and individual responsibility, it was still infused with the belief that the federal government can positively affect the lives of its citizens through active intervention. Whether in protecting the environment, enforcing civil rights, helping family farmers, safeguarding workers' rights, or guaranteeing health insurance to all, government was seen as a basically positive force.

Libertarian: The Libertarian Platform of 1992

The Libertarian party, which first ran a candidate for president in two states in 1972, espouses the most consistent—some would say extreme—version of the libertarian perspective. In 1980 its candidate, Ed Clark, received nearly 1 million votes (Judis 1980). In 1984 and 1988 the libertarian vote declined, perhaps because the Republicans co-opted part of the party's economic agenda. The party's 1992 candidate, Andre Marrou, received 291, 612 votes (*Congressional Quarterly Weekly Report*, 23 January 1993, 191).

The libertarian platform began by stating: "As Libertarians, we seek a world of liberty: a world in which all individuals are sovereign over their own lives, and no one is forced to sacrifice his or her values for the benefit of others" (all details and quotations from *1992 National Platform of the Libertarian Party* 1991). Taxation, in the libertarian view, is such a compulsory sacrifice, so the party advocated repealing "all criminal and civil penalties against tax evasion," in effect making the payment of taxes voluntary. The resultant drop in revenues would hardly bother a libertarian administration, since the party advocated abolishing most existing federal domestic programs, including social security, welfare, Medicare and Medicaid, farm subsidies, and the postal service. It also called for the abolition of the Federal Reserve System (see Chapter 12) and government-printed money, for the sale of highways to private enterprise, and for the removal of all controls on wages, prices, rents, and interest rates. Education should ultimately also be privatized, argue libertarians, but the 1992 platform supported school "voucher" plans that allow parents to choose their child's school as an interim measure.

The libertarians are not anarchists—they called for strong measures to protect citizens against crime. However, they opposed all penalties for "victimless" crimes, such as prostitution, drug use, or pornography. Their platform upheld a woman's right to choose abortion but also the right to keep and bear arms, including concealed weapons. Holding that "human rights should not be denied or abridged on the basis of nationality,"

they advocated repealing all immigration restrictions and allowing all who want to do so to enter the United States. At the same time, they called for abolishing all government programs to aid immigrants, just as they oppose such aid for citizens.

On foreign policy, the libertarians called for "the elimination of intervention by the United States in the affairs of other nations." Accordingly, they supported withdrawal of all American troops stationed abroad, the termination of the North Atlantic Treaty Organization (NATO) and all other alliances with other countries, withdrawal from the United Nations, and an end to all government foreign-aid programs. At the same time, they advocated repealing laws that prevent private citizens from aiding people fighting for freedom abroad. All restrictions on international trade and travel should be eliminated, and U.S. "colonial dependencies," such as Puerto Rico, the Virgin Islands, Samoa, and Guam should be granted "self-determination." The platform ended by stating that "our silence about any other particular government law, regulation, ordinance, directive, edict, control, regulatory agency activity, or machination should not be construed to imply approval." Indeed, there were few government activities immune from disapproval in the 1992 libertarian platform.

Populist: The Harkin, Buchanan, and Perot Campaigns

Nineteen ninety-two was a banner year for populists in the presidential election campaign. In the primaries, Iowa's Senator Tom Harkin, who ran for the Democratic nomination, represented left populism, while Patrick J. Buchanan, who opposed George Bush as a Republican, represented right populism. In the general election, H. Ross Perot combined elements of both versions of the populist perspective.

Of the three populists, Harkin stressed most the populist conviction that "the people with money in this country are not pulling their weight" (*Almanac of American Politics, 1992,* 440). He called, as Jesse Jackson had in 1988, for increases in spending for social programs financed

by greater cuts in defense spending. National health insurance was also a high priority for Harkin, who advocated a prevention-oriented plan he claimed would cost no more than what the government was already spending for health care.

Harkin's differences with traditional liberals came out most clearly in his positions on foreign policy. Unlike most liberal candidates, he took a protectionist stance toward trade, especially with Japan. He also broke with the liberal consensus by opposing aid to the former Soviet Union, arguing that the poor in the United States deserved the money and commenting that he "hadn't seen any thin Russians" on the television coverage of the August 1991 attempted coup. He opposed the Persian Gulf War but also criticized Bush's halting of military action short of overthrowing Saddam Hussein, comparing the president's policy to "juvenile lovemaking—too quick in and too quick out."

Pat Buchanan's views were opposed to Harkin's on many issues. Buchanan opposed new taxes on anyone, including the rich, and advocated massive budget cuts to eliminate the deficit. His attacks on immigration and affirmative action programs placed him clearly on the right wing of populism, with its concern for majority rights as against racial and ethnic minorities. Buchanan did reflect some of the economic side of populism, however, criticizing Wall Street takeovers as "vulture capitalism" and promising to protect American workers from job competition by illegal aliens. Buchanan and Harkin were closest on foreign policy and trade issues. Both backed protectionism and opposed the Persian Gulf War as an unnecessary foreign entanglement. While Harkin opposed aid to the ex-Soviets, Buchanan pledged to do away with foreign aid entirely and establish an "America First" foreign policy (*Christian Science Monitor*, 13 April 1992, 9). Such views, rarely heard in American presidential politics in recent years, suggest a resurgence of the isolationist themes in populism (see Chapter 11).

Ross Perot was more successful than the other two populist candidates, perhaps because he borrowed from both populist traditions and, spending $69 million of his own money, picked up support from both. Despite being one of the richest U.S. citizens, he criticized tax breaks for the wealthy and called for ending social security and Medicare benefits for "people like me." Perot relied more heavily, however, on general anti-Washington and antigovernment themes that appealed to both types of populists. He suggested a constitutional amendment requiring a popular referendum to approve tax increases, a stance agreeable to right-wing populists (*New Republic*, 15 June 1992, 29). On the other hand, he backed legal abortion, a heresy to the populist right. Like the other two populist candidates, Perot displayed an "America First" orientation to foreign policy. He opposed a free trade treaty with Mexico (see Chapter 11), criticized the Persian Gulf War, and demanded that Europe and Japan pay the United States $100 billion a year for being defended by American military forces (*New Republic*, 15 June 1992, 19–23, 29).

Perhaps Perot's most unusual idea was that national problems could best be solved by holding televised "national town meetings" during which different solutions to problems like health care could be debated and the public could vote for one directly through interactive television. This proposal appeared to move toward advocacy of a direct as opposed to a representative democracy, a common populist theme (*New Republic*, 15 June 1992, 29). While Harkin attacked the rich and Buchanan bashed liberals and minorities, Perot tapped into resentment of politicians and the public's lack of direct control over the government.

Marxist: The Socialist Workers Platform of 1992

Perhaps owing to the disarray within Marxism following the fall of the Soviet Union, the Communist party and some other long-standing Marxist parties did not field presidential candidates in 1992. One that did was the Socialist Workers party, which has existed in the United States since the 1920s. The Socialist Workers are followers of Leon Trotsky, an associate of Vladimir Lenin who stressed the need for simultaneous revolutions in the industrial nations, as opposed to Joseph Stalin's call for "socialism in one country." In 1992 the Socialist Workers nominated James Warren, a forty-year-old steelworker, for president, and Estelle DeBates, a journalist, for vice-president. Had DeBates been elected, she would have been unable to serve since she was only thirty-two years old.

The Socialist Workers platform called the Democratic and Republican parties "the parties of war, racism and economic depression" (all details and quotations from Socialist Workers 1992 Campaign 1992). Claiming to be the only party that represents working people, the Socialist Workers called for eliminating unemployment, which they said was "the greatest single scourge of capitalism," and reducing the work week to thirty hours with no reduction in wages. The party also strongly supported labor unions and strikes to halt wage concessions to corporations.

The Socialist Workers believe that the major parties use race to divide the workers. Accordingly, they came out strongly against racism and for affirmative action as "the only way to organize a united fight" against capitalism. The party strongly attacked right populists like Pat Buchanan, who, they conceded, "stress the real and perceived concerns of millions, but with solutions that spell disaster for the working people." On social issues the party took two libertarian stances: supporting abortion rights and full equality for women. Notably, all but one of the party's national committee members are minorities or women.

As might be expected, international affairs are a major concern for the Socialist Workers. Now that the Soviet Union (which they did not support) has collapsed, they predict that capitalist nations will go to war against each other for markets and sources of raw materials. The platform stated their fear that capitalists "will drag humanity into World War III unless workers and working farmers the world over organize to resist their assaults at home, oppose their military interventions abroad and build a massive movement to take power out of the hands of the warmakers." Insisting that "the working class is international," they called for Marxists around the world to work together. They have acted accordingly. Presidential candidate James Warren has visited Grenada and Nicaragua to learn more about the revolutionary process in those nations. Vice-presidential candidate Estelle DeBates has worked against apartheid in South Africa and has visited Cuba to show support against the U.S.-led economic boycott of that country.

The Socialist Workers party's "socialist alternative" candidate received 23,087 votes in 1992 (*Congressional Quarterly Weekly Report*, 23 January 1993, 191). Judging from its platform, however, the party is not easily discouraged and is likely to be back for future elections.

Feminist: The Gender Gap

Although women won the right to vote when the Nineteenth Amendment was passed in 1920, it has only been in recent elections that the women's vote has diverged sufficiently from the men's vote to attract the attention of political professionals. Feminists point to this gender gap (*American Enterprise*, January/February 1993, 98–104) as a major reason why the major parties are beginning to pay more attention to issues of importance to women, but they contend that the two major parties are still controlled by males.

Traditionally, feminist concerns have received more attention from the Democrats than from the Republicans. Democratic platforms have supported both the Equal Rights Amendment and choice on the issue of abortion (*National Review*, 3 August 1992, 16). The Democrats were the first to argue that civil rights statutes protected women, and they have championed policies supporting working women, including parental leave, affordable day care, and freedom from sexual harassment (*Congressional Quarterly Weekly Report*, 18 July 1992, 2087). In contrast, the Republican party at first failed to support feminist initiatives and finally offered alternatives that feminists viewed as antagonistic or insufficient (*Congressional Quarterly Weekly Report*, 22 August 1992, 2519–20). Democratic women outnumber Republican women in the House by more than 2:1. Five of the seven women members of the Senate, and four of the five women elected senators in 1992 and 1993 are Democrats. The first woman vice-presidential candidate from a major party, Geraldine Ferraro in 1984, was also a Democrat. The National Organization for Women has supported every Democratic presidential candidate since its inception in 1966.

To say all this is not to say that feminists are uniformly happy with the Democratic party. Feminists criticized the Democratic party for taking their votes for granted and for allowing the Republicans to take the "family" issue away from them. Democrats largely ignored issues like parental leave until 1990, when polls indicated that family-related issues were "hot." Even when the Democratic leadership decided to work actively for

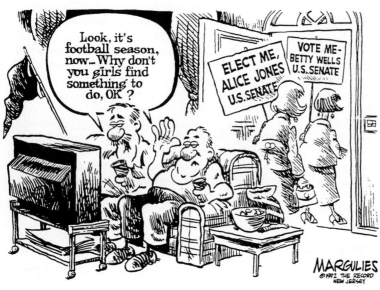

Jimmy Margulies. Courtesy *The Record*.

the passage of a day-care bill in 1991, party conservatives, by cooperating with Republicans, forced major compromises. Thus, although most Democrats (as liberals and left populists) are likely to be receptive to many reform feminist concerns, most often conservative and right populist Democrats, in cooperation with the Republican minority, undermine the legislation that feminists might like to see passed (*National Journal*, 2 June 1990, 1333–37).

This dissatisfaction prompted Ellie Smeal, former president of NOW, to establish the Fund for a Feminist Majority in 1987 and to advocate the creation of a new party. In 1988, some two thousand feminists from all over the United States voted at the NOW convention to establish a commission to explore such a possibility. The commission reviewed provisions passed by European social democratic and Green parties requiring floors for the least-represented gender that ranged from 25 to 50 percent. Although gains in the 1992 election may force recalculation of their figures, feminists concluded that at the current rate of increase of women representatives in the United States, it would take another sixty years for women to gain parity in Congress. Efforts to establish a minor party were unsuccessful, and in 1992 feminists turned to the Democratic party again, increasingly appealing on account of the strong presence of Hillary Rodham Clinton (Smeal 1992, 189–90).

Feminists argue that when women get into power, they do make a difference. Women are interested in issues different from those that interest men, and they vote in a significantly different manner. But getting women elected in sufficient numbers to shape legislative outcomes in the current two-party system is not easy. Advantages of incumbency and the need for compromise within parties and between branches of government are two major obstacles to the success of women's priorities. Feminists, like blacks, are victims of the lack of available options within a two-party system. They usually support the Democrats because that is the most likely arena within which their positions will receive both serious consideration and the possibility of becoming public policy.

DO PARTIES AND ELECTIONS WORK?

If American political parties are collapsing, as some political scientists believe, the consequences could be serious, given the important role parties play in a democracy. In some ways, parties are indeed weaker than they were in the past. We are impressed, however, with the evidence of party growth at state and national levels and tend to accept the view that parties are growing rather than declining. At the same time, we are concerned that the two-party system gives insufficient attention to minority views.

Regarding elections, we are alarmed by the low rates of voter turnout and the low level of political knowledge displayed even by those who do vote. Blaming the public for apathy is accurate but not a solution. We need to find out more about the causes of low voter turnout and find ways to encourage participation. We would like to see candidates address major issues in campaigns but realize that the public often votes against issue-oriented candidates.

These qualifications aside, electoral competition between parties is alive and well in the United States and still represents the best way to hold the government accountable for its actions. Some areas of the world where one-party systems have been the rule are now moving toward democracy. Criticism of the system should be tempered with awareness of the benefits of having viable choices and opportunities for participation.

SUMMARY AND REVIEW

Political candidates and factions in the United States have been organized into several different party systems. In the late 1800s, libertarians enjoyed widespread popularity. The Republican party came to depend on a coalition of conservatives and libertarians, while the Democrats successfully combined the rural and urban working class with the intellectual community into a liberal-populist coalition.

The Democrats became the majority party in the late 1930s, largely as a result of the Great Depression. The party's civil rights efforts in the 1960s, together with the divisive Vietnam War, eventually split the liberal and conservative wings. Many disaffected conservative Democrats have since joined the Republican party. Populists had mixed emotions. Despite the setback of Watergate, Republicans have won five out of the last seven presidential elections. Yet, the Democratic party now controls the presidency and both houses of Congress and remains the majority party in the United States.

At the apex of the Democratic and Republican party organizations are the national committees, which have become much more active in recent years. The Republican National Committee in particular has developed a sophisticated fund-raising operation. The activities of today's state party organizations include fund-raising, voter education, and candidate recruitment. Local party election activities revolve around the precinct and include registering voters, making sure voters get to the polls, and working for party candidates. In contrast to national and state party organizations, the importance of local party organizations has dwindled in recent years.

Once a party gets its candidate elected, of course, its influence can be felt only if its officials work together to achieve party goals. Few mechanisms exist, however, for enforcing party discipline; party leaders usually resort to persuasion. Still, there is a significant degree of party solidarity. Party is, for example, the best predictor of congressional voting.

In the electorate itself, libertarians and conservatives have generally adhered to the Republican party, while liberals and populists tend to be Democrats. Strong Democratic identifiers today include blacks, low-income groups, Hispanics, unionized workers, Jews, and intellectuals. The Republicans have been more attractive to business, professional people, and farmers; and sometimes the party has had to attract a large number of independent voters to win elections. The number of independents and ticket-splitters, however, has increased dramatically in recent decades.

The unique two-party nature of the U.S. system is best explained by the general consensus on Lockean values, which has tended to preclude the success of either radical or reactionary minor parties. Furthermore, minor parties face difficulties in getting on the election ballot and are discriminated against by the single-member district system of election. In spite of these difficulties, significant minor parties occasionally arise when the two major parties neglect the interests of one of the perspectives. Generally, they run more as a means of educating the public, recruiting support, and pressuring the major parties to deal with certain issues than for the sake of victory.

It is the responsibility of the parties to narrow the field of candidates in an election through a system of primaries and/or conventions or caucuses. Under the primary election system, voters of the state or local area choose among several party candidates for each office, and the winner becomes the party's nominee for that office in the general election. Both major parties select their presidential and vice-presidential nominees in national conventions—largely media events—which come after six months of state primaries and caucuses.

Voter turnout in the United States has been low and has generally declined since the 1960s, although it was up slightly in 1992. Research has correlated education with voting, though secondary factors exist. Turnout could prob-ably be increased if restrictive election requirement laws were changed, but would be unlikely to change most election results.

Locke's idea of popular sovereignty called for rational, self-interested participation in the electoral process. Today, however, voting can be determined most effectively by the party identification of the electorate, though the issues have become increasingly important. In the age of television, a candidate's image and perceived leadership qualities have played a large role in voter preference. Given this triumph of style over substance, it is comforting to learn that voters also judge elected officials by how the country fares under their leadership. Nevertheless, the increasing reliance by candidates on modern electronic media has opened up whole new areas of problems for Locke's concept of popular sovereignty. Presidential candidates must deal with the differing strategies needed to win their party's nomination on the one hand and the national election on the other. In the national election, each state is accorded electoral votes equal to the number of that state's senators and representatives. Traditionally, all of a state's electoral votes are awarded to the candidate who wins the state's popular vote, regardless of how slim the margin. Thus it is possible for the overall popular vote winner to be defeated in the electoral vote and thereby lose the election. In congressional elections, especially in the House, there is the added dilemma of the nearly unbeatable advantage of incumbency.

The need for money is important in modern elections, and candidates must be prepared to work to obtain it. Individuals, political parties, and political action committees are major sources of funding. Some public funding is available to presidential candidates, but not to congressional candidates. A significant controversy today centers around the legitimacy of PACs. Noting that House candidates receive a full third of their funding from PACs, critics complain that members of Congress now owe their first loyalty to PACs rather than to their constituents. Most research shows, however, that PAC contributions have little effect on congressional voting patterns since they are given to members who already agree with PAC interests.

Despite the problems with party structure in the United States, parties remain the single most important vehicle for assuring a stable form of government. Their roles in recruiting candidates, advancing alternative points of view, and helping to achieve compromise among various interests make parties an essential element in American democracy.

IMPORTANT TERMS

blanket primary
caucus
closed primary
coattail effect
convention
Democratic party
divided government
electoral college
faction
franking privilege
image
incumbent
independent expenditure
independent voter
interest group
Jim Crow laws
midterm election
minor party
national committee
national convention
nonpartisan election
open primary
parliamentary system
party identification

party in the electorate
party in government
party organization
party platform
party-unity voting
patronage
plurality
political action committee (PAC)
political machine
political party
political spectrum
popular vote
"pork-barrel" project
precinct
presidential primary
primary election system
progressive movement
proportional representation system
Republican party
single-member district system
soft money
ticket-splitter
Twenty-third Amendment
voter turnout

PUBLIC OPINION

"They have been over us like a swarm of locusts," stated one House committee staff member, speaking of interest group lobbyists expressing their opinions on legislation being considered by his committee *(Washington Post, 16 June 1987, A14).* **Interest groups** *(or* **lobbies***) are organizations of people who join together voluntarily to influence public policy in their favor on the basis of a shared interest or objective. They may be potato farmers, workers in the same industry, or gay rights advocates. They may seek to change public policy to benefit their cause, or they may simply wish to preserve the status quo. As the statement of the staff member illustrates, interest groups often work so hard to influence legislation that they consume a great deal of legislators' time.*

Individual opinions organized into interest groups are an essential part of the process of government. Indeed, Americans affect public policy even if they choose not to belong to an interest group, because their opinions are measured by pollsters and considered by politicians. But where do individuals get their opinions? They are shaped by the political and social system through a process called socialization and refined or sustained at least in part by the media's messages. This chapter will consider public opinion and its measurement in public opinion polls. It will also consider the origins of public opinion through the process of socialization and demonstrate how the media and interest groups also contribute to the shaping of public opinion.

PUBLIC OPINION AND POLLS

Public opinion is the sum of individual perspectives or beliefs. It is generalized but not unanimous; often one group has an opinion quite different from another. Women, for example, have been found to have a stronger commitment to organized religion than do men. In democracies, public opinion is expressed through elections, initiatives, referenda, the media, and interest group activities (*People and Politics* 1985, 217).

The most specific descriptions of how opinions differ among groups are found in opinion polls. George Gallup, Archibald Crossley, and Elmo Roper developed modern polling techniques by using personal interviews with relatively small samples from groups being studied (*People and Politics* 1985, 217). These **public opinion polls**, first devised in the 1930s, sample the opinions of small numbers of people to measure public thinking on selected public policy issues. The normal size of these survey groups is five hundred to two thousand. One poll, the Times Mirror Survey of the American Electorate, started to track George Bush in 1988 and continued to do so through the 1992 presidential election. During this time, it surveyed approximately one thousand American voters on a regular basis (*People, Press and Politics*, 15 November 1992, 15).

For a sample to be accurate, it must match the characteristics of the population surveyed. In a survey of the American population generally, the sample must be approximately 12 percent black, 52 percent female, 75 percent urban-suburban, and so forth, replicating in miniature the characteristics of the American people as a whole. Polling agencies have made a profession of scientific polling and accurate results (Dye and Ziegler 1986, 130–31).

But even with a representative sample, there is still a "margin of error" of plus or minus a few percent. Reasons for error include shades of meaning in the wording of questions and differing definitions of key terms. For example, a question asking whether you consider yourself a Democrat, a Republican, or an independent will produce a considerably different outcome from one asking whether you normally vote a Democratic or Republican party line. The word "independent" may mean one thing to one respondent and something else to another (*Vital Statistics on American Politics*, 1990, 142). With responses so easily manipulated by wording, polls must be regarded

with caution. Yet their very plasticity makes them useful to the media, politicians, and interest groups seeking support for their positions. When a politician or an interest group pays a professional polling agency to conduct the poll, it may choose to release only the results it wants. Polls paid for by a politician or an interest group can also be designed to elicit a very specific response. Because of such considerations, public opinion polls do not always reflect public opinion so much as the opinions of those paying to have the poll conducted.

Even with a margin of error and the possibility of skewed results, the success of virtually every public political action depends on the strength of opinion behind it as measured by public opinion polls. Polls are usually most effective before an election to show who is ahead and why. Politicians then use the results to make adjustments in their campaign strategies. During the 1988 presidential race, polls revealed that George Bush needed more support among populist voters. With information that many populists were concerned about the crime and lawlessness in their communities, the Bush campaign took steps to appeal to populists (*Washington Post National Weekly Edition*, 1–7 May 1989, 9–10). Republican political commercials gave statistics on the number of crimes committed by prisoners released under a Massachusetts program while Michael Dukakis was governor. The message about the program's irresponsibility was unambiguous and repeated over and over in the weeks before the election. Many observers were upset that this issue became so important, but the Bush campaign had done its homework. Polls later indicated that Bush had been successful in swaying the votes of populists, among whom he won a majority. In 1992, Bush was less fortunate in his efforts to keep populists loyal by appealing to life-style issues regarding the Democratic candidate's character. Bill Clinton's message of bad economic times, coupled with promises of more jobs and better health care proved to be a campaign message that had greater impact among independents and populists (*Washington Post National Weekly Edition*, 9–15 November 1992, 7; *Christian Science Monitor*, 27 October 1992, 1, 4).

When races are perceived by voters to be very close, polls can create momentum for a candidate. In the 1980 election, for example, Jimmy Carter and Ronald Reagan retained the services of two different polling agencies. Polling was done up until the day before the election. Both candidates used polls to refine their messages. The voters were told that the election would be close but that Reagan would probably win. The momentum from published poll results, Reagan's recent debate victory, and the ambiguous situation in the negotiations for the release of the American hostages in Iran helped Reagan surge at the end and win by a decisive margin (Ladd and Ferree 1980–81, 13–20; *Public Opinion*, December 1980/

January 1981, 2–12, 21–44, 63–64; see also *Gallup Opinion Index*, December 1980, 10–11).

Polls taken on election day as voters leave polling places are called **exit polls**. The effect of exit polls on voting has been particularly evident on the West Coast, where the voters can watch the election returns on television while their polls are still open. If people know who is going to win, they may be more inclined to vote for the winner, or not to vote at all. Because of this tendency to favor the leading candidate, called the **bandwagon effect**, in the last two presidential elections the news media have voluntarily chosen not to predict a winner until the polls on the West Coast have closed or an electoral victory has been certain (Patterson 1990, 176–83; *Congressional Quarterly Weekly Report*, 20 May 1989, 1208; *Broadcasting*, 9 January 1989, 70). Polls that track public opinion across time are called **tracking polls**.

Rob Rogers. *Courtesy Pittsburgh Press* and United Media.

Polling organizations, for example, closely tracked opinions about George Bush from the time of his inauguration until his 1992 election defeat (*American Enterprise* July/August 1992, 82–83; *American Enterprise* November/December 1992, 100–101). This tracking continues today with President Clinton. In important elections, tracking polls are taken on a daily basis by the major candidates.

Ordinary citizens take polls less seriously than do candidates for public office. Voters sometimes voice specific reservations or general skepticism. Most pollsters have encountered people who express distrust of polling. Other people complain that they have not been interviewed and wonder how representative the samples can be. Still others say the size of the samples is too small. Yet in the 1992 race nearly all the major tracking polls were accurate, within their margins of error, in predicting Clinton's electoral victory (Asher 1992, 14; see also *Washington Post National Weekly Edition*, 9–15 November 1992, 37; *Washington Post National Weekly Edition*, 5–11 October 1992, 37).

Critics of polling do have some legitimate objections. They contend that the opinion research technique itself is artificial in the sense that polls prompt people to express views on issues about which they may never have actually thought seriously (Cantril 1991, 208). They also point out that public opinion reported only in terms of summary percentages has no means of gauging the intensity with which opinions are held. The consequences of mistaking the amount of energy behind an expressed opinion has to be real enough to prompt politicians and news organizations to measure intensity through thermometer graphs, which ask people to say how "hot" or "cold" they feel toward a candidate (Cantril 1991, 206). Indeed, even meticulous attention to all potentials for error in polling methodology cannot eliminate the charge that the polling technique is flawed in nature and unable to represent public opinion accurately (Cantril 1991, 204). Such a charge must be taken seriously but must be balanced by the facts that the vast majority of polls are

reported accurately and that pollsters strive for improvement.

The most serious criticism leveled at polling is not related to techniques but to their impact on elections and election coverage. The argument is often made that polls contribute to the "packaging" of candidates and, indeed, aspiring leaders do consult the polls and then stake out their positions on issues accordingly (Asher 1992, 15). In 1992 George Bush, for example, moved rapidly to the right side of the political spectrum when it became evident that Patrick Buchanan would embarrass him during the early primaries. In response to polling data on Buchanan's following in Georgia, Bush fired the moderate chair of the National Endowment for the Arts and replaced him with a far more conservative appointee. The implications of polling for leadership and commitment in a democracy are worrisome to many.

Despite occasional anger and some skepticism about poll results, Americans generally think polls are accurate and fair. While they sometimes resent the intrusiveness and presumed power of the polls, they nevertheless eagerly consume the latest findings on all sorts of topics. This ambivalence is probably inevitable. We want our opinions registered, and when polls do not confirm what we think we say they undermine genuine citizen influence. Still, in a nation as large as the United States, polling may be the best way to get at the diversity of public opinion. The fact that polls strive to sample the public objectively usually makes their results acceptable in a democratic society (Asher 1992, 17). In sum, polls contribute to the give-and-take of political life by acquainting one group with another point of view and making the public at large an important player in the competition among interests vying for power in government (Cantril 1991, 238).

POLITICAL SOCIALIZATION

But why do people hold different opinions? After watching a movie with a friend, have

1990 less than 2 percent—about 4.6 million people—were farm residents (*Statistical Abstract, 1992*, 642; see also "Farm Problems" 1987, 13; and *USA Today*, 10 June 1992, A3). In reality this number is probably considerably lower because the Department of Agriculture, which keeps these figures, is interested for budgeting purposes in having them as high as possible. This small number does not, however, make agriculture an unimportant constituency, for agriculture remains a vital American industry. A significant percentage of the labor force works in agriculture-related industries, ranging from meat-packing plants to restaurants.

Agricultural groups representing farmers fall into three categories: umbrella organizations, commodity associations, and social action groups, the latter two of which are more specific interest groups. Six umbrella organizations represent the interests of all types of farmers and farm workers—the American Farm Bureau Federation, the National Grange, the National Farmers Union (NFU), the National Farmers Organizations (NFO), the American Agriculture Movement (AAM), and, perhaps the best-known farm labor group, the late Cesar Chavez's United Farm Workers (UFW)—but from sharply different perspectives. The Farm Bureau, the largest of the umbrella groups, is conservative and actually supported President Ronald Reagan's efforts to phase out farm subsidy programs. The NFU and the NFO are liberal, favoring greater government subsidies and collective bargaining between farmers and food processors. The Grange is less active politically, but moderate; the AAM is populist; and the UFW tends to be liberal (Wilson 1981, 17–33; see also Levy 1975).

Like business, agriculture is divided by conflicting interests. For example, higher grain prices are good for corn farmers but bad for livestock producers. Hence many farmers have turned to commodity groups to represent their interests. Groups like the American Soybean Association, the National Cattlemen's Association, National Milk Producers Federation, and the Peanut Council focus not on general farm problems but on government policy affecting a specific commodity. While commodity groups are becoming more influential, the influence of umbrella farm organizations is limited by the divisions among them (Browne 1988). Farm workers have been traditionally difficult to organize due to the seasonal and itinerant nature of their employment (*Encyclopedia of Associations, 1992*, 448).

The recession that hit the farm sector in the early 1980s spawned several social action groups to assist distressed farmers. These groups, which have received substantial support from nonfarmers, tend to be active on the state and regional levels. They have worked to provide farmers with counseling, financial and legal advice, and sometimes limited financial assistance. Examples of such groups include Farm Aid, which was started by country musicians, and Catholic Rural Life ("Farm Problems" 1987, 10–11).

Racial, Ethnic, Religious, and Gender-Based Groups   Blacks and other minorities have formed interest groups to fight against discrimination. The first major black interest group was the National Association for the Advancement of Colored People (NAACP), founded by W. E. B. DuBois in 1909. The NAACP has historically taken a moderate approach to protecting black rights and relied on legal action. The 1950s and 1960s gave birth to some new organizations, including Dr. Martin Luther King's Southern Christian Leadership Conference (SCLC), which was aided by nonviolent political activist groups like the Student Nonviolent Coordinating Committee (SNCC). Today the Reverend Jesse Jackson's People United to Serve Humanity (PUSH) attempts to advance the position of blacks through nonviolent activities and self-help skills (Wald 1987, 252; Williams 1987; King 1987).

Other minorities also have formed groups to protect their interests. The Hispanic League of United Latin American Citizens (LULAC) and the Mexican American Legal Defense and Education Fund (MALDEF) have fought to stop discrimination against job seekers who appear to be foreign. With Hispanics now accounting for 8–9 percent of the American population, these organizations also seek to prevent "second-class treatment within the civil rights community" (*National Journal*, 19 May 1990, 1210). The National Congress of American Indians lobbies to support Native American concerns such as government adherence to historic treaties (*Encyclopedia of Associations, 1992*, 1704).

Churches and other religious groups have long been active in national politics. Before the Civil War, northern evangelical Protestants spearheaded the antislavery movement. Later Protestant churches across the country united to support the prohibition of alcoholic beverages. Church-state relationships have historically been a primary concern of religious groups, with some favoring strict separation and others favoring more cooperation (Reichley 1985).

Although church members tend to be conservative, the majority of American church organizations today take a liberal position in politics. Catholic and some Protestant activists were heavily involved in the civil rights and anti–Vietnam War protests and more recently have strongly opposed U.S. involvement in Central America. Many churches attacked President Reagan's cuts in social programs and increases in military spending, even though most of their members voted for him in 1980 and 1984. The Roman Catholic church, though conservative on social issues, has issued pastoral letters calling for a halt to the arms race, greater efforts at nuclear disarmament, and major increases in antipoverty programs (Reichley 1985, 53–242; Catholic Bishops 1983).

The American Jewish community is often identified with Middle East issues, but Jewish Americans also have an active coalition of organizations lobbying on social and economic policies. Examples include the American Jewish Committee, the Anti-Defamation League of B'nai B'rith, and the American Jewish Congress. Although the Union of American Hebrew Congregations is the only organization representing temple members, the Jewish lobby as a whole has supported religious freedom and the separation of church and state (Hertzke 1988, 38–40).

Black churches are represented by several black Baptist and Methodist organizations. The black religious experience in the United States paved the way for such religious and political leaders as Martin Luther King, Jr., and Jesse Jackson, and the Progressive National Baptist Convention, formed in 1961, helped lead the movement for racial equality (Hertzke 1988, 42–43). Such churches also turned out the black vote for Jesse Jackson in his 1984 and 1988 bids for the presidency.

The leadership of religious interest groups has been mostly liberal in a political and theological sense. It has been dominated by the **mainline churches** (the term "mainline" refers to the largely Protestant suburbs lining the "main" railroad line into the center of Philadelphia; see Hutchison 1989, 1–5). In the 1920s, the seven establishment churches constituted 76 percent of American Protestants, but this preponderance has been changing. Since 1960 the mainline churches have been rapidly losing members, and recently a great deal of publicity has been given to the so-called **New Christian Right**, a coalition of evangelical Christian groups with political views opposed to those of the mainline churches. The New Christian Right, combining conservative and populist positions, vehemently opposes abortion, homosexual rights, and the Equal Rights Amendment for women; it favors prayer in public schools, tax breaks for parents who send their children to religious schools, and new right interpretations of Christian values in foreign policy, such as limits on American funds for birth control in Third World countries. Examples of New Christian Right organizations include Concerned Women for America, the Family Research Council, and the Christian Coalition, founded by the Reverend Pat Robertson (Reichley 1985, 311–31; *Encyclopedia of Associations, 1994*, 1277, 1749, 2036; Cromartie 1993).

As women have sought equal rights and a wider role in society, women's groups have become more nationally important. The National Organization for Women (NOW), with 250,000 members in 1992, is one of the most active (*Public Interest Profiles, 1992–1993*, 169). It lobbies for abortion rights, the Equal Rights Amendment, equal pay for work of comparable value, and the removal of remaining legal discriminations against women (*Encyclopedia of Associations, 1989*, 1515; Hayes 1986, 137–38). NOW took the lead in the successful drive to defeat President Reagan's nomination of Robert Bork to the Supreme Court in 1987, as Bork's literal interpretation of the Constitution was thought to put affirmative action laws and *Roe v. Wade* (1973), which struck down laws prohibiting abortions, in danger of being overturned (see the Controversy in Chapter 8). In opposition to NOW and other feminist groups, conservative women have formed groups like Concerned Women for America and Phyllis Schlafly's Eagle Forum (*Encyclopedia of Associations, 1992*, 1688).

Public Interest Groups **Public interest groups** claiming to represent the public interest press for the reform of society. Reform is a long-standing tradition in the United States. Before the Civil War, reform groups supported causes ranging from antislavery to the abolition of dueling. Of course such groups define the "public interest" according to their political perspectives. Groups called "public interest groups" by those who have a stake in the group are sometimes thought of as "special interest groups" by those who either oppose

Bob Gorrell. Courtesy *The Richmond News-Leader*.

or do not have a vested interest in the cause. A group made up of libertarians, for example, would see deregulation of business and removal of controls on the market as a vital "public interest," while a liberal group would call deregulation a "special interest." Public officials often have difficulty sorting out the public interest and satisfying all who claim to represent it (see Controversy).

Like other types of interest groups, public interest groups may have a broad or specific focus. Mothers Against Drunk Driving (MADD), for example, concentrates on a single issue, while Common Cause has stressed reform of the rules of politics over policy issues. Its leading concern is campaign reform, and it has declared war on the growing power of political action committees (see Chapter 4). Common Cause has also lobbied against "spe-

CONTROVERSY
Jobs v. the Environment in the Bush Administration

George Bush (UPI/Bettman)

Interest group struggles over solutions to problems in a public policy area like the environment are rarely neat and simple. President Bush's attempts to assuage environmentalists angered by Reagan administration stands are a good illustration. Bush wanted to gain the support of environmentalists by cooperating with Congress in reauthorizing the Clean Air Act, listening to "green" concerns about declining wetlands, and recognizing the role of old forests in the Northwest in preserving endangered species. But the honeymoon was brief. By 1990, as economic conditions in the United States began to deteriorate, Bush found himself having to stake out positions that offended environmentalists on many issues.

Although the Reauthorization of the Clean Air Act did reaffirm the nation's commitment to keeping the air quality from getting worse, sections of the bill made major concessions to Detroit's automakers and unions by keeping emissions standards the lowest in the industrialized world. The cost of higher standards, said the Bush administration, would be three hundred thousand jobs.

The wetlands controversy stemmed from this same standoff between environment and jobs. Wetland areas in the United States have been shrinking rapidly as they are filled in and developed. San Francisco Bay, for example, was once ringed by vast wetlands that were spawning areas for fish and wild birds. Wetlands, however, provide more than protection for wildlife. They are giant purification ponds for underground water tables as well as traps for large amounts of decomposition-created carbon dioxide, which is otherwise released into the atmosphere, contributing to global warming. No one doubts the value of wetlands. But most wetlands are privately owned.

cial interests'' on policy issues like tax reform, dairy subsidies, and environmental protection (McFarland 1984, 6–35).

Public interest groups, whatever their focus or perspective, are often handicapped by what economists call the **free rider problem**. If, for example, MADD succeeds in passing legislation that reduces the number of drunk drivers, the roads will be safer for everyone, not just those who joined or contributed to MADD. The average person, however much as he or she sympathizes with MADD's goals, has an incentive to be a "free rider," collecting the benefits of the group's work without paying any costs. Other groups have free riders, too—farmers do not have to join an agricultural group to get the subsidies the group presses for—but the problem is particularly severe for

They can be lucrative if filled in, but their value as real estate depends on the federal government's not stepping in to restrict development.

On this issue the Bush administration attempted to thread its way among environmentalists, developers, and agricultural interests by redefining what was meant by "wetland." Environmentalists became outraged, accusing the president of forsaking his pledge to not allow any net loss of wetlands. But in a period of economic slowdown, Bush was, again, looking for ways to encourage the investment and development that can lead to jobs.

Bush discovered that the jobs issue also cut across his determination to protect endangered species. The 1973 Endangered Species Act required a hold on projects that threatened the existence of any species of wildlife, no matter how small or apparently insignificant. In 1990 the spotted owl, which nested in old-growth forests in the Pacific Northwest, was placed on the endangered species list. The listing required that steps be taken to protect the owl's habitat, which happened to be more than 6 million acres of old-growth forest that the lumber industry hoped to harvest. Even though the Bush administration tried to cut back on the number of acres set aside to ensure this species' survival, Interior Department spokespersons predicted that at least thirty-one thousand lumbering jobs would be lost over the next twenty-five years. Yet many logging jobs will ultimately be lost whether or not the spotted owl receives protection, for lumbering is a declining industry. Still, the spotted owl produced a face-off between major corporate representatives like the National Association of Manufacturers and unions like the United Brotherhood of Carpenters and Joiners on the one hand and environmental groups like the Sierra Club and Greenpeace on the other.

During the 1992 election, George Bush and Bill Clinton both tried to straddle the jobs v. environment controversy but differed in their basic approaches. Bush argued that we can keep existing jobs and have a cleaner environment if we are willing to compromise. Clinton argued that environmental cleanup and protection will create new jobs. There is truth in both positions; interest group conflict on public policy issues rarely pits a right side against a wrong side. One thing seems certain: there will be some pain before we see substantial gain in either the economy or environmental protection.

President Clinton now is working to resolve the jobs v. environment controversy. He will not have an easy time as indicated by mixed reaction to his summer 1993 proposals on old growth forests. His original budget proposals include major reductions in timber cutting, mining, and grazing subsidies on federal lands. When these cuts were scaled back to accommodate senators from western states, environmentalists were unhappy. Clinton is now advocating a middle-of-the-road approach. It will be interesting to see if he is more successful than Bush.

Source: Congressional Quarterly Researcher, 15 May 1992, 411–20; *New York Times*, 31 March 1993, A1, A21; *Congressional Quarterly Weekly Report*, 3 July 1993, 1726–27.

---

public interest groups. Those who do join public interest groups tend to be upper- and middle-class professionals with the money and time for political involvement, but most members are not active in group affairs. A number of interest groups have no membership at all but consist solely of a staff in Washington, D.C., who are paid with contributions from foundations or other interest groups (Olson 1982, 17–35; McFarland 1984, 38–58; Berry 1977, 27–28).

Techniques

Interest groups pursue goals in a manner most likely to yield favorable results for their members. Many focus on a single strategy or technique, but the most successful are those with

WHO CAN TAKE OUR GOVERNMENT BACK FROM THE SPECIAL INTEREST GROUPS? THE AMERICAN VOTER, THAT'S WHO—

Dick Locher. Reprinted with permission: Tribune Media Services.

the resources and skills to use the entire arsenal of political pressure (*National Journal*, 4 July 1987, 1607–11).

One of the most effective interest groups is the American Israeli Public Affairs Committee (AIPAC) (see Profile). With only fifty-five thousand members, a staff of one hundred, and a budget of $12 million (*Public Interest Profiles, 1992–1993*, 605), it is not the largest or best-financed interest group in Washington, but it is vigorous and well managed and an important reason the United States has supported Israel. Its effectiveness is in part the result of its ability to employ a variety of techniques, such as those described below.

Direct Lobbying   Lobbying is still conducted on a face-to-face basis. During Senate Subcommittee on Intergovernmental Relations hearings, a veteran Washington lobbyist told the committee: "I still think that the lobby is substantially one man, one buttonhole. It is that personal eye-to-eye contact that has the maxi-

mum effect (quoted in *Congress and Pressure Groups* 1986, 17). A recent study showed that **direct lobbying**, involving personal interaction and including congressional testimony, is still the most popular method among the various lobbying techniques (Schlozman and Tierney 1986, 290–91; see also Smith 1988).

Analysts suggest at least three reasons why direct lobbying remains the technique of choice. First, it assures the lobbyist that the message has been delivered and was not misinterpreted. It also gives the lobbyist the opportunity to answer questions. Second, it reinforces and enhances the personal relationship between the lobbyist and the official. Third, it conveys to those the lobbyist represents that the lobbyist is informed and has the right connections (*Congress and Pressure Groups* 1986, 17–18).

What qualities define a good direct lobbyist? Emanuel Celler, a Democrat who served in the House of Representatives from 1923 to 1973, wrote:

Gary Trudeau. Doonesbury © 1978, G. B. Trudeau. Reprinted with permission of Universal Press Syndicate.

The man who keeps his appointment, presents his problem or proposal and lets the congressman get on with his other work comes to be liked and respected. His message has an excellent chance of being effective. The man who feels that it somehow adds to his usefulness and prestige to be seen constantly in the company of one legislator or another, or who seeks to ingratiate himself with congressional staffs, gets under foot and becomes a nuisance. He does his principal and cause no good (quoted in "Lobbies" 1986, 82).

Interest groups have found that the most influential and effective lobbyists are former members of Congress who, one year after leaving office, can be employed as lobbyists for private organizations. These lobbyists' insider perspective assists them in deciding when and what kind of pressure to exert on behalf of their clients. As former colleagues, they frequently enjoy easy access to members of Congress and their staffs. They also have in-depth knowledge of the subject matter of legislation. Moving from a government position to employment with an interest group in this way is what has been described as the **revolving door process**. Such movements from the public to the private sector are frequent. Because of such personal connections, however, the public sector often finds it difficult to regulate the private sector. President Clinton has been critical about the quick return of public officials to

lobbying roles in the private sector and made his high-level political appointees agree to refrain from lobbying for five years after they leave government.

During the last presidential election campaign, there was much discussion of the **gridlock** that existed between the White House and Congress. With government divided between Republican President George Bush and Democratic majorities in both Houses of Congress, both sides had trouble getting their programs enacted into law. An equally sound explanation for gridlock is the tight set of relationships that exist between incumbent members of Congress of both parties and the special interest groups with which they deal regularly and on which they depend for campaign donations to reassure their reelection (*Washington Post National Weekly Edition*, 10–16 August 1992, 6, 7; *Washington Post National Weekly Edition*, 16–22 November 1992, 24). Events during the Clinton administration, with a Democrat in the White House and a Democratic majority in both houses of Congress, should clarify which explanation is more valid.

Lobbyists seek to testify at congressional hearings and are frequently asked to do so by senior members of congressional committees. The hearing provides the lobbyist with a virtually unparalleled forum for representing an issue publicly (Oleszek 1989, 98). Hearings are also an opportunity for contact with key mem-

The American Israeli Public Affairs Committee: An Effective Interest Group

AIPAC Symbol (Courtesy AIPAC, Washington, D.C.)

WASHINGTON, July 6—The Reagan administration notified Congress at 5:57 P.M., Friday, May 29 [1987], of its intention to sell 1,600 Maverick antitank missiles to Saudi Arabia.

Within half an hour, lobbyists from the American Israeli Public Affairs Committee, the most important group registered to lobby Congress on legislation affecting Israel, were on the telephone about the proposal.

Over the next thirteen days, the committee mobilized its nationwide network of supporters with a series of memorandums and telephone calls urging them to lobby Congress.

Though it is unclear whether the committee, known as AIPAC, can take all the credit, more than 260 members of Congress co-sponsored resolutions to block the sale, prompting President Reagan to withdraw it.

AIPAC began as the American Zionist Emergency Council, founded by Rabbi Abba Hillel Silver in 1943 to lobby for American support for a Jewish state in Palestine (for more on Middle East issues, see Chapter 11). After Israel gained its independence in 1948, the organization, which changed its name in 1959, began to focus on lobbying for economic and military aid to Israel and for a pro-Israel Middle East policy. Particularly since the late 1960s, AIPAC has been considered Israel's

bers that lobbyists may not have been able to get in touch with in any other way. In their testimony, lobbyists try to develop a favorable public image of the interests and organizations they represent.

The day-to-day operation of interest groups may be less exciting than the resolution of big issues, but it is important. If an issue can be resolved before it attracts the attention of opposing interest groups, direct lobbying can be particularly effective. A knowledge of the complexities of government organization can en-

able the resourceful group to influence an agency or court decision with action that beats an opposing interest group to the punch. Experienced lobbyists often are masters of working quietly to promote their objectives. Japanese companies have been particularly successful with quiet lobbying due, in part, to their ability to retain many of the best lobbyists available. In 1992, Ross Perot accused the campaigns of both Bill Clinton and George Bush of employing persons who were on leave from law firms where they served as lobbyists for

informal representative in Washington, even though AIPAC emphasizes that its members are Americans.

Despite its name, AIPAC is not a political action committee that contributes directly to candidates, but it is perceived as influencing the decisions of many pro-Israel PACs that are important contributors. In 1984 pro-Israel PACs contributed $3.6 million to House and Senate candidates who were identified as either pro-Israel or opponents of candidates who were anti-Israel. Paul Simon, who defeated Charles Percy of Illinois for a U.S. Senate seat in 1984, received $270,000 from pro-Israel PACs. Many other Jewish organizations, such as the American Jewish Congress, B'nai B'rith, and the Union of American Hebrew Congregations, take their cue from AIPAC where the Middle East is concerned, and politicians who oppose AIPAC may alienate themselves from leaders who can influence a large bloc of votes.

Although the number of AIPAC members is fairly small, many are prominent and respected citizens of their communities, likely to be listened to by their members of Congress. Morris Amitay, former director, points out that its members give the group influence even in states with small Jewish populations because of their generally higher social status.

AIPAC also has a reputation for supplying accurate and timely information. Republican Congressman Henry Hyde of Illinois calls AIPAC lobbyists "professionals in every sense of the word" who "bring clarity of purpose with passionate commitment to everything they do."

Even with all it has going for it, AIPAC does not always win. In 1981 it failed to stop a sale of AWACS (Airborne Warning and Control System) planes to Saudi Arabia despite an intense lobbying effort. Yet AIPAC has consistently been able to persuade Congress to increase aid to Israel above administration budget requests, while aid to other countries usually is cut sharply. Congress also has made the interest on Israeli bonds tax deductible (American Jews provide the Jewish state with $1.4 billion a year in gifts and loans, on top of $2.6 billion in official U.S. aid) and closed the offices of the Palestine Liberation Organization (PLO) in the United States. Recently, it has had the more difficult job of keeping American public opinion and the Congress sympathetic to Israel's national security and financial concerns during negotiations for the Middle East settlement, initiated through pressure by the Bush administration following the Persian Gulf War. A determined president can probably overpower AIPAC, as President Bush did on some aspects of the Middle East settlement, but the political costs of the struggle make it unattractive. As long as AIPAC maintains its effectiveness, Israel will have a powerful voice in Washington.

Source: Tivnan 1987; Crabb and Holt 1992; Feuerwerger 1979 news quote from *New York Times*, 7 July 1987, A8.

foreign governments, a connection he likened to making an enemy officer privy to your army's strategic plans (*New York Times*, 10 October 1992, 20).

Grass-Roots Lobbying   Most lobbying on major issues includes wide-ranging efforts to involve the "grass roots"—the people at the local level. Massive propaganda drives seek to mobilize public opinion, often urging citizens to contact members of Congress to support or oppose a particular bill. This **grass-roots lobbying** assumes that individual constituents have more effect on politicians than well-paid lobbyists. Computerized mass mailings, mentioned above, are often used in grass-roots lobbying, and consultants who specialize in mail and phone campaigns are sometimes hired to help generate responses.

The National Rifle Association (NRA), which protects the right to bear arms and promotes safe firearm use, has been especially successful in single-issue grass-roots lobbying. Despite statistics indicating that a majority of

Jerry Robinson. Robinson/Cartoonists & Writers Syndicate.

Americans want to see gun control strengthened, most efforts aimed at stricter gun control legislation have been stifled by the NRA. Between 1988 and 1993, Maryland, New Jersey, and Virginia tightened handgun regulations. Such victories remain the exception rather than the rule, however, often because members of the NRA hold their views intensely and are extremely vocal about them (*Congressional Quarterly Weekly Report*, 18 March 1989, 579–82; *New York Times*, 7 April 1992, B6).

Interest groups also attempt to display grass-roots support through marches and demonstrations, especially in Washington, D.C., where they attract more media attention than elsewhere. The effectiveness of civil rights demonstrations during the 1960s encouraged other "outsider" interest groups to adopt similar tactics. Indeed, the civil rights movement may be regarded as both model and impetus for the growth of the consumer, environmental, antinuclear, peace, and women's movements in the late 1960s and early 1970s.

Grass-roots mobilization demands careful organization, communication, and timing. Not even large and wealthy groups can charge up their troops simply by passing orders down the line. And even if they could, mail that appears artificially generated may be ignored altogether by some politicians.

Electioneering   Interest groups also try to influence government policy by electing people who support the group's goals. This method,

known as **electioneering**, involves voter registration drives, general campaign assistance, and campaign contributions. In close races, interest groups may give money to both candidates to ensure support or access no matter who wins.

The AFL-CIO is experienced at electioneering. The organization's political arm, called the Committee on Political Education (COPE), is one of the most effective mass-membership interest groups in the United States today. Using a computer list of all members of AFL-CIO unions, COPE conducts massive voter registration drives, offers political education to union members, and works to get union members to the polls during each election. COPE also turns out tens of thousands of volunteers to work for its favored candidates. Individual AFL-CIO unions conduct similar efforts on their own (Wilson 1981, 41–43). COPE's efforts may explain why unionized workers are more likely to vote than nonunion workers. However, as with almost any group, members do not always vote as suggested by the leadership.

Increasingly, interest groups are forming political action committees (PACs) as channels for their financial contributions to candidates (see Chapter 4). As Tables 5.2 and 5.3 reveal, PAC giving is substantial, constituting 48 percent of all political donations to Democratic candidates for the House and 32 percent of all donations to Republican candidates for the House in 1990. Corporate and trade association PACs gave the largest percentage of that total. Political parties play a far less significant role in campaign funding (*Vital Statistics on Congress, 1991–1992*, 156). Of total contributions to House races in 1990, Democrats received more money than Republicans, largely because PACs expect that most incumbents will be reelected and the Democrats held the most seats in the House. In Senate races, because challengers have a better chance of defeating incumbents, corporate PACs favored the Republicans by a small margin. Both be-

TABLE 5.2   PAC CONTRIBUTIONS TO CONGRESSIONAL CANDIDATES, 1989–90 (IN MILLIONS)

	CORPORATE	*LABOR*	*TRADE ASSOCIATION*	*OTHER**	*TOTAL*
House Democrats	19.1	26.1	19.3	8.9	73.4
House Republicans	17.1	1.8	13.4	4.6	36.9
Senate Democrats	8.4	6.2	5.2	5.1	24.9
Senate Republicans	13.5	0.6	6.5	3.3	23.9
Total	58.1	34.7	44.4	21.9	159.1

* Includes PACs classified by the Federal Election Commission as cooperatives, corporations without stock, and nonconnected.

Source: Vital Statistics on American Politics, 1992, *182–83.*

cause Democrats have traditionally been the protectors of labor and because they control both houses of Congress, they received more money from labor PACs in both the House and the Senate. According to some analysts, the growing dependence of Democrats on business PAC funds is making Democrats in Congress more conservative, eroding party competition, and hurting those interest groups without the resources to establish PACs. The majority of campaign funds, however, still come from individual contributors, who may contribute a maximum of $1,000 to a candidate per election. (Godwin 1989, 125–31; *Vital Statistics on Congress, 1989–1990*, 88–91; *Vital Statistics on Congress, 1991–1992*, 156).

Education   Collecting information is an important interest group activity. Lobbyists spend more than a quarter of their time and resources preparing and presenting research results. This research function has expanded with the growth of government and the increasing complexity of issues. One Washington lobbyist states, "Insofar as a great deal of the legislation we deal with is technical, we're doing a lot more providing of research results and technical information. We often think of ourselves as educators" (quoted in *Congress and Pressure Groups* 1986, 16). To be effective, the information must be correct and complete. One member of Congress has cautioned: "It doesn't take very long to figure out which lob-

TABLE 5.3   CONTRIBUTIONS TO CONGRESSIONAL CANDIDATES, 1990 (PERCENT)

	TOTAL PARTY COORDINATED CONTRIBUTIONS	*POLITICAL ACTION COMMITTEES*	*INDIVIDUAL; CANDIDATE TO SELF; AND OTHERS*
House Democrats	3	48	49
House Republicans	5	32	63
Senate Democrats	6	22	72
Senate Republicans	9	21	70

Source: Vital Statistics on Congress, 1991–1992, *91–92.*

byists are straightforward, and which ones are trying to snow you. The good ones will give you the weak points as well as the strong points of their case. If anyone ever gives me false or misleading information, that's it—I'll never see him again" (quoted in Ornstein and Elder 1978, 77).

Public image is extremely important, and interest groups launch campaigns to convince the general public of the advantages of their views and the righteousness of their cause. Press releases may describe, for example, how a particular union has improved factory working conditions or explain how a certain industry is leading the fight against pollution. Advertising may seek to win public support. An environmental group may explain why a 10-cent deposit should be required on all soft drink and beer containers. Interest groups also spend large amounts of money for advertising on television, in magazines, and in newspapers.

Often lobbies create or support research institutions, commonly called **think tanks**, to conduct and present research supportive of their viewpoint. A good lobbyist will make use of this information and emphasize the educational aspects of the job. Interest groups that emphasize education over direct political influence can qualify for tax-deductible contributions, thus easing their fund-raising efforts.

Although there is often intense competition among similar interest groups, some groups prefer to cooperate and spend a good deal of time in consultation with other groups that have similar goals (Huckshorn 1984, 301–2). For example, while environmental groups may have differing interests, they share a common concern for a healthy environment and recognize that government officials should not receive too many contradictory signals.

Regulation of Interest Groups

The First Amendment protects interest groups from strict government regulation, but at-tempts have been made to control some of their activities. Congress passed a major lobby regulation law in 1946, requiring organizations whose principal purpose was lobbying to register with the clerk of the House of Representatives and the secretary of the Senate. But the law was full of loopholes. It excluded corporations whose "principal purpose" was their business activities but that still took part in active lobbying. Only direct lobbying of members of Congress, not of bureaucrats and congressional staffers, was regulated. Because no formal agency was assigned to enforce the law, only one violator was prosecuted over the next thirty years (Ornstein and Elder 1978, 103–4; *Washington Lobby* 1987, 35–65).

Despite many efforts, the disclosure provisions of the 1946 law have not been significantly tightened. Congress has, however, restricted lobbying by former executive branch officials and foreign governments. Two former Reagan administration officials, Michael Deaver and Lyn Nofziger, violated this new regulation. Deaver was convicted of perjury in connection with a formal investigation of his lobbying activities (*Washington Lobby* 1987, 36, 41–46). Nofziger was found in violation of a provision that prohibits officials from lobbying former colleagues for at least one year. Such provisions are meant to prevent a **conflict of interest**, a situation in which a present or past public official might take advantage of experience or position for private gain. Conflicts of interest have been more strictly regulated in the past two decades. The new restrictions do not, however, apply to former members of Congress, and many of them now engage in the same practices that got Deaver and Nofziger in trouble.

The most recent attempt to limit lobbying came with the 1989 Ethics Reform Act, which restricts honoraria, privately financed domestic travel, and certain gifts to government officials. The effectiveness of the law remains to be seen. As Kenneth A. Gross, a lawyer interviewed by *National Journal*, pointed out, there are "exceptions in place for getting around [the] rules" (*National Journal*, 12 May 1990, 1138–43). Congress has also passed legislation that requires foreign governments to disclose any lobbying activities in which they participate within the United States.

Moreover, campaign contributions by interest groups are regulated by the Federal Election Campaign Act of 1974 (see Chapter 4). While these restrictions are more effective than the lobbying regulations, they, too, can be avoided. The Supreme Court has ruled that independent expenditures by a PAC, in support of but not coordinated with a candidate's campaign, cannot be limited.

Individual actions by interest-group supporters can be important as well. Groups can also avoid the $5,000 per candidate contribution limit established in FECA by forming a large number of PACs to represent one interest. In 1984, one California Jewish activist spent $1.6 million independently to help Illinois Democrat Paul Simon defeat Republican Charles Percy for a Senate seat following Percy's call for U.S. recognition of the Palestine Liberation Organization (Findley 1985, 111–12).

Interest group money can also enter the political system as soft money, channeled through state and local parties to finance party-building activities (see Chapter 4). In recent years, Congress has cut the budget and enforcement powers of the Federal Election Commission, making finance laws harder to enforce. Moreover, because there are always three Republicans and three Democrats on the commission, tie votes often prevent investigations (*New York Times*, 18 March 1988, D22).

The PAC example illustrates the difficulties of regulating interest groups. With the exception of Common Cause and a few others, most interest groups across the political spectrum do not want to be regulated and work to oppose effective regulation. Politicians—who receive important support from interest groups —often are not interested in effective regulation either. Finally, too much regulation may impair constitutional rights. There has been increasing talk of PAC reforms, but at this writing details were still being debated in Congress.

Good or bad, interest groups are a reality in American political life. James Madison wrote in Number 10 of *The Federalist Papers* that "the latent causes of faction are sown in the nature of man" (*Federalist Papers* 1961, 79). Even more than this view of human nature, the great size and complexity of American government necessitate the existence of interest groups on some level to attempt representation in ways that elected officials either cannot or do not provide. Interest groups remain the major means by which public opinion is collected, expressed, and made known to government officials and lawmakers.

PERSPECTIVES

One of the first definitions of interest groups in the United States comes from James Madison: "By a faction, I understand a number of citizens, whether amounting to a majority or minority of the whole, who are united and actuated by some common impulse of passion, or of interest, adverse to the rights of other citizens, or to the permanent and aggregate interests of the community" (Number 10, *Federalist Papers* 1961, 79). Clearly Madison believed interest groups contrary to both other citizen rights and community interests, and his opinion is still held by many today.

In contrast to the picture of interest groups as powerful and dangerous, many analysts believe that interest groups are a necessary element in any thriving political system. Interest groups represent the public in Washington between elections when politicians might otherwise be tempted to ignore those who put them in office. They give people a chance to participate in government, though most forfeit the chance by not joining a group. Lobbying teaches group members about government and keeps them informed about political decisions. Interest groups also provide information that government officials need to make intelligent policy decisions (*Congress and Pressure Groups* 1986, 13).

All six perspectives are represented by interest groups. The extent to which interest groups are beneficial, and indeed which groups are most worthy of respect, is one of the major issues dividing the perspectives. Consequently interest groups are the primary focus of this Perspectives section. The six perspectives also have differing ideas about the impact of the media. Marxists are especially skeptical of socialization. Feminists worry about the continuing socialization of children

"HE'S QUITE INDEPENDENT — OF POLITICAL LEADERSHIP, THAT IS"

Herbert Block. From *Herblock on All Fronts* (New American Library, 1980).

into traditionally male and female roles. There are different ways for a group to seek influence, as well as different purposes for which that influence may be sought. The following discussion illustrates different types of groups as well as the six perspectives.

Conservative

James Madison wrote that one of the main purposes of the new Constitution was to "brake and control the violence of faction" (Number 10, *Federalist Papers* 1961, 77), a view that sums up what

conservatives think of interest groups today. Conservatives, with their skeptical view of human nature, believe that when people combine into groups for political action their goals are likely, as

Madison warned, to affect adversely both the rights of other citizens and the community. Fortunately, conservatives say, the Constitution set up a system that, by dispersing power, minimizes the negative aspects of interest group factionalism. In a free society, interest groups cannot be outlawed, but the separation of powers and the federal system help prevent any one group from dominating government at all levels and oppressing the others.

Unlike liberals, conservatives do not see business and the rich as the group most likely to accumulate excessive power. For them the greatest threat to liberty comes from what Madison called the "superior force of an [self] interested and overbearing majority" (Number 10, *Federalist Papers* 1961, 77). Such a majority is likely to consist of the underprivileged and less talented who are intent on invading property rights. Most liberal "reforms" aimed at controlling interest groups would heighten rather than alleviate this danger. For example, limiting campaign contributions and publicly financing elections would cripple the political power of business while helping labor interests, which can turn out volunteers and provide other resources not included in the limits. Tighter conflict of interest regulations would keep businesspeople out of government service and leave power in the hands of those who lack understanding and sympathy for the business community. As usual, say conservatives, liberal reforms are aimed against the most productive members of society.

Theodore J. Lowi, a political scientist who studies the effectiveness of the American political system, argues that interest groups actually negate democratic power. Interest groups appear to represent the public interest but actually do not because they are subject to less and less popular control. Lowi warns that democracy, as conceived by the framers and believed in by most Americans today, is threatened by interest groups that compete to be heard. With the enormous number of interest groups today, government officials have difficulty responding with fairness and doing their jobs (Lowi 1969, 288, 293).

Lowi believes that the areas of public concern most in need of regulation end up being regulated by related interest groups and professional associations that have specialized knowledge. Transportation industry managers, for example, know the most about how regulation could help or hurt their industry. Consequently transportation specialists are asked to sit on the government advisory groups and independent regulatory commissions (see Chapter 10) that make and enforce industry regulations. Embedding these interests in their own regulation grants them a legitimacy Lowi believes they do not deserve. Putting it most simply, the fox has been put in charge of the henhouse (see Lowi 1979). It should be noted that while Lowi's argument about the dangers of interest groups agrees with conservative views, this text is not characterizing him as anything other than a political scientist.

While conservatives are suspicious of interest groups, they have not hesitated to create and use them effectively to achieve their political goals, especially in the last twenty years. Business interest groups have become much more effective and well financed as government regulation and the activities of liberal public interest groups have increased (Wilson 1981, 54–82). Conservatives have also created an array of nonbusiness ideological groups, including PACs, grass-roots lobbying organizations, and legal foundations.

The Free Congress Research and Education Foundation, led by Paul Weyrich, is one of the new breed of conservative groups. Weyrich, a longtime conservative activist, modeled his group on those created by the left populist lawyer Ralph Nader. Instead of relying on campaign contributions and lobbying, as many other conservative groups do, the Free Congress Foundation is involved in information gathering and public education. One of the group's recent tasks was a judicial reform project. Desiring that Reagan leave a conservative legacy through the appointment of conservative judges, it pushed for the selection of such nominees and was a leader of the unsuccessful fight for the confirmation of Robert Bork to the Supreme Court (see Controversy in Chapter 8).

The Free Congress Research and Education Foundation differs sharply from libertarian groups like the Cato Institute on social and foreign policy issues. It backs laws against abortion and pornography, opposes the Equal Rights Amendment, and supports prayer in schools. It is more vehemently anticommunist than many other conservative groups. Several years ago it was one of the first to advocate aid to anticommunist guerrillas like the Nicaraguan *contras*. After receiving little support, it published *Combat on Communist Territory* (1985), a story of so-called freedom-fighter movements. The book helped generate debate among conservatives, and eventually the Reagan administration made aid to anticommunist guerrillas a major part of its foreign policy (Moser 1985; National Committee for a Free Congress 1987).

Although they seem to have found a place in interest group activity and influence, conservatives look to the media with frustration, for they perceive them to be liberally biased. William Rusher, a media analyst and publisher of the *National Review*, sought to prove liberal bias in the media in *The Coming Battle for the Media* (1988). He cited studies demonstrating that a large and often overwhelming majority of media personnel vote more heavily Democratic and hold far more liberal views than the American public on such issues as welfare, abortion, and extramarital sex. Other studies conclude that in the presidential elections of 1968 and 1984, the media depicted Republican candidates more negatively than Democratic candidates. The interesting thing about both of these elections, however, is that the Republican candidates won (Rusher 1988, 45–48, 67–74; Robinson 1981, 160–65; see also Thimmesch 1985, 1–36).

Liberal

Liberals believe in a government that is both active and responsive to its people. Interest groups play an important role in this vision. If government is to manage the economy and reform society, as liberals believe it must, the people need to control the government. Otherwise government might become the oppressive Goliath feared by libertarians. Since citizens cannot expect to participate in each decision directly, they need to organize groups that can make their influence effective (Dahl 1982, 31–40).

Unfortunately, liberals say, American democracy has allowed a significant imbalance to develop between the power of business interests and that of other groups. This disparity arises primarily from control by business over financial resources that are not usually available to labor or liberal public interest groups. Whether used to back conservative candidates, hire lobbyists to influence Congress and the executive, or employ attorneys, money gives business such disproportionate influence over politics that other groups are often forced to settle for crumbs from the table. As a result, the United States has done much less to address inequities by redistributing wealth and income from the rich to the poor than other democracies (Dahl 1982, 171–74). Without government redistribution, business and the rich gain more political advantage and political equality becomes even more distant.

In his farewell address to the nation on January 14, 1981, President Jimmy Carter asserted that the growth in the number of interest groups "tends to distort our [national] purposes, because the national interest is not always the sum of all our single or special interests" (quoted in *Washington Lobby* 1987, 1). Charles Peters, editor of the *Washington Monthly*, a political journal, voiced the same concern: "America is no longer a nation. It is a committee of lobbies. Politicians no longer ask what is in the public interest, because they know no one else is asking. Instead they're giving each group what it wants" (quoted in *Washington Lobby* 1987, 1). Liberals were concerned that the Reagan years heightened inequities. While Marxists see the solution as the abolition of private property and economic inequalities, liberals favor reforms to limit the power of money in interest group competition. They suggest limiting campaign spending, banning large contributions, and publicly financing elections. They argue that lobbying needs to be more carefully regulated. The private activities of former public officials should be limited by stricter conflict of interest regulations to check the revolving door process by which officials move from the public to the private sector and back again, thus blurring the distinction between sectors. At the same time, government needs to support and encourage organization by groups representing the underprivileged. Under

interested groups, as Jane Kimble did, and they work for media coverage of their activities. Informing and involving constituents can help dispel lack of trust in government or at least promote trust on an individual basis. In all, the job of communicator often takes up one-third of a member's time as well as the largest portion of the member's staff's time (Frantzich 1986).

The Ombudsman Role

A member of Congress, particularly of the House, is expected to serve as an **ombudsman**, or middleperson between constituents and the federal government who receives and acts to resolve complaints. For example, a scientist teaching at a university in a congressperson's district may have applied for a grant from the National Science Foundation after the deadline for applications has passed. A widow may not have received her social security benefits after moving, even though she has sent in her change-of-address form. In cases like these, the member asks the department or agency involved to investigate the matter to make sure the constituent was treated properly and to see if the constituent can be helped, then reports the result to the constituent. If done with diligence, this work takes considerable effort, sometimes as much as one-third of a member's and his or her staff's time.

Members occasionally provide services to individuals by sponsoring **private bills**, which are introduced at constituent request to correct a problem resulting from government action or address a matter not covered in public law. If passed, private bills apply only to those named in the bill. These bills might be a special exception to immigration laws or the resolution of an unusual claim not subject to normal procedure. Congressional leaders have tried to reduce the number of such bills, and they rarely pass without strong effort by the sponsoring member (Johannes 1984). Interestingly enough, it was the ombudsman role in spon-

"How Do I Know This Is a Good Honest Bribe and Not One of Those Underhanded Abscam Things?"

Wayne Stayskal. Reprinted by permission: Tribune Media Services.

soring private bills that led to the so-called Abscam scandal of 1979–81. The Federal Bureau of Investigation (FBI) suspected some members of Congress of wrongdoing and conducted an investigation during which agents posed as Arabs seeking sponsorship of a private bill by offering bribes. Eight members of Congress accepted the offers, were revealed by the press and the FBI, and generally did not fare well thereafter in the courts and before the public.

Balancing the Roles

With these various duties, do members really have sufficient time for legislation? Whatever the answer, members of Congress do not want to give up nonlegislative duties. Ombudsman work usually makes individual constituents happy, and communication provides the information necessary for the other roles. Leadership and votes on controversial legislation generally makes some people happy and others unhappy. All three roles are important in reelection. Even if voting records are not communicated to constituents, votes are published in the *Congressional Record*. Because controversial votes can be used against incumbents during the next election campaign, members like to see controversial issues decided in committee, with the floor vote serving as a ratification of the committee decision.

As a rule, representatives are more frequently reelected than senators. Only three times in the last twenty-four years has the percentage of senators reelected been higher than that of representatives (*Vital Statistics on Congress, 1991–1992*, 58–59; *National Journal*, 7 November 1992, 2555). Three considerations may help explain this difference. First, representatives undertake the ombudsman role for a larger proportion of their constituency than senators. Second, the voting records of senators are better known than those of House members, and popular knowledge of voting records works to one's disadvantage, as every vote will displease some person or group. Finally, a state is more diverse and difficult to represent than a congressional district. In addition, the Senate is more attractive than the House to well-known challengers. Still, the vast majority of senators who choose to run again are reelected.

Congressional Staffs

As the roles of communicator and ombudsman have expanded, and as the complexities of legislation have increased, members of Congress have acquired larger staffs to help with their workload. In 1938 Senator Harry Truman employed a secretary and one administrative assistant to serve Missouri. In 1988 this same suite of offices was occupied by Senator David Pryor of Arkansas, who had a staff of more than twenty—small by current Senate standards (*Christian Science Monitor*, 13 May 1988, 3). Between 1957 and 1989 total personal staff on the Hill employed by senators grew from 1,115 to more than 3,800. The House personal staff grew from 2,441 to more than 7,500 (*Vital Statistics on Congress, 1991–1992*, 133). In 1990 the legislative branch employed almost 37,500 people and spent $2.2 billion for its operations (*Statistical Abstract, 1992*, 322, 331). About one-third of these employees were on the personal

"Look! One of the Senators Is Briefing His Staff."

Jim Berry. Reprinted by permission of NEA, Inc.

staffs of members; the rest worked for committees or agencies, like the Library of Congress, within the legislative branch.

There is little doubt that large staffs are needed today if Congress is to be the effective check on the executive branch that the framers intended. Without staff help, members would simply not be able to gather the information they need to evaluate proposals coming from the executive, and Congress could become a rubber stamp for the president. Committee staff members are particularly important since they spend most of their time working on legislative issues rather than communicator or ombudsman activities. Congressional research agencies like the Congressional Budget Office (see Chapter 10) and the Office of Technology Assessment, which advises Congress on science issues, further increase a member's ability to deal competently with legislation and to challenge the president.

On the other hand, the staff explosion has caused problems. While some staffers see themselves as neutral experts, merely passing information to their congressional bosses, others are policy activists, looking for opportunities to get members to back policies they favor. And because members' time is so limited, they often rely on staff briefings and vote accordingly. As the opinions of staff become more powerful, Congress becomes less democratic, and some observers fear that legislation is being turned over to "the experts" (Price 1971, 316–36; see also Malbin 1980, 239–51).

Another problem with the staff explosion is that staffers, to prove themselves to their boss, spend time developing new bills and amendments to sponsor and gathering information on other members' bills. Thus the workload in Congress has expanded as the number of staffers has increased. Abner Mikva, a former Democratic representative from Illinois, used to say that he did his best work when he concealed himself in a hidden office where his staff could not find him and interrupt his reading and thinking by bringing him new papers and problems (Malbin 1980, 7). One might assume that the logical solution to the burgeoning workload would be to reduce staff. Most members, however, believe they need a small bureaucracy of their own in order to complete their work and both monitor and control the huge bureaucracy in the executive branch.

POWERS AND CONSTRAINTS

If members of Congress must perform a multitude of duties, so must Congress as an institution. These duties, in turn, add to the complexity of duties facing the members.

The Major Legislative Powers

The major **legislative powers**, or law-making powers of Congress, are listed in Article I, Section 8, of the Constitution (see Table 6.2

TABLE 6.2   POWERS OF CONGRESS

LEGISLATIVE (ARTICLE I, SECTION 8)

Levy and collect taxes
Borrow money
Regulate foreign and interstate commerce
Make naturalization and bankruptcy laws
Coin money and punish counterfeiting
Establish a post office and post roads
Make patent and copyright laws
Establish courts below the Supreme Court
Meet obligations of international law
Declare war
Raise armies and navies and regulate them
Call out militia to suppress insurrections and
    enforce federal laws
Control the District of Columbia and other federal
    property
Make all laws "which shall be necessary and
    proper" for carrying out the powers listed above
    (Elastic Clause)

OTHER CONSTITUTIONAL POWERS

Approve treaties and appointments (Senate only)
Propose constitutional amendments
Impeach and try officials
Regulate congressional operations and members

EXTRA-CONSTITUTIONAL POWERS

Investigate areas within the scope of legislative
    powers
Reject actions of bodies delegated authority by
    Congress (legislative veto, which is constitu-
    tionally uncertain)

and Appendix A; see also Appendix B for a list of significant legislation enacted by Congress). Several important powers deserve special attention.

Tax and Appropriate   Congress has the **power of the purse**, the authority to raise and spend money. Legislation that raises revenue to pay for government is **taxation**. Once a tax law has been passed, Congress decides how much money to authorize or spend in support of a specific program or piece of legislation. This is the power of **appropriation**. Congress

Robert Dornfried. © Dornfried/Rothco.

can also earmark appropriations for specific programs and uses within an agency. Earmarking has become increasingly common in recent years because it gives Congress more control over agency spending. Unfortunately it also promotes pet projects and, on occasion, inefficiencies.

Regulate Commerce and Money   Under the Constitution, Congress has the power to regulate all commerce among the states and with other nations. Congress also has the power to borrow and coin money.

Establish Courts   The Constitution gives Congress the authority to set the appellate jurisdiction of the Supreme Court, determining what types of lower court cases and decisions can be reviewed by the Court, as well as the entire jurisdiction and structure of the lower courts. As part of its legislative functions, Congress also determines the structure and jurisdiction of executive branch departments, executive branch agencies, and independent regulatory commissions.

Declare War   Congress has the power to declare war, raise armies, and provide for a navy. While the power to pass a **declaration of war** remains important, it has to some extent been

eclipsed by the rapid pace of warfare made possible by technological advances. Moreover, since World War II, covert operations have often been carried out without the approval of Congress (see Chapter 7).

The Elastic Clause   Article I, Section 8, of the Constitution also states that Congress has the power to "make all Laws which shall be necessary and proper for carrying into Execution the foregoing Powers, and all other Powers vested by this Constitution in the Government of the United States, or in any Department or Officer thereof." This Necessary and Proper Clause—also called the **Elastic Clause**—is one of the most widely used provisions of the Constitution and has been subject to continued interpretation by Congress and the Supreme Court. While Congress has used this clause to justify legislation in areas not specified by the Constitution, the Supreme Court has ruled that the clause does not give Congress any new powers but that Congress can act in a new area (such as banking or minimum wage regulation) in order to carry out one of the original functions (enumerated powers) of the United States government (see Chapter 2).

Other Constitutional Powers

Other powers granted to Congress elsewhere in the Constitution deserve special attention.

Approve Treaties   The Senate must approve all **treaties** (formal agreements between two or more countries) negotiated by the president by at least a two-thirds vote. The framers gave this power exclusively to the Senate because they deemed the Senate better able than the House to take a long-term view of issues. While the Senate rarely rejects treaties, the president is sometimes forced to withdraw those that lack its support. President Jimmy Carter, for example, withdrew the Strategic Arms Limitation Treaty (SALT II) he had nego-

Ed Uluschak. Courtesy *Edmonton Journal*. Reprinted by permission of the artist.

tiated with the Soviets after they invaded Afghanistan in 1979. Sometimes the Senate adds conditions or reservations to treaties, as it did with the 1978 treaty returning the Panama Canal Zone to Panama.

The most famous example of the Senate's power over treaties is its rejection of the Treaty of Versailles, which ended World War I and created the League of Nations. President Woodrow Wilson made major contributions to writing the treaty for the World War I victors, but the U.S. Senate modified it to such an extent that Wilson actually ended up opposing the modified treaty. In the end the treaty was defeated, and the United States was the only major power never to join the League of Nations. (For elaboration on executive-legislative relations, see Chapter 7.)

Approve Appointments   The Senate has the power to "advise and consent" to presidential nominations to offices, including cabinet posts, top-level agency positions, ambassadorships, the Supreme Court and lower federal courts, and positions like United States attorney and marshal. According to the custom of **senatorial courtesy**, the president consults the senators of his party from the state concerned when making a nomination to a federal office located in that state. Most presidential nominations are approved. When they are rejected, as was that of John Tower, nominated by George Bush as secretary of defense, or are hotly contested, as was Clarence Thomas, nominated by Bush to the Supreme Court, or when the nominee is forced to withdraw, as was Zoë Baird, nominated by Bill Clinton as attorney general, the controversies make news.

Propose Constitutional Amendments   Congress has the power to propose, by a two-thirds vote of both houses, amendments to the Constitution. Alternatively, two-thirds of the state legislatures may petition Congress to call a constitutional convention to propose amendments (see Figure 2.4). Proposed amendments must be ratified by three-fourths of either the legislatures or conventions of the respective states, at the option of Congress. All amendments to date have been proposed by Congress. Although thirty-two states had called for an amendment requiring Congress to balance the federal budget, this proposal was rejected for a third time by Congress in the summer of 1992 (Budd interview 1992).

Impeach and Try Officials   Another power of Congress is removal from office, for "Treason, Bribery, or other high Crimes and Misdemeanors," of all United States civil officials except military personnel and members of Congress. A majority vote in the House results in **impeachment**, a procedure whereby a civil official is formally accused and brought to trial in the Senate. Here, after the trial, a two-thirds vote is required for actual removal from office. Only sixteen government officials have been impeached since 1789, including one president (Andrew Johnson), one cabinet officer, one senator, and thirteen federal judges. Of these, fifteen were brought to trial in the Senate and seven were ultimately convicted (*Guide to Congress* 1991, 293).

Housekeeping   Congress also has the responsibility to police itself. Both House and Senate have committees charged with inquiring into violations of ethical standards by members. Expulsion from the body is the ultimate penalty, which may be imposed by a two-thirds vote. Recent ethics inquiries have led to the expulsion of two members involved in the Abscam scandal and the resignation under pressure of House Speaker Jim Wright. The House or Senate may also **censure**—officially reprimand or condemn the activities of a member of Congress without any sanctions—for misconduct by a simple majority vote.

A related housekeeping role is judging contested House and Senate elections when the outcome is uncertain. The last contested election occurred in Indiana's Eighth Congressional District in 1984 between Frank McCloskey, the incumbent Democrat, and Richard McIntyre, his Republican challenger. It has been called the closest House race in this century. The final count by Indiana gave McIntyre the victory by 34 votes; a recount increased his margin to 418 votes. But the Democratic-controlled House refused to seat McIntyre and appointed a Democratic majority task force to investigate the election. The task force gave McCloskey the victory by 4 votes, leaving 32 absentee ballots uncounted, and the House approved, 236–190, with 10 Democrats siding with the Republicans. When McCloskey was sworn in, House Republicans walked out in protest. The solution left visible partisan scars on the House (*Congressional Quarterly Weekly Report*, 4 May 1985, 821–25).

Extra-Constitutional Powers

Congress also engages in several activities that are not clearly specified in the Constitution. Two of these **extra-constitutional powers** are investigation and the legislative veto.

Investigation   Since the writing of the Constitution, Congress has assumed a power of **investigation**, undertaking study of anything from the executive branch to an ordinary citizen, so long as the investigation is within the scope of its legislative powers. For example, the congressional investigation of the Watergate scandal (see Controversy in Chapter 7) used as its basis a law designed to prevent campaign abuses. More recently Congress used the Boland Amendment (prohibiting direct or indirect support to the Nicaraguan *contras*) and the Congressional Oversight Act of 1980 (requiring the president to give "timely" notice to Congress of any covert operations) as a basis for the investigation into the Iran-*contra* affair (see Controversy in Chapter 11). As a result of its investigation, a new and more specific forty-eight-hour notification deadline was written into the 1988 amendments to the 1980 oversight law (Cohen and Mitchell 1988). Congress often uses this investigative power in execution of its duties of overseeing the operations of the executive and judicial agencies it creates and finances. While it does not often invade the technical aspects of an agency, Congress does attempt to make sure the money it appropriates for agency use is not wasted. Such oversight can improve government's performance.

The Legislative Veto   In certain cases Congress has tried to retain control over functions it has delegated to the executive through the use of the **legislative veto**. This power permits either house of Congress, within a given time period, to reject, and in effect veto, actions of bodies that have been delegated authority by Congress.

The legislative veto is constitutionally uncertain and the subject of much controversy. The 1983 Supreme Court decision, *Immigration and Naturalization Service v. Chadha*, declared that the practice was unconstitutional unless it involved approval of a **joint resolution** by both houses of Congress and submission to the president for his approval or veto, as dictated by Article I, Sections 1 and 7, of the Constitution. This procedure, requiring Congress to, in reality, pass a new law when controlling the actions it has delegated, would eliminate the usefulness of the legislative veto. The decision affects several hundred pieces of legislation Congress has passed requiring the president or other members of the executive branch to obtain the consent of Congress before taking specified actions. For example, a provision in the War Powers Resolution of 1973 requires the president to consult with Congress whenever possible before committing U.S. military forces abroad in an undeclared war situation or, in any event, to report to Congress within forty-eight hours of the commitment. Congress can order the force withdrawn by **concurrent resolution**—a measure passed by one house of Congress with the agreement of the other, not requiring the president's signature. If both houses of Congress do not expressly approve of a military action within sixty days, and in special cases ninety days, the troops must be withdrawn. It is possible that this provision, in essence a legislative veto, will be declared unconstitutional if tested (Cooper 1985, 364–89).

Constitutional Restraints

Not only does the Constitution delegate certain powers to Congress, it also specifically restricts certain actions. The writ of **habeas corpus** (a court order requiring that police officials explain why a person has been arrested and jailed) cannot be suspended except in cases of rebellion or invasion. **Bills of attainder** (legislation punishing specific individuals rather than kinds of behavior) and **ex post facto laws** (legislation punishing people or changing penalties for actions committed before the law was passed) are also prohibited. Although interstate commerce can be regulated, it cannot be taxed. Other important restrictions on congressional action are detailed in constitutional amendments, including the Bill of Rights (see Chapters 2, 9, and Appendix A).

THE ORGANIZATION OF CONGRESS

The organization of Congress is a result of the Great Compromise. An upper house, the **Senate**, represents all states equally, and a lower house, the **House of Representatives**, has representatives allocated according to population (see Chapter 2).

The House of Representatives

Since membership in the House of Representatives is based on state population, delegations from states with large populations dominate the House. At first, as the Constitution guarantees each state at least one representative, House membership grew with the nation. Since 1912, after admission of the forty-eighth state, the membership of the House has been set at 435. To accommodate population growth and shifts, congressional districts are reapportioned following the census. Every ten years the Census Bureau determines the number of representatives each state will receive, and the state legislatures are given the task of **redistricting**, or redrawing single-member district lines. The majority party in a state legislature will usually redraw electoral district lines to favor its chances in the next election. For example, California gained two seats in the House after the 1980 census. While most of the population growth had been in Republican areas, Democrats, who controlled the California legislature and governorship, were able to draw boundaries so that their margin in the House actually increased by seven members (*Congressional Quarterly Weekly Report*, 21 January 1989, 140).

The Democrats were not so fortunate in 1990. A provision added to the Voting Rights Act in 1982, intended to secure more equitable representation for minorities, required that redistricting following the 1990 census work to give minorities a majority status in individual districts. As a consequence, minorities gained twenty-two seats in the House of Representatives in the 1992 election. Although most of the minorities elected were Democrats, Republicans also gained because new strongly Democratic minority districts diluted Democratic strength elsewhere. The practice of redistricting to achieve partisan or factional advantage is called **gerrymandering** (*USA Today*, 8 June 1992, A8–A9; *Washington Post National Weekly Edition*, 9–15 November 1992, 8). In June 1993, however, the Supreme Court ruled that states could be sued for gerrymandering on the basis of race, without regard to geographic and political boundaries unless there is a compelling reason to the contrary (*Shaw v. Reno*). The Court did not rule that the particular district in question needed to be redrawn, leaving that question to a federal district court (*Washington Post National Weekly Edition*, 5–11 July 1993, 32).

Members of the House of Representatives are popularly elected by the voters of their districts every two years. To be elected to the House, one must meet the qualifications stipulated in the Constitution: be at least twenty-five years old, a citizen of the United States for at least seven years, and a resident of the state represented.

With a membership of 435 individuals, all of whom face an election every other year, the House of Representatives needs to be highly organized to accomplish anything. Some sort of consensus must be arrived at among 435 lawmakers with widely divergent constituencies, and substantial amounts of legislation must be addressed in a short two-year period—the length of a House term as well as the length of one session of Congress. Any legislation not completed by the end of each Congress must be initiated all over again in both houses in the next Congress, or dropped.

The House is organized along party lines. At the beginning of each Congress, the majority party votes as a block to elect the **Speaker of the House**, who is second in succession to the presidency, behind only the vice-president, and whose position may be second only to the president in terms of power. The Speaker is the leader of the majority party as well as the presiding officer of the House. Although the powers of the Speaker are not as great as in past years, this leader still wields great personal influence in the chamber.

The Constitution specifically mentions only the Speaker when it refers to officers of the House of Representatives. Each party, however, has found it necessary to choose floor leaders, whips, and other leaders from among their number (see Table 6.3). The majority and minority party **floor leaders** are chiefly responsible for guiding their party's programs through the House. The majority and minority party **whips**, as the name implies, have the job of "whipping up" partisan support for their party's legislative initiatives (Sinclair 1983).

The Senate

The Senate is composed of two senators from each state, for a total of one hundred. Wyoming, with 450,000 citizens, is entitled to two senators, just as is California, with a population of around 30 million (*World Almanac, 1993*, 129). To become a senator, one must be at least thirty years of age, a citizen of the United States for at least nine years, and a resident of the state represented. Senators serve six-year terms, which are staggered so that one-third of the Senate comes up for election every two years. In this sense the Senate, unlike the House, is a continuous body.

As a continuous body, the Senate avoids the automatic reorganization and rule implementation the House must go through every two years. Moreover, the Senate has fewer members to organize. Whereas most House action is guided by strict rules of procedure, the Senate is characterized by a more relaxed atmosphere and **gentlemen's agreements**, or informal but binding understandings. For example, the Senate's Rules and Administration Committee does not decide how a bill will be debated on the floor the way the House's

voters of the Eighth District, mostly working-class Poles and Hispanics with strong loyalty to the Democratic party, kept reelecting him with large majorities, and his seniority steadily increased. In 1981 he finally reached his goal, the chair of Ways and Means. ´

During his first years as chair, Rostenkowski showed little interest in reforming the tax code, once called "a disgrace to the human race" by President Jimmy Carter because of its thousands of loopholes and benefits for every interest group with influence in Congress. When tax reform became a major issue in 1985, many of its proponents feared that this Chicago politician would never allow a real reform proposal to get through Ways and Means. At first he was reluctant, but once President Ronald Reagan and many members of Congress from both parties got on the tax reform bandwagon, Rostenkowski decided that reform was both good policy and good politics. Declaring "I want to be a patriot, too," the chair of Ways and Means used all his political skills to shape a reform bill acceptable to both parties and move it through Congress. Overcoming his preference for private politics, he appeared on national television urging citizens to "write Rosty" with their own tax reform ideas. The new tax code, which went into effect January 1, 1987, lowered tax rates more than Rostenkowski had wanted, but it also contained, at his insistence, provisions eliminating business tax loopholes. Many of the industries adversely affected had contributed generously to Ros-

tenkowski's past campaigns. Some Republicans accused President Reagan of deferring too much to Rostenkowski, but without his help the bill could not have passed.

Despite the frustrations of changing committee membership and a restless constituency, despite rumors of retirement and legal problems, Rostenkowski seems resolved to stay on in Congress and in Ways and Means in his role of ward healer turned statesman. Democratic President Bill Clinton will need his help to pass an economic program, and although scandal (see Controversy) might derail Rostenkowski, as it has some past House members, his determination remains strong.

Rostenkowski's career illustrates the strengths and weaknesses of the modified seniority system that determines power in Congress. The system creates strong leaders who have the independence to defy pressures from special interest groups— when they want. This independence, in turn, preserves Congress's role as a representative institution. But does it serve democracy to concentrate so much power in the hands of one member of Congress who is effectively unaccountable to anyone except a relatively small number of constituents?

Source: Politics in America 1987, 435–39; *National Journal*, 21 December 1985, 2898–2901; *Congressional Quarterly Weekly Report*, 6 July 1985, 1316–19; *Congressional Quarterly Weekly Report*, 5 June 1993, 1403–10.

---

est. Legislators often introduce bills in response to pressure from interest groups and to requests from the executive branch. The interest group provides Kimble with a summary of the merits of the bill and helps her staff write it. She then introduces the bill, and the Speaker of the House assigns it to the appropriate committee. The subject of legislation usually

determines its committee, but the Speaker's decision can be important when the subject concerns multiple committees.

House Committee and Subcommittee   The committee system usually serves to differentiate between the best and the worst bills. If a committee, and especially its chair, considers a

Figure 6.1   How a Bill Becomes Law

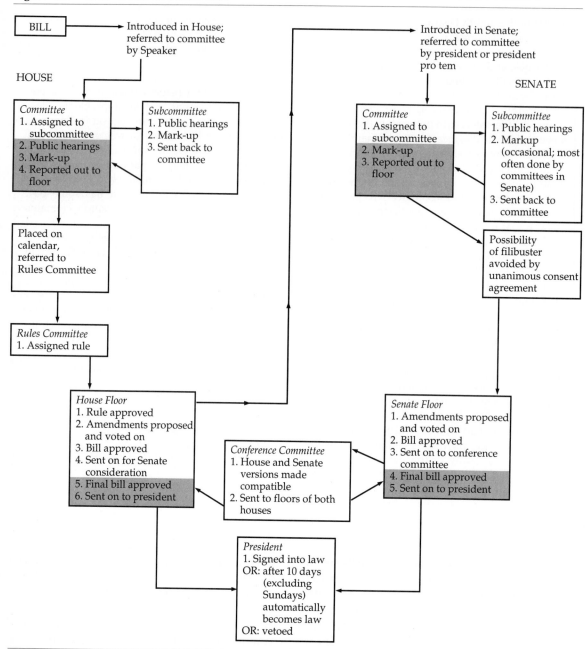

Note: This chart shows the path of Congresswoman Kimble's bill from introduction to presidential action. Please note that the route taken by this bill is much smoother than that of a "real" bill, which is subject to defeat at every step along the way. The possibility of parallel House and Senate introduction is also left out, as is an override of a presidential veto.

bill to have little merit, it is immediately **pi-geonholed**—set aside and forgotten. Kimble's bill, however, has considerable support within the committee, and, realizing this, the committee chair immediately assigns it to a subcommittee for further work.

Business is always piling up at the subcommittee level in Congress, so it is some time before the subcommittee chair has a chance to hold **public hearings** on the bill, which serve to inform both the public and the subcommittee members about its merits and problems. Experts concerned with the legislation are called in to give testimony; the interest group from which the idea for the bill originated also sends experts to testify. Other experts testify against the bill. The number of subcommittee members in attendance at each hearing varies greatly, depending on office work, constituent meetings, press interviews, and other committee schedules. As a result, members seem to come to and leave hearings at random, but they are actually trying to meet competing demands. After considering the testimony, the subcommittee members then discuss the merits of the bill among themselves in what is known as a **mark-up** session. Suggestions for changes in the wording may be made, and then the subcommittee sends the bill to the full committee.

More hearings are held on the bill at the committee level. Then the full committee meets in another mark-up session. Often a bill emerges from such a session in a form completely different from its original submission. The committee finds little wrong with the Kimble bill, however, and, after a final vote of approval, the bill is **reported out** of committee (sent on) to the floor of the House of Representatives.

House Rules Committee   Once a bill is reported to the floor, it is placed on one of five calendars: **union** (revenue and appropriations bills), **house** (public bills), **private** (private bills), **consent** (noncontroversial bills), and **dis-**charge (removes a bill from committee even if the committee has not passed it). Most bills then wait for consideration on the House floor, often for many weeks. Bills on the consent calendar, however, are normally sent directly to the floor, as well as bills that deserve special privilege, such as the annual budget or major appropriations bills.

Most controversial bills are first sent to the **House Rules Committee** before being reported to the House floor. A bill cannot continue to the floor until granted a **rule** (a statement regulating how a bill may be amended, debated, and considered) by the Rules Committee. An **open rule** permits unlimited amendments, or changes, to a bill on the floor; a **modified-closed rule** limits the number of amendments; a **closed rule** means that no amendments may be offered on a specific bill. An amendment to a House bill must be related to the subject of the bill. Some bills may avoid House rules if they are considered on the floor on special time-saving days when the rules are not enforced—under **suspension of the rules**.

The Kimble bill has developed little opposition in the House; it is sent to the floor under an open rule, as extensive debate is not expected.

House Floor   The rule given a bill must be approved by the entire House before action on the bill can continue. Normally, and especially under open rules, this approval is only a formality.

After the bill is read to the entire House, a period of time is set aside for amendments to be offered. Often, amendments are considered by a **committee of the whole** procedure, which allows the House to consider amendments with freer debate and fewer members in attendance than allowed under regular House rules. Actions taken in the committee of the whole must then be approved by the House. Strict time limits govern House debate, and after a few amendments are offered and rejected, the members of the House of Representatives vote to approve Kimble's bill and send it on to the Senate.

Often debate on the floor involves only a few members. Indeed, an average citizen visiting the Capitol to see Congress in action may be disillusioned by the small number of members present and listening to what is taking place. Absence does not mean, however, that members are not working, but that they may be working on legislation where it usually matters most—in their committees. They may also be meeting with constituents.

A system of bells warns members in their offices or other parts of the House office complexes to hurry from other duties so as not to miss the actual vote. Usually fifteen minutes is allowed for a member to get over to the floor to cast a vote once voting has begun. To avoid criticism from challengers, most members try to be present even for trivial votes like the fictional salamander bill that took members away from Kimble's subcommittee hearing. Concern for their voting record, rather than fondness for their mothers-in-law, probably explains why, in 1981, the House voted 306–66 to establish Mother-in-Law Day (Easterbrook 1984, 61).

Senate

A bill passed in the House follows a similar route through the Senate. Of course bills can also be introduced first in the Senate.

Introduction   The first step again is to find a sponsor who will introduce the legislation. Kimble asks the chair of the Senate committee that will consider the bill, Senator Peter Sanders, to sponsor it in the Senate. She knows that if Sanders consents to sponsor the bill, its passage will almost be guaranteed, since the sponsorship of the chair almost always assures the necessary support in the subcommittee and committee stages. Once again, the fate of the bill lies in the hands of a single person. Sanders feels that the bill may not be successful in

the Senate, so he tells Kimble that he will support it in his committee but does not want to sponsor a bill he is not sure will pass. Kimble then convinces a member of the subcommittee that will handle the bill, Senator George Wilkes, to introduce the bill into the Senate.

Senate Committee and Subcommittee   As Kimble expected, the bill is referred to Sanders's committee, and, as Sanders expected, opposition to certain provisions surfaces. Subcommittees are less important in the Senate than in the House owing to the absence of a Subcommittee Bill of Rights and to a lesser desire among senators to specialize in a narrow area of legislation. Hearings are usually held on a bill in a subcommittee, but mark-up is usually done only in the full committee (Smith and Deering 1984, 134). This procedure is followed with Senator Wilkes's bill. When the bill reaches full committee for mark-up, its opponents succeed in inserting several amendments that Kimble and Wilkes oppose, though the bill's major points remain.

Senate Floor   As in the House, bills are placed on calendars in the Senate, but the Senate does not have a committee that can effectively block bills and it has fewer rules than the House. When bills arrive on the floor for discussion, they can receive a **unanimous consent agreement**, a time-saving procedure used to adopt noncontroversial bills without submitting them to a vote, or they can be debated for days. Bills can also be set aside one week and picked up again the week after. In addition, they may be subject to unlimited debate, or **filibuster**. Usually a filibuster occurs when a group of individuals not large enough to defeat a piece of legislation tries to hold up action—sometimes for weeks—to gain concessions on a bill and possibly defeat it or force its withdrawal. Members have been known to read from the Bible, telephone directories, and cookbooks. In 1993, the Republican minority in the Senate effectively used the filibuster to block passage of a $30 billion public works jobs bill backed by President Clinton and the Democratic majority. A filibuster can be ended by the vote of **cloture**, which limits further debate, but cloture requires the approval of sixty senators, a majority that, in a matter of some controversy, can be hard to get. In the case of the jobs bill, cloture could not be obtained because forty-three Republicans were firmly united against the bill. To attempt a cloture vote, sixteen senators must first sign a petition requesting such a vote. Even if sixty votes are secured, each senator is still allocated one additional hour to continue to debate and clarify his or her position. There have been several attempts to reform filibustering over the years (Vogler 1980, 27–29). To avoid paralyzing the government for extended periods, filibusters are not allowed to block the annual budget resolution.

Senator Wilkes's bill arrives on the floor by a unanimous consent agreement, which precludes a filibuster. Amendments are proposed, including one that would return the bill to its original form. The Senate allows any amendment to be attached to a bill—thus a popular bill on agriculture may face an attempt to attach a controversial amendment on abortion. Such an amendment is called a **rider** because it would find passage difficult on its own. For Wilkes's bill, however, each floor amendment fails to pass. It is generally much easier to pass an amendment in a committee or subcommittee than on the floor, as most members of Congress abide by the decisions of the committee members who have had an extended chance to study the bill and are generally knowledgeable in areas covered by their committee. Wilkes had hoped, however, that the Senate's being less likely to accept committee work intact than the House might have enabled him to get his bill passed closer to its original form.

Senator Wilkes's bill is passed by the Senate after the defeat of floor amendments. The Sen-

ate version of the bill, because of the changes made by the committee, is different from its House counterpart and, as such, is not yet ready to leave Congress. Both bills are submitted to a conference committee, which is set up expressly to resolve differences between the House and Senate versions of the bill.

Conference Committee

The conference committee is composed of several members of both houses, most of whom have worked on the bill. Senior members of the standing committees that originally considered the bill, of both the majority and minority parties, and those with special interests in the bill are often included. Members of conference committees are officially appointed by the presiding officers of each house, but in actuality most are chosen by the chairs of the standing committees involved. If no compromise is reached, the bill dies. After a good deal of bargaining, some House language and some Senate language are accepted in the Kimble-Wilkes bill. The conference committee then reports this compromise bill back to the floor of each chamber. In both, the compromise bill is approved after short discussion. The Speaker of the House signs the bill, as does the president, or president pro tem, of the Senate. Finally the bill is sent to the desk of the president of the United States for consideration.

Presidential Action

Most bills that reach the desk of the president become law. He signs them into law or, if he takes no action for ten days, excluding Sundays, while Congress is still in session, the bills automatically become law. Sometimes, though, the president **vetoes** (rejects) a bill and sends it back to Congress with his objections. A presidential veto kills a bill unless a two-thirds majority in each chamber votes in favor of the bill and **overrides** the president's veto, making the bill law in spite of the president's opposition. Sometimes Congress modifies a vetoed bill in order to meet the president's objections.

If, however, by the tenth day, excluding Sundays, Congress has adjourned, the president's decision to take no action constitutes a **pocket veto**. Because Congress is not in session, there is no chance for an override, and the bill, in effect, dies. Presidents sometimes prefer not to take action on a piece of legislation because it is not in their political interest to invite any more publicity than absolutely necessary. President George Bush used vetoes effectively; of forty vetoes, only one—a bill to regulate cable television rates—was overridden (*Congressional Quarterly Weekly Report*, 19 December 1992, 3854–70, 3925–26).

The compromise Kimble-Wilkes bill is promptly signed into law by the president. Its road through Congress uncharacteristically avoided many of the problems that could have derailed it: committee refusal to hold hearings, a committee mark-up that changed the bill drastically, committee refusal to report the bill to either full chamber, House Rules Committee delay or refusal to grant a rule, intense opposition, leadership opposition in the House or Senate (particularly from the majority party, usually reflected in the attitudes of the Speaker of the House and the Senate majority leader), a filibuster in the Senate, failure of a conference committee to reach a compromise, or a presidential veto. Many individuals can kill a bill, and that explains why so few pass and why even successful ones can take so long. Relatively few members of Congress were deeply involved in considering the Kimble-Wilkes bill, however. The specialization enforced by the committee system limits participation and thus lends some efficiency to an otherwise cumbersome process. At the same time, it ensures that a few members will make the key decisions on any given issue, with no guarantee that what comes out reflects what most members of Congress want (Redman 1973; Birnbaum and Murray 1988).

REFORMING CONGRESS

Since the first session of Congress, members have sought ways to reform the institution. Usually these reforms have been advanced by liberals and populists, who are prone to see flaws and weaknesses in institutions, and are opposed by conservatives. The net effect has clearly been to make Congress a more democratic institution than it was in the past, but also to make it more complex and unwieldy. A short history of congressional reform illustrates both points (Rieselbach 1986).

In the early nineteenth century, Congress did away with numerous special committees by consolidating them into permanent standing committees. In the Senate, the chairs of these committees became the most powerful members because they could control the fate of legislation put before their committees.

In the House of Representatives, the Speaker gradually obtained new powers until, by the early 1900s, he was nearly a dictator. The Speaker had the right to appoint members to all standing committees and to chair the Rules Committee, which regulates the flow of legislation to the floor. On the House floor, he had the power to recognize members, a power used to control who could speak on any issue.

The Speaker at that time, Joseph Cannon of Illinois, was a conservative Republican, so liberal programs had little chance in the House. In 1910 liberal and populist members of both parties staged a successful revolution against Cannon. Subsequently the Speaker was stripped of many powers; he could no longer appoint members to standing committees, and he lost his position on the Rules Committee and much of his discretion in recognizing members to speak. The revolt of 1910 shifted many of the Speaker's powers to the committee chairs and members of the Rules Committee (see *Guide to Congress* 1982, 7–120).

By the 1950s liberals were unhappy with the system their predecessors had created. Many committee chairs, who held most of the power

list Caucus are left populists, far more liberal socially than their nineteenth-century counterparts. It should be remembered, nevertheless, that populism has been a perspective whose adherents in the general population have come from working-class backgrounds and have had lower levels of education than the population generally. As Americans become more highly educated and the number of jobs in agriculture and traditional industries decline, the dominant populist ideology in both the electorate and its representatives may well accord with the viewpoints of the Populist Caucus, which calls for progressive taxation, easy credit policies, and low interest rates that would reduce the political influence of big business and its control of energy prices (Congressional Populist Caucus 1987). However, right populists are likely to continue to claim the populist mantle and maintain pockets of strength in Congress.

The new Congress elected in 1992 was younger and more diverse than any in recent history, including an increased number of women, blacks, Hispanics, and Asians. In addition, for the first time the majority of House members had not served in the military. Thirty-one of the new House members had never been elected to a public office. What impact the changing profile of legislators will have on the future of populist politics in the House remains to be seen (*USA Today*, 5 November 1992, A15).

Marxist

Marxists look at Congress in the same negative light in which they view other American political institutions. Like the other two branches, it is seen as an instrument for maintaining elite dominance. Marxists argue that the check-and-balance system is a very effective way to prevent the popular will from being carried out and that Congress plays an important role in this process. The Marxist indictment of Congress has several parts. First, Marxists point out that while Congress may be elected, the institution is hardly representative of the American people. Many senators and representatives may have been born into the middle class (few rise from the lower), but by the time they are elected they are almost always from the top 10–15 percent of the occupational and income brackets. In the 103d Congress (1993–94), 181 of 435 representatives (42 percent) and 58 of 100 senators were lawyers. One hundred thirty-one representatives (30 percent) and 27 senators were businesspeople or bankers. Not a single member of either house was a blue-collar worker, though two had been labor officials (*Congressional Quarterly Weekly Special Report*, 16 January 1993, 13, 160–68; see also Domhoff 1983, 126–28).

Marxists concede that many members of Congress think they serve the ordinary people of the country but argue that the members' judgment as to what policies will serve the people are bound to be biased by their upper-class social position. Thus Republicans and conservative Democrats— the conservative coalition—have almost always been the majority in Congress since the 1930s, even though most Americans hold liberal or populist views on economic issues. According to Marxist scholars, liberals have been able to pass modest reforms like civil rights or Medicare legislation only when they have gained the support of moderate conservatives (Domhoff 1983, 143–46).

Even if a member of Congress wanted to challenge the capitalist elite, he or she could not persist for long. For one thing, campaign money is raised privately, primarily from business PACs and wealthy individuals unlikely to support true —that is, socialist—reform of the system. Once in Congress, a member has limited independent sources of information. Often he or she relies on elite, business-funded policy analysis groups (often called think tanks) for ideas and information. Examples of such groups include the Council on Foreign Relations and the Trilateral Commission (on foreign policy), and the Committee for Economic Development and the Conference Board (on domestic policy). Studies produced by such groups invariably reflect a basic support for the corporate capitalist system, often combined with moderate reform proposals—the kind of advice Congress wants and usually follows (Domhoff 1983, 84–98).

If, as Marxists claim, Congress is always elite-dominated, why do we see such intense conflict on Capitol Hill among conservatives, liberals, lib-

PROFILE

Hank Brown: A Libertarian in Congress

Hank Brown (Courtesy Senator Hank Brown)

Senator Hank Brown from Colorado, formerly a member of the House of Representatives, is a good example of a person holding a libertarian perspective in Congress. Although he usually sides with conservatives on issues involving government efficiency and fiscal responsibility, his civil rights and civil liberties record, as well as his record in the area of defense and foreign affairs, sets him apart from his conservative Republican colleagues.

The *Almanac of American Politics* characterized Brown's former House district as Republican "by heritage and usually by inclination," adding, "Brown's record in the Congress is partisan but not lockstep. Conservative generally, he is more moderate on some culture issues (abortion, wilderness), on foreign policy, and even on economics."

In May 1985 Brown voted with a majority of Democrats to sanction the Justice Department for failing to enforce a law offering an unsuccessful bidder to a federal contract the right to protest discrimination. He also voted with the Democrats to uphold a prohibition against tampering with affirmative action plans once they had been set in motion. In March 1987 he opposed an amendment offered by William Dannemeyer of California, a

ertarians, and populists over such a broad range of issues? According to Marxists, such conflicts are real, but of little relevance to the working masses, for they concern the division of wealth and power within the ruling class. At the state and local level, capitalist elites can be cohesive and cooperative and politics can be very dull (see Chapter 3). At the national level, cohesion is not possible since the business community nationwide contains too many diverse interests. Some companies want protection from foreign competition; others, with factories abroad, want free trade. Insurance companies want stricter product safety standards to minimize claims, while manufacturers resist such regulations. Low-wage industries oppose minimum wage laws, while their higher paying counterparts favor such laws as a means of limiting competition. All these special interests bring their claims to Congress, which balances and adjusts them through the legislative process. The majority of Americans are affected, positively or negatively, by the clash of special interests, but their interests are rarely represented.

Currently Marxists have no hope that their views will ever be advanced through the legislative process. Due to the obstacles placed in the way of minor party candidates (see Chapter 4), only a few democratic socialists have ever been elected to Congress, one of whom, Bernard Sanders from Vermont, is currently serving. Since he is

Feminists believe that once women are fairly represented in legislatures, issues of concern to women (such as comparable worth, more and better day care, and strengthened parental leave legislation) will receive a priority they have not been given in legislatures dominated largely by older white males. The failure of the Equal Rights Amendment to be passed by thirty-eight state legislatures is an often-cited example of how legislative imbalance hurts women's political agenda. More than three-quarters of all women legislators supported the ERA, compared to less than half of their male counterparts (Mansbridge 1986, 149–64). In another example, feminists argue that the presence of at least one female senator during the Clarence Thomas hearings (see Controversy in Chapter 8) in 1991 would have changed the treatment of Anita Hill and the tone of the questioning on both sides of the aisle ("Refusing to Be Silenced" 1992; see also Hill 1992, 32–33). More recently, charges against Senator Bob Packwood of Oregon have pointed to a pattern of sexual harassment on Capitol Hill itself (Sharpe 1992, 28–31; *Washington Post National Weekly Edition*, 13–20 December 1992, 23). Because Congress has exempted itself from the very civil rights statutes regarding sexual harassment it has passed (Sharpe 1992, 28–31), feminists argue that until women's representation in Congress reflects their percentage in the population, the internal checks on member behavior set up by each house will not be adequate to protect the rights of women employees.

In sum, from a feminist perspective, female membership in Congress, although increased by the class of 1992, remains both less numerous and less powerful than male membership. No woman chairs a major authorization or appropriation committee in either the House or the Senate. The position of women in Congress is exemplified by Patricia Schroeder of Colorado (see Profile in this chapter). Although first elected in 1972, she does not have the power that one would expect of such a senior member. Perhaps she has taken on so many different women's issues that she has not had time to become an insider. In any case, the relative lack of power of women in Congress has been a disappointment to feminists ever since the Twentieth Amendment gave women the right to vote. Early feminists assumed that enfranchisement would lead to immediate significant gains in political power. Feminists now realize that until the status of women changes in society as a whole, Congress will fall short of what most feminists envision it as some day becoming: an institution that fairly represents all Americans.

DOES CONGRESS WORK?

To the casual observer, Congress often seems like a huge truck spinning its wheels in the mud, getting absolutely nowhere. The degree of debate, compromise, and emphasis on procedure that makes Congress democratic also makes it somewhat inefficient in law-making. This very inefficiency, however, is perhaps what the framers intended in a government of checks and balances. The structure of Congress certainly ensures that many views are considered and that compromises are reached.

Still, persisting incumbency advantage in the face of the term-limitation movement forces some hard questions about the nature of representation in a democracy and especially in the House of Representatives, which the framers intended to be the more responsive to the people. We are sharply divided on the issue of how to assure representativeness in Congress. One of us thinks that the high number of incumbents reelected indicates that members are responsive to the people and interests the people care about. The two other authors believe that term limits may be the only rein on a Congress that has distanced itself from the people and become too beholden to special interests. If members of Congress, however, emphasize their communicator and ombudsman roles at the expense of their legislator role, then the electorate has the responsibility either to approve that emphasis by reelecting incumbents or to reject that emphasis by electing a challenger.

Yet, Congress is more responsive to well-organized interest groups than are the executive and judicial branches of government, and this responsiveness can be a problem given inequalities among groups (see Chapter 5). One constructive way to decrease the power of interest groups is to strengthen the party system in Congress instead of diffusing so much power among committees and subcommittees.

In the end, the very complexity of the legislative branch provides ways for the major perspectives to be heard by members of Congress and to be reflected in policy. Members vote on many issues, but they have an incentive to settle controversial issues in committee lest a floor fight expose votes that lose rather than win the support of groups. In essence, Congress works better than first glance might suggest, though certainly less well than it could.

SUMMARY AND REVIEW

This chapter examines the duties and structure of Congress, the supreme legislative body of the United States. Members of Congress perform a vast number of difficult duties every day to meet three different sets of expectations: legislating for, communicating with, and serving as ombudsmen for their constituents. Most of the important legislative work is handled at the committee level. Unable to be experts in all areas, most legislators try to obtain seats on committees that are well suited to the interests of their districts. When taken to an extreme and involving federal expenditures, promotion of district interests is known as "pork-barreling." It is essential for a member of Congress to keep open communications with those he or she represents; accordingly, huge volumes of mail flow in and out of Congress, legislators make frequent visits to their districts for all types of events, and many members take time out of their busy schedules to talk with visiting groups of constituents. Finally, members of Congress act as ombudsmen between constituents and the federal government, making inquiries of federal agencies on behalf of constituents or sponsoring private

bills. All these activities are essential to a member's reelection prospects—though House members in particular are almost always returned to office—and take huge amounts of time. The size and importance of congressional staffs have increased dramatically in the last few decades.

Specific congressional powers as laid out in Article I, Section 8, of the Constitution include the power to tax and appropriate money among authorized uses, regulate commerce and money, establish courts, and declare war. The Elastic Clause empowers Congress to make all laws that are "necessary and proper" for executing the powers of the government; the clause has been interpreted by the Supreme Court to mean that Congress can act in a new area in order to carry out one of its original functions in the government. Other powers of Congress include investigation, proposal of amendments, congressional housekeeping, and Senate appointment approval and treaty approval.

The membership of the House of Representatives is set at 435, and members are popularly elected every two years. The House is organized along party lines, and the House majority party elects the Speaker of the House, a powerful leader of the majority party as well as the presiding officer of the House. Each party also has floor leaders, whips, and other leaders to help guide party programs through the House.

The Senate is composed of two senators, serving staggered six-year terms, from each state regardless of population. The president of the Senate is the vice-president of the United States; in his absence, the president pro tempore serves as the presiding officer. The Senate also has majority and minority party floor leaders, whips, and other leaders.

Both houses have standing committees to deal with specific areas of legislation and to work out the details of a bill before bringing it up for general debate in the full chamber. Many of the bills that come before a committee are initially passed on to an appropriate subcommittee. Committee appointments are decided on the basis of seniority and along party lines; the ratio of Democrats and Republicans on each committee is roughly equivalent to the ratio for the entire body. Committees usually are chaired by the member of the majority party with the longest service on the committee. A committee chair is a powerful position, although much power has been diffused to subcommittees in recent years, especially in the House. Subcommittee chairs also go to senior or favored members of the majority party.

Relatively few bills are passed in any given session of Congress, for the path they must take to become law is long and full of obstacles. Many bills are introduced by members of Congress at the suggestion of interest groups or the executive branch. Once introduced in the House of Representatives, for example, new bills are assigned to the appropriate committee, whose chair then sends the bill to a subcommittee for further work. The subcom-

mittee holds hearings on the bill to inform the public and the subcommittee members of the merits and problems of the bill. After all changes are agreed upon in a mark-up session, the subcommittee sends the bill back to the full committee, where the bill is again the subject of public hearings and marked up. A bill could emerge from mark-up in essentially the same form as when it was introduced, or it might be completely transformed. After final committee approval, the bill is placed on a floor calendar. In order to be discussed on the floor, major bills are assigned a rule that spells out rules for debate and conditions for amendments. Eventually, amendments may be offered and debate heard before the bill comes to a final vote.

At the same time—or before or after the House is acting—a similar bill must wind its way through the Senate. Senate business is handled quite differently from that of the House: there are far fewer rules and some unique practices like the filibuster.

After both houses have passed bills, a conference committee reconciles the differences between the House and Senate versions. The compromise bill is then sent back to both chambers for final approval. If it passes, it goes to the president; who can sign it into law or veto it. A veto override requires the approval of two-thirds of both houses.

Congressional reforms have usually been spearheaded by liberals. In the early twentieth century, power was taken from the Speaker and given to committee chairs. In recent decades, committee chairs have lost power to subcommittee chairs and to the House Democratic Caucus. Reform has made Congress more democratic, but also slower in passing legislation. The Senate has undertaken less reform than the House. More recently, additional reforms have been suggested to make both houses of Congress more democratic and more efficient.

IMPORTANT TERMS

appropriation
bill of attainder
censure
closed rule
cloture
committee chair
committee of the whole
communicator
concurrent resolution
conference committee
consent calendar
conservative coalition
declaration of war
delegate theory of representation
discharge calendar
divided government
Elastic Clause
ex post facto law
extra-constitutional power
filibuster
first-term members
floor leader
franking privilege
gentlemen's agreement
gerrymandering
gridlock
house calendar
House Democratic Caucus
House of Representatives
House Rules Committee
impeachment
investigation
joint committee
joint resolution
legislative power
legislative veto
legislator
logrolling
mark-up
modified-closed rule

ombudsman
open rule
override
partisan committee
party-unity voting
pigeonhole
pocket veto
"pork-barreling"
power of the purse
president of the Senate
president pro tempore
private bill
private calendar
public hearing
ranking minority member
redistricting
report out
rider
roll call vote
rule
safe district
secret ballot
select committee
Senate
senatorial courtesy
seniority
Speaker of the House
standing committee
subcommittee
Subcommittee Bill of Rights
suspension of the rules
taxation
treaty
trustee theory of representation
unanimous consent agreement
union calendar
veto
whip
writ of habeas corpus

7

THE PRESIDENCY

On November 3, 1992, Bill Clinton was elected president of the United States. He carried thirty-two of fifty states for an electoral vote margin of 370 to 168 over incumbent George Bush. At the same time, Clinton's Democratic party sustained small losses in the House and in the state legislatures. Still, for the first time since 1980, the United States has the same party controlling the White House and both houses of Congress. **Divided government** *was at an end. Nevertheless, the president has experienced difficulty getting some of his programs passed, while others have failed.*

What has accounted for the failure of the most powerful man in the world to get what he wanted? The answer may lie partially in weaknesses and failures peculiar to the Clinton administration, but it is also due to the nature of the office itself. If the presidency is the most powerful office in the world, the constraints placed upon it by the Constitution and the other institutions of government also make it the most difficult. (For a list of those who have held this powerful, albeit trying, office, see Appendix C.)

POWERS AND CONSTRAINTS

According to Article II, Section 1, of the Constitution, "The executive Power shall be vested in a **President**." When the framers outlined the important, yet limited powers of the president in 1787, they did not realize how much the office would grow. Since 1789 the president has assumed extra-constitutional roles that rival in importance those originally delegated.

Presidential Roles

An examination of the six major presidential roles gives an idea of the magnitude of the job.

Head of State   As **head of state**, the president is the chief representative of the United States. Although this role is mostly ceremo-

CONTROVERSY

The Case of the Missing Missiles

John F. Kennedy (Library of Congress)

Nikita Khrushchev (AP/Wide World Photos)

It was October 1962, and President John Kennedy was angry. First, the Soviet Union, in violation of a pledge by its leader, Nikita Khrushchev, had se- cretly delivered forty-five missiles that could be equipped with nuclear warheads to Cuba. Then, confronted with indisputable evidence from U-2

---

nial, it can be important in both foreign and domestic affairs. Like the queen of England, the president can use his position as head of state to improve relations with other countries, as when he plays host to visiting heads of state at the White House or attends ceremonies in other countries. He can also use the position to cement relations with important domestic interest groups, as when he speaks before meetings of civic, religious, labor, business, or veterans' organizations.

Head of Government   As **head of government**, the president has the **executive power**, the responsibility to enforce the laws of the land. Of course only the guidelines for execut-

ing policy can be set at the White House; for actual implementation, the president depends on the federal **bureaucracy**—the civil servants and political appointees who work mostly within the executive branch.

The president has the authority to appoint approximately 650 people to high-level positions within the executive branch, including the White House staff, the secretaries of the cabinet departments, and top officials in the departments and independent agencies (Edwards III and Wayne 1985, 368). These presidential appointees can, in turn, fill several thousand mid-level jobs. Through his control over the jobs of top officials, the president can assure, to some extent, that his policies will be

spy plane photographs, the Soviets claimed that the presence of their missiles in Cuba was justified by the presence of fifteen American missiles in Turkey, a U.S. ally just south of the Soviet Union, missiles Kennedy had ordered to be withdrawn several months before because they were obsolete. Faced with such a challenge, Kennedy felt that he had little choice but to order a U.S. naval quarantine of Cuba to prevent the installation of more missiles and to begin preparations for a possible air strike against those already there.

What Kennedy did not know at first was that the Soviets had a point. He had indeed ordered the missiles withdrawn from Turkey—but the order had not been carried out. State Department bureaucrats, concerned that withdrawing the weapons might be interpreted as a weakening of U.S. commitment to Turkey, asked the army, which controlled the missiles, to delay carrying out the president's order. When Kennedy found that the missiles were still there, providing the Soviets with a pretext for their actions in Cuba, he was understandably furious. His advisers counseled him not to withdraw the missiles now, even though they were militarily worthless, as such action would appear to reward the Soviets for putting the missiles in Cuba.

With war looking more and more likely, the Soviets finally made two proposals. The first promised to withdraw the missiles from Cuba in return for a U.S. pledge not to invade Cuba, a move the Kennedy administration was not planning anyway. The second, received later, called for a withdrawal of the missiles from both Cuba and Turkey. Kennedy accepted the first proposal publicly, but privately he assured the Soviets that the U.S. missiles would be removed from Turkey. The Soviets agreed, and the crisis was resolved. The bureaucracy had not caused the crisis, but it had seriously complicated the effort to resolve it. As Kennedy observed at the time, no matter how many orders a president issues or how hard he tries to monitor his subordinates, "There is always some S.O.B. who doesn't get the word."

Recent analysis has concluded that Khrushchev's reason for sending the missiles to Cuba was to improve the Soviet position in the world power balance. Regardless of the exact motives, the crisis illustrates the awesome responsibilities facing world leaders in the nuclear age.

Source: Allison 1971, 226–30; Cline 1989, 190–96.

---

implemented. However, the 3.1 million federal civilian employees covered by the merit-based civil service system (see Chapter 10) do not owe their jobs to the president, nor do most of the 1.6 million military personnel, though the president, as commander in chief, may remove commanders at will. Most civil service appointments and military positions are independent of the president, and the people who fill them feel less compelled to follow a president's wishes than do political appointees. Their independence can be an important limitation on presidential power and can have serious consequences, as President John Kennedy learned during the Cuban missile crisis (see Controversy).

Unlike Britain's ceremonial queen, the president as head of government has the power to negotiate agreements with foreign governments. He may do this through either a **treaty** or an **executive agreement**. The difference between the two is that treaties require the approval of two-thirds of the Senate. Executive agreements, on the other hand, may be kept secret when necessary (during wartime, for example) and are negotiated and binding by the power and authority vested in the president. Some executive agreements can be implemented without congressional approval, while others require funding, and votes on funding must achieve a majority in both houses. Executive agreements are now more common than treaties, even for fairly important matters, and the president sometimes uses them to circumvent the Senate's treaty powers (Crabb Jr. and Holt 1992, 15–16).

Commander in Chief   Article II, Section 2, of the Constitution makes the president "**Commander in Chief** of the Army and Navy of the United States." American presidents have assumed leadership in every war the United States has conducted. Although the Constitution grants to Congress the power to declare war, presidents have used their power as commander in chief to involve the nation in a large number of undeclared military actions. The Korean and Vietnam conflicts are the best-known examples. The president also has the authority to order military maneuvers or "shows of force" to assist diplomatic efforts. Several times, most recently in the early 1970s, Congress believed that the president had overstepped the legal bounds of his authority and it passed legislation to curb his discretion in this area.

Legislative Leader   The power to legislate belongs to Congress, but the president, whose signature makes a bill a law, is the single most important person in the legislative process—the **legislative leader**. Early presidents rarely initiated legislation, but today the president is expected to have a plan for the country that requires changes in the law. Since the 1940s presidents have employed more and more as-

sistants to lobby Congress and have involved themselves more and more in the details of lobbying (Wayne 1978).

When the president takes a position on a legislative issue, he usually wins. Since 1961, only two presidents, Reagan and Bush, were unable to have their way on more than 50 percent of the votes in Congress on which they took a stand each year (Edwards III 1989, 26–33; *Congressional Quarterly Weekly Report*, 19 December 1992, 3842). Reagan's success rate dropped to 43.5 percent in 1987 and rebounded only slightly to 47.4 in 1988, largely because both the House and Senate were controlled by the Democrats for the first time since he took office (*Congressional Quarterly Weekly Report*, 16 January 1988, 91–100; *Congressional Quarterly Weekly Report*, 19 November 1988, 3323–33). President Bush never had a majority in either the House or Senate, and his success rate dropped below 50 percent in 1990 and 1992, both highly charged partisan election years. In 1992, Bush's success rate dropped to a record low of 43 percent as the Democrats accused him of misguided priorities and sought to seize control of the national agenda, with the goal of defeating him in the presidential election (*Congressional Quarterly Weekly Report*, 19 December 1992, 3841–43). Dwight Eisenhower and Richard Nixon had similar difficulties toward the end of their terms, though they still won a majority of votes each year.

The presidential record of success is deceptive, however. Presidents frequently compro-

Tom Curtis. Courtesy artist.

mise with congressional opponents and end up supporting legislation that is far from what they originally wanted. Just as frequently, presidential proposals die in committee and never come to a vote, or they are not even introduced in Congress because the president recognizes that they will not pass. Moreover, many presidential "successes" are minor, non-controversial bills that artificially elevate the success rate while major proposals are defeated (Edwards III 1989, 16–25). In the end, Congress is an effective check upon the president, just as the framers intended.

While all presidents have trouble with Congress, some have more trouble than others. Presidents usually do better when their party has a majority in Congress and when they have strong public support (Edwards III 1989, 98, 114–25). Republican presidents have had more difficulty than Democrats since World War II, presumably because they have usually faced Democratic-controlled Congresses.

While party may be more important than personality, the president's style and legislative skills, along with those of his aides, can also affect his ability to influence Congress.

During his campaign for president Jimmy Carter criticized members of Congress as part of the "Washington establishment." In office, he offended Democratic congressional leaders by failing to extend customary courtesies like phone calls and patronage appointments or support for bills they favored. Despite his poor record at managing Congress, Carter got many of his proposals through, but often they were substantially amended (Glad 1980, 423–25). Reagan and his staff generally got better marks for skill in handling Congress (Buchanan 1987, 80–86), but his overall success rate was lower (Jones 1988, 53), suggesting that legislative skill cannot fully compensate for a hostile congressional majority.

If all else fails, the president has the power to **veto** legislation by returning the bill to Congress unsigned and with the reasons for his objections. Gerald Ford made frequent use of his veto power. Presidential vetoes require a two-thirds majority in both houses of Congress to be overridden. But although they rarely are, there is less to the presidential veto power than meets the eye. The problem from the president's point of view is that he must

DON'T WORRY, FOLKS! I'LL WORK WELL WITH THESE GUYS...

CONGRESS

Jeff MacNelly. Reprinted by permission: Tribune Media Services.

sign or veto an entire bill; he cannot reject sections he opposes. Knowing this, Congress often puts provisions the president disapproves of into bills he is likely to sign. Faced with such a bill, the president often signs it into law rather than jeopardize many programs he favors for the sake of a few he wants to eliminate. Each recent president has advocated strengthening the veto power by adding an **item veto**, which would allow him to reject some parts of a bill and accept others. Although forty-three states have given governors an item veto, permitting the president to use this device could possibly require a constitutional amendment. Since it would enhance the president's power over legislation at the expense of Congress, it has not gathered much support in Congress.

Party Leader   The president is considered the national leader of his party. Presidents are expected to support the election bids of party members at congressional and state levels, although, as noted in Chapter 4, the coattail effect of a president's victory on other races seems to be declining. As **party leader**, the president has a good deal of control over the national party committee. This control and the prestige of his office give him a major advantage in running for renomination. Only two presidents in recent times—Harry Truman and Lyndon Johnson—chose not to seek renomination, and both pulled out of the race early after a disappointing showing in the New Hampshire primary. The president, through his control over the national committee, also has a major voice in writing the party platform.

Presidential control does not extend to the state and local parties. Apart from the ability to grant or withhold some financial assistance, neither the president nor the national party committee has much leverage over state and local party organizations. Nominations for Congress are usually in the hands of primary voters and not subject to presidential control either. This diffusion of power makes it difficult for the president to function as national party leader. Since members of Congress from the president's party owe him little, they will not automatically support his policies if they are not convinced that it is in their interest to do so, from either a personal or a public policy standpoint.

National Leader   The president is the **national leader**. As such, he is able to set the national agenda and is expected to lead in times of crisis. While this function is not specifically mentioned in the Constitution, it best explains the growth of presidential power.

"They Can't Say I'm Not Doing Anything"
Herblock. From *Herblock on All Fronts* (New American Library, 1980).

Franklin Roosevelt was an effective national leader because he produced programs, like social security, that alleviated the effects of the Great Depression. Opponents criticized his New Deal programs but offered no alternatives. His leadership continued during World War II, and when he died in 1945 he was at the beginning of an unprecedented fourth term as president. The Republican-initiated Twenty-second Amendment now limits presidents to two four-year terms.

Ronald Reagan had admired Roosevelt in the 1930s, but by 1960 was a Republican. Although President Reagan (1981–89) had reservations about New Deal programs, he recognized that Republican talk of a balanced budget was no match for Democratic promises of program benefits. Reagan redefined the debate by supporting a tax cut for all, thus forcing the Democrats into the uncomfortable position of having to say no or maybe. Again, the president was acting as the national leader.

Opponents of Roosevelt and Reagan had an impact, but these presidents set the framework for a national agenda and defined the nature of the opposition. No one but the president in the American political system has such power or influence (see Profile of Lyndon Johnson).

The president is also expected to be a moral leader for the nation. President Reagan was particularly skilled at articulating the ideals of patriotism, faith, and family, treasured by many Americans, despite strains in his own family relationships (Muir Jr. 1992). The notion that the president must stand for important national and moral values explains, in part, the increasing focus on the personal lives of presidential candidates during the campaign. During the 1992 campaign, for example, Bill Clinton was damaged by accusations of adultery and draft evasion, but he addressed the charges to the satisfaction of enough voters—ultimately more concerned about the economy than about personal qualities—to win.

Some Restraints

Presidential power is not static and unchanging, and in a government with separate institutions sharing powers, constitutional conflict is inevitable. At some periods the **imperial presidency**, a contemporary term describing the misuse or abuse of presidential powers, seemed to usurp the powers of Congress and threaten the foundation of American democracy (Schlesinger Jr. 1973). At other times congressional and constitutional restraints seemed to deprive the president of his "power to lead" (Burns 1984). Different people may see both trends at the same time. The difficulties in defining the limits of presidential power are evident in the struggles over three important presidential powers: the war powers, the power to conduct covert operations to advance foreign policy, and the power over spending.

The War Powers   The first draft of the Constitution granted Congress the power to "make" war. Some delegates to the Constitutional Convention pointed out that response to a surprise attack would have to wait until Congress could be called into session. So "make" was changed to "declare," allowing the president the right to repel attacks on the United States or its citizens abroad, while reserving to Congress the right to initiate offensive military operations (Crabb Jr. and Holt 1992, 49–51). The **war powers** are thus divided between the executive and legislative branches.

The first military action conducted without a formal declaration of war was ordered by George Washington, who sent troops to the frontier to fight hostile Indians. His successor, John Adams, used the navy to attack French ships in retaliation for attacks on American ships, and the next president, Thomas Jefferson, fought an undeclared war against the Barbary pirates of North Africa, who had also attacked American shipping. These early presidents believed that these limited military ac-

Lyndon Johnson and the Civil Rights Revolution: The Use of Presidential Powers

Lyndon Johnson (Library of Congress)

"We have talked long enough in this country about equal rights. We have talked for one hundred years or more. It is time now to write the next chapter—and to write it in the books of law."

The idea was not new. It had been proposed many times in the previous ten years—by civil rights leaders, liberal politicians, and even by the last president. What was new was the accent. This was the voice of a southern president, Lyndon Baines Johnson, speaking to Congress and the nation at a time of tragedy—November 27, 1963, just five days after an assassin's bullet had claimed the life of President John Kennedy and elevated Johnson to the presidency. In the next two years Johnson presided over the most sweeping civil rights legislation in the nation's history. While he certainly was not solely responsible for the nation's civil rights revolution, his actions show how presidential leadership can resolve an issue dividing the country.

Dwight Eisenhower, who was president when the civil rights movement began in the 1950s, enforced federal court orders requiring school integration but otherwise showed little enthusiasm for the movement. Without his active support, two civil rights bills were passed, one in 1957 and one in 1960, but they were greatly weakened to meet southern objections. President John Kennedy strongly supported civil rights legislation but did not actively lobby for it in Congress, and his civil rights bill was stalled on Capitol Hill when he died. Civil rights advocates feared, and segregationists hoped for, another weak compromise that would leave "Whites Only" signs posted outside southern hotels and many southern blacks without the right to vote.

At first glance Johnson seemed an unlikely person to break the civil rights deadlock. As a House

tions, which had the support of Congress, did not require a declaration of war. Their actions set a precedent, and from 1789 to 1970 American forces engaged in more than two hundred military actions without a declaration of war. Most of these were small-scale operations against Indians, pirates, bandits, or other countries that were threatening American lives, property, or interests (Foreign Affairs Division 1970, app. 2, 50–57).

Controversy over war powers usually develops when a president uses military force on a large scale over the opposition of a significant part of Congress and the public. In 1846, for example, President James K. Polk sent troops into territory disputed between the United

member and later a senator from Texas, he had at first stood with other southern members of Congress against civil rights. But during his years as Senate majority leader, and later as vice-president, he had concluded that strong legislation was both politically necessary (to hold onto the Democratic party's black support) and morally right. The word went out from the White House: this time there would be no compromise.

Since the civil rights bill had majority support in the House of Representatives, the main battle would be in the Senate, where southern senators could filibuster (see Chapter 6). To end a filibuster, Johnson needed a two-thirds vote (today a 60 percent vote is required), and for that he needed the support of the Senate minority floor leader Everett Dirksen, Republican from Illinois, who was undecided. Johnson deployed the full resources of the presidency to win Dirksen over; Vice-President Hubert Humphrey later claimed he courted Dirksen almost as persistently as he had his wife. While Humphrey appealed to Dirksen's "sense of fairness and spirit of nation," Johnson offered the Illinois senator help in getting federal funding for projects in his state and federal jobs for his friends. On June 10, 1964, Dirksen came out in favor of the bill, dooming the southern filibuster. Less than a month later, on July 2, Johnson signed into law the Civil Rights Act, which outlawed discrimination in employment, education, and public accommodations.

After his decisive victory over Barry Goldwater in 1964, Johnson ordered the Justice Department to begin work on a bill that would eliminate literacy tests and other barriers southern states used to keep blacks from voting. On March 15, 1965, Johnson appeared before a joint session of Congress to give a televised address proposing the toughest voting rights bill ever. "It is not just Negroes," he told the assembled members and the nation, "but really it is all of us who must overcome the crippling legacy of bigotry and injustice." Then he invoked the theme song of the civil rights movement: "And we shall overcome." Johnson's eloquence impressed both Congress and the public; a few months later the Voting Rights Act of 1965 became law.

Lyndon Johnson's civil rights accomplishments transformed race relations in the United States. Segregated public facilities disappeared. A million blacks were enfranchised. In Mississippi alone, black registration increased from 29,000 in 1964 to 330,000 in 1980. Of course, Johnson did not do it all himself. Without the protest and agitation by the civil rights movement, little would have changed. It helped that Johnson had a Democratic majority in Congress, cooperation from many Republicans, and the memory of Kennedy, which he often invoked to rally support. But without a president willing and able to use the full powers of his office, from influence over public opinion to old-fashioned "pork barrel" rewards for supporters, Congress might have chosen to evade the issue as it had before. Often no one but the chief executive is in a position to provide moral leadership and political direction.

Source: Wicker 1968; Bornet 1983, 98, 232; Kearns 1976, 229.

States and Mexico, drawing the Mexicans into a fight that forced Congress to declare war (see Controversy).

President Abraham Lincoln, faced in 1861 with the greatest crisis the nation has ever seen, delayed calling Congress into special session for three months following the Confederate firing on Fort Sumter and in the intervening period virtually ran the country alone. He enlarged the army and navy, assembled the militia, spent public money without congressional appropriation, and in other ways ignored the Constitution. In defending his actions, Lincoln argued that the Constitution could not be preserved if the Union was lost; it was therefore his duty to preserve the Union

CONTROVERSY
Mr. Polk's War

James K. Polk (Library of Congress)

When James K. Polk took office as the nation's eleventh president, he had one thing on his mind —expansion. His predecessor, John Tyler, had just annexed the Republic of Texas despite the fact it was still claimed by Mexico. But Polk was not satisfied. He wanted the Mexican provinces of California and New Mexico (including today's New Mexico and Arizona plus parts of Colorado, Nevada, and Utah) as well as the Oregon Territory claimed by both the United States and Great Britain. Polk's use of his powers as commander in chief led the nation into war with Mexico, provoked a storm of controversy, and reinforced the broad interpretation of the president's military powers.

Polk was no warmonger. He first sent an envoy, John Slidell, to Mexico with instructions to obtain California and New Mexico peacefully. Slidell was authorized to offer the Mexicans $25 million for California, $5 million for New Mexico, and, in return for Texas, the U.S. government would assume its citizens' claims in lawsuits against Mexico. But Slidell got nowhere; the Mexicans, enraged at the annexation of Texas and crippled by political divisions, refused to meet with

him and dispatched troops to the Rio Grande. Frustrated, Slidell wrote back to Washington, "We can never get along with them until we have given them a drubbing."

Polk was not sure he could get a declaration of war through Congress; many northerners feared that expansion would mean the extension of slavery. But he could command the army. In March 1846, acting on Polk's orders, General Zachary Taylor advanced with three thousand troops to the Rio Grande, occupying territory north of the river that had been in dispute between the United States and Mexico. Polk ordered Taylor not to fire first, but he clearly realized that the arrival of U.S. troops in the disputed area could trigger a battle. It did; on April 24–26 the Mexicans crossed the river and attacked Taylor's army.

By the time word of the fighting reached Washington, Taylor had already defeated the Mexicans and driven them back across the Rio Grande. But Polk had his justification. On May 11 he sent a message to Congress, proclaiming that "Mexico has invaded our territory and shed American blood upon the American soil." He asked Congress not to declare war but to declare that it had already begun "by the act of Mexico." Many members of Congress, including Abraham Lincoln, later denounced the president for provoking a war without consulting Congress, but they had no choice but to support the army by voting for the declaration. Opposition continued throughout the war. Ulysses S. Grant, who served with Taylor as a lieutenant, called the war "one of the most unjust ever waged by a stronger against a weaker nation." Although there was much regional disagreement regarding the wisdom of the war, the American military effort was strong enough to win a decisive victory over the weak and divided Mexican government. The peace treaty in 1848 gave Polk the territory he wanted for $15 million. With this purchase, the United States also assumed up to $3 million in claims against Mexico by American citizens.

Source: Bauer 1974; quoted in Polk 1988, 310–11; Nevin 1978; Weems 1988.

even if that meant violating specific provisions of the Constitution temporarily (Corwin 1984, 229–34).

Between the Civil War and World War II presidents regularly sent troops to other countries without a declaration of war. But no president, after Lincoln, used his powers as commander in chief so extensively until Franklin Roosevelt. Realizing that he lacked the popular support to lead the country into the war that had already broken out in Europe and Asia, Roosevelt nevertheless persuaded Congress to allow the transfer of American ships to the British navy and the loan of military equipment to the British forces. He also authorized

"THAT FELLOW ABE LINCOLN WHO OPPOSED THE MEXICAN WAR — CAN YOU IMAGINE A GUY LIKE THAT AS COMMANDER-IN-CHIEF?"

Herblock. Copyright 1992 by Herblock in *The Washington Post*.

convoying ships carrying war materials to England. The last measure involved the United States in an undeclared naval war against Germany by mid-1941, several months before the Japanese attack on Pearl Harbor on December 7 of that year. Much of what Roosevelt did clearly stretched the president's power to, if not beyond, its constitutional limits (Schlesinger Jr. 1973, 100–14).

Postwar presidents, mindful of Roosevelt's example and faced with aggressive Soviet actions, further expanded presidential authority in war making, and Congress generally acquiesced. Few voices were raised in dissent when President Harry Truman ordered U.S. forces to Korea in 1950, and in 1964 only two dissenting votes were cast when President Lyndon Johnson requested authority to use American forces in Southeast Asia after a reported attack on two U.S. destroyers in the Gulf of Tonkin off the coast of North Vietnam (Crabb Jr. and Holt 1992, 142–43).

The Tonkin Gulf Resolution in 1964 represented the high-water mark of presidential war powers. As years passed and casualties in Vietnam mounted, liberals in Congress turned against the war and began to call for a reassertion of Congress' right to consent to war making. In 1973, with President Richard Nixon embroiled in the Watergate scandal (see Controversy), Congress passed over his veto of the War Powers Resolution, which aimed at restoring the balance between the branches.

The War Powers Resolution sought to limit presidential war making in three different ways. First, the president is required to notify Congress whenever troops are committed to action and to consult congressional leaders in advance "in every possible instance." Second, the president is limited to committing troops to action for a maximum of sixty days without congressional approval; if approval is not forthcoming within this time, a maximum of thirty days is allowed to withdraw the troops. Third, Congress reserved to itself the power to direct, by concurrent resolution, that troops be

CONTROVERSY

Watergate: Presidential Power against the Law

Richard M. Nixon (UPI)

While making his normal rounds in the Watergate office complex in Washington, D.C., in the early morning of June 17, 1972, security guard Frank

Willis noticed that a lock on the door to one of the offices was taped open. Suspecting a burglary, Willis called Washington police, who arrested five intruders in the offices of the Democratic National Committee. The greatest political scandal in modern American history had begun.

The five burglars turned out to be employees of President Nixon's reelection staff, led by James McCord, a former FBI agent. They were trying to install a tap on the phone of Larry O'Brien, chair of the Democratic National Committee. Two others, former CIA agent E. Howard Hunt and Nixon campaign committee attorney G. Gordon Liddy, were also implicated. The White House dismissed the case as "a third-rate burglary," but presiding Judge John Sirica of the Federal District Court in Washington was not convinced. Sirica, a Republican, put pressure on the convicted burglars by threatening them with the maximum sentence—forty years in prison—unless they cooperated. McCord cracked. On March 23, 1973, Sirica read a letter from McCord acknowledging that others had been involved. McCord later testified before a Senate hearing that the head of the Nixon Committee to Re-Elect the President, former Attorney

withdrawn even before the time limits had expired (Fisher 1985, 307–14). This power to reject the action of the executive or an administrative agency delegated authority by Congress is known as the **legislative veto**.

The provisions of the War Powers Resolution have still not been fully tested. Only four military actions since 1973 have lasted more than sixty days—the ill-fated Marine mission to Lebanon in 1983–84, the Persian Gulf crisis in 1987–88, Operation Desert Shield–Desert Storm in 1990–91, and the deployment of troops to Somalia in 1992–93. In Lebanon, Congress granted permission for an eighteen-month deployment, but the troops were withdrawn when opposition to the mission mounted. In the Persian Gulf crisis of 1987–88, U.S. ships patrolled the Persian Gulf to protect oil tankers until the 1988 cease-fire between Iran and Iraq. In the Persian Gulf War of 1991, troops were deployed after the Iraqi invasion of Kuwait in 1990. In Somalia, the president deployed troops to assist in a United Nations humanitarian relief operation that ultimately led to hostilities against Somali "warlords," whose forces were hindering relief efforts.

Some members of Congress sought to

General John Mitchell, and White House attorney John Dean had authorized the break-in and other illegal activities, and that he had been offered a presidential pardon and $100,000 to keep quiet.

Throughout 1973 and into 1974, inquiries by the courts, Congress, and the press uncovered more and more illegal or questionable activities. These included other burglaries, illegal campaign contributions, and efforts to disrupt the campaigns of Democratic presidential candidates. Much of the damaging information was revealed by *Washington Post* reporters Bob Woodward and Carl Bernstein, who had an informer in the Nixon administration known as "Deep Throat" (the title of a pornographic movie of the period). Other damaging revelations came in Senate hearings, where John Dean testified that the president had known of efforts to cover up his and Mitchell's involvement. Nixon denied it.

Whether Nixon or Dean was lying might never have been known had it not been revealed in July 1973 that the president kept tapes of all official conversations. When he refused to surrender the tapes, special prosecutor Archibald Cox petitioned the courts to force their release. After Nixon fired Cox on October 20, 1973, the House Judiciary Committee began an impeachment inquiry. The end came for Nixon when the Supreme Court, including four of his own appointees, ruled on July 24, 1974, that he had no right to withhold the tapes. The tapes, released after the Judiciary Committee had voted on August 3 to recommend impeachment, showed clearly that Nixon had approved the cover-up. On August 8, Richard Nixon announced his resignation, the first chief executive in United States history ever to do so. He was granted a pardon a month later by his successor Gerald Ford, but many of his top aides went to prison for Watergate-related crimes.

Watergate is both a warning of the dangers of presidential abuse of power and a vindication of the checks and balances system. The courts, Congress, people of both parties, and the press all worked to rein in a president who initially failed to control his aides and later covered up their crimes. On the other hand, it reminds us of the role chance plays in human affairs. Watergate might never have been uncovered but for the alertness of Frank Willis, who at last report was unemployed in Washington.

Source: Watergate 1975; Ervin Jr. 1980; White 1975; Bernstein and Woodward 1974.

---

amend or rewrite the War Powers Resolution after court proceedings failed to apply it to the 1987–88 Persian Gulf crisis. Moreover, the legislative veto provision of the resolution is now apparently null and void as a result of the Supreme Court's decision in *Immigration and Naturalization Service v. Chadha* (1983) declaring such vetoes unconstitutional (Fisher 1985, 178–83). Presidents Ford and Carter did notify Congress when they sent forces to rescue Americans in danger—Ford in the case of the freighter *Mayaguez*, which had been seized by Cambodian communists; Carter in the ill-staged Iranian hostage rescue mission. Neither president consulted Congress in advance, however (Fisher 1985, 314–18). Reagan followed a similar pattern when he used military force against Libya, Iran, and Grenada during his presidency (Carpenter 1986, 13–16).

The 1991 Persian Gulf War once again revealed the extent of the president's power over war, despite the War Powers Resolution. In response to Iraq's invasion of Kuwait (see Chapter 11), President Bush ordered U.S. troops to Saudi Arabia in August 1990 without consulting Congress in advance. Congress approved the deployment after it occurred, but more dissent arose after Bush set a deadline for

Iraqi withdrawal and prepared for offensive action. The U.N. Security Council adopted several firm resolutions, with U.S. support, that strongly condemned Iraq's invasion of Kuwait and called for withdrawal. After lengthy and heated debate both houses of Congress finally approved the war, four days before it started on January 16, 1991 (*Congressional Quarterly Weekly Report*, 12 January 1991, 65–70). However, Defense Secretary Richard Cheney and other top Bush advisers indicated that the president felt he had the power to begin hostilities without congressional approval, so a negative vote in Congress might not have prevented the war.

Congress may be more effective in controlling the president's war powers when it uses its power of the purse (discussed further below). In 1973, military involvement in Southeast Asia finally ended when Congress cut off funds for bombing operations in Cambodia (Crabb Jr. and Holt 1992, 144). On the other hand, Congress may push the executive toward military action. In December 1989, two months after congressional leaders criticized President Bush for not intervening against Panama's drug-dealing strongman Manuel Noriega, Bush sent in troops to oust him (see Chapter 11). The 1992–93 deployment of troops to Somalia on a mission to restore order so that food could be distributed to the hungry had the support of both the Bush and Clinton administrations and most congressional leaders.

Cover Operations   Before World War II, when the United States intervened in foreign countries, it usually landed troops. During World War II, however, the Office of Strategic Services (OSS) was created to gather strategic information and conduct **covert operations**, or conventional low-intensity warfare, ranging from propaganda to sabotage to organizing guerrilla forces behind German and Japanese lines. The OSS was shut down after the war, but in 1947 Congress created the Central Intelligence Agency (CIA) as the nation's first peacetime intelligence organization. Although the law creating the CIA mentioned only intelligence gathering and analysis, a few months later President Truman authorized the agency to conduct covert operations. Without clear authorization from Congress, the executive thus claimed a new power in foreign affairs not envisioned in the Constitution (Prados 1986).

Every president since Truman has employed covert operations, with decidedly mixed results. The CIA helped prevent a communist victory in the Italian elections of 1948, overthrew anti-American (but not necessarily pro-Soviet) governments in Iran in 1953 and Guatemala in 1954, and helped thwart communist attempts to seize power in Portugal in the mid-1970s. While these operations were successful, there have also been some spectacular failures. The worst occurred when Presidents Eisenhower and later Kennedy ordered the CIA to recruit a force of Cuban exiles to oust Cuba's Marxist dictator, Fidel Castro. After this force suffered a humiliating defeat at the Bay of Pigs in April 1961, the agency made several plans to have Castro assassinated, even exploring the possibility of employing "hit men" from organized crime for the purpose, but none of the plans were successful.

The uproar over Watergate and other presidential excesses in the early 1970s prompted a major congressional investigation of the CIA, which uncovered the Castro assassination plots and other improper activities, including drug experiments on unwitting U.S. citizens. Congressional liberals seeking a less interventionist foreign policy secured the passage in 1974 of the Hughes-Ryan Amendment, which required that all major covert actions be reported to representatives of eight different congressional committees. Armed with information, Congress began to exercise more control over covert operations. In 1976, Congress barred the Ford administration from aiding anti-Marxist forces in Angola.

Covert operations were scaled back during the Carter administration, but revived by the conservative and strongly anticommunist Rea-

Figure 7.1   The Structure of the Executive Branch

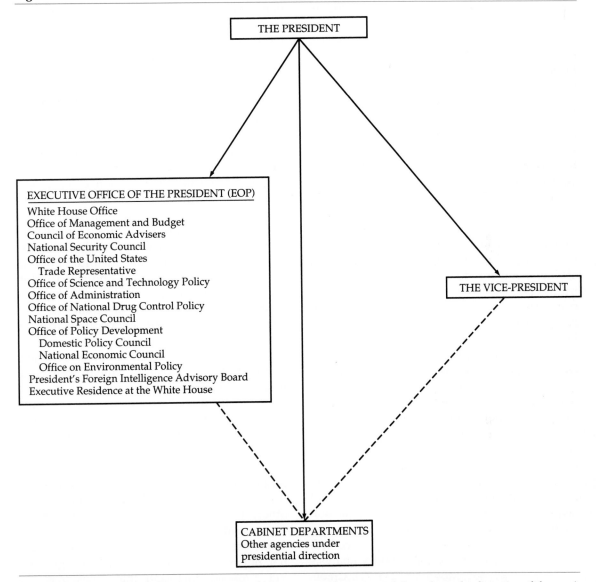

Note: The extent to which the EOP and the office of the vice-president are used depends on the discretion of the president. The president also determines which mechanisms will be used to coordinate the various agencies. This figure does not include vice-presidential offices or offices the Clinton administration has proposed to eliminate.

Source: Adapted from United States Government Manual, 1988–89 *and communications from the Clinton White House.*

and organizational strategies to manage their growing staff. Under Franklin Roosevelt, Kennedy, and Carter, control of the staff was centralized in the sense that many top staffers reported directly to the president and were assigned work by him; at the same time control was decentralized in that the top presidential aides had less control than previously. Such an arrangement allows the president to draw on information and advice from many independent sources. It also tends to encourage competition and backbiting among staffers, as each tries to gain the president's confidence. Both Eisenhower and Nixon, who did not want such conflicts on their staffs, used a more hierarchical system, with staffers reporting to a chief of staff who took the main responsibility for giving advice to the president (Kernell and Popkin 1986). Reagan attempted to use a hybrid system that contained elements of both approaches (Campbell 1986, 80–112).

The growth of the White House staff has clearly contributed to the loss of influence of cabinet members in the last forty years. It is easy for a president to surround himself with loyal staffers in the White House who, unlike cabinet members, do not have to be confirmed by the Senate or testify before congressional committees (Rossiter 1960, 274). President Nixon virtually turned foreign policy over to Henry Kissinger, the national security adviser, cutting off Secretary of State William Rogers. Domestic policy was put in the hands of White House aides H. R. Haldeman and John Ehrlichman, who frequently intervened in agency policymaking, giving orders that contradicted those of the agency heads (Nathan 1975). In such a situation, the lines of communication and authority can become very muddled.

Choosing White House staff members can be very challenging for a president. They must share the administration's views on public policy but should be willing to express their opinions, for their diversity and experience will increase the scope of available policy analysis (Mondale 1989, 465; Moe 1985, 235–71). Chiefs of staff are particularly important. Bush's first chief of staff, John Sununu, was widely believed to be too assertive and abrasive for the job. In late 1991, Samuel Skinner was brought in to replace Sununu, but he proved unable to get the administration on a constant course. The August 1992 return of James Baker, who had served in the position for President Rea-

gan, raised hopes for Bush's reelection. President Clinton appointed an Arkansas business leader, Thomas "Mack" McLarty, who is likely to be much more of an honest broker among viewpoints than a forceful figure like Sununu. Most observers agree that, as in the case of the national security adviser, an honest broker is the preferred mode (Pfiffner 1993, 77–102).

During the Clinton administration, First Lady Hillary Rodham Clinton has played a more active role in her husband's presidency than any other first lady. Her most visible impact has been in health care reform, as she headed a Health Care Task Force that was charged with determining the direction of the health care system in the future. Her involvement was controversial at first, but she has proved knowledgeable and helpful. Prior to becoming first lady, Hillary Rodham Clinton made a lot more money as a lawyer than her husband did as governor of Arkansas. This fact caused quite a stir among the Japanese when the first couple traveled to Japan in 1993 for an economic summit, for it is generally unheard of for a Japanese woman to make a higher salary than her husband.

The **institutional presidency**, the network of bureaucratic agencies on which the president depends for policy-making decisions, presents a difficult challenge to the modern president. On the one hand, a large staff and numerous agencies are needed to handle the complex issues facing the president. On the other, the size of the staff can create problems. The president must rely on agencies and his staff to settle most disagreements among cabinet departments and independent agencies. Yet a presidential staff that takes over too much policy-making will undermine the rest of the government and create an overly busy president. The president has to manage the White House staff and resolve disagreements without being a mere coordinator. Now that the nature and problems of the institutional presidency are beginning to be recognized, solutions may be forthcoming.

FOREPLAY

Jim Borgman. Courtesy artist and *Cincinnati Enquirer*.

EVALUATING PRESIDENTS

Despite a given office framework and set of duties, each president is an individual who deals with the position and its power in a personal way. What makes some presidents great and others below average? Previous political experience is not a major factor. The most important determinant seems to be what happens once a president takes office.

A war clearly offers an unusual chance for leadership, and most wartime presidents are rated high by historians. Prosperity likewise helps the ratings. So does solving a crisis, particularly one inherited from another president. Reelection is an indicator of success. Those presidents who were assassinated have also been rated higher but the reasons are uncertain. A president who is chosen by the people in an election at the start of a political realignment toward his party is also clearly helped (Simonton 1987; Holmes and Elder Jr. 1989, 529–57). There is no magic formula for achieving a high rating.

Ratings are low for presidents who defer action on what later is seen as a major crisis. Presidents who served in the 1850s are rated near the bottom, while Abraham Lincoln, who took forceful action to solve the issues of slavery and civil war, is rated at the top. A major scandal is certain to bring down one's rating. Popularity in the short term, however, may not be an indicator of success in the long term.

When campaigning, each presidential candidate tries to persuade voters that his election will bring numerous benefits to the nation, while the election of his opponent will bring disaster. Considering that all presidents face somewhat similar problems in dealing with Congress, the people, the bureaucracy, and their own staffs, such assertions are clearly exaggerated. Does a change in the occupant of the White House make a big difference? Scholars disagree about how much the president's personal style and character can affect his policies and, through them, the future of the country.

Style

Some presidents have been power brokers. James K. Polk, for example, manipulated events to serve his goal of expansion and during his term of office, 1845–49, managed to almost double the size of the United States (see Controversy earlier in this chapter). Richard Nixon, another power broker, received high marks in foreign policy from most observers but had to relinquish the presidency for his manipulations in domestic affairs revealed in the Watergate scandal (see Controversy earlier in this chapter).

Some presidents place a priority on being popular and are more likely to lead by making use of friends and maintaining strong ties with the electorate. Ronald Reagan was a master of this technique (see Profile). Although many people disagreed with his policies, most liked him as a person. Warren G. Harding, another president who liked to be popular, died in office in 1923 in an aura of scandal, unable to control friends who took advantage of their positions.

Some presidents just plod along and manage to survive over the long term. Harry Truman, for example, in office from 1945 to 1953, was a practical man who recognized what needed to be done and stuck to it. Other plodders, like Herbert Hoover and Jimmy Carter, were unable to solve the larger issues. They were generally admired for their honorable instincts but criticized for not turning intentions into reality.

To some extent crises create leaders. Some presidents, like Abraham Lincoln, faced national crises that inspired their greatness. Andrew Jackson and Theodore Roosevelt are presidents in the same mold, as they addressed important issues that needed attention.

Character

The political scientist James David Barber argues that personality traits shaped by childhood and early adult experience have a profound influence on the behavior of a president in office. He delineates four presidential character types: active-positive, active-negative, passive-positive, and passive-negative (Barber 1985, 1–11; also see Pederson 1989;

Barber 1988, 156–80). Barber uses "active" and "passive" to describe the amount of energy a president puts into his job; he uses "positive" and "negative" to describe personal satisfaction from being president.

The active-positive president invests considerable effort in his work and gains positive satisfaction from it. According to Barber, such presidents are likely to have been raised by parents who stressed independence, responsibility, and achievement, and these traits show through in office. The active-positive seeks power and enjoys wielding it, but primarily as a means of carrying out what he views as good policies for the nation. Barber places Franklin Roosevelt, Harry Truman, and John Kennedy in the active-positive category and attributes many of their policy successes to their upbringing and personality. Sometimes, however, the active-positive can get into trouble by placing too much faith in human nature and expecting others to seek achievement for its own sake as he does.

The active-negative president has a passion for power but ends up gaining little satisfaction when he gets it, due to a suspicious and basically hostile nature. Active-negative personalities are shaped by cold, demanding, perfectionist parents who drive their children to achieve but provide them little love or reward for doing so. As president, an active-negative will see enemies everywhere, a view not altogether paranoid, for his aggressive power seeking tends to create enemies. Barber places Woodrow Wilson, Herbert Hoover, Lyndon Johnson, and Richard Nixon in the active-negative category and attributes many of the failures of their administrations to personality structure. Internal needs are likely to impel an active-negative to persist in policies that are clearly failing: Wilson's refusal to compromise on the Versailles Treaty, Hoover's refusal to grant federal relief to the unemployed during the Great Depression, and Johnson's refusal to cut back on American involvement in Vietnam. Even worse, their belief that others are probably out to get them may lead them, as it

PERSPECTIVES

Every president is an individual, and presidents with similar political views can have very different styles and personalities, yet there is a strong relationship between a president's perspective and his attitude toward the office.

Conservative

Conservatives, who see government as primarily charged with keeping order rather than making changes, see a correspondingly limited role for the president. A conservative president will not try to force the country to go in bold, new directions the way Franklin Roosevelt did, for such a course could threaten the two most important values: order and liberty. Hence conservative presidents rarely try to stake out new territory for themselves or their successors to dominate.

This does not mean that a conservative president will be inactive. Ronald Reagan, for example, made some major changes in the policies of the federal government, but they were made in the name of contracting rather than expanding government's power. Some of Reagan's proposals advocated returning responsibility from the national government to the states (see Chapter 3). Thus, although Reagan made changes, he made them in the cause of a conservative view of government. However, it must be noted that almost any president will defend his power when challenged, and Reagan was no exception.

In keeping with their view of order, conservatives believe the transition between presidential administrations, particularly when a change in political party is involved, needs to be much smoother. Each new administration brings new ideas; however, the experiences and expertise of former presidential employees should be tapped to ensure an efficient transition.

The Detached Management Style...

MacNelly. Reprinted by permission: Tribune Media Services.

The major exception to the conservative preference for a limited presidency is in the area of foreign policy, as demonstrated in presidential efforts to contain communism. George Bush was also much more active in foreign policy than in domestic policy. To conservatives, it is imperative that the president be given broad powers to act on his own in the interests of national security. Hence they usually defend the right of presidents to use troops or initiate covert operations without congressional approval, though they might strongly oppose similar assertions of authority in the domestic sphere (Ford 1989, xxvii–xxxiv).

Liberal

The essence of liberalism is active government for the benefit of the disadvantaged. This principle requires a strong executive, for bold new initiatives and programs are unlikely to come out of Congress, a body of 535 individuals in which the natural tendency is always toward compromise.

MacNelly. Reprinted by permission: Tribune Media Services.

(The Supreme Court has a better track record as an originator of liberal social policy, but it lacks the power to enforce its decisions.) It is thus logical for liberals to champion a powerful presidency to lead the nation forward to a better life.

Franklin Roosevelt is the prototype of an assertive president pursuing a liberal policy agenda. Faced with an inherited economic disaster and limited constitutional powers to deal with it, Roosevelt maneuvered skillfully to stretch his powers as far as they would go within the system. He encouraged his advisers to compete with each other in supplying him with ideas and information, but used this competition to keep decision-making authority in his own hands. For example, Roosevelt frequently assigned two subordinates to deal with the same problem, then stepped in to decide the policy when they began to disagree. He also opened channels to lower-level officials in the bureaucracy, bypassing his cabinet secretaries to get information they might have wanted to keep for themselves. In dealing with Congress, he was able to unite northern and southern Democrats with

different interests behind a broad program of social reforms. His only major defeat came when he tried to reshape the Supreme Court, an effort many saw as an attempt to grab powers not rightfully his (Neustadt 1980, 115–18; see also Chapter 8).

From the liberal perspective, the advantage of the activist approach is that it can overcome the inertia and barriers to change built into the checks and balances system (see Chapter 2). The conservative framers cleverly structured the government so as to block radical changes; only the president is given enough power to push through reforms when they are needed (Burns 1984, 101–19). Liberals saw Roosevelt's approach to presidential leadership as essential to dealing with the problems created by the Depression. It was no wonder that liberal presidents after Roosevelt pursued the same activist course, even coining catchy titles for their programs, like Fair Deal, New Frontier, and Great Society, in imitation of the New Deal.

The disaster of Vietnam caused liberals to temper their enthusiasm for active presidents. They were dismayed when a liberal president like Lyndon Johnson escalated a war without involving Congress and when they learned that John Kennedy had approved efforts to assassinate a foreign leader. Convinced that the president could no longer be allowed to launch overseas interventions on his own, liberals spearheaded the campaign for the War Powers Resolution and restrictions on covert operations and aid to the *contra* rebels in Nicaragua (Wormuth and Firmage 1986).

Despite their dismay over Richard Nixon's activism, revealed in the Watergate scandal, liberals still favor an active presidency. The president is still the only official in the country elected by all the people; while he may make mistakes, say liberals, he is less likely to be captured by narrow special interests than is Congress, the bureaucracy, or the state legislatures, and thus has a duty to challenge such interests. Jimmy Carter was seen as a failure by many liberals because he did not use the powers of the office to challenge the rich and powerful. Perhaps a liberal's idea of heaven would be a president with the policies and political skills of Franklin Roosevelt and the popularity of John Kennedy. Liberals want President Clinton to come as close to such an ideal as possible.

Libertarian

The last truly libertarian president was Herbert Hoover. Indeed his devotion to libertarian principles was so great that he sacrificed his political future to uphold them. A dedicated humanitarian, Hoover had supervised famine relief efforts that saved millions of lives in Europe after World War I. Yet, faced with the suffering created by the Great Depression, he opposed extending emergency federal relief to the unemployed because it would have expanded the powers of the national government and the presidency in a way not envisioned in the Constitution. Though Hoover gave substantial amounts of his own considerable fortune to poor relief and urged others to do the same, his reluctance to use his powers to deal with the crisis brought a harsh public reaction: makeshift shantytowns erected by the unemployed were derisively called "Hoovervilles" (Smith 1970; Burner 1978, 245–83).

Today's libertarians would not all agree with Hoover's opposition to emergency relief, but they see his warnings about executive power as prophetic. The corrupting effects of power are evident, libertarians say, in the careers of all the post-Hoover presidents, liberal or conservative. Among the liberals, Franklin Roosevelt, the liberal "man of the people," swept aside constitutional liberties and interred one hundred thousand Japanese-Americans (later found entirely innocent of any wrongdoing) in camps during World War II. Harry Truman trampled upon property rights by seizing the steel industry during the Korean War. John Kennedy used his powers to plot assassinations and intimidate businesspeople who tried to exercise their right to raise prices. Jimmy Carter deprived American farmers of their livelihood by imposing a useless grain embargo on the Soviet Union. The record of conservative presidents is only slightly better. Dwight Eisenhower, Richard Nixon, Ronald Reagan, and George Bush all claimed unconstitutional powers in both foreign and domestic affairs. Nixon was, of course, the worst offender, but his much-publicized Watergate activities were mild compared to his imposition of wage-price controls in 1971, which deprived all Americans of their economic liberties for the next three years (Carpenter 1986, 22–23).

What do libertarians want to do to put the presidency back in its place? They endorsed Reagan's efforts to cut back the bureaucracy and return powers to the states, but they believe that conservative support for an "imperial" presidency in foreign affairs is foolish and a threat to domestic liberties. "The Founders," says one libertarian analyst, "would likely be mystified at recent presidential contentions that, although Congress declares wars, the President has a right to wage them with or without formal declarations. Executive supremacy in foreign affairs was not set forth in the Constitution" (Carpenter 1986, 23). Libertarians want Congress to enforce the War Powers Resolution and rules on covert action so that presidents use force only when the nation's security is really at stake.

Likewise, libertarians want Congress to reclaim authority delegated to the president over the domestic economy so that no future chief executive can seize industries or dictate what goods and services will sell for in the marketplace. What is most needed, however, is a change in public attitude. People need to realize that the president is not the national problem solver but the holder of an office with limited powers and responsibilities under the Constitution. Only by returning to the ideals of self-reliance and individual freedom on which it was founded, say libertarians, can the United States break free of the imperial presidency.

Populist

While the libertarian sees presidential power as a threat to freedom, the populist sees it as a two-edged sword that may cut either for or against the rights of the majority. Being elected by a majority of the people can give a president the ability to challenge the concentration of power in the hands of the wealthy minority. Andrew Jackson, the most populist president, challenged the wealthy so effectively that his enemies dubbed him "King Andrew" and accused him of concentrating all power in his hands (Remini 1984, 125, 137). Later presidents like Theodore Roosevelt and Franklin Roosevelt have also used the office to check the abuses perpetrated by the wealthy under the cloak of "free enterprise" and to aid the underprivileged majority. Harry Truman, arguably the most populist of recent presidents, once remarked that the richest 10 percent of Americans did not need a president for they had thousands of Washington lobbyists looking out for their interests; the president's job was to represent the other 90 percent.

While the president has the potential to counterbalance the pro-business, pro-wealth bias that populists see in American government, such a happy result is by no means inevitable. The problem is that presidents, by the nature of their office, cannot help but become somewhat remote from the concerns of average people. This tendency is accentuated by the reliance of presidential candidates on the support of wealthy contributors (particularly in the early stages before the candidacy is officially announced and federal funds are available) and by the method of filling top positions in the executive branch. Presidents look to those who have served in such posts before or gained prominence in other ways, and this tendency introduces an inevitable bias toward selecting the rich and powerful. A study of the early Reagan administration by Ralph Nader's populist organizations, for example, shows that the overwhelming majority of the top one hundred officials were wealthy businesspeople or professionals. Voicing a populist complaint, Nader charged that Reagan had created a "homogenized government by elites" who were "reluctant to mix with ordinary people" and showed "little idealism for alleviating the agonies of human beings" (quoted in Brownstein and Easton 1983, xvii, xx, xxi). The capture of presidents by the elite did not begin with the Reagan administration, however, for the rich have occupied many of the top posts in Democratic administrations as well. Understanding this connection, many Americans responded positively to Ross Perot's attacks on the Bush and Clinton presidencies and his claims that presidents were out of touch with ordinary people.

Marxist

Marxist writers on the presidency echo the populist critique. Marxists point out that presidential candidates of both parties rely on wealthy donors, that most high-level appointments go to corporate executives or rich lawyers, and that the president operates through a vast bureaucracy that insulates him from ordinary people (Greenberg 1986, 220–50). Unlike populists, Marxists do not see any

8

THE JUDICIARY

Imagine nine people in a dark basement viewing a grainy motion picture full of explicit sexual activity. The gathering may sound like a late night stag party or a wild fraternity bash, but these are nine Supreme Court justices, in the Supreme Court Building on Capitol Hill, determining what is obscene or pornographic and whether such materials should be outlawed. Making judgments on such matters is often difficult; Justice Potter Stewart once acknowledged the problems in defining obscenity but contended "I know it when I see it" (quoted in Woodward and Armstrong 1979, 194, see also 198–99).

Why do Supreme Court justices watch pornography? How does a case like this make it to the Supreme Court? To answer such questions, one must understand the judicial branch of the federal government as an institution. That is the subject of this chapter. The substance of pornography and similar cases are discussed in the next chapter, which concerns civil liberties.

POWERS AND CONSTRAINTS

The **judiciary**, the system of courts and judges, is the branch of government that has **judicial power**, the responsibility to render judgments according to the laws of the land. In Number 78 of *The Federalist Papers*, Alexander Hamilton referred to the judiciary as "the least dangerous" branch of the new government; it was, he assured his audience in New York, the least likely to endanger the rights and liberties of the people (*Federalist Papers* 1961, 465). A glance at Article III of the Constitution, which states the powers of the judiciary, appears to support his claim. Only one court, the **Supreme Court** of the United States, is created by the Constitution; establishment of other federal courts inferior to the Supreme Court is left to Congress. The Supreme Court is granted **original jurisdiction**—the right to hear a case when it first arises—over only a few, relatively unimportant types of cases (see Figure 8.1). All

Figure 8.1   Jurisdiction of State and Federal Courts

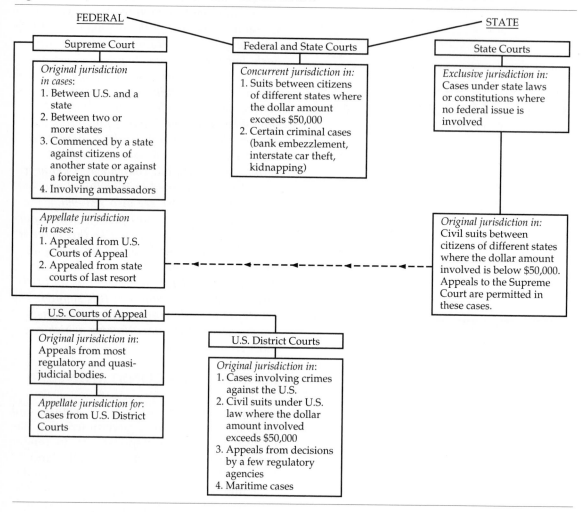

FEDERAL · STATE

Supreme Court

Original jurisdiction in cases:
1. Between U.S. and a state
2. Between two or more states
3. Commenced by a state against citizens of another state or against a foreign country
4. Involving ambassadors

Appellate jurisdiction in cases:
1. Appealed from U.S. Courts of Appeal
2. Appealed from state courts of last resort

Federal and State Courts

Concurrent jurisdiction in:
1. Suits between citizens of different states where the dollar amount exceeds $50,000
2. Certain criminal cases (bank embezzlement, interstate car theft, kidnapping)

State Courts

Exclusive jurisdiction in:
Cases under state laws or constitutions where no federal issue is involved

Original jurisdiction in:
Civil suits between citizens of different states where the dollar amount involved is below $50,000. Appeals to the Supreme Court are permitted in these cases.

U.S. Courts of Appeal

Original jurisdiction in:
Appeals from most regulatory and quasi-judicial bodies.

Appellate jurisdiction for:
Cases from U.S. District Courts

U.S. District Courts

Original jurisdiction in:
1. Cases involving crimes against the U.S.
2. Civil suits under U.S. law where the dollar amount involved exceeds $50,000
3. Appeals from decisions by a few regulatory agencies
4. Maritime cases

other cases must originate in lower courts and be appealed to the Supreme Court, and the Court's **appellate jurisdiction**—power to review the decision of a lower court—may be limited by Congress. The president is also granted an important power over the courts—the right to appoint judges with the advice and consent of the Senate. While the Supreme Court is the final authority on all the cases it chooses to hear, the broad powers over the judiciary held by other branches suggest that the framers of the Constitution had little desire to see a strong court system.

Yet, a closer examination of the intent of the framers reveals that the opposite is the case, for the Constitution laid the foundation for a powerful judiciary. The framers wanted a strong national government that would keep order and eliminate state barriers to the expansion of commerce. To ensure that states would not reassert their independence, they stated in Article VI that the Constitution and acts of

Congress passed under it "shall be the supreme Law of the Land; and the Judges in every State shall be bound thereby."

The Growth of Judicial Power

One basis for judicial power not spelled out in the Constitution is the concept of **judicial review**. In the English tradition, courts have felt bound to apply whatever laws Parliament sees fit to enact, without inquiring into their justice or fairness. But in the United States, courts in several states refused to enforce laws that openly contradicted provisions of the new state constitutions. By the time of the Constitutional Convention in 1787, a majority of the delegates who spoke on the issue stated that the Supreme Court should have a right to declare acts of Congress unconstitutional, and Hamilton so argued in *The Federalist Papers*. Still, the power of judicial review was not written into the Constitution (Abraham 1993 301–5; Hamilton, Number 78, *Federalist Papers* 1961, 464–72).

Marbury v. Madison   Early in 1801, President John Adams appointed his secretary of state, John Marshall, chief justice of the Supreme Court. Marshall, a prominent Virginia lawyer before he entered politics, found himself the chief justice at a critical time for the young Supreme Court and nation. Marshall was only one of many appointments made during the final months of John Adams's presidency. In December, Adams learned he had lost the presidential election to Thomas Jefferson, a Democratic-Republican. One of the last acts of the Federalists was to pass the Judiciary Act of 1801, which, among other things, enlarged the federal judiciary. To assure the Federalists some political power in the years to come, Adams appointed several dozen federal judges in the last two weeks of his term, which ended March 3. Because he was reputedly up until midnight, or later, signing these commissions, these appointments came to be known as the **midnight judges**.

Adams's efforts to ensure Federalist power led to one of the most important cases in American judicial history. Ironically, the case that led Chief Justice Marshall to assert authority for the Supreme Court resulted from his own inaction. Some of the judges Adams appointed had not received their official commissions because Marshall, who continued to act as secretary of state until the end of Adams's term and so had the responsibility of delivering such commissions, had not had time to see to it and assumed the incoming administration would do so.

Thomas Jefferson ordered his secretary of state, James Madison, not to deliver these commissions. One of the midnight judges, William Marbury, appealed to the Supreme Court under Section 13 of the Judiciary Act of 1789, which authorized the Supreme Court to issue **writs of mandamus**, a court order that would require Madison to deliver Marbury's commission, according to Madison's duty under the law.

Marshall seemed to be trapped in a "Catch 22" situation. If he and the Supreme Court ruled in favor of Marbury, Madison would probably ignore the decision, which would be a severe blow to the future prestige and power of the Supreme Court. If they ruled in favor of Madison, the Court would be backing down before the power of the presidency.

Marshall's solution was a political master stroke. Speaking for a unanimous court in 1803, he contended that, while Marbury was entitled to his commission, the Supreme Court could not help him because, in spite of the Judiciary Act of 1789, it had no authority over the case. The Constitution specified the areas in which the Supreme Court had original jurisdiction, and Congress could not add to these; thus Section 13 of the Judiciary Act, which gave the Court original jurisdiction over requests for writs of mandamus, was unconstitutional and could not be enforced by any court. Jefferson chose to do nothing because the Court had ruled in his favor on the narrow issue of the appointments. The Supreme Court

Wayne Stayskal. Reprinted by permission: Tribune Media Services.

had traded the relatively minor power of issuing writs of mandamus for the power to strike down acts of Congress as unconstitutional. Thus Marshall had seized the broad policy-making power that the Supreme Court has today right from under the very noses of his political opponents. (For a selective list and explanation of important policy-making Supreme Court cases, see Appendix D.)

The Fourteenth Amendment   After *Marbury v. Madison* the Supreme Court used its newly won power of judicial review cautiously, primarily to strike down state laws that unconstitutionally restricted interstate trade. The only other case prior to the Civil War in which a federal law was declared unconstitutional was *Dred Scott v. Sandford* (1857); in it the Court ruled that Congress could not prohibit slavery in federally administered U.S. territories. This decision caused a violent reaction in the northern states and contributed to the outbreak of the Civil War. As a result, by the end of that war the Court's prestige was at a low ebb.

The **Fourteenth Amendment**, adopted in 1868, restored the importance of the judiciary. Designed to protect the rights of the newly freed blacks, it made all persons born or naturalized in the United States citizens and barred any state from depriving "any person of life,

liberty, or property, without due process of law" or denying "any person within its jurisdiction the equal protection of the laws." **Due process** refers to established legal proceedings that act as safeguards, ensuring individuals that laws are reasonable and applied in an equitable manner and protecting them from the arbitrary denial of life, liberty, or the free use of property. Although the amendment was not used effectively to protect blacks for a long time, it provided a basis for challenging many laws alleged to deprive an individual of life, liberty, or property, particularly after the Supreme Court decided, in *Santa Clara County v. Southern Pacific Railroad Co.* (1886), that business corporations were "persons" and entitled to the same Fourteenth Amendment protection as individuals. The amendment thus greatly increased the power of the Supreme Court to make law and policy through constitutional interpretation.

Around the turn of century, the Supreme Court heard many cases interpreting the application of the Fourteenth Amendment to property rights. It usually took a libertarian position. In 1905, the Court ruled that a law restricting hours of employment in bakeries was an unconstitutional interference with an employer's rights of contract and property (*Lochner v. New York*). In 1895 it had declared a federal income tax unconstitutional (*Pollock v. Farmers' Loan and Trust Co.*). This decision led to the passage of the Sixteenth Amendment, which granted Congress the right to tax incomes.

The 1930s brought a change in judicial policy. After first resisting President Franklin Roosevelt's New Deal, the Supreme Court began to abandon its stand against regulation of business. At the same time it began to scrutinize laws that appeared to infringe upon the individual's Fourteenth Amendment right to liberty. The most dramatic changes took place during the years 1953 to 1969, when Earl Warren served as chief justice. Besides extending civil liberties and rights in a variety of cases,

Jeff MacNelly. Reprinted by permission: Tribune Media Services.

the Warren Court required reapportionment of state legislatures on a "one person, one vote" basis (*Reynolds v. Sims*, 1964, among others), giving liberal urban voters more political power. Under Chief Justices Warren Burger (1969–86) and William Rehnquist (1986–), the Court has become more conservative. But it has not yet reversed any of the major precedents set during the years of the Warren Court.

The Limits of Judicial Policy-Making

One of the most famous chief justices of the Supreme Court, Charles Evans Hughes, once said that "the Constitution is what the judges say it is" (quoted in Graglia 1982, 138–39). Yet the judiciary cannot dictate government policy at will any more than the other two branches; checks and balances, both written and unwritten, act as restraints on the Supreme Court, just as they restrain both Congress and the president.

The Appointment Power   The president's power to nominate federal judges is significant. So is the Senate's power to "advise and consent" to these nominations of judges, with a majority vote required for confirmation. Consent is not always forthcoming, as President Ronald Reagan learned in 1987 when a coalition of liberal and moderate senators rejected Robert Bork, a conservative legal scholar Reagan had nominated to fill the seat left vacant by the retirement of Justice Lewis F. Powell, Jr. In 1991, Clarence Thomas was nominated for the Supreme Court by President George Bush. Thomas appeared on the brink of approval when allegations of sexual harassment were brought by Anita Hill, a former colleague. Confirmation hearings were extended so that her testimony could be included, and a political battle followed. In the end, Thomas was confirmed, but by a very small margin (see Controversy). The public followed the hearings through the media, and many, from all political perspectives, were disgusted by the

CONTROVERSY
Confirmation Battles: Bork and Thomas

Robert Bork (Richard Johnson)

Clarence Thomas (Reuters/Bettmann)

Neither Robert Bork nor Clarence Thomas were strangers to controversy before they were nominated to the Supreme Court. Yet neither could have been prepared for the storm that was to come. The Bork and Thomas battles illustrate the political nature of Supreme Court appointments and the Senate confirmation process.

Robert Bork was nominated to fill Lewis Powell's seat when Powell retired from the Supreme Court in July 1987. Undoubtedly President Reagan chose the former Yale Law School professor because of his strongly conservative views on legal issues. Bork had criticized the *Roe v. Wade* (1973) decision legalizing abortions as "a serious and wholly unjustifiable judicial usurpation of state legislative authority." He also criticized Supreme Court decisions that limited police powers. In a

1963 article that he later disavowed, Bork had said that while racial discrimination was an "ugly" practice, proposed civil rights legislation would impair freedom of association and mean "a loss in a vital area of freedom." In a 1971 article he wrote that the First Amendment protected only political speech, raising the possibility that a state could limit nonpolitical expression.

Bork had other problems. During the Watergate scandal in the early 1970s he had served as acting attorney general and obeyed President Richard Nixon's order to fire Special Prosecutor Archibald Cox after two superiors had been fired for refusing to do so (see Controversy in Chapter 7). This action made him a marked man to liberals. Bork also was nominated at an inauspicious time, while President Reagan was struggling with the

Iran-*contra* affair (see Controversy in Chapter 11). A coalition of liberal groups, including the American Civil Liberties Union, the National Association for the Advancement of Colored People, and the AFL-CIO, formed to oppose the nomination. In response, conservative groups mobilized for a pro-Bork campaign.

When Bork appeared before the Senate Judiciary Committee in September 1987, several senators remained undecided. Under questioning, he gave complicated, legalistic explanations for his views, which often appeared insensitive to minorities and women. Much of what Bork said apparently did not please the committee, which issued a negative report to the Senate. In November, the Senate rejected the nomination, 58–42.

President Bush narrowly escaped a similar defeat in 1991, when he nominated federal circuit judge Clarence Thomas to the Court. Thomas, a black conservative, had been outspoken in his views prior to the nomination, especially in criticizing affirmative action as a demeaning policy that, in his view, did not help minorities. The same groups that opposed Bork rallied against Thomas. However, learning from Bork's experience, Thomas refused to answer many questions from the Senate Judiciary Committee and was vague in responding to others. The committee split 7–7 on Thomas but by the end of the hearings in late September he appeared headed for confirmation, with most senators unwilling to oppose the president without a clear reason to do so.

Suddenly, the situation changed when an FBI report was leaked to the press by Senate staff aides seeking to block the nomination. Professor Anita Hill, an assistant to Thomas while he served as head of the Equal Employment Opportunity Commission, had told FBI agents that Thomas had persistently made sexual remarks to her on the job. The Judiciary Committee was forced to reopen its hearings, calling both Hill and Thomas as witnesses.

The sexual harrassment allegations trans-formed the ideological debate over Thomas into a test of personal credibility. After Hill graphically described the alleged advances, Thomas denied all the charges, emotionally describing the committee hearing as a "lynching" of "an uppity black man." With no effective corroborating witnesses on either side, it came down to Hill's word against Thomas's. By a narrow margin, the Senate believed Thomas: he was confirmed in October 1992 by a vote of 52–48. However, the vote may have produced a backlash among women; Alan Dixon, a Democratic senator from Illinois who voted for Thomas, lost in the 1992 primary to Carol Moseley Braun, who made the hearings her main campaign issue.

The Bork and Thomas nominations demonstrate how partisan judicial appointments have become. Bork was a more experienced legal scholar than Thomas, but neither would have been nominated if he had not shared the president's political perspective. The majority of the Senate had a different perspective but rejected Bork while reluctantly accepting Thomas. Bork's legalism and past record of taking unpopular positions worked against him in much of the same way it might against a candidate for elective office. Thomas, like many successful political candidates, won support by appealing to emotions while being short on specifics. One result of the Thomas hearing may have been to mobilize women in the liberal camp. The nomination fights also show that, while the president has the initiative in shaping the Supreme Court through power of nomination, the Senate has an effective check if it chooses to use it.

Source: Bork 1990, 267–349; Pertschuk and Schaetzel 1989; Kaminar 1992, 59–70; *Congressional Quarterly Weekly Report*, 21 September 1991, 2689–92; *Congressional Quarterly Weekly Report*, 28 September 1991, 2786–87; *Congressional Quarterly Weekly Report*, 12 October 1991, 2948–57.

entire process and called for change. Since George Washington's presidency, one in every five presidential nominations to the Supreme Court has been rejected (Tribe 1985, 94). Still, 80 percent of the time the president's first choice reaches the Supreme Court, and the vast majority of presidential appointments to federal district and circuit courts are confirmed.

It is not surprising that judicial appointments should reflect the president's partisan political and ideological interests. In the last century more than 90 percent of those chosen for federal judicial positions have been members of the same political party as the president who appointed them (Carp and Stidham 1985, 99). Ronald Reagan was especially vigilant about ensuring that his nominees shared his conservative political philosophy; he refused to consider some Republicans because they supported abortion rights or gun control. His

ideological criteria led to charges that he was "packing" the court with conservative appointees (*New York Times*, 29 September 1985, D21; see also Schwartz 1988, 94).

Once on the court, do justices continue to reflect the president's ideas? According to two studies, about three-fourths of the justices have generally followed the political philosophy of the president who appointed them. Thus presidential appointments can clearly affect the course of events on the Court, but there are no guarantees. Lifetime appointment serves just as the framers intended: it gives judges a substantial measure of independence. Justice Sandra Day O'Connor (see Profile), while agreeing with Ronald Reagan, the president who appointed her, on many issues, has nonetheless contradicted him on social issues. Earl Warren, whom President Dwight Eisenhower believed would be a moderate chief justice when he made the appointment, led one

Charles Bissell. Courtesy *The Tennessean*.

THE STEALTH JUDGE: ABLE TO SWEEP THROUGH SENATE CONFIRMATION HEARINGS WITH HIS IDEOLOGY UNDETECTED

SOUTER

John Spencer. Courtesy artist. Reprinted with permission of *Philadelphia Business Journal*.

of the most liberal courts in history (Scigliano 1971, 96–99, 146–60; Tribe 1985, 60–65, 89–92, 128–34). As Harry Truman once put it, "Whenever you put a man on the Supreme Court he ceases to be your friend" (quoted in Abraham 1993, 74).

Congressional Power   In addition to the Senate's power to "advise and consent" to judicial appointments, three important checks Congress has on the judiciary are the power to pass laws, the power to propose constitutional amendments, and the power to determine the jurisdiction of the federal courts. When a federal court makes a decision based solely on a law passed by Congress, Congress may nullify the decision simply by amending the law in question. In *Ward's Cove Packing Co. v. Antonio* (1989) the Supreme Court ruled that the 1964 Civil Rights Act, which banned job discrimination by private companies, applied only if a plaintiff could show that there was no "business justification" for the firm's employment practice. Thus, if a company required all em-

ployees to have a high school diploma, a qualification that would tend to reduce the number of blacks hired, there was no violation of law unless the requirement could be proven unjustified. This decision, which reversed an earlier case, angered liberals in Congress, who in 1991 managed to pass a new Civil Rights Act, which put the burden of proof back on the employer to justify employment practices (*Congressional Quarterly Weekly Report*, 8 June 1991, 1500–01; *Congressional Quarterly Weekly Report* 7 December 1991, 3586–87).

If the Supreme Court bases a decision on some provision of the Constitution, a constitutional amendment is usually required to overturn it. Constitutional amendments require the support of two-thirds of both houses of Congress and three-fourths of the states (see Figure 2.4), a level of support very difficult to obtain unless the decision is unpopular throughout the country. Nevertheless, five amendments have been passed specifically to reverse Supreme Court decisions: the Eleventh, which overruled a decision allowing

Sandra Day O'Connor: First Woman on the Supreme Court

Sandra Day O'Connor (Courtesy United States Supreme Court)

Sandra Day O'Connor, the first woman to be appointed to the Supreme Court, was born on March 26, 1930, the first child of ranchers Harry and Ada Mae Day, who owned the three-hundred-acre Lazy B ranch on the New Mexico–Arizona border. By age ten, she could drive a tractor, brand a steer, and shoot a rifle. Her father, an inventive and resourceful type who designed a solar water heater for the ranch fifty years before such heaters became common, taught his daughter individualism, independence, and Republican politics. O'Connor is not only the first woman justice, but the only one in the Court's history who can talk at length on the subject of how to make adobe bricks

by hand, a trade she learned helping her parents add rooms to the ranch house.

A brilliant student, O'Connor graduated from high school at sixteen, then breezed through Stanford University and law school in just five years. While there she briefly dated William Rehnquist, later to be chief justice, but married John O'Connor, a fellow editor of the law review. Despite her stellar academic record, however, Sandra Day O'Connor could not get a job in any major law firm when she graduated in 1952. "None had ever hired a woman as a lawyer," she recalls, "and they were not prepared to do so." After her husband joined a law firm in Phoenix, Arizona, she became a housewife and raised three sons. It was not until 1965 that she got a job, as an assistant attorney general for the state of Arizona.

O'Connor rose in Republican circles after being appointed to fill a vacant seat in the Arizona Senate in 1969. After becoming Senate majority leader, she ran for and won a job as a state trial judge, earning a reputation as a stern law-and-order advocate. Once, a mother of two young children, guilty of passing bad checks, came before O'Connor for sentencing. She asked for mercy for the children's sake. O'Connor sentenced her to two years in prison—then went to her chambers and wept.

State trial judges are usually not appointed to the Supreme Court. However, Ronald Reagan had pledged to appoint a woman to the Court, and when Potter Stewart retired in April 1981, there were few Republican women jurists available. O'Connor had the backing of Rehnquist and Arizona's libertarian senator, Barry Goldwater, and on July 7, 1981, Reagan announced her nomination. Sandra Day O'Connor, who once could not

federal courts ever reach the United States Supreme Court, the top of the judicial pyramid (see Figure 8.2). About 4 percent of these involve major constitutional issues; the rest relate to federal law (*Statistical Abstract, 1992,* 193; O'Brien 1986, 204). This textbook concentrates on constitutional issues because of their importance to the governmental system, but it is important to remember that most cases involve issues relating to the administration of justice or the meaning of laws and regulations in individual instances.

The Supreme Court, the court of last resort, consists of nine justices including a chief justice presiding. All nine hear each case that comes before the Court, and each has one vote. Until 1925 the Court heard all cases appealed to it from the lower courts. In that year Congress acted to trim a growing caseload by granting the justices the power of **certiorari**—the right to decide which appeals have enough merit to warrant a further hearing. Only four of the nine justices must vote to grant certiorari for a case to be placed on the Court's docket; still, 85–90 percent of the more than two thousand appeals reaching the Court are denied certiorari. In 1990 only 114—a little less than 2 percent of the six thousand or so cases requesting a grant of certiorari—received a full hearing with oral argument before the Court (*Statistical Abstract, 1992,* 193). A case is much more likely to be granted a hearing if it in-

Figure 8.2   The U.S. Judicial Process

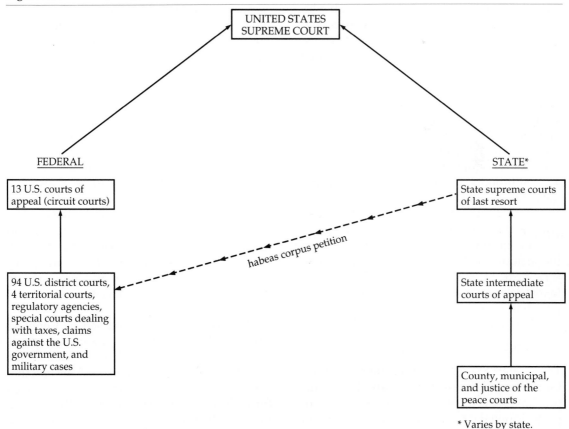

volves a major public policy issue, especially a civil liberties issue, than if it concerns only or primarily the parties to the case. The Court is also inclined to hear cases where a state or the national government is appealing an adverse lower court decision (Provine 1980, 74–103).

Once a case is accepted, attorneys for the two sides submit written briefs arguing their positions. In most important cases, persons or interest groups concerned about the issue file **amicus curiae** (friend of the court) briefs stating their views. After briefs have been submitted, oral argument is heard from counsel on both sides. The justices then deliberate, considering each case collectively. Decisions are reached by majority vote.

Often a clear majority develops quickly; at other times no point of view commands a majority in the beginning, and considerable bargaining and compromise may be necessary. After reaching a decision, the Court issues a written opinion supporting its ruling, but dissents by the minority are common and are published along with the majority opinion. In many cases the Court simply reaffirms the lower court's ruling without issuing a written opinion. If a decision is based on constitutional grounds, it is binding on lower federal and state courts until the justices reverse it or until a constitutional amendment is passed (Rehnquist 1987; see also O'Brien 1986, 213–75).

The chief justice has only one vote, like the other justices, but has the power to assign the task of writing the Court's opinion when in the majority. Often, but not always, chief justices have been leaders on the Court. Chief Justice Warren was more dominant, for example, than Chief Justice Burger.

The Rule of Law

The United States, like other democracies, is said to live under the **rule of law**. This phrase can have several meanings. One is that the people are to be treated in accordance with the general principles embodied in the law, not according to the arbitrary decisions of govern-

ment officials. Another is that government officials as much as ordinary citizens are bound to obey the laws and subject to penalties for failing to do so. In the Watergate scandal, the rule of law brought down a president and sent many of his aides to jail (see Controversy in Chapter 7). A third meaning is that the laws themselves must apply equally to people regardless of considerations like race and gender; this meaning has posed the greatest problems for Americans (see Chapter 9).

Law in the United States has several sources. One, obviously, is the bills enacted into law by Congress and the state legislatures as well as ordinances passed by local governments. This type of law is known as **statute law**. However, judges in the United States also follow the **common law**, a set of principles derived from past judicial decisions, some of which go back to England in the Middle Ages. For example, common law dictates that contracts made voluntarily between individuals are to be respected and enforced by the courts, except under unusual circumstances (R. Epstein 1992, 20–27).

Under American legal procedure, common law rules unless and until it is overridden by statute law. For example, laws against racial discrimination override the common law presumption that contracts are to be enforced: a court will no longer enforce a contract between two whites that calls for discrimination against blacks. For example, housing covenants, formal agreements common before the 1950s in which buyers promised that if and when they sold their houses they would sell only to whites, are no longer enforceable and are actually illegal.

However, the statutes passed by Congress and state legislatures also require interpretation by the courts, and such interpretations are law unless they are superseded by another law enacted by the legislature. Laws created through such interpretations as well as judicial interpretations of the Constitution and administrative agency decisions form **case law**.

Since the emergence of the common law in

England, judges have relied for guidance on **stare decisis** (to stand by decided matters), or **precedent**, the principle that new cases should be decided in the same manner as similar, previous cases. In England, where the courts have little policy-making power, stare decisis is followed fairly strictly. In the United States, and especially on the Supreme Court, a more flexible pattern has emerged as judges respond to pressure to use their much greater powers to promote policy goals. Precedent is still important, but its application is colored by the political perspectives of the judges. One study of the Supreme Court in the early 1970s found that 85 percent of the decisions could be predicted in advance by the past record and political philosophy of the Court's members (Rohde and Spaeth 1976, 145–51: see also Tribe 1985, 122–23). On the other hand, surprises can happen. Many observers were shocked when, in *Texas v. Johnson* (1989), a Supreme Court believed to be conservative ruled that flag burning was protected by the First Amendment.

Problems of the Judicial Process

In 1960, 79,200 cases were filed in U.S. district courts, and 3,765 appeals were made to the circuit courts (Posner 1985, 61). In 1990, 269,900 cases were filed—an increase of 293 percent—and the number of appeals was up to 40,898—an increase of 920 percent (*Statistical Abstract, 1992,* 193). Some of the caseload increase is the result of decisions to get tough on crime by making more crimes a federal offense. But the federal caseload explosion is only one element in an overcrowding affecting all courts that has resulted from the exponential increase in litigation. Among the causes of this increase are a crime rate that rose dramatically during the 1960s and 1970s, leveled off in the early 1980s, and then rose again; a relaxation of rules governing the types of suits that could be filed; and an increasingly litigious public ready to go to court to settle disputes that were once privately adjusted. Among its

effects are sharply rising liability insurance rates, delays in dispensing of cases, and general frustration with the judicial system.

One effect of crowded courts at both state and federal levels is the widespread resort to **plea bargaining** in criminal cases. More than 90 percent of criminal cases nationwide are now settled by negotiations between the prosecutor and the defense attorney instead of by trial. Someone charged with several offenses, for example, may plead guilty to one in return for dismissal of the others; alternatively, a prosecutor can agree to a lesser charge for one defendant who testifies against another defendant. Plea bargaining may serve the cause of justice and efficiency by settling cases quickly, but it also permits some guilty defendants to receive light sentences while others, who exercise their constitutional rights to trial, are penalized with severe sentences if found guilty. Sometimes defense attorneys even advise innocent defendants to plead guilty rather than risk trial and conviction (Fine 1986, 76–84). The federal government, as well as some states and cities, has recently moved to place limits on the practice of plea bargaining. Such restrictions, however, add to the number of persons in prison and the expense of their maintenance.

Justice is not only slow; it is also expensive. While the high cost of justice is not entirely new, it has attracted more attention in recent years as demands for equal justice have grown. Wealthy individuals and well-financed interest groups have always been able to pay for high-priced legal talent. In recent years state-subsidized legal services have continued to make legal aid available to the poor, despite cutbacks during the Reagan administration. Still, legal services are often beyond the reach of middle-income people, who cannot qualify for government help and cannot afford a private lawyer.

And sometimes justice is not achieved. While research indicates that juries usually try to render a fair decision, they are not immune from prejudices that exist in society, and in heavily publicized cases an unpopular jury

CONTROVERSY
Justice and Juries: The Rodney King Cases

Rodney King (Reuters/Bettmann)

"Not Guilty. Not Guilty. Not . . ." The jury foreman's words rang out through the courtroom and across the nation, producing disbelief and outrage. A Simi Valley, California, jury had decided that four Los Angeles police officers had been justified in beating Rodney King, a black man they had stopped for drunk driving. The case was already front page news throughout the country, due to a videotape of the beating made by bystander George Halliday and widely shown on television. The jury's 1992 verdict would trigger the nation's worst riot since the New York draft riot of 1863, with fifty-three people killed and more than $1 billion in property damage. How could the jury have reached a verdict so apparently out of line with the evidence?

The story of the King trial begins with Judge Stanley Weisberg's decision to accept a defense request for a change of venue—a procedure that allows a trial to be moved from the place where the crime was committed to another jurisdiction. The policemen's attorneys argued that because of the massive publicity about the case, an "impartial jury," required by the Sixth Amendment to the Constitution, could not be selected in Los Angeles. However, moving the trial to Simi Valley, an affluent suburb with a population only 2 percent black, meant that few blacks would be called to serve.

Once a pool of jurors is assembled for a case, the attorneys for both sides are allowed to question them and to challenge any juror they feel would be biased. The attorneys may also remove a certain number of jurors without giving a reason (known as a peremptory challenge). In the King case, the few blacks in the pool were all eliminated, leaving a jury of ten whites, one Hispanic, and one Filipino American.

In posttrial interviews, all jury members denied that race played any role in their decision. They insisted that there was more to the case than most Americans had seen on George Halliday's videotape. King had been drunk, had led officers on an

---

verdict can have serious consequences. In April 1992, a suburban Los Angeles jury acquitted four policemen on state charges of assaulting Rodney King, a black motorist stopped for drunk driving. Popular indignation about the verdict, which seemingly contradicted a videotape of the beating, led to the worst riots in the United States since the Civil War; fifty-three people were killed (DiPerna 1984; *Time*, 11 May 1992, 30–32). A second trial on federal civil rights charges led to the conviction of two of the policemen in April 1993 (see Controversy).

The United States may come closer than

eight-mile chase, and had resisted arrest after finally stopping, at one point throwing four officers off his back as they tried to handcuff him. None of that appeared on the tape. Defense attorneys argued successfully that the tape showed that King continued to resist and try to get to his feet, forcing the officers to hit him.

However, many blacks and whites found it impossible to believe that there had not been prejudice. They remembered earlier cases like that of fifteen-year-old Latasha Harlins, shot dead by a Korean store owner in a fight over a bottle of orange juice. A judge gave the store owner, Soon Ja Du, five years probation because she had no prior record. Clearly more than racial injustice was involved in the Los Angeles riots—60 percent of those arrested were found to have criminal records, and organized criminal gangs were responsible for much of the violence. But just as clearly, perceptions of an unjust judicial system played a major role.

In the aftermath of the riots, President George Bush ordered federal prosecutors to investigate whether the four officers could be retried. Ordinarily retrial would be impossible due to the Fifth Amendment's ban on a person's being tried "for the same offence . . . twice put in jeopardy." However, the 1964 Civil Rights Act makes it a federal crime to act "under color of law" to deprive any person of his or her civil rights—and not being beaten is a civil right. Using this justification, the federal government brought civil rights charges against the officers.

The federal case, tried in March and April 1993, took place under conditions different from those of the first trial. The jury, selected from throughout the federal court district of southern California, had two blacks, one Hispanic, and nine whites. Most observers felt that the federal prosecutors put together a much better case than the state prosecutor had at the first trial. For one thing, Rodney King himself testified to refute the police version of the events. Although they were instructed to disregard it, the second jury could not help knowing that another not guilty verdict might trigger another riot. On April 18, 1993, they reached a verdict: guilty for Sergeant Stacy Koon, who commanded the other officers, and Officer Laurence Powell, who struck the most blows. Officers Timothy Wind and Theodore Briseno were again found not guilty. There was no recurrence of rioting.

Was justice done in either of the Rodney King cases? Most Americans thought the police had used excessive force in subduing King, and many thought that the first verdict had proved that the judicial system was racist. On the other hand, in the second case the government used a loophole in the law to retry individuals acquitted by a jury of their peers. Was this fair to the police officers or to members of the second jury, faced with making a decision that might cost dozens of lives and millions of dollars? Given the situation, what choices were available to the government?

Source: DiPerna 1984; *Understanding the Riots* 1992; *U.S. News and World Report,* 31 May 1993, 35–57.

most other nations to achieving the motto inscribed above the entrance to the Supreme Court: "Equal Justice under Law." The judicial system is not, however, a model of efficiency. The federal system, with fifty-one different court systems, and the judicial process, with extensive safeguards to guarantee individual rights, do not make for swift, easy, or cheap resolution of disputes. Average citizens involved in litigation may take cold comfort from the knowledge that the judges and lawyers who run the system often share their frustration.

PERSPECTIVES

Adherents of all six perspectives tend to judge the judiciary by its effects on public policy. As judicial policy changes, views regarding the courts also change.

Conservative

From the conservative perspective, the courts should play an important but limited role in American government. Conservatives revere the Constitution, and they expect the courts to uphold the basic principles of fundamental law against invasion by the executive or legislative branch through, for example, laws destroying private property rights or denying freedom of religion.

Conservatives contend that the liberal Warren Court and, to a lesser degree, the Burger Court went wrong by playing a major policy-making role. They contend that judges have little special knowledge of policy issues and no direct contact with the people whose lives may be affected by their decisions. Moreover, conservatives believe the intent of the framers must govern constitutional interpretation and that the framers never intended the courts to make laws for the nation. The liberal courts of the 1960s and early 1970s, by employing liberal interpretations of the Constitution, have enforced liberal policies such as integration by busing, the right to an abortion, and an expansion of the rights of criminal defendants. While the courts have become more conservative since then, most of these liberal policies remain in place. This kind of policy-making is dangerous, conservatives say, because judges do not represent the people and there is little reason to believe that their values conform to what most Americans want. Antonin Scalia, a conservative justice appointed to the Supreme Court by Ronald Reagan, wrote in 1984, "Where the courts do enforce adherence to legislative policies that the political process itself would not enforce, they are likely to be enforcing the prejudices of their own class" (quoted in Vigilante 1984, 23). Conservatives fear that checks on judicial power have become so weak that the nation is in danger of being governed by unelected judges rather than by representatives of the people.

What do conservatives want to see the judiciary do? First and foremost, they want judges, and especially Supreme Court justices, to interpret the Constitution in accord with the original intent of its authors. Conservatives recognize that not everything in the Constitution can be taken literally, but they believe that "the meaning of the Constitution can be known" and that "the meaning can be understood and applied" (Meese III 1986, 33). Sticking to original intent is vital because it is the only way judges can keep from usurping the power of Congress and state legislators to make the laws. Today, sticking to original intent would require overruling some precedents. Generally, however, conservatives believe the courts should stick as closely to precedent as to original intent in interpreting the Constitution. The conservative William Rehnquist (see Profile), appointed to the Supreme Court by President Richard Nixon and promoted to chief justice by President Ronald Reagan, is a firm believer in original intent.

During their terms in office, Ronald Reagan and George Bush appointed five justices to the Supreme Court, and their effect will be felt in the 1990s. On issues ranging from abortion to civil rights, the Supreme Court's recent decisions (often by a vote of 5–4) have had a fairly conservative slant. Three Reagan-Bush appointees, however, have been willing to part with the views of the presidents who appointed them. Sandra Day O'Connor (see Profile earlier in this chapter), Anthony Kennedy, and David Souter have taken more centrist positions than had been expected. In 1992, Kennedy returned to the conservative fold, and Souter voted more liberal (*Christian Science Monitor*, 1 July 1993, 1, 4).

In addition to the presidential appointment power, conservatives troubled by judicial activism in support of liberal policies have sought to activate other checks on the judicial branch. During the 1960s, some conservatives sponsored efforts to impeach Chief Justice Earl Warren. More recently they have pushed for restrictions on the Supreme Court's jurisdiction and for constitutional amendments to reverse court decisions on school prayer, abortion, busing, and flag burning—efforts that appear to contradict the conservative reverence for established institutions.

Liberal

Since the 1950s and the Warren Court, liberals have favored an activist, reform-oriented judiciary. In defending this position they challenge virtually every point made by the conservatives. First, they deny that judicial policy-making is incompatible with democracy. It is too narrow a view of democracy, they say, to regard democracy simply as a system by which the majority rules. To fulfill its promise, American democracy must guarantee to minority groups and individuals the rights granted to them in the Constitution. If the legislative branch, swayed by a passing popular mood, could deny or abridge these rights, the will of the enduring majority expressed in the Constitution would be frustrated. The judiciary, by being insulated from public pressure, is uniquely qualified to protect individual and minority rights (Dworkin 1977, 137–49; see also Rostow 1952, 193–224; Tribe 1985, 23–25). In fact, liberals point out, politicians are often happy to have the courts decide inflammatory issues like busing and abortion, freeing them from making a choice between the "right" and the politically popular course.

Second, liberals also question the conservative assertion that original intent should be the governing principle in constitutional interpretation. One problem with this standard is that it may be impossible to determine what the framers intended with regard to a contemporary issue. For example, cases involving the public schools can hardly be decided on the basis of original intent, since few public schools existed in 1789.

Even when original intent is fairly clear, however, liberals do not believe it should always be followed. Applying the original meaning of the Constitution under greatly changed conditions can lead to unjust or absurd results. For example, the authors of the Fourteenth Amendment probably did not intend to grant women the right to abortions, although some states did allow abortions at the time the amendment was passed, 1868. They could not have foreseen, however, the development of safer procedures for abortions, health problems resulting from unregulated illegal abortions, and the entry of middle-class women into the paid work force. In the liberal view, it is entirely appropriate for the courts to reinterpret the Constitution in the light of twentieth-century realities, so long as basic constitutional principles—such as separation of powers and freedom of expression—are maintained (*New York Times Magazine*, 23 February 1986, 42, 59–60, 67–68; see also Levy 1988, 350–87). Justice William O. Douglas (see Profile), who served from 1937 to 1975, is an excellent example of a liberal justice who felt that interpreting the Constitution to meet the needs of contemporary society was the proper role of a judge. What liberals want from the judiciary is continued protection and extension of individual and minority rights, especially the freedoms of religion, press, speech, and assembly in the First Amendment and the right against racial discrimination in the Fourteenth Amendment. What they fear is a narrowing of these protections by an increasingly conservative judiciary. Eight of the nine justices now serving on the Supreme Court were appointed by Nixon, Ford, Reagan, or Bush. The retirement of more elderly justices could begin to

"I SAID, 'I HAVE GOOD NEWS, DEAR!'...."

Jim Borgman. Courtesy artist and *Cincinnati Enquirer*.

PROFILE
William Rehnquist: A Conservative on the Supreme Court

William Rehnquist (Courtesy United States Supreme Court)

The current chief justice, William Rehnquist, exemplifies the conservative ideal for the Supreme Court. Rehnquist was born in Wisconsin in 1924 to an activist Republican family. He went on to obtain a master's degree in political science from Harvard University in 1950 and finish first in his class at Stanford University Law School in 1952. He moved to Arizona and entered Republican politics, and in 1969 he was recruited by the Nixon administration as deputy attorney general. In 1971 President Nixon put Rehnquist on the Supreme Court, and in 1986 President Reagan made him chief justice, following the retirement of the more moderate conservative Warren Burger.

"I'm a strong believer in pluralism," Rehnquist once told an interviewer. "Don't concentrate all the power in one place. . . . You don't want all the power in the Federal Government as opposed to the states." Rehnquist believes that federalism is an important part of the Constitution ignored by liberal justices. At almost every opportunity, he votes to uphold state power in disputes with the national government. For example, in *Garcia v. San Antonio Metropolitan Transit Authority* (1985) he dissented from a 5–4 decision that required state and local governments to pay the federal minimum wage to their workers, arguing that the federal government had no business interfering in relations between the states and their employees.

While opposed to concentration of power, Rehnquist has been a strong "law and order" advocate throughout his years on the Court. He supports the death penalty; has backed decisions that narrow the *Miranda* rule, which requires police to warn suspects of their rights; and opposes the exclusionary rule, which bans the use in court of illegally seized evidence. He supports pretrial detention for dangerous suspects, arguing that "society has a right to protect its citizens, for limited periods, from persons who pose a serious threat to life and safety." Rehnquist has attacked Warren Court decisions in this area so strongly that liberals accuse him of ignoring precedents he dislikes.

Perhaps the most controversial aspect of Rehnquist's career has been his record on racial issues. During the early 1960s he opposed laws desegregating public accommodations, arguing that "a measure of our traditional freedom" would be lost if restaurants were forced to serve blacks. He later did concede that a Phoenix antidiscrimination law had "worked really well," but he still opposes affirmative action programs and busing to achieve school integration.

In his early years as a justice, Rehnquist was known for his acidic dissents from liberal rulings. When the Court ruled in 1977 that minors had a right to buy contraceptives, he wrote, "It is hard to imagine the reaction of those who valiantly, but vainly defended the heights of Bunker Hill in 1775, if they could have lived to know that their efforts had enshrined in the Constitution the right of commercial vendors of contraceptives to peddle them to unmarried minors through vending machines located in the men's room of truck stops." Such absurd results, in Rehnquist's view, could only come from the liberal effort to disregard original intent and invent new constitution "rights" for every situation.

For most of his career Rehnquist's conservative views isolated him on the Court. Then Reagan's judicial revolution made Rehnquist's views respectable, even mainstream. As chief justice, Rehnquist has not been the leader as much as some earlier chief justices have been, primarily because the Court has other articulate conservatives like Justice Antonin Scalia. However, Rehnquist remains an important player on the Court's right wing.

Source: Guide to the U.S. Supreme Court 1979, 865; Rehnquist quoted in Boles 1987, 16, 64, 76, 85; Alderman and Kennedy 1991, 334.

shift the balance of power in a liberal direction, since Democrats have recaptured the presidency. Liberals would like to see a return of an activist court like that led by Earl Warren. With President Clinton's first appointment going to a moderate, Ruth Bader Ginsburg, the return to a Warren-type Court may seem unlikely to some liberals. However, as vacancies open up in the future, many expect President Clinton to make more activist-minded appointments.

Libertarian

Libertarians combine elements of conservative and liberal thinking in their view of the judiciary and their interpretation of the Constitution. Like conservatives, they believe that the courts have little justification for legislating under the guise of settling disputes. Libertarians particularly oppose large-scale judicial intervention in the private economy to correct social problems, as in the case of judicially mandated affirmative action programs. On the other hand, they sympathize with the liberal desire to protect individual and minority rights from government intrusion. On issues like abortion and pornography, they usually side with the liberals in supporting judicial decisions that prevent government from enforcing moral legislation regulating private behavior.

Most libertarians agree with liberals in rejecting original intent as a guide to interpretation, arguing that it leads to an excessively restrictive view of individual rights. They also reject the conservative argument that the majority's moral values have a status superior to those of minorities as a whole or of individuals (Macedo 1986, 15–31). On the other hand, libertarians cannot accept the liberal view that the Constitution can be shaped and molded according to the perceived "needs" of the times because they believe that the eternal principles of individual freedom embodied in the Constitution should not be at the mercy of popu-

Herblock. From *Herblock on All Fronts* (New American Library, 1980).

William O. Douglas: A Liberal on the Supreme Court

William O. Douglas (Courtesy United States Supreme Court)

Born in Main, Minnesota, on October 16, 1898, to an impoverished family, William O. Douglas went on to become one of the greatest liberal justices ever to sit on the Supreme Court. After suffering a polio attack as a child, Douglas hiked in the mountains near his home to increase strength in his legs. This activity stimulated an early interest in the outdoors that carried over into his adult life. After graduating from Columbia Law School in 1925, Douglas became known as a top financial lawyer. An ardent supporter of the New Deal, Douglas served as chair of the new Securities and Exchange Commission, formed to regulate the stock market after the 1929 crash. When a vacancy appeared on the Supreme Court in 1937, Roosevelt chose Douglas to support his liberal programs against the libertarian justices who dominated the Court in the 1930s. Douglas did so, voting to uphold strong antitrust laws and other economic regulations against what he called "the vicious powers of the corporate world."

Douglas won his greatest fame, however, as a defender of individual civil rights and liberties. In *Griswold v. Connecticut* (1965) he got the majority of the Court to strike down a Connecticut law that banned the use of birth control devices. Acknowl-

lar majorities. Some of these principles, like property rights, have been neglected by liberal judges, while others have been elevated. What is needed, say libertarians, is a "principled judicial activism" in which the judiciary uses its power to protect the rights of Americans against oppressive majorities (Macedo 1986, 43–50). One libertarian justice who strongly believed that the judiciary should practice this kind of activism was George Sutherland (see Profile).

Libertarians are responsible for the development of the new form of legal analysis called "law and economics." The law and economics approach contends that, in deciding cases, judges should begin with the presumption that free markets and voluntary contracts between individuals are to be upheld. To justify interference with individual choices, legislators should have to show that government regulation produces a more desirable result for more people than would unregulated relationships. Ordinarily this will not be the case, because individuals generally enter into a contract only if it brings them benefits (R. Epstein 1992, 15–27). For example, a zoning ordinance that restricts what individuals may do with their property would be held unconstitutional unless the community can prove that some imperfection in the market makes regulation necessary. Today the law requires only that the state show a "rational" basis for intervention. Libertarians believe in general that the courts' function is to guard against government infringement on the rights of citizens.

edging that the Constitution contained no explicit right to use birth control, Douglas argued that the Supreme Court had the duty to create new rights to give "life and substance" to the Bill of Rights under conditions not foreseen by the framers. Noting that the Constitution did protect citizens from unreasonable search and seizure, Douglas asked rhetorically, "Would we allow the police to search the sacred precincts of the marital bedrooms for telltale signs of the use of contraceptives?"

On many other issues, Douglas fought for the liberal doctrine that the Constitution must grow and change. A strong opponent of U.S. cold war policies (see Chapter 11), he argued successfully that the Supreme Court should hear cases brought by people who argued that the Vietnam War was unconstitutional because Congress never declared war. The majority of the Court thought the issue was a political question, outside their jurisdiction, but Douglas noted that the Court had forbidden President Truman to seize steel mills during the Korean War. "A man whose life may be taken," he remarked, "or whose legs may be shot off in Vietnam has as high a right to judicial protection as have the steel mills," Douglas said.

An outdoorsman and early environmentalist, Douglas also fought against clear-cutting of Western forests. Douglas abhorred racial discrimination and strongly supported the Warren Court's decisions against segregation. On the other hand, he also surprised some of his liberal colleagues by sympathizing with whites subject to reverse discrimination. Some critics charged that Douglas, like Rehnquist, was more a politician than a judge, but he rejected the idea of a politically "neutral" Supreme Court, saying, "On most issues, the Constitution is not neutral. It vigorously champions freedom of expression, not censorship; it declares against self-incrimination, not for inquisition; it proclaims against the establishment of a religion by the state. . . . The Constitution is not neutral when it comes to race: and a Court, therefore, that undertook to pose as neutral would not be faithful to the constitutional scheme."

Source: Guide to the U.S. Supreme Court 1979, 852; Douglas 1975, 55, 137, 166; Douglas quoted in Alderman and Kennedy 1991, 318.

Populist

Since the judiciary is the branch of government least responsive to majority control, it is not surprising that populists have severe disagreements with the courts. In the last century these centered on economics: populists strongly opposed libertarian Supreme Court decisions limiting the regulation of big business.

In the early nineteenth century Jacksonians worked for the popular election of judges, a practice adopted by most states though never by the national government. In the early twentieth century populists helped pass the Sixteenth Amendment, allowing an income tax on the wealthy, after the Supreme Court had declared such a tax unconstitutional. More recently, right populists resisted Court orders to integrate schools and to end public support of religion.

From the populist perspective, the problem with a powerful judiciary is that it is based on the theory that someone knows better than the people what is the best. If judges are going to exercise the power of judicial review, populists, like conservatives, want it exercised with restraint. Their reason, however, is not that past decisions or the original intent of the framers deserve veneration; it is because unelected judges should not try to control other people's lives. Justice Hugo Black (see Profile) held to this view while he served from 1937 until 1971.

PROFILE
George Sutherland: A Libertarian on the Supreme Court

George Sutherland (Courtesy United States Supreme Court)

From the Civil War to the 1930s, libertarians dominated the Supreme Court. One of the last eminent libertarian justices was George Sutherland, who served on the Court from 1922 to 1938. The son of a poor English Mormon immigrant, Sutherland dropped out of school at twelve but later worked his way through Brigham Young University and the University of Michigan Law School. Many of his teachers were libertarians, and the self-made Sutherland found their philosophy congenial. After becoming a successful lawyer, Sutherland entered politics as a Republican and served Utah in both Houses of Congress from 1900 to 1916. In 1922 he was tapped by President Warren G. Harding for a Supreme Court seat.

Sutherland showed his libertarianism in one of his first cases, *Adkins v. Children's Hospital* (1923), writing an opinion that struck down a law passed by Congress setting minimum wages for women workers in the District of Columbia. He pointed out that, since market forces set wages, the law actually discriminated against women by causing them to be fired if their work was not worth the minimum. Denying that women needed special protection from Congress, Sutherland almost sounded like a modern feminist: "The ancient in-

Marxist

No branch of our national government has been significantly influenced by Marxists, but at least recently the judiciary has been kinder to them than have the other branches. Beginning in the late 1950s the judiciary protected the rights of unpopular Marxist groups to speak and assemble against restrictions by the states and the federal government. The Warren Court also advanced some causes that Marxists had long supported, notably that of racial equality.

Nevertheless, Marxists remain basically as critical of the judiciary as they are of the other branches of American government. From the Marxist perspective, liberal reforms by the judiciary are aimed not at correcting fundamental injustices but at preserving an unjust system. Apparently progressive Supreme Court decisions have usually represented minor changes that tend to pacify the discontented without really altering their condition. For example, giving poor defendants the right to counsel has the appearance of making the legal system more equitable but does not really correct the inequality between the poor person with a court-appointed attorney and the wealthy person with an experienced and expensive lawyer. Similarly, school integration decisions have led to some integration and probably made blacks less dissatisfied with the system, but they have not improved the inferior education offered low-income children (Roelofs 1982, 249–66).

equality of the sexes has . . . come now almost, if not quite, to the vanishing point. . . . We cannot accept the doctrine that women of mature age require, or may be subjected to, restrictions upon their liberty of contract which could not lawfully be imposed upon men under similar circumstances."

Sutherland often used federalism to limit congressional restrictions on business. In *Schechter Poultry Company v. United States* (1935) he voted to declare President Roosevelt's National Recovery Administration (NRA) unconstitutional because it regulated wages and prices for small businesses not directly involved in interstate commerce. Unlike conservatives, however, Sutherland was willing to check state actions as well when they contravened his notion of economic or civil rights. In *Powell v. Alabama* (1932) he wrote the opinion in the first case in which the Supreme Court struck down a state criminal conviction as a result of an unfair trial. Noting that Powell, one of nine black youths accused of rape, had been tried without proper counsel and under threat of a lynching if not convicted, Sutherland accused the state of Alabama of deciding "not to proceed promptly in the calm spirit of regulated justice but to go forward in the haste of the mob." Overall, Sutherland's career shows a highly activist stance toward the

Constitution, driven by a belief that individual rights (especially, but not exclusively, property rights) need judicial protection from the tyranny of the majority. While still a senator, he expressed this libertarian philosophy succinctly:

> The written constitution is the shelter and the bulwark of what might otherwise be a helpless minority. Tyranny is no less hateful in the hands of the people than in the hands of the despot, and the oppression of the minority by the majority is tyranny no less than the arbitrary oppression of the king. The forward march of democracy will be of little avail if in the end it delivers us to the absolutism of the majority.

Source: Paschal 1951, 3–36; Sutherland quoted in Paschal 1951, 78, 120–21, 216.

Unfortunately, little more can be expected from the judiciary, say Marxists, since American judges usually come from affluent backgrounds and accept the basic principles of capitalism without question. According to Marxists, judicial intervention may reduce some forms of oppression, but the way to social justice lies through transforming the economic system, not through judicial policymaking. A Marxist would argue, in fact, that by alleviating the most blatant symptoms of an oppressive system, the Court prevents the revolutionary outburst necessary to begin this transformation.

Feminist

Feminists recognize the importance of the judiciary in either impeding or facilitating women's progress. The Court's refusal to include women as a category for protection under the Equal Protection Clause of the Fourteenth Amendment until the 1970s was a major roadblock to the progress of

PROFILE
Hugo Black: A Populist on the Supreme Court

Hugo Black (Courtesy United States Supreme Court)

Relatively few populists have sat on the Supreme Court. One who did, and became one of the most respected jurists in American history, was Hugo Black of Alabama. Black was born in February 1886, and twenty years later, in 1906, he had obtained his law degree from the University of Alabama. For two years in the 1920s he was a member of the Ku Klux Klan for its political and social benefits, an association he later regretted. Black became an ardent supporter of Franklin Roosevelt's New Deal while serving in the Senate in the 1930s. Like William O. Douglas, Black was tapped by Roosevelt in 1937 to change the majority that had dominated the Court up to then. Although not a consistent populist, Black comes the closest of any recent justice to representing this perspective.

Black agreed with the liberal Douglas about upholding economic regulation and many individual liberties. Unlike most populists, he opposed limits on freedom of speech and press because a literal reading of the Constitution does not appear to allow for such limits. Black is famous for his argument that when the First Amendment says "Congress shall make no law abridging freedom of speech, I read 'no law abridging' to mean 'no law abridging.'" He felt upholding the Constitution, even at the cost of allowing pornography (which he detested), was vital to the freedom of ordinary people.

women. Similarly, the court appointments of Ronald Reagan and George Bush, with the possible exception of Sandra Day O'Connor (see Profile earlier in this chapter) were not welcomed by feminists concerned about abortion rights.

Feminists have criticized the legal system of the United States as male in conception and operation. They do not see male domination as the result of a conspiracy on the part of men against women, however, and are pleased by the many gains made by women within the legal profession and as a result of legal decisions during the last twenty years.

Still, this change is slow, resisted, and often brought on by forces outside the judiciary's control. The civil rights movements of the 1960s and Civil Rights Act of 1964, feminists point out, were instrumental in the Supreme Court's reinterpretation of the Equal Protection Clause as applying to women, following years of case precedents holding that a special standard for women precluded their protection under this clause (see Chapters 2 and 9). Radical feminists continue to see the legal system and its case precedents as based on an earlier paternalistic conception of women as weak and inferior to men (Baron 1987, 474–503). Evidence that justice is still rendered unequally can be found in the application of criminal law. For example, although arrests of women doubled during the period between 1970 and 1980, men were four times as likely to be given a death sentence for committing a violent crime resulting in death.

At the same time, Black strongly rejected the liberal argument that the Supreme Court had the responsibility to change the Constitution to fit the times. As a populist, he contended that only the people could correct injustices not forbidden by the Constitution. In the *Griswold* case (1965), he agreed that the Connecticut law against birth control was silly but argued that the state had a right to pass such a law because there was no constitutionally guaranteed right to "marital privacy." Dissenting from Douglas's majority opinion he remarked, "I like my privacy as well as the next one, but I am nevertheless compelled to admit that the government has a right to invade it unless prohibited by some specific constitutional provision." This was exactly the view expressed by the conservative Robert Bork more than twenty years later.

On other issues as well, Black sided sometimes with liberals, sometimes with conservatives. Despite his background, he became convinced that school segregation was unconstitutional and voted for the *Brown* decision in 1954, a vote that ruined his son's chances of being elected to Congress from Alabama. On the other hand, he contended that private property owners had the right to exclude blacks from their restaurants and hotels until Congress legislated otherwise. Generally, Black was more aligned with Court liberals in his early career and grew more conservative in his later years as he saw the Warren Court challenge traditional social values. He summed up his belief in popular control of government and a limited role for the unelected Supreme Court as follows in his dissent on the *Griswold* case:

> I realize that many good and able men have eloquently spoken and written . . . about the duty of this Court to keep the Constitution in tune with the times. The idea is that the Constitution must be changed from time to time and that this Court is charged with a duty to make those changes. For myself, I must with all deference reject that philosophy. The Constitution makers knew the need for change and provided for it. Amendments suggested by the people's elected representatives can be submitted to the people or their elected agents for ratification. That method of change was good for our Fathers, and being somewhat old-fashioned I must add it is good enough for me.

Source: Black quoted in *Guide to the U.S. Supreme Court* 1979, 390; Yarbrough 1988, 241; Black quoted in Yarbrough 1988, 23, 59; Berman 1967, 75–95.

Men were also more likely to receive longer sentences for similar crimes; women were more likely to be given probationary sentences (Moulds 1982, 205–31).

In essence, say feminists, traditional patterns of socialization that treat women as children (less dangerous and less responsible) are still embedded in the American judicial system. Special treatment is, in the words of a song by Marlo Thomas, "the kind of help we all can do without." The types of discrimination that women have traditionally experienced at the hands of the legal system will be difficult to weed out of a legal code grounded in ancient custom and tradition. Laws enacted by legislatures and decisions of courts have set the tone for the inferior regard of women held by much of society by helping institutionalize assumptions that are at the bases of such laws. Most of the judges and lawyers who have participated in this process have been male. Even in 1990 only 10 percent of state court judges at all levels were women. Similarly, only 10 percent of all sitting federal district court judges and 13 percent of all sitting appellate and bankruptcy court judges were female. The recent appointment of Ruth Bader Ginsburg to the Supreme Court makes it, with two female justices (or 22 percent female), the most representative level, in terms of gender, in the federal judicial system (McPherson interview 1993).

O'Connor, appointed by President Ronald Reagan, and Ginsburg, appointed by President

Bill Clinton, both illustrate the point made by some feminists that women often are able to resolve the questions on issues that have proved divisive to male peers. Although O'Connor is a moderate conservative and Ginsburg a moderate liberal, both have been termed centrist and have the respect of colleagues on the courts on which they sat. In her decade on the Supreme Court, O'Connor helped to mold the new centrist majority on the court in regard to reproductive rights. Moving away from the "trimester" provisions delineated by Justice Harry Blackmun in his majority opinion in *Roe v. Wade* (1973), O'Connor convinced several justices of the importance of balancing the needs of state government against the needs of the individual by stating that although the state has an interest in regulating the area of abortion, it cannot place an undue burden on a woman's right to procure an abortion. It is much too early to know what role Ginsburg will play on the Supreme Court, but her role as a respected centrist on an appellate court split between more liberal Carter appointees and more conservative appointees named by Ronald Reagan and George Bush has been attested to by colleagues from both perspectives.

O'Connor and Ginsburg know what it is like to be a woman in this largely male profession. Each graduated number one in her law school class (O'Connor from Stanford and Ginsburg from Columbia); neither was able to procure a job with a national law firm after graduation (*Wall Street Journal*, 5 June 1993, A1, A6). In a speech given in 1985, O'Connor, in her own understated way, suggested, "Women's equality under law does not effortlessly translate into equal participation in the legal profession" (quoted in Stewart 1993, 48). O'Connor, who has raised three children with her lawyer-husband, maintains without rancor that women professionals still have the primary responsibility for children and housekeeping. "The choices that women must make in this respect," she explains, "are different from the choices that men must make" (quoted in Stewart 1993, 48).

Although an increasingly large number of women are law students or practicing law (43 percent of all law students and 24 percent of all lawyers in 1993 and 1990 respectively) (McPherson

interview 1993), they suffer considerable discrimination in what remains an occupation still dominated by men. In a study of gender bias within the judicial community of Massachusetts, two-thirds of the women attorneys responding reported that they had been asked within the court whether they were in fact an attorney. Only 14 percent of male respondents practicing within the courts of Massachusetts had been asked the same question. Thirty-nine percent of all attorneys surveyed had observed at least one other attorney make inappropriate comments of a sexual or suggestive nature to a female attorney. Sixty percent of the judges responding reported observing incidents in which gender affected the relationship between opposing counsel, including belittling remarks made to female attorneys, improper address by first name or terms of endearment, and not allowing female attorneys to speak. Women attorneys also received fewer state appointments to hear cases and lower rates of pay when they were so assigned (Frug 1992, 1–60).

Some feminist scholars hope that gender bias in the judicial process will diminish as the legal work force becomes more equally divided between women and men. Others point to the positive effect of a growing number of female voices on the American legal tradition. Echoing Carol Gilligan's distinction between women's and men's ways of knowing (Gilligan 1982, 24–63), some suggest that perhaps the adversarial we-they, right-wrong approach to law that has emerged from a male-dominant way of thinking will gradually be refined by increasing numbers of female practitioners of the law who are less inclined toward hierarchical order. Once in charge, women lawyers will be more likely to account for all parties' needs (just as O'Connor has attempted to do on the issue of reproduction rights) and will emphasize communication rather than third-party arbitrated debate as the way of resolving legal claims and cases. Already many minor cases are submitted to dispute resolution (Baron 1987, 474–503). When women are well positioned at all levels of the judiciary, they will contribute to a transformation of American jurisprudence (Atkins and Hoggett 1984, 1–5).

DOES THE JUDICIARY WORK?

Democracy is capable of turning into a tyranny of the majority. The framers feared this tyranny and designed the Supreme Court as a check on the power of the majority. Unfortunately, for much of its history the Court ignored the rights of some oppressed minorities. The Warren Court remedied many serious injustices perpetuated by majorities, but Americans continue to disagree on its legacy. Two of the authors think the Warren Court occasionally went too far in creating new rights, while the third author is disturbed about the conservative trend of the recent Court.

It is important that the Supreme Court itself be subject to checks and balances. The Bork nomination shows that the president cannot put anyone he wants on the Court; the choice must be acceptable to the Senate. Other, more drastic checks like impeachment (see Chapter 2) and court packing (see Chapter 9) are available if the Court strays too far from the popular consensus.

The everyday administration of justice is as important as the resolution of constitutional issues. Securing access to the Courts has been a major problem for many Americans. Many avenues for legal representation today available to the poor and middle class did not exist thirty years ago. We believe, however, that the provisions for legal assistance need to be improved to achieve "Equal Justice under Law."

The judiciary is the least democratic part of the American political system. Yet, paradoxically, it has an important role to play in sustaining democracy. On the whole, we believe it has fulfilled this role effectively.

SUMMARY AND REVIEW

Originally considered the least dangerous branch of government, the judiciary has since experienced a tremendous growth of power. Most of the time courts are engaged in interpreting the meaning of laws, not in determining their constitutionality, but the Supreme Court does have the power to declare acts of Congress unconstitutional, as well as laws and even the constitutional provisions of the states. This power, known as judicial review, is not spelled out specifically in the Constitution but has evolved from perhaps the most significant court case in American history, *Marbury v. Madison* (1803). It remained for the passage of the Fourteenth Amendment in 1868, however, to legitimate the power of the Supreme Court to make law and policy by the process of constitutional interpretation. Around the turn of the century the Court used the Fourteenth Amendment to advance the libertarian economic cause of property rights; not until later did the justices apply that amendment to individual rights. Under Chief Justice Earl Warren (1953–69), the Court extended civil liberties.

As with the other branches, the judiciary is restrained by various checks and balances. Under the Constitution, the president is given the important power to appoint judges with the advice and consent of the Senate. Congress also has the power to pass laws, propose constitutional amendments, and determine the jurisdiction of the federal courts. The judiciary must wrestle with the difficult problem of enforcement; the courts frequently face foot-dragging obstructions or even outright defiance of their decisions by officials in federal and state government. In the end the courts are forced to rely on the cooperation of the executive branch to remedy noncompliance. In an effort to avoid interbranch controversy and excessive work loads, the judiciary has also imposed certain restraints on its own power. Some judges practice judicial activism, reshaping the meaning of the law to fit the times. Others espouse judicial restraint, deferring, for the most part, to the legislative branch.

The administration of justice in the United States is still primarily in the hands of the states and localities. The federal judiciary has original jurisdiction over most cases arising under the Constitution or federal law and in a variety of other cases. The bulk of the civil and criminal cases enter the federal system through the ninety-one U.S. district courts and four territorial courts or through special courts established by Congress to handle other types of cases. Above the district courts are the thirteen U.S. courts of appeal, which have appellate jurisdiction over all cases from the district courts and from various regulatory agencies. Only a tiny fraction of the cases initiated in federal courts advance to the U.S. Supreme Court which is also the court of last resort for appeals from state courts where a federal issue is involved. The Supreme Court consists of nine justices including a chief justice presiding; each has one vote. The Court has the power of certiorari, or the right to decide for itself which appeals have enough merit to warrant a further hearing. A Supreme Court deci-

sion is binding on lower courts until the justices reverse it, a constitutional amendment is passed, or Congress changes the law. The people of the United States live under the rule of law. Statute law, common law, and case law make up the sources of law. In the United States the application of the traditional legal principle of stare decisis, or precedent, is colored by the political perspectives of the judges, which in turn relates to whether a judge is inclined toward judicial restraint or activism.

Due to a dramatic increase in the number of cases filed in U.S. district courts, there is widespread overcrowding in the federal court system. This overcrowding has created problems such as excessive plea bargaining and a lack of access to the courts by some people. It has also led to a slower and more expensive system of justice.

Gradually the Supreme Court has become a third policy-making branch of government. In case after case, the responsibility of interpreting the Constitution has allowed it to make public policy—and its judgments are formed largely by the perspectives of the individual justices.

IMPORTANT TERMS

For a list and explanation of important policy-making Supreme Court cases, see Appendix D.

advisory opinion	district court
amicus curiae	due process
appellate jurisdiction	Fourteenth Amendment
case law	habeas corpus petition
certiorari	judicial activism
circuit court	judicial power
class-action suit	judicial restraint
common law	judicial review
concurrent jurisdiction	judiciary
county court	justice of the peace court
court of appeal	midnight judges
court packing	municipal court

original intent
original jurisdiction
plea bargaining
political question
precedent
rule of law
standing

stare decisis
state court of appeal
state supreme court
statute law
Supreme Court
test case
writ of mandamus

9

CIVIL RIGHTS
AND LIBERTIES

"Do you want to die?" asked the state's attorney. "When the Lord is ready to take me," replied twelve-year-old Pamela Hamilton. Pamela and her parents were in Campbell County Tennessee's Juvenile Court in September 1983 because she had a rare form of bone cancer known as Ewing's sarcoma. The doctors believed her chances for survival were good if chemotherapy was started immediately. But Pamela's father, the Reverend Larry Hamilton, was pastor of the Church of God of the Union Assembly of La Follette, Tennessee, a church that rejects modern medicine in favor of faith healing. After the Tennessee Department of Human Services was unable to change Hamilton's mind, the state of Tennessee filed suit to remove Pamela from the custody of her parents. Pamela, her parents, and their attorney were now in court arguing that the First Amendment prohibits laws infringing on "free exercise" of religion, making it unconstitutional for Tennessee to compel a person to receive treatment against her religious beliefs. The state's attorney conceded that adults have the right to such a claim, but argued that this right should not apply to minors. "She ought to have the opportunity to form her own religious convictions when she becomes an adult," he argued. "Therefore, she should be given an opportunity to live" (quoted in Newsweek, *3 October 1983, 57). The state wanted a quick decision from Judge Charles Herman, for delay would lessen the effectiveness of the treatment (*Newsweek, *3 October 1983, 57;* America, *15 October 1983, 201–2).*

"Free Speech for Whites" read the signs Frank Collin and his eleven followers wanted to display in Skokie, Illinois. Collin, the self-styled "fuehrer" of a tiny neo-Nazi faction called the National Socialist Party of America (NSPA), applied for a permit to demonstrate in Skokie in 1977 because nearly half the city's seventy thousand residents were Jewish, and several hundred were survivors of

the Nazi concentration camps where 6 million Jews died. The date selected for the demonstration was April 28—Adolf Hitler's birthday. Outraged survivors and other Jewish residents promised violence if the Nazis appeared, and the town of Skokie went to court to block the demonstration. Collin contended that the First Amendment's protection of "freedom of speech" and "the right . . . peaceably to assemble" gave him the right to demonstrate in Skokie (Hamlin 1980, 1–52; Downs 1985, 19–83).

Theodore Choplick, assistant principal of Piscataway High School in New Jersey, thought he was just doing his job when, on March 7, 1980, he opened the purse of a fourteen-year-old student accused of smoking in the girls' lavatory. Choplick found that the purse contained cigarettes, marijuana, and a list of customers; the girl was involved in selling drugs to other students. Under New Jersey law, Choplick had to call the police, and the student was arrested. Her parents asked that the case be dismissed on the grounds that Choplick had not had "probable cause" to search their daughter's purse and that the seizure of the evidence had violated the Fourth Amendment's ban on "unreasonable searches and seizures." When the New Jersey Supreme Court agreed, the state of New Jersey took the case to the United States Supreme Court, contending that the Fourth Amendment was not intended to apply to school authorities, who, they said, needed to be able to search students and their belongings to maintain order and discipline (Flygare 1984, 294–95).

How would you decide each of these cases? Does a twelve-year-old have the right to risk death for her faith? Is freedom of speech for Nazis, too? Do students have the same right to privacy as adults? American judges have to decide such controversial issues, for American courts have a policy-making role not per-formed by courts in most other countries. The independent political power of American courts, especially the Supreme Court, is a product of unique historical circumstances.

THE BILL OF RIGHTS

The framers of the Constitution were aware of the need for protection from such legislative practices as **ex post facto laws** (legislation punishing people for actions committed before the law was passed) and **bills of attainder** (legislation punishing specific individuals without a trial). Those who believed that the new Constitution did not sufficiently protect individuals against actions by a strong central government secured an agreement that ten amendments protecting their rights, the **Bill of Rights**, would be added to the Constitution shortly after its ratification (see Chapter 2 and Appendix A). These rights, or freedoms from government interference, are known as **civil liberties**. **Civil rights** are rights protected by the Thirteenth, Fourteenth, and Fifteenth Amendments to the Constitution, which were aimed against racial discrimination by the states.

Until the 1920s the Supreme Court consistently ruled that the Bill of Rights limited only the power of Congress and that state legislatures could still pass laws restricting freedom of speech, religious freedom, or any of the other civil liberties guaranteed in the Bill of Rights (Cortner 1981, 3–7). As a result, individual rights were much better protected in some states than others. For example, black defendants in some southern states were routinely denied anything resembling **due process**, legal procedures to safeguard equality before the law. In *Gitlow v. New York* (1925), however, the Court suddenly declared that the freedoms of speech and the press were "incorporated" through the post–Civil War **Fourteenth Amendment**, which guaranteed "equal protection of the laws," and that they applied to the states as well as the federal government.

At first the Court was reluctant to use this doctrine of **incorporation** to make other rights in the Bill of Rights applicable to the states as well as the federal government. During the 1950s and 1960s, however, a liberal majority of justices led by Chief Justice Earl Warren made dramatic moves to apply more and more rights guaranteed by the Bill of Rights to the states, especially the rights given to criminal defendants and suspects in the Fourth, Fifth, Sixth, and Eighth Amendments. Conservative legal scholars have never fully accepted the doctrine of incorporation, and Attorney General Edwin Meese, who served in the Reagan administration, once called for its abandonment (Meese III 1986, 32–35). For now, incorporation seems solidly entrenched. Only five of the rights in the Bill of Rights have not been applied to the states, among them the Fifth Amendment's requirement of a grand jury indictment in all criminal cases, the Seventh Amendment's provision for a jury trial in all civil cases in which more than $20 is at stake, and the Eighth Amendment's prohibition of excessive bail (Schwartz and Lesher 1983; Abraham 1988, 113–14).

While incorporation has greatly increased the power of the federal courts to protect individuals from government infringements of their rights, it has also greatly increased the power of judges to decide what those rights shall be. If the provisions of the Bill of Rights could be taken literally as written, and any state or federal law contradicting them declared unconstitutional, judges would not have to decide. Such an approach would, however, quickly lead to chaos. A literal reading of the First Amendment prohibition against "abridging the freedom of speech," for example, would protect false advertising or threats of violence. If, literally, no law could prohibit the "free exercise" of religion, the Aztec religious practice of mass human sacrifice could be revived. To avoid such disastrous outcomes, courts must seek standards for interpretation outside the bare words of the Consti-tution. Although most constitutional scholars agree that the purpose of the framers must have some weight, **original intent** is frequently unclear. Hence the meaning of constitutional rights and liberties ranges within some very broad limits, and judges must decide complex issues of interpretation.

It should be noted that the courts are not solely responsible for protecting rights. Several constitutional amendments, including the Thirteenth, Fourteenth, and Fifteenth Amendments, explicitly confer on Congress the right to enforce the amendment by "appropriate legislation." In addition, Congress and state legislatures may, by using their normal legislative powers, create new rights not envisioned by the Constitution, such as the right to public education or the right to protection from discrimination by private individuals (the Fourteenth Amendment protects only against discriminatory actions by states). In many instances, state constitutions confer more rights than the U.S. Constitution. Many states, for example, have passed their own Equal Rights Amendments against gender discrimination.

As a last resort, the U.S. Constitution may be amended if the Supreme Court refuses to recognize a right desired by the majority. The Twenty-fourth Amendment, which bans poll taxes (taxes that must be paid before a person may vote) in national elections was passed after the Supreme Court upheld the states' right to levy such taxes (the Court later declared poll taxes unconstitutional in state elections as well). Thus, Americans who believe their rights have been violated have many channels through which to seek redress, though most of the discussion below focuses on the courts and on rights guaranteed by the Constitution rather than by statute.

Freedom of Religion

The **First Amendment's** guarantees of "free exercise" of religion and freedom from "an establishment of religion" (for example, a tax-

Jeff Stahler. Copyright 1993, *The Cincinnati Post*. Reprinted with permission.

supported church) did not originally apply to the states. In the Mormon cases (see Controversy) the Supreme Court upheld the right of the federal government to regulate religious behavior, as opposed to religious belief.

It was not until the 1940s that the **Free Exercise Clause** became an issue again. By that time, the Court was becoming more liberal and more sympathetic toward religious minorities. In 1940 the Court ruled in *Cantwell v. Connecticut* that Jehovah's Witnesses in New Haven, Connecticut, had a constitutional right to distribute religious literature door-to-door even though the city had an ordinance prohibiting door-to-door solicitation without a license. This was the first time an action motivated by religion was given constitutional protection.

In the same year the Court faced another case involving the Jehovah's Witnesses, *Minersville School District v. Gobitis*. Because their doctrine forbade the worship of "graven images," some of their members instructed their children not to pledge allegiance to the flag in school. When a Pennsylvania school board expelled several children of the denomination for not saluting the flag, the Supreme Court upheld its decision by an 8–1 vote. Justice Felix Frankfurter, speaking for the majority, argued that the flag salute requirement was a legitimate way for the state to foster national unity, an integral part of national security, and thus overrode the religious freedom of a minority. The Jehovah's Witnesses still refused to comply, and when waves of expulsions followed, several justices apparently were shocked into changing their minds. In 1943, in *West Virginia State Board of Education v. Barnette* the Court reversed its earlier decision and ruled 6–3 that the state's interest in promoting patriotism through the flag salute was not sufficient to justify infringing on freedom of speech. Although the case was decided on the grounds of speech rather than religion, the victory of the Jehovah's Witnesses signaled that religious behavior as well as belief would be protected, unless the Court found a compelling public interest to justify restrictions (Goldberg 1984, 18–34).

Since the 1940s the courts have tended to widen the scope of the Free Exercise Clause. In 1972 the Supreme Court ruled in *Wisconsin v. Yoder* that members of the Old Order Amish, a Christian sect that mandates a traditional way of life, could not be made to send their children to school past the eighth grade because schooling past that age would tend to undermine the group's chosen life-style. Not all claims made under the Free Exercise Clause have been sustained, however. One that was not was the Reverend Larry Hamilton's attempt to prevent his daughter from being treated for cancer. Following past Supreme Court precedents, both the Campbell County Juvenile Court and the Tennessee Supreme Court ruled that the state's interest in the lives and health of children justified a limitation on the Hamiltons' religious freedom (Goldberg 1984, 18–34; *Newsweek*, 3 October 1983, 57). (Despite the treatments, Pamela died in 1984.) The Court has approached religious expression matters without issuing broad-ranging or sweeping opinions. Some practices that would be illegal outside of religious rites have been upheld, but the Court has affirmed the rights of states to make some regulations. While some observers argue the Court is muddled in its thinking, others argue it has maintained judicial restraint (*Christian Science Monitor*, 1 July 1993, 1, 4). The distinction between religious belief and action is still important, although the emphasis is now more on individual rights of conscience than it was a hundred years ago.

The **Establishment Clause** of the First Amendment, which prohibits Congress from making any law respecting an establishment of religion and essentially requires the government to act in a neutral manner regarding religion, was not applied to the states until *Everson v. Board of Education of Ewing Township* (1947). This case involved a New Jersey law that provided state funds for bus transportation of students attending parochial (mostly Catholic) schools. Protestant groups opposed to such aid united with civil libertarians and taxpayer groups to challenge the law as an unconstitutional "establishment" of religion. By a 5–4 vote, the court upheld the bus law on the grounds that it did not aid the parochial schools but only the students by providing safe transportation. At the same time, however, the Court warned that "neither a state nor the Federal Government" can "pass laws which aid one religion, aid all religions, or prefer one religion over another."

The double-edged *Everson* ruling invited a surge of new cases under the Establishment Clause. Obviously, almost any aid to a church-affiliated institution, be it a school, college, hospital, soup kitchen, or day care center, could be interpreted as either an unconstitutional effort to "aid one religion" or as constitutionally permissible assistance to the people benefiting from the institution's work. The issue is highly political; most liberals favor limiting aid to religious organizations, fearing a danger to freedom in too close a relationship between church and state. Most conservatives (and most Catholics of all political perspectives) are inclined to favor such assistance, particularly for religious schools that are increasingly seen as desirable alternatives to the public schools (Levy 1986; Cord 1982).

Having assumed responsibility for this thorny issue, the Supreme Court has produced a series of seemingly contradictory decisions. Aid to institutions like hospitals and day care centers has been upheld, as have grants and loans to students attending religious colleges and even direct government aid to such colleges. But the Court has severely restricted the kind of aid that can be given to religious elementary and secondary schools; it has allowed, for example, provision of mathematics

CONTROVERSY
The Court and the Politics of Polygamy

Brigham Young (Library of Congress)

Theoretically, the courts are supposed to decide controversies about civil rights and liberties in a nonpolitical manner. The fifty-year controversy between the United States government and the Church of Jesus Christ of Latter-Day Saints, commonly known as the Mormons, suggests otherwise.

The Mormons, founded by Joseph Smith in Fayette, New York, in 1830, had had to leave settlements in Missouri and Illinois because of conflicts with residents of those states that ultimately led to the murder of Smith in Illinois in 1844. In 1846–47 the sect moved west under the leadership of Brigham Young to a remote part of Mexico they called Deseret. The United States acquired the Mormon kingdom in 1848 at the conclusion of the Mexican War and renamed it the Utah Territory. By the 1860s Utah had enough people to become a state, but it was not admitted to the Union until 1896, after much of its original land had been given to Nevada and Colorado. The reason had nothing to do with any lack of law and order, as law and order were more prevalent in Utah than anywhere else in the West. It had to do with the Mormon church's sanctioning of polygamy.

A Mormon man who could afford it was allowed to have more than one wife, if his first wife approved. Polygamy shocked most Americans, especially those concerned about the role of women, and Congress passed a law against it in 1869.

books but not salary supplements for math teachers. The justification given for this apparent inconsistency is that college students are more "mature" than elementary and secondary students and better able to resist religious indoctrination. Yet this argument about maturity conflicts with other Supreme Court decisions giving more rights to minors and certainly with the decision in the Amish case, which allowed minors to withdraw from school altogether. Political considerations may be a good explanation for the disparate treatment of schools and colleges. Most major American churches have affiliated colleges and would object to a Court move against aid to religious higher education, but parochial elementary and secondary schools, which are mostly Catholic and fundamentalist Protestant, do not have as wide or influential a political constituency (M. Schwartz 1984, 192–93).

Perhaps the most bitter conflict over the Establishment Clause concerns the issue of organized prayer in public schools. Until 1962, prayer was a routine practice in many states

Shortly thereafter, the territorial chief justice disqualified all Mormons from jury duty, knowing convictions of church members would be hard to obtain if Mormons served on juries. The Mormons sued, and the Supreme Court ruled in 1872 that Mormons could not be excluded from juries based on their religious beliefs. Then, a Mormon named George Reynolds challenged the whole antipolygamy law as a violation of his First Amendment right to free exercise of religion. Like so many other social problems in the United States, this one ended up before the Supreme Court.

The Court was in one of its most conservative periods, and the justices proved very unsympathetic to the unorthodox life-style of the Mormons. They ruled unanimously in *Reynolds v. United States* (1879) that, while religious "opinion" was constitutionally protected (thus Mormons could not be banned from juries just for being Mormons), Congress could prohibit religious "actions" that were "in violation of public duties and subversive of good order." Polygamy was an action, not an opinion, and could be prohibited because it was "odious" and antagonistic to the monogamous family "on which society may be said to be built." Furthermore, allowing Mormons to practice polygamy would actually give them a preferred status in comparison to other religions, since citizens belonging to other churches would still be breaking the law if they practiced polygamy.

After the *Reynolds* decision federal authorities in Utah began to pursue Mormons suspected of polygamy, and many Mormons went to prison. Congress went on to pass other laws seizing Mormon church property used by polygamists and requiring voters to take an antipolygamy oath. These laws were upheld in court. With many of its leaders in jail or in hiding, the Mormon church finally repudiated polygamy in 1890, clearing the way for the admission of Utah as a state six years later.

The Mormon cases raise troubling questions about the role of the courts in protecting the rights of citizens. Religious freedom is not absolute, and polygamy was considered morally outrageous by most Americans at the time. Yet in this case the courts allowed the government to, in effect, compel otherwise law-abiding citizens to change one of their basic religious beliefs. Wasn't this the kind of situation the First Amendment was designed to prevent? And if the courts will not defend an unpopular group from legislative attacks, whose rights are safe?

Source: Reynolds v. United States, 1879; Reichley 1985, 121–22; Stone 1956.

---

and accepted so long as the prayers were "nondenominational" and voluntary. In that year the Supreme Court ruled that, even if voluntary, such prayers were an unconstitutional establishment of religion (*Engel v. Vitale*). Reaction to the decision was vigorous. The Court was accused of taking God out of the classroom and having "deconsecrated the nation" (Goldberg 1984, 65–66). Repeated attempts by conservatives and populists to reverse the prayer decision through constitutional amendments or appeals to the Court

have failed, but some schools continue to defy the decision and permit voluntary prayer at the beginning of each school day. Other public schools have included prayers in graduation ceremonies at the request of a school official, despite the fact that, in 1992, the Supreme Court declared such prayers to be unconstitutional (*Lee v. Weisman*). In other cases, students have taken the initiative to lead prayers on their own. Student religious groups are permitted to use school facilities if nonreligious groups are allowed to do so.

"Class Will Confine Its Style of Classroom Prayer to the Normal, Proper, Accepted, Conservative, All-American, Right-Wing Christian Variety!"

Pat Oliphant. Courtesy Universal Press Syndicate.

Freedom of Speech, Press, and Assembly

Few cases involving freedom of speech, press, and assembly reached the Supreme Court until World War I. During the war Congress passed an Espionage Act that punished not only spying but also political speech and activities designed to disrupt the war effort. Charles Schenck, a member of the American Socialist party, which strongly opposed the war, sent letters to fifteen thousand draftees urging them to "assert your rights" and not report for military service (Abraham 1988, 195). After being convicted under the Espionage Act, Schenck and his associates appealed to the Supreme Court, alleging that the Espionage Act violated the First Amendment's guarantee of freedom of speech and the press. In a unanimous decision in *Schenck v. United States* (1919) the Court rejected this argument. Justice Oliver Wendell Holmes, who wrote the opinion, articulated what came to be known as the **clear and present danger doctrine**, which allows limitations on free speech when such speech threatens public order or national security. Holmes explained that:

We admit that in many places and in ordinary times the defendants in saying all that was said in the circular would have been within their constitutional rights. But the character of every act depends upon the circumstances in which it is done. The question in every case is whether the words used are used in such circumstances and are of such a nature as to create a clear and present danger that they will bring about the substantive evils that Congress has a right to prevent. When a nation is at war many things that might be said in time of peace are such a hindrance to its effort that their utterance will not be endured so long as men fight and that no Court could regard them as protected by any constitutional right.

The *Schenck* decision appeared to limit freedom of speech and expression, but its long-term effect was just the opposite. Along with the *Gitlow* case a few years later, which applied provisions of the First Amendment to the states, it invited future court challenges to state and federal laws on the grounds that they restricted First Amendment rights without the justification of a "clear and present danger" to public order.

This right to privacy may need elaboration in light of the selling of information about individuals by private companies (see Controversy).

The Right to Remain Silent

The **Fifth Amendment** states that no person "shall be compelled in any criminal case to be a witness against himself" and protects private property rights (discussed later). The roots of the former are religious. Before the Constitution, the common law allowed a defendant to refuse to testify under oath in order not to force him or her to choose between admitting guilt and facing divine punishment for perjury (Morgan 1984, 93–94). In recent times, however, most cases under the Fifth Amendment have dealt with the right of a suspect under police interrogation to refuse to answer questions. Not until 1936 did the Supreme Court rule that confessions produced by physical coercion—the "third degree"—were not admissible as evidence (*Brown v. Mississippi*). From then until 1966 confessions were judged according to their "voluntariness"; if a suspect freely confessed to a crime, the confession could be used as evidence even if he or she had not known of the right against self-incrimination. In 1966, in *Miranda v. Arizona*, the Court laid down a set of new rules governing interrogations. Now police were required to tell suspects of the **right to remain silent** and to speak with an attorney and to warn suspects that anything they said might be used against them in court. If a suspect was not notified of any or all of these rights, the exclusionary rule would apply and any confession would be inadmissible, even if voluntary.

Like the exclusionary rule, the *Miranda* decision is unpopular among conservatives, right populists, and some law enforcement officials, who see its protections as contributing to a sharp increase in crime during the 1960s and 1970s (Morgan 1984, 74–76). Yet studies of the effects of *Miranda* indicate that most defendants eventually confess anyway, either during interrogation or as part of a later plea bargain, and that many do not understand their rights even after hearing them read (Walker 1985, 98–101). Apparently *Miranda* has neither secured the right to remain silent, as many liberals and libertarians hoped, nor handcuffed the police as the right populists and conservatives feared.

The Right to Counsel

The **Sixth Amendment** requires defendants in federal criminal cases to be granted the right "to have the Assistance of Counsel" for their defense. This right did not originally mean that government should provide a lawyer for a defendant unable to afford one; it merely specified that defendants should be allowed to retain their own counsel. By the early 1960s the federal government and most states had programs to provide legal assistance to indigent defendants in felony cases (crimes punishable by death or imprisonment for more than a year), but some states still did not. In 1963, in *Gideon v. Wainwright*, the Supreme Court ruled that all states had to provide lawyers to defendants in all felony cases. This **right to counsel** was later extended to misdemeanor cases (minor criminal offenses) in which there was a likelihood of imprisonment upon conviction, but not to minor offenses like traffic violations (Lewis 1964; Abraham 1988, 155).

Unlike some of the other new rights created by the Warren Court, the right to counsel was already widely accepted. However, requiring that each defendant have a lawyer is one thing; ensuring effective representation is another. Many states and cities provide representation through a public defender's office staffed by lawyers assigned full time to defense work, but these offices are frequently overworked and usually employ young and inexperienced attorneys. In other communities private attorneys are assigned to represent poor defendants, but the best attorneys may try to avoid

CONTROVERSY
Is Anything Still Private?

(Courtesy Apple Computer, Inc.)

Ernie Trent of New Orleans, Louisiana, is an experienced oil field worker, but for three years he could not get work. Trent's problem was not the weak economy. When he appealed to a friend who owned an oil-service company for a job, the friend said, "Ernie, I can't hire you. Nobody can. You're on the list."

"The list" is a file in the computers of Employers Information Service (EIS), a data bank set up by the oil and gas industry to screen employees. Trent got on it because he collected worker's compensation for an injury suffered while working on an oil rig in the Gulf of Mexico. Using EIS's data, employers can—and some apparently do—screen out any worker who has ever filed a worker's compensation claim. (Trent finally found work—as a security manager for Burger King.)

How can this happen? Doesn't the Constitution protect the right of Americans to privacy? Not so; in fact, the word "privacy" never appears in the Constitution. While the Supreme Court has recognized certain aspects of privacy as implied in the Constitution, these rights do not extend to information about a person gathered legally and stored in computers. Moreover, the Constitution protects us only against government, not other citizens.

It is not only employers who have access to information about us. Credit bureaus have files on every American who has ever borrowed money, and they sell these records not only to banks and other lenders but also to anyone willing to pay the fee. The Federal Bureau of Investigation's National Crime Information Center (NCIC) has information on more than 20 million Americans, accessible instantly via computer to any police department in the country.

such assignments whenever possible because they are unpaid or poorly paid. In addition, the right to free counsel does not extend to civil cases, although legal aid societies providing representation for some indigent persons and lawyers often take cases on a "contingent" basis, accepting a percentage of whatever damages are collected instead of collecting a fee before the case is settled. Despite court decisions on the right to counsel, access to legal assistance is far from equal for all Americans.

Private Property Rights

In addition to protecting against self-incrimination, the Fifth Amendment guarantees that private property shall not "be taken for public use, without just compensation." The amendment thus gives the government the power of

Usually these records are accurate, but when they are not the results can be damaging or even disastrous to individuals. The entire population of Norwich, Vermont, was denied credit temporarily when a computer error caused the records to show that everyone in town had failed to pay taxes. Terry Rogan of Saginaw, Michigan, has been arrested five times for crimes he did not commit, because an escaped murderer stole his wallet and used his identification, which then went into the NCIC computer. James Russell Wiggens lost his $70,000 job as a sales representative because a computer mixed him up with James Ray Wiggens, a convicted cocaine dealer. Michael Engelhardt, one of the authors of this text, once got a letter from his state driver's license bureau accusing him of drunk driving in New York, even though he had never lived or driven a car there. The computer had him confused with another Michael Engelhardt born on the same day.

Has the government done anything to protect the privacy of Americans in the computer age? A Fair Credit Reporting Act, passed in 1968 and strengthened in 1992, gives consumers the right to see their credit files on demand and to correct any errors they find. However, the law does nothing to restrict the sale of information, and even accurate information, as in Ernie Trent's case, can be misused. Television evangelist Oral Roberts once used credit histories that he purchased to target people with heavy debts for fund-raising appeals, promising that God would relieve their problem if they donated to his ministry. A Privacy Act passed in 1974 makes many government records confidential, but this law has many loopholes. For example, it allows computer matching, thus allowing computer checks of lists of federal employees against lists of welfare recipients to see if there are employees illegally drawing welfare. The Selective Service Administration once matched its files with lists of eighteen-year-olds who were given birthday discounts by ice cream parlors to see if any of those listed had failed to register for the draft.

Privacy advocates argue that tougher regulation is needed to deter unjustified snooping by business, government agencies, and others including con artists who use computer-accessible information to target easy marks for scams. However, there is another side to the story. Restricting the flow of credit information could make life easier for deadbeats who do not pay for what they buy, raising prices for honest consumers. Surely employers have a right to know something about the backgrounds of their employees, and no one wants to deny the police access to information that would help them catch criminals. As more and more information about all of us has become available from computers, balancing individual rights of privacy with public needs has become much more complicated than it was for the authors of the Bill of Rights.

Source: Rothfeder 1992.

eminent domain, the power to seize the property of individuals or groups for public purposes, provided adequate compensation is paid; the courts must determine what level of compensation is "just." Some of the most interesting cases arising under this provision have involved Indian tribes, who in the nineteenth century frequently sold their land for far less than its value (see Controversy).

The issue of defining a legitimate "public use" for property that may be taken by the government has faced the courts many times. In *Poletown Neighborhood Council v. Detroit* (1981) a Michigan court ruled that the city of Detroit could take a citizen's private property and turn it over to a private corporation to build a factory, because significant public benefits in the form of jobs and tax revenue would result (Alderman and Kennedy 1991, 191–205). The courts have also ruled that if the govern-

CONTROVERSY
The Sioux Indian Claims

Sioux Indians (AP/Wide World Photos)

"There's gold in the Black Hills!" As the word spread through the West in the fall of 1874, miners picked up their tools, pulled up stakes, and headed for Dakota Territory. Within a few months twelve thousand prospectors were swarming over the highlands of what is now southwestern South Dakota. Few cared that the land they were invading was sacred to the Sioux (also known as Dakota) Indian nation and guaranteed to them by the United States government in a treaty signed just six years before, in 1868.

For a year, the administration of President Ulysses S. Grant tried to protect the Sioux lands by sending troops to drive the miners out of the Black Hills. The task proved hopeless, however; there were simply too many miners and not enough soldiers. Then the government tried to buy the Black Hills from the Sioux for $6 million, but the Indians refused to sell. Crazy Horse, war chief of the Oglala band of Sioux, spoke for many when he said, "One does not sell the earth the people walk on!" To pressure the Sioux to sell, the government finally withdrew the troops from the Black Hills, allowing the whites to overrun the area, while cutting off rations to the Sioux until they signed the treaty.

Enraged, many Sioux took to the warpath, and on June 25, 1876, they annihilated Gen. George A. Custer and 225 soldiers from his Seventh Cavalry at the Little Big Horn, the worst defeat for the U.S. Army in Indian warfare in sixty years. (Ironically, Custer himself was the source of the original Black Hills gold rumors.) Still, the struggle was hopeless: by 1877 the Sioux had been defeated and an act of Congress had ratified the seizure of the Black Hills, with little compensation to the Sioux. Deprived of their best lands and exiled to reservations on the prairies of North and South Dakota, the Sioux have become the poorest of the nation's poor. Today, only one-third of the Sioux adults on the reservations have a job, and nearly half are alcoholics.

In 1961, attorneys Marvin Sonosky and Arthur Lazarus began trying to correct this injustice. They

ment goes beyond a certain point in regulating the use of private property (for example, prohibiting the only profitable use), it must pay compensation to the owner.

No Cruel and Unusual Punishment

In banning **"cruel and unusual punishments,"** the authors of the **Eighth Amendment** clearly

filed suit on behalf of the Sioux in federal court, alleging that in seizing the Black Hills the government had violated the Fifth Amendment, which states that "private property shall not be taken for public use, without just compensation." Of course, almost all the land making up the United States was originally acquired from Indians, often by ethically dubious means. Since 1946, however, an act of Congress had given Indian tribes the ability to sue the government for compensation with interest. Sonosky and Lazarus argued that the government owed the Sioux what the land was worth in 1877, plus eighty-four years of interest.

The Black Hills case took many years to be resolved, in part because it involved so many complicated legal issues. Sonosky and Lazarus claimed that the Black Hills had been worth $27 million in 1877, while the government estimated only $4.7 million, less than the Sioux had been offered. The government also contended that it had done its best to protect the Sioux from an ultimately irresistible tide of white settlement and that expenditures for food, education, and health care for the Sioux after 1877 should be allowed to offset any claim. The tribe's attorneys responded that the government had been obligated by the 1868 treaty to protect the Sioux lands, and that if whites had not destroyed the Indians' buffalo-hunting economy and seized their land, no government aid would have been necessary.

Impatient with the slow pace of the case, some Indians took matters into their own hands. In 1973, militants of the American Indian Movement (AIM) seized the village of Wounded Knee, site of the last Sioux defeat in 1890, demanding, among other things, the outright return of the Black Hills to the Sioux. The siege of Wounded Knee ended peacefully after seventy-one days, but the AIM continued to be a force in Sioux politics.

On June 13, 1979, the U.S. Court of Claims finally handed down its decision: the government had illegally taken the Black Hills and owed the Sioux $17.5 million plus interest, a total of $106 million. Then the case took a surprising twist: the Sioux tribal councils reversed a decades-old stand and embraced the AIM's view, rejecting the money. Proclaiming, in the echo of Crazy Horse's defiance, that "the Black Hills are not for sale!" the Sioux now insisted that they would only be satisfied with a return of the Hills, now inhabited by more than one hundred thousand white residents, plus $3.1 billion in "damages" for misuse of their property.

The land return demand generated an anti-Indian backlash among many South Dakotans, many of whom had previously sympathized with the Sioux claim. Whites contended that any land giveback would violate their property rights and subject them to the jurisdiction of a tribal government for which only Indians could vote. When Senator Bill Bradley of New Jersey introduced a bill to return the federal land in the Hills (about a million of the seven million acres) to the Sioux, Senator Larry Pressler of South Dakota threatened to introduce legislation giving New Jersey back to the Indians. Bradley's bill did not pass. Meanwhile, the Black Hills compensation money, invested by the government for the Sioux, had reached $300 million by 1991. Perhaps someday the Sioux will have enough to buy the Black Hills back, if they decide that land can be bought and sold.

Source: Lazarus 1991; Ambrose 1975; Prucha 1984.

did not intend to halt capital punishment, which was widely practiced at the time the Bill of Rights was adopted. Most Americans today still support the death penalty, but there is also widespread and determined opposition, particularly from liberals. One reason for liberal opposition to capital punishment is that minorities have tended to be executed more frequently than whites for similar crimes. In 1972 the Supreme Court in *Furman v. Georgia* declared that then-existing capital punishment statutes were unconstitutional because there were no guidelines for judges or jurors to follow in determining whether to impose the death sentence. Justice Potter Stewart called the death penalty, as then administered, "cruel and unusual in the same way that being struck by lightning is cruel and unusual" (quoted in Alderman and Kennedy 1991, 299).

The victory for death penalty opponents was short-lived. By 1976 thirty-five states had passed revised death penalty laws designed to comply with *Furman v. Georgia*. By this time as well, the Court, with four Nixon appointees, had become more conservative. In *Gregg v. Georgia* (1976) the justices voted 7–2 to uphold a death sentence under Georgia's new law, which gave jurors specific criteria by which to judge whether a murderer deserved to be executed. Since then 143 prisoners have been put to death, but more than two thousand remain in death row cells awaiting the outcome of their appeals (Alderman and Kennedy 1991, 310; *Statistical Abstract, 1992*, 200).

RACE AND THE CONSTITUTION

Race and race relations have shaped the American national experience. Race was at the heart of the constitutional crisis that led to the Civil War and since then has exerted an enormous influence on politics and the Constitution. The shifts in judicial policy on race show how changes in public opinion are reflected in judicial decisions. They also show how difficult and complex race relations have been in the United States.

Following the Civil War, the Thirteenth, Fourteenth, and Fifteenth Amendments were passed to outlaw slavery and confer citizenship, including the right to vote, on former slaves. Among the most critical statements in the Constitution is the Fourteenth Amendment's **Equal Protection Clause** which says,

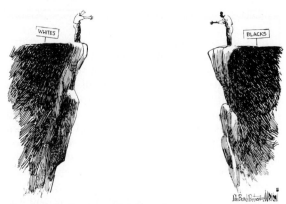

Don Wright. Courtesy *The Palm Beach Post*.

"No State shall . . . deny to any person within its jurisdiction the equal protection of the laws." The meaning of this clause is perhaps the most disputed in the entire Constitution, and racial discrimination has been the most important constitutional issue in American politics.

School Segregation and Integration

Following the Civil War, schools in the South, like most institutions, services, and accommodations, became segregated, at first by custom and then by law. These laws were known as **Jim Crow laws**. The practice of segregation was upheld by the Supreme Court in *Plessy v. Ferguson* (1896), which ruled that separate facilities were not unconstitutional as long as they were equal. Although this case dealt with railroad cars rather than schools, it became the precedent justifying the **separate but equal** school system in the South and was supported by both right populists and conservatives.

Separate but equal turned out to be anything but equal. White-controlled state governments quickly moved to assure whites of preference in school funding and facilities. Not until 1954, in the case of *Brown v. Board of Education of Topeka*, was the separate but equal doctrine overturned. Issued shortly after Earl Warren became chief justice and by a Court still staffed by some of Franklin Roosevelt's appointees, the decision almost certainly ignored the original intent of the framers of the Fourteenth Amendment, which was probably not to require integration in school (Fairman 1971, 1207–1300). Instead the *Brown* decision acknowledged the validity of sociological evidence that black children were damaged psychologically by segregation, which branded them as unfit to associate with white children. Stressing this point, Chief Justice Warren wrote in his opinion that "in the field of public education the doctrine of 'separate but equal' has no place. Separate educational facilities are inherently unequal." **De jure segregation**— that is, segregation imposed by law rather than resulting from location of residence—had to be eliminated (Cortner and Lytle 1971, 406–9).

At first glance the Court's decision appeared to settle the issue of school segregation, but in fact the struggle had only begun. Southern states resorted to a wide variety of tactics to delay and obstruct the decision. Many areas devised so-called transfer or freedom-of-choice plans, which allowed white students to stay in an all-white school or to transfer from a school about to be integrated. In some areas schools were closed to evade the order, and in others state funds were given to all-white private schools. As a result of these delaying tactics, the percentage of students attending integrated schools was little higher in 1966 than it had been in 1954, before the *Brown* decision (Carter 1969, 56–84).

By 1971 the Court decided that the time for delay had passed. In *Swann v. Charlotte-Mecklenburg County Board of Education*, the justices ruled that schools had to be integrated immediately, if necessary by assigning students to schools on a racial basis and busing them out of their neighborhoods. The *Swann* case led to much more rapid progress in desegregation in the South, but it also had implications for the North. While northern states had not segregated schools by law, local school boards had often adopted policies that led to majority black schools. These policies were also de jure

segregation. Soon liberal civil rights groups were charging northern school districts with discrimination and calling for busing of students to remedy the effects of discrimination and achieve racial balance. Many libertarians, populists, and conservatives objected, arguing that forced busing represented a perversion of the *Brown* principle: instead of forbidding assignments to schools on a racial basis, the Court was now requiring it. An antibusing backlash spread from the South to the rest of the country.

As before, the Supreme Court began to reflect the change in public attitudes. By 1974, under the influence of justices appointed by Richard Nixon, the Court had become more conservative. In *Milliken v. Bradley*, it overturned a lower court decision requiring busing of suburban students to inner-city schools in Detroit, Michigan. Although the Detroit school system had discriminated against blacks, the suburban districts where few blacks lived had not; thus they did not need to be included in the busing plan. This ruling did not eliminate the use of busing, but it limited the scope of the integration. With whites moving out of inner-city areas, urban schools in both the North and the South are becoming resegregated (*Lansing State Journal*, 26 March 1989, A8). In 1991–92 the Supreme Court ruled that the cities of Oklahoma City and Denver could cease busing because their school boards had done all they could to eliminate the effects of past de jure segregation (Traub 1991, 24–37). Rising **de facto segregation**, resulting from the fact of where people choose to live, appears beyond the reach of the courts, unless the justices choose to alter the basic principles they have tried to follow since *Brown* in 1954.

Job Discrimination and Affirmative Action

The 1964 Civil Rights Act, which bans discrimination by employers on the basis of race, religion, nationality, and gender, opened up many areas of employment formerly closed to minorities and women. In the last forty years the number of blacks employed in professional and managerial jobs has increased from 187,000 to 1.9 million, a 1,000 percent increase, while the black population only doubled (Edsall and Edsall 1991, 55). Some of this progress is due to **affirmative action** programs adopted by corporations and other institutions under pressure from the government. These programs aim to reverse a pattern of past discrimination by setting goals and timetables for making the workplace more representative through preferential hiring. Companies with government contracts or universities that receive federal aid have been required to set up affirmative action programs.

Allan Bakke, a white male with a superior academic record, was turned down when he applied to the University of California at Davis Medical School in 1972. After discovering that the school had a policy of allocating sixteen of the hundred places opened each year to nonwhites, Bakke sued the state for denying him equal protection on the basis of his race. After losing in the lower courts, the state of California appealed to the Supreme Court in *Regents of the University of California v. Bakke* (1978) (O'Neill 1985).

Like the nation, the Supreme Court ended up split on this thorny issue. In a 5–4 vote, the Court ruled that the university's plan was a racial "quota" that unconstitutionally discriminated against whites. The deciding vote, however, was cast by Justice Lewis Powell, who added in his opinion that a university could "take race into account" in its admissions policy to "achieve educational diversity," so long as a quota was not applied (U.S. Commission on Civil Rights 1979, 55).

Bakke was admitted to medical school, but the affirmative action issue was hardly settled. Institutions continued to grant preferences to minorities, claiming that these preferences were not "quotas" but merely "took race into account" to achieve "diversity." Whites continued to sue, claiming they were being subjected to "reverse discrimination." Increasingly, the conservative majority on the Supreme Court has sided with the whites, but not consistently. For example, in *Fullilove v. Klutznick* (1980) the Court upheld a federal law that set aside 10 percent of government construction contracts for minority contractors, but nine years later, in *City of Richmond v. J. A. Croson Co.* (1989), it struck down a similar requirement by a city, saying that past discrimination against minorities must be proven before such a plan is used.

Voting Rights

The **Fifteenth Amendment**, passed in 1870, explicitly forbids the states from restricting voting rights on the basis of race. However, from the end of Reconstruction until the 1960s, southern states used all kinds of methods, legal and illegal, to keep blacks from voting. The most successful was the literacy test, which supposedly required aspiring voters to prove that they could read and write. In fact, whites were routinely permitted to register without taking the test, while blacks were forced to answer such questions as, "How many bubbles are there in a bar of soap?" Blacks who persisted in trying to register were harassed, fired from jobs, jailed, or even killed. Some states like Mississippi, where nearly half the population was black, had almost no black voters (Thernstrom 1987, 11–18).

Such outrageous denial of a clearly defined constitutional right was ended by the Voting Rights Act of 1965, which was pushed through Congress by President Lyndon Johnson (see Profile in Chapter 7). This act banned the use of literacy tests in states where less than 50 percent of the population was registered to vote (a subsequent amendment banned such tests nationwide) and authorized the president to send federal registrars into areas where voting rights had been denied to register voters. The act also required states and localities previously practicing discrimination to submit future changes in their voting laws for "pre-clearance" by the Justice Department to prevent them from developing new methods of keeping minorities from voting.

The Voting Rights Act is one of the most successful pieces of legislation ever passed by Congress. Within a few years after its passage, blacks were as likely as whites to be registered to vote in the South, and thousands have been elected to public offices where none served before. Today, debate over voting rights revolves not around the individual's right to vote but around whether minorities have a right to have districts apportioned so as to give them a better chance of winning office. For example, if a state has a 30 percent black population but only 10 percent of state legislators are black, should the state have to redraw legislative districts to create more black majority districts? Many leaders of minority groups favor "affirmative apportionment," but it clearly goes beyond a guarantee of the equal right to vote.

In *City of Mobile v. Bolden* (1980) the Supreme Court ruled that no right to affirmative apportionment existed. The city of Mobile, Alabama, was allowed to keep an "at large" election system for its city council (one in which all voters voted for all members of the council, rather than dividing the city into districts), although this provision allowed the white majority to elect all the council members. Two years later, however, the more liberal Congress passed amendments to the Voting Rights Act that overturned the *Bolden* decision and outlawed apportionment practices with "discriminatory effects," regardless of the intent behind such practices. These amendments have forced major changes in legislative apportionment. After the 1990 census, congressional districts across the country were redrawn with the object of creating as many minority-dominated districts as possible. Ironically, these affirmative apportionment measures are strongly backed by Republicans, who hope that redistricting minorities into minority-majority districts will create more heavily white

districts likely to vote Republican in future elections (Brown 1991, 302–5). However, in *Shaw v. Reno* (1993) the Supreme Court tightened the restrictions on these affirmative apportionment initiatives (*Washington Post National Weekly Edition*, 5–11 July 1993, 32).

WOMEN AND THE CONSTITUTION

The rights of women have evolved as much since the founding of the nation as have the rights of blacks. The Constitution of 1787 did not mention women, thus leaving intact common law traditions and state laws denying them several rights, such as voting, the right to own property after marriage, and the right to serve on juries. Although the Fourteenth Amendment forbade the states, after 1867, from denying equal protection to "any person," the courts got around applying equal protection to women because of their "natural" role as wives and mothers. In the case of *Bradwell v. Illinois* (1873) the Supreme Court upheld an Illinois law that barred women from practicing law. A concurring opinion said that "the natural and proper timidity and delicacy which belongs to the female sex evidently unfits it for many of the occupations of civil life" and a legal career required "decision and firmness which are presumed to predominate in the sterner sex."

Special Protection

In the early twentieth century legislatures passed and the courts upheld laws that required special treatment for women because their roles as wives and mothers necessitated special protection. In *Muller v. Oregon* (1908), for example, the Supreme Court ruled that states could limit working hours of women without applying the same limits to men because of women's greater physical vulnerability (Kerber and De Hart-Mathews 1987, 481–83). In *Quang Wing v. Kirkendall* (1912) the

Supreme Court upheld a law exempting women running small laundries from paying taxes. Though women got the right to vote through the **Nineteenth Amendment** in 1920, constitutional interpretation was slow to change. As late as 1961, the Court in *Hoyt v. Florida* (1961) upheld a Florida law allowing women with children to claim exemption from jury duty, on the grounds of preserving the traditional female role.

Equal Protection

The recent revolution in women's status began, not with a Supreme Court decision but with the Civil Rights Act of 1964, which prohibited job discrimination on the basis of sex as well as race. Some who supported this provision were southern segregationists who had hoped that including women would serve to discredit the whole concept of civil rights and kill the bill (Steiner 1985, 12). Congress later prohibited sexual harassment in the workplace, discrimination in granting of credit, and other acts seeking to assure women the equal protection of the laws.

Lagging behind Congress, the Supreme Court took until 1971 to move toward gender equality. In *Phillips v. Martin Marietta Corp.* it struck down a company policy of not hiring women with young children as a violation of the Civil Rights Act. The same year, it extended the Fourteenth Amendment's Equal Protection Clause to women for the first time in *Reed v. Reed* (1971), throwing out a state law favoring men over women as administrators of wills. The Court continued, in 1973, to oppose gender discrimination by ruling in *Frontiero v. Richardson* that the Air Force had acted improperly by not allowing female members automatically to qualify for allowances for dependent spouses as did male members. The Court declared the need for stricter judicial scrutiny in cases involving classifications based on sex (Leeson and Foster 1992, 639–47).

Since the early 1970s the courts have struck down a host of local, state, and federal laws originally aimed at "protecting" women as inconsistent with either the Fourteenth Amendment or the Civil Rights Act. The most famous such case was *Roe v. Wade* (1973) in which the Supreme Court declared that laws against abortion violated a woman's right to "privacy"—a right not stated in the Constitution but that the Court found to be implied. However, recent decisions by the more conservative Rehnquist Court have significantly narrowed the scope of *Roe*. States are now allowed to require that parents be notified when a minor child requests an abortion and to prohibit abortion of "viable" fetuses beyond the twenty-fourth week of pregnancy (Savage 1992, 288–98).

As with minorities, affirmative action for women has become controversial. In *Johnson v. Transportation Agency of Santa Clara County* (1987) the Court upheld a policy that resulted in a woman's being hired over a man with slightly higher job qualifications because the difference was not "significant." Generally, women have moved into professional jobs faster than minorities (except Asians) have, and disparities in qualifications are less of an issue.

Males have also benefited from the egalitarian reinterpretation of the Constitution, be-

Rob Rogers. Reprinted by permission of NEA, Inc.

Hank McClure. Courtesy *The Lawton Constitution*.

cause many laws that favored women have been revised or discarded. In *Craig v. Boren* (1976) an Oklahoma law that allowed females to drink at eighteen but set the drinking age for males at twenty-one was declared unconstitutional even though the state showed that young men presented the greater drunk-driving problem. In *Caban v. Mohammed* (1979) the Court threw out a law that allowed an unwed mother, but not an unwed father, to block adoption of an illegitimate child.

An Equal Rights Amendment?

The Nineteenth Amendment in 1920 gave women the right to vote. In 1923 the National Woman's party first introduced an Equal Rights Amendment (ERA), and though it was regularly introduced into Congress thereafter, it did not receive widespread support. Many women hoped that application of the Equal

Protection Clause to laws discriminating on the basis of sex would be sufficient to remove legal obstacles to equality, but by 1970 they were ready to turn to a constitutional amendment to get the job done. The version passed by Congress in 1972 and submitted to the states said, "Equality of rights under the law shall not be denied or abridged by the United States or by any state on account of sex." Feminists who advocated an ERA in the 1970s pointed to the protective legislation enacted in the late nineteenth and early twentieth centuries as an indication of the inequality women have been forced to endure.

Submission of the amendment to the states drew fire from conservatives and right populists, who argued that such a broad amendment could upset gender-related insurance premiums, alimony (*Congressional Record*, 17 August 1983, S11918–24), and other female-support awards. The Reverend Jerry Falwell called the amendment "vague and undefined" and feared that it would compel "women to serve in the military force and to go into combat zones" (Falwell 1980, 155–56; see also Steiner 1985). Liberals argued that the amendment was long overdue and that most legal distinctions between males and females were outmoded and discriminatory.

The ERA had majority support in the mid-1970s, but also dedicated opposition. With passage in thirty-eight states needed for ratification, supporters had to win several conservative states. In the end the task proved impossible. The amendment originally had a 1979 deadline, but even after a thirty-nine-month extension time ran out. Many states have, however, passed their own ERAs.

PERSPECTIVES

Issues of civil rights and liberties are among the most emotional and divisive in American politics. Accordingly, it is hardly surprising that the six perspectives are as divided here as anywhere. All six claim to champion the rights of the people, but in very different ways.

Conservative

Conservatives respect American traditions, including civil rights and liberties. However, they are generally discontented with the way civil rights and liberties have recently been interpreted, in part because some rights they value highly have been downgraded. Once, defense of property rights was a high priority with the Supreme Court, but since the 1930s the Court has basically left the definition of such rights to the legislative branch. Conservatives also believe freedom of religion has been eroded by decisions like the school prayer cases that restrict religious expression in public places.

Even more distressing to conservatives, however, has been what they see as the unreasonable extension of other rights, particularly those of criminal defendants. To conservatives, multiplying procedural safeguards for suspects (most of whom are guilty) is hardly a high priority in a society where rising crime is the biggest threat to the rights of most citizens. Conservatives also believe that imposing judicial standards of due process on the routine decisions of employers, local governments, police departments, and school boards tends to impair the effective functioning of these institutions. The New Jersey school search case is the kind conservatives believe should never have come to court in the first place. School administrators cannot be expected to maintain effective discipline if they have to worry about whether they are doing something that may be held later to violate student "rights." Such judicial activism, say conservatives, has promoted the national government's interference into all kinds of issues best left to the states or private institutions, while paradoxically weakening the government's ability to perform its legitimate functions (Morgan 1984, 134–61, 191–214).

Joe Thibodeau. Courtesy *Arkansas Democrat-Gazette.*

In contrast to many conservatives prior to the 1960s, today's conservatives agree with liberals that racial discrimination is wrong and should be illegal. However, conservatives are increasingly impatient with blacks and other minorities who blame discrimination for their problems. Conservatives are strongly of the opinion that blacks especially have failed to take advantage of the opportunities offered them by American society, preferring instead to blame whites and demand more government aid and affirmative action (Sowell 1984; Taylor 1992). Moreover, such programs do not always serve to advance minorities. For example, 80 percent of the blacks admitted to the University of California at Berkeley under the "special admissions" (affirmative action) program failed to graduate. Nationally, blacks and Hispanics are twice as likely as whites to drop out of college for academic reasons (D'Souza 1991, 33). Such racial preferences, conservatives say, should be ended as soon as possible so that all Americans learn that self-reliance is as important as equal rights. Moreover, problems like crime and family disintegration in the black community need to be honestly confronted, not concealed out of fear of the charge of racism (Taylor 1992, 217–79). Conservatives also want the government to stop trying to integrate schools by busing, since this policy clearly has not worked and has added to racial tensions.

On issues concerning sexual bias, conservatives caution that there are certain inherent differences between men and women and that each sex has its own strengths and weaknesses which assign men and women to different roles. Conservatives warn that trying to ignore these differences has led to the breakdown of family values in today's society (Thornton 1993, 33–34).

In contrast to the Warren Court, when some conservatives called for the impeachment of the chief justice, conservatives have been mildly encouraged by recent Supreme Court decisions on civil rights and liberties. None of the major Warren decisions has been overturned, but the death penalty is back and the restrictions on police searches have been eased. Still, the persistence of most Warren Court decisions indicates that the United States has a long way to go before a sensible interpretation of civil rights and liberties is restored.

Liberal

Liberals believe that civil rights and liberties have advanced dramatically in recent decades, largely due to their efforts. Their view of the Warren Court, for instance, is exactly the opposite of that of the conservatives. Prior to the Warren era, blacks were segregated by law in a large part of the United States, "third-degree" police methods and warrantless searches were routine, and states could put a person on trial without an attorney. All these injustices have been removed, thanks to the resolute stance of the Supreme Court and of liberal groups such as the American Civil Liberties Union and the National Association for the Advancement of Colored People in protecting individuals and minority groups from government oppression.

Liberals also contend that conservatives have grossly exaggerated problems stemming from increased protection of rights. The exclusionary rule barring the use of illegally seized evidence is one example. While some unquestionably guilty people are set free because of the rule, only about 0.4 percent of felony cases have such an outcome (Walker 1985, 94). Surely this is a relatively small price to pay for enforcing the constitutional ban on unreasonable search and seizure. Liberals were alarmed by Reagan era Court decisions that narrowed the scope of protections for criminal defendants and hope that new justices appointed by President Clinton can restore some of these rights.

One of the top liberal priorities is the enforcement of rights against race and sex discrimination. Since their central belief is in equal opportunity, not necessarily equal results, most liberals are not entirely comfortable with programs like affirmative action that grant preferences to minorities. However, they contend that there is no alternative to such programs if the damage done by centuries of pervasive discrimination is to be overcome (Jencks 1992, 24–69). Liberals also place a very high priority on protecting the right of women to have an abortion. Much of the opposition to the Bork and Thomas nominations (see Controversy in Chapter 8) came from liberals who feared that these men would roll back abortion rights.

Liberals are divided on some issues concerning the freedom of speech. Those associated with the American Civil Liberties Union argue that this freedom must be absolute, even for racist groups such as the Nazis and the Klan, which liberals abhor (Hamlin 1980). Other liberals have moved toward a stance once embraced by the conservatives: that, at least in some circumstances, the content of speech should be regulated to uphold community values, in this case the value of racial equality. For example, liberal administrators of some college campuses have sought to ban expressions of hostility to minorities, an effort derided by conservatives as "political correctness."

Recently liberals have been preoccupied with

defending previously established civil rights and liberties against conservative assault. If liberals had their way, some new rights would be created. Unlike Marxists, liberals do not believe in economic equality, but they do believe the courts should protect some economic and social rights in addition to civil and political ones. For example, states should not be allowed to maintain education systems that disadvantage poor students; unequal funding for education clearly violates the Fourteenth Amendment's guarantee of equal protection of the laws (Kozol 1991, 206–33). Since the courts are now dominated by conservative and libertarian judges appointed during the Reagan–Bush years, extending rights will be difficult, but still essential for achieving justice in the United States.

Libertarian

For libertarians, government exists to protect rights—economic, civil, and political. Libertarians sympathize with the liberal desire to protect individuals and minorities from government intrusions; hence, they support many Supreme Court decisions conservatives oppose, particularly *Roe v. Wade.* Indeed, many libertarians would like to see the courts go much further in protecting individual rights. They believe that, for example, laws against drug use are not only ineffective but in violation of individual rights. Libertarians and conservatives have, in fact, had some bitter exchanges over the role of the government in enforcing morality. George Bush's conservative education secretary William Bennett called libertarian economist Milton Friedman and former Secretary of State George Shultz "stupid" for urging that drugs be legalized (Bennett 1992, 115–121).

Where libertarians clash with liberals is in the area of economic rights. To libertarians the rights that need to be protected are not rights to aid from the government at someone else's expense but the right to private property and freedom of contract. From the 1880s to the 1930s, the Supreme Court was dominated by libertarians who frequently struck down laws they thought violated such economic rights. Libertarians today believe the courts should again look at whether laws setting minimum wages or controlling prices violate constitutional rights.

One of the less popular stances taken by some libertarians is opposition to laws forbidding discrimination. This opposition does not stem from any theory of racial superiority but from the conviction that government has no place legislating and enforcing behavior with regard to race or gender. The libertarian legal scholar Richard Epstein contends that freedom of contract—the right to hire and do business with whomever one chooses—should be a basic constitutional right. He claims, "An antidiscrimination law is the antithesis of freedom of contract, a principle that allows all persons to do business with whomever they please for good reason, bad reason, or no reason" (R. Epstein 1992, 3). Epstein also argues that market forces, which reward those who produce a superior product at a better price regardless of their race or sex, would erode discrimination as fast or faster than coercive laws (R. Epstein 1992, 59–87). Libertarian politicians typically do not attack antidiscrimination laws because of their wide support, but they do strongly oppose government-mandated affirmative action.

Populist

Advocates of civil liberties have long worried about populists, who were thought to have an intolerant attitude toward dissent. This view is based on surveys done in the 1950s, which showed that working-class and less-educated Americans, the main populist constituency, rejected freedom of speech for people with unpopular views or life-styles, such as commu-

IMPORTANT TERMS

affirmative action
bill of attainder
Bill of Rights
civil liberties
civil rights
clear and present danger doctrine
content-neutral
cruel and unusual punishment
de facto segregation
de jure segregation
due process
Eighth Amendment
eminent domain
Equal Protection Clause
Establishment Clause
ex post facto law
exclusionary rule

Fifteenth Amendment
Fifth Amendment
First Amendment
Fourteenth Amendment
Fourth Amendment
Free Exercise Clause
incorporation
Jim Crow laws
Nineteenth Amendment
original intent
probable cause
right to counsel
right to remain silent
Second Amendment
separate but equal
Sixth Amendment
unreasonable search and seizure

10

THE BUREAUCRACY

At one point during his term of office, President Jimmy Carter began to have trouble with mice. Many American homes have mice problems, but to have mice in the White House was unacceptable. The General Services Administration (GSA), the government agency responsible for the upkeep of federal buildings, claimed that the mice were getting into the White House from the grounds outside, which are under the jurisdiction of the Department of the Interior's National Park Service. The Park Service, meanwhile, laid the blame for the mice on GSA, since the mice were now living inside. At this point President Carter got tough, calling in the heads of the two agencies and angrily suggesting that someone had better take responsibility for ridding the White House of mice quickly. Miraculously, it seems, major progress was soon made on the mice problem (New York Times, *11 November 1977, A18).*

Unfortunately, neither the president nor most other Americans usually have their bureaucratic problems solved so easily. On the other hand, Americans cannot seem to get along without bureaucracy, judging by its enormous size and the growth of state and federal bureaucratic budgets during the decades prior to the 1990s. In spring 1993, President Bill Clinton presented Congress with a requested budget outlay of $1.5 trillion, including defense (*Wall Street Journal*, 9 April 1993, A4). About 1.2 percent of this budget was to cover the operation of the core institutions of government—the president, Congress, and the federal judiciary (*Budget Baselines* 1993, 324). The rest was for the programs of what some refer to as the "fourth branch" of the U.S. government, the bureaucracy.

The **bureaucracy** consists of the agencies and people who administer the government's programs. Congress appropriates the money the bureaucracy spends, and the bureaucracy operates under presidential direction unless otherwise specified by Congress. While Congress supplies the executive and the subordinate bureaucracy with guidelines, it lacks the expertise to write every regulation needed for a policy to be carried out. Most regulations are written by **bureaucrats**, the people who administer government agencies and programs. Staff in the Occupational Safety and Health Administration (OSHA), for example, write and enforce regulations that protect the safety of American workers in the workplace (Mendeloff 1979, 1–3). The bureaucracy's task of spending such vast sums of money, coupled with its large degree of discretion in **policy implementation** (carrying out the policies set by the president and Congress), gives it a role far beyond the technical execution of the laws under presidential direction. That is why the bureaucracy merits a chapter of its own in this volume.

To most Americans, "bureaucracy" evokes images of "red tape" and secret schemes, and "bureaucrats" are associated with displays of arrogance, self-interest, or unintelligent behavior. From the standpoint of political scientists or public administrators, "bureaucracy" denotes the formal, structural elements of an organization that are arranged in a hierarchical manner for the accomplishment of routine tasks. The term was first used by the sociologist Max Weber to describe modern organizational structures. Weber distinguished modern bureaucrats from their traditional counterparts by the fact that they were specialists rather than generalists. He also described their authority as based on a legally established, impersonal set of rules rather than on their ascribed status or charisma. In other words, the authority of modern bureaucrats supposedly comes neither from their family histories and connections nor from their personalities. Modern administrators have a more limited (specialized) function than their predecessors, and their authority to perform this function is vested not in themselves or their

Malcolm Hancock. © MalEnt, Inc.

families but in their offices or ranks. Bureaucrats hold offices or ranks based on merit and experience (Stillman II 1984, 45–55).

Bureaucracy grows as an organization becomes more complex. The United States government has a large bureaucracy because it serves a large and complex society. Although the public bureaucracy constituted 14.7 percent of the civilian work force in 1990 (including state, local, and federal government employees and the military) and spent 40 percent of the nation's gross national product (GNP) (*Statistical Abstract, 1992,* 280, 304, 381, 431), parts of it are still proportionately smaller than the bureaucracies of most developed nations. The real question, however, is the effectiveness of the bureaucracy, an issue explored later in this chapter.

EVOLUTION OF THE AMERICAN BUREAUCRACY

The size of the bureaucracy and the amount it has available to spend are major issues dividing the six perspectives. Liberals and Marxists generally find adequate justification for additional programs (and thus additional spending and bureaucrats) to meet the human needs of an urban industrial society. Libertarians, responding to the burgeoning of government power and influence during the twentieth century, argue for decreased government management of both the economy and their own personal lives. Conservatives and populists seek government intervention on what they consider to be moral questions and differ with each other on the degree of government intervention necessary for economics and defense. Feminists decry the underrepresentation of women at the higher levels of the bureaucracy and believe this is a reason why it has a limited understanding of women's needs.

The Growth of Government

Table 10.1 shows the growth of the federal civilian work force and spending across time. In 1841, 18,038 persons were civilian employees of the federal government. In 1990, there were 3.1 million. In 1841, government expenditures were $26.6 million. In 1990, federal government expenditures were $1.393 trillion or 25 percent of the gross national product (*Historical Statistics of the United States* 1975, 1103, 1114–15; *Statistical Abstract, 1992,* 279, 431). How did the U.S. government come to be so big and spend so much?

Modernization is the principal cause of government expansion; modern, technologically advanced societies both require and can afford more government than simple, traditional societies (Huntington 1968). In some instances technology makes the need for more government obvious. For example, the invention of radio gave rise to the problem of two stations trying to broadcast on the same frequency, a problem that led to the creation of the Federal Communications Commission in 1934. Later the commission's regulatory authority was extended to television.

Some functions of government arise from the need to regulate modern industry. In the 1870s and 1880s, as larger and larger concentrations of capital in the form of corporations came into being, some businesses conspired to set artificially high prices. Others took advantage of the impersonal nature of modern retailing to market unsafe food and drugs (Woll 1977, 40–43, 51, 93; Plano and Greenberg 1989, 406).

Pressure from farmers and consumers caused government to create the Interstate Commerce Commission (1887) and the Federal Trade Commission (1914), which regulate trade by preventing artificial restraints, monopolies, and unfair practices. The Food and Drug Administration (1906) prevents unsafe food or drugs from getting on the shelves of retail stores (*Vital Statistics on American Politics* 1992, 270). In some cases businesses also pressed for the creation of such regulatory mechanisms to secure their market share.

Industrialization gradually concentrated the nation's growing population into urban areas. Older children who in the past would have stayed on or near the family farm left home for city jobs. Improvements in transportation promoted mobility that, in turn, separated families by even greater distances. Life expectancy increased, and more and more of the nation's elderly spent the later years of their lives with neither family nor private pensions to support them (Wells 1982, 120–27, 241–63).

The dispersal of extended families was one factor in the establishment of social security, a self-funded insurance program that provides income security for older Americans. In 1935 the Social Security Administration was created to administer this system, which has since been extended to include medical benefits for the elderly and stipends to young dependents who have lost a parent. These programs now cost Americans about $468.1 billion a year, including the Medicare program (see Table 10.2). Today even conservatives believe government should provide a **"safety net"**—a backup system of support—for the needy.

Wars and international involvement are a second cause of the increased size and cost of

TABLE 10.1   THE GROWTH OF THE FEDERAL GOVERNMENT

YEAR	POPULA-TION (Millions)	BUDGET (Millions)	FEDERAL EMPLOYEES	CABINET DEPARTMENTS AND SELECTED AGENCIES ESTABLISHED
1821	9.9	$15.8	6,914	War, State, Treasury, Attorney General (1789) Navy (1798)
1841	17.7	$26.6	18,038	
1861	32.3	$66.5	36,672	Interior (1849)
1881	51.5	$260.7	100,020	Agriculture (1862) Justice (1870) Post Office (1872)
1901	77.6	$524.6	239,476	*Interstate Commerce Commission (1887)
1921	108.5	$5,061.8	561,142	Food and Drug Administration (1906) Commerce, Labor, *Federal Reserve Board (1913) *Federal Trade Commission (1914)
1941	133.4	$13,254.9	1,437,682	**Federal Deposit Insurance Corporation (1933) *Federal Communications Commission, *Securities and Exchange Commission (1934) *National Labor Relations Board, Social Security Administration, Soil Conservation Service (1935) *Civil Aeronautics Board (1940)
1961	183.7	$97,794.6	2,435,804	Defense (1947; replaced War and Navy) **Central Intelligence Agency (1947) Health, Education and Welfare (1953; renamed Health and Human Services in 1979)
1970	205.1	$195,600.0	2,928,000	Housing and Urban Development, *Equal Employment Opportunity Commission (1965) Transportation (1966)
1980	227.8	$590,900.0	2,987,000	**Environmental Protection Agency (1970) *Consumer Product Safety Commission (1972) Energy (1977) Education (1979)
1990	252.7	$1,393,000.0	3,105,000	Veterans' Affairs (1989)

* Independent regulatory commission.
** Other agencies, not in cabinet department.

Note: The Post Office has existed since 1789, but did not become a cabinet department until 1872. In 1970 the Post Office became a government corporation. The Commerce and Labor Departments were formed in 1903 as one department but split into two in 1913. The Department of Agriculture, created in 1862, became a cabinet-level department in 1889. Population figures from 1941 on include U.S. Armed Forces personnel overseas.

Source: Historical Statistics of the United States 1975, 8, 1102–3, 1114–15; Statistical Abstract, 1990, 7, 309, 324; Statistical Abstract, 1992, 8, 279, 305; Vital Statistics on American Politics, 1990, 247; World Almanac, 1990, 289–95; World Almanac, 1991, 75, 139, 143.

budget cycle in order to provide more time for deliberation on important issues. The federal budget restrains the operation of the bureaucracy, but its problems are more political than administrative.

Judicial Controls   The federal courts also exercise control over the bureaucracy through their power to interpret the law. Many agencies, especially regulatory commissions, have the authority to make regulations that have the force of law and their own judicial system of administrative law judges to settle disputes (see Chapter 8). There is always, however, a right of appeal to the federal courts for anyone wishing to challenge an agency's decision. Just as interest groups exert leverage over the bureaucracy through their supporters in Congress, they also seek to change bureaucratic decisions through lawsuits or the threat of lawsuits.

Self-Constraints   Despite the many ways the president, Congress, and the courts can exert control over the bureaucracy, a good argument could be made that, more often than not, the bureaucracy controls itself without effective interference from the rest of the government. Bureaucracies compete with one another for the resources being appropriated by Congress, and in this sense they become checks and balances on one another.

Individual bureaucracies also restrain themselves. The Agriculture Department's Forest Service and the Interior Department both deal with a variety of users of government lands, including environmentalists, ranchers, and lumber companies. To prevent potential clashes among these groups that may have repercussions on the floor of Congress as interests make their influence felt through appeals to members, these agencies often seek to compromise. They failed to prevent congressional involvement in early 1993, however. President Clinton's proposal to phase out below-cost timber sales on federal land was dropped in the Senate in response to lobbying by lumber interests that gained the support of influential senators from western states. The agencies also seek to respond to constituencies with conflicting interests by holding public meetings whenever land-use changes are proposed (Culhane 1981, 232–62).

EVALUATING THE BUREAUCRACY

No part of government is so constantly criticized, by so many people, as the federal bureaucracy. Perhaps, considering its size, such criticism is inevitable; some agency or another is bound to offend someone practically all the time. But criticism of the bureaucracy is not limited to those outside it. Those who work in it have their share of complaints, too.

Complaints from the Outside

In recent years Americans have expressed increasing dissatisfaction with the performance of presidents, Congress, and the judiciary; it is not surprising, then, that the bureaucracy should have its critics. Indeed, bureaucrats are probably more apt to draw criticism, both fair and unfair, than are elected officials. All of the common complaints against bureaucracy have some validity when applied to the bureaucracy in the United States; fortunately none is fully supported by the evidence.

"Red Tape" and Unresponsiveness   Jimmy Carter's experience with the White House mice represents a humorous example of the possibilities for overlap, buck passing, and confusion among government agencies. It can be very difficult for civil servants themselves, let alone outsiders, to fix responsibility for resolving a problem. Most Americans have probably heard stories of people who have telephoned government offices seeking assistance, only to be referred to other offices until referred back to the number called the first time. The complexity of bureaucratic procedures often goes under the name of **"red tape"**—from the red tape formerly used to tie up legal documents in England—and can be a source of profound frustration, not to mention delay.

For example, suppose that, while watching television, you see a bank loan advertisement that you feel is misleading. Being a concerned citizen, you naturally want this type of advertising eliminated. Since banks are regulated by the national government, you consult the *Washington Information Directory, 1993–94* (249–50) to find out who has jurisdiction in such cases.

After finding the section on "Consumer Affairs: Advertising," you discover that one of three economic agencies covers the advertising practices of banks, depending on whether the bank involved is a national or state bank. If it is a national bank, you contact the Comptroller of the Currency in the Treasury Department. If it is a state bank that is a member of the Federal Reserve System, you contact the Federal Reserve System. If it is a savings and loan association that is not a member of the Federal Reserve System but whose deposits are federally insured, you contact the Office of Thrift Supervision. In this case, it is also possible that two different independent regulatory commissions—the Federal Communications Commission, which regulates broadcasting, and the Federal Trade Commission, which polices advertising—might become involved, as well as the Justice Department, which would be responsible for prosecuting the offending bank. Obviously you will have to make a few phone calls to make sure you take the proper action. Without a good reference source, you might become confused enough to drop the matter entirely.

This example is by no means atypical—overlapping jurisdictions exist throughout government and can lead to conflicting and contradictory policies. Even if only one agency is involved, complying with the bureaucracy's

procedures can be onerous, especially for people in highly regulated industries. A pharmaceutical manufacturer once complained, "Our application to the FDA [Food and Drug Administration] for a drug for treatment for arthritis consisted of 120,000 pages. About 25 percent of these pages—or 30,000 of them—contained information that was important to the evaluation of the drug by FDA. The other 90,000 pages contained incredibly detailed records." The same manufacturer stated that his company spent more time preparing government reports each year than on cancer and heart disease drug research (Richard D. Wood quoted in Kaufman 1977, 10).

Defenders of the bureaucracy argue that examples like this one have been overplayed, especially by the media, which tend to highlight unusual "man-bites-dog" stories about government malfeasance. People who have dealt with government agencies report that they usually receive good service—even the often-criticized Postal Service is rated "excellent" or "very good" by nearly half the people surveyed (Goodsell 1985, 2–6, 30). This evidence suggests that the American people probably are much happier with the individual civil servants with whom they deal personally than with the bureaucracy as a whole. Unfortunately, responsiveness is less newsworthy than unresponsiveness, so the image of bureaucrats suffers, often unfairly.

Waste   Americans of all perspectives agree on one thing: the federal bureaucracy wastes a great deal of money. A 1981 public opinion poll showed that 88 percent of those surveyed thought the bureaucracy was wasteful (*Business Week*, 18 May 1981, 132–36). Of course the agreement is more apparent than real, because one's political perspective determines what one sees as "waste." Libertarians and conservatives tend to see social programs they oppose as "wasteful" no matter how efficiently they are administered. Liberals who want resources diverted from defense to aid the

regulation of others. Conservatives point to some successes in this area. Jimmy Carter's deregulation of commercial airlines, an industry that had effectively captured its regulatory commission, at first led to an overall decline in air fares by reducing underutilized services to smaller airports (Schwieterman 1985, 36–37). In the 1990s, fare wars between competing airlines drove a number of small airlines into bankruptcy, but overall prices for tickets between major airports were low enough to be generally good for the customer. Still, they may not have been good for the industry. Even airlines not in bankruptcy were losing money, causing delays in orders for new planes that hurt aircraft manufacturers. Conservatives viewed these troubles as "needed adjustments." Deregulation of oil prices, say conservatives, also brought benefits. They increased exploration efforts and contributed, along with international events, to a surplus and falling prices for several years. Conservatives also support privatization and praised Reagan's efforts to contract out government services.

Conservatives are not consistently or uniformly critical of bureaucracy. Reagan repeatedly spoke of the need to maintain a safety net for those truly in need, which in itself would imply a substantial bureaucracy, even as he criticized certain programs. Conservatives stress that government must protect society against enemies internal and external; they support bureaucracies whose purpose is to catch criminals (the Federal Bureau of Investigation), enforce moral rules against objectionable individual behavior (the Drug Enforcement Administration), and guard against foreign enemies (the Defense Department).

Liberal

American liberals are both critical and supportive of bureaucracy. The critical aspect of their thinking comes from a recognition that bureaucracy can threaten personal liberty, which liberals value most highly. The support comes from their belief that big government and an active bureaucracy are tools available to both check the abuses of business and help it compete in a global economy. In addition, liberals want government to extend economic opportunity to the underprivileged and those in need. Though liberals concede that bureaucracies may at times be inefficient, they still defend them from conservative attacks.

Conservatives, say liberals, define any program they dislike as "waste" and ignore many efficient programs that have achieved their goals. During the 1960s and 1970s, for example, poverty among elderly Americans dropped substantially due to increases in the social security program, which delivers the overwhelming majority of its money directly to older Americans. After Medicare and Medicaid were introduced in the mid-1960s, infant mortality among poor people in some areas was cut nearly in half (Schwarz 1988, 38–40). Not all programs can claim similar success, but not every private enterprise is a model of efficiency either,

say liberals. If it were, many American firms would not be calling for protection from foreign competitors while simultaneously condemning "excessive regulation."

Concerning government regulation of business, liberals are again critical but supportive. Some liberals joined in efforts aimed at deregulation of airlines and other industries, in part because they preferred deregulation to regulatory agencies captured by industry and special interests. They were, however, highly critical of Reagan's and Bush's efforts to reduce environmental and safety regulations, believing that these administrations put economic costs above life and health. Liberals are also cautious about privatization, fearing that it might lead to removing services from public control and create the potential for abuses by private enterprises. This issue was raised most clearly by the debate in the mid-1980s over proposals to contract out the management of state and federal prisons to private firms (*U.S. News and World Report*, 2 July 1984, 45–46).

Liberals fear most the parts of the bureaucracy that conservatives fear least: the agencies concerned with internal and external security. Liberals were in the forefront of efforts to curb the

Central Intelligence Agency (CIA) when, for example, it was discovered in 1975 that the agency had hired American dissidents to infiltrate foreign dissident groups, bypassing the necessary chain of command (*Commission on CIA Activities 1975*, 149). Today liberals are leading an attack on such Defense Department programs as the Strategic Defense Initiative (also called "Star Wars"), arguing that tax money should support social programs rather than unnecessary or ineffective weapons (*Congressional Quarterly Weekly Report*, 28 December 1991, 3765; *National Journal*, 3 April 1993, 822; *Congressional Quarterly Weekly Report*, 20 March 1993, 678).

Liberals believe that one way to keep bureaucracy from abusing its powers is to keep it out of the business of enforcing morality, and they guard vigilantly against invasions of civil liberties by government agencies, particularly police agencies. Liberals also favor strict laws to prevent conflicts

Carl Moore. Courtesy artist.

of interest in the bureaucracy and limit the revolving door process that often ties bureaucrats too closely to private interests.

Libertarian

Libertarians share the criticism of bureaucracy voiced by conservatives and liberals, but more intensely. While conservatives back selective deregulation and privatization, libertarians insist that only radical surgery, leading to a drastically scaled-down national government, can save the United States from becoming hopelessly bureaucratized. Conservative proposals are not only too timid but hypocritical, say libertarians, and invariably exempt wasteful programs that serve conservative constituencies or value preferences. When the libertarian David Stockman served as Reagan's budget director (see Profile in Chapter 1), he found conservatives lobbying him not to cut out programs ranging from peanut subsidies to military bases to an "experimental" nuclear reactor that was already out of date before its completion. Stockman privately called Republican leaders "piranhas" and alleged that "there are no real conservatives in Congress"—meaning no conservative is really serious about shrinking the government (quoted in Greider 1981, 44, 50).

Stockman's views reveal what libertarians think about the growth of bureaucracy (see Chapter 1). Government has grown, they say, not because of need but because of greed—the desire to use government to gain an advantage in the marketplace or obtain part of someone else's earnings. While individual pursuit of self-interest in the economy brings public benefits, group pursuit of self-interest in politics leads to each organized group's grabbing subsidies, monopoly privileges, and bureaucratic protection from competition at the expense of other groups and those not organized. Large government thus benefits not the poor but the already privileged who have the resources to participate in the political process. This abuse cannot be prevented by liberal or conservative tinkering but only by returning to the limited concept of government advanced by John Locke and Adam Smith.

In searching for ways to minimize bureaucracy's role in society, libertarians have come up with some interesting ideas that have been supported by others. The economist Milton Friedman developed the idea of a "voucher" system that would allow parents to choose the school their children would attend, forcing public schools to compete on an equal basis with private ones for students (Friedman 1962, 85–107; see also Bolick 1985, 207–21). During the 1992 election campaign, Bill Clinton said that while he did not favor choice between public and private schools, he did think permitting parents to have some choice among public schools could improve school performance. Although vouchers have been tested in some areas and limited programs allowing parents to choose among public schools have been tested in Minnesota and Iowa, Friedman's proposal has not been widely adopted. He has also proposed a "negative income tax" to replace all existing welfare programs and get money to poor people without large intervening bureaucracies: a guaranteed income would be established, and the government would simply ensure that everyone had a base income by giving individuals the amount of money they were deficient. Both Friedman's ideas have gained support from some liberals and conservatives seeking ways to promote their social objectives without creating new bureaucracies.

Populist

Of the four major perspectives, populism is perhaps the most ambivalent about bureaucracy. On the one hand, populism stands for the "ordinary person" who wants and needs services from government. Nineteenth-century populists were not afraid to call for government ownership of railroads and public utilities, which would have meant more bureaucracy. Today populists generally favor the big government entitlement programs like social security and Medicare, which benefit middle-class Americans and create the need for a large bureaucracy.

On the other hand, both left and right populists are suspicious of bureaucracy. Left populists are impressed with the evidence that bureaucracies tend to be captured by special interests. An example frequently cited by populist farm groups involves the U.S.-Soviet wheat deal of 1972. That year, cold weather killed much of the Soviet Union's wheat crop. The Department of Agriculture arranged a massive sale of U.S. wheat to the Soviets but "forgot" to tell farmers. Major grain companies were able to buy wheat from farmers at $1.25 a bushel and sell it to the Soviets for $2.25 before the information became public. Clarence Palmby, the Department of Agriculture official who had arranged the sale, resigned to become vice-president of one of the grain companies (Boyte, Booth, and Max 1986, 138–39).

Right populists also tend to see bureaucracy as insensitive and out of touch with ordinary people. For example, many in the New Christian Right argue that the public education bureaucracy has adopted a "humanist" outlook and methods of teaching that contradict Christian values (Schlafly 1984).

While populists distrust bureaucrats, they fear that the libertarian alternative—deregulation— may be worse. When government relaxes its regulations, private abuses of economic power can grow, as illustrated by the savings and loan industry collapse. Partial deregulation of the savings and loans in the early 1980s opened the way for swindlers and "rip-off" artists to infiltrate the industry. Through 1992, the bankruptcies cost $250 billion (Seidman 1992, 34), and that figure may more than double over the next thirty to forty years (Krugman 1992, 135–41). Sixty percent of the losses in 1989 alone may be due to fraud on the part of these "world class con men" (*Time*, 21 May 1990, 67). Fortunately, another government program guaranteed that small depositors would not lose their savings.

There is no body of populist theory about bureaucracy comparable to that developed by conservatives, libertarians, and liberals, but it is clear that populists would make some changes if they had the power. In general, both right and left populists would favor as much decentralization of authority as possible, with programs at the local level. If neighborhood leaders would be less subservient to special interests in the federal bureaucracy, then average Americans could participate once again in decisions that affect their lives, as their ancestors did in town meetings. Obviously new forms of participation are needed for today's society. Left populists have had their greatest success when they organized local citizen groups to pressure the bureaucracy on issues like utility rates and farm foreclosures. Ironically, if conservatives succeed in reducing federal bureaucracy, they could make such groups more important and effective (Boyte, Booth, and Max 1986, 47–68, 186).

Marxist

While conservatives and libertarians see the bureaucracy as a threat to business and the free market and liberals see it as a necessary regulator of that system, American Marxists believe that it is simply another mechanism for maintaining the capitalist system and the control of elites over society's resources. Given the constant complaints about bureaucracy from business, how can the Marxists maintain this position? According to them, many such complaints are crocodile tears, for the growth of bureaucracy often serves capitalist interests that business could not take care of itself. For example, welfare programs do not cost business very much because benefits are so low, but they make it possible for government agencies to control the poor by granting or withholding benefits. If such programs did not exist, the poor would not even have a minimal stake in the system and would be more likely to rebel (Piven and Cloward 1971, xv–xvii).

Marxists concede that there are real conflicts within the bureaucracy and between the bureaucracy and the other branches of American government. They insist, however, that these conflicts reflect disputes within the ruling class rather than effective participation by other groups. Some agencies, like the Office of Management and Budget, or security agencies like the military, the Federal Bureau of Investigation, and the Central Intelligence Agency, are more independent of specific interests and work to maintain the basic structure of capitalism, even if some capitalists have to be inconvenienced by taxes or regulations. According to most Marxists, the security agencies are not subject to the same controls as other agencies (Greenberg 1986, 270–81).

What would American bureaucracy look like if the United States became a Marxist country? Karl Marx predicted that after the revolution, government, including bureaucracy, would eventually fade away because without class oppression there would be no need for coercive power to preserve order. In practice, until the mid-1980s and with the exception of Yugoslavia, countries that adopted Marxism created highly centralized and admittedly unwieldy bureaucratic structures that had responsibility for planning the whole economy as well as providing services. Indeed, bureaucratic abuses were a major cause of the anticommunist upheavals in Eastern Europe in 1989. The old Eastern European system is not, however, the model most American Marxists would like to imitate. Somewhat surprisingly, many of them agree with conservatives and libertarians that power in government should be decentralized as much as possible to the local level, where people can participate directly in decision making (Parenti 1987, 319–21). Of course, Marxists differ from conservatives in wanting local public control of economic as well as political decision making; they would clearly reject deregulation or privatization as solutions to the problems of bureaucracy.

Feminist

The dominant feminist critique of the bureaucracy focuses on jobs. Feminists are quick to point out that though women represent a majority of job holders in the federal service, they are overwhelmingly overrepresented in clerical categories that are paid less than comparable jobs in the blue-collar federal labor force. Though women's computer and quasi-administrative skills are at least as important as men's labor skills, largely female working categories such as "clerical" are paid less than jobs at the lower levels dominated by men or shared more equally by both men and women. In the bureaucracy only one in four federal supervisors is female, and only one in ten senior federal executives is a woman. Conversely, women hold two-thirds of the lower graded positions (GS-1–GS-8) and account for 86 percent of all clerical jobs (*Statistical Abstract, 1991*, 329). This critique applies to the private sector as well.

Moreover, women in the civil service are held back by the "glass ceilings"—a level above which they are not promoted—just like women in the private sector. Studies of both the private and the public sector work force in 1991 and 1992 indicate that these ceilings seem to exist at a much lower level of most organizations than was first thought. What surprised members of both research teams— and angers some feminists—is that women are weeded out long before they have the opportunity to compete for supervisory positions. The principal barriers seem to occur at the GS-9 and GS-11 level, below the GS-13 level, considered the entry level to federal supervisory jobs (*Washington Post National Weekly Edition*, 9–15 November 1992, 34). The author of the study conducted by the Merit Systems Protection Board was startled to find that women were less likely to win promotions in their first five years in federal government than men with similar qualifications and background. "If you can't get through the prerequisite hoops at the GS-9 and GS-11 levels in the early part of your career, you will never have them [women] in the SES [Senior Executive Service]" (Evangeline Swift quoted in *Washington Post National Weekly Edition*, 9–15 November 1992, 34). In response to the assertion that things are getting better in the federal service, Lynn Eppard, legislative director of Federally Employed Women, an organization of current and retired federal workers, believes there has been a frightening disregard for the rights of women and minorities during the 1980s and early 1990s. Eppard says, "We had been doing a better job in the 1970s. I often like to say that the glass ceiling is a new label put on an old problem: race and sex discrimination." She is hopeful that the Clinton administration will move quickly to improve the situation for women (Eppard interview 1993).

High-level political appointments have also been closely monitored by feminists and women's studies scholars. Although women can and do receive appointments to significant executive branch positions (see Profile of Carla A. Hills in this chapter and Profile of Alice Rivlin in Chapter 12), such appointments remain the exception rather than the rule. For example, over sixteen presidential terms between 1932 and 1990, only ten women have held thirteen cabinet-level positions (Stetson 1991, 55). In several instances one woman occupied at least two different positions. These thirteen positions represent only about 2 percent

of the individuals who served in presidential cabinets during this time. Since then, President Bush appointed two more women, while President Clinton broke this pattern in 1993 by appointing three women to cabinet positions—Janet Reno as attorney general, Donna Shalala at Health and Human Services, and Hazel O'Leary at the Department of Energy—and three others to cabinet-rank positions, which permit them to sit in on cabinet meetings though they are not officially members of the cabinet. (*Congressional Quarterly Almanac, 1992*, 209; *Congressional Quarterly Weekly Report*, 23 January 1993, 169). In the past, however, many appointees suffered the worst effects of tokenism—high visibility but little support. Token appointments are often manipulated by powerful men or are isolated and ignored. Feminists hope this will not be the case in Clinton's administration. Sometimes women married to men with powerful political connections receive appointments to key positions. Elizabeth Dole, the wife of Senate minority floor leader Robert Dole, is one example, serving in cabinet posts in both the Reagan and Bush administrations. While Elizabeth Dole was highly qualified, she might not have been chosen had she not been married to Robert Dole.

Another major area of concern to feminists is how bureaucracies affect government policies and programs that pertain especially to women, such as child care, family and medical leave, and civil rights. Bureaucratic structures and attitudes, formed decades ago, when the public sphere was dominated by men, typically reflect the male lack of emphasis on relationships, compromise, and caring. Even today, bureaucracy continues to emphasize hierarchy and formality. It is, at its best, authoritative and at its worst, authoritarian. Feminists argue that because women are more empathetic, relationship oriented, and egalitarian, they experience bureaucrats as callous and uncaring, and bureaucracies, in fact, behave in self-serving and uncaring ways. Foster care and child care programs are examples. These programs, administered by state and local governments, are marred by mistreatment and poor delivery of services, and feminists believe more federal controls and funding are needed (*National Journal*, 27 February 1993, 512–16).

The federal executive branch, including both elected and appointed officials and career civil servants, may be a powerful force for mischief or creative change and problem solving. But policy solutions are likely to reflect female orientations and conclusions primarily the extent that women occupy significant positions of power in the executive branch. Feminists applaud the careers of women like Carla A. Hills and Alice Rivlin (see Profile, Chapter 12) but would like to see change in the gender balances at the top levels of the bureaucracy occur more quickly. They remain convinced that changes in the gender balance will be reflected in changed priorities in the making of public policy (Stetson 1991, 55–58; *Washington Post National Weekly Edition*, 9–15 November 1992, 34).

DOES THE BUREAUCRACY WORK?

Few Americans are pleased with the performance of all parts of the federal bureaucracy. There is some reason for their discontent, and striving for improvement is an admirable and useful endeavor. On the other hand, the bureaucracy probably does better than most of us are inclined to admit. Many of its problems and errors are due to its size and complexity, which in turn are owing to the demands of Americans for government services. Barring a sharp swing in public sentiment toward libertarianism, we are likely to continue denouncing our bureaucrats while asking more from them, ensuring that the "fourth branch" continues to grow in size and influence.

The system provides a bureaucracy that responds to the needs of the public, as defined by a combination of the four major perspectives. The bureaucracy is composed of civil servants who have diverse viewpoints and an awareness of the rules. We believe most programs meet real needs, though each of us has our own list of programs that we think are wasteful and should be eliminated. We encourage you to compile your own list and vote for candidates whose views match your own. Ultimately, the bureaucracy is subject to the control of our elected representatives.

We are concerned that current annual federal deficits in the $200–$300 billion range are passing on a major burden to future generations. Two of us want to cut spending first in the tradition of conservatives and libertarians, while the third wants to raise taxes, especially on the wealthy, to pay for needed programs in the tradition of liberals and populists.

SUMMARY AND REVIEW

As the American population grew and the nation became more industrialized and active in world affairs, government functions expanded to include practically everything from defense to social welfare and the regulation of commerce and industry. The number of government workers and the size of the federal budget also grew at dramatic rates to meet these needs.

Today Americans cannot seem to get along without bureaucracy—those agencies and people who administer programs for the U.S. government. Over the years, all four major perspectives have influenced the evolution of American public administration. This development has occurred in phases that include the conservative elitism of the early Republic, the populist upsurge that came with Andrew Jackson's presidency and brought in the spoils system, the liberal drive for moral reform and the libertarian emphasis on efficiency in the late nineteenth and early twentieth centuries, and the modern trends toward decentralization.

Today the bureaucracy serves four major

functions: social welfare, which consumes the largest portion of the budget; national defense and foreign policy, which include the Department of Defense, the Department of State, and the Central Intelligence Agency; other government service functions; and regulation, the impact of which is out of proportion to the relatively few dollars spent on it. All told, the national government proposed to spend around $1.5 trillion for 1994.

It is the president's responsibility to control and direct the bureaucracy so that the goals laid down in the laws will be met. He does this by appointing trusted heads of departments and agencies and coordinating his dealings with these bureaucracies with the aid of his White House staff. On occasion his department and agency appointees are able to effect the changes he wishes. Sometimes, however, political appointees become advocates of the very agencies the president has asked them to control. The president often has trouble with White House staffers as well. As the Watergate scandal and the Iran-*contra* affair have demonstrated, there are few checks on the activities of these people, and scandals can result from an overreliance on their services. Since the Senate must approve presidential appointments, both houses of Congress hold periodic oversight hearings. Congress also appropriates any and all money that agencies spend. Therefore, bureaucrats must in effect serve two masters—executive and legislature. The federal courts also exercise control over the bureaucracy through their power to interpret the law. Despite these limitations, the superior command of information enjoyed by bureaucrats is a powerful advantage, and it can be argued that the bureaucracy effectively restrains itself more often than not.

Although the bureaucracy initiates the budget process each year, it is largely at the mercy of the Congress and its power of the purse. Until the mid-1980s, the governing principle of budgeting was incrementalism, but the Gramm-Rudman-Hollings Act modified this principle. Under this law, Congress was committed to producing a balanced budget through a series of successively lower deficit limits. Gramm-Rudman-Hollings proved unsuccessful in lowering the deficit and was replaced by the Omnibus Budget Reconciliation Act of 1990. The passage of both acts resulted from an unlikely alliance of liberals and conservatives and in response to the huge federal deficit. At this present time, Congress and the Clinton administration are struggling to cut in half the $300 billion plus deficit from the last year of the Bush administration by the end of President Clinton's current term. President Clinton and Vice President Gore are working to eliminate waste and reinvent government. As a part of this reform, Clinton has proposed a two-year budget cycle.

There are many common complaints against bureaucracy, including "red tape" and unresponsiveness. Yet, bureaucrats rarely get credit for their generally positive and successful efforts, and they probably suffer much unfair criticism. Although most Americans agree that the federal bureaucracy wastes a great deal of money, Reagan's Grace Commission was unable to find many ways to eliminate inefficiency without changing policy. Many also complain that the bureaucracy has been captured by special interests, is biased by exchanges of personnel with the private sector, and effectively protects bureaucratic interests. Again, these criticisms are only partially valid.

There are complaints, issues, and problems coming from within the bureaucracy, too. The Senior Executive Service (SES) established by the Civil Service Reform Act of 1978 sought to create a more flexible, accountable, and satisfied core of senior executive bureaucrats. Unfortunately, with a large number of employees leaving the SES, it does not appear that the federal administration is benefiting as much from this service as hoped.

Most employees of the federal bureaucracy are chosen by the civil service merit system. This system seeks, by means of examinations and other criteria, to determine the most-qualified applications for a job in a politically unbiased way. Whether the system actually secures merit is open to question. The federal work force, some argue, should be representative of the public it serves, including women, minorities, and handicapped people. Discrimination in the workplace is often monitored by federal regulatory agencies. At the same time, federal employees are also subject to restrictions, on and off the job, imposed by their role as public servants. Federal employees and most state and local employees are not permitted to strike because of their ongoing responsibility to the public. Sexual harassment is not permitted in the workplace, although it is reported to occur. All civil servants are barred from extensive political involvement through the Hatch Act of 1939. They are also required to act in accord with the Ethics in Government Act (1978), and former employees are restricted in their use of advantageous connections formed as civil ser-

vants. Whistle-blowers, who expose waste within the bureaucracy, are increasingly protected. Drug testing presents the civil service with a difficult issue because it involves the question of individual privacy versus the responsibility civil servants have to the public they serve.

The bureaucracy probably achieves more good than most Americans are willing to admit. Many problems perceived to be widespread actually occur in only a few agencies and stem from poor management that can be improved. Some problems are due to venality and greed, but many result from a failure to adapt new technologies quickly. It must be remembered that checks and balances protect democracy but make it cumbersome, and that the expansion of government itself has been generated by the seemingly unending demands Americans make for services.

IMPORTANT TERMS

affirmative action
bureaucracy
bureaucrat
conflict of interest
consent decree
economy and efficiency movement
executive regulatory agency
gridlock
incrementalism
independent regulatory commission
iron triangle

merit system
net interest on the federal debt
policy implementation
privatization
"red tape"
revolving door process
"safety net"
scientific management movement
"smoke-and-mirror games"
spoils system
whistle-blower

11

AMERICAN FOREIGN POLICY

A missile fired by accident slams into the side of a U.S. Navy frigate, killing thirty-seven sailors. A nation the United States has regarded as its worst enemy for decades becomes a friend—and begins receiving American food aid as its economy collapses. An Eastern European country liberates itself from communist dictatorship—and falls into a bloody civil war. Americans worry about foreign competition and urge each other to "buy American," while the Japanese build factories in the United States. The dictator of a small Middle Eastern nation threatens to cut off the president's nose.

To the average American, such events—all drawn from news reports of the past several years—may seem frightening or simply incomprehensible. If most Americans are not well informed about the actions of government within the nation's borders, they know even less about what the nation is doing in the world and why. The institutions that conduct foreign policy include Congress, the president, and many agencies in the bureaucracy (see Chapters 6, 7, and 10). This chapter emphasizes the foreign policy problems the United States faces today and the historical roots of these problems. The last few years have seen major changes all over the world to which American foreign policy has had to adjust. As might be expected, the six perspectives offer very different explanations of how the nation arrived at its current position in foreign policy and where it should go in the future.

INSTRUMENTS AND INSTITUTIONS

The sign President Harry Truman placed on his desk, "The Buck Stops Here," applies more to foreign policy than to any other issue. The president has greater authority in dealing with the rest of the world than with domestic problems. However, the American system of government divides and separates power over

"YOUR NAME CLINTON?"

Herblock. Copyright 1992 by Herblock in *The Washington Post.*

foreign policy as well as over domestic policy. Indeed, the Constitution has been called an "invitation to struggle" over control of foreign affairs (Edward S. Corwin, quoted in Crabb Jr. and Holt 1992, ix). The following section surveys the current status of the various participants in this struggle and notes the instruments available to those who make foreign policy.

Instruments

International relations is a system for interactions and relations among nation-states and other independent political communities and the elements that affect them. A nation's basic goals in its international relations and the actions taken to achieve those goals are its **foreign policy**.

Each nation has a number of instruments it can employ in implementing its foreign policy. The first of these is **diplomacy**, or the process by which nations carry out political relationships with other nations and possibly reach an agreement. Such agreements can be formal or informal. Formal agreements often involve **alliances**, agreements whereby two or more nations with common goals agree to join in defending their interests on an issue to improve their power position. Foreign aid, both military and nonmilitary, can further foreign policy goals. Nations can also use force at a low level with **covert operations** (concealed actions approved by the president and carried out by intelligence agencies) or at a high level with open **war** (see Chapter 7). **Economic sanctions**—limits on trade such as boycotts and embargoes—can also be directed toward foreign policy goals.

Sometimes governments go over the heads of other governments and appeal directly to the people through information or propaganda campaigns. Nations also work to find out information about one another by means of intelligence gathering. In the modern age, with the world becoming increasingly interdependent, people-to-people efforts can have an impact. Nations can also appeal to international law and organizations. Even in international organizations, however, each nation retains final authority—**sovereignty**—over its own foreign and domestic affairs.

The American experience as a nation is unique. The United States has never been as comfortable with the traditional instruments of foreign policy as are most other modern nations. As a country that was isolated from world power centers before 1945 and has been a superpower ever since, it is accustomed to projecting its values on other nations. In its immediate geographic area, the United States has seen itself as having a "manifest destiny" to expand from coast to coast. Yet from 1800 until 1949, the country avoided forming alliances with powerful nations because they were seen as "entangling" by President George Washington. Generally, U.S. foreign policy could be described as **isolationism**, for outside the Western Hemisphere, the country usually sought to minimize political and military involvement with foreign nations. At the same time the country eagerly entered into trade relations with other nations.

When the United States was assertive, it was for the sake of economic advantage or in the name of a defensive principle like the **Monroe Doctrine**, which, issued in 1823, demanded that European nations establish no new colonies in the Western Hemisphere. U.S. involvement in activities in Latin America and East Asia was more acceptable than involvement in Europe, which was seen as too power hungry and war prone. When the United States did get involved in international politics, the goal was often to get the world to accept the American way of thinking (Hunt 1987; Holmes 1985; Rainey 1975; Dallek, 1983). At times American enthusiasm alienated allies, as in its efforts to contain communism. Now that world communism has collapsed, the United States is adjusting its foreign policy to deal with a world no longer divided into two hostile camps.

Institutions

In *The Federalist Papers* John Jay noted that in foreign policy "perfect secrecy and immediate dispatch are sometimes requisite" (Number 64, *Federalist Papers* 1961, 392). Since a single person is much more capable of acting quickly and secretly than a large legislative body, the framers of the Constitution gave the president power to negotiate treaties, to send and receive ambassadors (and thus recognize or refuse to recognize foreign governments), and to command the armed forces. At the same time, ever mindful of the potential for abuse of power, they subjected the president to restrictions

such as requiring a two-thirds majority for Senate approval of treaties and a majority vote of both houses of Congress for a declaration of war (Crabb Jr. and Holt 1992, 11–19, 39–58). Congress also restrains the president through its power of the purse. It appropriates funds for foreign policy activities and for war making, and in recent years it has used this power in policy-making ways.

As noted in Chapter 7, presidents have used their constitutional powers to the full extent and asserted new powers. Among these are the power to conclude executive agreements (which do not require Senate approval), to use troops without a declaration of war, and to conduct covert operations. Why has Congress, for the most part, acquiesced in these assertions of executive power? The reason may be that Congress is too large and decentralized to develop its own foreign policies as an alternative to the president's—and certainly not with the "perfect secrecy and immediate dispatch" often required. Congress can do little more than halt executive initiatives, but even this action involves taking the blame if perceived American interests are jeopardized. For example, many Democrats in Congress switched their votes in 1983 and supported U.S. aid to the government of El Salvador after President Ronald Reagan publicly threatened to charge them with "losing El Salvador to the Communists" (Wiarda 1990, 203). By giving the president what he wants, Congress can put the blame on him if policies fail. This strategy may be one reason that George Bush, who never enjoyed a majority in either house of Congress, found it much easier to lead in foreign than in domestic policy.

Despite its tendency to defer to the president, Congress has become more assertive in foreign affairs over the past twenty-five years. The most visible results are the War Powers Resolution and restrictions on covert operations (see Chapter 7). Congress has also become more assertive on issues of foreign aid and trade, seeking to protect domestic industries from foreign competition and increasingly

Steve Sack. Courtesy *Minneapolis Star Tribune.*

making American aid conditional on eliminating human rights abuses. On such issues, Congress has frequently prevailed over the executive, which tends to favor free trade and maximum discretion in disbursing aid funds (Crabb Jr. and Holt 1992, 197–224).

Congressional assertiveness in foreign policy has a strong base because Congress has acquired expertise in foreign affairs. In recent years the House Foreign Affairs Committee and Senate Foreign Relations Committee have, like other committees, greatly increased the number of their staff, some of whom are foreign policy experts (Crabb Jr. and Holt 1992, 272). Their expertise frees members of Congress from having to rely on the executive branch for information and advice and makes them more likely to question presidential policies. Twelve years of divided government (1981–93), with liberal Democrats controlling one or both houses of Congress and a conservative Republican in the White House, also encouraged congressional assertiveness. Because President Bill Clinton now leads a government in which one party controls both Congress and the presidency, Congress may become less assertive.

Agencies in Conflict   The State Department is charged by law with the responsibility for conducting foreign relations. In fact, however,

its position has been eroded in recent years (see Chapter 10). Part of the reason is competition from other agencies, which often view the career diplomats of the Foreign Service as suffering from "clientitis"—being too sympathetic to the views of the countries in which they work. For example, the Latin American Bureau of the State Department opposed Jimmy Carter's human rights policies because they strained relations with some Latin American regimes. Later, it opposed Ronald Reagan's hard-line policies because they irritated other Latin American regimes (Rubin 1987b, 182, 218–31). Not surprisingly, neither administration fully trusted the professional diplomats in the State Department.

Yet the State Department's weakness is also its strength; its employees are the people who deal with foreign governments on a day-to-day basis and thus understand their interests and concerns. When presidents bypass the State Department, as they often do, those with the most knowledge can be cut out of policy-making. The ill-fated arms-for-hostages deal with Iran, for example, was conducted against the advice of the State Department (see Controversy).

Theoretically, the armed services are not supposed to be policy-making bodies; they are only to carry out the policies set by the civilian branches of government. In practice, because foreign policy after World War II has frequently involved the threat or use of force, military leaders, by virtue of advising the president on when and how American military power is to be used, have become involved in policy-making. Contrary to common belief, these leaders are often more reluctant to use military force than are civilians. For example, during the Reagan administration the joint chiefs of staff (the heads of the four armed services) and Secretary of Defense Caspar Weinberger often opposed proposals by the State Department and the national security adviser to use troops, particularly in the Middle East and Central America (Weinberger 1990, 30–32, 133–74). At the same time, the services

Jack McLoed. Reprinted permission courtesy *Army Times*, Army Times Publishing Co., Springfield, Va.

constitute, along with civilian defense industries, a permanent lobby for a strong military and high defense spending.

The role of the secretary of defense, who by law must be a civilian, has varied from one administration to another. Some secretaries, like Robert McNamara in the 1960s, have tried to act as a check on the services, vetoing the funding of weapons they thought too costly or not needed. Others, like Weinberger and George Bush's secretary of defense, Richard Cheney, have tended to reflect the military's point of view (Stubbing and Mendel 1986, 259–398). President Clinton's secretary of defense, Les Aspin, is likely to fit in the middle.

A relatively new player in the foreign policy arena is the **national security adviser (NSA)**. Created in 1947, the NSA is authorized to provide the president with advice on foreign policy independent of any department and to manage the staff of the National Security Council (see Chapter 7). Some presidents, however, have used the national security adviser and the adviser's staff to carry out foreign policy, sometimes without the knowledge of other departments. The high point of this arrangement occurred in the Nixon administration, when national security adviser Henry Kissinger negotiated the reopening of relations with China without informing William Rogers, the secretary of state. Nixon and Kissinger feared that opponents of the new policy in the State Department might leak it to the press and stop the negotiations (Kissinger 1979, 163–94, 684–787). Giving such authority to the national security adviser is worrisome to Congress because the position does not require Senate confirmation and lacks accountability to anyone but the president. No national security adviser since Kissinger, however, has been so powerful (Inderfurth and Johnson 1988).

The Central Intelligence Agency (CIA), like the military, has no formal responsibility for policy-making; instead, it is supposed to gather and analyze intelligence. However, since the agency frequently has more information about a problem than the State Department or the military, the CIA director can be an influential adviser. This position puts pressure on intelligence agents and analysts to produce in-

---

CONTROVERSY
The Iran-Contra Affair

Oliver North

When Congress halted Ronald Reagan's program of assistance to the Nicaraguan *contras* in October 1984, it looked like the end for the anti-Sandinista forces. The president could try to get the decision reversed the next year, but the troops needed weapons, food, and support on an ongoing basis. To "keep the *contras* together body and soul," Reagan turned to his national security adviser, Robert McFarlane. He, in turn, handed the job to Lieutenant Colonel Oliver North, a decorated Vietnam War hero and zealous anticommunist who worked on the National Security Council staff.

Over the next two years, North built a covert operations network to aid the *contras.* He and McFarlane solicited funds from private donors, and Saudi Arabia and other countries. North recruited retired Air Force General Richard Secord, who created a group of corporations, known collectively as the "Enterprise," to buy arms and ship them to the *contras.* All this was done without informing the House and Senate Intelligence Committees, as required by law in covert operations. On several occasions, North and McFarlane lied to Congressman Lee Hamilton of Indiana, chair of House Intelligence, in denying reports about their activities.

Eventually the *contra* operation intersected with another North was running: the secret shipment of arms to Iran. Over the objections of several of his top advisers, including Secretary of State George Shultz and Secretary of Defense Caspar Weinberger, Reagan had agreed to a risky plan to sell Iran the weapons it needed in its war with Iraq. In return, Iran, still overtly anti-American, agreed to open negotiations and help free six American hostages held by pro-Iranian terrorists in Lebanon. When North was put in charge of this operation, he used Secord's "Enterprise" to ship the arms to Iran. In January 1986, North and McFarlane's successor, Admiral John Poindexter, decided to divert to the *contras* some of the profits made on the weapons sales to Iran. (Poindexter later testified that he did so without Reagan's knowledge.)

---

telligence reports that support the director's policy preferences. Reagan's CIA director William Casey was accused of "demanding" intelligence that would support continuing aid to the *contras* in Nicaragua (McNeil 1988, 206–24). Generally, however, CIA analyses are highly respected in the foreign policy community and actually more important than the agency's much publicized covert operations.

Other agencies are also becoming increasingly involved in foreign policy. The Treasury Department has always competed with the State Department for control of economic diplomacy, and it may be winning. The plan

With one man running so many secret operations, the Iran-*contra* affair looked a little like a comic opera. At one point, a $10 million contribution from the leader of a friendly Asian nation was lost due to clerical error; it later turned up in the account of a Swiss businessman unconnected with the "Enterprise." North took money from the funds to build a security fence around his home, and Secord and other arms dealers reaped substantial profits. In May 1986 a mission led by North and McFarlane carried a Bible signed by the president as a gift to the Ayatollah Khomeini, Iran's political and spiritual leader, along with a cake for one of the Iranian negotiators, purchased in Israel. The delegation never got to meet with the top Iranian leader, however, and Iranian guards stole and ate the cake. Three hostages were eventually released, but more were taken in Lebanon.

The operation began to unravel in October 1986, when one of Secord's planes carrying arms to the *contras* was shot down and a crewmember, Eugene Hasenfus, was captured. Hasenfus revealed the *contra* part of the operation, and further investigation soon led to the exposure of the Iranian arms sale and diversion of funds to the *contras*.

Unlike Richard Nixon in the Watergate scandal (see Controversy in Chapter 7), Reagan cooperated with the congressional investigating committee assigned to probe the affair. Nonetheless, talk of impeachment was heard until North testified before the joint House-Senate investigating committee in July 1987. North's air of sincerity and patriotism so impressed the public that the committee members found themselves, rather than the administration, on the defensive. North and Poindexter were both eventually convicted, however, on charges connected with the affair, but Weinberger and others were pardoned by President George Bush just before he left office. This action led to charges that Bush was trying to cover up his own involvement. The degree of knowledge that Bush had had of the affair as vice-president was a matter of controversy in the 1992 presidential election.

Just who was involved and to what degree, as well as the rights and wrongs of aiding the *contras* or seeking better relations with Iran, may be debated indefinitely. The abuse of power and inept performances of many of the Iran-*contra* players, however, illustrate the potential for danger in the power to conduct covert operations if these operations are not properly supervised by Congress and the president. Perhaps the clearest judgment was made by the majority report of the Iran-*contra* investigating committees:

> The concept of a covert company to conduct covert operations with funds not appropriated by Congress is contrary to the Constitution. The decision to use the "Enterprise" to fight a war with unappropriated funds was a decision to combine the power of the purse and the power of the sword in one branch of government.

Source: Majority report quoted in *Report of the Congressional Committees Investigating the Iran-Contra Affair* 1988, 413; Cohen and Mitchell 1988; *New York Times Magazine*, 29 April 1990, 46–78.

proposed by the United States for dealing with the debt problems of Third World countries was prepared by President Bush's secretary of the treasury, Nicholas Brady. The Justice Department is concerned about gaining the cooperation of other countries in checking the international drug trade. The Agriculture Department runs its own Foreign Agricultural Service (FAS) to promote the sale of American agricultural products abroad. With the world economy having an even larger impact on the lives of Americans, the number of agencies concerned with foreign policy, and the conflicts among them, are likely to grow.

Interest Groups and Public Opinion   Interest groups have less opportunity to affect foreign policy than domestic policy for several reasons. First, foreign policy is mainly determined by the executive branch, which is less accessible to interest group pressures than is Congress. Second, many foreign policy decisions are made secretly and may even be carried out secretly, eliminating the opportunity for influence. Third, interest groups usually do not have as much information and expertise on foreign policy as they have on many aspects of domestic policy, so their advice is not as valued by the decision makers (McCormick 1985, 264). Finally, the opinion held by foreign governments and world conditions restrict the influence of interest groups.

Nevertheless, some interest groups can significantly influence foreign policy. The American Israeli Public Affairs Committee (see Profile in Chapter 5), for example, is a well-organized group that faces less effective activity on the other side of Middle East issues. Some foreign policies, moreover, have direct domestic impact and so may be of great concern to interest groups. For example, stopping construction of a new weapon becomes harder after contracts are awarded and companies and workers develop an interest in lobbying for the project's continuation. Groups also become more influential when they have a popular cause. In 1986, when black groups and human rights groups asked Congress to pass economic sanctions against South Africa over Ronald Reagan's veto, the *apartheid* (racial separation) regime was so unpopular that more than half the Republicans in Congress voted against the Republican president (*Almanac of American Politics, 1988*, xix–xx). Usually interest group success in foreign policy depends on getting Congress involved in the issue.

While most observers agree that public opinion has more effect on foreign policy in the United States than in most other countries, some dispute about the influence of public opinion relative to other policy considerations remains. Some critics point out that most Americans are poorly informed about foreign policy. Polls on the Central American issue showed that, even in the late 1980s after several years of heavy news coverage, only 38 percent of the public knew that the United States was on the side of the *contras* against the Sandinistas in Nicaragua and one-fourth had not heard of the war there at all. Only 20 percent of Americans in 1988 even knew that Nicaragua had a leftist government (Asher 1992, 127).

Skeptics also point out that the president can usually shift public opinion to his side of any foreign policy issue, at least temporarily. Polls taken during the Vietnam War showed the majority of Americans consistently supported whatever policy the president was pursuing, whether it was escalation or withdrawal (Mueller 1973, 69–74). During the Persian Gulf War support for the president was also high. In addition, much foreign policy is made by bureaucrats. Knowing how ill-informed and changeable public opinion is, many of these bureaucrats agree with the State Department official who told an interviewer, "To hell with public opinion! We [the State Department] should lead and not follow" (quoted in Cohen 1973, 62).

Some (including two of this textbook's authors) contend that, no matter how well or ill informed the public, the public's "mood," or general attitude toward foreign affairs, is important in influencing policy. For example, before Pearl Harbor most Americans wanted to avoid involvement in "foreign wars," and the public mood of isolationism made it hard for Franklin Roosevelt to give the British as much assistance as he wanted to in the war against Adolf Hitler (Klingberg 1952, 248–49). In the early 1960s fear of communist expansion was high, and that made it difficult for John Kennedy and Lyndon Johnson to contemplate "losing" Vietnam by withdrawing. After Vietnam, polls showed strong public opposition to military involvement abroad, and Congress responded by checking executive attempts to become involved in Angola, Central America, and elsewhere. A strong public mood can override the influence of the president; despite limited knowledge of the issues involved, the public remained strongly opposed (by 80 percent or more in most polls) to direct U.S. intervention in El Salvador or Nicaragua during the 1980s (Sobel 1984, 117–18). In addition, foreign policy options were even more limited by strong opinions in Congress. Recently, the public has been permissive regarding U.S. involvement in troubled areas throughout the world. The major problem with using public mood to direct foreign policy is that policy matters are too complex to be decided by simple attitudes like "avoid foreign wars" or "stop communism." The effect of following public mood may be to cause the United States to go to extremes in its foreign policy (Holmes 1985, 70–108, 140–60).

While political scientists do not agree regarding the extent of public influence, it is important to remember that effective American leaders must have the support of the people. How they obtain that support—through manipulation, catering to public wishes, or some combination of the two—is also the subject of disagreement among political scientists.

THE RISE AND FALL OF THE SOVIET THREAT

For four and one-half decades Americans worried more about their relationship with the Soviet Union, comprising Russia and fourteen other states, than about any other foreign policy issue. Both superpowers had enough nuclear weapons to destroy civilization several times over. Some thought the weapons themselves were the problem, and pushed for arms control or disarmament. (**Arms control** refers to measures to restrict the number of weapons and their continued production, while **disarmament** refers to actual reduction in the number of existing military forces or weapons.)

Today, however, it is clear that it was the deep differences in values and political perspectives that divided the two nations and peoples. The presence of weapons does not, in and of itself, represent a threat to peace; the Russian government still has most of the former Soviet Union's weapons, but the probability of war with the United States has declined dramatically because Russia no longer poses a challenge to the Western democratic political system. The former Soviet Union now is divided into fifteen nations. The United States and the new Russia are moving closer together, though problems remain.

Indeed, it is largely because of the Soviet Union that the United States has become so deeply engaged in world affairs. Before the period of the U.S.-Soviet tension, U.S. foreign policy outside the Western Hemisphere was often isolationism, especially in relation to Europe. (Isolationism did not apply to economic issues; the United States has always tried to expand trade with other nations and to make money abroad.)

When the Communist party seized power in Russia in 1917, President Woodrow Wilson sent a small force to help the anticommunists in the ensuing civil war. American troops had little effect on the war, however, and Communist party control was secure by 1920. The United States refused to recognize the Soviet government until 1933. Conservatives and libertarians detested the Soviet system for its suppression of private property rights and religious freedom; liberals admired some Soviet social programs but were horrified by police terror and the lack of civil liberties. The situation was, in fact, worse than most Americans knew. The Soviet dictator, Josef Stalin, is estimated to have caused the death of 20 million Soviet citizens in his ruthless effort to force peasants into collectivized agriculture and eliminate opposition within the Communist party (Conquest 1968). The Soviet Union was not seen as a serious threat to the United States at that time, though there was exaggerated concern about the small pro-Moscow Communist party of the United States as a subversive influence.

Differences were buried during World War II when the United States and the Soviets found themselves on the same side against Nazi Germany; wartime propaganda even presented a favorable view of Soviet society. But attitudes quickly changed with the coming of peace. Just before the war ended in 1945, the United States, Britain, and the Soviet Union signed an agreement at the city of Yalta in the Soviet Union stating that countries liberated from the Germans would be allowed to choose their own governments in free elections. Elections were held in Western Europe, which was occupied by U.S., British, and French troops, but in Eastern Europe Soviet occupying forces helped local communists crush all opposition and establish what were, in effect, **puppet governments**, ostensibly sovereign states actually controlled by Moscow. Since the Communist parties in Western Europe were dominated by pro-Soviet leaders, Americans feared that the Soviets wanted to dominate the whole continent. Communist control of Western Europe would have negated the gains for democracy hoped for from the defeat of the Nazis and presented the United States with a dangerous military threat. The Soviets also demanded large war reparations from Germany, which the United States feared would impede the world's economic recovery from the war, and territory from Turkey and Iran, which to the United States looked like a threat to the oil fields of the Middle East. Observers began to speak of a U.S.-Soviet **cold war**—an ideological conflict between the superpowers without direct violence (Gaddis 1972).

The policy response of the United States to these aggressive Soviet moves was to help noncommunist states perceived to be threatened by Soviet expansion. The goal was to "contain" communism, and the policy was first advocated in an article published anonymously in *Foreign Affairs* in 1947. The author,

George F. Kennan, urged the United States to use **containment**—stopping Soviet expansion by supporting countries that were threatened with Soviet control. This strategy, Kennan predicted, would work "to force upon the Kremlin a far greater degree of moderation and circumspection than it has had to observe in recent years, and in this way to promote tendencies which must eventually find their outlet in either the break-up or gradual mellowing of Soviet power" (Kennan 1947, 582; see also Kennan 1972, 5–21; Kennan 1982).

Certainly the policy of containment had some of the results Kennan envisioned, but the road paved by that policy from 1947 to 1989 was long and rocky. Indeed, Kennan himself has disagreed with some of the actions taken in the name of containment. Containment included a variety of policies. Starting in 1948, Western Europe received billions of dollars in economic aid through the **Marshall Plan**, named for Secretary of State George C. Marshall. Economic aid, it was hoped, would reduce the appeal of communism to the people of these nations and build loyalty to the United States. The government of Greece received military aid to put down a communist revolt. In Iran and Turkey, President Harry Truman simply warned the Soviets to stay out, and they did. But in other cases force had to be used, as when the pro-Soviet, North Korean government invaded South Korea in 1950. Chinese communist forces, which had recently won a civil war in China and established the People's Republic, were ultimately drawn into this war, which lasted three years and, including both combat and noncombat deaths, cost fifty-four thousand American lives. In 1949 the United States entered into a defense agreement with Europe, called the **North Atlantic Treaty Organization (NATO)**, in which the members pledged to defend each other against any outside (presumably Soviet) attacks.

Many of these containment efforts were successful, but there were also some reverses. U.S. aid could not halt communist revolutions

Step on It. Doc!

Roy Justus. Courtesy *Minneapolis Star Tribune.*

against weak or unpopular governments, as demonstrated by the victory of Mao Zedong's Chinese communists over Chiang Kai-shek's corrupt Nationalist government in 1949 and Fidel Castro's triumph over the dictator Fulgencio Batista in Cuba in 1959. The containment policy placed the United States in opposition to almost all Marxist movements and may have precluded its exploiting the differences among the communists, particularly between Stalin and Mao. Containment also forced the United States to rely on nuclear weapons as a deterrent, since American troops could not be stationed everywhere in sufficient numbers.

President Harry Truman even considered using nuclear weapons against the Soviets when they blockaded Berlin in 1948, but he chose instead to resupply the city with an airlift. President Dwight Eisenhower rejected recommendations from advisers to use nuclear weapons against Vietnamese communist

forces fighting the French in 1954 (Kaku and Axelrod 1987, 49–94). Perhaps the closest the world ever came to nuclear war was in 1962, when the Soviets placed missiles in Cuba (see Controversy in Chapter 7). The missiles were withdrawn after President John Kennedy quarantined the island and threatened a nonnuclear air strike, but for a while the fear of escalation to nuclear war was high. The crisis spurred a desire in both countries for some improvement in the relationship. In 1963 an agreement between the United States and the Soviet Union banned the testing of nuclear weapons above ground. It was followed by agreements banning nuclear weapons in space and on the ocean floor.

Perhaps the most controversial American foreign policy in the last forty years was involvement in the Southeast Asian country of Vietnam from 1954 to 1975. What started as a limited commitment by the Eisenhower administration to aid a shaky anticommunist government in South Vietnam grew to sixteen thousand "advisers" helping the South Vietnamese army against communist guerrillas (the Viet Cong) by the end of the Kennedy administration. Although Vietnam itself had little strategic significance, American leaders felt that a defeat there would encourage communist revolutions elsewhere in Asia. Their fear that the fall of one nation would cause the fall of others was known as the **domino theory.** When the South Vietnamese army proved unequal to the task, President Lyndon Johnson sent the first U.S. ground combat units to South Vietnam in 1965. Communist North Vietnam, which up to this point had merely been aiding the Viet Cong, then sent some of its own troops to the South, and a cycle of escalation began. By 1968, 540,000 American troops were in South Vietnam, with no victory in sight (Karnow 1983; see also U.S. Department of Defense 1971).

By that time the American people had started to turn against the war. President Richard Nixon gradually reduced the number of American troops, and in 1973 a peace settlement was signed. By 1975 the North Vietnamese communists had taken over all of Vietnam—the very result the United States had fought to avoid. The experience of Vietnam had a profound effect on American foreign policy (Holmes 1985, esp. 100–03). In Asia in particular the United States became less assertive and more multilateral, but in all areas of the world policymakers sought to avoid "another Vietnam."

Relations with the People's Republic of China improved steadily through most of the 1970s, though differences remained. Relations with the Soviet Union improved further in the early 1970s when President Nixon signed agreements with the Soviet leader Leonid Brezhnev limiting the number of nuclear missiles and drastically limiting antiballistic missiles (ABMs), designed to shoot down attacking missiles. Nixon also sought to open up trade between the two countries, hoping to give the Soviets a "vested interest in peace"

with the United States. For a while it looked as though this policy, known as **détente** (French for "relaxation of tensions"), might bring a permanent improvement in relations. Indeed, from 1968 to 1978 the percentage of the American gross national product devoted to national defense was reduced from 9.5 to 5.0, a clear indicator of a less assertive American stance, as well as a reflection of the American withdrawal from Vietnam (Foreign Policy Association 1980, 12).

Détente broke down because of lack of trust and differences in values between the two countries. The Trade Act of 1974 and the Jackson-Vanik Amendment to this law denied the Soviets equal trading rights (nations with these rights are confusingly referred to as having **most favored nation status**) with the United States until Soviet citizens were allowed to emigrate freely. To the Soviets, this condition looked like American interference in internal affairs. On the other hand, Americans were angry that the Soviets, despite their expressed wish for peace, kept trying to extend their influence. In 1973 the Soviets backed the Arabs in a war with Israel that nearly led to another dangerous confrontation between the superpowers (Quandt 1977, 165–206). In 1975 the Soviets transported Cuban troops to Angola to back a pro-Soviet faction there. In 1978 the Cubans, again with Soviet support, appeared in Ethiopia helping that Marxist government in its war with neighboring (and also Marxist) Somalia.

Détente was already fraying at the edges when, in December 1979, Soviet forces invaded Afghanistan. While Afghanistan itself was not vital to the United States, the Soviet move was widely perceived as a threat to the oil-producing areas of the Middle East. Stating that "my opinion of the Russians has changed considerably in the past week," President Jimmy Carter then imposed economic sanctions, including a grain embargo, on the Soviets; withdrew U.S. athletes from the 1980 Olympic Games in Moscow; and began sending aid (later greatly expanded by the Reagan administration) to Afghan rebels.

No one expected Ronald Reagan to take a soft line with the Soviet Union, and he did not. His conservative administration increased defense spending 33 percent (in constant dollars, adjusted for inflation) (*Budget Baselines* 1993, 370–71) and used harsher anti-Soviet language than had been heard in Washington since the 1950s. In one early speech Reagan called the Soviet government "the focus of evil in the modern world" (Dallin and Lapidus 1987, 228). He also aided anticommunist resistance forces under the so-called **Reagan Doctrine**, which called for helping people under communist rule to liberate themselves. Naturally, this position produced very chilly U.S.-Soviet relations during Reagan's first term.

Unexpectedly, the U.S.-Soviet relationship improved dramatically during Reagan's second term, largely as a result of initiatives taken by the Soviet president, Mikhail Gorbachev. Gorbachev's policies of *glasnost* (Russian for "openness") and *perestroika* (economic restructuring) were originally intended as moderate reforms of the communist system. However, Gorbachev found he could not control the reform process, which initiated fundamental changes in Soviet foreign policy. When the Eastern European peoples demanded the removal of their Soviet-imposed puppet gov-

Vic Harville. Courtesy *Arkansas Democrat-Gazette*.

ernments in 1988–89, Gorbachev gave in, provoking similar demands in the Soviet Union. Seeking to take U.S. pressure off while internal reforms went ahead, he signed arms agreements favorable to the West and permitted Germany to reunite in 1990. By the end of his term, Reagan was no longer talking about an "evil empire" to the east—in fact, he and Gorbachev were friends (Balzer 1991; Mandelbaum and Talbot 1987; Cohen and Vanden Heuval 1989; Gorbachev 1991).

American friendship could not save Gorbachev, however. After an attempted coup by communist hard-liners in August 1991, Gorbachev was discredited among most of the Russian people, who followed ex-communist Boris Yeltsin (see Profile). Yeltsin allowed non-Russian nationalities to secede and form their own states, and on January 1, 1992, the Soviet Union was replaced by a loose Commonwealth of Independent States. Two members of the Commonwealth, Armenia and Azerbaijan, promptly went to war with each other, and tensions also appeared between other republics, especially Russia and the agriculturally rich Ukraine. All the new nations pleaded for economic aid from the West. By mid-1993 some

Clyde Wells. Courtesy artist.

PROFILE

Boris Yeltsin: Founder of a Free Russia?

Boris Yeltsin (Reuters/Bettmann)

The Russian nation has endured for eleven hundred years, more than five times as long as the United States. During those years there have been tsars and commissars, but only one democratically elected president—Boris Yeltsin, a former high official of the Soviet Communist party. Can Yeltsin, born into poverty under the Soviet regime, lead his people on the path to economic prosperity under a market economic system? Or will Russia's authoritarian tradition reassert itself, with him or someone else as the new tsar?

Boris Yeltsin was born February 1, 1931, the son of a construction worker in Sverdlovsk, a province in Siberia. Famine gripped much of the Soviet Union then, and Yeltsin remembers his childhood as "a fairly joyless time. There were never any sweets, delicacies or anything of that sort: we had only one aim in life, to survive." In the repressive Stalin period, young Boris showed early signs of independence. As top student in his elementary school graduating class, he used his graduation speech to denounce a tyrannical teacher. He was expelled from school temporarily, but he got the teacher fired.

Like most future Soviet bureaucrats, Yeltsin entered a technical field—engineering—and became director of construction work in Sverdlovsk province. From there he advanced to the post of Communist party chief of the province in 1976 and gained a reputation for opposing corrupt bureaucrats. In need of support for his fledgling reform efforts, Mikhail Gorbachev summoned Yeltsin to Moscow in 1985 to take a seat on the party central committee. A few months later Yeltsin became head of the important Moscow party, replacing the notoriously corrupt Viktor Grishin. Under the Soviet system, this in effect made Yeltsin mayor of Moscow.

In his new position, Yeltsin once again won popular acclaim by cracking down on official corruption but made enemies in high places of the party. Communist hard-liners pressured Gorbachev into censuring Yeltsin at a November 1987 party conference and finally into removing him from his post in Moscow in June 1988. Up to this time Yeltsin had been a communist reformer, but once outside the party his views became more radical. He sought and won the support of intel-

aid was arriving, but economic conditions remained grim. The former "evil empire" was now a charity case, and the United States was the world's only superpower.

The waning of the cold war did not solve all world's problems; in fact, it created some new ones. Many Americans worried about what might happen if the internal conflicts in the former Soviet Union got worse. Perhaps nuclear weapons once aimed at the United States would be used by Russians against the Ukrainians, or by Russians against each other in civil

lectuals who wanted to discard communism in favor of democracy as well as workers fed up with increasing shortages and Russian nationalists who felt Russia might be better off without the other Soviet republics. When Gorbachev held the first free elections in Soviet history in March 1989, Yeltsin won a seat in the Congress of People's Deputies and became leader of the opposition Inter-Regional Group. The following year, he was elected president of the Russian Republic and began to push for a new Union treaty giving the individual republics more control over their own affairs.

The day before the Union treaty was to be signed, on August 19, 1991, the hard-liners struck. Declaring Gorbachev to be "ill," they formed an emergency committee and attempted to seize power. They failed to seize Yeltsin, however, who gathered thousands of followers around the Russian parliament building and resolved to hold out. Troops refused to fire on the people, and on August 21 the coup collapsed. Yeltsin was the hero of the hour, while Gorbachev was discredited because his closest advisers had been involved in the coup. Discredited, too, was the Communist party, which Yeltsin ordered banned without consulting Gorbachev.

After the coup attempt, the Soviet Union disintegrated rapidly, with Yeltsin's encouragement. Republic after republic declared its independence, and at the end of 1991 a new Commonwealth of Independent States, with ill-defined powers, was formed to replace the old Union. Gorbachev resigned, leaving Yeltsin to inherit most of what was left of Soviet power as president of Russia.

Yeltsin's popularity, soaring after the coup, took a sudden nose dive when he began moving Russia toward a free market economy. In January 1992, initial steps toward a market economy including removal of some price controls resulted in the prices of basic necessities skyrocketing, with the average family spending 60 percent or more of its income for food. Most economists said such measures were essential for the long-term revival of the economy, but many people were naturally angry. Soon ex-communists and others organized demonstrations in which they displayed pictures of Lenin and Stalin and called for a return to the old system. Russians living in other republics were also bitter, since many had been denied citizenship there by the new governments despite years of residence. By early 1993, the Russian Parliament, most of whose members were former communists like Yeltsin, was pressuring him to slow down reform.

Boris Yeltsin helped lead a peaceful revolution in Russia, but observers wondered if he could handle the consequences. A Communist party bureaucrat for most of his life, Yeltsin knows little about running a modern economy. For that matter, no one knows how to manage the transition from communism back to capitalism, a task likened by one popular Russian joke to turning fish soup back into fish. Yeltsin pleaded for more aid from the West, but the United States and other former enemies, with their own economic problems, were reluctant and slow to help. Many feared that, to hold his increasingly chaotic country together, Yeltsin would be forced to resort to traditional authoritarian methods of rule or be replaced by someone who would. Indeed, he dissolved the Russian Parliament in September 1993 and forcefully occupied it in October 1993. The Constitutional Court was also dissolved. His challenge now will be to retain popular support.

Source: Yeltsin 1990; Malia 1992, 21–28; *USA Today*, 6 October 1993, A1, A8.

---

war, or sold to a leader like Iraq's Saddam Hussein (see Profile later in this chapter; *Strategic Survey, 1992–93*, 5–28). If so, the United States could hardly escape environmental and other consequences, and many thought the United States and other countries needed to send aid to the Commonwealth of Independent States to preserve stability and prevent future problems. Others thought aid could do little good and that the Russians and others had to solve their own problems. Despite these worries, most Americans welcomed the end of the cold war, seeing a need to turn government's attention to national and other international problems.

Two of the most important questions facing the United States are whether it will remain a great power and what to do about the need for power adjustments. In 1987 Paul Kennedy argued that great powers rise and fall and that the United States has entered the decline stage (Kennedy 1987). In 1990 Joseph Nye argued that the United States was "bound to lead" and would continue to do so for some time to come (Nye 1990). Speculating who is right is beyond the scope of this textbook. What seems to be the consensus, however, is that the United States is the only nation that can claim to be a great power both militarily and economically. The real question is whether the nation will shift its emphasis from power center to interaction and cooperation within an interdependent world system. Since the seventeenth century, international relations have been guided by the **balance of power** theory, which seeks peace and security through an equilibrium of power distributed among groups of nations. In the early twentieth century, Woodrow Wilson and the League of Nations introduced the notion of **collective security,** in which peace and security would be achieved through multinational organizations acting to condemn any nation that commits aggression, using force if necessary. The 1991 Persian Gulf War, in which a UN-sponsored coalition of troops forced Iraq to withdraw from Kuwait, is an example. Multilateral peacekeeping forces can also be dispatched to deal with low-level conflicts. In the future, international relations may be increasingly guided by the notion of **complex interdependence** in which war is no longer seen as a real possibility among nations bound by trade and economic relationships. Other analysts argue that the future could involve clashes of civilizations (Huntington 1993).

Brian Duffy. Courtesy artist.

RELATIONS WITH INDUSTRIAL DEMOCRACIES

Compared to past problems with the former Soviet Union, American relations with other industrial democracies seem placid enough. The threat of war has disappeared, even with old enemies like Germany and Japan. Goods and people flow from country to country more freely than at any previous time in history. Yet cooperation and peace have not meant the end of problems between the United States and the other advanced nations. Indeed, there is a whole new set of concerns.

Trade Issues

As World War II drew to a close, many policymakers feared peace would bring a return of the Depression that had gripped the world in the 1930s. Since government-imposed **tariff barriers** to trade (taxes on imported goods) were widely believed to have contributed to the economic crisis, the United States and its allies began discussions aimed at creating a freer world trading system. At a meeting in Bretton Woods, New Hampshire, in 1944, representatives of these nations reached a set of agreements. One provided that the rate at which one nation's currency was exchanged for another's would be fixed rather than allowed to fluctuate. This agreement was aimed at preventing countries from promoting their exports at the expense of others by devaluing their currencies. Another agreement set up an **International Monetary Fund (IMF)** to loan money to nations experiencing economic problems. Later the United States promoted the **General Agreement on Tariffs and Trade (GATT)**, an international agency that sponsors talks and agreements aimed at reducing trade barriers among nations. As a result of GATT, tariff barriers worldwide were cut substantially; the average duty on goods entering the United States dropped from 39 percent before World War II to around 11 percent in 1978 (U.S. State Department figures cited in Kegley and Wittkopf 1981, 175).

The postwar economic reforms led to a vast expansion of world trade, and the United States shared in the benefit. In fact, the United States exports more goods to other nations than any other country in the world. Unfortunately, it imports even more than it exports. The result by 1993 was a trade deficit of $84.3 billion, the latest in a series of such trade deficits (*New York Times*, 19 February 1993, D2). Faced with this troubling imbalance and the decline of many once-dominant American industries, an increasing number of Americans are calling for changes in the world trading system (*U.S. News and World Report*, 1 January 1990, A6).

Why is the United States buying so much more than it sells to its trading partners? Part of the reason is that other nations have simply gotten better at producing things; the label "Made in Japan," once a synonym for low-quality goods, is now taken by many consum-

ers as a sign of superior quality. The problem is exacerbated because Americans are more inclined to spend and less inclined to save than citizens of some competing countries. Another factor is that the fixed-exchange system established at Bretton Woods broke down in 1971, and exchange rates now fluctuate sharply. Between 1980 and 1984 the dollar rose in value by more than 50 percent, which made imports to the United States cheaper, made exports from the United States more expensive, and contributed to the growth of the trade deficit (see Chapter 12). Since then, the dollar has fallen significantly, and so has the trade deficit, from more than $152 billion in 1987 to $84.3 billion in 1992, as noted above (*New York Times*, 19 February 1993, D2; *Statistical Abstract, 1992*, 796). The third reason, and the one that aggravates Americans the most, is that the tariff reductions under GATT have not always secured an open door for American goods overseas. Many U.S. trading partners use so-called **nontariff barriers** to limit imports of American products; these range from unnecessary "safety" inspections to subsidies for the domestic industry to outright bans on imports. For example, American farmers can grow rice much less expensively than Japanese farmers, but Japan excludes most foreign rice from its market, arguing that it cannot afford to depend on imports for its basic food supply. In January 1992, President Bush traveled to Japan to urge its government to lift its trade barriers but made only limited progress (Council of Economic Advisers 1992, 416). The United States has some nontariff barriers of its own, but they have apparently not been as effective at limiting imports. President Clinton has pledged to take a tougher stance toward Japan and other countries that restrict American goods.

According to opinion polls, most Americans want to deal with the trade problem by imposing high protective tariffs or other trade barriers on foreign goods (Schneider 1987, 63–66). In a few cases, the Reagan administration responded to this pressure by imposing restrictions on some European and Japanese imports until restrictions on American goods were removed and other unfair practices like **dumping** (selling goods for less than they cost in order to put a competitor out of business) were ended (*Time*, 13 April 1987, 28–36). On the whole, however, Reagan, like previous presidents, remained committed to **free trade,** a policy of minimizing trade barriers among nations. Many economists agreed, contending that trade restrictions would hurt American consumers by raising the price of imported goods, damage the export industries because trading partners would retaliate with new barriers of their own, and bring on a world depression like the one of the 1930s (*Time*, 13 April 1987, 30–31). But if free trade is to be preserved, the problem of nontariff barriers must be solved by negotiation between the United States and other industrial nations. So far, there has been much talk but little progress.

Military and Strategic Issues

The United States is tied to other nations by defense agreements as well as by trade, and these relationships can also create problems. During the cold war, the United States often complained that it was carrying too great a share of the burden of defending the noncommunist world against the Soviets. In 1984, for example, the United States spent 6.9 percent of its gross national product (GNP) on defense, compared to 3.6 percent spent by the other members of NATO (Posen and Van Evera 1987, 98; Huntington 1987–88, 453–77; *Statistical Abstract, 1991,* 330). Japan, which has a U.S.-imposed provision in its constitution forbidding any military action outside its borders, spends only about 1 percent of its GNP for defense.

With the end of the cold war, the United States is cutting its defense budget, but complaints about unequal burdens persist. When the United States appealed for support against Iraq in the Persian Gulf, Britain sent forty-two

Steve Kelley. Courtesy Copley News Service.

thousand troops and France fourteen thousand, but other allies sent only token forces (Dunnigan and Bay 1992, 401). Even with Arab allies, the United States contributed nearly two-thirds of the victorious coalition forces (Watson et al. 1991). From the European and Japanese perspective, of course, the situation looks different. Germany and Japan contributed more than $17 billion to the effort.

Among Europeans and Japanese, there is gratitude for American military protection, but there is also the feeling that the United States claims the right to make policy decisions without consulting its allies. For example, before sending the troops to Saudi Arabia in August 1990, President Bush consulted British Prime Minister Margaret Thatcher but not the leaders of other major allies. His action may account for Britain's being more supportive of the United States than other nations were at the time. If the United States wants greater burden sharing in future military conflicts, it may have to give its allies a greater role in decision making.

By 1992 the NATO alliance was searching for a new role. With the Soviet threat gone, the United States was cutting its forces in Europe by two-thirds, from three hundred thousand to one hundred thousand, but critics charged that even the lower figure was too high and that the United States was wasting money defending Europe from a nonexistent threat. Defense commitments to Japan were even more controversial, given that country's position as chief economic competitor of the United States (Calleo 1992, 175–80). On the other hand, problems in Europe, such as civil war in Yugoslavia and turmoil in former Soviet republics, led the Bush administration and many scholars to argue that NATO should be maintained against the possible emergence of new threats to peace (Dunn 1990). Even as some Eastern European countries are becoming interested in joining NATO, U.S. policy can still best be described as cautious, awaiting future developments.

Relations with Canada

The United States' relations with its northern neighbor have usually been so good that Canada is often ignored in discussions of foreign policy. Some recent issues in U.S.-Canadian relations may be important for the future, however. Factories and power plants on both sides of the border pollute the air on the other side, but since the United States is the larger country, Canada receives the bulk of the pollution and is lobbying hard for Congress to impose tough, costly antipollution controls. This issue suggests the increasing importance of international environmental problems. For industrialized nations like the United States and Canada, acid rain and polluted waters along shared borders can spark disputes. Third World countries, on the other hand, seek development first and do not give high priority to pollution controls. U.S. foreign policy on environmental issues is likely to grow increasingly complex as the issues themselves multiply (see Controversy in Chapter 13).

Another issue in U.S.-Canadian relations is free trade. Both the Reagan administration and the conservative government in Canada favored free trade between the two countries and reached an agreement in the fall of 1987

(Aho and Levinson 1987, 143–55). The American-Canadian Free Trade Agreement was approved by Congress and in Canada following a hard-fought national election in 1988. It went into effect in January 1989, but opposition still exists, especially in Canada where some businesses have been adversely affected by free trade and the falling American dollar.

A third issue is the real possibility that Canada may break up, due to tensions between English-speaking Canadians and French speakers, many of whom want a separate nation in Quebec. If such a breakup occurred peacefully, the United States would not be seriously affected, but a violent split would concern American policymakers. Like trade and defense problems with Europe and Japan, U.S.-Canadian relations show that foreign policy can be complex and difficult even between friends.

THE THIRD WORLD AND REGIONAL CONFLICTS

Most of the world's 6 billion people do not live in the United States, or in the other advanced industrial democracies, or in the former Soviet Union. More than two-thirds live in the less economically developed nations, most of which are in Asia, Latin America, and Africa. While these nations have little in common with one another culturally, ethnically, or politically, the vast majority of them share one common characteristic—poverty. For this reason such countries are often grouped together under the name **Third World** to distinguish them from the advanced capitalist **First World** and the formerly communist **Second World**. The gap between the living standards advanced nations enjoy and those in the Third World is only imperfectly illustrated by Table 11.1.

What do such statistics mean? For one, they mean massive differences in health; an estimated 7 million children die each year in the Third World from diarrhea caused by polluted

**TABLE 11.1   THE RICH AND THE POOR: PER CAPITA GNP IN TEN
COUNTRIES, 1989**

FIRST WORLD (Current U.S. Dollars)		THIRD WORLD (Current U.S. Dollars)	
Japan	$23,730	Bangladesh	$ 180
United States	21,100	Zaire	260
Germany	20,750	India	350
France	17,830	Egypt	630
Great Britain	14,570	Brazil	2,550

Source: World Resources, 1992–93, 236–37.

water because their countries lack the money for the water purification facilities Westerners take for granted. Most children born in Third World countries are not inoculated against diseases like diphtheria, measles, or tuberculosis, as American children must be, again because of lack of funds. The statistics also mean hunger; current estimates are that 500 million of the world's people are suffering from malnutrition. They mean illiteracy; nearly half of the people in poor countries cannot read (Pearson and Rochester 1988, 448–60). Not everyone in the Third World is poor; there are some rich people, and some Third World countries, especially in Latin America and Asia, have significant middle classes, ranging from one-tenth to one-fourth of the population. However, on the whole, the people of the Third World are separated from advanced nations by a great economic gulf.

Yet more than income differences divide the United States from the Third World: the politics and cultures are very different. American liberals, conservatives, libertarians, and populists all accept the basic principles of John Locke's early liberalism: government exists to protect individual rights and should be limited to that purpose. They disagree mostly about *which* rights are more important and *how* they should be protected. Except during the Civil War and Reconstruction period, Americans have been able to assume that free citizens

would be loyal to a just government that protected their rights; freedom and order have not been seen as in conflict.

These assumptions are simply not valid for much of the Third World. In many countries, loyalty to the nation is very weak, in part because national boundaries were artificially drawn by European colonial powers and often do not conform to ethnic or cultural divisions. People are inclined to value the interests of their family, ethnic, or religious group or region first and the nation second, if at all. To hold the nation together, Third World governments often resort to dictatorial methods—or leaders willing to use such methods win out over others. One of the largest Third World

Josh Beutel. Courtesy artist.

countries, India, has maintained a democracy, and all Latin American countries except Cuba and Haiti now have elected governments, but authoritarian rule by one or a few is the norm.

Of course such arbitrary government power opens the way for egregious abuses. Uganda's Idi Amin ordered the deaths of more than three hundred thousand of his own people before he was ousted by an invasion from neighboring Tanzania in 1979. Argentina's military government made at least nine thousand opponents "disappear" in the late 1970s; their bodies were found in unmarked graves after civilian rule was restored. Nicaragua's Anastasio Somoza and the Philippines' Ferdinand Marcos killed fewer people, but both looted their countries of billions of dollars. Yet dictators can be popular in Third World countries if they are skillful in appealing to the people. Dean Acheson, President Truman's secretary of state, once said that Argentina's rabble-rousing strongman of the 1940s, Juan Perón, was "detested by all good men—except Argentinians" (quoted in Rubin 1987b, 75). The same might be said of others like Libya's Muammar Qaddafi or Iraq's Saddam Hussein (see Profile), both of whom seemed to retain the support of their people despite actions that seem outrageous to the rest of the world. It should be noted, however, that most Third World leaders are more responsible than leaders mentioned in this paragraph and that, indeed, Third World leaders often criticize the United States for concentrating on the negative examples.

It is fair to say that the United States' most serious foreign policy failures have come in its dealings with Third World states. The nation's first defeat in a war, in Vietnam, came at the hands of a tough, authoritarian communist government that mobilized and motivated its people far more effectively than the American military thought possible. A similar blindness to Third World realities—and consequent ineffectiveness—is often evident in U.S. policies in the Middle East and Central America.

The Middle East

American oil companies began exploring in the Middle East as early as the 1920s, but the United States did not become deeply involved in the politics of the region until after World War II. At first President Truman was concerned with countering Soviet pressures on Iran and Turkey, but in 1948 he had to face the question of support for the creation of a Jewish state in Palestine. A United Nations commission had recommended that Palestine, then under British control, be divided between the native Arab population and the Jews who had been settling there since the early part of the twentieth century, hoping to restore the biblical state of Israel. The Palestinian Arabs and neighboring Arab states angrily rejected the plan and prepared for war. Perhaps wanting to support the new United Nations or the idea of a Jewish homeland, or perhaps wanting Jewish-American support in the 1948 presidential election, Truman decided to recognize the new state of Israel (Spiegel 1985, 16–49). Israel won the ensuing war, and several hundred thousand Arabs fled Palestine and became homeless refugees. Since the 1948 war, Israel has won four more wars against its Arab neighbors (in 1956, 1967, 1973, and 1982) and now occupies most of Palestine plus part of Syria (see Figure 11.1).

Support for the Jewish state is one point on which most American politicians, whatever their perspective, agree. Israel is a democracy while the Arab countries are not; it is a Western nation; and many Jewish-Americans work hard to rally support for the Jewish state in Congress (see Profile of the American Israeli Public Affairs Committee in Chapter 5). Arab states have been slow to recognize Israeli's right to exist, and U.S. support for Israel has been an irritant in its relations with the Arabs. An oil embargo by the Arab countries against the United States during the 1973 war failed to damage the U.S. economy, though it did produce lines at gas stations in some places. In the

PROFILE

Saddam Hussein: Third World Dictator

Saddam Hussein (Reuters/Bettmann)

Saddam Hussein has become the man Americans love to hate. Since his invasion of Kuwait in August 1990, editorial writers, politicians, and ordinary citizens have called him everything from "the butcher of Baghdad" to "another Hitler." Unfortunately for the United States, Hussein is not a second Hitler whose demise would solve the problems his career has created. Rather, he is an extreme example of a type of leader that frequently arises in the Third World. A look at his career may tell us something about why developing nations

so frequently find themselves in the grip of despots—and why the United States finds it so hard to deal with such leaders.

Saddam Hussein was born April 28, 1937, in the impoverished Iraqi village of Tikrit. Reportedly abused by his stepfather, who was known as "Hasan the liar," young Saddam ran away from home at ten to live with his uncle, an army officer and fervent Arab nationalist. At eighteen Saddam sought to follow in his uncle's footsteps by becoming an officer but failed the entrance examination for Iraq's military academy. With the legal path to power closed, Saddam joined a revolutionary group, the Ba'ath (Arabic for "renaissance") party in 1957 at the age of twenty.

The Ba'ath party preached pan-Arabism and called for the unification of all Arab countries. These ideas appealed to Saddam because of his upbringing, but his main interest was power, not ideology. After the Ba'ath came to power in 1968, Saddam began to work his way up in the government, partly by "exposing" non-Ba'athists and rival party leaders as "traitors." Many of his opponents were publicly hanged in the streets of Baghdad before cheering crowds. By 1979, Saddam was in full control of Iraq.

Under Saddam and his Ba'ath predecessors, Iraq achieved substantial economic development fueled by the revenues from its vast old fields. This progress was put in jeopardy, however, when he launched his attack on neighboring Iran in September 1980. Saddam evidently thought Iran, whose Islamic revolutionary government was then embroiled in the embassy hostage crisis

future, however, the United States is likely to become increasingly dependent on Arab oil. The willingness of the United States and its European allies to go to war with Iraq over Kuwait is evidence of unwillingness on the part of the industrial nations of the world to be

held hostage by the "oil weapon" a second time, but the power of oil as a weapon will probably continue to grow.

To make matters worse, the Palestinian refugees have understandably become very embittered toward both the United States and

with the United States, would be easy prey. Seizing its oil fields, which lie close to the border, would have made Iraq the dominant power in the Persian Gulf region.

Saddam miscalculated. Iranian resistance was fierce, and the leader who failed to get into military school interfered with and mismanaged the Iraqi forces. By March 1982 the Iraqis had been forced back beyond their own borders and feared being overrun. At this point a rare community of interests among the United States, the Soviet Union, and the other Arab countries saved Saddam. Fearing the consequences of a victory for the fundamentalist Muslims of Iran, the Americans and the Soviets both began supporting Iraq with weapons and intelligence. Saudi Arabia and Kuwait loaned Saddam billions of dollars to pay for arms. Even so, the Iraqi army could not win, but it finally fought the Iranians to a standstill and forced a truce in 1988. Also in 1988, Saddam put down a revolt by Iraq's oppressed Kurdish minority by massacring more than one hundred thousand Kurds.

The United States might not have supported Saddam in the war if it had known how he would try to pay for it. Iraq, which entered the war with $35 billion in cash reserves, finished it $80 billion in debt. To solve his economic crisis, Saddam began pressuring the tiny oil-rich principality of Kuwait to cancel his debts and give him more money. When the Kuwaitis refused, he moved troops up to the border. Perhaps encouraged by ambiguous statements from Americans indicating that the United States might not defend Kuwait, Saddam sent his troops in on August 2, 1990. Within forty-eight hours, Kuwait was overrun, and Iraq controlled 20 percent of world oil reserves.

Once again, Saddam had miscalculated. The United States, his former ally, turned against him, and his forces were crushed by a United Nations coalition under American leadership. When the guns fell silent on February 28, 1991, few expected Saddam to remain in power, but the Iraqi leader proved to be a better dictator than he was a general. Popular uprisings did break out across Iraq, but they were ruthlessly suppressed by Saddam's remaining troops, while the Americans, fearful of being trapped in another Vietnam if they interfered, looked on. Two years later Saddam continued to rule Iraq. After Bush left office in early 1993, Saddam Hussein launched a "charm offensive" aimed at getting President Clinton and other world leaders to relax sanctions, but with few results.

Saddam Hussein's survival is due to several factors. One clearly is sheer terror: telling a joke about the president is punishable by death in Iraq. Another, however, is admiration for Saddam's assertion of Arab aspirations against an allegedly hostile West. While not a popular ruler, Saddam does have support of Arabs both inside and outside of Iraq, who believe a strong leader is necessary to give them independence from the United States. His greatest weakness is his penchant for taking on militarily superior foes, which may yet bring him down. Until it does, Saddam Hussein will continue to pose problems for the United States and the world.

Source: Karsh and Rautsi 1991; Berman and Jentleson 1991, 115–24; Committee against Repression and for Democratic Rights in Iraq 1986; al-Khalil 1990.

Israel. In 1964, some of them formed the Palestine Liberation Organization (PLO), which has carried out bloody terrorist attacks against both Israelis and Americans. In 1988, after a wave of violent Palestinian protests against Israeli occupation, the PLO indicated willing-

ness to recognize Israel if an independent Palestinian state was also recognized. Israel rejected the gesture as the United States began talking with the PLO.

Jimmy Carter was more successful in his efforts to settle the Arab-Israeli conflict than

Figure 11.1   The Middle East

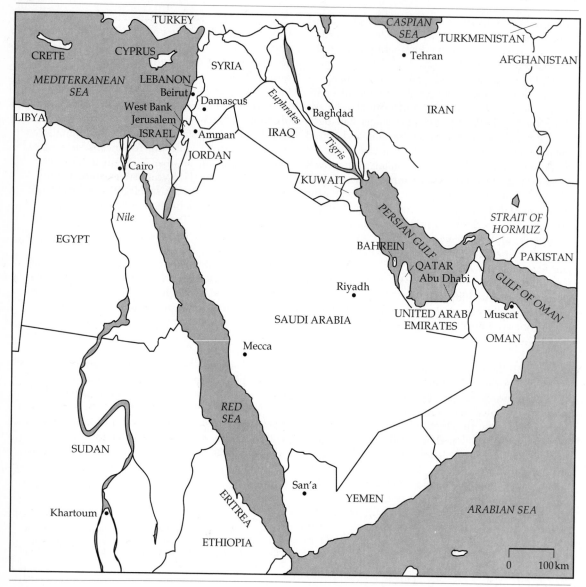

any previous president. In 1978 he was able to get Egypt and Israel to sign an agreement at Camp David in Maryland, whereby Egypt would recognize Israel in return for Israel's withdrawal from Egyptian territory captured in the 1967 Six Day War. So far this **Camp David Agreement** has held up.

After the Persian Gulf War, the Bush administration managed to arrange for the first negotiations between Israel and all of its Arab neighbors as well as a Palestinian delegation (Bannerman 1992–93, 145– 57; Atherton 1992, 114–33). Negotiations resulted in a fall 1993 agreement between the PLO and Israel for the

Ed Stein. Reprinted by permission of *The Rocky Mountain News.*

PLO to be given the Gaza Strip and Jericho as a prelude to a peaceful general settlement.

In August 1990 world attention had focused on a different region of the Middle East, as Iraq invaded and occupied Kuwait. While Iraq had long claimed the oil-rich principality as part of its territory, the invasion was viewed in the United States as a bid by Saddam Hussein (see Profile earlier in this chapter) to dominate the Persian Gulf and control world oil supplies and prices. Unwilling to accept such an outcome, President George Bush dispatched more than one-quarter of America's military strength (a total of 540,000 armed personnel) to Saudi Arabia, where they were joined by a quarter-million coalition troops.

While U.S. troops poured into Saudi Arabia, both sides engaged in diplomatic maneuvering. Saddam Hussein took seemingly contradictory positions, sometimes acting defiantly and sometimes hinting at a compromise. Mindful of the prestige any deal would give the Iraqi dictator, Bush, backed by the United Nations, insisted on unconditional Iraqi withdrawal from Kuwait.

When Iraq refused to withdraw unconditionally by January 15, 1991, the coalition went into action. After a crushing five-week air bombardment, a ground attack drove the Iraqis from Kuwait in four days. The coalition lost only 234 armed personnel, while 86,000 Iraqis surrendered and thousands more died (Freedman and Karsh 1993, 408).

The Persian Gulf War remains a hotly disputed topic in American foreign policy. Some critics charged that the United States went too far in using military force before all other options were exhausted (Menos 1992). Others made the opposite criticism, that the coalition forces stopped too soon, leaving Saddam Hussein in power (*Commentary*, June 1991, 15–19). Defenders of the Bush policy said that the outcome was the best that could have been achieved and that prolonging the war could have led to a Vietnam-style quagmire (Petre and Schwarzkopf 1992, 496–500).

Trouble with Iraq continued through 1992 and 1993, as Hussein's attempts to preserve a nuclear weapons program in defiance of the coalition's cease-fire terms brought various

U.S. air and missile attacks. In June 1993, President Clinton launched further military strikes against Iraq, charging that Iraqi intelligence had attempted to kill former President Bush while he was visiting Kuwait. As much as Americans wished for Hussein's demise, few wanted to invade and occupy Iraq, the only reliable way of removing the Iraqi dictator. Like their allies the Israelis, the Americans found it was easier to win victories on Middle Eastern battlefields than it was to achieve a stable peace in the region.

Still another problem in the Middle East is the smoldering civil war between religious factions in Lebanon. An attempt by the Reagan administration to resolve this problem cost the lives of 241 marines, sent to the country as part of a multinational peacekeeping force. A related problem is the increasing influence of fundamentalist Islamic movements in the Middle East, many of which are hostile to Western and especially American policy. Relations with the fundamentalist-dominated Iran, broken in 1979 after the taking of American hostages by the revolutionary government, have still not been fully restored.

The Middle East seems to present the United States with one dilemma after another. The existence of Israel is an irreversible fact. The Israelis demand their rights as a nation, but until recently they have refused to concede the same rights to the Palestinians. Religion, friendly or neutral toward American foreign policy in most parts of the world, often works here against the United States. Similarly, the reliance of the United States and other industrial nations on Middle Eastern oil creates a dependency on an unstable region of the world. Giving up and withdrawing from this region may be impossible for the United States, given the entanglements of Israel and oil.

The Caribbean and Mexico

The nations of Central America and the Caribbean (see Figure 11.2) are very poor. The richest, Costa Rica, had a per capita income of only $1,780 in 1991 (*World Development Report 1991*, 205). Except for Costa Rica and some former British colonies in the Caribbean, most have been under military rule for most of their history. They are largely agricultural, and most of the land has been owned by a small number of families. In El Salvador in 1975, the top 1 percent of farm owners owned 40 percent of the land, while 40 percent of the rural families owned no land and eked out a living as farm laborers (North 1985, 48; see also Booth and Walker 1989, 15–46). Population growth in recent years has been rapid, aggravating the land shortage.

American involvement in Central America goes back more than a century and a half. In 1823, President James Monroe issued the Monroe Doctrine, which declared that the United States would consider any European attempt to colonize additional territory in the Western Hemisphere "an unfriendly act." In turn, the United States would stay out of European affairs. The doctrine was applied irregularly after the middle of the nineteenth century. Late in the century, however, the United States became increasingly active in Central America and the Caribbean and went to war against its rival for influence, Spain.

In the twentieth century the Monroe Doctrine was reinterpreted by President Theodore Roosevelt, who in 1904 asserted that the United States would exercise a right under international law to intervene if Central and South American governments engaged in "chronic wrongdoing" that threatened American or European lives and property. Under this so-called **Roosevelt Corollary**, the United States stationed marines in Central America to collect revenues and at times practically ran the governments of Panama and Nicaragua (LeFeber 1984, 49–67). President Woodrow Wilson tried to affect the course of the Mexican Revolution between 1913 and 1917, but he was met with much resistance in Mexico. Many of these American actions were, of course, resented by Latin Americans.

The Roosevelt Corollary was repudiated by

Figure 11.2   Central America and the Caribbean

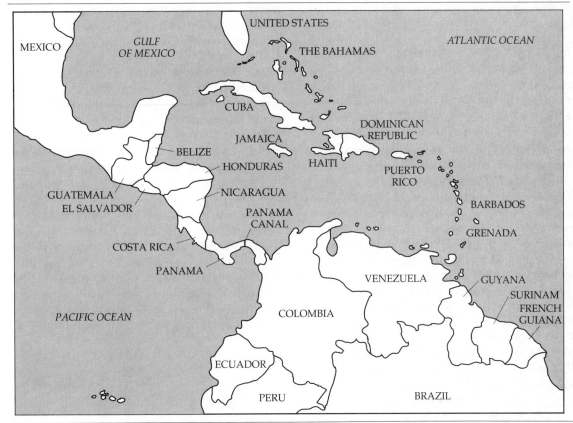

the administrations of Herbert Hoover and Franklin Roosevelt in the late 1920s and early 1930s. The Organization of American States (OAS) was formed in 1948 after the good neighbor era of the 1930s, a feeling which continued into the 1940s. The United States returned to interventionist policies again in the mid-1950s. This time the reason was less to protect foreign property than to stop communist governments from gaining hold in the region. The effort was not entirely successful: Fidel Castro established a communist dictatorship in Cuba and defeated U.S. attempts to overthrow him in the early 1960s (Smith 1987, 13–67). However, U.S. troops checked a revolution in the Dominican Republic in 1965 and ousted a Marxist regime on the island of Grenada in 1983.

The United States was particularly active in Central America during the Reagan and Bush administrations, which were alarmed about the emergence of the Marxist Sandinista government in Nicaragua in 1979. Reagan backed anti-Sandinista guerrillas called *contras* in Nicaragua, while supporting the government in neighboring El Salvador against another leftist guerrilla movement (LeMoyne 1989, 105–25; Rubin 1984, 299–318). Both policies were unpopular, but by 1992 the tide had turned in favor of the United States. The Sandinistas were pressured into holding a free election and voted out of power in 1990, while the guerrillas in El Salvador and the government reached a peace agreement including some redistribution of land to the poor (*Des Moines Register*, 27 February 1990, A1–A8; Karl 1992,

147–64). For the first time in history, all the Central American and Caribbean countries except Cuba and Haiti now had freely elected governments, though the economy of the region was badly damaged by the years of war.

With Marxism no longer a threat, one might think intervention in Central America would no longer be necessary. However, pressure to suppress drug trafficking, which is often tolerated by corrupt or frightened government officials in Latin America, is creating a new cause for intervention. In December 1989 the U.S. military ousted and captured Panama's drug dealing military strongman, Manuel Noriega, who was once a U.S. ally. Promoting democracy may also be a cause for intervention; some in Congress criticized President Bush for *not* intervening when the elected president of poverty-stricken Haiti was overthrown by the military. Following the coup thousands of Haitians attempted to flee to the United States and were turned back.

While there is wide consensus on some aspects of Middle East policy such as support for Israel, policy toward Central America and the Caribbean has generated much controversy. Liberals generally opposed President Reagan's aid to the *contras,* contending that the United States had no right to subvert a sovereign government and that another Vietnam might result. On the other hand, intervention to promote democracy and social reform often gains liberal support (Lowenthal 1991). Most conservatives, on the other hand, supported intervention to stop Marxism and drug trafficking but not for the purpose of reforming Central American societies. Libertarians and populists tended to oppose both kinds of intervention. The issue of how much to involve itself in the affairs of its southern neighbors is likely to perplex the United States for a long time, despite the downfall of communism.

One reason for U.S. concern over Central America was the fear that trouble there might spread into Mexico. For the last half-century, the United States has benefited from having a stable neighbor to the south. Now rapid population growth has created severe unemployment; half of Mexican workers do not have full-time jobs (Ridding 1985). Many resort to crossing the border to work illegally in the United States, a flow immigration laws passed in the 1980s were unable to stop. The Bush administration pushed for a free trade agreement with Mexico similar to the one already made with Canada, hoping this would boost the Mexican economy and head off social unrest that might trigger even more illegal immigrants (see Controversy). However, environmentalists, labor unions, and populist politicians opposed the agreement as a threat to the environment and American jobs (Morici 1992, 88–104). President Clinton obtained some side agreements prior to supporting the part. Whether free trade passes or not, economic development in Central America, the Caribbean, and Mexico may turn out to be a greater concern for U.S. policymakers in the 1990s than Marxist revolution was in the 1980s.

THE UNITED NATIONS

One institution that many Americans believe should be strengthened to deal with world problems is the **United Nations (UN)**. Organized in 1945, at the end of World War II, the United Nations made a strong commitment to prevent another war and "to solve economic problems, to assure justice, to promote respect for human rights, to encourage transcultural understanding and to aid those in need" (United Nations Charter 1986, v). The ultimate objective of the United Nations, though, was to promote international peace and security.

The central body of the United Nations is the **General Assembly**, which provides a meeting place for the 184 member nations to express their opinions and concerns. The General Assembly reflects the liberal's desire for equal opportunity in the international arena, as each nation has one vote. As former colonies of the developed nations became independent, they were permitted to join the United

Nations, and critics say that the Third World now exerts too much control over the assembly. Balancing the equal representation in the General Assembly is the **Security Council**. Its fifteen members include five permanent members—France, China, Russia, the United Kingdom, and the United States—and ten nations elected for two-year terms. The Security Council is responsible for maintaining international peace and security, but at any point one of the five permanent members may effectively veto a substantive motion, an arrangement that often makes it very difficult to get any measure through the council. For example, until 1990, the United States consistently vetoed proposals to impose sanctions on Israel for its treatment of Palestinians.

The United Nations was formed with a great deal of optimism, but it has disappointed those who hoped it would play a dominant role in the international arena. However, recent concerted UN action against Iraq for its invasion of Kuwait has again raised hopes that the organization may become more effective through greater cooperation among the major powers.

The United Nations attempts to halt conflicts by deploying peacekeeping forces to trouble spots. In 1992, more than fifty-thousand UN troops were involved in thirteen peacekeeping operations at a cost of $3.6 billion (*Congressional Quarterly Weekly Report*, 6 March 1993, 526–28). However, UN forces frequently operate under rules that prevent them from acting effectively if peace agreements break down (Michaels 1992–93, 93–4). For example, in the Yugoslavian civil war that began in 1991, both sides broke truce after truce and the United Nations could do little to stop them. Under the circumstances, President Clinton has declined to involve American troops except to prevent the conflict from expanding into Macedonia.

Some Americans favor an expanded UN role because the United Nations could relieve pressure on the United States to become involved in unpleasant foreign entanglements.

YUGOSLAVIAN CEASEFIRE...

Jim Todd. Copyright the Southam Syndicate.

This may not always be the case, however. In late 1992, President Bush sent thirty-one thousand American troops to Somalia after the United Nations proved unable to halt the factional fighting that was interfering with famine relief operations (Clark 1992–93, 109–23). Many Americans were replaced by UN troops, but American support was still needed. The situation was particularly difficult in the fall of 1993 as Americans debated what action was best in the face of resistance from a Somali warlord. The debate was intensified as U.S. and UN efforts in Haiti met resistance.

Other principal organs of the United Nations are the **Economic and Social Council (ECOSOC)**, the International Court of Justice (ICJ), the Trusteeship Council, and the Secretariat. ECOSOC, which coordinates economic and social work, has emphasized the economic and social concerns of Third World nations, and through it the United States has provided a considerable amount of aid. But in recent years critics have questioned the size of the U.S. contribution. While in the past the United States has supplied the United Nations with as much as 40 percent of its budget, today the United States pays about 25 percent, a figure approximating its share of the combined GNP of member nations (*Facts on File Yearbook, 1992*, 145–46). Dependence on the United States brought about major budgetary problems for the United Nations in 1985 when Congress

CONTROVERSY

NAFTA: Job Boom or Environmental Bust?

In August 1992, trade representatives of Mexico, Canada, and the United States signed the North American Free Trade Agreement creating the framework for the largest market on the globe, with more than 360 million consumers and $6 trillion in annual output. The two-thousand-page treaty follows the 1989 American-Canadian Free Trade Agreement, which increased the total trade between the two countries by 8 percent. However, NAFTA has ignited a debate in the United States concerning its effect: will it cost or create jobs, and what impact will it have on the environment of the countries that arrived at this historic agreement? Congress was to debate the new treaty in 1993, but an overturned court ruling requiring an environmental impact statement delayed consideration for months. President George Bush viewed NAFTA as an agreement with no losers, expanding markets and increasing jobs. But his vision is not shared by a coalition of environmentalists and labor unions, who view NAFTA as a zero-sum game with the environment and U.S. jobs as losers. President Bill Clinton supports NAFTA but only after he revised some specific provisions.

President Bush and Mexican President Carlos Salinas de Gortari aggressively pursued NAFTA in hopes of creating new jobs in their respective countries. Indeed, there is no dispute that new jobs will be created by the treaty but great disagreement over where and what kind of jobs. Advocates of free trade point to predictions that

Mike Luckovich. By permission of artist and Creators Syndicate.

Mexico's economy could double its growth rate to 6 percent and by that growth prompt an increase of U.S. exports to Mexico of more than 26 percent, versus 3.6 percent without the treaty. With predictions for increased growth and greater exports, NAFTA supporters cite a study by the University of Maryland that predicts nearly forty-five thousand new jobs in the United States during the first five years of an agreement, mainly in nonlabor-intensive sectors.

On the other hand, groups such as the AFL-CIO have led the fight against NAFTA, arguing

passed the Kassebaum Amendment withholding the U.S. contribution until budget reductions and reform of the Secretariat were accomplished. Although the United Nations enacted some reforms, the United States was slow to pay its back dues. This action angered some UN members, including some U.S. allies.

Like all foreign policy stands, U.S. participation in the United Nations is subject to political compromise. In 1988, for example, Congress did not appropriate as much to international organizations, including the United Nations, as the president initially requested (*Congressional Quarterly Weekly Report*, 2 January 1988, 17), but it increased the president's

that although new jobs may be created, they will not be for American workers. Pointing to statistics showing the average wage is one-seventh that of the average American manufacturing job, the AFL-CIO fears that U.S. factories will move to Mexico to take advantage of the cheap labor there. Labor-intensive industries such as textiles, construction, and agriculture would be among the losers. Vulnerability of these sectors has created a coalition including both labor unions and one of their traditional enemies, conservative Senator Jesse Helms, whose opposition to NAFTA is based on an attempt to protect a sizable North Carolina textile industry. With the Mexican minimum wage around 59¢, many unskilled and semiskilled manufacturing jobs would most likely head south in the years following the agreement. The AFL-CIO claims that low-wage Mexican labor has already cost more than five hundred thousand U.S. jobs in the manufacturing sector. Ross Perot opposes NAFTA as an agreement that will cost American jobs.

Environmentalists take the side of the AFL-CIO, but not for the sake of U.S. jobs. They fear large-scale migration of U.S. corporations looking to take advantage of weak environmental regulation in Mexico. Indeed, the environmental protection record of the *maquiladoras*, the more than two thousand factories south of the border that already enjoy barrier free trade, is quite poor. Environmental groups such as Friends of the Earth, Sierra Club, Greenpeace, and Environmental Action all oppose NAFTA, fearing increased pollution in border rivers. Mexican environmental standards appear strict on paper, but enforcement has been lacking. Treaty proponents argue that it will improve with the free trade treaty.

Transcending arguments on the immediate economic impact of NAFTA are the long-term implications of regional free trade agreements. With the current round of the General Agreement on Tariffs and Trade (GATT) stalled over European subsidies, the NAFTA debate has occurred at a delicate time for world trade. Regional blocs, which would set tariff barriers against outside goods, are the fear of some analysts. If NAFTA is concluded before the current Uruguay round, it may lead to hardening of world trade positions between the North Americans and the European Economic Community. This hardening would force Southeast Asia to form its own bloc in order to compete, further restricting world markets. NAFTA supporters deny that NAFTA will destroy GATT, pointing out that nearly three-quarters of the U.S. trade occurs outside North America. Further, they point to the European Economic Community as the model for the future of world trade and see NAFTA as a necessary response to the European Economic Community.

Whatever the final outcome, the evolution of the American-Canadian Free Trade Agreement and NAFTA has changed the look of world trade, and the debate over jobs versus the environment will continue to shape discussions of trade and its impact on the United States.

Source: Baer 1991, 132–49; *U.S. News and World Report,* 13 September 1993, 61.

---

budget request for the United Nations Development Program (UNDP) and the United Nations Children's Fund (UNICEF) (*Congressional Quarterly Weekly Report,* 5 December 1987, 2984). The Democrat-controlled Congress had priorities different from those of the president, and it had the power of the purse. Both President Bush and President Clinton were more inclined to support the United Nations than was President Reagan. At the same time, the role of the United Nations was becoming more important with the end of the cold war.

PERSPECTIVES

Thirty years ago the perspective approach presented in this book would not have been applicable to foreign policy. During the 1950s and early 1960s, American liberals, conservatives, libertarians, and populists shared a consensus dictating resistance to a Soviet Union presumed to be aggressive. Only American Marxists stood outside this consensus. The Vietnam debacle shattered the consensus and made foreign affairs a topic of heated debate among the perspectives.

Although the consensus of the past has broken down on foreign issues, American foreign policies are usually supported by most Americans. For example, Americans do not like authoritarian leaders; there still is a consensus that democratic governments are desirable. This support might come for different reasons, but it is support nonetheless.

More than in most other countries of the world, where foreign policy is regarded as the province of the educated elite, American policy depends on public support. Long-term American foreign policy moods fluctuate on a regular basis, and Jack Holmes has described how these moods can make it difficult for the United States to respond to world power realities (Holmes 1985; see also Klingberg 1952, 239–73). In view of the importance of public thinking and the breakdown of consensus, the Perspectives section in this chapter is longer than in others.

Conservative

For forty years conservatives focused their foreign policy agenda on what they saw as the deadly menace of Soviet power and expansionism. Conservatives differed among themselves on strategy for containing the Soviets. Some, like President Richard Nixon, believed military strength and firmness could be combined with negotiations, while others rejected any kind of accommodation with communists. All conservatives, however, agreed that security for the West required a U.S. military second to none and a firm resolve to resist aggression. Some, like President Ronald Reagan, went further, promoting the liberation of communist countries. Many conservatives argue that Reagan's policies were responsible for the ultimate success of the West because, as one Republican senator put it, "The Soviet Union was driven to the wall economically in an unsuccessful attempt to match the United States militarily" (Lugar 1992, 87).

How, in view of the collapse of the Soviet Union, do conservatives think American foreign policy should change? Predictably, they favor less change than other perspectives, because of the conservative view of human nature. Since human beings are naturally selfish and aggressive, say conservatives, war and conflict cannot be expected to disappear with the collapse of communism. Not all aggressors threaten American interests, but some will, as Saddam Hussein's invasion of Kuwait shows. It is therefore as important as ever for the United States to remain the strongest country in the world, though doing so may now be less costly.

A 1992 Pentagon study of future defense needs endorsed by the Bush administration reflects the conservative approach to foreign and defense policy. This document, authored by a team headed by Paul Wolfowitz, then undersecretary of defense for policy, argues that presently friendly nations, especially Germany and Japan, could become a threat to American security if they remilitarize and develop nuclear weapons. To prevent these developments, the United States needs to continue to provide defense for these nations and eliminate the need for them to rearm, thereby "discouraging them from challenging our leadership or seeking to overturn the established political and economic order" (quoted in New York Times, 8 March 1992, A1). In short, the Pentagon team called for maintaining a "one superpower world" in which no nation is capable of challenging the United States militarily and the United States can deal with any security problems without the aid of other nations.

The Pentagon planners also foresaw a growing threat from "irrational" leaders, such as Saddam Hussein of Iraq, Fidel Castro of Cuba, or Kim Il-Sung of North Korea. The experience of Iraq shows that such small nations headed by dictators are capable of developing nuclear and other weapons of mass destruction. The report warns that in the future the United States "may be faced with the question of whether to take military steps to prevent the development or use of weapons of mass destruction"—in other words, the United States might need to be ready to attack such nations to stop them from acquiring nuclear weapons. The Wolfowitz study also warns of a possible "nationalist backlash" in Russia and suggests that the United States cooperate with European nations to "plan to defend against such a threat" should it arise. All of this, the report argues, can be done with a military of 1.6 million personnel and a defense budget of around $250 billion— about 25 percent less than in the cold war years (*New York Times*, 8 March 1992, A14). In identifying so many possible threats, the Wolfowitz study clearly reflects the pessimistic conservative view of human nature as well as, of course, the military's desire to be prepared for contingencies, which require its budget to be as high as possible.

Conservatives admit that the military, like other government bureaucracies, often wastes money and operates at an unacceptably low level of efficiency (Luttwak 1984). However, waste in defense is not nearly as serious as underfunding in terms of its potential effects. If unnecessary weapons are built, Americans will pay more taxes than they should, or have fewer social services, and that is regrettable. If necessary weapons are not built, Americans may lose their lives or their freedom, and that would be disastrous.

As for relations with the Third World countries, conservatives believe the main goal of U.S. policy should be to encourage them to adopt the free market economic policies that led to development in the rich countries. But conservatives do not believe the United States should assume the responsibility of bringing economic development to the Third World. If poor countries follow the

U.S. example of a free economy with protection for private property rights, they will achieve development without much direct American aid, say conservatives. Indeed, Third World capitalist countries like Taiwan, South Korea, Hong Kong, and Singapore are now tough competitors for the United States and well on their way to joining the developed world. Promoting democracy in the Third World is also a low priority for most conservatives. Most Third World countries are not culturally equipped to practice democracy, say conservatives, as they lack the tradition of freedom under the law that exists in Western nations.

For conservatives, often the best to be hoped for in a Third World country is an "authoritarian" government—one that may rule without popular consent but at least respects private property and other personal rights like freedom of movement and freedom of religion (Kirkpatrick 1979, 34–35). Even with regimes they dislike, conservatives favor maintaining relations if the regimes recognize American interests, as does the People's Republic of China. On the other hand, conservatives back tough action against Third World leaders like Manuel Noriega or Saddam Hussein who threaten U.S. interests.

Finally, conservatives value close relations with nations allied with the United States during the cold war and advanced industrial democracies but are often frustrated by the behavior of these friendly nations. During the cold war, they often complained that Western Europe and Japan did not spend enough on defense and were too eager to trust the Soviets. Today, they still complain that these allies do not pull their military weight, citing the Persian Gulf War as an example, while at the same time worrying about what might happen if, for example, Japan *did* become a military superpower. Conservatives support the free world trading system that has grown up since World War II but argue that free trade cannot be a one-way street. When even "friendly" countries engage in unfair trade practices against the United States, retaliation may be necessary. Conservatives believe that both friends and foes need to know that the United States will deal fairly with all nations but accept abuse from none.

Liberal

The present international system is far from compatible with liberal values. Liberals cherish equality of opportunity, but what could be more unequal than the opportunities available to a child growing up in the United States and one growing up in Bangladesh? Nor are the individual rights prized by liberals protected in a world whose governments are allowed, most of the time, to do whatever they choose to their citizens. Liberals are realistic enough to know they cannot remake the world in their own image, but they believe the United States can play a major role in making things better if it changes some of its policies.

Most liberals supported the anti-Soviet policies of Harry Truman after World War II, believing that the Soviet Union was a threat to world peace and freedom. After Vietnam, many liberals became critical of U.S. policy, contending that American mistakes helped produce the cold war. Some liberals point to the Marshall Plan to rebuild Germany, as raising legitimate Soviet fears, for the people of the Soviet Union had suffered two devastating German invasions in less than thirty years. Most liberals also believe that the credit for ending the cold war should go to Mikhail Gorbachev, Boris Yeltsin, and the other Soviet reformers rather than to Reagan's hard-line policies (Deudney and Ikenberry 1992, 123–38).

Today, say liberals, the military threats of the cold war are a thing of the past. The primary foreign policy problem for the United States is to be economically competitive with its friends, especially Germany and Japan, and not to compete militarily with enemies (Bergsten and Prestowitz Jr. 1992, 3–24, 67–87). Therefore resources need to be massively redirected from defense to domestic programs, particularly education and economic development. Unfortunately, say liberals, conservatives are preventing this "peace dividend" by maintaining a defense establishment far bigger than necessary. Long before the cold war ended, liberals were calling for defense cutbacks; now that it is over they see nothing standing in the way of reductions far greater than the 25 percent contemplated by the conservative Bush adminis-

tration or even the steeper reductions implemented by the moderate liberal Clinton administration.

Liberals acknowledge that there will be threats to the peace in the post–cold war world, just as conservatives predict. However, they argue that the way to deal with such threats is not by maintaining the "one superpower world" advocated in the Wolfowitz report (*New York Times*, 8 March 1992, A1, A14), but through collective security and multilateral peacekeeping forces. During the 1990–91 crisis in the Persian Gulf, many liberals opposed the use of military force, claiming that economic sanctions would work, given more time. If military force was to be used, however, they wanted it to be a multilateral UN action. Most liberals believe the United States needs to rely more heavily on multilateral arrangements for dealing with aggressors like Saddam Hussein and preventing troubled situations from getting out of hand. One liberal defense analyst argues that the U.S. defense budget could be reduced to $70 billion if the United States relied on the support of the other major powers, acting through the United Nations, to deal with any aggression other than direct attack (Forsberg 1992, 5–9). Not all liberals would trust so much in collective security and peacekeeping forces or cut defense so drastically. The Clinton administration has proposed far more modest cuts and endorsed elements of the conservative "second to none" military approach. This policy, however, reveals the gulf in thinking between liberals and conservatives, who would contend that other nations cannot be trusted and the United States needs the power to handle security unilaterally.

In addition to collective security, liberals place greater faith in arms control as a means of advancing the cause of peace. Even before the end of the cold war, some liberals were calling for negotiations with the Soviet Union to reduce nuclear weapons by 90 percent or more (*New York Times Magazine*, 16 November 1986, 70–75). Today liberals support wider arms control agreements, particularly those aimed at preventing more nations from obtaining nuclear weapons. They might question, however, the conservative approach of using force to prevent nuclear proliferation.

In regard to the Third World, liberals believe one of the most important U.S. interests is a negative one: it must never again send forces to suppress an internal revolution or national liberation movement—"no more Vietnams." Opposing aggression by one state against another is different; many liberals supported Ronald Reagan's efforts to aid the Afghan resistance and George Bush's deployment of troops to Saudi Arabia. But if a government is about to fall to domestic revolutionaries, even communists, most liberals argue that it cannot be saved by shedding American blood. Covert operations by the Central Intelligence Agency, like the one tried in Nicaragua, are usually ineffective and violate international law; they cannot be ruled out, but they should be the exception.

Yet liberals do not want to keep the United States out of the Third World. On the contrary, liberals promote increased steps to reduce the gap between rich and poor abroad, as they do within the nation's borders. To liberals, it is little short of disgraceful that the United States gave only $9.86 billion in economic development aid to the poor countries in 1989 while in the same year Americans spent $22 billion on cigarettes (*Statistical Abstract, 1991*, 802; Hancock 1989, 43). Of course the government's first responsibility is to its own people, but much more aid should be given to poor countries. Most liberals also supported aid to Russia and the other republics of the former Soviet Union in 1991–92, while criticizing President Bush for not also boosting spending on domestic social programs (Wofford 1992, 106–13).

Another major concern for liberals regarding the Third World is the promotion of human rights and democracy. Liberals are appalled at the conservative argument that "authoritarian" governments are good enough for Asia, Africa, and Latin America. Conservatives may not be conscious of it, liberals say, but they are displaying racism by

Jack Ohman. Courtesy artist.

using this argument and collaborating in the worst kind of oppression and corruption. Ferdinand Marcos, the Philippines dictator who received U.S. support until the final days of his regime, is estimated to have stolen between $2 billion and $20 billion from his country in his twenty years in power, while the proportion of Filipinos living in poverty rose from 28 percent in 1965 to 70 percent in 1986. Marcos's wife accumulated nearly three thousand pairs of shoes, some of which cost more than the average Filipino's yearly income. To contend that supporting such a person is necessary to "stop communism" is ludicrous. In fact, Marcos's oppression drove people into supporting a communist insurgency that grew from eleven people in 1968 to a guerrilla army of twenty thousand in 1985 (Kessler 1986, 41–42). Fortunately the United States distanced itself from Marcos in the end and helped a democratic government take power, but

backing him for so many years hurt both its integrity and the Philippines and may yet contribute to a successful communist revolution. Of course, liberals also oppose repression by leftist regimes; they strongly condemned the communist Chinese government of Deng Xiaoping for its massacre of protesting students in Beijing in June 1989.

The views of liberals and conservatives are perhaps closest on the U.S. relationship with Western Europe and Japan. Like conservatives, liberals believe the United States must maintain its military commitments in these regions, though the allies should take more responsibility for their own defense. On trade, liberals have been growing more militant in their demands that some American industries be protected from foreign competition, particularly Japanese. Still, they are not ready to abandon the goal of free trade (see Chapter 12).

Libertarian

Only in recent years has a distinct libertarian position on foreign policy emerged. During the 1950s and 1960s politicians like Senator Barry Goldwater of Arizona, who held libertarian positions on other issues, were solidly behind conservative and anticommunist policies. Over the past decade and a half, however, a growing number of libertarians have begun to question the active role the United States has played in the world since 1945 and to call for a return to a noninterventionist policy.

From the perspective of these libertarians, there are two problems with interventionist foreign policies, liberal or conservative. First, like the civilian side of government, intervention has simply become too expensive. In 1988, 60 percent of the U.S. defense budget—$669 for every man, woman, and child in the United States—was allocated to U.S. forces in Europe or to forces intended to reinforce Europe in a war (Armed Services Committee figures cited in Schroeder 1989, 170). Many other U.S. forces are intended for missions in distant areas of the world such as keeping the Persian Gulf open for oil shipments that go mostly to Europe and Japan. Clearly government spending is far higher than it would be if the United States were concerned only with defending itself. Just as clearly, money for defense spending comes

out of the pockets of hard-working, productive Americans and burdens the economy as much as other government spending.

The second problem with U.S. commitments to defend other nations is that, like domestic welfare, it has bred dependency in its recipients, the so-called allies of the United States. During the cold war, Europe and Japan let the United States do most of the work of containing the Soviet Union and spend most of the money to do it (Krauss 1986). Now that the cold war is over, there is no threat of communist expansion to justify bearing such a burden. In the view of many libertarians, both the liberal ideal of collective security and the conservative quest for military superiority are dangerous. The effect of both is the same—to involve the United States in other people's wars.

Libertarians differ in how, and how far, the United States should withdraw from overseas military commitments. Some libertarian scholars advocate a phased withdrawal, giving allies a few years to build up their own defenses; after that, the United States would fight only if its own territory were attacked (Ravenal 1979). Others believe the United States should maintain a defensive umbrella over the Western Hemisphere (Hospers 1981, 372–74). Libertarians acknowledge that U.S.

withdrawals might create some problems. Persian Gulf oil might be cut off by a future Saddam Hussein, but if it were, the free market system would encourage Americans to conserve energy and develop alternative sources of energy. If the allies did not improve their defenses they might be threatened by a resurgent Russia or by each other, but the United States would retain its nuclear deterrent to preserve its own freedom, which is all it is obligated or entitled to protect. Some businesses would lose money as defense contracts dried up, but more would gain as Americans paid lower taxes and had more to spend on consumer goods. Most important, Americans would be much more secure from the threat of nuclear war because the nation would no longer be committed to situations in which war is likely to break out. Overall, libertarians seem to be close to the isolationist stand that guided U.S. foreign policy throughout much of its history.

At the same time, libertarians support the free and unfettered flow of goods and people across national boundaries, unhindered by tariffs, nontariff barriers, or other government-imposed restraints. Actually, trade barriers do not "protect" American jobs, libertarians argue, but protect some jobs at the expense of others as well as of consumers. A clear example is the "voluntary" import quota on Japanese automobiles, which Ronald Reagan pressured the Japanese government to impose to head off even stricter protectionist legislation. The quota "saved" forty-four thousand jobs in the auto industry but raised the price of a Japanese car by an average of $1,500 and the price of an American car $650, as lack of competition allowed the American manufacturers to raise prices, too (*Washington Post National Weekly Edition*, 11 March 1985, 27; Barnes 1987, 32). Of course consumers who paid those higher prices had less money to spend on other goods, and so American workers in other industries lost their jobs to "protect" the auto workers.

Trade barriers also provoke retaliation by other countries, say libertarians, and particularly hurt the Third World, as the losses to many poor countries from U.S. restrictions on imports greatly exceed the value of American foreign "aid" (Sewell and Contee 1987, 1029–30). Politically inspired restrictions on trade, whether against the communist countries or right-wing dictatorships, are just as bad from the libertarian point of view. They hurt innocent people, in both the United States and the target country, and have not been effective in changing the admittedly abhorrent policies of these governments. For example, making a major public issue of Chinese human rights practices will hurt more than it will help.

As might be expected, libertarians do not support American foreign aid to poor countries—not because they do not care about the suffering but because they believe such programs do not promote development. Aid merely channels resources to corrupt and repressive governments and not to the people in need or to private businesses that might provide them with jobs. Besides direct misuse of American funds, foreign aid has a broader negative impact; it enhances the authority of the state, distorts the market, and encourages socialist policies that do not work. For example, free grain donated by the United States often lowers grain prices in a country to the point that farmers are discouraged from planting, thus creating a permanent dependency. Nor has aid been effective in preserving "friendly" governments, as conservatives hoped; many countries received large amounts of U.S. assistance and still turned communist (China and Nicaragua) or hostile (Iran). Some emergency famine relief might be justified, and the United States should certainly help the poor countries (and itself) by lowering trade barriers. But poor nations can advance without burdening American taxpayers with another government program. Poor nations should follow market-oriented economic policies; after all, the United States and other rich countries were poor once, and they developed without receiving aid from anyone (Bauer and Yarmey 1983, 115–35).

Libertarian ideas have not been as influential in foreign policy as in other areas, and most libertarians have been more concerned with shrinking government's domestic role than its international role. Libertarian voters have usually supported the Republican party despite its interventionist, conservative orientation toward foreign policy. However, since many domestic social programs have now been cut significantly, it is possible that more libertarians may turn their attention to reducing foreign commitments. If so, the move could produce a serious split in Republican ranks.

Populist

While focusing primarily on domestic issues, populists have given some attention to foreign policy. Usually, their orientation has been isolationist, even more so than libertarians. Tom Watson, an important southern populist leader from the 1890s to the 1920s, opposed nearly every U.S. foreign policy initiative of the period, including the Spanish-American War, World War I, the League of Nations, and interventions in Latin America. Watson argued that the only purpose behind foreign policy was to serve selfish business interests (Woodward 1938, 463–65). Huey Long, a populist leader of the 1930s, was equally isolationist, opposing U.S. membership in the World Court (Williams 1981, 800).

During the cold war, populists, like most other Americans, accepted the idea of a more active foreign policy to contain the Soviet Union. They still felt, however, that the government was giving too much attention to foreign concerns and not enough to the needs of ordinary people back home. Polls taken during the Vietnam War showed that populists were the first to turn against the war. Populists backed a strong defense to deter the Soviets but were reluctant to see American resources go to expensive international commitments (Schneider 1987, 63–66).

The end of the cold war seems to have strengthened populist isolationism. All three of the populist candidates in 1992—Pat Buchanan, Tom Harkin, and Ross Perot—sounded isolationist themes in their campaigns. All were vocal opponents of the Persian Gulf War. All three supported protectionist trade policies to some extent and opposed the free trade pact with Mexico.

Harkin sharply questioned aid to the former Soviet Union, while Buchanan condemned all foreign aid and urged tough restrictions on nonwhite immigration (see Profile in Chapter 1). These positions clearly indicate populist opposition to foreign involvement of all kinds, but populists are not necessarily hostile to foreigners. Rather, they believe that the upper-class political leaders who usually run American foreign policy are too concerned about problems far away and too oblivious to suffering here at home. Tom Harkin expressed this view pungently in one of his campaign speeches: "For nearly half a century, the American people have given their money, their blood and their lives to defend the world from communism. But now the Cold War is over. And we won! Just look at what we've done for Europe, and South Korea, and Taiwan, and Japan. Well, now its *our* turn" (quoted in Alden and Schurmann 1992, 109–10).

Populists can be differentiated from both traditional isolationists and present-day libertarians by their opposition to free trade. In fact, this sentiment surfaced among populists long before U.S. industry began having trouble competing with imports. Apparently, populists see the issue as moral rather than economic, believing that it is wrong for one American to benefit from cheap imports at the expense of another American's job (Schneider 1987, 63–64). While the populist view has been underrepresented in foreign policy-making, the end of the cold war may allow populists to gain greater influence and restrain interventionist policies that they think carry too many costs for the average American.

Marxist

To understand the Marxist view of American foreign policy, one must look at the writings of Vladimir Lenin, leader of the Russian Revolution, whose work forms an important basis of the Marxist view of international politics. In a book written just before the revolution (Lenin 1972), Lenin sought to explain why the capitalist system

was maintaining itself longer than Karl Marx had expected and why the major industrial nations had all acquired colonies. According to Lenin's theory, capitalists in all industrial nations were making high profits but not paying their workers enough to buy all the goods that could be produced. Their greed produced a surplus of capital—profits above those that could be reinvested because the new goods produced would find no market. In one country after another, capitalists solved the problem by pressuring their governments to expand into the underdeveloped regions of Asia and Africa in brutal imperialist campaigns costing hundreds of thousands of native lives. Once conquered, the colonies made a profitable outlet for surplus capital because they needed railroads, factories, and mines, and labor was cheaper than at home. The gains from imperialism also allowed capitalist countries to treat their workers a little better and thus stifle discontent.

Fortunately, Lenin argued, capitalist imperialism is bound to fail in the end. Since there is a finite number of new countries to be colonized, the capitalist nations will eventually go to war with each other over colonies; Lenin believed that World War I, which was raging when he wrote his book, was the first in a series of imperialist wars. But war would eventually weaken public support for the system and increase support among the workers for socialist movements.

Applying Lenin's analysis with some modifications to the United States, Marxists say that the United States reached the stage of surplus capital somewhat later than Europe, around the turn of the century. The nation engaged in some minor imperialist ventures, like the conquest of the Philippines and interventions in Latin America, but not until Germany and Japan threatened U.S. access to markets and investment opportunities in Europe and Asia did the United States really become involved in world politics. After World War II the Soviet Union extended its control over Eastern Europe, denying that area to U.S. business. According to most Marxists, the Soviets were motivated primarily by national security concerns, but the U.S. leadership used the "Soviet threat" as a justification for a policy of "containing" communism—which in practice meant preserving an open door for American investment everywhere outside the Soviet sphere (Gardner 1976, 157–202; Kolko and Kolko 1972).

American foreign policy is, then, according to Marxists, imperialist foreign policy. Yet its tactics are different from those of the European imperial powers of the past. Because U.S. policymakers see Marxism as the main enemy, the United States has allied itself with the other capitalist countries instead of going to war against them, as Lenin predicted. And because the American people believe in freedom and democracy, U.S. leaders cannot openly conquer underdeveloped nations and make them colonies. Instead the United States supports "friendly" governments (in fact, puppet governments) in Third World countries, propping them up with economic and military aid and, when necessary, covert operations and military intervention. In return, U.S. business gets the same right to invest and trade as it would if a colonial relationship existed.

American imperialism may be more subtle than the old-fashioned variety, but according to Marxists its human costs are just as great. American corporations in the Third World pay higher wages than local companies, but they also take profits out of the country and put less efficient local firms out of business, adding to unemployment and widening the gap between rich and poor. If a government, communist or not, seeks to control such corporations, the United States may find a reason to declare the government "communist" and intervene, overtly or covertly. In Guatemala in the early 1950s, for example, a nationalist military government seized and redistributed nearly four hundred thousand acres of unused land owned by the American United Fruit Company. President Dwight Eisenhower and his secretary of state, John Foster Dulles (who had ties to the company), authorized a CIA covert operation that overthrew the government and installed a rightist regime, which gave the land back to the United Fruit Company (Schlesinger and Kinzer 1983).

Obviously Marxists see no merit in the conservative view that the United States needed to contain the Soviet Union after World War II. Most American Marxists acknowledge that the Soviet government cruelly mistreated its own people and others. However, such Soviet actions are simply irrelevant to the economic forces that really drive U.S. imperialism. The Persian Gulf War showed that with Soviet power gone, the United States will be even more imperialistic, using military power to impose its domination on the economically vital Middle East.

If conservatives are deceptive, say Marxists, liberals and libertarians are blind. There is no use saying, as liberals do, that the United States should act more humanely in its dealings with other countries, for as one Marxist scholar put it, "Imperialism is not a matter of choice for a capitalist society; it is the way of life of such a society" (Magdoff 1969, 26). Liberals are probably sincere in their desire to promote human rights, but they are unable to stop support for tyrants like Marcos or the Shah of Iran because of U.S. corporate economic interests. Nor can the United States retreat to its own shores and mind its own business as libertarians want; their cherished free market system would sink under the weight of surplus capital with no place to go.

Marxists continue to predict the downfall of capitalist imperialism, though the timetable has been pushed back many times. If capitalism falls, they say, most of the problems outlined in this chapter would be solved. American workers would be paid enough to buy all they could produce, so there would be no need to send young Americans abroad to fight for investment opportunities. Poor countries, freed from imperialism, would develop rapidly, especially if they adopted socialism, so "aid" would soon be not needed. The United States would still be an important nation in the world, but its influence would, for the first time,be exerted for the betterment of humanity.

Feminist

Feminists argue that American foreign policy reflects male concerns because there are so few women in important foreign policy positions. Men's tendency is to emphasize competition. Rarely is the international arena seen as a place where everyone can be a winner. Even talk of free trade clouds efforts on the part of each participant to reach agreements that secure advantage. In speeches and debates in 1992 during the presidential campaign, Ross Perot used such terms as "global war" and "economic treason" to describe the economic competition emerging between the United States and other countries and the willingness of some leaders in Congress and the executive branch to become lobbyists for foreign countries after leaving office. Perot's metaphors, say feminists, reveal a male point of view, which clearly diverges from the more tolerant, inclusive, and relational manner in which women view the world. These different world views explain the gender gap on issues relating to defense and foreign policy. Women are concerned about aid and assistance; men are concerned about defense. Perot's authoritarian military manner may be responsible for his failure to garner large numbers of women's votes, despite his support for some feminist issues like choice (*Time*, 16 November 1992, 47).

American women have always been more active than men in promoting peace. The only member of Congress to vote against both world wars was Jeanette Rankin, a Montana Republican, suffragette, and active participant in peace movements. With the resurgence of feminism during the Vietnam War, defense spending and nuclear weapons have emerged as foreign policy issues examined in light of a feminist critique.

Feminists believe that some of the money spent on defense could be better applied to domestic social programs, to aid for women and children in the Third World, or to reducing the federal budget deficit. If women were in positions of power, say feminists, they would bring different priorities to foreign policy. Many feminists, for example, were among those who wanted to see economic sanctions carried out longer in the 1990–91 Persian Gulf crisis. Because the major players in that conflict were men, say feminists, it escalated into a military conflict more quickly than necessary. Until a critical mass of feminist women ascend to important positions in foreign policy and defense policy, women who do have authority will be forced to make policy decisions in the context of male agendas.

Although the United Nations has always promoted equal rights, in the 1970s a series of world conferences began to acknowledge the key role of women in population control and economic development and to encourage major changes in Third World development policies (Pietila and Vickers

1990, vii–ix; see also Chodorow 1993, 82–91). As U.S. feminists sought common ground with women from other regions of the world, they found the task of overcoming obstacles to equality much more difficult in the global setting than in the United States. The world offers a wide variety of settings within which women live and work, including differing cultural, economic, class, and political contexts (Adler 1991, xii–xxi).

Feminists in industrialized countries acknowledge that they operate from a privileged position vis-à-vis their Third World sisters. They also define gender roles in different ways. Because they already have procured greater job opportunities and legal protections than their Third World counterparts, they sometimes appear to the latter to be trying to push things too far, too fast, and in wrong directions.

One important common ground is concern for the status of women. The poorest portions of the populations in many First World and Third World countries are increasingly families maintained by women. This trend, known as the feminization of poverty, results from a breakdown in cultural traditions manifested by increases in divorce rates and out-of-wedlock births (Schaffer 1988, 223–46). In the Third World, male migrations and war fatalities are also contributing factors. Because they lack power, women are first to experience health problems when plague or famine strikes. Indeed,

despite their greater longevity in the First World, mortality rates for women, although falling in many Third World countries, remain almost as high as those of men.

Third and First World feminists also share concerns about the negative impact of the development programs created by Western countries (Stuadt and Jaquette 1988, 263–81; see also Schaffer 1988, 223–46). Although women play important economic roles in most rural Third World societies, aid programs from the 1950s to the 1970s addressed them only as mothers. Resources were always transferred from men to other men, overlooking women's involvement in traditional agriculture or their roles as heads of households. Analysts must focus, say feminists, on ways aid programs relate to women's roles and change in developing societies (Pietila and Vickers 1990, 17).

Although feminists may differ on how women in the Third World should utilize grants or legal protections once they have been provided, few would disagree that Third World women and children need more protection than currently exists. Military, trade, and aid policies continue to be dominated by men. Feminists believe that until the uneven nature of women's rights and status around the world changes, allowing for more meaningful contributions by women to policy processes, feminist criticism of American foreign policy will continue to have an important role.

DOES AMERICAN FOREIGN POLICY WORK?

Assessments of whether U.S. foreign policy is working vary with how well things are going for the United States at the time. With the benefit of hindsight, we believe that the United States was right in attempting to contain Soviet influence in the world, and this policy was clearly successful. We also think that forging close relations with the other industrial democracies has been a major achievement and that such ties should be preserved and strengthened. U.S. policy toward the Third World has frequently been inept and occasionally disastrous. Unlike the Marxists,

who perceive a conscious desire to exploit, we attribute this failure to American self-absorption and lack of understanding of cultures different from our own.

Perhaps, as Marxists claim, the United States could get along better with the rest of the world if it had a different economic system. Perhaps, as libertarians argue, it could get along better with much less involvement in the world. If, as seems likely, either liberal or conservative assumptions guide foreign policy, the issues discussed in this chapter are likely to persist.

The legacy of communism is a baffling array of problems in the former Soviet Union, most of which are beyond American power to solve. The United States will probably retain leadership of the Western bloc, but its allies will not always be prepared to follow the leader, whether the direction is liberal or conservative. The Third World will continue to frustrate and baffle U.S. policymakers with intractable problems.

All these complications are no excuse for poor foreign policy, and all six perspectives agree that the United States should be more intelligent in its foreign relations than it has been. But just as clearly, the solution to all the world's problems does not lie in the hands of one nation, even a very powerful one, with only 5 percent of the world's people. The United States could destroy the world tomorrow, but it cannot control the world because its power is limited by the power and sovereignty of other countries. Whichever perspective American leaders adopt, they need to temper it with realism about how much the United States can do to make things better. The public needs to do the same and not expect miracles from foreign policy.

SUMMARY AND REVIEW

The United States has never been as comfortable with the traditional instruments of foreign policy as most other modern nations. As a country that was for the most part isolated from great power struggles before 1945 and then became a superpower, it is used to projecting its values on other nations. Both president and Congress have important constitutional powers in the realm of foreign affairs, and since 1945 both have striven to assert new powers. Over the past twenty-five years Congress has become increasingly assertive.

Many agencies assist the president in formulating foreign policy. With the world economy having an ever greater impact on the lives of Americans, the number of agencies concerned with foreign policy, and the conflicts among them, are only likely to grow.

Interest groups have less opportunity to affect foreign policy than domestic policy, but some interest groups do have a significant influence in foreign affairs. Usually, success depends on getting Congress involved in the issue. Public opinion has more effect on foreign policy in the United States than in other countries, though public knowledge of foreign affairs is very limited. But the general attitude toward foreign affairs may be more important than whether people are informed and interested in specific issues, for American leaders must have popular support for their foreign policy initiatives.

For most of the period since World War II, the United States was preoccupied with containing the Soviet Union. The United States and the Soviet Union had been allies during the war, but relations deteriorated afterward, mainly due to Soviet policies in Eastern Europe. The containment policy produced the Marshall Plan and the North Atlantic Treaty Organization (NATO), which committed the United States to rebuild and defend Europe against the Soviets. The worst setback for containment was the failed war in Vietnam. During the 1970s relations between the superpowers improved for a while under détente, but détente broke down with the Soviet invasion of Afghanistan. After a period of confrontation under President Reagan, reforms initiated in the Soviet Union led to the end of the cold war.

Relations with international friends have not been easy for the United States either. After years of prosperous international trade, the United States now has a huge trade deficit and a long list of declining industries, and many Americans are calling for changes in the world trading system. There is disagreement among the allies on defense issues as well. One of the biggest complaints is that the

United States is carrying too great a share of the European and Japanese defense burden; lack of allied support for certain U.S. foreign policy initiatives is also disturbing. On the whole, the United States has had a difficult time with the Third World throughout the postwar period. Even foreign policy with neighbors can be complicated; current issues in U.S.-Canadian relations include acid rain and the free trade agreement effective in January 1989.

The United States first became deeply involved with the Middle East after it recognized the state of Israel in 1948. Support for Israel is one point of agreement for American politicians of all major perspectives—a consensus that profoundly irritates the Arab states and has damaged U.S. relations in the Middle East. In 1978 Jimmy Carter succeeded in helping Israel and Egypt reach a peace accord, and the Bush administration tried to broker a similar agreement between the Israelis and the other Arabs following the Persian Gulf War. In that war, the United States led a UN coalition to force Iraq from Kuwait. Most Americans hoped that the fall 1993 agreement between Israel and the PLO would lead to a reduction in tensions and further agreements. The United States will continue to involve itself in Middle Eastern affairs because of its ties to Israel and the dependence of industrial nations on oil from the region.

In Central America and the Caribbean, American interests date back to the Monroe Doctrine of 1823. In the 1980s the Reagan administration intervened in Central America and Grenada to stop Marxist movements. More recently, the United States has been concerned about eliminating drug trafficking and illegal immigration from Latin America. A free trade agreement with Mexico may help solve some of these problems, but it has also generated much opposition.

The United Nations was formed after World War II to promote peace, check aggression, and solve other world problems. In the General Assembly each nation has one vote, but in the Security Council five nations—France, China, Russia, the United Kingdom, and the United States—each have veto power. During the cold war, the United Nations was often paralyzed by the veto system. Now it is able to act more effectively, but the organization still has only the power its members are willing to give it. The United Nations was effective in the Persian Gulf crisis but has been less so in resolving problems in Somalia and the former Yugoslavia.

Not too long ago, Americans of all perspectives shared a foreign policy consensus that dictated an active American foreign policy and resistance to an aggressive Soviet Union. This consensus was shattered by Vietnam, and now foreign policy is a topic of great debate. The power of the United States is limited by the power of other countries. Much of U.S. foreign policy has been successful, but the United States cannot control world events; it must live and work in a community of nations.

IMPORTANT TERMS

alliance
arms control
balance of power
Camp David Agreement
cold war
collective security
complex interdependence
containment

covert operations
détente
diplomacy
disarmament
domino theory
dumping
Economic and Social Council (ECOSOC)
economic sanctions

First World
foreign policy
free trade
General Agreement on Tariffs and Trade
  (GATT)
General Assembly
International Monetary Fund (IMF)
international relations
isolationism
Marshall Plan
Monroe Doctrine
most favored nation status
national security adviser (NSA)

nontariff barrier
North Atlantic Treaty Organization (NATO)
puppet government
Reagan Doctrine
Roosevelt Corollary
Second World
Security Council
sovereignty
tariff barrier
Third World
United Nations (UN)
war

12

NATIONAL ECONOMIC POLICY

John Q. Saccos's hair glistened as the sun shone through the glass telephone booth. His dark hair and tan contrasted with his lightly colored swim trunks. John absentmindedly flicked sand from his arm as he listened to the phone ringing in his exclusive suburban home many miles away. Spring break '93 in Florida had been wild, and last night had been the wildest of all. Unfortunately, all the partying had left John broke, and, as usual, he was calling his father to get "bailed out." As one of the top vice-presidents of the International Division of A-Z Industries, John's father had often wondered why the financial genes of the family had not been passed along to his profligate son, but he had never denied John's requests when the phone calls came.

John's mother picked up the telephone, and after an exchange of pleasantries John made his pitch and received the following reply: "It hurts us to say this John, but your father lost his job a week and a half ago when A-Z's International Division was sold to another company. We may have to move, and we're not even sure we can cover tuition next year unless we take out one of those student loans they talk about. At the very least, you'd better put off the European study tour planned for fall semester that you talked to us about at Christmas."

In answer to questions as to how his father lost his job, John learned that it was not really his father's fault. The International Division was showing a profit, but A-Z needed liquidity (cash) and was forced to sell one of its better divisions. When the new manager came in, he wanted his people at the top. Now, it seemed, because of the adverse market for oil, businesses were laying off employees all over the city, and John's father could not even get a serious interview. John's father chimed in to conclude the conversation by saying, "#$! Washington! I'm so mad at the politicians and their foot-dragging policies I could spit. If Treasury and the Fed had stimulated the economy a year earlier, it *might have made A-Z International's job more difficult, but we wouldn't have been in a cash crunch and I might still be employed."*

Although the example is fictional and perhaps oversimplified, situations like this do occur. The impact of national and international economic policies on the economy and, in turn, the impact of the economy on people, make this area of concern to all six perspectives. Libertarians and conservatives, with certain exceptions, want to protect producers through limited government intervention at home and few restrictions on international trade. Liberals and populists believe that the economy in a capitalist society is inherently unstable and that various forms of economic intervention are necessary to protect both producers and consumers. To Marxists, economic policy in the United States is antithetical to their central doctrine of equality: the existence of private property and free enterprise as presently organized are inherently unjust and should be restructured. Feminists view capitalist institutions as hierarchical and male dominated. Like Marxists, they point to the fact that the contribution and productivity of certain groups (males in the work force) are rewarded far more than the contribution and productivity of other groups (females in the home). Moreover, in the work force alone, males are paid more for the same types of jobs and achieve promotion more quickly than females (*Washington Post National Weekly Edition*, 9–15 November 1992, 34).

Every government has some sort of economic policy at the national level, even if it is to allow free trade. All governments also create legal systems that provide the framework for economic arrangements. In the United States, as early as the presidency of George Washington, an interventionist economic policy was being formulated on the national level. Alexander Hamilton, secretary of the treasury, in 1791 proposed a variety of measures, including a protective tariff and the creation of a national bank, designed to place the new government on a sound financial footing and stimulate the growth of industry. Only in relatively recent times, however, has the national government accepted a general responsibility for keeping unemployment low and monitoring the economy on a month-by-month basis. The nation's failure to regain prosperity in the period of falling prices, output shrinkage, and unemployment following the stock market crash of 1929 led to considerably greater interest in ways and means of producing better economic conditions. The move toward conscious government management of the economy was ratified by the Employment Act (1946), which directs the president to pursue policies that "promote maximum employment, production, and purchasing power."

As **inflation** (a sustained general rise in the price level or cost of living, as opposed to price increases for individual products) began to be a serious problem in the mid-1960s, the government also accepted responsibility for maintaining a stable price level. The nation's recent history makes clear that such goals are easier stated than achieved. The variety of ideas that emerged from President-elect Bill Clinton's December 1992 economic conference in Little Rock indicates that there is no scarcity of alternative strategies. The problem is that there is an equal abundance of problems and obstacles associated with carrying out those policies.

THE INSTRUMENTS OF ECONOMIC POLICY

Economic policy can be described as occurring on two separate but interrelated levels. On the **microeconomic** level, government affects the economy through laws and regulations applying to specific industries and sectors or to particular problems affecting many sectors. Such policies include tariffs, import quotas, subsidies, tax incentives, and job retraining to improve worker skills. While this type of economic legislation may have a substantial cumulative effect on the performance of the economy, it is usually framed with regard to specific problems rather than the needs of the whole economy. Some of President Clinton's advisers, notably Robert Reich, secretary of labor, and Laura D'Andrea Tyson, chair of the Council of Economic Advisers, have indicated that microeconomic variables are of equal or greater importance than macroeconomic ones. Most economists still assert the primacy of macroeconomics in providing a relatively stable environment within which the business community and financial markets can function effectively. Some argue that a primarily microeconomic approach to solving the country's economic problems is not feasible until major macroeconomic issues are addressed. On the **macroeconomic** level, which is the level emphasized in this chapter, the government attempts to influence the behavior of the total economy through the use of three basic policy tools: monetary policy, fiscal policy, and incomes policy. It will be valuable to examine how these three policy tools work and the problems they entail before discussing alternative perspectives on their use in the struggle for, as the Employment Act hopes, "maximum employment, production, and purchasing power" (*Washington Post National Weekly Edition*, 19–25 October 1992, 12–13; *Washington Post National Weekly Edition*, 16–22 November 1992, 9, 10; *Washington Post National Weekly Edition*, 30 November–6 December 1992, 31; *Congressional Quarterly Weekly Report*, 23 January 1993, 169, 171).

Monetary Policy: The Federal Reserve Board

Article I, Section 8, of the Constitution grants Congress the power to "coin Money" and "regulate the Value thereof." Nevertheless, it is not the Congress but private banks under the guidelines set forth by the Federal Reserve Board, as established by Congress in 1913, that are the major producers of money in the United States. Until the Civil War, state-chartered banks could actually print their own money and issue it to the public. Today the government monopolizes the printing of currency, but the banks under the Federal Reserve System still control **monetary policy**— government policy designed to affect the amount of currency and the availability of credit—by creating most of the nation's money supply when they extend credit. To control the money supply effectively, the United States, like other nations, has been compelled to create its own "superbank"—the **Federal Reserve System**.

The Federal Reserve System was created by the Federal Reserve Act in 1913, primarily to stem the periodic waves of bank failures that had plagued the nation in the late nineteenth and early twentieth centuries. It was widely felt that an institution was needed which could provide private banks with emergency funds when they were faced with a "run" (worried depositors withdrawing their money) and, at the same time, exercise some control over banking practices to keep bank runs from happening. To this end Congress created twelve "banker's banks," each in a different region of the country and linked together by a **Board of Governors** in Washington, whose seven members are appointed by the president with the advice and consent of the Senate. The Federal Reserve banks were to make credit available to those banks that voluntarily agreed to become part of the Federal Reserve System and to accept some supervision over their activities. Even today not all banks belong to the system, but it does include most of the country's largest financial institutions, and since 1980 all banks and thrift institutions are subject to its supervision (*Federal Reserve System* 1974; see also Greider 1987; Kettl 1986).

During its early years, the Federal Reserve's power over the money supply, and therefore over the economy, was not fully understood even by those running the system. Until 1971 the country was on a **gold standard**—a system in which currency is "backed" by a fixed quantity of gold. In fact, despite the gold standard, by the early twentieth century credit had already become more important than gold or paper currency as a source of purchasing power, giving the Federal Reserve and other central banks in the Western world much more power over the economy. Many observers had already noted the link between a rising or falling supply of money and rising or falling prices, but few had appreciated the link between an expanding money supply and a high level of economic activity on the one hand and a contracting money supply and declining production on the other. Between 1929 and 1933, the Federal Reserve Board allowed the money supply to decline by one-third, and some economists have argued that this drop was the primary cause of the Great Depression (Friedman and Schwartz 1963, 299–419). Since at least the 1950s, however, the importance of money in the economy has been more clearly recognized and the Federal Reserve's role has become primarily one of managing the nation's money supply, with some attention to the direct control of interest rates.

The "Fed," as the Federal Reserve Board is commonly known, has three major tools with which to control the volume of money and credit in the economy. It has the power to establish **reserve requirements** for most banks and thrift institutions—requiring them to keep a specific percentage of their funds on hand to satisfy the demands of depositors seeking to withdraw money. By raising or lowering this requirement, the Fed can decrease or increase the amount of money banks can lend to their borrowers. The Fed can also raise or lower the **discount rate** at which it lends money to its member banks to meet emergency needs; this rate, in turn, will affect the rate the banks charge their customers and ultimately the amount of money borrowed. The third method used by the Fed to control the money supply,

open market policy, has evolved into the primary mechanism for managing monetary policy. Open market policy involves the Fed's buying and selling of United States government bonds. Buying bonds and paying for them with dollars—Federal Reserve notes printed for that purpose—releases money into the economy; selling bonds absorbs money from the economy. Open market policy is handled by a committee consisting of seven governors of the system and five presidents of the twelve regional banks, serving in rotation.

The Fed wields greater power, and yet it is less susceptible to executive and legislative oversight and control than most executive branch agencies. The seven members of the Board of Governors are chosen for fourteen-year terms, with one member's term expiring every two years, making it difficult for the president or Congress, with their shorter terms, to control the board by replacing uncooperative members. The chair of the board, who customarily exercises a leadership role, is appointed for four years from among the other members (Kettl 1986, 14–15). His or her tenure does not, however, coincide with that of the president, and the president may thus have to put up with a chair whose views conflict with his or her own.

In recent years the operations of the Federal Reserve Board have grown more controversial. Some authorities blame the board for the severe inflation of the 1970s, accusing it of letting the money supply grow too quickly. Other experts fault it for being too concerned about inflation and oblivious to the problem of unemployment. Certain critics, for example, argue that Alan Greenspan, the Federal Reserve chair, lowered interest rates too little and too hesitantly and thus prolonged the recession that began in 1990 (*Business Week*, 30 March 1992, 22; *Business Week*, 14 December 1987, 35). All observers recognize that the board's influence over economic conditions is formidable and that it acts as a major constraint on the

Mark Cullum. Courtesy *Birmingham News.*

power of the elected branches in shaping economic policy.

Fiscal Policy: The Heritage of Keynes

Ever since it began to collect taxes and spend money, the government has had a **fiscal policy**. Fiscal policy in the sense of using taxes and spending as a tool of economic management, however, is of even more recent vintage than monetary policy. Until fairly recent times governments tended to follow fiscal policies that remained constant in the face of changing economic conditions; an effort was made to keep the budget balanced regardless of the state of the economy. For the last fifty years, however, the growing belief that the government should work toward a strong economy and prevent high levels of unemployment has reduced the importance of a balanced U.S. budget. In the 1960s fiscal policy became particularly activist, seeking to influence economic performance through tax and spending cuts (Stein 1969, 413, 416).

The roots of activist fiscal policies lie in the theories of John Maynard Keynes, an English economist of the 1920s and 1930s (Keynes 1935). Keynes identified the cause of economic instability as a tendency on the part of consumers either to overspend or underspend. When people chose to save too much of their incomes and spend too little, business activity declined for lack of consumer demand and the increased savings tended to go to waste for lack of profitable investment opportunities. When people chose to spend more and save less, the economy might recover, but the increased demand for goods would push prices up. According to Keynes, capitalist economies are inherently unstable because they depend on unstable consumer preferences, and therefore government action is needed to ensure stability. A believer in private ownership, Keynes did not advocate socialism as a solution; instead he called on governments to adopt policies to counteract the cycles of inflation and recession. Keynes believed that during a depression the government should run a deficit, spending more than it took in to make up for reduced private spending and get the economy moving again. During an inflationary period, it should raise taxes, cut spending, and run a surplus.

When Franklin Roosevelt was elected president in 1932, he promised to balance the budget and cut spending. This goal proved impossible, however, since the government was unable to collect enough taxes to pay for routine operations, let alone the new social welfare programs that Roosevelt introduced. Roosevelt thus stumbled into the policy proposed by Keynes almost without intending it, and he never accepted Keynes's argument. Spending for the New Deal programs during the 1930s was not large enough to bring the country out of the Depression, but when the dramatic deficit spending for World War II did lead to recovery, Keynes's theories appeared vindicated (McElvaine 1984, 329, 331). Countercyclical policies involving tax cuts and/or spending increases have been employed in nearly every recession since, although the other half of the Keynesian prescription—fiscal restraint during booms—has proven far less popular. That is not surprising in a democracy in which voters benefit from government spending.

Although the Constitution grants the power of the purse to Congress, the initiative in fiscal policy has gravitated to the president as a result of budgetary legislation passed following World War I. By the very nature of his position as the single head of a vast bureaucracy, the chief executive is much better equipped to formulate coherent policies than a body of 535 individuals, each with limited access to advice and information. The president submits a budget to Congress each year for its approval, and the most that legislators can usually do is make incremental changes, leaving the basic structure intact (see Chapters 7, 10). For their part presidents also find it difficult to make substantial change in the policies of the past, as demonstrated by the resistance both Presi-

dents Ronald Reagan and George Bush encountered in trying to enact their budget proposals. Tax policy has also been an area of contention. Bush attempted unsuccessfully to lower capital gains taxes that, according to conservative and libertarian economists, would release funds for reinvestment and spur economic growth. President Clinton had been interested in investment tax credits, which give tax breaks only to businesses that meet certain criteria. These should have a better chance of passing the Democratic Congress, but opposition from those who do not benefit is likely (*New York Times*, 29 March 1992, sec. 3: F12–F13; *New York Times*, 12 February 1992, D1, D8; *Washington Post National Weekly Edition*, 30 November–6 December 1992, 21–22; *Congressional Quarterly Weekly Report*, 19 June 1993, 1617).

The president has the assistance of several executive agencies in shaping economic policy. The Office of Management and Budget (OMB) in the Executive Office of the President advises the president on budget matters and reviews the spending proposals of various government agencies with an eye toward their effect on the economy as well as their immediate objectives. The Treasury Department, in addition to raising the money needed for expenditures, advises the president on tax policy and international economic issues such as tariffs and the balance of payments. Since 1946 the president has also benefited from the advice of a Council of Economic Advisers—three economists with general advisory duties.

In Congress the members who have the most say in determining fiscal policies are those serving on important committees dealing with fiscal matters—chiefly the Appropriations, the Budget, and the Ways and Means Committees in the House, and the Appropriations, the Budget, and the Finance Committees in the Senate. The preferences of leading members of Congress such as Dan Rostenkowski (see Profile in Chapter 6), longtime chair of the Ways and Means Committee, always have to be taken into account by a president who wants to submit tax legislation, even if on exceptional occasions, such as one Bush effort in 1989, the president has the votes to overrule them (*Politics in America* 1991, 439). Rostenkowski's cooperation was essential to both the Reagan tax reform of 1986 and the Clinton tax plan of 1993.

Since 1975, the Congressional Budget Office (CBO) has helped to offset the executive branch's superior expertise at the Office of Management and Budget. The CBO's role is to provide Congress with the same type of expert economic analysis that the president receives from the executive fiscal agencies. Often the OMB and CBO make different assumptions, which affect projections of economic figures, including interest rates, unemployment, economic growth, or inflation for a given year; thus their forecasts for the future of the American economy are likely to differ.

Incomes Policy: The Visible Hand

Incomes policy—direct or indirect government intervention aimed at controlling wages and prices—has been widely used in the United States in times of war. Price and incomes policy usually become important in such times because prices shoot up (inflation) when a demand for weapons is added to the already existing demand for other goods and services, thus reducing the availability of these consumer goods and raising their prices. Laborers must then struggle to keep their salaries rising in order to be able to pay for the rising costs of goods. During World War II and the Korean War, wages and prices were controlled by the government, but controls were lifted soon after (World War II) or just before (Korea) the hostilities ended.

Incomes policy has not been entirely neglected in time of peace, however. During the early 1930s the National Recovery Administration, in an unsuccessful effort to keep prices from falling further, established "codes of fair competition" for many industries. In the postwar period both John Kennedy and Lyndon Johnson suggested guidepost prices for certain products. In 1971 the Nixon administration imposed a ninety-day freeze on wages and prices, followed over the next three years by alternate loosening and tightening of controls. In 1974 these controls were finally lifted completely, except for energy prices, which were lifted later under the Reagan administration.

The United States has not established a permanent incomes policy. However, the government has not been altogether willing to leave wages and prices to Adam Smith's "invisible hand" of the marketplace (see Chapter 1). Sometimes presidents have attempted to influence wage and price decisions, without the use of formal controls, through the power and prestige of their office. The practice of **jawboning**—publicly approving or condemning wage and price increases as they affect the national economy, especially inflation—was launched in earnest by John Kennedy and has been used to some extent by most presidents since. Jimmy Carter also created wage-price guidelines based on appeal to voluntary restraint. Ronald Reagan's lack of interference in the area of wages and prices, even in the form of jawboning, was at first criticized by some as a weakness in his economic strategy (*New York Times*, 12 July 1981, sec. 4: E1). Later the point became moot as reduced inflation tempered demands for large wage increases. Early in his term President Clinton indicated his willingness to speak out by publicly attacking drug companies for the high prices of their vaccines.

THE PROBLEMS OF ECONOMIC POLICY

Today the United States government has a somewhat better understanding of the economic policy tools available than did governments in the past. Yet economic management

TWO ECONOMISTS ENGAGING IN A HEATED DEBATE:

BOOM!   BUST!

Malcolm Hancock. © MalEnt, Inc.

is not necessarily any easier. While economists can explain some aspects of how the economy works, wide areas of disagreement remain about the effects of alternative policies. For example, numerous explanations were advanced for the 508-point drop in the stock market on October 19, 1987 (*Facts on File Yearbook, 1987*, 773). Few analysts publicly predicted this crash, and fewer still agree on exactly what regulatory changes (microeconomic) and revenue or budget adjustments (macroeconomic) need to be made in order to prevent it from happening again.

Moreover, the experts may answer questions about what can be done, but the political process decides what actually will be done in an attempt to achieve the results society wants. As with foreign policy, the voting public has the final word in judging the economic policies of an administration or Congress. Thus economic management is a political problem as well as an economic one. If the stock market's problem was computer trading, technical corrections would suffice. If the nation's budget and trade deficits are a major reason, as some have suggested, for the loss in investor confidence, the changes required to restore confidence may be politically very painful. Some populists and most liberals argue that

social programs have already been cut as far as feasible; further cuts would be crippling. Recent polls indicate that even voters not benefiting from such programs seem unwilling to cut them further. How can politicians who depend on these voters for reelection be expected to resolve such an economic crisis themselves, even if they agree that reducing the deficit is the proper solution? Even with more than 120 new House and Senate members in Congress and Democrats controlling both Congress and the White House, limited knowledge, combined with sharply diverging views on what values should be pursued, can make doing what is theoretically the right thing to do politically impossible to achieve. Economic policy is much harder to implement in practice than to understand in theory.

Monetary Policy

Monetary policy has a number of features that make it attractive to policymakers attempting to deal with economic instability. As an independent body, the Federal Reserve Board can act much more quickly than the elected branches to deal with problems because no changes in the law are required for the Fed to change monetary policy. The board's insulation from political pressures has another advantage; with their long terms, the governors can afford to carry out unpopular policies, like credit tightening, that might not pass Congress. Typically, the governors are themselves well versed in economics, while the president and Congress must rely on the advice of others. Although Reagan's support for lower inflation rates is sometimes credited for the dramatic reductions in inflation between 1982 and 1984, informed citizens realize that a far more important factor was the monetary policy of the Federal Reserve led by Chair Paul Volcker.

Along with these advantages, however, monetary policy faces some serious technical difficulties. Although changes in policy can be

TABLE 12.1   PERCENTAGE CHANGES IN PRODUCTIVITY AND RELATED DATA, 1973–1976

QUARTER	OUTPUT (Per Hour)	OUTPUT	HOURS	EMPLOYMENT	UNEMPLOYMENT RATE
1973:1	3.9	11.3	7.1	7.0	5.0
2	− 3.5	0.8	4.4	4.0	4.9
3	0.8	1.4	2.2	2.5	4.8
4	− 2.4	0.3	2.7	3.7	4.8
1974:1	− 4.1	− 4.1	0.1	2.4	5.0
2	− 5.0	− 3.4	1.7	2.3	5.1
3	− 2.2	− 4.0	− 1.7	−0.9	5.6
4	− 2.3	− 9.1	− 7.0	−4.8	6.7
1975:1	1.1	−11.0	−11.9	−9.3	8.2
2	10.2	6.5	− 3.4	−3.3	8.9
3	9.1	12.5	3.1	2.5	8.5
4	− 2.4	3.7	6.2	4.0	8.3
1976:1	3.7	11.5	7.5	5.9	7.7
2	5.0	5.7	0.7	3.4	7.5
3	2.7	2.5	− 0.2	1.3	7.7
4	− 0.9	1.2	2.1	2.0	7.8

Source: Blinder *1979, 66.*

included. Suppose you were trying to decide whether to work for an additional $1,500 of income and realized that $750 would be lost in taxes. Would you decide to work in order to purchase more expensive consumer items, or would you make do with what you have? Would you use your time to work and therefore contribute to an increase in "taxable income," or would you use your time to pursue a hobby or relax in your backyard? Your answer might vary according to your overall income, but the Reagan reforms were aimed at encouraging more persons to work.

Added elements in the economic picture that worked as a disincentive to productivity were **loopholes** in the federal tax code. By the 1970s the code had become a veritable cornucopia of tax breaks for enterprising tax avoiders and interest groups. Many of these loopholes encouraged using money in economically unproductive ways. For example, ownerships in unproductive ventures in oil or real estate yielded large tax savings for eligible

individuals but had negative or neutral effects on the productivity of the economy as a whole (Boskin 1987, 139–76).

At the same time that a number of disincentives to productivity were being caused by inflation, price controls, and the tax code, the role of government in the economy as a whole was becoming more and more activist. Commitments to protecting consumers and ensuring worker safety were being added to the regulatory chores of the federal bureaucracy. Each program had laudable goals, but the net effect was an additional burden on the economy. In 1979 one cost-benefit study placed the total cost to the economy of complying with government rules at almost $100 billion a year (Boskin 1987, 19; *Grand Rapids Press*, 26 June 1989, A1).

Government commitments to reducing poverty caused dramatic spending increases in the domestic areas at the same time that the tax system and other forms of government intervention were creating disincentives to produce. This increase in spending was not for the purchase of goods and services, which can have a large **multiplier effect** (stimulate more economic activity), but for transfer payments from wealthier groups of individuals to poorer groups of individuals, which involve less net gain for the economy than government purchases. All government spending (including state and local governments) was 33 percent of gross national product (GNP) in 1970 and 35 percent in 1980. A $92 billion federal budget in 1960 (18 percent of GNP) had grown to $617 billion in 1980 (23 percent of GNP). Transfers between groups of individuals, as a percent of transfers plus purchases of goods and services, increased from 28 percent of the federal budget in 1960 to 55 percent in 1980 (*Statistical Abstract, 1992*, 279, 315, 431; Boskin 1987, 17).

Government was becoming a larger and larger player in competition for the money necessary to stimulate economic growth; yet a smaller and smaller amount of government expenditures was being used to purchase private sector goods that would, in turn, stimulate such growth. In addition, less money was available in the private sector for savings and investment, and Americans were already notoriously bad savers compared to citizens in many industrialized nations.

The results of government efforts to end poverty were initially successful. By some estimates, abject poverty in the United States declined by at least half, from 22 percent in 1960 to 11 percent in 1977. Although the decline leveled somewhat as a result of the inflation of the mid to late 1970s, the aging segment of the American population was better secured against impoverishment than at any time in the twentieth century (*Statistical Abstract, 1992*, 8; Goldsmith and Blakely 1992, 30; *Historical Statistics of the United States* 1975, 15, 340–41).

But the net effect of the government's controlling a larger share of the GNP was negative for economic growth. As a result of the policies described above, the average working, taxpaying American's standard of living improved at a much slower rate in the 1970s than in the 1960s. Growth in total productivity and wealth came from more people entering the labor force. Because of shrinking investment caused by uncertainty about inflation and the regulatory climate, high taxation of individual incomes, and less savings, the industrial sector was not being modernized and American workers were working less. American per-worker productivity actually declined in the early 1970s (see Table 12.1), a phenomenon almost unheard of in advanced capitalist societies. Between 1973 and 1980, increases in American productivity per worker shrank to a flat zero (Boskin 1987, 21). The nation was mired in an economic state that has come to be known as **stagflation**—a situation in which zero real per capita growth, higher than average levels of unemployment, soaring inflation rates, and rising interest rates for those who wished to borrow and invest exist simultaneously. It was in this context that Ronald Reagan was elected with what he perceived as an electoral mandate that allowed him to implement decisive changes in American economic policy.

The Reagan-Bush Years

Reagan and his advisers were determined to take a different approach. During the presidential campaign, Reagan attacked the forty years of liberal economic policies that he said had caused stagflation; he wanted to change "the failed policies of the past." Too much government regulation and spending, coupled with too high a level of taxation, were seen as the twin causes of the nation's economic malaise (Derthick and Quirk 1985, 19–22).

Reaganomics   Reagan modeled his economic recovery program on John Kennedy's ideas that cutting taxes and freeing the economy of excessive government regulation would stimulate economic growth. Although there might be a short time when government expenditures would outweigh tax receipts, the resulting economic expansion would eventually provide more tax revenues than before the tax cut (*Business Week*, 23 February 1981, 128–29). This idea is known as **supply-side economics**.

Reagan's policies had some detractors. George Bush, Reagan's opponent in the 1980 Republican primaries, had called them "voodoo economics." Liberal Democrats led by Speaker of the House Thomas P. ("Tip") O'Neill attacked Reagan for his "callous" behavior in cutting social spending. Alice Rivlin, director of the Congressional Budget Office (now deputy director of the Office of Management and Budget under President Clinton), criticized both the president and Congress for ignoring implications in regard to the budget and deficits (see Profile). Even a number of southern or border state moderate to conservative Democrats, like Congressman James Jones of Oklahoma, expressed doubts. Jones, explaining to his conservative constituents why he was voting against the tax cut of 1981, predicted a $90 billion yearly deficit if the cuts went through. Jones was wrong on his numbers, of course. The deficits were higher than even he had imagined, but he had the right

idea (*Washington Post National Weekly Edition*, 29 February–6 March 1988, 31; see also *Wall Street Journal*, 2 September 1981, 20; *Detroit News*, 22 November 1992, B1, B6).

Reagan coupled his tax cuts with requests for cuts in social spending. At the same time, however, he also successfully argued for the largest peacetime military spending increases in American history (see Profile of David Stockman in Chapter 1). Although Democrats in Congress muttered about irresponsible behavior in the White House, Reagan's popularity, especially after the 1981 assassination attempt, made it impossible for them to fight his basic economic program. Leading a fight against a tax cut can be political suicide, as Congressman Jones discovered when he ran for the Senate and lost in 1986, a year when most Democrats did well in Senate races. Polls showed that American voters agreed with Reagan that a defense buildup was necessary. Reagan also sought to reduce government regulation of the economy. Left populists and liberals in Congress could do nothing more than try to prevent major cuts in social spending for the poor. They were somewhat successful, but

Rob Rogers. Reprinted by permission of NEA, Inc.

PROFILE
Alice Rivlin: Independent Public Servant

Alice Rivlin (AP/Wide World Photos)

Often people appointed to high-level posts in a new administration are Washington insiders, old faces on the Washington scene. Alice Rivlin, President Bill Clinton's appointment to the deputy directorship of the Office of Management and Budget, is a case in point. This Radcliffe Ph.D.'s career in government or government-related think tanks spans nearly forty years and includes positions as assistant secretary of the Department of Health, Education and Welfare (HEW) during the 1960s and at prestigious Brookings Institution (a liberal Washington think tank) during portions of the past four decades, and leadership of the Con-

gressional Budget Office from its inception in 1975 until 1983.

Rivlin is known for her neutral excellence as an economist and for standing tough in the face of political pressures from Republicans and Democrats, members of Congress and presidents. She has published widely in economics and economic-related areas. At sixty-two she is a member of Washington Women Outdoors, at athletic association that emphasizes outdoor sports, and her special interests include skiing, cycling, swimming, and running.

Rivlin joined the Brookings Institution in 1957. She served as consultant to the House Committee on Education and Labor during 1961–62, and to the secretary of the treasury from 1964 to 1966. She entered government service full time as an assistant secretary at HEW in time to participate in Lyndon Johnson's Great Society program. Returning to Brookings during the Nixon administration, she published, along with several colleagues, a three-volume series entitled *Setting National Priorities* that analyzed the Nixon budgets for 1971, 1972, and 1973 and suggested alternatives to White House budget priorities.

Rivlin's analysis of the Nixon budgets caught the attention of Democrats in Congress who recommended her to head the Congressional Budget Office when it was established to counter the presidentially controlled Office of Management and Budget (OMB). Although she had competitors (House members preferred a safer choice; Republicans claimed her liberal bias would make CBO statistics unreliable), she proved herself the most competent candidate for the job and was offered the position. She accepted, staying in office for eight years. At times she angered Democrats by affirming, in their eyes, too many of the Republican presidents' predictions. At different times, she embarrassed both Carter and the Democratic Congress.

Rivlin was often at loggerheads with the White House because the CBO figures almost always differed dramatically from figures produced by the more politically motivated OMB. For example, late in her first year of office, Rivlin discovered that the House version of the defense bill was $932 million more than even Gerald Ford had recommended. CBO's findings, reported in the press, indicated that she—and not Congress or the president—had done the math correctly. In the early 1980s CBO began to project the massive budget deficits that are now so worrisome in the 1990s. "We have taken no policy position, nor will we ever," said Rivlin in response to Republican criticism. Reagan shot back: "That's them, practicing what they've been preaching the last 30 years. Their figures are phoney." Rivlin's figures have long since been proven correct. Reagan supporters in the Senate like Orrin Hatch (see Profile in Chapter 1) tried to get Rivlin to resign, but she insisted on the nonpartisanship of her organization and continued her self-professed role of official purveyor of bad news to Congress with her annual reports on the economy and its implications for the federal budget. Her office's conclusions were always more pessimistic than the OMB's, no matter which party was in office. "Administrations always take the optimistic range of uncertainty. We don't. We take the middle range," she said. Her objectivity and strength of character in the face of political pressure has established the reputation of the CBO as a nonpartisan technical office of the Congress beholden to neither political party.

For the next ten years Rivlin was back at Brookings. Her most recent book, *Reviving the American Dream*, has tried to rethink some of the problems facing American government in ways that, if not unconventional, are politically unpalatable. Rivlin suggests that the federal government is doing too many things to do any of them well, and she calls for a reordering of priorities and trading off of responsibilities with the states. For example, the federal government may need to take over the administration and cost of health care, says Rivlin, but, if it does so, it must shift responsibility for education, training, and economic and infrastructural development back onto the states, where capacity to adapt to local conditions and accountability to on-the-scene officials are more necessary.

Bill Clinton was impressed by Rivlin's research and her wealth of institutional memory about the U.S. budget crisis. He was also aware, in appointing her to OMB, that he was taking a chance by putting such a strong person in a place with high visibility. If she thinks the president is misleading the country, she just might say so. Her outspokenness could embarrass Clinton, who promised to be more honest and forthright than the president he replaced. Rivlin may already have given Clinton some pause to reflect. Recently she stated, "If he only does the short-run stimulative things he can make the long-run deficit problem much worse." Rivlin has been honest with presidents for several decades, and she's not about to stop now.

Source: Current Biography Yearbook 1982, 355–58; *Wall Street Journal,* 19 November 1992, A1, A6; *National Journal,* 3 October 1992, 2255–57; Rivlin 1992a; Rivlin 1992b, 5.

they continued to believe that additional programs were necessary.

By late 1981, **Reaganomics** had passed Congress. Conservative Republicans were muzzled by their desire for a successful presidency and attracted by Reagan's defense policies. Liberal Democrats feared losing their party's majority in the House of Representatives if they opposed defense increases and tax cuts by this popular Republican president. In addition, even though House Democrats outnumbered Republicans by a large margin, conservative Democrats sometimes voted with the president, and their defections made it difficult for Democrats to control House votes.

In 1988, President Reagan's vice-president, George Bush, was elected president, and he continued Reagan's economic policies with one major exception. In 1990, to control the federal deficit, he agreed to a compromise with Democrats in Congress that raised taxes and set some spending limits. The measure was a stopgap. When Bush left office in 1993, the country was already experiencing the consequences of the Reagan-Bush years: increased budget deficits and national debt, an increased trade deficit, and, arguably, a recession in 1990–91.

Budget Deficits   One result of Reaganomics is now pretty much common knowledge. The large tax cuts, combined with the peacetime military buildup, created massive **budget deficits** (the annual amounts by which expenditures exceed receipts) (see Controversy; Rauch 1989, 36–42). Between 1981 and 1982, despite cuts in domestic programs, the annual deficit doubled (*Washington Post National Weekly Edition*, 29 February–6 March 1988, 31). Between 1980 and 1992, the **national debt** (the total of all the yearly budget deficits) owed by the government to those who have loaned it money increased more than fourfold—from $908.5 billion to $4.1 trillion (*Statistical Abstract, 1992*, 315).

Reagan's fiscal policy solution might have been successful in "stimulating" the economy

and bringing in needed revenues to close the deficit gap had it not been for the fact that inflation (the rising cost of living) was still quite high in 1981. Stimulating the economy would have caused inflation to rise at an even faster rate. In fact, Paul Volcker, appointed chair of the Federal Reserve Board by Jimmy Carter and reappointed by Ronald Reagan in 1983, was committed to following a "tight" monetary policy (Fleisher, Ray, and Kniesner 1987, 577). Volcker contained any inflationary impact that Reagan's highly "stimulative" fiscal policy might have had (*Washington Post National Weekly Edition*, 25–31 January 1988, 22; Greider 1987).

The Fed had begun to tighten the money supply as early as 1979 and simply continued its policies despite the pleas of some of Reagan's advisers. Interest rates, already high because of the inflation of the 1970s, did not move downward as a result of the Fed's actions; 1982 saw a recession and record high levels of unemployment as the Fed focused on "squeezing" inflation out of the economy. This situation made it impossible to expect the increases in revenue that "supply-siders" had initially predicted. In addition, increased government expenditures for defense widened the

Rob Rogers. Reprinted by permission of NEA, Inc.

gap between revenue and spending, even though domestic expenditures had begun to level off. At the same time that deficits were beginning to increase, however, other indicators of economic health did begin to improve. Employment increased, inflation dropped dramatically, and interest rates began to fall, albeit slowly, from the unprecedented heights of the late 1970s (*Washington Post National Weekly Edition*, 29 February–6 March 1988, 20; *Washington Post National Weekly Edition*, 25-31 January 1988, 22; see also Greider 1987). Despite this strong recovery from the 1982 recession, by 1986 yearly federal deficits had increased to $238 billion.

Why are these yearly deficits so dangerous? One might argue that debt in itself is not bad if it is wisely invested to yield a return higher than the interest needed to repay it, but Americans were consuming rather than saving with the money they did not pay in taxes. In addition, at least the interest on what one has borrowed must be paid back. Because the federal debt more than tripled from 1982 to 1992, the amount of interest that must be paid to finance the debt grew from just over $53 billion in 1980 to projections of $231 and $251 billion in 1995 and 1996 (*Federal Debt and Interest Costs* 1993, 54). If social security trust funds are excluded from the calculations, the deficit would be some $60 billion higher. Budgetary slights of hand risk giving Americans the idea that, if they turn their backs, this problem will go away (Gist interview 1988). In 1990 the interest on the national debt was almost as large as the annual budget deficit (*Statistical Abstract, 1992*, 315, 317). This is the money that must be collected from taxpayers (or borrowed from willing lenders) and hence cannot be invested by private individuals or spent on government programs for defense, education, the environment, or social services. The massive debts keep interest rates higher than they would otherwise be, as the private sector and government compete for the funds of people who have the money to lend. Whatever the general economic situation, the demand for money,

and thus interest rates, is higher than otherwise would be the case. It also makes the United States more dependent on foreign sources of money in order to pay the interest (*National Journal*, 9 January 1988, 63). Many views exist about the deficit (Penner 1987; Phelps 1987; Rauch 1989). Liberals and left populists fear the deficit puts social programs at risk. They believe that is unacceptable, since, although the number of poor people decreased from 40 million in 1960 to 24 million in 1969, it has been in the range of 32 million–35 million from 1983 to 1990 (Goldsmith and Blakely 1992, 30).

Managing the Deficit   How can government manage the deficit? One option is through monetary policy. The Federal Reserve Board might use a "loose money" policy to fight recessions—in effect, creating lots of money. Such a policy is called **monetization**. By lowering the member banks' reserve requirements, lowering the discount rate, or buying up government securities (U.S. Treasury notes and bonds) on the open market, the Fed can increase the availability of money and credit.

Inflation can be most advantageous to a government or a private citizen with unpaid debts that were incurred when dollars were worth more. As long as debtors are not required to compensate for the inflation by paying higher interest rates, they are able to pay off their debts with increasingly cheaper dollars. This "loosening" of the money supply should drop interest rates because more money is around to borrow. Banks, however, tend to charge a premium on new loans to compensate for the losses they are taking on the old loans and in anticipation of future inflation. This practice works to keep interest rates higher than one might expect. The Federal Reserve System seems committed to holding down inflation; therefore, getting the Fed to agree to a substantial loosening of the money supply was out of the question. Thus the government did not elect to follow the monetary policy alternative because it would have retriggered inflation

CONTROVERSY

National Debt and Annual Deficits: How Would You Start?

During the past twelve years (since 1981) the U.S. national debt has grown from under $1 trillion to about $4 trillion. To put this growth in perspective, look at it this way: it took 190 years for the debt to reach almost $1 trillion; it took only twelve years to quadruple it. Annual deficits, the amount of shortfall in each year's budget, during this period have been around $200 billion each year and increasing. How did this happen?

At the beginning of the 1980s, in a poor economy, government attempted to do three things simultaneously: end high inflation, reduce taxes on corporations and consumers to provide for greater investment and more buying power, and preserve most government programs while increasing spending on defense. The Federal Reserve lowered inflation and raised above-inflation interest rates. Annual deficits added to the total debt. Consequently, borrowing money cost the government more than previously. At the same time, the government became less capable of collecting revenue from taxpayers because of the tax cuts for corporations and individuals initiated by President Ronald Reagan and passed by Congress. Nevertheless, defense spending was raised, and the government kept most existing programs at the insistence of Congress.

There were other reasons that the government lost revenue. High-paying manufacturing jobs were leaving the country. Workers were not able to pay the amount of taxes that they used to pay. Runaway costs of entitlement programs (guaranteeing certain, qualified individuals particular benefits from the government) such as Medicaid, Medicare, and agricultural subsidies, also added

Jeff MacNelly. Reprinted by permission: Tribune Media Services.

to the deficit. What has happened results from a simple truth that families and individuals learn early on: you cannot spend more than you earn, unless the debt incurred represents a good investment. If income decreases, it is not possible to continue spending the same amount. By lowering taxes, raising the rate of interest borrowing money costs after adjustment for inflation, and continuing to fund government programs at previous or higher levels, the U.S. government guaranteed it would end up in trouble.

The trend of having annual deficits of over $200 billion continued under President George Bush. At the end of Bush's term in office the deficit neared $300 billion as the election approached and deficit spending increased during difficult economic times. These annual deficits, highlighted in the 1992 election campaign by Ross Perot, helped

similar to that in the 1970s and kept interest rate levels unreasonably high; indeed the Reagan administration had promised, when elected, to try to reduce both the interest rates and inflation.

A second path that government can take in such circumstances is to try to reduce the deficit as quickly as possible through cutting costs and raising taxes. This is the approach President Clinton followed during his first months in office. These steps require negotiating compromises among different political groups to achieve a voting majority. Such negotiations have met with only limited success even in

Bill Clinton become president. President Clinton, also realizing the need to reduce the annual deficits and the debt, has proposed to narrow the annual shortfall of about $300 billion to about $200 billion by 1997. His plan includes tax increases for the rich, some taxes on social security benefits, and new energy taxes. Spending on defense will be lowered, as will some other programs, but entitlement programs and cost of living adjustments will be protected. Government employees, with smaller raises, will also feel the pinch.

President Clinton was careful with his plan. You are younger and might be bolder. The easiest way to bring spending and revenues into balance would be simply to freeze spending increases until revenues catch up with expenditures. Alternatively, taxes might be increased across the board. However, both these moves would alienate large numbers of voters, and you would suffer if you were an elected leader.

If you are not bold, there still is the need to reduce the budget another $200 billion after President Clinton's actions. Achieving this reduction will be much more difficult than the first reductions were. Even if the annual budget deficit is eliminated, a $4 trillion debt still exists and must be paid off. Since the debt is almost as large as the entire gross national product for a year, reducing the debt could be an even greater challenge.

What would you do to get the U.S. government's finances back in order? Look at the budget in Chapter 10, Table 10.2 and Figure 10.2, especially the percentage of income from each source. How would you make up the difference between what is spent and what is being taken in? Rewrite the budget in accordance with your priorities. Would you continue to have $200–$300 billion annual deficits and leave reductions for the next generation? If so, your children will have a major

obligation and problem. Would you tax more or spend less? If so, think about the problems noted in the fiscal policy sections of this chapter. What taxes would you use and why? Remember a few things about taxes: the poor cannot always afford higher taxes, the rich can move their money around to end up being taxed less, and the middle class votes. Which programs, if any, would you cut? Would you initiate any new programs by shifting money from others? Which of the six perspectives do your decisions tend to support? List the programs that you would not cut under any circumstances. Do you think that your class could reach a compromise that would still save over $200 billion *and* preserve essential programs?

Perhaps you believe, like some economists, that deficits are not that bad because they stimulate economic activity and that borrowing a year's income is not alarming. If so, difficult decisions can be delayed, but for how long?

Unfortunately, the United States government is not some abstract entity. It is us. Citizens of the United States, not just its representatives in the legislative and executive branches of government, must be held accountable for the country's problems. The choices that will have to be made to reduce the deficit are difficult and will prove painful to all groups of Americans one way or another. Even so, they must be made if we are not to end up like a family or business that, because of irresponsible financial decision making, has to declare itself bankrupt. Everyone has some idea of what he or she would do with the budget if given the opportunity. Assume you have the opportunity. What would you do?

Source: Statistical Abstract, 1992, 279, 315; Congressional Quarterly Weekly Report, 10 April 1993, 886; Federal Debt and Interest Costs, May 1993, 11.

recent times due to election year politics and fundamental differences of opinion among conservatives, liberals, libertarians, and populists over defense and social program priorities. Although Gramm-Rudman-Hollings has since been superseded by the 1990 Ominbus Budget Reconciliation Act (see Chapter 10), it achieved

many one-time savings and was the major means of stemming the flow of government red ink through the 1980s (*Fortune*, 7 December 1987, 36; *Where the Money Goes*; 7 December 1991, 392).

A third way of dealing with a growing national debt is to allow people from other countries to finance the debt while a political compromise is being negotiated. This arrangement keeps a lid on inflation and prevents interest rates from creeping too high because the debt is being financed neither by monetizing it (inflationary) nor by using available American money (recessionary). It also releases real national resources for more productive purposes, although whether such resources are invested or utilized for additional consumption is always questionable. It was this policy that the Reagan and Bush administrations pursued, more or less by default, while trying to reach political compromises on the budget crisis with Congress.

The Trade Deficit   Beginning in 1982 the Fed's tight money supply, combined with the U.S. Treasury's willingness to support a strong dollar on foreign markets, began to attract a great deal of foreign investment to the United States. A strong dollar buys more abroad. The foreign individuals who are left holding dollars spent by Americans must find somewhere to spend or invest them in order to make additional money. Since a strong dollar makes American goods cost a great deal, foreigners holding American dollars may choose to buy, instead, high-yielding U.S. government securities—thus financing the federal deficit. Some of the U.S. national debt is being financed by foreign capitalists who feel that investing in U.S. securities, as opposed to buying American goods, is the best way they can invest these dollars (see Prestowitz Jr. 1988, 305–33).

Because of the dollar's buying power, American consumers initially felt only positive effects from the influx of cheap foreign products coming into the American marketplace. Between 1982 and 1985 they also began to travel overseas in record numbers as European vacations became true bargains. But it was not long before the strong dollar, combined with high interest rates, began to hurt the American economy. American steel plants, already un-

able to compete with countries like Japan, began to shut down. The American auto industry watched its share of the American market shrink as Japanese and Korean models flooded the market with inexpensive, high-quality imports. American farmers and exporters were also badly hurt because the stronger dollar made American products less and less competitive (too expensive) in foreign markets.

In 1980, before the dollar's meteoric rise, the United States had experienced a **trade deficit** (the excess of imports over exports) of $24 billion. By 1987 the per-year trade deficit had grown to $152 billion (*Statistical Abstract, 1992*, 796). Once the Reagan administration made a decision to weaken the dollar in 1985, excess American dollars left overseas flowed back into the United States at an even more rapid rate in the form of stock market investments, American industry and real estate purchases, and further financing of the growing federal debt. Some would argue that the United States was being purchased by the dollars that Americans had spent on foreign products because these same dollars were being used by foreign interests to purchase American real estate and businesses. The strong value of the dollar also exacerbated shifts within the American work force from higher- to lower-paying jobs, as some major industries shrank, unable to compete against cheaper imports in domestic markets.

It is important to note that the Reagan strategy did not produce only negative consequences. The United States had fallen out of the number one spot of worker productivity in the late 1970s. Although American businesses screamed loud and hard about the inequity of the dollar and argued for protection from "unfair" foreign competition, they also were forced to cut back on unproductive facilities, keep wage increases to minimal levels, and modernize outmoded facilities in an effort to meet the unprecedented levels of foreign competition that increased productivity (Feldstein 1988, 322–28).

Signe Wilkinson. Courtesy Cartoonists & Writers Syndicate.

By 1985 it was clear to the Reagan White House that the strong dollar could no longer be maintained. The issue of competitiveness and lost jobs was becoming a political hot potato. It was also causing a decline in investor confidence, as an imbalance of payments in international trade totaling nearly $357 billion (1981–85) had now been added to the internal deficit (*Business Week*, 16 November 1987, 160); *Statistical Abstract, 1992*, 796). Some argued for **protectionism**, policies that would protect American business by limiting foreign competition. Protectionists led by Richard Gephardt, a liberal Democrat from Missouri, were growing stronger and more emphatic in their demands for **tariff barriers**, taxes on imported goods (see Chapter 11). Many Democrats and even some Republicans began to argue that the only way the trade deficit could be dealt with was through tariff or nontariff (see Chapter 11) barriers or **economic sanctions** (limits on trade such as boycotts or embargoes) against foreign governments, which they accused of subsidizing the exports of their country's businesses in order to keep the prices of their goods sold in the United States artificially low (*Congressional Quarterly Almanac, 1988*, 209–22). The stage

was set for the dramatic weakening of the dollar that took place as conscious policy during the last three and one-half years of the Reagan administration (*Congressional Quarterly Weekly Report*, 22 February 1986, 460–64; *Statistical Abstract, 1990*, 804).

American exports had to be stimulated in order to erase the trade deficit. Between 1982 and 1987, a $400 billion positive balance in assets possessed by Americans overseas had become a $600 billion debt owed to creditors overseas. The United States has become a **debtor nation**, with its **internal debt** (money owed to Americans) and **external debt** (money owed to foreigners) increasing yearly. Between 1985 and 1987 the Reagan administration encouraged the dollar's fall. During this time the dollar declined 50 percent against other major foreign currencies. With the cost of foreign goods some 50 percent higher, it was anticipated that Americans would purchase fewer foreign goods and foreigners would purchase more American exports (*Business Week*, 16 November 1987, 160–61; *Congressional Quarterly Weekly Report*, 22 February 1986, 460–64; *Statistical Abstract, 1990*, 804; see also Feldstein 1988, 322–28).

Such changes in monetary policy take time to trigger results. Gradually, by the middle of 1989, three and one-half years after the shift in policy on the dollar, the massive trade deficit began to shrink. Export of American manufactured goods rose 94 percent from 1985 to 1991, while imports increased in this period by only 44 percent (*Information Please Almanac, 1993*, 71). Was this intentional deflation of the dollar a partial solution to the fiscal policy problems triggered by the Reagan tax cuts and budget deficits? Only for so long as foreign investment in government securities and the stock market remained high, attracted by interest rates on U.S. government securities and good investment opportunities in the stock market. A stock market crash was a possibility if the interest rates continued to slide lower and American stocks continued to be overpriced in terms of earnings being made by the companies they represent.

The shrinkage of high-paying jobs that started with the strong dollar in the 1980s continued during the early 1990s. Spurred by the need to be competitive at the international level, major industries adopted new technologies and sought production opportunities abroad that permitted them to reduce their work forces.

By 1992, the United States again had a dominant lead in labor force productivity. It has the highest per capita and total gross domestic product in the world. It is ranked second on the world competitiveness scoreboard compiled by the Institute for Management Development, which takes into account 330 criteria including research and development spending, capital formation, work force attitudes, long-term management orientation, and economic trends to rank countries on their ability to compete in international markets (*Fortune*, 26 July 1993, 96). This achievement, however, has been a two-edged sword, for heightened productivity has been achieved by reducing the work force. Many of those formerly employed have been unable to find work or forced to take lower-paying jobs in service industries. They buy less, and thus American industry has suffered. As long as American goods could be exported overseas, heightened productivity could prove positive for the country as a whole, although not for some Americans. It would also make American prosperity more dependent than ever on the prosperity of the rest of the industrialized world (Barlett and Steele 1992).

The Recession of 1990–91   The recession that began in 1990 followed the longest peacetime economic growth in the history of the United States. Some felt that the recession was caused by economic policies in the 1980s. Others felt that the recession was an inevitable downturn in the economic cycle. The recession was marked by not only blue-collar layoffs but also white-collar, middle-management layoffs, many the result of private industry's efforts to achieve greater efficiency. IBM, a bastion of stability, laid off workers for the first time in its history. The strongly competitive global economy gave big business an impetus to reduce costs by eliminating white-collar middle management. Computer technology has made such reductions easier than previously. Once one company reduces costs, others have no choice but to follow.

The recession technically ended in 1991 (Schnorbus and Bergman 1992, 1), but at this writing the recovery is exceedingly slow in comparison to past recessions. Many workers who were laid off have not been rehired. Without jobs, these workers are spending less on goods and services. Higher unemployment and reduced consumption lengthen the recovery time.

The current unemployment situation is complex. In the past, the largest burden of unemployment was on blue-collar workers, since their jobs depended on demand; most white-collar workers continued to be needed during slow times. But unemployment actually rose from 6.7 percent in 1991 during the recession (*Statistical Abstract, 1992*, 399) to 7.4 percent in 1992 following the recession (*Congressional Quarterly Weekly Report*, 27 February 1993, 465). These figures reflect, in addition to the streamlining already noted, the cutbacks in defense industries that followed the end of the cold war.

The Clinton Dilemma

Bill Clinton is like the man who wanted to play poker so much that he picked up a losing hand in a poker game for the player who had to leave for home earlier than anticipated. He has been dealt an unenviable set of economic cards. He inherited a massive national debt, a large trade deficit, and an economy that is growing slowly.

It is in this context that Clinton's early effort to simultaneously stimulate the economy and reduce deficits must be understood. He believes that more people must be given jobs because higher rates of unemployment mean lower purchasing power, which slows economic growth. He also believes that American productivity and competitiveness in the future will be based on the nation's capacity to keep modernizing or repairing its immense infrastructure of roads and high-tech lines of communication. Consequently he first attempted to pass a bill that would have cost more in the form of spending and taxes but put unemployed American workers back to work and improved the country's transportation and communications network. Lacking the votes in Congress to pass such legislation in 1993, he was forced to withdraw this portion of his economic plan. He also would like to institute an **industrial policy** to give the government a greater role in promoting economic growth. The nation's number one economic competitor, Japan, currently has an industrial policy that appears to work well (see Controversy).

The deficit issue has always been important

Don Wright. Courtesy *The Palm Beach Post*.

CONTROVERSY

Is Japan's Economy a Model for the United States?

Some economists proclaim Japan to be the new number one in the world economy. Others predict a coming Japanese collapse, with serious consequences for many countries, including the United States. How does the economy of the leading competitor of the United States work? Is it a model for the United States to follow or avoid?

The part of the Japanese economy most Americans recognize are the large corporations whose names appear on products for sale all over the United States—Honda, Toyota, Sony, and Mitsubishi. These firms are marvels of efficiency. Chrysler Corporation has sent researchers to Honda in Japan to learn how to produce cars more efficiently. Yet most Japanese work in small, family-owned businesses that are protected by the government from the rigors of competition. For example, department stores are illegal in most of the country, so Japanese must do their shopping in millions of tiny shops. Owners of such shops usually agree to sell the goods of only one or two Japanese companies, and any new company entering the market must build its own network of stores. Hence, American and other foreign companies find it difficult to penetrate the Japanese market, while the Japanese can readily sell their goods in the United States. This policy of the Japanese government is one reason that approximately two-thirds of the U.S. trade deficit of $84.3 billion is with Japan.

The Japanese Ministry of International Trade and Industry (MITI) works more closely with private business than does any agency in the U.S. government. While American businesspeople can go to jail for cooperating to fix prices and divide up markets, MITI actually encourages cooperation between competitors through a process called "administrative guidance." Working together, Japanese companies can often outdo American and other competitors in research and development of new products. At the same time, they are free to disregard MITI's advice if they choose. For example, in the 1960s MITI, seeking to protect

Ed Stein. Reprinted with permission of *The Rocky Mountain News.*

to Clinton, but challenges from Ross Perot and Republicans regarding the need to focus on spending cuts have forced him to pay attention to an election promise to reduce the annual deficit by half during his first year in office through some combination of spending cuts and tax increases. Once in office, he decided that the budget deficit could not be cut in half during his first year and promised to do so by

1998. He also promised that the tax increases would fall on the wealthiest Americans, then revised this promise by planning to increase taxes on the middle class while still placing the bulk of the tax burden on the wealthy. To achieve narrow margins of victory in the House and the Senate, Clinton had to sacrifice certain portions of his own tax plan and accept more cuts in Medicare than he might have

Toyota and Nissan, tried to discourage Honda from producing automobiles, but Honda went ahead and has been highly successful.

The Japanese people have contributed to their nation's economic success by saving prodigiously. On the average, Japanese save 15 percent of their income, while Americans save only 4 percent. As a nation, Japan now saves more total than the United States, which has twice as many people. Japanese young people, prodded by ambitious parents, put their studies ahead of fun, often attending private "cram" schools in the evening and on weekends in addition to public school. Japanese high school graduates often outscore American college graduates on standardized tests, and they provide Japanese industry with a steady supply of skilled workers.

Should the United States try to be more like Japan? If economic growth is the goal, the answer may be yes. Japan's economy has grown at an average rate of around 4 percent for the last twenty years, compared to 2.5 percent for the United States. If this trend continues, Japan will someday outproduce the United States with only half the population. Unemployment in Japan rarely goes above 3 percent, even in recessions, and problems like homelessness and drug addiction are practically unknown.

On the other hand, restrictions on competition have made the cost of living in Japan twice as high as in the United States, while wages are now about the same. Due to restrictions on food imports, apples cost $5 apiece, and a single melon can cost as much as a truckload would outside Japan. Even products made in Japan cost an average of 20 percent more there than in the United States. The average Japanese home is less than half the size of the average American home. Japan could well run into competitive pressures from the world economy that would require even more sacrifice.

Under a system known as "lifetime employment," workers in large companies are protected against layoffs but are also effectively denied the right to leave the company, since no other employer would hire such a "disloyal" worker. Women, even if they are college graduates, are largely restricted to menial jobs as "office ladies," pouring tea for their male superiors.

Admirers of the Japanese way contend that the United States must adopt at least some of Japan's policies or be left behind in the economic race. Detractors argue that to do so would actually reduce the American standard of living and trample cherished American values like free competition and gender equality. They would rather pressure Japan to be more like the United States by saving less, consuming more, and opening its markets. Admirers question why the Japanese should do so, when their economy is doing so well. The United States, they say, needs to begin stressing cooperation over competition, saving over spending, and group interest over individual rights. What do you think?

Source: Reading 1992; Prestowitz 1988; Huntington 1988–89, 76–96; Krugman 1992, 115–32; *Washington Post National Weekly Edition,* 5–11 July 1993, 16; *New York Times,* 19 February 1993, D2.

---

wished. He did, however, keep his promise to place the bulk of the tax increases on the wealthy. His total package of spending reductions and tax increases totals more than $500 billion and is projected to reduce the deficit by half by 1998.

Clinton has also inherited a health care system burdened by high costs. By reforming the system, he hopes to cut health care costs to levels similar to those of the United States' competitors. First Lady Hillary Rodham Clinton headed a special task force that prepared proposals for health-care reform.

Clinton will continue to press for passage of legislation he feels will rebuild and revitalize the nation's economy. Supporters have hailed the president's proposals as "a pervasive effort across the federal government" (*Washington*

Post National Weekly Edition, 1–7 March 1993, 29). Not all share the president's vision, however. The response of conservatives on Capitol Hill has been critical, with the Republicans attacking the spending proposals as wasteful. Others have been more blunt. According to Herbert Stein, who headed the Council of Economic Advisers in the Nixon administration, "It sounds to me like a bunch of kids have got loose in Toys R US and they want one of everything" (*Washington Post National Weekly Edition*, 1–7 March 1993, 21). Critics like Stein emphasize the importance of letting the free enterprise system work on its own.

It is clear that Clinton's program will continue to face stiff competition from Republicans in Congress who would prefer to cut spending than use government programs for economic stimulation (*USA Today*, 6 July 1993, A5, A8). In addition, critics have charged that the wealthy will avoid the higher taxes by earning less, moving their money into tax shelters, or finding other loopholes. Some of these critics even predict that the new taxes will actually result in decreased revenue, though the Clinton administration is convinced revenue will increase (*Vail Daily*, 19 July 1993, 15).

One longtime observer of the economy, Brian Berry, suggests that Republicans usually do well following difficulties such as the stagflation of the Carter years and Democrats usually do well following difficulties such as the recession during Bush's term (Berry et al. 1992, 2–15; see also Berry 1991). President Clinton may lead the United States in important new directions during his first term as he works toward an industrial policy to promote the economy, renovating the infrastructure, and hiring workers who lost their jobs during the recession while simultaneously trying to reduce the massive national debt. In the 1992 election, the American people looked for a leader who could bring prosperity. Most observers believe that the economy was the crucial issue in the election, and the American people hope Clinton will deliver.

The 1990s: Economics and You

How will economics affect you in the 1990s? Whether you become prosperous, just survive, or go broke, even what you do for a living may be the direct result of decisions on economic policy made by your country or other countries. Economic policies always benefit some groups more than others.

Looking for a Job   The national economic policy, influenced by many major factors, greatly affects the job market. An aspect of the economy that has little effect on one sector might mean disaster to another. For example, a weak dollar makes American farm products more competitive in global markets, benefiting farmers. But consumers benefit from a strong dollar when they buy foreign goods, because the buying power of the dollar is much higher. The same consumer might find an American car more attractive with a weak dollar, but lack of foreign competition could hurt American industry in the long run. The U.S. economy is influenced by the economies and policies of other nations in several ways.

As the U.S. share of the world's GNP gradually contracts due to considerations discussed earlier in this chapter, the American work force will have to become more mobile. Employers are increasingly willing to reach across national borders to find the skills they need, and the greatest relocations will involve young, well-educated workers like yourselves who will flock to cities in the developed world.

Several factors are creating an international work force. First, the world is now a smaller place. Jet airplanes have only recently started to make their greatest impact. Between 1960 and 1988, for example, the real cost of international travel dropped nearly 60 percent. During this same period, the numbers of foreigners in this country on business increased 2,800 percent. Second, economic policy is becoming more international. Sure to accelerate this trend is the North American Free Trade

Agreement (NAFTA), signed by President Bush and supported by President Clinton (see Controversy in Chapter 11). If implemented, NAFTA will allow products and materials to cross the borders of Mexico, Canada, and the United States without being subject to tariffs. Third, as the physical barriers to transporting products decrease, information barriers have all but disappeared. Improvements in computer technology have moved along at lightning speed, and networks of supercomputers tie world business, financial, and labor markets together. National competition is being replaced by international interdependence.

Yet this growing interdependence in the international job market has had negative effects on certain employment sectors in the United States. As you begin your job search, it will be important to note the changes that have occurred and are occurring. In 1950, manufacturing jobs accounted for nearly 40 percent of all private industry employment, but by 1990, that percentage had been cut nearly in half (Fabricant and Burghardt 1992, 7). In contrast, the service sector grew from 17.5 percent in 1950 to 37.1 percent in 1990. While the net number of jobs has increased, a more critical evaluation points to a major shift in the job market. A service job pays about $12,500 on the average, slightly more than one-half that of a manufacturing job. Thus, those who lack the skills to be competitive in the job market will discover that the jobs they find may not pay nearly as much as they did in the previous decades (Fabricant and Burghardt 1992, 7). Inflation-adjusted hourly wages of a factory worker in private employment from 1947 through 1973 increased more than 70 percent. From 1973 through 1987, however, real hourly wages fell 5 percent. There is evidence that the trend toward lower wages will continue (Goldsmith and Blakely 1992, 37).

While manufacturing has suffered a steady decline throughout the last four decades, recent trends in corporations have hurt white-collar workers as well. Prominent firms experiencing financial difficulties, such as General Motors and IBM, have laid off thousands of middle managers in efforts to streamline. Rising health care costs have contributed to further white-collar layoffs (Schnorbus and Bergman 1993, 3). White-collar workers now account for 40 percent of the total unemployed, a higher percentage than in the recessions of 1975 and 1982. The vulnerability of white-collar jobs, once viewed as secure employment, has contributed to a lingering lack in consumer confidence that started with the 1990–91 recession (Kosters 1992, 20–23).

All is not gloom and doom, however. If you have the skills to be competitive and possess the drive to work, you can find ample opportunity in the United States of the 1990s. The Bureau of Labor Statistics points to computer technology and health care as the fastest growing job sectors into the next century. The number of computer systems analysts and scientists is expected to increase by nearly 80 percent, leading in percentage growth. Demand for managers, nurses, and home health providers is expected to increase with the reform of the health care system. Overall, the bureau predicts that between 1991 and 2005, 23.3 million new jobs will be created, a total increase of more than one-fifth (*Fortune*, 12 July 1993, 52).

Responding to the changing nature of the U.S. work force, the Clinton administration began reshaping relations between government and the private sector. Clinton has promised $17 billion in increased spending for civilian research and development and intends for the Commerce Department to spearhead the high-tech revival (Beltz 1993, 29). These new emphases from government could affect your job prospects.

If you know a foreign language, are in the fields of computer technology, health, or engineering, and are using your college education as a chance to prepare yourself for life in the multicultural United States, there will be plenty of options for your future. The authors believe that there is also a good future for well-prepared students in political science. A person who understands political science is skillful at analyzing overall trends and opinions. Individual initiative will continue to be important, but college graduates will have an obvious advantage when entering the work force (*Fortune*, 26 July 1993, 96). It is likely that the rapid changes now taking place in the global economy will continue at an accelerated pace. The work force will need to adjust to such changes, and college graduates have an advantage in a world of such rapid change, where a high school diploma means less and less.

Regional location will also influence your job prospects. In recent decades, decaying industrial complexes in the Midwest and Northeast combined with high business taxes and high unionized labor salaries in those areas to force many businesses to relocate, either elsewhere in the United States, usually the South or Southwest (see Chapter 3), or abroad. Relatively speaking, the South continues to do well today. Figure 12.1 suggests that in March 1992, states in the Southeast, with the exception of Mississippi, Alabama, and Florida, continued

to have unemployment levels well below the national average of 7.3 percent. Agricultural states in the central United States, like Iowa, Nebraska, and the Dakotas, have also begun to attract industry. These states are also among those with the lowest unemployment rates of the fifty states (*Where to Live and Look for Jobs* 1992, 11). Conversely, wages in the Northeast and Midwest continued to fall through the 1980s and 1990s, and so did well-paying jobs. Young workers in jobs in industrial mill towns of Massachusetts, Illinois, or Michigan were insecure during much of the past decade. As of March 1992, job prospects in all three of these states remained worse than in most southeastern states.

International competition may be felt more keenly in some sections of the country than others. In the 1970s and early 1980s the heightened efficiency and productivity of Japanese industry in combination with supportive efforts of Japanese government gradually undercut the ability of the United States to compete with Japan in producing cars and steel. Many autoworkers and steelworkers in the Northeast and Midwest, both blue-collar and white-

Chip Bok. By permission of artist and Creators Syndicate.

Figure 12.1 Unemployment Rates by State, March 1992 (seasonally adjusted)

(U.S. average = 7.3 percent)

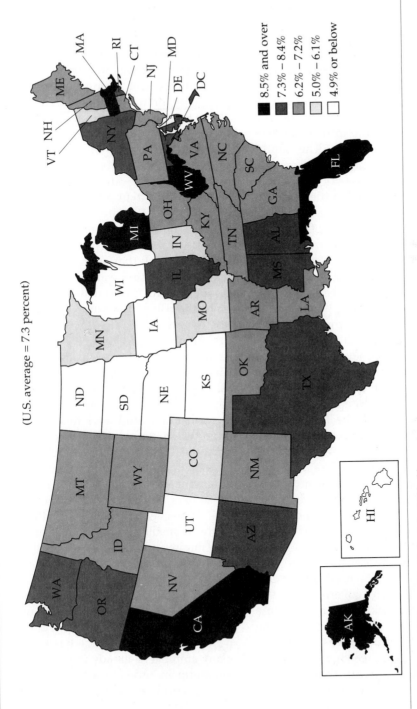

8.5% and over
7.3% – 8.4%
6.2% – 7.2%
5.0% – 6.1%
4.9% or below

Source: Where To Live and Look for Jobs 1992, 11.

collar, were displaced by this international economic competition. One ad in a Michigan newspaper during this period of high unemployment in the auto industry read: "Will the last person to leave Michigan please turn out the lights?" (Steingraber 1987, 758–62; see also Weidenbaum 1987, 46–54).

On the other hand, jobs can be affected by totally arbitrary decisions made outside the United States that have little to do with economic efficiency or productivity. The Southwest absorbed many Michigan workers because it was experiencing an energy boom due to the high price of foreign oil in the 1970s. In a sense this region was prospering from a situation that was hurting the rest of the U.S. economy. The Organization of Petroleum Exporting Countries (OPEC) had set an artificially high price for oil. Its policies made drilling the harder-to-get-at American oil economically more feasible and triggered a boom in the American Southwest. When the oil bubble burst in the early 1980s, reducing international oil prices to more realistic levels, these same Michigan workers who had moved to the Southwest found themselves out of jobs again because of the lack of competitiveness of American crude oil against the lower OPEC prices. Texas has still not recovered fully from the oil shocks of the early 1980s. More recently the West Coast has become a less desirable area to look for good jobs, due to the growth of competition from Mexico and adjoining states and reductions in defense-related industries (*Where to Live and Look for Jobs* 1992, 1, 5–9, 11).

Getting Paid   Over the last few years your wages have also been influenced by government economic policy. The government sets a **minimum wage** that employers in most sectors of the economy are required to pay. In the 1950s, before the dramatic increase in the required minimum wage, teenage unemployment was not all that high. In the mid-1950s the minimum wage began to increase rapidly, from 75¢ to nearly $3.35 an hour by 1981, and the number and type of jobs covered by the minimum wage expanded as well (*Statistical Abstract, 1992*, 415). All teenage unemployment began to rise, but black teenage unemployment rose to nearly 50 percent. High unemployment was in part explained by the large numbers of young people seeking employment for the first time. These were the "baby boomers," born in the post–World War II baby boom.

Liberal advocates of a higher minimum wage argue that it is beneficial to young workers and all Americans. Figures such as those cited in regard to high teenage unemployment of the early 1970s are used by conservatives and libertarians to argue that the costs and benefits of raising the minimum wage for the poor are not all that clear. Employers may attempt to do with fewer employees in order to compensate for the increase in salaries brought on by the rising minimum wage. The poor and less educated are often the last hired and the first fired (Banfield 1974, 107–14).

In 1989, in part due to the erosion in the value of the dollar, Congress raised the minimum wage for the first time in nearly a decade. During the 1992 campaign, Bill Clinton indicated that he would work to see that the minimum wage would rise to keep pace with inflation (Clinton and Gore 1992, 126). Business owners continue to argue that a higher minimum wage will lead to higher prices for consumers and more unemployment. This time, however, the adverse effect on jobs might be smaller for several reasons. First, the 1989 minimum wage law exempted some small businesses from having to raise wages. In addition, the number of young people entering the labor market is currently on the decline. Finally, because of the shrinking numbers of younger laborers and the length of time during which the minimum wage has not increased, many employers already pay wages above the minimum in order to attract young workers (Devine and Wright 1990, 50–54; *Business Week*, 19 October 1987, 146; see also *Congressional*

saw Clinton's economic proposals as a confirmation of their worst fears. By relying upon higher taxes on the "rich" to balance the budget, conservatives say, Clinton was engaging in class warfare and penalizing the efforts of the country's most hard-working and productive citizens. They agreed that the deficit needed to be cut but urged that reductions be accomplished primarily, or if possible exclusively, with spending cuts.

While conservatives have faith in the market economy, they warn Americans that people do not live by bread alone. They see economic prosperity as a product of values as much as correct policies. Societies like present-day Japan (see Controversy in this chapter) and the United States in the nineteenth century, which encourage people to value hard work and take pride in what they do, prosper; those without a strong work ethic fail. If traditional values (meaning, in the United

States, Judeo-Christian values) no longer hold the loyalty of the people, economic decline is sure to follow, even in a market system. Charles Colson and Jack Eckerd, two evangelical Christian conservatives, express the conservative view this way: "Since the beginning of our nation, Americans have understood these truths to be self-evident—that thrift, industry, diligence, and perseverance are all qualities to be cultivated and respected in society. It's called the work ethic, and these are the American ideals that set us apart for centuries" (Colson and Eckerd 1991, 26). Colson and Eckerd believe that the work ethic in the United States is derived from religious beliefs. They reason that the United States has lost the work ethic that it once had and that while "we can recover [it] . . . first we have to understand what it is, where it came from, and how we lost it" (Colson and Eckerd 1991, 27).

Liberal

While libertarians generally promote a hands-off policy in regard to government intervention in economic affairs and conservatives emphasize the need for government intervention only as a means of obtaining a strong and stable economy for the country as a whole (within a capitalist framework), liberals are more likely to support interventionist forms of government policy aimed at assuring equal opportunities for all individuals and direct and indirect assistance to the less fortunate. Clinton is more fiscally conservative in some areas than most liberals would like, but they still prefer him for the highest office than any likely Republican candidate. They might have hoped that he would have fought harder for his energy tax and increases in social spending, but they strongly supported his attempt to concentrate tax increases on the wealthy. The liberal's solution to the budget deficit is to cut back on defense spending and increase taxes on corporations and on the wealthy. Liberals also argue that reducing the deficit too quickly will slow the already anemic economic growth by reducing the spending power of the American consumer.

Liberals express greater concern for those who have been born into poverty or have been unable

to win in the economic game. Therefore liberals have favored economic policies designed to create jobs and reduce the rate of unemployment, often at the expense of balanced budgets (Rothenberg 1984, 160–72). For example, liberals were the strongest supporters of Clinton's failed economic stimulus package early in 1993. Unemployment is seen as demeaning to the individuals who lose their jobs and as a waste of productive resources. While libertarians and conservatives would not disagree with achieving equal opportunity or the alleviation of large-scale homelessness or unemployment, liberals have been more willing to favor government action in the creation of welfare programs like social security, Medicare, Medicaid, unemployment insurance, federal deposit insurance, and public housing. In order for such benefits to be provided to the poor, the less fortunate, the old, and the sick, a redistribution of resources is sometimes necessary. Based on the belief that "the poor are needier than the rich," liberals have generally supported progressive taxation.

While liberals continue to have these concerns, they are not as inclined to raise taxes and to target and initiate government-run programs as they have been in the past. Prior to the Reagan years, liberals tended to favor economic policies based on Keynesian theory, including deficit spending and tax cuts. The current trade and budget deficits have attracted the attention of liberals and caused a change in the methods they see necessary to achieve their goals. It is safe to assume that liberals today see a dire need to reduce the trade and budget imbalances but do not agree on the necessary means. Most liberals, like most conservatives, favor some sort of government-invoked protection of U.S. industries from foreign competition to stimulate production and create jobs. They differ from conservatives by calling for cuts in defense spending and increases in taxes. Liberals also are more willing to come down on the side of loosening the money supply, lowering interest rates, and risking 1 or 2 percentage points more inflation than are libertarians or conservatives.

Sound economic policy is not often politically acceptable. The liberal economist Alan S. Blinder contends that most liberal politicians are "soft-hearted" or compassionate, which is good, but that their policies are often "soft-headed" in allocating money to programs while failing to count the total cost or recognize all side effects. Liberal support of rent controls, for example, ignores the destructive effects controls have on housing. But some libertarians and conservatives are "hard-hearted" and "soft-headed." Blinder claims Reagan betrayed his math teachers, but not his political supporters, when he promised to cut taxes, raise defense spending, and shrink the budget deficit all at the same time. Blinder calls on people of all political viewpoints to make economic policies more "hard-headed" by paying attention to the facts, respecting efficiency, thinking logically rather than wishfully, and obeying economic laws. The best economic policy would also be "soft-hearted." New liberals, like Blinder, believe that public policymakers from all perspectives "must start thinking with [their] minds and feeling with [their] hearts, rather than the other way around" (Blinder 1987, 15, 23).

Libertarian

In the early twentieth century, any form of active government management of the economy was an abomination to libertarians. Recalling the destructive effects of meddlesome regulations in precapitalist England as described by Adam Smith, they insisted that government confine itself to maintaining a stable framework of laws and an economic infrastructure, leaving the direction of the economy, including production, wages, and pricing decisions, to market forces. To be sure, libertarians did not always behave in a manner consistent with their beliefs; some libertarians, along with conservative allies, supported protective tariffs restricting foreign goods in competition with American goods and subsidies to certain industries like railroads. Economic management at the macroeconomic level, however, was held to be both harmful and unnecessary.

Such classic libertarian perspectives can be found today, along with more moderate libertarian views. Economic libertarianism is expressed in this pure form by spokespersons from the Libertarian party (see Chapter 4). Problems that have faced the American economy in the twentieth century are always framed in terms of mistakes made by the federal government's macromanagement (Bergland 1984, 160–72).

Libertarians often start from the works of their intellectual godfather, the Austrian economist Ludwig von Mises. In *A Critique of Interventionism*, von Mises demonstrated the impossibility of economic calculation in planned economies. He argued that a planned economy would do nothing but flounder continuously because without a free market for goods and services there was no market-pricing mechanism to tell producers and entrepreneurs what consumers desired most (von Mises 1977, 15–35).

For example, in a capitalist economy, if many people want VCRs, we will learn a VCR's true worth by the price they are willing and able to pay. In the early 1970s, seeing the prices people were willing to pay for good VCRs, many companies began to produce them. As large quantities of VCRs became available, the companies producing them were forced to adjust prices downward. As demand for VCRs has leveled, profits have shrunk and total production has slowed. The market-pricing mechanism has controlled the industry. Von Mises argued that planned economies fail because they do not pay attention to the level of consumer demand. Thus production and pricing bear little relationship to the actual need for or worth of a given product.

Libertarians have also disagreed with the government's methods of controlling the money supply. They point to von Mises's accurate prediction of the initial contraction that brought on the Great Depression of the 1930s. In the 1920s von Mises argued that the Federal Reserve was allowing unrealistically large amounts of money to circulate in the economy (a practical equivalent to legalized counterfeiting) and that the artificial boomlet of the period would automatically lead to overexpansion of facilities and production and a subsequent economic bust. In the Great Depression, the free market did not fail, they reason; it just was not allowed to work. The Libertarian party advocates a return to the gold standard as a basis for U.S. currency because it would keep politicians from interfering with the value of the people's money. A less drastic alternative favored by moderate libertarians calls for tighter economic controls on the Federal Reserve Board (Friedman and Friedman 1980, 70–90).

In the area of fiscal policy, libertarians also take a hands-off view. Their guideline is that any control of individual economic choices leads to a shrinking of the economic pie. Whether it is government's decision to tax (all taxes), protect domestic industries (protective tariffs), bail out sick companies (subsidies), stabilize prices (wage and price controls), or raise wages (minimum wage laws), the net result will always be less productivity and growth for the economy as a whole (Bergland 1984, 19–20). Libertarians also oppose monetary policy and argue that decisions made by the Fed hurt the economy more often than they help.

Libertarians view deficits as resulting from too much government spending. Generally, they favor contracting the sphere of government influence in as many areas of economic life as possible as the most productive means to achieve the deficit reduction. Taxes are an abhorrence to libertarians. They view Clinton as a more moderate liberal and are in sympathy with some of his views on social issues, but they side with conservatives when it comes to his views on the value of industrial policy. Further, Clinton's decision to tax the wealthy segment of society will not increase revenue, say libertarians, because the wealthy will find ways to shield their money from taxes.

Another example cited by libertarians as demonstrating the unintended consequences of government interference is the minimum wage. The summer 1991 minimum wage was $4.25 per hour, and it was a crime for two people to agree that one will work for the other for less than that amount, unless the employee receives a gratuity from the general public on top of the hourly wage, as is the case for waiters and waitresses, among others. The intention of the minimum wage is to prevent young or weak (in terms of bargaining power) wage earners from being taken advantage of by unscrupulous employers. The effect is, according to libertarians, to make unemployable the youngest or least-skilled members of the work force because employers hesitate to pay totally unskilled workers that much money, although they might be willing to pay them less during training. The net result of a minimum wage is fewer hands at work, more unemployment, and lowered productivity (Bergland 1984, 17–18).

Libertarians continually point to the great differences in economic development between controlled and free societies. Hong Kong, a free city in which the British have imposed minimal controls, is cited as a prime example of how many people can be supported on limited amounts of land when market choices have not been limited by government caprice. The opposite result is clearly true of the planned segments of China's economy.

Libertarians' first priority is the reduction of the

total governmental take from the private economy. After that, they would free most forms of economic activity from the prospect of government interference through specific limits on state and local governments. Next they would provide for taxation at a flat rather than a progressive rate and a consistent monetary policy on the part of the Federal Reserve that would allow for rational planning by businesspeople and protect against inflation (Friedman and Friedman 1980, 298–310, app. B). Libertarians sometimes refer to themselves as "market liberals" to distinguish them from conservatives, who are willing to accept somewhat more government intervention in the economy.

Populist

"God hates monopoly," declared a populist leader of the 1890s, "and so do we, and heartily endorse his condemnation of it" (Tedford 1967, 259). If there is a common thread running through populist writings on economic issues, it is fear and distrust of concentrated economic power. Both brands of populism share it, but apply it in different ways.

Right populism may be described as "Jacksonian" in its economic aspects. A self-made man, Andrew Jackson believed that the common folk could hold their own in economic competition if no one was granted special privileges by the government. Hence he destroyed the Second Bank of the United States, a private bank that had been favored by the government, and sought to open up government lands for sale directly to small farmers instead of speculators (Hofstadter 1974, 56–85). Acknowledging that "equality of talents, of education, or of wealth cannot be produced," he went on to contend:

> When the laws undertake to add to these natural and just advantages artificial distinctions and exclusive privileges, to make the rich richer and the potent more powerful, the humble members of society—the farmers, mechanics and laborers—who have neither the time nor the means of securing like favors to themselves, have a right to complain of the injustice of their Government (quoted in Hofstadter 1974, 77–78).

Like Jackson, right populists today believe in the free enterprise system, but they criticize the way its rules have been rewritten to favor dominant elites. Richard Viguerie, a right populist organizer, warned in 1981 that "big business has become far too cozy with big government" and "comfortable with red tape, regulations, bureaucracy—these things freeze the status quo, impede newcomers and hold down competition" (Viguerie 1981, 107). Viguerie went on to condemn government bailouts of failing corporations like Lockheed and Chrysler, call for tough restrictions on business trading with the Soviet Union, and denounce special tax loopholes for corporations (Viguerie 1981, 116–17, 149). During his years in Congress Jack Kemp, later George Bush's secretary of housing and urban development and thought to be a potential candidate for president in 1996, was a longtime advocate of eliminating special tax preferences and lowering tax rates to ensure a "level playing field" in the economy before this principle was incorporated into a 1986 tax bill (Kemp 1979, 49–76). In 1984 right populist groups opposed U.S. contributions to the International Monetary Fund, contending that such contributions only went to bail out big banks that had made bad loans to Third World countries instead of lending to Americans. In 1992 Ross Perot argued that the proposed free trade agreement with Mexico was another scheme to benefit powerful industries. If implemented, it would produce a "giant sucking sound," for American companies would rush to move plants to Mexico to take advantage of cheaper labor.

Left populists agree with the traditionalist attacks on special privilege but carry them further. They regard the very existence of large private corporations, with or without unfair government assistance, as a major threat to economic freedom and prosperity. Without any government subsidies at all, large firms still can and have hired workers to work under unsafe conditions, moved plants abroad in search of cheaper labor leaving Americans unemployed, invested profits in mergers and takeovers instead of in job-creating activities, and disregarded the rights of individuals and local communities (Boyte, Booth, and Max 1986, 176–87). Worse, say left populists, selfish corporate values tend to infect the general culture, producing a "radical individualism and dog-eat-dog morality" that subverts the sense of community required for effective democracy (quoted in Boyte, Booth, and Max 1986, 186; see also Pollack 1962, 467–534). Left populists do not believe such problems can be addressed simply by abolishing corporate privileges; rather, the government must actively intervene in the economy to break corporate power over the lives of citizens.

Left populist strategies for curbing corporations have varied with the times but consistently been more radical than those advanced by liberals. Late nineteenth- and early twentieth-century populists advocated government ownership of some industries, such as railroads and banks, not as a step toward socialism but as protection for small farmers and businessmen against exploitation. North Dakota, a state not noted for recent radicalism, still has a state-owned bank and state-owned grain mills dating from the heyday of the populist Nonpartisan League (Morlan 1955).

What measures do left populists favor today to curb business power? Breaking up large firms through antitrust action is a popular idea; during the energy crisis of the 1970s, left populists called for the dissolution of the major oil companies into smaller and, they hoped, more competitive firms. When corporations cannot be broken up, left populists want them subjected to much greater control by workers and local communities as well as the government. Local communities and union pension funds might, for example, buy stock in corporations instead of simply extending tax breaks and other favors, thus gaining a role in corporate decision making in return for their money (Boyte, Booth, and Max 1986, 108, 181; see also Harris 1973, 55–143). These suggestions are considerably more radical than those advanced by most liberals, but retain the capitalist system.

Left populists also differ from populists of the right in favoring government regulation to protect small entrepreneurs from competition. Senator

"YOU HAD A VERY PROFITABLE YEAR. LET'S SEE—AFTER SPECIAL TAX BREAKS AND SUBSIDIES, WE OWE YOU…"

Herblock. From *Herblock through the Looking Glass* (W. W. Norton, 1984).

Tom Harkin of Iowa, a Democrat and a left populist, has advanced a plan that would allow farmers to fix farm prices and production by majority vote, guaranteeing that family farms could make money and stay in operation (Boyte, Booth, and Max 1986, 142). A right populist like Richard Viguerie or Jack Kemp would probably condemn such a proposal as a violation of the individual farmer's economic freedom.

One point on which right and left populists agree is in criticism of the Federal Reserve Board and the banking system generally. Ordinary people depend on bank credit to carry on their economic activities, yet they have no control over the cost and availability. These are determined not by market forces but by the unelected bankers who sit on the Federal Reserve Board and alone have the right to produce money. The long terms granted to board members give them the power to do almost anything they want. Since most Fed members come out of the banking community and will return to it when they leave the board, it is virtually inevitable that their policies will reflect the interests of banks, especially the large ones. Usually these interests mean tight money and high interest rates, which hold down inflation and protect the value of the money banks lend to the people. Such policies are good for lenders but bad for borrowers, and most Americans owe more than they lend. Most populists would like to see the Fed brought under the direct control of elected officials, whom the voters could hold responsible if money became too tight (Harris 1973, 157–58; see also Greider 1987, 243–67).

In sum, all populists want to end policies that give the rich an advantage in the economy. They believe that economic policy should be made more open, more subject to majority control, if the United States is to live up to its democratic ideals. Left populists would go further and restructure the economy to reduce the power of large corporations.

Marxist

Marxists share many of the liberal and populist criticisms of the American capitalist economy, but they carry these criticisms much further. While reform liberals see capitalism as capable of reforming itself, Marxists see it as a system not only grossly unjust but doomed by its own internal contradictions. Capitalist economies produce enormous wealth, but this wealth is so unequally distributed that desperate poverty persists in the midst of plenty. The contradiction between the productive capacity of industry and the weak buying power of the workers guarantees the persistence of instability, recession, inflation, and unemployment regardless of all efforts by the capitalist state to mitigate these evils. Meanwhile the capitalist system must turn to military spending and foreign investment to absorb the surplus of capital and productive capacity, embroiling the country in overseas imperialist adventures. In the view of Marxists, the continued existence of American capitalism endangers not only economic well-being but world peace (Baran and Sweezy 1966; Block et al. 1987, 1–43).

Contemporary American Marxists put less stress than traditional Marxists on the labor theory of value, which holds that the worth of a product comes from the amount of time spent on it by a laborer. They have recognized that worth is determined by demand, but they continue to believe that capitalism is an exploitative system and that government economic policies simply support the capitalist way of life by alleviating its worst excesses (Gintis 1982, 53–81). They would heartily concur with populists and some liberals that institutions such as the Federal Reserve Board are simply techniques created by the wealthy class to assure a stable economic environment within which profit taking can occur. Similarly, they would concur with early Marxists, like Lenin, in their suggestion that economic "colonies" in Third World countries help perpetuate the United States as a world economic power. The economic machinations and ultimate military intervention that forced Panama's Manuel Noriega from power and drove Saddam Hussein from Kuwait are clear examples, say Marxists, of economic imperialism (see Chapter 11; *Time*, 1 January, 1990, 26–31).

American Marxists have broken with European Marxists in some significant ways. Whereas European Marxists have concentrated primarily on economics, American Marxists have pointed to the American family and educational system as important forces in sustaining capitalist economic relationships. The patriarchal (male-dominated) American family sets the tone for male domination in American industry. The grade-oriented, competitive, time-oriented, hierarchical educational system is the perfect preparation ground for operating within a capitalist business hierarchy. One American Marxist has argued that the major role of higher education is to sanction the types of job and salary classifications that justify control of the workers by managers. Acceptance of the system makes it easier for capitalists to pay workers less than their true worth—the only way to make a profit (Gintis 1982, 62–68).

American Marxists see a fundamental contradiction in the role of government in advanced industrial societies like the United States that accounts for the sustained sluggishness of the economy. They suggest that the effectiveness of working people as a political force, as a political pressure group, has raised worker benefits to the point where capitalists' ability to make profits has been threatened by taxation. Moreover the government, in its efforts to legitimate capitalism by refining its roughest edges, has created a social "safety net" that makes workers less vulnerable and so more difficult for employers to control.

Budget deficits and a rising national debt are inevitable.

American Marxists generally do not hold Cuban, Chinese, or the former Soviet forms of Marxism to be positive examples of how their ideas work in practice. They argue that heavily centralized, managed economies were perversions of Marx's dream of a worker utopia, which is why they became vulnerable to capitalist reforms. American Marxists do argue strongly for changes in American priorities, including shifts in spending from defense to social programs and greater worker control of the workplace as steps toward the realization of Marx's dream.

Feminist

Feminists have generally taken two approaches to analyzing the role women play in the American economic system. They first argue that many laws involving the welfare of women and children, including social security, were first passed on the assumption of a two-fold division of labor: the man was the breadwinner and the woman was an economic dependent who stayed at home and cared for his children, contributing little economic value to the gross national product. Women who did not earn wages received no social security credit for the work they contributed within the home to their family's well-being. At the same time, women in the work force were still governed by laws that made their social security payments dependent on their husbands' wages. Amendment to the tax code retained "dependent" deductions, institutionalizing language reflecting women's inferior economic position in society. Even after women achieved increasing autonomy, and despite statutes forbidding discrimination, banks and other financial institutions continued to treat women as economically dependent on males (Lewis 1986, 85–100).

All feminists are aware that financial autonomy for women may not result in a higher quality of life for women until reasons for continued inequality of wages and position are confronted and overcome. The second approach feminists take results from the snail-slow rise of women to po-

sitions of economic power in the private sector. In a 1978 study of 1,300 major companies undertaken by *Fortune,* only 10 of 6,400 officers and directors of these corporations were women. A follow-up study in 1990 counted 19 women in 799 corporations with 4,000 officers, or less than 1 percent (*Fortune,* 30 July 1990, 40). All explanations aside, few disagree that discrimination still significantly impedes the path of women to the top of the corporate ladder. Eighty percent of 241 chief executive officers in a survey conducted by an agency concerned with women in the workplace acknowledged that there are identifiable barriers to women's advancement in their corporations. Of those admitting such barriers exist, 81 percent say that stereotyping and preconceptions limit female advancement (*Fortune,* 30 July 1990, 42). No such discrimination impedes women in lower-level positions such as secretarial work (where women make up 99.1 percent of the total). However, across the private sector, women earn an average of 70 percent of the salary of a male in the same position (Stetson 1991, 155).

While private sector advancement for women in important economic positions has been slow, recent presidents have offered hope for feminists in the appointment of women to key economic posts. Alice Rivlin (see Profile in this Chapter), the deputy director of the Office of Management and Budget, and Laura D'Andrea Tyson, the chair of the Council of Economic Advisers, have achieved key economic policy positions. Susan M. Phillips, a Bush appointee, is one of twelve members of the Federal Reserve Board. Feminists are quick to point out, however, that a woman has never occupied the cabinet-level position of treasury secretary.

Women in recent years have begun to suffer far more than men from changes in social values and recurrent periods of economic recession. Divorce has increased; more women are in the work force. Many women are now raising children alone, with little or no support from former husbands (Norris 1987, 80–82; Kaus 1988, 212–19). The late 1980s were particularly hard on women with small children because welfare benefits from the 1970s did not keep up with inflation. In fact, unmarried women with children and widowed women over the age of sixty-five are now the most impoverished groups of persons in American society. Moreover, as the American economy has slowed and the number of high-paying manufacturing jobs has declined, women have been squeezed into low-skilled manufacturing service-sector jobs. The consequence of these social and economic trends is a new concept in the U.S. public debate: the feminization of poverty. Not only do women constitute a majority of the poor, but they suffer from poverty more keenly than men as they must often care for children on wages that are already lower than men's. Feminists argue that unless public policy practitioners begin to view policy through the eyes of women, the economic condition of women and children compared with white males will continue to decline (Stetson 1991, 233–34). During the 1980s the National Feminist Coalition and the Congressional Caucus on Women's Issues attempted unsuccessfully to pass an economic equity bill that would have addressed equity in pensions, insurance, child support, day care, and tax reforms (Stetson 1991, 342–45; see also Reid 1992, 86–89). Although reforms in the area of pension benefit rights, day care, and parental leave are now on the books, other aspects of the bill remain blocked.

Although outside observers might suggest that women have come a long way since the times when they were regarded as totally dependent on husbands or fathers and devoid of economic rights, the pace of change from a feminist viewpoint remains glacially slow. All feminists agree that society must find a way to recognize the contributions of women's work in the home and stop punishing women at work because they are also wives and mothers. Radical as well as social feminists are somewhat encouraged by the presence of the Clintons in the White House. They do, however, remain convinced that women's relative lack of political power, along with the economic impact of family responsibilities, low levels of education, and lack of job-related supports and benefits will keep American women at the low end of the economic ladder for decades to come (Renszetti and Curran 1992).

DOES NATIONAL ECONOMIC POLICY WORK?

Since the 1970s, economic management has been an increasing concern of the national government. While some progress has been made, no policy or set of policies has ensured full employment and price stability. The U.S. government, by its very nature, is greatly affected by what can be considered politically expedient decisions in the process of economic policy-making. No perfect combination of monetary, fiscal, incomes, or some other policy has yet been found, and until it is, the search for economic stability and prosperity will continue to be prominent on the national agenda.

Managing the economy is a difficult task. Is the American system up to it? As in the case of foreign policy, the answer might depend on whether one is talking of the long or short term. There may be no way that a democratic system can avoid the type of short-term problems discussed in this chapter. Leaders are often under pressure to do what is politically popular rather than what is economically sound. Unfortunately, they often yield to such pressure.

In the largest sense, the American economic system has worked well and is now the envy of most of the world. Even the Japanese, who have been doing better than the United States in some areas the past few decades, were started on their course by the United States, and the Japanese economy now has some problems of its own. As Americans learned from Clinton and Perot in 1992, the American economy also has problems, but they simply are not of the magnitude of most other countries. Certainly they are not of the fundamental kind the country faced during the 1930s.

The three of us disagree on just how well the American system works in the area of economic policy. The most liberal of the authors believes that much more should be done by government to extend equal economic oppor-

tunities to the less fortunate and protect U.S. manufacturing jobs. The other two authors are relatively more concerned about the United States' competitive position in the world compared to rising stars like Japan and South Korea. These disagreements do not keep us from feeling that the American system has, relative to other industrialized countries, done a good job with the economy over the long term.

As with most Americans, the authors disagree as to how to solve the debt crisis. One would not hesitate to raise taxes and make some spending restrictions. The other two are inclined to want to reduce spending by putting a cap on spending increases until the budget is balanced or making it possible for citizens to propose and vote on spending limitation measures, as they already can in several states. All three recognize such proposals are easier to make in a textbook than to accomplish in Washington, D.C.

SUMMARY AND REVIEW

In relatively recent times the national government has accepted a general responsibility for the health of the national economy. Government attempts to influence the behavior of the economy on the macroeconomic level through the use of three basic policy tools—monetary policy, fiscal policy, and the wartime or postwar use of incomes policy.

The main instrument of monetary policy is the Federal Reserve System, whose primary role is to manage the nation's money supply, with some attention to the control of interest rates. The Federal Reserve Board influences the economy in three ways: by establishing reserve requirements, raising or lowering the discount rate, and, most directly, through open market policy. Despite the fact that it wields great power, the Federal Reserve System is relatively immune from legislative or executive oversight and control, primarily be-

cause of the long terms of the seven members of its Board of Governors.

Fiscal policy—using taxes and spending as a tool to influence economic performance—has become the accepted approach in the last forty years. John Maynard Keynes argued that governments should adopt policies to counteract the cycles of inflation and recession, but only the politically palatable aspects of his equation have been used. The initiative in fiscal policy lies with the president, although members of Congress serving on the fiscal committees have some say in the matter. Incomes policy—direct or indirect government intervention aimed at controlling wages and prices—has been most frequently employed during times of war, though peacetime use has occurred. Economic policy is clearly much harder to implement in practice than in theory.

Despite definite advantages, monetary policy faces some serious difficulties as well. The close relationship between the money supply and the price level has proven particularly difficult for policymakers, who are often faced with the unappealing possibility of easing inflation at the cost of higher unemployment. In addition, monetary policy often has unpleasant and destabilizing short-term effects on interest rates. Consequently the Fed is largely engaged in an unpopular inflation-unemployment balancing act, rather than pursuing a consistent course. In the realm of fiscal policy, only half of the Keynesian strategy has been adopted with enthusiasm; increasing spending while reducing taxes during hard times is politically painless and generally successful, but tax increases coupled with spending cuts are especially unpopular during inflationary times and as such have rarely been tried. For similar reasons, the elimination of deficits by running a surplus in prosperous times can rarely occur because of political considerations. Highly touted in the writings of John Kenneth Galbraith, incomes policy attracted much interest in the 1970s. Since then, however, much of the early support for wage-price controls has disappeared, due largely to an awareness among policymakers that price controls are liable to create serious distortions and inefficiencies in the economy.

During the troubled economy of the 1970s, a number of disincentives to productivity were caused by inflation, wage and price controls, and the tax code even as government became increasingly involved in the economy. While efforts to reduce poverty were initially successful, the overall effect of the government's controlling a larger share of the gross national product was negative for economic growth, and the standard of living improved hardly at all as productivity failed to increase. In short, the United States was in a period of stagflation, and it was in this context that Ronald Reagan won the presidency.

Reagan seemed to accept the idea put forth by Jack Kemp and certain supply-side economists that cuts in taxes and a decrease in government regulation would stimulate economic growth to such an extent that tax revenues would actually increase. Reaganomics emphasized lower taxes, increased defense spending, and decreased spending on domestic programs, although Reagan was unable to cut many domestic programs due to gridlock with the mostly Democratic Congress. The result of lower taxes with dramatic increases in defense spending and maintained spending on domestic programs led to an annual deficit of around $200 billion. The tight monetary policy of the Fed—seen as proper to fight the high inflation of the late 1970s and early 1980s—worked to counteract Reagan's stimulative fiscal policy. The annual deficits continued under George Bush, growing to around $300 billion during the 1992 election year and the debt grew from nearly $1 trillion when Reagan took office in 1981 to more than $4 trillion in 1993 when Bush left office. Attempts to reduce annual deficits and the debt, such as Gramm-Rudman-Hollings legislation and a 1990 budget compromise, kept the situation from getting worse but did not make the difficult choices required to solve the problems.

From 1982 to 1985 the tight money supply of the Fed attracted a great deal of foreign investment, but it was not long before the strong dollar began to hurt the American economy. The yearly trade deficit has grown disturbingly high, and some feared that too much American real estate and too many American companies were being bought by foreign investors. To counteract this trend, in the late 1980s the government moved to decrease the value of the dollar in order to reduce the trade deficit. Between 1985 and mid-1989 the dollar fell 50 percent and the trade deficit had begun to shrink. The challenge to the Federal Reserve Board was then to control the dollar's descent and prevent drops in value that would lead to investor flight. The stock market crash of 1987 may be viewed as a possible result of the increasing skepticism with which investors were viewing the American economy. The economy reversed, and the stock market grew until mid-1990. By this time, U.S. products were more competitive than they had been in the mid-1980s in international markets, but, unfortunately, one result of increased productivity was greater unemployment.

The rising federal deficit has meant increasingly larger interest payments that will necessitate postponing many kinds of government programs. Despite dramatic reductions of interest rates by the Fed in 1991–93, it is likely that the deficit will cause interest rates to rise eventually, further slowing the economy. Alternative solutions to the deficit dilemma continue to include the monetization of U.S. debts, a quick reduction by cutting costs or raising taxes (steps that proved politically impossible in the middle of the 1980s and led to the Gramm-Rudman-Hollings Act), or the financing of the debt by foreign investors, which is the path that the United States continued to pursue more or less by default while Congress and the president were trying to achieve political compromises. While the recession officially ended in 1991, high unemployment and decreasing numbers of well-paying jobs continue to plague the American work force.

The recession can be viewed as a result of Reagan-Bush policies or as an inevitable cyclical downturn. Whatever its cause, recovery was slow, and Arkansas's Governor Bill Clinton was able to defeat President George Bush in the 1992 election on the basis of economic policy.

Clinton attracted voters by promising to improve the economy. His program emphasizes cutting the size of the annual deficit in half, or about $500 billion over five years; this reduction still might not meet his objective. He also hopes to put unemployed Americans back to work. His economic stimulus package was defeated, but the great bulk of his deficit reduction plan was approved. Many economic challenges continue to face the American government.

Economic policy affects everyone, no matter what age, job, or place of residence in the United States. All economic policies help some people while hurting others. For example, the government makes policies regarding minimum wages and acts against discrimination in the workplace due to race, gender, and age. Finding policies that produce the most good for the greatest number of people in the long run is difficult. Implementing such policies may be even harder, because political leaders are often tempted to do what is politically popular rather than what is economically sound.

Economics are becoming more interdependent and global in focus. They must adjust to new realities on short notice. Well-educated workers can be expected to be more flexible than their less-educated peers. Your future will be affected by government economic policies. Almost whatever your career choice, an understanding of government will be beneficial.

IMPORTANT TERMS

Board of Governors
bracket creep
budget deficit
comparable worth
debtor nation
depression

discount rate
dual economy
economic sanctions
external debt
Federal Reserve System
fiscal policy

gold standard
hedges against inflation
incomes policy
industrial policy
inflation
internal debt
jawboning
loopholes
macroeconomic
microeconomic
minimum wage
monetarism
monetary policy
monetization

multiplier effect
national debt
open market policy
protectionism
Reaganomics
recession
reserve requirement
stagflation
supply-side economics
tariff barrier
trade deficit
velocity
wage and price controls

13

THE FUTURE
OF AMERICAN
GOVERNMENT

*In 1981 President Ronald Reagan called the
Soviet Union an "evil empire"; in 1988, with
one arms control agreement signed and another pending, he visited Moscow. A year later,
the Berlin Wall came down. In the 1960s
young people across the country demonstrated
and rioted against a war or dropped out of
conventional society; in the 1980s they voted
Republican and went to business schools in
record numbers. In March 1991 George Bush
had approval ratings of almost 90 percent,
having successfully guided the multinational
effort to drive Saddam Hussein from Kuwait.
By November 1992 his approval ratings had
fallen into the 30s, and, with a lower percentage of the popular vote in his bid for reelection
than even Herbert Hoover, Bush headed for
Houston with his wife to build a retirement
home (Gallup Poll Monthly, March 1991, 4–5;
National Journal, 9 June 1990, 1413–14). Such
turnarounds illustrate the difficulty of predicting political events. Nevertheless, political
science seeks to give some ideas for the future
as well as to describe the present. The con-
cluding chapter of this textbook looks both
back and ahead: back to how the six perspectives view recent American politics and ahead
to suggest how trends in public opinion may
shape the political future.*

LOOKING BACK: PERSPECTIVES ON THE LAST DECADE AND A HALF

The fifteen years since 1980 saw the ascendan-
cy of the Republican party at the presidential
level for three terms, continued Democratic
domination of Congress and state legislatures,
and, for the most part, retrenchment in new
national government initiatives. Interna-
tionally, the period began in confrontation
with the Soviet Union and ended with good
prospects for peace and cooperation among
the major powers. How do the six perspectives
see these years?

WHAT A BEAUTIFUL EVIL EMPIRE !

Frank Evers. Courtesy New York *Daily News.*

Conservative: Fragile Gains, New Fears

Given their view of human nature, conservatives should be pessimists. During the Reagan administration, however, they saw reasons to be more optimistic than usual. To conservative eyes, Reagan was the first president in many years to recognize the seriousness of the Soviet threat and respond with a rearmament program capable of meeting it. Domestically, lower taxes and less regulation opened up opportunity for inventive, intelligent, and hard-working Americans—the "natural aristocracy" conservatives prize. The result was an improved economy, a stronger defense, and a surge of national self-confidence, itself a major gain in the eyes of the conservatives.

As the Reagan era wound down, however, conservatives saw threats on the horizon. Their major worry from the beginning of Bush's term was his failure to hold the line on federal spending, which had continued to increase all during the 1980s despite "conservative" administrations. From 1980 until 1992, federal outlays rose from $590.9 billion to $1.382 trillion, an increase of 134 percent (*Budget Baselines* 1993, 477). During the same period the national debt increased from less than $1 trillion to more than $3 trillion. This surge was

the result of tax decreases, defense increases, and economic recessions in the early 1980s and again in the early 1990s. But Reagan's and Bush's inability to restrain the greed of various special interest groups was also a factor. Conservatives had never fully trusted Bush to carry on the "Reagan revolution." His positions on social issues like abortion had changed across time, and some believed he put expediency above principle. In addition, Bush alienated the conservative wing of his party with his willingness, despite his famous campaign promise—"Read my lips. No new taxes"—to raise taxes to control the deficit. Although the Persian Gulf War gave Bush a brief respite from conservative attacks, some Republicans and right populists turned first to Pat Buchanan and then to Ross Perot. During the primary season leading up to the 1992 election, Bush supported an unsuccessful attempt to pass the Balanced Budget Amendment and then returned to his pledge of no new taxes during the primaries and at the Republican convention. Some conservatives, however, continued to view Bush with distaste and voted for him in 1992 only as the least of three evils.

Conservatives have also remained cautious about improved relations with the former Soviet Union and Eastern Europe. While agreeing that conditions are changing, they point to the darker portents of the breakup of the former Soviet empire, which include destabilization of the nuclear balance and increasing ethnic turmoil. For these reasons most conservatives are less willing than liberals to scale down the U.S. military dramatically. Conservatives disagreed among themselves about the wisdom of the Persian Gulf War. They suggested that false hopes for permanent peace in either Europe or the Middle East might lead the United States to neglect its defenses and fail to see new threats to national security in the midst of a rapidly changing international scene. Although some were disappointed by Bush's failure to take a firmer stand on independence for Lithuania

First the Good News...

Eldon Pletcher. Courtesy artist.

and other dissident Soviet republics, most supported his more cautious approach to relations with the Commonwealth of Independent States and Eastern Europe.

Finally, conservatives are concerned that little of their social agenda was accomplished during either the Reagan or Bush administrations. Despite eloquent presidential statements, abortions remain legal, drugs and pornography are widely available, and organized prayer is banned in public schools. This lack of movement on social issues was clearly a factor in right populist Pat Buchanan's challenge to President Bush in the Republican presidential primaries of 1992 (see Profile in Chapter 1). The Clinton administration's moves to protect the rights of homosexuals in the military and rescind previous executive orders forbidding abortions at government hospitals overseas and counseling in regard to abortion at any institution receiving government funds represent a conservative's worst nightmare come true. Although conservatives would still rate the years between 1980 and 1992 as better than either the 1960s or 1970s, the years to come may not bode well for those holding a conservative agenda.

Conservatives increasingly trace their disappointments to general adverse trends in American society. While they reject Marxist hopes of

transforming human nature, they stress the need for religion and morality as a discipline to human self-interest and greed. In a society like that of the United States where an increasing number reject higher moral law other than "do your own thing, as long as you don't hurt anybody else," the capitalist economic system may still function well while the society it serves so efficiently remains sick. Conservatives hope the electorate will see the wisdom of their argument in years to come.

Liberal: Disappointment, Then Hope

For liberals, the period from 1980 to 1992 was rough. Ronald Reagan, whom they long considered a right-wing fringe figure, emerged to capitalize on the failures of the Carter administration. After eight years of trying to preserve their programs from Reagan's "budget ax," liberals initially hoped for more cooperation from a "kinder, gentler" George Bush. They found Bush no easier to work with than Reagan on issues from civil rights to the environment, although compromise measures were finally passed in both areas. A weak economy, including vulnerable banks and savings and loan institutions along with a recession and recurring deficits, made it difficult to justify social programs because there was no money

"HEY, LISTEN – THEY'VE HAD ME DEAD AND BURIED SO MANY TIMES! – "

Herblock. Copyright 1993 by Herblock in *The Washington Post.*

to fund them. With the pay-as-you-go principles of the budget accords negotiated with the Bush administration 1990 firmly in place, major new initiatives became politically impossible.

However, Bush's inability to sustain his popularity in the year following the Persian Gulf War, combined with the lingering effects from the recession and increasing internal strife between the moderate and conservative wings of the Republican party, gave liberals some reasons to feel hopeful by the summer of 1992. During the fall election campaign, Bill Clinton successfully accused George Bush of having lost control of the economy and being

out of touch with the ordinary American's feelings about issues such as abortion, the environment, and health care. Clinton's centrist liberal message convinced a plurality of voters that all had not been well on the Reagan-Bush watch and that domestically things had actually gotten worse under Bush. The longest period of growth in the twentieth century followed by a long recession and slow recovery left Americans feeling betrayed and angry. Hunger, homelessness, and deprivation among poorer Americans had increased. An increasing gap between the richest Americans and the rest of the population was also evident. Polls showed that the majority of Americans wanted problems such as jobs and health care addressed and believed the wealthiest Americans should pay a higher percentage of the tax burden. Clinton promised action in these areas, and liberals rejoiced at his victory in the 1992 presidential election.

Unfortunately voters, stirred by the campaign rhetoric of populist Ross Perot, also want to see deficit and spending reductions during the new Clinton administration. For the remainder of the century, the hopes of liberals may be frustrated by the limited amount of funds for new and existing programs. Liberals of all stripes agree that solving economic and social problems will require a more active and interventionist government. Although there will continue to be ample scope for private enterprise, liberals want a national government whose priorities lie with the majority at the bottom and in the middle of society. With both houses of Congress and the White House controlled by the party most sympathetic to their cause, liberals should be more optimistic than at any time in the last two decades.

Libertarian: Hope and Disillusionment

Libertarians have some of the same concerns as conservatives about the course of recent American politics, and some different ones.

Mike Peters. Reprinted by permission: Tribune Media
Services.

Like the conservatives, they applaud the Reagan administration's efforts to shrink the domestic role of government, yet they regret the limited success of those efforts. Compared with the 1960s and 1970s, the libertarian view of the state received a much more sympathetic hearing in the 1980s; government has actually stopped regulating some industries, like trucking and airlines, and cut back regulation of others, like banking, steps libertarians once believed were impossible. But libertarians now fear that the United States may move away from the free enterprise system. They point out that conservatives and liberals have poured vast amounts of money into the defense of other regions of the world such as Europe or of specific countries such as Kuwait or Somalia. Such actions have been a threat to the economy, while other actions, such as Oliver North's attempts to thwart Congress in the Iran-*contra* affair (see Controversy in Chapter 11), have threatened the right of the people to determine the overall direction of foreign policy through their elected representatives. In addition, attempts to enforce conservative social morality, such as restricting abortion and the use of drugs, have been equally futile and threaten freedom of choice and expression.

On the whole, Americans with libertarian proclivities joined with conservatives in backing the Reagan administration. The need to maintain this coalition accounted for the low priority Reagan placed on social issues, which clearly had the potential to split it. This is exactly what happened in 1992 when right populist Pat Buchanan challenged George Bush in the primaries. The prominent roles

Chuck Asay. Courtesy *The Gazette Telegraph*, Colorado.

given Buchanan and evangelist Pat Robertson at the Republican convention—Bush's attempt to repair the split—further alienated "economic" libertarian Republicans.

The protest vote for the Libertarian party (931,000 votes in 1980, 228,000 in 1984, 432,000 in 1988, and 291,612 in 1992), as well as the size of the protest vote for Ross Perot in 1992, show that some libertarians remain unhappy with Republican candidates who support a conservative social and foreign policy. If the Republican party in 1996 nominates a candidate with clearly conservative or libertarian social credentials, the split may break into the open, with serious consequences for the supporters of both perspectives (*Chicago Tribune*, 8 November 1992, C2; *Congressional Quarterly Weekly Report*, 23 January 1993, 191.)

Populist: A Time for the People

Populists on the right probably had the most reason to like the turns taken by American politics during the 1980s, but what they witnessed during Bush's presidency did not please them. Under Reagan, tax rates were sharply reduced in 1982, and then reduced again by tax reforms in 1986. These reductions lightened the burden on lower-income workers and removed many poor people from the tax rolls altogether. But large numbers of blue-collar jobs continued to be exported to Asia and Latin America, and millions of Americans, including many populists, saw their standards of living decrease during the 1980s. In the area of social questions, right populists were glad to see fewer government initiatives like busing or affirmative action but were disappointed that more restrictions were not placed on abortions or pornography.

Populists on the left today see things somewhat differently. To them, the bromides of Robertson- or Buchanan-style populism are too simplistic. While low taxes and less government might have helped some people to move up the ladder, the granting of more freedom and power to rich individuals and powerful corporations has made life harder for many. Viewing themselves as defenders of the economic interests of the common folk against the rich and powerful, left populists have portrayed the 1980s and early 1990s as painful times when cutbacks in social programs hurt poor marginal members of society. During the presidential primaries in 1992, Senator Tom Harkin of Iowa and former Governor Jerry Brown of California attempted to harness left populist dissatisfaction.

Harkin had taken George Bush to task as early as May 1991, saying, "Bush thinks the threat to the United States is halfway around the world—but the real threat is right down the street. . . . I don't think that Bush is that popular. He's got feet of clay and I'm going to go after him" (quoted in *Politics in America* 1991, 525). Harkin introduced fiery rhetoric into the early primaries. Later Brown carried forward the populist cause, criticizing the American political system as a gravy train for powerful interests and arguing that politicians of all stripes were captured by those interests. Brown carried this critique of American politics right through to the Democratic convention (*New York Times*, 15 July 1992, 1).

Left populists want some of the social programs cut by Reagan and Bush to be restored. They also want mandated job retraining programs for workers who have lost their jobs, comprehensive health care for all Americans, and an end to the power of monied interests in the political process. Clinton forces were able to contain left populists like Jackson and Harkin and to attract their support during the election. As a southerner, Clinton was aware of the power of populist rhetoric, and he adopted the slogan of "People First" in his campaign. Although right populists fear the moral decline that may occur during a Clinton presidency, all populists agree that the prospect of a moderate liberal in the White House provides hope that some of the worst economic inequities of the

Reagan-Bush era will begin to be addressed (*Detroit Free Press*, 15 July 1992, 1; *New York Times*, 13 July 1992, 1).

Marxist: Darkness before Dawn?

For Marxists, the twelve Reagan-Bush years seemed like a tunnel with no end in sight. The strong reformist and radical movements in the 1960s, though not Marxist themselves, seemed to hold the promise of revolutionary change. By the 1990s all such hopes seemed to have vanished. According to Marxist analysis, the Reagan-Bush program served the interests of capitalists well: cutting social welfare, forcing the unemployed to compete harder for jobs, and driving wages down while ironically winning applause from many working people who believed "welfare chiselers" were the cause of their problems (see Block et al. 1987). Far from being a tragic error, as liberals believed, Reagan-Bush policies appear to Marxists as a clever and largely successful capitalist strategy, however morally repugnant. Similarly, conservatives have been able to use race and religion to keep the people divided over issues like affirmative action or prayer in schools, while corporate profits rose and the standard of living eroded. Most depressing of all to Marxists was that these trends produced few mass protests—at least until the April 1992 riot in Los Angeles (see Controversy in Chapter 8).

Despite the repudiation of communism in the former Soviet empire, Marxists continue to believe that history is on their side. The collapse of governments that labeled themselves Marxist and yet were perverted totalitarian despotisms actually has many Marxists feeling more optimistic because such governments were not what they purported to be and gave Marxism a bad reputation. At a forum in Amherst, Massachusetts, during the fall of 1992, Marxist scholars Bertell Ollman and Stephen Cullenberg stated: "A lot of people have taken the wrong lessons from the collapse of the so-called socialist systems, and that's propagated by the capitalist-owned media. . . . We never endorsed that kind of Marxism. For us, it's kind of an albatross that's been removed from our political and theoretical necks." A third scholar suggested: "We don't have history to confirm our politics, but we can look back at some of the failures . . . and try to reconstruct our Marxist politics. . . . That's what Marxism has always been about" (quoted in *Chicago Tribune*, 15 November 1992, B18).

Marxists still see capitalism as fraught with contradictions, particularly between what managers and owners are paid in the form of profits and the gradually deteriorating standard of living of workers in advanced nations such as the United States. To Marxists it is obvious that the capitalist engine of growth is sputtering throughout the industrialized world and no solution is likely to return growth rates in societies in Europe and the United States to what they were earlier in the century. Marxists still believe that capitalism will eventually fail. They realize that it may take much longer than Marx or Lenin or many Marxist scholars predicted and that the form that government may take in its aftermath may be closer to democratic socialism than to the communism that existed in the Soviet Union and Eastern Europe prior to the 1990s.

Feminist: Heightened Expectations, New Anxieties

Feminists spent most of the 1980s pushing their agenda to a somewhat indifferent political system. The fact that female voters tended to be more Democratic than their male counterparts kept both parties interested in the women's vote, but feminist causes often were considered to be on the fringe of the political spectrum.

After Bill Clinton's 1992 victory, feminists began to celebrate. This young president and his feminist wife Hillary Rodham Clinton, a well-known lawyer, support many of the viewpoints feminists have been fighting for since the 1970s: gay rights, choice regarding abortion, the family leave bill passed by Congress, and the appointment of a higher percentage of women for top-level positions in the executive branch. The 1992 elections gave feminists other reasons to celebrate. Thousands of women ran for elective office, and the seven female senators and forty-seven female representatives in the new Congress represent an all-time record. After years of being outsiders, derided by Republican administrations as "far out liberals" and even characterized by one conservative in the mass media as "feminazis" (Limbaugh 1992, 202), reform feminists faced the heady prospect of being supported by a president who knows that the electoral gender gap was one factor that helped him defeat George Bush.

So why the anxiety? With less opposition, feminist organizations may have more difficulty generating money and support. With abortion rights somewhat secure and the family leave bill signed into law, feminists fear that liberals will begin to expend more time, resources, and energy on issues such as the environment. It is possible that many feminists will be absorbed into the major perspectives, leaving those who remain outside more hard core and not as powerful.

As the Clinton administration began, feminists leading three women's interest groups described plans that reflect feminist thinking in Washington. The National Abortion Rights Action League is anxious to take advantage of gains from the election of 1992. Kate Michelman, president, stated, "We expect the election of a pro-choice President and our significant incremental gains in Congress to mean that we can very quickly undo some of the most egregious damage done by President Bush" (Michelman 1992, 3). Diane Dodson of the Women's Legal Defense Fund suggests, "People are more interested in making real-world progress than protesting. They want to

see their agenda move forward" (Dodson interview 1993). Patricia Ireland of the National Organization for Women (NOW) sees one of her main goals as improving upon compromises made in the 1993 Family and Medical Leave Act that set the minimum number of employees for businesses subject to the legislation at fifty instead of fifteen. Unfortunately, it is hard to translate such goals into provocative slogans that attract support and money.

Radical feminists find less to celebrate than reform feminists, recognizing that there are many social and political institutions to change before full equality can be secured. With some reform goals achieved, their larger cause may suffer just as victories appear to have been won (*Washington Post National Weekly Edition*, 7–13 December 1992, 19).

LOOKING AHEAD: THE 1990s AND BEYOND

The first twelve chapters of this textbook have provided an introductory account of United States government. Chapter 1 identified the major perspectives on American government, and the following chapters described government institutions and policies and evaluated them according to six political perspectives. Will the electorate still be divided in the same way ten or twenty years from now? Will Republicans include, as they do now, libertarians, conservatives, and a number of disgruntled right populists? Will Democrats still be fighting to maintain the liberal-populist coalition forged during Franklin Roosevelt's New Deal? Although it is always difficult to predict the future, a closer look at trends within the electorate may produce an educated guess.

The Changing American Electorate

A Times Mirror survey taken in November 1992 sliced the electorate into a statistical pie with nine classifications (see Profile). The core groups of the Democratic and Republican parties come close to representing the four major perspectives (conservative, liberal, libertarian, and populist) analyzed in this textbook, although the pollsters did not use the same terms. The Republicans' core constituency is 28 percent of the electorate, divided between Enterprisers (12 percent) and Moralists (16 percent). At first glance these two groups look very much like libertarians and conservatives as we have described them in this book. But Moralists come in large numbers from the South, reflecting the Republican party's inroads in presidential elections into the right populist wing of the southern Democratic party. The Democratic party's core constituents are 33 percent of the electorate. This core is divided among '60s Democrats (10 percent), New Dealers (6 percent), and Pocketbook Democrats (17 percent) and closely resembles the liberals and left populists discussed in this text. They favor government intervention to address inequities and ensure social and economic justice.

Republican core groups have generally been more loyal than Democratic core groups. When the Democrats won the presidency in 1992, their core constituents voted for Clinton at about a 75 percent rate, compared to the 97 percent rate Bush got from Republican core groups when he won in 1988 (*People, the Press and Politics*, 15 November 1992, 14; *People, the Press and Politics*, November 1988, 69, 82). Viewed another way, Republicans in 1992 were almost as loyal to their defeated candidate as Democrats were to their victorious candidate (see Table 13.1).

In terms of issues of importance to the perspectives presented in this textbook, the Democrats' core constituencies, although not in total agreement, were less fractionalized on their economic priorities in 1992 than they were in 1988. Whereas New Dealers and Pocketbook Democrats differed to a substantial degree with '60s Democrats regarding job protection in 1988, all three Democratic constituencies saw jobs as quite important in 1992. They also saw the North American Free Trade Agreement as producing a net loss of jobs. New Dealers and Pocketbook Democrats were only slightly more likely than '60s Democrats to see control of health care as a dominant issue that government needed to address. No Democratic constituency saw foreign policy as an important issue. Deficit reduction was seen as an important issue by a majority of all Dem-

TABLE 13.1   THE AMERICAN ELECTORATE AND THE 1992 VOTING RESULTS

CONSTITUENT GROUP	ACTUAL VOTE			
	Voters in Electorate	Bush	Clinton	Perot
Enterprisers	12%	69%	9%	21%
Moralists	16	68	12	13
Upbeats	11	45	32	17
Disaffecteds	9	26	36	27
Seculars	9	9	69	10
'60s Democrats	10	12	66	17
New Dealers	6	14	71	11
Pocketbook Democrats	17	5	83	10
Bystanders/Others	10	23	44	30

Source: People, the Press and Politics, *15 November 1992, 14, 17.*

PROFILE

The American People in 1992

The November 1992 Times Mirror survey of Americans supports the thesis of this textbook: there are not just two perspectives on politics, but several. However, the Times Mirror survey distinguishes nine different major groups instead of the four in this textbook. Some are clearly associated with one or the other of the major political parties, while others are more independent or apathetic.

CORE REPUBLICAN CONSTITUENCIES

Enterprisers (12 percent): Fiscal conservatives, likely to be male, who favor business and oppose welfare. Enterprisers are affluent, well-educated, and well-informed. They are more likely than other Americans to disagree with the popular notion that the rich get richer and the poor get poorer. Enterprisers do not agree that too much power is concentrated in the hands of big companies or that society should make sure that everyone has an equal opportunity.

Moralists (16 percent): Social conservatives who are highly religious and show low levels of concern for personal freedoms. Moralists are less affluent and older than average Americans. A vast majority of them live in the South and agree that books with dangerous ideas should be banned from public schools, setting them firmly to the right of center on the issue of censorship.

CORE DEMOCRATIC CONSTITUENCIES

'60s Democrats (10 percent): Strong believers in peace and social justice. More than any other segment of the population, '60s Democrats disagree with the idea that the best way to preserve peace is through military strength. Two-thirds of them completely agree that society should guarantee everyone an equal opportunity. This is a heavily female, middle-class, middle-aged group that supports most of the policy positions of the Democratic party.

New Dealers (6 percent): Older Democrats who experience little financial pressure and are more socially conservative than the national Democratic party. Drawn heavily from the South, many of these old-time Democrats have party roots that go back to Roosevelt. Despite the end of the cold war, New Dealers still universally agree that the best way to ensure peace is through military strength.

Pocketbook Democrats (17 percent): Believers in social justice and an active government role in solving the problems of socio-economic minorities. Most Pocketbook Democrats have less than a high school education and agree that they don't have enough money to make ends meet.

---

ocratic constituencies, except Pocketbook Democrats, the poorest and least-educated Democratic constituency (*People, the Press and Politics,* 15 November 1992, 15–17).

The Times Mirror survey of the 1992 electorate offers interesting insights on how the four major perspectives relate to the core of the Republican and Democratic electorate. This survey also suggests the importance of the independent groups or the "leaning" groups

(Upbeats, Disaffecteds, and Seculars) whose inclination to support one party or the other heavily influences the outcome of elections. Other surveys underscore the importance of these groups to winning. For example, the *National Journal* 1992 election day survey reported solid Democrats at 39 percent of voters, solid Republicans at 34 percent, and independents at 27 percent. Both Republicans and Democrats clearly need the votes of the "leaning"

INDEPENDENT GROUPS

Seculars (9 percent): Democrats who identify more closely with the GOP on certain issues. Seculars are strongly supportive of personal freedoms. It is the liberal Democrat's commitment to choice in sexual preference, abortion, speech, and lifestyle that attracts these voters, who might best be described as social libertarians. Seculars are well-informed, relatively affluent, and more often found on the East and West Coasts. Their defining characteristic is an almost total lack of religious conviction. While 87 percent of the rest of the public says that prayer is an important part of their daily life, only 12 percent of seculars hold this view. Their support for personal freedoms is best reflected in their feelings about censorship: 97 percent disagree with banning books containing dangerous ideas from public school libraries, compared with 48 percent of other Americans.

Disaffecteds (9 percent): Mostly middle-aged, these voters are personally alienated, financially pressured, and deeply skeptical of politicians. Many Disaffecteds are blue-collar workers. They are nearly twice as likely as other groups to agree that hard work offers little guarantee of success. Their political distrust is such that three-quarters of them believe that elected officials care little about what people like them think. They leaned toward the Republicans in 1988 but in 1992 gave their votes to all three candidates, with more going to Bill Clinton than any other. Often they lean toward whichever candidate appears to be ahead.

A decade ago many were "Reagan Democrats." Ideologically, they most closely resemble populists.

Upbeats (11 percent): Independents who leaned to the GOP in 1992, but their attitude profile is almost the opposite of Disaffecteds. Upbeats are primarily young people who tend to be uncritical of government and other institutions. They also believe the United States is a uniquely virtuous and favored nation. Most upbeats agree that Americans can always solve their problems. This group gave Republicans the edge in 1988 and gave Bush 45 percent in 1992 with 49 percent split between Clinton and Perot.

Bystanders/Others (10 percent): Mostly young singles of the urban, lower socioeconomic group having an almost total lack of interest in politics and public affairs. Forty-six percent of Bystanders say they seldom vote, although the style of campaigning used in the 1992 election caused higher than anticipated numbers of this group to go to the polls. The remaining are classified as Others. They have a mixture of views that make it virtually impossible to put them in any one of the other categories. These people seem to represent the group having no discernible ideological preference (see Chapter 1).

Source: The People, the Press and Politics, 15 November 1992, 15–17; Maddox and Lilie 1984.

groups or independent groups to win at the polls (*National Journal*, 7 November 1992, 2543). Sometimes the independent percentage is higher during a campaign than on election day, when voters have often made up their minds and usually support one of the major parties. In most surveys, Democrats are ahead of Republicans by 3–9 percentage points, and independents constitute up to one-third of the electorate.

The Future of the Major Political Parties

Although Republicans made significant gains during the early years of the Reagan administration, party identification has remained fluid since the mid-1980s (see Chapter 4).

Of particular significance for the future of the two parties is their respective appeal to populists. Democrats seem to draw well from populists when economic issues are at the

Figure 13.1 Profile of the American People, 1992

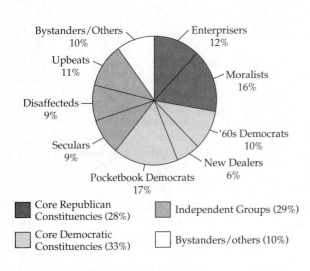

Bystanders/Others 10%
Enterprisers 12%
Upbeats 11%
Moralists 16%
Disaffecteds 9%
'60s Democrats 10%
Seculars 9%
New Dealers 6%
Pocketbook Democrats 17%

■ Core Republican Constituencies (28%)
■ Independent Groups (29%)
□ Core Democratic Constituencies (33%)
□ Bystanders/others (10%)

Source: People, the Press and Politics, *15 November 1992,* 17.

forefront, as they were in 1992. Bill Clinton's selection of Al Gore for vice-president, southerner and Baptist with strong credentials on some family issues, obviously helped the Democratic election effort. George Bush's difficulties in 1992 stemmed from his need to balance tensions between the right populist–conservative (Moralists) and libertarian (Enterprisers) wings of his party, while appealing to independents who tend to be somewhat more liberal on social issues. Internecine strife was already present in 1988, but better times economically allowed Bush to concentrate on social issues, and conservative populists voted overwhelmingly for him. In 1992, economic conditions made these appeals less successful. Democrats maintained the same advantage in the Senate and gained in the governorships, coupled with only modest losses in the House. Republicans did show some gains from the reapportionment process, as they picked up seats in some state legislatures in both the South and Midwest.

Democrats remain the dominant party in

terms of officeholders at the federal and most state levels of the political system and they now hold the presidency as well. What looked to be a threatened decline into minority party status was prevented by the selection of moderate liberals to head the ticket, coupled with economic hard times that the electorate associated with George Bush.

Democrats cannot become complacent, however. Although initial postelection polls showed George Bush and Bill Clinton essentially even in numbers of votes received from white voters (39 and 40 percent, respectively), more intensive analysis in the week following the election had Bush polling 43 percent of the white vote while Clinton took only 38 percent, with the remainder going to independent Ross Perot. Black majorities of 82 percent in the nation as a whole were responsible for the Democrats' victory (*Chicago Tribune*, 15 November 1992, 3; *National Journal*, 7 November 1992, 2542–44).

Voter alienation from politics continued to be evident, as only 55 percent of all Americans old enough to vote cast a ballot for one of the three candidates. Although this percentage represents the first increase in voter turnout since the Goldwater election in 1964, it took millions of dollars of purchased television time by an appealing independent candidate and a major shift in how the candidates communicated with the electorate (see Chapter 4) to achieve this result. Such alienation will only mount if the Democratic president and Congress do not act decisively to formulate policies for dealing with pressing economic and social issues.

In addition, members of what once was the Democrats' largest voting bloc, the New Dealers (older Catholics and unionized workers), are aging or, in the case of southern New Dealers, leaving the party. Younger Catholics as a whole are becoming more highly educated and are among the wealthiest groups in the electorate, while unionized labor represents a smaller and smaller segment of the American industrial work force and is being replaced by greater numbers of service-oriented white-collar workers. Between 1970 and 1990, the percentage of blue-collar workers in the federal civilian work force shrank from 20 percent to 12 percent, while the percentage of white-collar workers grew from 80 percent to 88 percent (*Statistical Abstract, 1992*, 517).

Polls among young people indicate that they have an open mind about party preferences and are likely to be influenced by performance. A June 1987 poll of teens aged thirteen to seventeen showed 48 percent of those questioned defined themselves as more likely to vote Republican. Only 34 percent labeled themselves as Democrats. But in the 1992 election, Bill Clinton led George Bush in both first-time voters and voters between the ages of eighteen and twenty-four by margins of 19 and 16 percent respectively. Clinton's appeal to young voters comes at a good time for Democrats, who must find alternative constituencies to replace the aging members of Roosevelt's New Deal coalition (*National Journal*, 7 November 1992, 2542–44).

To hold together a coalition that the Times Mirror survey suggests is even more self-contradictory than that of its Republican counterparts, Democrats did what was needed in 1992. They emphasized their common belief that government could and should address economic bad times and the inequities that exist in American society. At the same time, Democrats downplayed their differences by deemphasizing policy changes or initiatives in morality- or defense-related areas. Clinton supporters often talked about a sign that hung in Clinton's Little Rock headquarters, "It's the economy, stupid!!" This emphasis did not mean that Democrats shied away from their commitment to choice for women or support for homosexuals. What it did mean was that other points on the party's agenda were subordinated to the economic questions on which all Democrats could agree. The Democrats also needed to win the presidency before an entire generation of young voters began to think that Republicans are the candidates Americans

usually elect as their presidents. Democrats managed to do just that in 1992.

Now President Bill Clinton must use the slightly improved economic climate and the Democrat-controlled Congress to stabilize the living standards of workers who have jobs and, through retraining, to expand the job prospects of lower- and middle-income Americans who have lost jobs because of the streamlining of American business or defense cutbacks. Clinton must also keep his campaign promises to scale back the deficit. These are tall orders in a less than healthy economic environment. If the underlying problems in the economy, especially spiraling health care and deficit costs, prove difficult for Clinton to resolve, the Republicans and Ross Perot will have an opportunity to gain support.

In 1992, Republicans needed to convince the American people to elect more of them to other offices if they were to have any chance of becoming the party of a majority of politically active Americans. The results of the 1992 election give little indication that they will be able to accomplish this goal. Divided government, which gave excuses to both parties in the 1980s, has now been ended at the national level. Americans will finally be able to hold one party accountable for the successes or failures of the mid-1990s. Which party will benefit from this unlocking of party gridlock remains to be seen.

The Future of the Four Major Perspectives

As noted in Chapter 1, survey research data from the early 1990s indicated that liberals, populists, and conservatives were slightly younger than libertarians, but that the libertarians were the largest group. These data seem to suggest that the future of American political perspectives is up for grabs. Other recent data support this assumption. Several social and demographic forces are reshaping the balance among the perspectives, but not in any clear direction. In addition, it is important

Dick Wright. Reprinted by permission of UFS, Inc.

to remember that people from different perspectives need to combine in order to form a majority.

For example, the electorate has become more supportive of both abortion and gay rights during the years between 1977 and 1992. In fact, a Gallup poll taken in 1991 and again in 1992 suggests that support for decriminalizing sexual activity between gay adults increased by 12 percent in one year's time, the largest single-year increase in fifteen years (*Gallup Poll Monthly*, June 1992, 2–6). Conversely, there are some trends running in the electorate that continue to favor right populist and conservative positions.

The so-called baby boomers, that portion of the population born between 1944 and 1964, is becoming politically more important as it ages. The median age of people who actually vote, as distinct from eligible voters, is now over forty (*Public Opinion*, November/December 1987, 22). People tend to develop more stable, tradition-oriented life-styles as they mature. They marry, have children, and often return to churches abandoned during adolescence or young adulthood. Baby boomers seem to be developing more conservative views on social issues as they grow older. Recent polls of boomer-aged Americans indicate a desire to spend more time with family, religious pursuits, and self-introspection (*Gallup Poll Monthly*, April 1991, 31–42). A 1991 analysis shows the number of Americans opposing prayer in the schools as generally decreasing across time, although a majority of Americans (58 percent) still oppose earlier Supreme Court decisions in this area (*American Enterprise*, March/April 1992, 102). Table 13.2 illustrates voter responses to some questions on social issues: a gradual drift toward liberalism on certain social issues is balanced by an increased interest in religious institutions.

TABLE 13.2   *VOTER OPINION ON SOCIAL ISSUES, 1977–1992*

	PERCENT SAYING GAY RELATIONS		PERCENT SAYING ABORTION	
	Should Be Legal	Should Not Be Legal	Should Be Always Legal	Should Be Never Legal
1992	48%	44%	34%	13%
1991	36	54	33	14
1990			31	12
1989			29	17
1988			24	17
1987	33	55		
1986	33	54		
1985	44			
1984				
1983			23	16
1982	45	39		
1981			23	21
1980			25	18
1979			22	19
1978				
1977	43	43	22	19

	PERCENT SUPPORTING	PERCENT SAYING	PERCENT SAYING
	Prayer Ban in Public School	Religion Important to Their Lives	Drug Use Most Important U.S. Problem
1992			
1991	38%	57%	12%
1990	40	58	10
1989	41	55	63
1988	37	54	16
1987		55	8
1986	37	55	2
1985	43	56	(not asked
1984		56	before 1986)
1983		56	
1982	37	56	
1981		56	
1980		52	
1979			
1978			
1977	33		

Source: Gallup Poll Monthly, *April 1992, 42*; Gallup Poll Monthly, *June 1992, 2–3*; Gallup Poll Monthly, *July 1992, 51–52*; American Enterprise, *January/February 1992, 101*; American Enterprise, *March/April 1992, 102*.

This growing drift toward liberalism and libertarianism in the social area should favor Democrats slightly in future elections and may require Republicans to soften the strongly conservative social rhetoric they used at their 1992 presidential convention. In addition, conservatives and libertarians may have to adjust to the greater willingness of Americans to use government to solve problems. One goal of the Reagan and Bush administrations was to get Americans to expect less from government and more from themselves, but a look at the varied things Americans still expect government to do, based on 1991 poll responses (see Table 13.3), suggests that expectations continue. In this survey, 75 percent of those polled said government should provide health care for the sick, and 60 percent said government should provide decent housing for those unable to afford it.

Clearly Americans want contradictory things: most want government to cost less and yet do more. They are frustrated with the size of government and the way it encroaches on

TABLE 13.3   PERCENTAGE OF AMERICANS EXPECTING THE GOVERNMENT TO:
(1991 data)

Provide a job for everyone who wants one	36%
Keep prices under control	63
Provide health care for the sick	75
Provide a decent standard of living for the old	74
Provide industry with the help it needs to grow	57
Provide a decent standard of living for the unemployed	43
Reduce income differences between the rich and poor	36
Give financial assistance to college students from low-income families	72
Provide decent housing for those unable to afford it	60

Source: General Social Surveys, *1972–91, 506–8.*

their lives, yet they want to protect the particular benefits that government gives to them. Americans want the government to assure them their rights, yet they are reluctant to endorse income redistributions that guarantee everyone the same rights to an equal extent. As an example of contradictions, many in Congress supported choice for women in the area of abortion rights yet voted for the Hyde Amendment that forbade the use of government funds by poor women desiring abortions. Democrat Karen Thurman of Florida, cosponsor of a freedom of choice bill that assures the right to choice on abortion for American women, says of her support of the Hyde Amendment, ''I don't think government ought to be involved in the area of reproduction and that includes financing. . . . I have a responsibility to my constituents not to members on this floor'' (quoted in *Holland Sentinel,* 4 July 1993, D12). While many Americans may desire less spending in general, they do not appear sympathetic to conservative-libertarian calls for decreased spending when specific issues are discussed. Table 13.4 shows the percentage of Americans who believe increased spending is essential to solve specific problems. An increasing number of Americans also believe that business and government should work together to provide social benefits such as day care and job security (Miller 1989, 9–11, 59; see also *National Journal,* 6 March 1993, 582; Sussman 1988, 57–73).

Table 13.5 indicates that a majority of Americans also believe the government causes more problems than it solves. While they believe that government finances and the economy are in trouble, they are optimistic about their futures. With so many different opinions, and so many contradictions in public opinion, conservatives and libertarians will have considerable room to maneuver.

These contradictions in public opinion might be perceived as part of a regularly changing cycle, and historians have often interpreted American history as cyclical. Arthur Schlesinger, Sr. (1949), and Arthur Schles-

TABLE 13.4 DOES GOVERNMENT SPENDING NEED TO INCREASE, DECREASE, OR REMAIN THE SAME FOR:

(1991 data)

	INCREASE	DECREASE	REMAIN THE SAME
The environment	50%	25%	25%
Health	60	21	19
The police and law enforcement	47	32	21
Education	62	20	18
The military and defense	11	31	58
Retirement benefits	40	34	26
Unemployment benefits	22	42	36
Culture and the arts	11	36	53

Source: General Social Surveys, *1972–91, 500–2.*

TABLE 13.5 ATTITUDES OF AMERICANS, 1991–1993

Federal government creates more problems than it solves	69%
Federal government solves more problems than it creates	22
(1993 Survey)	
Future generations will be worse off than people today	40
Future generations will be the same as people today	31
Future generations will be better off than people today	25
(1992 Survey)	
Would stay in the United States if had the chance to settle another country	90
Would leave the United States if had chance to settle another country	9
(1991 Survey)	
U.S. economy is not good or poor	85
U.S. economy is excellent or good	15
(1993 Survey)	
Personal finances are not good or poor	51
Personal finances are excellent or good	49
(1993 Survey)	
Optimistic about opportunities to get ahead	60
Pessimistic about opportunities to get ahead	33
(1993 Survey)	

Source: American Enterprise, *July/August 1993, 88–89, 91–92.*

inger, Jr. (1986), have suggested an alternation of public or liberal and private or conservative periods of political orientation. Public-oriented periods (in this textbook's terms, liberal-populist) emphasize reform as opposed to the self-interest–free market emphasis of the private-oriented periods (libertarian-conservative). Frank L. Klingberg (1952) and Jack E. Holmes (1985) describe alternating introvert and extrovert foreign policy mood phases (Klingberg 1952, 239–73; Holmes 1985; Holmes and Elder 1987). Proponents of such theories say that changes often take place around the time people start taking the old way of thinking for granted. While few political scientists perceive strict cycles, the vast majority recognize the constantly changing nature of politics. An intelligent observer of the political scene should have a good sense of history and be prepared for the unexpected.

Of the four perspectives, populism, which is socially conservative but economically liberal, appears best positioned in the 1990s to cast "swing" votes. However, populism is split between left and right varieties. In addition, some traditional themes are no longer acceptable. Racism is still alive, but it is no longer possible to use it overtly in the public policy arena as George Wallace did in 1968. David Duke, a former leader of the Ku Klux Klan, faced the limits of his appeal in his run for the

Randy Wicks. © *The Signal* (Valencia, CA).

governorship of his home state of Louisiana in 1992 and in his foundered presidential campaign of that same year. Patrick Buchanan was only slightly more successful at using anti-immigrant themes in his primary campaigns against Bush in the same year. The lower-middle and lower classes, which are the natural home of populism, have become more educated and thus more tolerant (Lipset 1987, 4–5, 57–58). Between 1940 and 1991 the percentage of adults with a high school diploma rose from 25 to 78 percent (*Statistical Abstract, 1992, 143*).

With women gaining greater economic independence, old-fashioned male chauvinist attitudes are also declining and are no longer possible as a campaign theme for anyone hoping to be successful in contemporary politics (*Statistical Abstract, 1992, 381, 452*). While overt appeals to racial hostility may not play well among today's voters, other populist positions seem to fit the public mood. Government intervention on behalf of the "little people," pro-

tection of American jobs from foreign competition, and the promotion of religious and moral values are some of these. Left populists like Jesse Jackson (see Profile in Chapter 1) and Lane Evans (see Profile in Chapter 6) are thus particularly well positioned. Both Democrats and Republicans recognize the need to appeal to the growing populist constituency (*Gallup Poll Monthly*, March 1992, 5–7; *Congressional Quarterly Weekly Report*, 15 February 1992, 369).

What will be the relative strength of the four perspectives by the year 2000? Events now unforeseen will affect public opinion, so all speculations must be made with caution. Based on current trends, however, it is possible that a chastened liberalism, together with a transformed populism, has the potential to hold the electoral majority in American politics. It is equally possible that libertarians and conservatives will remain significant segments of the electorate; they could even become the majority if they can form coalitions with right popul-

Dana Summers. © 1993, Washington Post Writers Group. Reprinted with permission.

ists on a regular basis. Thus, much will depend on how coalitions are formed. Whether Republicans or Democrats will hold the presidency and Congress depends on which party senses and capitalizes on tendencies toward social liberalism, economic restraint, and an assertive but not aggressive foreign policy.

Certainly one of the most important immediate determinants of the future strength of the two parties will be the performance of President Bill Clinton and the Democratic majorities in the Congress. If they perform well, Democrats can add to their strength in the American political system. Reviews of Clinton at the time this book was put to press were mixed. Some observers have dwelled on problems, while others noted the potential of important new beginnings. Clearly the president will need to deal with special interests in Congress if he is to keep his promises. If he puts his promises aside, Clinton may, like Bush, who suffered from breaking his promise not to raise taxes,

be a one-term president. By the time this book is in your hands, the picture should be clearer.

Government and Your Future

Most of the disagreements among the six perspectives discussed in this textbook revolve around the proper role of government in the lives of the American people. Adherents of all perspectives can agree on one thing: government involvement has increased tremendously within the lifetimes of many people now living. In 1902 government spending at all levels consumed 7.7 percent of the gross national product (GNP). By 1990 government spending at all levels accounted for an estimated 40 percent. By 1992 the United States had experienced twelve straight years of a conservative-libertarian administration committed to tight budgets and limited government; yet overall government spending had actually increased. The federal government alone was estimated

Auth. Courtesy Universal Press Syndicate.

to consume 25 percent of the GNP in 1990, up slightly from 23 percent in 1980, before Ronald Reagan took office (Dye 1981, 234; *Statistical Abstract, 1992,* 279, 431). One area in which there has been an increased call for government regulation has been the environment, illustrated by the concern about the greenhouse effect (see Controversy).

The challenge to young people starts with the observation of many analysts that the current college generation collectively is going to have to work harder than their parents just to provide for their families what their parents have given them. Since many will try to improve their situation, both spouses will have to be in the work force. Housing offers one example of the decline in the rate at which the standard of living has been increasing. Home ownership rose more than 15 percentage points between 1920 to 1960, but between 1960 and 1990 it rose less than 4 percentage points (*Statistical Abstract, 1992,* 716). It will be difficult for the current generation to improve upon the current percentage of 68.

More than half of American marriages already end in divorce (*Statistical Abstract, 1992,* 44; *USA Today,* 9 December 1992, 12A). Environmental, politico-military, and economic problems remain. Being behind one baby boom and ahead of another means that a political system responsive to numbers of voters could be hard on the current college generation. The future indeed presents a hearty challenge (*Business Week,* 25 September 1989, 90–181).

One particular challenge to today's college generation is the national debt, which political leaders to date have proved unwilling to address. It is growing by the hundreds of billions of dollars each year (*Statistical Abstract, 1992,* 315). Efforts to reduce spending have been met with objections from groups benefiting from the expenditures involved. Raising taxes never is popular. However, there will come a time when the bill must be paid, and the current generation of college students are likely to be taxpayers at that time (see Controversy, Chapter 12).

Neil Howe and Bill Strauss, analysts who

have studied American generational change over the span of American history, believe that the generation born between 1961 and 1981 will have generational conflicts with their baby-boomer parents, be fairly conservative, need to deal with greater multiculturalism, not get or receive much from government, and bear a heavy leadership burden in terms of making people aware of future needs (*U.S. News and World Report,* 22 February 1993, 57–58). Of course one cannot predict the future, but it surely holds opportunities for those who are able to recognize them.

Most college students do not have to face the full impact of American tax laws—not quite yet, at any rate. All students, however, will have to deal with government influence in their chosen areas of work. A brief look at several fields of study will emphasize the vast role of government in American life today. It should become clear that all students, not just political science majors, must have a basic understanding of American government, for it will be encountered at just about every turn on the road of life.

Students of medicine and health care will have to deal with heavy government regulation in their fields. According to Syracuse Hospital administrator David M. Beers, 164 different government agencies claim some regulatory jurisdiction over his hospital (*National Journal,* 6 January 1979, 20). These regulations would be a tremendous burden even to someone with a vast knowledge of government; the complexities could be insurmountable to one with little such knowledge. With plans for some form of national health insurance or mandatory health benefits being discussed in Washington, the prospects for increased government involvement in medicine and health appear strong.

Those who plan to conduct research in the various fields of science, such as chemistry and geology, would do well to remember that the national government finances a little less than half of the research conducted by American

colleges and universities each year (*Statistical Abstract, 1992,* 586). Good relations with government and an understanding of research policy are a must for scientists doing basic research, especially when some programs are being eliminated from the federal budget.

Students who plan futures in business administration or economics should be aware of the tremendous amount of government paperwork they will be required to complete. Government regulations in areas like safety, pollution, and fair trade practices affect most businesses, especially larger ones. A working knowledge of the government can be invaluable to a student entering business management. Economics majors must show a special concern for the government sector, due to the influence of economic policy and government spending, which accounts for 40 percent of the nation's GNP (*Statistical Abstract, 1992,* 280, 431).

Government regulations will also be a major concern of future engineers and architects. The results of the Americans with Disabilities Act of 1990 can be seen in the new ramps to public buildings and doors to mass transit buses that meet the needs of Americans in wheelchairs. Automobiles sold in the United States must have certain safety features, including restraints such as seat belts or air bags, and must meet fleet gasoline mileage standards. Architects and engineers will likely see government assume an increasing role in encouraging buildings that are designed to conserve energy, possibly using solar and other renewable sources of energy.

Government involvement in social programs has grown rapidly in recent decades, and social workers are likely to be employed by government. Governments spent about $41 billion on public assistance (not including social security) in 1975, and the figure increased to $127 billion in 1989 (*Statistical Abstract, 1992,* 354). Social workers can expect a close relationship with the government in the coming years.

CONTROVERSY

The Greenhouse Effect: A Problem for the Future

"Everybody talks about the weather," wise-cracked Mark Twain, "but nobody does anything about it." Twain's observation may no longer be true. If current scientific theories are accurate, human activities may be altering the earth's climate more drastically than anything since the last Ice Age. As the world's most powerful nation, the United States will play a key role in determining how humankind will respond to this global problem.

The scientific explanation for the so-called greenhouse effect (which has little to do with the operation of a greenhouse) is generally agreed on. Carbon dioxide (CO_2), a minor component of the atmosphere, keeps the earth warm enough to sustain life by trapping heat from the sun that would otherwise leave the earth's surface. But use of fossil fuels (coal, oil, and natural gas), as well as the clearing of forests, is increasing the amount of carbon dioxide in the atmosphere by about one part per million per year. If Third World nations industrialize using primarily fossil fuels for energy, the amount of carbon dioxide could double within a century. This increase would raise global average temperatures, but how much is unclear—the increase could be less than two or as much as nine degrees Fahrenheit, depending on the behavior of other factors such as clouds and ocean currents. Emissions of other manufactured "greenhouse gases" like methane could significantly speed the warming.

If it were occurring over several centuries, a warmer climate would not necessarily be bad. Large northern areas in Canada and the Soviet Union, for example, might be opened up to agriculture. It is the speed of the projected change that alarms many scientists. Since plants and trees migrate slowly, forests might die as they become trapped in the "wrong" climate. Drier conditions in some agricultural areas could, according to one authority, "cause millions to starve (in the short term) even if in the end more food could be grown." While forecasts of total melting of polar icecaps are science fiction, partial melting would raise sea levels several feet, flooding some low-lying areas. At least one sovereign nation, the Maldive Islands in the Indian Ocean, would be eliminated by a three-foot rise in sea level.

What can be done to slow global warming? In theory, the industrialized world could dramatically reduce its use of fossil fuels. Prototype automobiles get as much as 138 miles per gallon. Using the most efficient technology already on the market would cut electricity use by three-quarters without depriving anyone of electric lights or refrigerators. However, incentives would be needed, and here the perspectives are likely to differ. For example, few consumers buy fuel-efficient cars because speed and horsepower are more valued. Conservatives and libertarians will probably favor higher gasoline prices, letting the market encourage conservation, while liberals and left populists may call for government fuel economy standards or rationing. Some experts like Amory Lovins of the Rocky Mountain Institute argue that the industrial nations must turn over energy-efficient technologies to the Third World to safeguard their own climates. In a competitive world, such a move is sure to be controversial.

The problem of global warming is international. Nations of the Third World are not ignoring it, but neither do they wish to sacrifice their plans for development. To respond to growing concerns about global warming and biodiversity, the United Nations Conference on Environment and Development sponsored an Earth Summit at Rio de Janeiro in June 1992, attended by more than 130 countries. The Bush administration refused to sign the biodiversity treaty, arguing that it would weaken patent protection for American biotechnology corporations. In a counterproposal Bush added $150 million to the funds the United States spends on conservation efforts for the world's forests. The Bush administration agreed to sign the treaty on global climate change, but only after target dates were made much less specific.

"*You Know, Harriet, Maybe It's Time We Worried about the 'Greenhouse Effect'...*"

Bruce Beattie. Courtesy *Daytona Beach News-Journal*.

While Rio was a success in bringing the world community to the negotiating table, it failed to develop real solutions.

If prevention efforts fail, people could try to adapt to warmer conditions—developing new irrigation systems, for example, or relocating settlements away from threatened coastal areas. Such policies would also generate political opposition, however. The most radical proposals call for intervening in the global climate to counteract the greenhouse effect, perhaps by dumping fertilizer on the oceans to grow algae (which absorb carbon dioxide), planting trees on a massive scale, or placing giant mirrors in space to reflect away sunlight. But even if such projects prove practical and safe, cooperation with other countries will again be required. As the Earth Summit made clear, such cooperation is only beginning.

Clearly, the issue of global warming has enormous implications for both domestic and foreign policy. Is the American political system capable of responding adequately? Environmentalists are more optimistic with the Clinton-Gore team in the White House. Not only did Clinton support the biodiversity treaty negotiated at the Earth Summit,

but Gore, as senator from Tennessee, had been one of the Senate's experts on the environment. He is convinced that environmental protection need not be pitted against jobs and looks to an expansion of environmentally oriented industries that will increase hiring (see Controversy in Chapter 5). Generally, however, politicians tend to respond to constituents, who in turn tend to focus on short-term issues. President Clinton proposed an energy tax based on the heat content of fuels, but it was changed to a gasoline tax in a compromise with Congress. Americans right now are more concerned about immediate job losses, but if they want to avoid painful disruptions in their lives and those of their children, they need to demand that their leaders develop workable solutions to long-term environmental issues.

Source: Gribben 1981; *New York Times*, 3 September 1989, E5; Schneider 1989, 70–79; Ruckelshaus 1989, 166–74; *New York Times*, 22 April 1993, A1, A10; Bailey 1993, 141–67; *Congressional Quarterly Weekly Report*, 18 September 1993, 2489.

Students of the arts and humanities can probably expect little government interference in their chosen careers; after all, one would think there is no place for government regulation of the arts and humanities in a democracy. For most of its history, the national government has given minimal support to these areas but in 1990 a total of $311.8 million was contributed by the federal government in its role as "a patron of the arts" (*Statistical Abstract, 1992*, 244). In the future some of the money may come with more strings attached because of the recent public outcry about subsidy for allegedly obscene art. Still, government support of projects in the various fields of the arts and humanities can be obtained by skilled people who know how to ask for it.

Education has received considerable attention in the past few years. The government plays a major role in funding education, with all levels of government spending at $343 billion in 1988 (*Statistical Abstract, 1992*, 141). For the most part, curriculum is determined at the state and local levels, but the federal government has increased its influence. Many people believe that U.S. education is lacking in quality compared to that of other industrial democracies, and they advocate major reforms. There is a need for good teachers at all levels. A person going into a career in education must understand government.

The importance of government to the legal and law enforcement professions is obvious. Government bodies make and enforce the laws. The energy industry has been heavily regulated by government for many years. Farmers receive considerable help from government (about $17.2 billion in 1992) but must comply with regulations on soil conservation, use of pesticides, and other matters (*Statistical Abstract, 1992*, 319). People in agriculture must also consider government policies regarding quality and selling of products, while those in leisure-time industries must consider government safety and trade standards.

Public administrators who carry out the laws at all levels of government usually do not receive salaries equal to those of high-level administrators in the private sector, but they do receive the satisfaction that comes with serving the public. Civilian government positions at the state, local, and federal level constituted 14.7 percent of the American work force in 1990 (*Statistical Abstract, 1992*, 304, 381), and some of you will fill these positions in the coming years. Political leaders do not have the time to learn all the details of the complex issues with which they must deal and hence must depend on public administrators to help. In addition, most politicians hire personal staffs. A congressional or state legislative staffer often has the opportunity to influence the political process in ways not appreciated by most Americans.

Those of you who pursue careers as elected officials will obviously have an important role in the American political process. Like the word "bureaucrat," the word "politician" has some bad connotations with many Americans, yet there is little evidence that dishonesty is more prevalent in politics than in most other fields. If it were, that would be an additional argument for honorable and capable citizens to seek elective office.

Finally, there are religious vocations. One of the founding principles of the United States concerns the separation of church and state; the American government cannot favor one religion over another or prevent people from expressing their beliefs. Yet, as in other areas, government brings at least some indirect influence to bear on religion. American taxpayers are allowed to deduct religious contributions from their taxable income, and in 1991 $65.8 billion in religious contributions (just over half of all charitable contributions) were deducted on federal income tax forms (*Statistical Abstract, 1992*, 375). This tax exemption encourages Americans to contribute to the religious organizations of their choice and provides some indirect support to religion. People who plan to follow religious vocations often are affected by property tax exemptions for religious organizations and the continuing debate over government aid to various kinds of private schools. Members of the religious community also deal with problems of their congregations (or parishes) and communities that often relate to government involvement in the ordinary lives of American citizens.

WILL THE SYSTEM WORK?

The American system of government was designed not to subject, but to be subject to, the people. "Government of the people, by the people, for the people" has stood the test of time in the United States and has come to represent freedom to people all over the globe. Nonetheless, many Americans today fail to take an interest in "their" government. "You can't fight city hall" is their slogan as they complacently accept rules passed down by others with which they do not agree. One thing that you should learn from this textbook, however, is that you can fight city hall—or at least change city hall so that you will not have to fight it.

Perhaps the most difficult question to ask regarding the working of the system is whether it will continue to work in what is certain to be a future more complex than the present. In accordance with the thrust of this textbook, our answer is yes. We must qualify this yes by noting that it is impossible to project the future with certainty.

What is possible is to project the present into the likely future noted in this chapter. Each of the four major perspectives has a fu-

Mike Luckovich. By permission of artist and Creators Syndicate.

ture. Whenever one or two are seen as having failed, others rise to prominence. The diversity of American government gives the four a variety of ways to push concerns regardless of which ones are on top at the moment. In addition, the four share a number of concerns and are conditioned to compromise. Feminists have enough support to have an effect on the competition among perspectives, but Marxists remain weak.

The likely continuation of the trend toward specialization means that government will have a lot of information available to it, and complexity will probably increase despite efforts at simplification. These two trends are likely to allow the system of checks and balances to continue, with some needed modifications of the kind that have been experienced regularly in American history.

At this writing, Americans are more pessimistic regarding the political system than they were at the time of our first edition. However, we have noted conflicting trends and wishes in this chapter. Thus we believe at least some of the frustration is the inevitable result of conflicting viewpoints that are difficult to satisfy. No one of the four major perspectives will get its way all of the time on all of the issues. Rather, policy will continue to be a compromise that starts from common ground and splits differences in areas of disagreement. That result is perhaps the best that can be expected from a system in which participants must compromise.

In closing, we want to emphasize that we reject views which see the American system either as perfect or as terrible, flawed in all respects. The latter view leads to premature cynicism, while the former leads to rejecting the validity of the dynamic interactions that propel the system. Rather, the informed observer needs to build on the basic information presented in this textbook by engaging in the process of government. Your participation makes the system work.

GLOSSARY

The terms defined in this glossary are those we have identified as key terms within the chapters and shown in boldface in the text. The number or numbers after each entry are those of the chapters in which the term is introduced.

We have not generally provided definitions more extensive than those in the text, although some terms have been expanded upon so that they can be understood in the context of the text. For elaboration on these terms, as well as others, consult Jack C. Plano and Milton Greenberg, *The American Political Dictionary*, 9th ed. (Fort Worth: Harcourt Brace Jovanovich, 1993).

Actuality An edited portion of a statement or speech provided to the media by a campaign office or officeholder. [5]

Advisory opinion A view on the constitutionality of a law offered by a court before an actual case on the issue has reached it. In the United States, federal courts do not issue advisory opinions. [8]

Affirmative action An effort to reverse a pattern of past racial or gender discrimination by setting goals and timetables for making workplaces, classrooms, or other areas more representative. Such action usually relates to hiring policy or admission standards designed to offset existing discrimination by increasing the percentage of nonwhite, female, or handicapped people in the workplace or student body. [9, 10]

Agenda setting The media's influence in deciding what is news and thus what the public agenda will be. [5]

Agricultural group An independent interest group of any size that represents farmers. Different categories of agricultural groups represent different interests within the agricultural field. [5]

Alliance An agreement whereby two or more nations with common goals agree to improve their power position on an issue by joining together in defense of their common interests. [11]

Amicus curiae A person (or group) permitted to advise a court on a matter of law in a case to which it is not a party. The document is called an amicus curiae (literally, "friend of the court") brief. [8]

Annapolis Convention A 1786 convention attended by delegates from five states who sought to establish uniform commercial regulations but concluded that they could not do so under the Articles of Confederation, which could be amended only by unanimous vote. The delegates called for a new convention to revise the Articles. [2]

Anti-Federalists Those who opposed the Federalists and the ratification of the Constitution, which Anti-Federalists believed gave too much power to the national government at the expense of the states. A key concern of the Anti-Federalists was that the new Constitution originally did not include a bill of rights. [2]

Appellate jurisdiction The power of a court to review the decision of a lower court. [8]

Appropriation The allocation of money by Congress to support a specific program or piece of legislation. [6]

Arms control Measures to restrict the number of weapons and their continued production, usually through a process of negotiation with an opposing country. [11]

Articles of Confederation Document outlining the first government of the United States. Written in 1776–77, it was ratified in 1781 by the thirteen original states. It gave the Confederation Congress an impressive list of powers, but action required agreement of nine states, and amendments required agreement of all thirteen. This confederation of sovereign states was replaced by the Constitution in 1789. [2]

Authoritarianism A government in which control is in the hands of an individual or group of individuals and freedoms are strictly limited. Authoritarianism emphasizes obedience, efficiency, and expediency over diversity, opinion, and feedback. [1]

Autonomy Independence from central control; the power to make final decisions, usually without the need for consultative or joint action. In the federal system, state and local governments have autonomy in some areas and partial autonomy in others. [3]

Balance of power A theory of international relations that seeks peace and security through an equilibrium of power distributed among groups of nations. [11]

Bandwagon effect An election phenomenon in which voters tend to favor the candidate who is already ahead. [5]

Bicameral legislature A legislature composed of two houses usually constituted according to different principles of selection. In the United States one house, the House of Representatives, is based on population, and the other house, the Senate, is based on the equal representation of the states. [2]

Bill of attainder Legislation punishing a specific individual, rather than a kind of behavior, without trial; prohibited by the Constitution. [6, 9]

Bill of Rights The first ten amendments to the Constitution, ratified by the states in 1791 and intended primarily to protect individual rights from arbitrary national government action. [2, 9]

Blanket primary Primary in which all registered voters may participate. A voter may vote in the primary of more than one party. [4]

Board of Governors The seven-member board that governs the Federal Reserve System; appointed by the president with the advice and consent of the Senate. [12]

Bracket creep A tax system phenomenon in which taxpayers are automatically placed in higher tax brackets as inflation raises their incomes. [12]

Budget deficit The amount by which expenditures in a given year exceed revenues. [12]

Bureaucracy Any group of people organized to accomplish a task in a routine hierarchical manner. The federal government's bureaucracy consists of the agencies and people—both civil servants and political appointees—who administer the government's programs. [7, 10]

Bureaucrat An administrative worker in a government agency who carries out everyday policy decisions. [10]

Business group An independent interest group of any size that represents businesses and protects their interests. [5]

Cabinet The body of persons appointed by a head of state to direct the executive departments of the government. They may or may not be close personal advisers. In the United States the cabinet usually includes the vice-president. [7]

Camp David Agreement A 1978 agreement between Israel and Egypt negotiated by President Jimmy Carter and signed at Camp David, Maryland, that resulted in Egypt's recognition of Israel in return for Israel's withdrawal from Egyptian territory captured in the 1967 Six Day War. [11]

Capitalism An economic system based on a supply and demand economy that includes private ownership of the means of production, free markets, and minimal government intervention. [1]

Case law Body of law created through judicial interpretations of the Constitution, statutes passed by Congress and state legislatures, and administrative agency decisions. [8]

Caucus The first form of delegate selection used in the United States, in which candidates were selected by state and county meetings composed of delegates chosen in local meetings. [4]

Censure The power of each house of Congress to officially reprimand or condemn the activities of a member of Congress without any sanctions. [6]

Certiorari Judicial authority of a higher court to decide which appeals from lower courts have enough merit to warrant a further hearing. In the U.S. Supreme Court a writ of certiorari is issued when at least four of the nine justices believe a case deserves review. [8]

Checks and balances System set up by the U.S. Constitution whereby the powers of each of the three branches of government are constrained by the powers of the others. The powers of the national and state governments are also mutually checked and balanced. [2]

Circuit court Another name for a U.S. court of appeal, so called because the judges used to ride from town to town on a regular circuit to try cases. Eleven of the thirteen courts of appeal cover the fifty states. These circuit courts have appellate jurisdiction over all cases from the district courts and the regulatory agencies. [8]

Civil liberties Rights or freedoms from government interference guaranteed by the Bill of Rights, the first ten amendments to the Constitution that protect individuals against actions by government. [9]

Civil rights Rights protected by the Thirteenth, Fourteenth, and Fifteenth Amendments to the Constitution, which were aimed against racial discrimination by the states. [9]

Class-action suit Lawsuit on behalf of a group of people who have a similar grievance against the same organization or individual. The class-action suit makes it possible for a number of small claims that might not individually have been worth pursuing to be combined into one case. [8]

Clear and present danger doctrine The doctrine that freedom of speech may be limited when it poses a threat to public order or national security. [9]

Closed primary A primary requiring that voters be registered as supporters of the party for which they vote. [4]

Closed rule A rule issued by the House Rules Committee that prohibits amendments on a bill while it is debated on the House floor. [6]

Cloture A vote that can end continual debate or filibuster in the Senate and bring the bill to a vote. Sixteen senators must first sign a petition to close debate and then three-fifths of the Senate (sixty senators) must vote in favor of the cloture. [6]

Coattail effect The tendency for the winning candidate at the top of the ticket (most often the president) to carry his or her party's candidates for lower offices to victory. [4]

Cold war An ideological conflict without direct violence between the superpowers that characterized post–World War II relations between the communist Soviet Union and the capitalist United States. [11]

Collective security A system in which nations agree to join together to oppose any nation that commits military aggression. [11]

Commander in chief The president's role in commanding the U.S. armed forces. The Constitution (Article II, Section 2) thus establishes the civilian control of the military. Presidents have assumed leadership in every war the United States has conducted and have often used their power as commander in chief to involve the nation in undeclared military actions. [7]

Commerce Clause The clause of the Constitution (Article I, Section 8) giving Congress the power to regulate foreign and interstate commerce. [2, 3]

Commerce Compromise A compromise at the Constitutional Convention between northern and southern regional interests whereby Congress could tax imports but not exports. [2]

Committee chair A majority party member who is in charge of a congressional committee. [6]

Committee of the whole A procedure used by the House of Representatives at the time of consideration of amendments in which formal rules are suspended to allow freer debate and a smaller quorum. The House needs only one hundred members to operate as a committee of the whole. [6]

Common law A set of principles derived from past

judicial decisions. Some of these principles go back to England in the Middle Ages. [8]

Communicator   A role of a member of Congress involving informing and collecting opinions of constituents on legislative actions and issues. [6]

Communism   An economic system based on a classless society and public ownership of the means of production. Communism is the goal of Marxist theory. [1]

Comparable worth   A criterion for measuring jobs held by men and women that attempts to ensure that there will be similar pay and benefits for jobs requiring similar types of skills. [12]

Complex interdependence   The idea that in the modern world, with its growing economic and social interrelationships, war will no longer be a real possibility and power relationships will increasingly resemble interdependent webs. [11]

Concurrent jurisdiction   The ability of more than one court to have jurisdiction over, or rule on, the same issue, usually different federal and state courts. [8]

Concurrent resolution   A measure passed by one house of Congress with the agreement of the other house. Concurrent resolutions do not have the force of law, are not given appropriations, and do not need the president's signature. [6]

Confederation Congress   Governing body of the United States during the period of the Articles of Confederation, 1781–89. It had impressive powers, but was dependent on states for revenue. Each state had one vote; legislation required a two-thirds majority. [2]

Conference committee   A temporary committee consisting of several members of the House and Senate, most of whom worked on a bill, constituted to resolve differences between House and Senate versions of the bill. [6]

Conflict of interest   A situation in which present or past public officials might take advantage of their experience or position for private gain. [5, 10]

Congress   The legislative body in American government. Congress consists of the Senate and the House of Representatives. [6]

Consent calendar   Schedule on which noncontroversial or minor House bills are placed when released from committee. For example, appropriations of less than $1 million may appear on the consent calendar. [6]

Consent decree   An agreement between the government and the offending entity to redress a perceived wrong. For example, an agency of the federal government found to be out of compliance with federal equal opportunity employment laws may have to sign a consent decree that initiates action to bring the agency back into compliance with federal law. Consent decrees often follow a government finding of noncompliance. [10]

Conservatism   A perspective that began as the opposition of European aristocrats to liberalism and the changes in society it advocates. Conservatism promotes the idea that people need the direction and structure tradition or religion provides. [1]

Conservative coalition   An alliance of Republicans and southern Democrats in Congress that for many years made it difficult for the Democratic majority in the House and Senate to accomplish its legislative agenda. [6]

Constitution   A written document that is the fundamental law of a country. [2]

Constitutional amendment   A method of modifying a constitution that involves a process of proposal and ratification; the document that results from this process. [2]

Constitutional Convention   Meeting called in Philadelphia in 1787 that drafted the United States Constitution, subsequently ratified by the thirteen original states. The Constitution has been amended twenty-seven times, including the first ten amendments (the Bill of Rights), which were part of a ratification compromise. [2]

Containment   A Truman administration policy begun in 1947 to stop the expansion of Soviet control by supporting those nations near the Soviet Union that were threatened by a communist takeover. [11]

Content-neutral   The doctrine that freedom of assembly can be limited only to protect the rights of those not participating and not to prevent the expression of particular ideas. [9]

Continental Congress   Governing body of the United States during the Revolutionary War. Delegates were appointed at first by revolutionary provincial congresses and later by state legislatures. [2]

Convention   An assembly of delegates and leaders of a party that selects candidates and carries out party business. [4]

County court   State court at the county level that has original jurisdiction over most major civil and criminal cases; often called a district, circuit, or superior court. [8]

Court of appeal A court above the U.S. district court and below the U.S. Supreme Court; also known as a circuit court, because judges used to ride from town to town on a regular circuit to try cases. Since most federal cases never reach the Supreme Court, the circuit court is usually the court of last resort. [8]

Court packing President Franklin Roosevelt's 1937 plan to increase the number of Supreme Court Justices from nine to fifteen. Had the plan succeeded, the additional posts would have allowed Roosevelt to "pack" the Court with liberals and secure Court agreement with his liberal-populist economic policies. More generally, court packing is a tactic sometimes used by the president during the judicial appointment process to ensure that federal justices hold political and ideological beliefs similar to his. [8]

Covert operation A concealed action in foreign policy approved by the president and carried out by intelligence agencies, usually the Central Intelligence Agency. [7, 11]

Cruel and unusual punishment A phrase in the Eighth Amendment to the Constitution that makes lingering torture and degrading treatment unconstitutional. It also requires that the penalty for crimes be appropriate for the act committed. [9]

De facto segregation Segregation that results from housing patterns and individual decisions, literally, "segregation following from fact." This type of segregation is not illegal. [9]

De jure segregation Segregation imposed by law; no longer permitted in the United States. [9]

Debtor nation Any country that borrows more money from other countries than it lends to them. The United States is now the world's largest debtor nation. [12]

Declaration of Independence Document that created the original confederation of the thirteen states in 1776. It proclaimed the independence of the American colonies from Great Britain and provided justification for the Revolutionary War. [2]

Declaration of war Official statement passed by Congress that a state of war exists between the United States and another country. The president can ask for war, but only Congress can declare war. [6]

Delegate theory of representation The theory that a legislator's duty is to reflect as accurately as possible the preferences of constituents. [6]

Democracy Rule by a majority of adults who decide to vote; a system that gives the people final political authority. [1]

Democratic party A major American political party that developed from the Democratic-Republican party of Thomas Jefferson established by the end of George Washington's years in office (1789–97); the majority party since 1932. The party is most strongly supported by minorities, low-income people, and organized labor groups, and intellectuals. [4]

Democratic socialism The combination of a political emphasis on liberalism and an economic emphasis on Marxism. Political institutions in a democratic socialist state are generally democratic and representative; economic institutions are heavily regulated and may even be owned by the state. [1]

Depression A long lasting down phase in the business cycle characterized by decreased purchasing power, currency deflation, and high unemployment. [12]

Détente A Nixon administration policy to improve relations with the Soviet Union through arms control measures and an expansion of trade. The French term means "relaxation of tensions." Détente ultimately broke down due to lack of trust and differences in values. [11]

Dictatorship A government in which one person makes all the major decisions and has little or no responsibility to the people he or she governs. [1]

Dillon's Rule A rule articulated by an Iowa judge in 1872 that exemplifies the state's authority and priority over local governments. The rule states that a municipal corporation may perform only those duties assigned to it by the state; if there is any dispute over who has power, the dispute will be resolved in favor of the state. [3]

Diplomacy The process by which nations carry out political relationships with other nations; includes dialogue in an effort to reach an agreement. [11]

Direct lobbying A lobbying technique involving personal interaction and often conducted on a one-on-one basis. [5]

Disarmament The reduction by a government of its own military forces or weapons. [11]

Discharge calendar A list of bills that have been

removed from committee for the purpose of being considered on the House floor. Bills may be moved to this calendar even if the committee has not passed them; the rarely employed procedure used to do so is called a discharge petition. [6]

Discount rate   The interest rate charged by the Federal Reserve on loans to member banks. [12]

District court   Federal court of original jurisdiction where most federal cases begin. There are ninety-four U.S. district courts. [8]

Divided government   Government with one party controlling the presidency and the other controlling Congress. [4, 6, 7]

Domino theory   The post–World War II theory that the fall of one nation to communism would have a domino effect—that is, cause other nations to fall to communism as well; the principle behind U.S. involvement in Vietnam. [11]

Dual economy   A theory, based on the role of large corporations and labor unions in an economy, which holds that a small number of large firms control most manufacturing industries and negotiates good wage settlements with their labor unions. The result is positive for these industries, but promotes inflation and ignores the rest of the economy and employees of small and medium-size companies. [12]

Due process   Established legal proceedings that act as safeguards, assuring individuals that laws are reasonable and applied in an equitable manner and protecting them from the arbitrary denial of life, liberty, or free use of property. For example, the Fifth Amendment protects individuals charged with a crime from testifying against themselves if they believe it is against their interests to do so. [8, 9]

Dumping   An unfair trading practice in which goods are sold below cost in order to put a competitor out of business. [11]

Economic and Social Council (ECOSOC)   The United Nations department that coordinates economic and social policies and programs. ECOSOC has called world attention to some economic and social conditions in the Third World. [11]

Economic sanctions   Economic measures, such as boycotts and embargoes, taken by one or more nations against others to impose foreign policy goals. These might include withholding aid or not allowing trade. [11, 12]

Economy and efficiency movement   Measures taken in the early 1900s to improve city and state services and to maximize the effectiveness of government resources by following corporate examples; applied privately endowed municipal research to government agencies. [10]

Eighteenth Amendment   Amendment to the Constitution (1919) that prohibited the manufacture, sale, or transportation of alcoholic beverages. It was repealed in 1933 by the Twenty-first Amendment. [2]

Eighth Amendment   Amendment to the Constitution (1791) that bans "cruel and unusual punishments" along with excessive bail and fines. [9]

Elastic Clause   The clause of the Constitution (Article I, Section 8) giving Congress the power to make any laws that are "necessary and proper" for carrying out the enumerated powers. [3, 6]

Electioneering   An interest group technique that emphasizes getting individuals elected who, the group hopes, will help its cause. Electioneering may involve voter registration drives, general campaign assistance, and campaign contributions to candidates who support the interest group's goals. [5]

Electoral college   A body of electors popularly chosen in each state and the District of Columbia who meet on the same day in their respective states and cast ballots for the president and vice-president. With the exception of Maine, the candidate who wins the majority of a state's popular vote wins all the electors from that state. Electors are usually not bound to vote for a certain candidate, but they almost always do. The electoral college was a compromise between those at the Constitutional Convention who wanted direct popular election of the president and those who wanted election by Congress or by state legislatures. [2, 4]

Eminent domain   The power of government to take private property for public use provided just compensation is given. [3, 9]

Enumerated powers   Powers specifically granted to the federal government by the Constitution. [3]

Equal Protection Clause   The clause in the Fourteenth Amendment that restricts setting classifications for different types of people to a reasonable, planned purpose. It says that a state may not "deny to any person within its jurisdiction the equal protection of the law." A reasonable classification is the different tax classes established according to what a person is able to pay. Unreasonable classifications such as race or national origin have been interpreted as denying people equal protection of the laws. [1, 9]

Equal Rights Amendment Proposed amendment to the Constitution stating that "equality of rights under the law shall not be denied or abridged . . . on account of sex." It was first offered in 1923 and has been offered almost every year since. In 1972 it was offered with a deadline for ratification of 1979, extended to 1982, but failed to pass the required three-quarters of the states. Some continue to work for its passage. [1]

Establishment Clause Clause in the First Amendment that prohibits any law favoring the establishment of religion and requires government to act in a neutral manner with regard to religion. The Supreme Court has construed this clause to erect a wall of separation between church and state but has been willing to make certain accommodations to religiously affiliated institutions. [9]

Ex post facto law A law that disadvantages the accused because it makes an act a crime after it has been committed, increases the penalty for the crime, or allows for an easier conviction by modifying rules of evidence. Ex post facto laws are forbidden by the Constitution (Article I, Section 9). [6, 9]

Exclusionary rule Principle that evidence obtained illegally cannot be used against the defendant in a criminal trial. [9]

Executive agreement An international agreement made by the president with a foreign nation similar to a treaty except that it can be implemented without congressional approval; it may, however, require funding by Congress. Such agreements may be kept secret when necessary (during wartime, for example) and are binding by the power and authority vested in the president. [7]

Executive branch The branch of government responsible for enforcement of the laws. This branch is also responsible for diplomatic representation and the appointment of government officials. In the United States it includes the president and his cabinet, their departments and agencies, the Executive Office of the President, and the bureaucrats who work within them. [2]

Executive Office of the President An office created in 1939 to assist the president that now includes twelve offices: the White House Office, Office of Management and Budget, Council of Economic Advisers, National Security Council, Office of Policy Development, Office of the United States Trade Representative, Office of Science and Technology Policy, Office of Administration, Office of National Drug Control Policy, National Space Council, President's Foreign Intelligence Advisory Board, and the Executive Residence at the White House. [7]

Executive power Power granted to the president; the responsibility to enforce the laws of the land. [7]

Executive regulatory agency A unit of government that imposes requirements or regulations on businesses. These requirements have a large impact on the economy. The agency may be assigned to a cabinet department or independent. Examples are the Occupational Safety and Health Administration of the Department of Labor and the Environmental Protection Agency. Each agency has a single head who is appointed and may be removed by the president. By contrast, heads of independent regulatory commissions are appointed by the president, confirmed by the Senate for fixed terms, and cannot be fired by the president. [10]

Exit poll A poll taken of voters immediately after they have voted. [5]

Exports Products going out of a country, especially for sale or trade to a foreign country; the total value of such products. [2]

External debt Money owed by the United States government to foreign individuals or institutions. [12]

Extra-constitutional power Activity of Congress or the president that is not clearly specified in the Constitution. Two extra-constitutional powers of Congress are investigation and the legislative veto. [6]

Factions James Madison's term for interest groups. He viewed them as inimical to the public interest and in need of control. [4]

Federal balance of payments The difference between the taxes collected in a state and the budgetary appropriations by the federal government spent in that state. [3]

Federal lands Real estate owned by the national government. [3]

Federal Reserve System A bank management system established in 1913 to prevent bank failures by providing that adequate emergency funds would be maintained and banking practices would be supervised. It comprises twelve banks, one for each of the twelve designated Federal Reserve districts across the United States. Each bank is governed by a board of directors. The Federal Reserve System as a whole is governed by a seven-person Board of Governors appointed by the president. [12]

Federalism   The division of political power between the national and state levels. [2, 3]

Federalists   Supporters of the Constitution who promoted its ratification and the formation of the Union. Many also became members of the Federalist pary, the first American political party. [2]

Feminism   The advocacy of women's rights to overcome discrimination against women. As a political perspective, feminism works for change in all aspects of society to improve the position of women. [1]

Fifteenth Amendment   Amendment to the Constitution (1870) that explictly forbids the states from restricting voting rights on account of "race, color, or previous condition of servitude." [9]

Fifth Amendment   Amendment to the Constitution (1791) that guarantees the right not to be tried twice for the same crime or made to testify against oneself. It also states that no one can be deprived of life, liberty, or property without due process of law and requires a grand jury indictment for major crimes. [2, 9]

Filibuster   A tactic used in the Senate to delay action on a bill by taking advantage of the unlimited debate authorized by custom and Senate rule 22, which also provides a mechanism for stopping such debate. [6] *See also* Cloture.

First Amendment   Amendment to the Constitution (1791) that guarantees freedom of religion, speech, press, assembly, and petition for redress of grievances; also prohibits an establishment of religion. [2, 9]

First-term members   Members of Congress in their first term of office who have less seniority than members who have been reelected. [6]

First World   The nations that are the most advanced economically; most have capitalistic economic systems. [11]

Fiscal policy   Government's use of its control over finances to regulate the national economy by means of federal taxes and spending. [12]

Floor leader   Representative or senator responsible for guiding his or her party's program through the House of Representatives or Senate, respectively. There is a majority party and a minority party floor leader in each chamber. [6]

Foreign policy   The goals of a nation's international relations, and the actions taken to achieve those goals. [11]

Formula grant   A type of federal aid given to states and localities generally allocated on the basis of a formula or set of criteria. For example, low-income housing money might be designated for urban areas with high minority populations and a low tax base. These three criteria would be used to figure the formula for distributing the available federal money. [3]

Fourteenth Amendment   Amendment to the Constitution (1868) that was designed to protect the rights of the newly freed slaves and restore the importance of the judiciary. It made all persons born or naturalized in the United States citizens and barred any state from depriving "any person of life, liberty, or property, without due process of law" or denying "any person within its jurisdiction the equal protection of the laws." Gradually interpreted to give the federal government the power to intervene when states permitted the violation of individual rights. [1, 3, 8, 9]

Fourth Amendment   Amendment to the Constitution (1791) that prohibits "unreasonable searches and seizures" of persons and their possessions. It requires that police present a judge with probable cause to obtain a search or arrest warrant. [9]

Franking privilege   Policy that gives members of Congress free mail by placing their signatures on mail instead of a postage stamp. [4, 6]

Free Exercise Clause   Clause in the First Amendment that guarantees the free exercise of religion. [9]

Free market economy   An economy that permits competition among businesses with minimal government control of economic activity. [1]

Free rider problem   Term coined to describe the problem public interest groups have with people who do not feel the need to join the group or pay the membership costs but will still benefit from the group's actions. [5]

Free trade   An economic policy aimed at minimizing trade barriers between nations. [11]

Frostbelt   The Northeast and Midwest of the United States. [3]

General Agreement on Tariffs and Trade (GATT) An international organization that sponsors talks and agreements that try to reduce trade barriers among nations. [11]

General Assembly The major body of the United Nations in which issues and problems are discussed by all members on the basis of equal representation. It is involved with almost every function of the United Nations. [11]

Gentlemen's agreement An informal, but binding, understanding between individuals, specifically members of the Senate. For example, decisions in regard to the rules governing debate in the Senate are not usually made by the Senate Rules and Administration Committee but informally by "gentlemen's agreement" between majority and minority floor leaders. [6]

Gerrymandering Drawing electoral district boundaries for partisan and factional advantage by creating majorities of one's own party in as many districts as possible while decreasing the potential legislative power of opposing parties. [6]

Gold standard A system in which currency is "backed" by a fixed quantity of gold. [12]

Government The authoritative allocator of resources for a society. Allocation is accomplished through formal institutions and processes. [1]

Grant-in-aid Funds Congress provides to state and local governments, or which state legislatures provide to local governments, for specified purposes and subject to accountability. [3]

Grass-roots lobbying Lobbying technique that focuses on the importance and effectiveness of individual constituents, as opposed to professional lobbyists in the capital, and that tries to win public support for a cause in order to influence legislators through pressure from home. Constituents are encouraged to write or call congressional offices in either the district or Washington and attend meetings that members of Congress hold for the public when they return to their districts. [5]

Great Compromise The agreement at the Constitutional Convention whereby the lower house of Congress was to be elected by the people according to population and the upper house elected by state legislatures, with the same number for each state; also called Connecticut Compromise. [2]

Gridlock A basic impasse within institutions often involving political parties and interest groups. Gridlock has a number of causes, including divided government, institutional jealousies, and interest group inflexibility. [5, 6, 10]

Habeas corpus petition An appeal from a prisoner seeking to be released. [2, 8] *See also* Writ of habeas corpus.

Head of government The president's role as leader of the executive branch of government. [7]

Head of state The chief representative of a country. In the United States this role, filled by the president, is primarily ceremonial, but it can be important in both foreign and domestic affairs. [7]

Hedges against inflation Investments believed to hold their value better during a period of high inflation, such as real property, precious metals, and objects of art. [12]

House calendar Schedule on which public House bills that do not involve appropriations or revenue are placed when released from committee. [6]

House Democratic Caucus Organization of all Democrats in the House of Representatives. This group can make important organizational decisions, as Democrats have controlled the House in recent decades. In 1971 the caucus voted to limit each House Democrat to one committee and one subcommittee chair. [6]

House of Representatives The lower house of the U.S. Congress, in which representatives are allocated according to population. Since 1912 the total membership has been fixed at 435, and each state has at least one representative. [6]

House Rules Committee A standing committee of the House of Representatives that receives major bills before they go to the House floor and provides rules for each bill in regard to length of debate and whether it may be amended on the House floor. [6]

Image Perceptions regarding the personal qualities of a candidate that can be an important basis for voting. [4]

Impeachment Procedure whereby a civil official is formally accused of commiting treason, bribery, or other crimes or misdemeanors or abusing the power of office. In the United States, the power of impeachment is assigned to the House of Representatives. Trial and removal from office is the responsibility of the Senate. Impeachment is a check Congress has over the president and the judiciary. [2, 6]

Imperial presidency A term coined in the 1960s

and used to describe kinds of abuse aimed at the enlargement of presidential powers that some argue might threaten the foundation of American democracy. [7]

Implied powers Powers not specifically granted by the Constitution, but that may be implied from the constitutionally delegated powers of the national government. In Article I, Section 8, the Constitution gives the national government the authority to do whatever is "necessary and proper" for carrying out the enumerated powers. [3]

Imports Products coming into a country from a foreign country, usually for sale or trade; the total value of such products. [2]

Impound An act by the executive branch to hold rather than spend funds appropriated by Congress. [7]

Incomes policy Direct or indirect government intervention to control wages and prices. [12]

Incorporation The judicial application of rights in the Bill of Rights to the states. The Supreme Court began to incorporate portions of the Bill of Rights into the Fourteenth Amendment's due process clause in the 1920s, thereby applying parts of the Bill of Rights to the states. [9]

Incrementalism A method of budget decision making in which the past year's budget for a program is a protected base and only upward revisions are considered. There is no discussion of whether spending can be cut or whether the program is still needed. Incrementalism as a method for determining the federal budget was disrupted in 1985 by the Balanced Budget and Emergency Deficit Control Act. [10]

Incumbent The current holder of an office. [4]

Independent expenditures Money spent by an individual or political action committee independently, without the knowledge or concurrence of the candidate being supported. It is aimed at helping the candidate win the election but does not count as a donation to the campaign; a major loophole in a 1974 amendment to the Federal Elections Campaign Act of 1971 after the Supreme Court held in *Buckley v. Valeo* in 1976 that money spent by individuals on behalf of a candidate is a form of free speech and cannot be restricted by the government. [4]

Independent regulatory commission A government agency created to regulate a part of the economy. Examples are the Interstate Commerce Commission and the Securities and Exchange Commission. These commissions operate without direct supervision from the president or Congress and often engage in executive, legislative, and judicial functions in the process of conducting their affairs. [10]

Independent voter A person who votes on a candidate's qualifications and position on particular issues rather than on party affiliation. [4]

Industrial policy A policy that gives the government a comprehensive role in promoting economic competitiveness and growth. While the United States has no such comprehensive policy, its leading competitor, Japan, does have an industrial policy that seems to be effective. Most Americans have been leery of industrial policy in the past, as it is similar to central planning, which is often associated with socialism. [12]

Inflation A sustained general rise in the price level or cost of living. This increase in prices usually strips a consumer of purchasing power, especially one on a fixed income. [12]

Initiative A method, used primarily at the state and local level of government, for giving the people greater power by allowing voters to recommend a law or constitutional amendment after presenting a petition with a specified number of signatures. They then vote on the proposal at election time. [3]

Insitutional presidency The network of bureaucratic agencies on which the president depends for policy-making decisions. The Executive Office of the President is part of this institutional presidency, as is the Office of Management and Budget, which helps the president plan the executive budget and shepherd it through Congress. [7]

Interest (or lobbying) group An organization of individuals who join together voluntarily to influence public policy on the basis of a shared interest or objective. [4, 5]

Internal debt Money owed to Americans by their government. [12]

International Monetary Fund (IMF) An international organization established in 1944 to loan money to nations experiencing economic problems. It is also concerned with stabilization of currencies, monetary exchange, and the expansion of economic trade. [11]

International relations A system for interactions and relations among nation-states and other independent political communities and the elements that affect them. [11]

Investigation An extra-constitutional power Congress has assumed, under which it studies anything from the executive branch to an ordinary citizen. The investigation must be within the scope of its legislative powers. [6]

Invisible hand Term associated with Adam Smith, the eighteenth-century economist who emphasized that a free market with limited government involvement would produce positive results. Smith argued that the process worked "as by an invisible hand" guided by self-interest because government was not interfering with it. [1]

Iron triangle The liberal critique arguing that bureaucracies, interest groups, and congressional committees form coalitions which work together to dominate policy-making. Different coalitions form around different issue areas. Agencies are captured by special interests, and there is little opportunity for overall policy coordination. [10]

Isolationism Policy directed toward minimal political and military interaction with foreign nations. Isolationism generally characterized American foreign policy until 1949, most often in relation to Europe and least often in relation to the Western Hemisphere. Isolationism did not apply to economic relationships. [11]

Item veto A proposal to permit the president to reject sections of a bill without vetoing the entire bill. Many governors have an item veto. [7]

Jawboning The president's ability to use the power and prestige of office to approve or condemn wage and price increases as they affect the national economy, especially to prevent inflation. [12]

Jim Crow laws Laws mandating racial segregation. These are no longer constitutional. [4, 9]

Joint committee Committee composed of members of both houses of Congress and convened for some joint purpose. [6]

Joint resolution A measure that, when passed by a simple majority in both houses of Congress and signed by the president, has the force of law. It is often used for single appropriations and for voicing congressional opinion of presidential actions in the area of foreign policy. If a joint resolution is used for a constitutional amendment, no presidential signature is required, but that is the only exception. [6]

Judicial activism Deciding cases on the spirit of the law with a willingness to test the boundaries of jurisdiction and play an active role in shaping public policy. Activist judges take an interventionist role in order to right what they see as economic or social injustice. [8]

Judicial branch The branch of government re-

sponsible for the interpretation of law and the administration of justice. In the United States it consists of a system of courts and judges. [2]

Judicial power The power granted to the judicial branch of the government to render judgments according to the laws of the land. [8]

Judicial reinterpretation Method of changing the meaning of a provision of the Constitution through a restrictive interpretation that in effect minimizes the provision. [2]

Judicial restraint Deciding cases on the basis of the intent of the framers and established legal precedent. [8]

Judicial review Court action to decide whether executive and legislative acts are in conflict with the Constitution. This authority is not granted specifically in the Constitution, but United States courts exercise it. [8]

Judiciary The system of courts and judges in the United States; that part of government whose primary role is to render judgments in regard to the laws of the land. [8]

Justice of the peace court A state court that handles minor matters, such as civil marriages and traffic offenses, matters that also may be handled by municipal courts. [8]

Labor union An organized group that represents workers in an industry, company, or trade and protects their interests. [5]

Laissez faire A French term meaning "hands off," that became an eighteenth-century economic doctrine calling for little or no government intervention in the economy. A laissez-faire economy is one in which self-interest and competition become the regulators of supply and demand. [1]

Layer-cake federalism A type of federal system in which national and state powers are separate and clearly defined. [3]

Left populism A version of populism focused on economic issues, including the concern that the privileged should not receive excessive favors from government. [1]

Legislative branch The branch of government responsible for making laws. This branch is also responsible for levying and collecting taxes and making financial appropriations. In the United States this branch consists of the Senate and the House of Representatives. [2]

Legislative leader The president's role as the single most important person in the legislative process. [7]

Legislative power   The lawmaking power of Congress established primarily in Article I, Section 8, of the Constitution. [6]

Legislative veto   An extra-constitutional power Congress has assumed, under which it may reject an action of the executive or an administrative agency by vetoing an administrative rule before it is put into effect. This veto does not require the agreement of the president, although the courts have usually held that Congress must either exercise or delegate its powers but cannot delegate them subject to a veto. [6, 7]

Legislator   A government official elected to pass or reject legislation. Members of the House and Senate are legislators. [6]

Liberalism   A political perspective that has as its goal of changing society through government intervention to promote fairness and to protect individual rights. [1]

Libertarianism   A political perspective that strongly supports individualism and capitalism, favors the limitation of government involvement in all areas of life, and stresses the importance of private property. [1]

Lobby   *See* Interest (or lobbying) group.

Logrolling   An exchange of favors among legislators, each of whom supports projects in other districts in the hopes that his or her district projects will likewise be supported. [6]

Loophole   A technicality by which the stated intent of a law may be evaded; specifically, a provision of the tax law that reduces someone's taxable income; usually applied to provisions that benefit the wealthy. [12]

Macroeconomic   A level of economics in which the government attempts to influence the behavior of the total economy through the use of three basic policy tools: monetary policy, fiscal policy, and incomes policy. [12]

Mainline church   Usually a long-established church whose leadership is usually theologically and politically liberal. The term comes from the suburban, largely Protestant, communities on the main rail line into Philadelphia in the early twentieth century. [5]

Mandate   An order sent from a higher to a lower level of government that has the status of an authoritative order or command. An example is a condi-

tion placed on a grant-in-aid being given by the national government to a state or local government. In another meaning, an elected official who has won by a resounding margin claims that she or he has received a mandate from the voters. [3]

Marble-cake federalism   A type of federal system in which the federal, state, and delegated local powers are not separate and clearly defined but mixed and constantly changing. [3]

Mark-up   The process of revising a proposed bill; also the session in which a committee or subcommittee focuses on making suggested changes in the wording of a proposed bill. [6]

Marshall Plan   A scheme proposed by Secretary of State George Marshall in 1947 to rebuild the economies of postwar Europe and gain their loyalty in the face of Soviet expansionism. As a result, in 1948 the European Recovery Program was created to assist sixteen nations. [11]

Marxism   The political perspective based on the teachings of Karl Marx that rejects the values of capitalism and private property and holds that inevitable class struggle in capitalist nations will cause the society to move from capitalism to socialism and eventually to communism. [1]

Marxism-Leninism   Vladimir Lenin's implementation of Marxist theory with qualifications, including the idea of a dictatorship "over" rather than "by" the proletariat; the form of government many Marxist countries have used over the past seventy years. [1]

Mass media   Means of communicating with mass audiences electronically and through print, including radio, television, newspapers, and magazines; also the organizations or institutions, such as networks, that utilize these techniques. [5]

Matching funds   Funds that the recipient of a grant must provide toward the total needed as a condition of receiving the grant. Aid from a higher level of government to a lower level of government may involve such a condition. [3]

Merit system   The practice of making appointments to government posts on the basis of qualifications rather than political affiliation or connections. About 90 percent of federal employees are chosen, retained, and promoted by the merit system. [10]

Microeconomics   A level of economics in which laws and regulations are aimed at specific areas of an economy such as real estate or the automobile industry. Microeconomics may also involve the attempt to maximize efficiencies within a specific business. [12]

Midnight judges   Judges appointed by President John Adams at the end of his term as president in 1801. Some of them did not receive their commissions because Jeffersonians feared courts with a strong Federalist slant. *Marbury v. Madison* (1803) is often called the "case of the midnight judges." [8]

Mid-term election   A general election occurring in an off-year between presidential elections. [4]

Minimum wage   The legislated hourly wage that employers in most sectors of the economy are required to pay; periodically adjusted by Congress. [12]

Minor party   A party organized on the basis of ideas or interests inadequately represented by the two major parties; also sometimes called a third party. Because its support is either too concentrated or too scattered, it is seldom able to win an election in the American system. [4]

Modified-closed rule   A rule issued by the House Rules Committee that permits a limited number of amendments on a bill while it is debated on the House floor. The rule usually sets strict limits on the number of hours for general debate. [6]

Monetarism   Economic theory in which monetary policy is stressed. Economists who subscribe to this theory emphasize that although monetary policy is an important factor in the economy, the Federal Reserve Board is wrong more often than not about what the economy is going to do and thus frequently makes policy errors. [12]

Monetary policy   Government policy regulated by the Federal Reserve System, which influences the amount of currency and credit available. [12]

Monetization   A method of reducing the deficit that creates more money which the government can use to pay debts; a type of monetary policy. [12]

Monroe Doctrine   A unilateral warning by President James Monroe in 1823 that the United States would oppose any intervention of European powers in the affairs of countries in the Western Hemisphere, primarily Central and South America. In turn, the United States would stay out of European affairs. [11]

Most favored nation status   Status granted through an agreement whereby the United States grants equal trading rights to another country. In turn, that "most favored" nation makes trade concessions to the United States. [11]

Muckraking   Journalism that concentrates on exposing scandal, often corruption in institutions and persons in power. [5]

Multiple-use land   Land devoted to multiple purposes, such as mining, grazing, farming, logging, recreation; includes many lands owned by the federal government. [3]

Multiplier effect   The stimulation of additional economic activity as money circulates through the economy. [12]

Municipal court   A state court that handles minor matters such as civil marriages and traffic offenses, matters that may also be handled by justice of the peace courts. [8]

National committee   The highest council of a national political party, consisting of representatives from each state. It provides money and other forms of assistance to party candidates and helps to organize and run the national convention at which presidential and vice-presidential candidates are nominated. The Democrats and Republicans have the most active such committees. [4]

National convention   An assembly of each major party held every four years to choose presidential and vice-presidential candidates, pass a party platform, and complete other party business. The first national convention took place in 1831. [4]

National debt   The total amount of money owed by the national government; it consists of accumulated yearly budget deficits not repaid. [12]

National leader   The president's role as leader of the nation. In times of crisis, such as war or natural disaster, the nation turns to the president for leadership. [7]

National security adviser (NSA)   A position created in 1947 to provide the president with advice on foreign policy independent of any department and to manage the staff of the National Security Council. Some presidents have used the national security adviser and staff to carry out foreign policy, sometimes without the knowledge of other government departments. [11]

National Security Council (NSC)   An executive agency created by the 1947 National Security Act to counsel the president on domestic and foreign affairs that affect American interests and national security. Members include the president, vice-president, secretary of state, and secretary of defense. At the president's discretion, other advisors can be added. In recent years the director of the CIA and the chair of the Joint Chiefs of Staff have been members. [7]

Nationalism   A bond felt by a group of people within a political system that encourages loyalty and love of country; the centralization of government powers at the national level. [2, 3]

Net interest on the federal debt   Payments by the government for money borrowed to finance the federal debt. [10]

New Christian Right   A coalition of evangelical and fundamentalist church groups opposed to the views of the mainline churches. Their perspective on political matters is most closely related to conservatism and right populism. [5]

New Jersey Plan   A plan proposed at the Constitutional Convention that would have modified the Articles of Confederation by giving Congress the power to tax and regulate trade and by creating an executive and a judicial branch. The structure of a single-house legislature elected by state legislatures with each state having one vote would have remained. [2]

News management   Attempt on the part of elected officials or others in the executive or legislative branch to channel the power of the media in directions designed for maximum benefit. [5]

Nineteenth Amendment   Amendment to the Constitution (1920) that gave women the right to vote. [1, 9]

Ninth Amendment   Amendment to the Constitution (1791) stating that rights not named in the Constitution shall not be construed to be denied to the American people. [2]

Nonpartisan election   An election in which people vote for candidates as individuals; party labels do not appear on the ballot. [4]

Nontariff barrier   A measure other than a tariff, to limit imports. They include, for example, unnecessary "safety" inspections, subsidies for the domestic industry, and outright bans on imports. [11]

North Atlantic Treaty Organization (NATO)   An organization created by treaty in 1949 to protect the nations of the North Atlantic region from attack. The original twelve nations signing agreed that an attack upon one nation in the alliance would be viewed as an attack upon all. NATO was created as a part of the U.S. policy of containment aimed at halting communist expansion. [11]

Nullification   A state's attempt to invalidate an act of Congress within its borders, sometimes by passing its own law voiding the federal law, thus making it null and void. South Carolina's 1832 rejection of "the tariff of abominations," passed in 1828, is one example of nullification. [3]

Objective journalism   Reporting the news without acknowledged bias. [5]

Office of Management and Budget   The principal budgeting arm of the executive branch. The OMB develops the president's budget in conjunction with the heads of various departments and agencies. [7]

Oligarchy   A government in which a small group of people make most of the decisions; rule by the few. [1]

Ombudsman   One who acts to redress individual grievances between private citizens and government agencies. In the United States, this duty falls to members of Congress. [6]

Open market policy   A method of regulating monetary policy by the purchase and sale of government bonds by the Federal Open Market Committee of the Federal Reserve System. [12]

Open primary   A primary that allows people to vote in any primary regardless of party affiliation. [4]

Open rule   A rule issued by the House Rules Committee that permits unlimited amendments on a bill while it is debated on the House floor. The rule also fixes the number of hours for general debate. [6]

Opinion molder   A leader who interprets what the media say to peers or institutional associates. Two good examples might be union leaders and ministers, although informal group leaders might also be opinion molders. [5]

Original intent   A standard for interpreting the laws, including the Constitution, by examining the purposes and thinking of those who wrote the law, especially the framers of the Constitution, and deciding cases accordingly. [8, 9]

Original jurisdiction   A court's authority to hear a case at its inception. [8]

Override   The power of a two-thirds majority vote in each house of Congress to pass a bill over a presidential veto. [6]

Pack journalism   The tendency of reporters and news organizations to adopt the same ideas about what is news and how it should be presented. [5]

Parliamentary system   A political system that concentrates power over both the legislature and executive in the prime minister and his or her cabinet. This system is both effective at making decisions and accountable to the electorate, and it allows for a more highly disciplined majority party whose members vote together and work with their leadership to achieve party goals. It stands in sharp contrast to the lack of party discipline in the U.S. party system. [4]

Partisan committee   One-party committee in Congress that takes care of either Democratic or Republican business; sometimes known as a party committee. Each party has a partisan committee on committees in each house to appoint party members to various authorization or appropriation subcommittees. [6]

Party identification   Loyalty of a voter to a particular political party. [4]

Party in government   Members of a party who have been elected or appointed to public office and seek to accomplish party goals. [4]

Party in the electorate   The citizens who identify with and support the party. [4]

Party leader   The president's role as the national leader of his or her party. [7]

Party organization   Structure created to set party policies and help get candidates elected. [4]

Party platform   A nonbinding statement of the goals and ideals of a party or candidate that is used to gain voter support. [4]

Party-unity voting   A vote in which a majority of one party's members in Congress oppose a majority of the other party's members. [4, 6]

Patronage   The placing of party supporters, personal friends, or close relatives in government jobs. Most civil officials, especially the president, hold some of this power for close advisers, though its general use has been limited by law and court decisions. [4] *See also* Spoils system

Per capita income   The total personal income earned in an area divided by the total population to determine the average personal income per individual in the area. [3]

Perspective   A system of thought or a viewpoint. Conservative, liberal, libertarian, and populist are the major political perspectives in the United States. [1]

Pigeonhole   The setting aside of a bill by the chair of a committee or subcommittee in order to avoid its consideration. Unless others are strongly interested

enough to oppose the chair's action, the effect is usually to kill the proposal. [6]

Plea bargaining   Negotiation of a settlement between prosecution and defense in which the accused person pleads guilty to a reduced charge. The deal settles the case without a trial and helps to alleviate court backlog. It develops out of the state's need for evidence to convict another accused person. [8]

Plurality   A greater number of votes than those received by any other candidate in an electoral contest but less than a majority of the votes cast. A plurality may be enough to win the election, but if a majority is required, a runoff election is necessary. [4]

Pocket veto   Action by the chief executive to kill a bill by withholding his signature. Once the legislature adjourns, if the president has not signed the bill within ten days of its passage, it constitutes a veto; possible only if a bill has been passed within ten days of a recess or adjournment. [6]

Police power   Law enforcement and criminal justice power exercised by the states under the Constitution in order to advance and ensure the well-being of their citizens. [3]

Policy implementation   The carrying out of policies set by Congress and the executive; the primary role of the bureaucracy. [10]

Political action committee (PAC)   An organization that gives financial support to candidates or parties of its choice by raising funds through its members; recognized by the Federal Election Campaign Act of 1974. [4, 5]

Political culture   The predominant outlook on government and politics in a society, state, or region. For example, political culture in the South is more conservative than elsewhere in the country. [3]

Political machine   A strong party organization ruled by a boss or small group of autocratic leaders. [4]

Political party   A group of interests and individuals who organize to gain control of political offices by helping their candidates win elections. In the United States, the Democratic and Republican parties are the two major political parties. [4]

Political question   A case that should be addressed by the legislative and executive branch rather than the courts. Cases are refused on the basis that they are "political" in nature. When a case of this nature is heard, the decision is usually framed as narrowly as possible. [8]

Political science   The systematic study of politics as an academic discipline. [1]

Political spectrum   The range of political perspectives among the public. For example, the American political spectrum ranges from conservatives to a few Marxists. These two ideologies could be said to exist at opposite ends of the political spectrum. Other perspectives described in the text fall between the extremes. [4]

Politics   The science or art of government. [1]

Popular vote   The actual number of votes cast for each candidate in a presidential election, as distinguished from the vote of the electoral college. [4]

Populism   A perspective that emphasizes majority rule and power in the hands of the "little person" in an effort to counterbalance large institutional concentrations of power, either public or private. Populism originally organized as a protest against large private corporations. [1] *See also* Left populism; Right populism.

"Pork-barrel" project   A project that benefits a particular state or congressional district for which federal funds are appropriated. Successful "pork-barreling," or securing federal support for projects in one's district, usually increases a legislator's chances for reelection. [4, 6]

"Pork-barreling"   *See* "Pork-barrel" project.

Power of the purse   Authority of Congress to raise revenue and allocate it. [6, 7]

Precedent   The principle that new cases should be decided in the same manner as similar previous cases. [8]

Precinct   A unit of two hundred to a thousand voters used to group voters for elections and party organization. [4]

President   The chief executive and head of state for the United States. [7]

President of the Senate   The presiding officer of the Senate. This position is usually held by the vice-president of the United States. The only time that the president of the Senate votes is in the case of a tie. [6]

President pro tempore   Presiding officer when the president of the Senate (the vice-president) is not present; traditionally the member of the majority party who has served in the Senate the longest. [6]

Presidential primary   A procedure used by most states and the District of Columbia to elect delegates to attend a party's national presidential nominating convention, which selects the presidential nominee. These delegates may or may not be bound to vote for a certain candidate. Most presidential primaries also allow voters to support their preferred candidate for president. [4]

Primary election system   A system for selecting each party's candidates for office in the general election or, especially in the case of presidential elections, selecting delegates to a party's nominating convention. [4]

Private bill   A bill that involves personal matters and individuals, introduced by members of Congress upon the petition of constituents. Private bills do not follow normal procedure and if passed become private law relevant only to those named in the bill. [6]

Private calendar   Schedule on which private House bills are placed when released from committee. [6]

Privatization   Utilizing the private sector to perform functions currently being performed by the government. Privatization can be contracting out services to a private firm, selling government property to private persons, or giving people money to purchase in the private market a service formerly provided by a government agency. [10]

Probable cause   Fourth Amendment guarantee that in order for the police to obtain a search or arrest warrant there must be reasonable grounds to believe a person is guilty of an offense. [9]

Product association   *See* Trade and product association.

Professional association   An independent interest group of any size that represents the interests of organized professional workers. Lawyers, doctors, and teachers are examples of professionals who have organized professional associations. [5]

Progressive movement   An early twentieth-century political movement that encouraged reforms such as greater regulation of big business and the introduction of social programs to help the needy. The progressive movement stimulated modern liberalism in the United States. [1, 4]

Project grant   A type of federal aid given to states and localities at the discretion of federal administrators and useful for experimental projects. [3]

Proportional representation system An electoral system not used in the United States but widely used in Europe in which the parties are given a number of seats in the legislature based on their percentage of the overall popular vote. This system gives small "third parties" a stronger voice. [4]

Protectionism Theory that advocates government protection of American business by limiting foreign competition through tariffs, import quotas, or other measures that make foreign goods more costly or unavailable. [12]

Public hearing An open meeting of a congressional committee or subcommittee, which gives both the general public and the committee members a chance to discuss a bill's merits and problems. [6]

Public interest group An independent organization, of any size, of people who band together to promote an issue they feel is in the public interest. Two examples are Partnership for a Drug-Free America and Mothers against Drunk Driving. [5]

Public opinion The sum of individual perspectives or beliefs. [5]

Public opinion poll A method for recording and reporting public thinking on certain issues, first devised in the 1930s. A pollster questions a small sample of people scientifically selected to be representative of a larger group. [5]

Public services Services rendered to the public by the government, such as education. Public service also describes government service by an individual. [3]

Puppet government A government that is controlled by another nation and is actually sovereign in name only. After World War II, most nations of Eastern Europe had puppet governments controlled by the Soviet Union. [11]

Ranking minority member The member of the minority party with the longest continuous service on a given House or Senate committee. This member is likely to become chair of the committee if his or her party becomes the majority. [6]

Reagan Doctrine Reagan administration policy that encouraged an offensive strategy to counter communist insurgencies and supported American aid for forces fighting for democracy in communist-ruled nations. [11]

Reaganomics A doctrine contending that economic growth is encouraged by reducing government involvement and regulation, making tax cuts, and reducing expenditures for social programs. It also included vast increases in military spending, so that one result was a large budget deficit. [12] *See also* Supply-side economics.

Recall A method whereby voters can remove an elected official from office before the end of his or her term. Voters must present a petition with a specified number of signatures to call a special election that will decide whether to remove the official. [3]

Recession A period of reduced economic activity lasting six months or more that is not as severe or prolonged as a depression. [12]

"Red tape" An excessive amount of bureaucratic paperwork and procedure that prevents (or delays) action; so called for the red tape formerly used to tie up legal documents in England. [10]

Redistricting The redrawing of single-member district lines by state legislatures or other bodies in following new census figures released every ten years. These lines delineate districts for the U.S. House of Representatives and for state House and Senate seats. [6]

Referendum A method whereby voters can veto or offer support for a public policy bill passed by their legislators by a yes-no vote. The referendum is used in many states and localities, but not at the national level. [3]

Regionalism A consciousness of regionally based interests, aims, or political beliefs. An extreme case of regionalism occurred during the Civil War; a new form of regionalism has appeared in the current conflict between frostbelt and sunbelt states. [3]

Report out To send a bill from committee or subcommittee to the floor of the House of Representatives or Senate for further consideration and debate. [6]

Representative democracy A government in which elected representatives make decisions by majority rule while guaranteeing certain fundamental rights to those holding minority opinions. [1]

Republican party A major American political party that developed in the 1850s out of the Free Soil and Whig parties and in opposition to slavery. Its strongest following comes from people from small Protestant towns and from management levels of large businesses. Although the party has done well in recent presidential elections, the Democrats have many more officeholders. [4]

Republicanism A political system in which delegates elected by the people run the government; also referred to as mixed or balanced government. In the United States, elected officials check and balance one another. [2]

Reserve requirement Under the Federal Reserve System, the percentage of total bank deposits that banks are required to keep on hand. [12]

Reserved powers Powers not constitutionally delegated to the national government or prohibited to the states and therefore, by the Tenth Amendment, reserved to the states or the people. [3]

Revenue sharing A federal program initiated by President Richard Nixon that sought to reduce the growth of the federal grant system by making national funds available to states and local districts with little restriction on their use. Under this system, the national government automatically gives a part of its tax yield to the states. [3]

Revolving door process The frequent movement of officials from the public to the private sector. [5, 10]

Rider A provision to a bill that may have little or no relevancy to the bill. The provision usually would not pass on its own merit, so it is attached to an important bill, usually an appropriations bill, in hopes that rider opponents and the president will accept the bill instead of rejecting the whole package. [6]

Right to counsel The right of a defendant to be provided legal counsel by the state or federal government in all felony and misdemeanor cases in which there is a likelihood of imprisonment upon conviction; derived from the Sixth Amendment. [9]

Right populism A version of populism most concerned with social issues such as the crime rate and moral decay. [1]

Right to remain silent Right derived from the Fifth Amendment and *Miranda v. Arizona* (1966) that a suspect does not have to answer questions in a police interrogation or make a statement until he or she has counsel present. A person accused of a crime must be informed of this right upon arrest. [9]

Roll call vote A vote in either house of Congress for which each member's vote is recorded individually. [6]

Roosevelt Corollary A revision to the Monroe Doctrine in which President Theodore Roosevelt asserted that the United States had the right to intervene in Central or South American affairs if corruption or violence endangered American or European lives or property. [11]

Rule A statement regulating how a bill may be amended, debated, and considered by the House. Rules are assigned by the House Rules Committee after a bill is reported out of committee and before it goes to the House floor. [6]

Rule of law Belief that people are to be treated in accordance with the general principles embodied in the law, not according to the arbitrary decisions of government officials. Government officials as much as ordinary citizens are bound to obey the laws and are subject to the penalties for failing to do so. Laws apply equally to all people regardless of irrelevant considerations such as gender and race. [8]

Safe district A voting district in which opposition parties rarely, if ever, offer a credible challenge to the incumbent. [6]

"Safety net" A backup system of support for the needy coined by the Reagan administration when it first began to cut programs in the early 1980s. The administration believed that a "safety net" for the truly needy still should, and did, exist. [10]

Sagebrush Rebellion The angry response of certain western states to the federal government's regulation of extensive federal lands within their boundaries. In Nevada, for example, 82 percent of the land within the state is federal land. [3]

Scientific management movement Measures taken in the early twentieth century to increase the efficiency of government by breaking tasks down into component parts and offering incentives such as work breaks and bonuses; also called "Taylorism" for Frederick Taylor, a private sector industrial engineer who introduced "time and motion" studies. The movement was short-lived; in 1912 stopwatches were outlawed at government facilities. [10]

Secession The withdrawal of a state from the Union, as several southern states did immediately prior to the Civil War. [3]

Second Amendment Amendment to the Constitution (1791) stating, "A well regulated militia being necessary to the security of a free state, the right of the people to keep and bear arms shall not be infringed." The extent to which this amendment protects firearms is a source of continuing debate. Courts have generally not applied this amendment

ty, underdevelopment, and lack of industry in common; includes a majority of all nations, most of them in Asia, Latin America, and Africa, relatively newly independent of colonial rule. [11]

Three-fifths Compromise A compromise at the Constitutional Convention between northern and southern regional interests whereby a slave was counted as three-fifths of a person for purposes of representation and taxation. It remained part of the Constitution until after the Civil War. [2]

Ticket-splitter Voter who crosses party lines to vote for two or more candidates of different parties. [4]

Tracking poll Poll that follows public opinion on the same political issue and contest across time. [5]

Trade deficit An excess of imports over exports. [12]

Trade and product association An interest group representing one particular industry or service. [5]

Treaty A formal agreement between two or more countries. In the United States, a treaty is negotiated by the president, approved by the Senate with a two-thirds vote, and made final by presidential ratification of the Senate version. [6, 7]

Trustee theory of representation The theory that a legislator's duty is to rely on his or her own judgment or conscience first, instead of on the preferences of constituents, especially since constituents cannot be well informed on all issues. [6]

Twenty-first Amendment Amendment to the Constitution (1933) that repealed the Eighteenth Amendment, which had banned the manufacture, sale, or transportation of alcoholic beverages. [2]

Twenty-third Amendment Amendment to the Constitution (1961) that gave the District of Columbia three electoral votes. [4]

Tyranny A form of government in which a group or individual holds absolute power and uses it in an oppressive manner. [2]

Umbrella organization An interest group consolidating groups that represent similar interests. The Leadership Conference on Civil Rights, which includes many civil rights groups, is an umbrella organization. [5]

Unanimous consent agreement Procedure used by both houses of Congress to save time on noncontroversial bills by permitting bills to pass without going through the vote-recording process. The Senate uses this procedure for major and minor bills. [6]

Union calendar Schedule on which House bills concerning revenue and appropriations are placed when released from committee. [6]

United Nations (UN) An organization formed in June 1945 for the promotion of international peace, security, justice, and human rights. The Charter of the United Nations was signed by 50 nations; today 184 nations are members. [11]

Unreasonable search and seizure Actions prohibited by the Fourth Amendment. An example of a prohibited action would be searching a person's house without a search warrant. [9]

Velocity The speed with which money circulates through the economy. [12]

Veto The authority of a branch of government to block the actions or proposals of another department. The chief executive, or president, has the power to reject a legislative act and return it to Congress with an explanation. [6, 7] *See also* Item veto; Legislative veto; Override; Pocket veto.

Vice-president of the United States The Constitutional office with the only powers assigned to it being to preside over the Senate and to assume the presidency in case of death, resignation, removal, or temporary disability of the president. The vice-president also has the privilege of breaking any tie votes in the Senate. [7]

Virginia Plan A plan proposed at the Constitutional Convention for a national legislature with the lower house to be elected by the people and the upper house to be elected by the lower house. Representation in each house was to be based on population. [2]

Voter turnout The number or percentage of eligible voters who actually vote. [4]

Wage and price controls A program of government regulation imposed to keep wages and prices from rising beyond a certain level and to halt inflation; a type of incomes policy. [12]

War A foreign policy instrument using military force openly rather than covertly. In the United States, a formal declaration of war is required and must be approved by a majority vote in each house of Congress. Prior to 1945, some wars were undeclared because of consideration for distance and poor communication. Since 1945, some wars have been fought without a declaration of war because such declarations can introduce a complicated international legal situation. [11]

War powers The authority granted Congress or the president by the Constitution to protect the

United States from foreign attack. The powers of Congress include taxing and spending for the common defense, raising and supporting armies and navies, and making rules for captures. Congress also has the authority to do what is necessary and proper in performing these duties. The president has the power to do what is necessary and proper for the protection of the nation, including asking Congress for a declaration of war. He also serves as commander in chief of the armed forces. [7]

Watchdog   The media's role in "checking" government by closely watching the manner in which the government performs and reporting governmental or individual malfeasance to the public. [5]

Whip   Representative or senator responsible for "whipping up" partisan support for his or her party's legislative initiatives in the House of Representatives or Senate respectively. There is a majority whip and a minority whip in each chamber. The Republican's minority whip in the Senate is called the assistant minority leader. [6]

Whistle-blower   Employee of a government organization who exposes improper or illegal behavior. [10]

White House Office   The most important division of the Executive Office of the President; staff members are usually closer to the president than are other members of the executive branch and have more influence on his decisions. [7]

Writ of habeas corpus   Court order requiring that police officials explain why a person has been arrested and jailed. [6] *See also* Habeas corpus petition.

Writ of mandamus   A court order requiring a government official to carry out his or her duty under the law. A writ of mandamus was at issue in the case of *Marbury v. Madison* (1803). [8]

Yellow journalism   A term coined in the late nineteenth century to characterize journalism that emphasized the sensational. The *National Enquirer* might be considered a current example of yellow journalism. [5]

Zoning   The set of regulations, usually established by local governments, that determines what can and what cannot be done with a particular piece of property. When making zoning decisions, local governments usually operate under state guidelines. An example of a zoning decision might be a rule that no establishment selling alcohol may be operated within two hundred feet of a church. [3]

APPENDIXES

APPENDIX A

The Constitution of the United States and The Declaration of Independence

WE THE PEOPLE of the United States, in Order to form a more perfect Union, establish Justice, insure domestic Tranquility, provide for the common defence, promote the general Welfare, and secure the Blessings of Liberty to ourselves and our Posterity, do ordain and establish this Constitution for the United States of America.

Article I

SEC. 1 All legislative Powers herein granted shall be vested in a Congress of the United States, which shall consist of a Senate and House of Representatives.

SEC. 2 The House of Representatives shall be composed of Members chosen every second Year by the People of the several States, and the Electors in each State shall have the Qualifications requisite for Electors of the most numerous Branch of the State Legislature.

No Person shall be a Representative who shall not have attained to the Age of twenty five Years, and been seven Years a Citizen of the United States, and who shall not, when elected, be an Inhabitant of that State in which he shall be chosen.

Representatives and direct Taxes shall be apportioned among the several States which may be included within this Union, according to their respective Numbers, which shall be determined by adding to the whole Number of free Persons, including those bound to Service for a Term of Years, and excluding Indians not taxed, three fifths of all other Persons. The actual Enumeration shall be made within three Years after the first Meeting of the Congress of the United States, and within every subsequent Term of ten Years, in such Manner as they shall by Law direct. The Number of Representatives shall not exceed one for every thirty Thousand, but each State shall have at Least one Representative; and until such enumeration shall be made, the State of New Hampshire shall be entitled to chuse three, Massachusetts eight, Rhode-Island and Providence Plantations one, Connecticut five, New-York six, New Jersey four, Pennsylvania eight, Delaware one, Maryland six, Virginia ten, North Carolina five, South Carolina five, and Georgia three.

When vacancies happen in the Representation from any State, the Executive Authority thereof shall issue Writs of Election to fill such Vacancies.

The House of Representatives shall chuse their Speaker and other Officers; and shall have the sole Power of Impeachment.

Sᴇᴄ. 3   The Senate of the United States shall be composed of two Senators from each State, chosen by the Legislature thereof, for six Years; and each Senator shall have one Vote.

Immediately after they shall be assembled in Consequence of the first Election, they shall be divided as equally as may be into three Classes. The Seats of the Senators of the first Class shall be vacated at the Expiration of the Second Year, of the second Class at the Expiration of the fourth Year, and of the third Class at the Expiration of the sixth Year, so that one third may be chosen every second Year; and if Vacancies happen by Resignation, or otherwise, during the Recess of the Legislature of any State, the Executive thereof may make temporary Appointments until the next Meeting of the Legislature, which shall then fill such Vacancies.

No Person shall be a Senator who shall not have attained to the Age of thirty Years, and been nine Years a Citizen of the United States, and who shall not, when elected, be an Inhabitant of that State for which he shall be chosen.

The Vice President of the United States shall be President of the Senate, but shall have no Vote, unless they be equally divided.

The Senate shall chuse their other Officers, and also a President pro tempore, in the Absence of the Vice President, or when he shall exercise the Office of President of the United States.

The Senate shall have the sole Power to try all Impeachments. When sitting for that Purpose, they shall be on Oath or Affirmation. When the President of the United States is tried, the Chief Justice shall preside: And no Person shall be convicted without the Concurrence of two thirds of the Members present.

Judgment in Cases of Impeachment shall not extend further than to removal from Office, and disqualification to hold and enjoy any Office of honor, Trust or Profit under the United States: but the Party convicted shall nevertheless be liable and subject to Indictment, Trial, Judgment and Punishment, according to Law.

Sᴇᴄ. 4   The Times, Places and Manner of holding Elections for Senators and Representatives, shall be prescribed in each State by the Legislature thereof; but the Congress may at any time by Law make or alter such Regulations, except as to the Places of chusing Senators.

The Congress shall assemble at least once in every Year, and such Meeting shall be on the first Monday in December, unless they shall by Law appoint a different Day.

Sᴇᴄ. 5   Each House shall be the Judge of the Elections, Returns and Qualifications of its own Members, and a Majority of each shall constitute a Quorum to do Business; but a smaller Number may adjourn from day to day, and may be authorized to compel the Attendance of absent Members, in such Manner, and under such Penalties as each House may provide.

Each House may determine the Rules of its Proceedings, punish its Members for disorderly Behaviour, and, with the Concurrence of two thirds, expel a Member.

Each House shall keep a Journal of its Proceedings, and from time to time publish the same, excepting such Parts as may in their Judgment require Secrecy; and the Yeas and Nays of the Members of either House on any question shall, at the Desire of one fifth of those Present, be entered on the Journal.

Neither House, during the Session of Congress, shall, without the Consent of the other, adjourn for more than three days, nor to any other Place than that in which the two Houses shall be sitting.

Sᴇᴄ. 6   The Senators and Representatives shall receive a Compensation for their Services, to be ascertained by Law, and paid out of the Treasury of the United States. They shall in all Cases, except Treason, Felony and Breach of the Peace, be privileged from Arrest during their Attendance at the Session of their respective Houses, and in going to and returning from the same; and for any Speech or Debate in either House, they shall not be questioned in any other Place.

No Senator or Representative shall, during the Time for which he was elected, be appointed to any civil Office under the Authority of the United States, which shall have been created, or the Emoluments whereof shall have been encreased during such time; and no Person holding any Office under the United States, shall be a Member of either House during his Continuance in Office.

Sᴇᴄ. 7   All bills for raising Revenue shall originate in the House of Representatives; but the Senate may propose or concur with amendments as on other Bills.

Every Bill which shall have passed the House of Representatives and the Senate, shall, before it become a Law, be presented to the President of the United States; If he approve he shall sign it, but if not he shall return it, with his Objections to that House in which it shall have originated, who shall enter the Objections at large on their Journal, and proceed to reconsider it. If after such Reconsideration two thirds of that House shall agree to pass the Bill, it shall be sent, together with the Objections, to the other House, by which it shall likewise be reconsidered, and if approved by two thirds of that House, it shall become a Law. But in all such Cases the Votes of both Houses shall be determined by yeas and Nays, and the Names of the Persons voting for and against the Bill shall be entered on the Journal of each House respectively. If any Bill shall not be returned by the President within ten Days (Sunday excepted) after it shall have been presented to him, the Same shall be a Law, in like Manner as if he had signed it, unless the Congress by their Adjournment prevent its Return, in which Case it shall not be a Law.

Every Order, Resolution, or Vote to which the Concurrence of the Senate and House of Representatives may be necessary (except on a question of Adjournment) shall be presented to the President of the United States; and before the Same shall take Effect, shall be approved by him, or being disapproved by him, shall be repassed by two thirds of the Senate and House of Representatives, according to the Rules and Limitations prescribed in the Case of a Bill.

SEC. 8   The Congress shall have Power To lay and collect Taxes, Duties, Imposts and Excises, to pay the Debts and provide for the common Defence and general Welfare of the United States; but all Duties, Imposts and Excises shall be uniform throughout the United States;

To borrow money on the credit of the United States;

To regulate Commerce with foreign Nations, and among the several States, and with the Indian Tribes;

To establish an uniform Rule of Naturalization, and uniform Laws on the subject of Bankruptcies throughout the United States;

To coin Money, regulate the Value thereof, and of foreign Coin, and fix the Standard of Weights and Measures;

To provide for the Punishment of counterfeiting the Securities and current Coin of the United States;

To establish Post Offices and post Roads;

To promote the Progress of Science and useful Arts, by securing for limited Times to Authors and Inventors the exclusive Right to their respective Writings and Discoveries;

To constitute Tribunals inferior to the supreme Court;

To define and punish Piracies and Felonies committed on the high Seas, and Offenses against the Law of Nations;

To declare War, grant Letters of Marque and Reprisal, and make Rules concerning Captures on Land and Water;

To raise and support Armies, but no Appropriation of Money to that Use shall be for a longer Term than two Years;

To provide and maintain a Navy;

To make Rules for the Government and Regulation of the land and naval Forces;

To provide for calling forth the Militia to execute the Laws of the Union, suppress Insurrections and repel Invasions;

To provide for organizing, arming, and disciplining, the Militia, and for governing such Part of them as may be employed in the Service of the United States, reserving to the States respectively, the Appointment of the Officers, and the Authority of training the Militia according to the discipline prescribed by Congress;

To exercise exclusive Legislation in all Cases whatsoever, over such District (not exceeding ten Miles square) as may, by Cession of Particular States, and the Acceptance of Congress, become the Seat of the Government of the United States, and to exercise like Authority over all Places purchased by the Consent of the Legislature of the State in which the Same shall be, for the Erection of Forts, Magazines, Arsenals, dock-Yards, and other needful Buildings;—And

To make all Laws which shall be necessary and proper for carrying into Execution the foregoing Powers, and all other Powers vested by this Constitution in the Government of the United States, or in any Department or Officer thereof.

SEC. 9   The Migration of Importation of such Persons as any of the States now existing shall think proper to admit, shall not be prohibited by the Congress prior to the Year one thousand eight hundred and eight, but a Tax or duty may be imposed on such Importation, not exceeding ten dollars for each Person.

The Privilege of the Writ of Habeas Corpus shall not be suspended, unless when in Cases of Rebellion or Invasion the public Safety may require it.

No Bill of Attainder or ex post facto Law shall be passed.

No Capitation, or other direct, Tax shall be laid, unless in Proportion to the Census of Enumeration herein before directed to be taken.

No Tax or Duty shall be laid on Articles exported from any State.

No Preference shall be given by any Regulation of Commerce or Revenue to the Ports of one State over those of another: nor shall Vessels bound to, or from, one State, be obliged to enter, clear or pay Duties in another.

No Money shall be drawn from the Treasury, but in Consequence of Appropriations made by Law; and a regular Statement and Account of the Receipts and Expenditures of all public Money shall be published from time to time.

No Title of Nobility shall be granted by the United States: And no Person holding any Office of Profit or Trust under them, shall, without the Consent of the Congress, accept of any present, Emolument, Office, or Title, of any kind whatever, from any King, Prince or foreign State.

SEC. 10   No State shall enter into any Treaty, Alliance, or Confederation; grant Letters of Marque and Reprisal; coin Money; emit Bills of Credit; make any Thing but gold and silver Coin a Tender in Payment of Debts; pass any Bill of Attainder, ex post facto Law, or Law impairing the Obligation of Contracts, or grant any Title of Nobility.

No State shall, without the Consent of the Congress, lay any Imposts or Duties on Imports or Exports, except what may be absolutely necessary for executing its inspection Laws: and the net Produce of all Duties and Imposts, laid by any State on Imports or Exports, shall be for the Use of the Treasury of the United States; and all such Laws shall be subject to the Revision and Control of the Congress.

No State shall, without the Consent of Congress, lay any Duty of Tonnage, keep Troops, or Ships of War in time of Peace, enter into any Agreement or Compact with another State, or with a foreign Power, or engage in War, unless actually invaded, or in such imminent Danger as will not admit of delay.

Article II

SEC. 1   The executive Power shall be vested in a President of the United States of America. He shall hold his Office during the Term of four Years, and, together with the Vice President, chosen for the same Term, be elected, as follows

Each State shall appoint, in such Manner as the Legislature thereof may direct, a Number of Electors, equal to the whole Number of Senators and Representatives to which the State may be entitled in the Congress: but no Senator or Representative, or Person holding an Office of Trust or Profit under the United States, shall be appointed an Elector. The Electors shall meet in their respective States, and vote by Ballot for two Persons, of whom one at least shall not be an Inhabitant of the same State with themselves. And they shall make a List of all the Persons voted for, and of the Number of Votes for each; which List they shall sign and certify, and transmit sealed to the Seat of the Government of the United States, directed to the President of the Senate. The President of the Senate shall, in the Presence of the Senate and House of Representatives, open all the Certificates, and the Votes shall then be counted. The Person having the greatest Number of Votes shall be the President, if such Number be a Majority of the whole Number of Electors appointed; and if there be more than one who have such Majority, and have an equal Number of Votes, then the House of Representatives shall immediately chuse by Ballot one of them for President; and if no Person have a Majority, then from the five highest on the List the said House shall in like Manner chuse the President. But in chusing the President, the Votes shall be taken by States, the Representation from each State having one Vote; a quorum for this Purpose shall consist of a Member or Members from two thirds of the States, and a Majority of all the States shall be necessary to a Choice. In every Case, after the Choice of the President, the Person having the greatest Number of Votes of the Electors shall be the Vice President. But if there should remain two or more who have equal Votes, the Senate shall chuse from them by Ballot the Vice President.

The Congress may determine the Time of chusing the Electors, and the Day on which they shall give their Votes; which Day shall be the same throughout the United States.

No person except a natural born Citizen, or a Citizen of the United States, at the time of the Adoption of this Constitution, shall be eligible to the Office of President; neither shall any Person be eligible to that Office who shall not have attained to the Age of thirty five Years, and been fourteen Years a Resident within the United States.

In Case of the Removal of the President from Office, or of his Death, Resignation or Inability to discharge the Powers and Duties of the said Office, the Same shall devolve on the Vice President, and the Congress may by Law provide for the Case of Removal, Death, Resignation or Inability, both of the President and Vice President, declaring what Officer shall then act as President, and such Officer shall act accordingly, until the Disability be removed, or a President shall be elected.

The President shall, at stated Times, receive for his Services, a Compensation, which shall neither be encreased nor diminished during the Period for which he shall have been elected, and he shall not receive within that Period any other Emolument from the United States, or any of them.

Before he enter on the Execution of his Office, he shall take the following Oath or Affirmation:—"I do solemnly swear (or affirm) that I will faithfully execute the Office of President of the United States, and will to the best of my Ability, preserve, protect and defend the Constitution of the United States."

SEC. 2 The President shall be Commander in Chief of the Army and Navy of the United States, and of the Militia of the several States, when called into the actual Service of the United States; he may require the Opinion, in writing, of the principal Officer in each of the executive Departments, upon any Subject relating to the Duties of their respective Offices, and he shall have Power to grant Reprieves and Pardons for Offenses against the United States, except in Cases of Impeachment.

He shall have Power, by and with the Advice and Consent of the Senate, to make Treaties, provided two thirds of the Senators present concur; and he shall nominate, and by and with the Advice

and Consent of the Senate, shall appoint Ambassadors, other public Ministers and Consuls, Judges of the supreme Court, and all other Officers of the United States, whose Appointments are not herein otherwise provided for, and which shall be established by Law; but the Congress may by Law vest the Appointment of such inferior Officers, as they think proper, in the President alone, in the Courts of Law, or in the Heads of Departments.

The President shall have Power to fill up all Vacancies that may happen during the Recess of the Senate, by granting Commissions which shall expire at the End of their next Session.

SEC. 3 He shall from time to time give to the Congress Information of the State of the Union, and recommend to their Consideration such Measures as he shall judge necessary and expedient; he may, on extraordinary Occasions, convene both Houses, or either of them, and in Case of Disagreement between them, with Respect to the Time of Adjournment, he may adjourn them to such Time as he shall think proper; he shall receive Ambassadors and other public Ministers; he shall take Care that the Laws be faithfully executed, and shall Commission all the Officers of the United States.

SEC. 4 The President, Vice President and all Civil Officers of the United States, shall be removed from office on Impeachment for, and Conviction of, Treason, Bribery, or other high Crimes and Misdemeanors.

Article III

SEC. 1 The judicial Power of the United States, shall be vested in one supreme Court, and in such inferior Courts as the Congress may from time to time ordain and establish. The Judges, both of the supreme and inferior Courts, shall hold their Offices during good Behaviour, and shall, at stated Times, receive for their Services, a Compensation, which shall not be diminished during their Continuance in Office.

SEC. 2 The judicial Power shall extend to all Cases, in Law and Equity, arising under this Constitution, the Laws of the United States, and Treaties made, or which shall be made, under their Authority;—to all Cases affecting Ambassadors, other public Ministers and Consuls;—to all Cases of admiralty and maritime Jurisdiction;—to Controversies to which the United States shall be a Party;—to Controversies between two or more States;—between a State and Citizens of another State;—between Citizens of different States;—between Citizens of the same State claiming Lands under Grants of different States, and between a State, or the Citizens thereof, and foreign States, Citizens or Subjects.

In all Cases affecting Ambassadors, other public Ministers and Consuls, and those in which a State shall be Party, the supreme Court shall have original Jurisdiction. In all the other Cases before mentioned, the supreme Court shall have appellate Jurisdiction, both as to Law and Fact, with such Exceptions, and under such Regulations as the Congress shall make.

The Trial of all Crimes, except in cases of Impeachment, shall be by Jury; and such Trial shall be held in the State where the said Crimes shall have been committed; but when not committed within any State, the Trial shall be at such Place or Places as the Congress may by Law have directed.

SEC. 3   Treason against the United States, shall consist only in levying War against them, or in adhering to their Enemies, giving them Aid and Comfort. No Person shall be convicted of Treason unless on the Testimony of two Witnesses to the same overt Act, or on Confession in open Court.

The Congress shall have Power to declare the Punishment of Treason, but no Attainder of Treason shall work Corruption of Blood, or Forfeiture except during the Life of the Person attainted.

Article IV

SEC. 1   Full Faith and Credit shall be given in each State to the Public Acts, Records, and judicial Proceedings of every other State. And the Congress may by general Laws prescribe the Manner in which such Acts, Records and Proceedings shall be proved, and the Effect thereof.

SEC. 2   The Citizens of each State shall be entitled to all Privileges and Immunities of Citizens in the several States.

A Person charged in any State with Treason, Felony, or other Crime, who shall flee from Justice, and be found in another State, shall on Demand of the executive Authority of the State from which he fled, be delivered up, to be removed to the State having Jurisdiction of the Crime.

No Person held to Service or Labour in one State, under the Laws thereof, escaping into another, shall, in Consequence of any Law or Regulation therein, be discharged from such Service or Labour, but shall be delivered up on Claim of the Party to whom such Service or Labour may be due.

SEC. 3   New States may be admitted by the Congress into this Union; but no new State shall be formed or erected within the Jurisdiction of any other State; nor any State be formed by the Junction of two or more States, or Parts of States, without the Consent of the Legislatures of the States concerned as well as of the Congress.

The Congress shall have Power to dispose of and make all needful Rules and Regulations respecting the Territory or other Property belonging to the United States; and nothing in this Constitution shall be so construed as to Prejudice any Claims of the United States, or of any particular State.

SEC. 4   The United States shall guarantee to every State in this Union a Republican Form of Government, and shall protect each of them against Invasion; and on Application of the Legislature, or of the Executive (when the Legislature cannot be convened) against domestic Violence.

Article V

The Congress, whenever two thirds of both Houses shall deem it necessary, shall propose Amendments to this Constitution, or, on the Application of the Legislatures of two thirds of the several States, shall call a Convention for proposing Amendments, which, in either Case, shall be valid to all Intents and Purposes, as Part of this Constitution, when ratified by the Legislatures of three fourths of the several States, or by Conventions in three fourths thereof, as the one or the other Mode of Ratification may be proposed by the Congress; Provided that no Amendment which may be made prior to the Year One thousand eight hundred and eight shall in any Manner affect the first and fourth Clauses in the Ninth Section of the first Article; and that no State, without its Consent, shall be deprived of its equal Suffrage in the Senate.

Article VI

All Debts contracted and Engagements entered into, before the Adoption of this Constitution, shall be as valid against the United States under this Constitution, as under the Confederation.

This Constitution, and the Laws of the United States which shall be made in Pursuance thereof; and all Treaties made, or which shall be made, under the Authority of the United States, shall be the supreme Law of the Land; and the Judges in every State shall be bound thereby, any Thing in the Constitution or Laws of any State to the Contrary notwithstanding.

The Senators and Representatives before mentioned, and the Members of the several State Legislatures, and all executive and judicial Officers, both of the United States and of the several States, shall be bound by Oath or Affirmation, to support this Constitution; but no religious Test shall ever be required as a Qualification to any Office or public Trust under the United States.

Article VII

The Ratification of the Conventions of nine States shall be sufficient for the Establishment of this Constitution between the States so ratifying the Same. Done in Convention by the Unanimous Consent of the States present the Seventeenth Day of September in the Year of our Lord one thousand seven hundred and Eighty seven and of the Independence of the United States of America the Twelfth In witness whereof We have hereunto subscribed our Names,

G^O Washington—Presid^t
and deputy from Virginia

New Hampshire	John Langdon Nicholas Gilman
Massachusetts	Nathaniel Gorham Rufus King
Connecticut	W^M Sam^L Johnson Roger Sherman
New York	Alexander Hamilton
New Jersey	Wil: Livingston David Brearley W^M Paterson Jona: Dayton
Pennsylvania	B Franklin Thomas Mifflin Rob^T Morris Geo. Clymer Tho^S FitzSimons Jared Ingersoll James Wilson Gouv Morris

Delaware	Geo: Read Gunning Bedford Jun John Dickinson Richard Bassett Jaco: Broom
Maryland	James M^{C}Henry Dan of S^T Tho^S Jenifer Dan^L Carroll
Virginia	John Blair— James Madison Jr.
North Carolina	W^M Blount Rich^D Dobbs Spaight Hu Williamson
South Carolina	J. Rutledge Charles Cotesworth Pinckney Charles Pinckney Pierce Butler
Georgia	William Few Abr Baldwin

Articles in addition to, and Amendment of the Constitution of the United States of America, proposed by Congress, and ratified by the Legislatures of the several States pursuant to the fifth Article of the original Constitution.

The first ten amendments went into effect December 15, 1791.

Amendment I

Congress shall make no law respecting an establishment of religion, or prohibiting the free exercise thereof; or abridging the freedom of speech, or of the press; or the right of the people peaceably to assemble, and to petition the Government for a redress of grievances.

Amendment II

A well regulated Militia, being necessary to the security of a free State, the right of the people to keep and bear Arms, shall not be infringed.

Amendment III

No Soldier shall, in time of peace be quartered in any house, without the consent of the Owner, nor in time of war, but in a manner to be prescribed by law.

Amendment IV

The right of the people to be secure in their persons, houses, papers, and effects, against unreasonable searches and seizures, shall not be violated, and no Warrants shall issue, but upon probable cause, supported by Oath or affirmation, and particularly describing the place to be searched, and the persons or things to be seized.

Amendment V

No person shall be held to answer for a capital, or otherwise infamous crime, unless on a presentment or indictment of a Grand Jury, except in cases arising in the land or naval forces, or in the Militia, when in actual service in time of War or public danger; nor shall any person be subject for the same offence to be twice put in jeopardy of life or limb; nor shall be compelled in any criminal case to be a witness against himself, nor be deprived of life, liberty, or property, without due process of law; nor shall private property be taken for public use, without just compensation.

Amendment VI

In all criminal prosecutions, the accused shall enjoy the right to a speedy and public trial, by an impartial jury of the State and district wherein the crime shall have been committed, which district shall have been previously ascertained by law, and to be informed of the nature and cause of the accusation; to be confronted with the witnesses against him; to have compulsory process for obtaining witnesses in his favor, and to have the Assistance of Counsel for his defence.

Amendment VII

In Suits at common law, where the value in controversy shall exceed twenty dollars, the right of trial by jury shall be preserved, and no fact tried by a jury, shall be otherwise re-examined in any Court of the United States, than according to the rules of the common law.

Amendment VIII

Excessive bail shall not be required, nor excessive fines imposed, nor cruel and unusual punishments inflicted.

Amendment IX

The enumeration in the Constitution, of certain rights, shall not be construed to deny or disparage others retained by the people.

Amendment X

The power not delegated to the United States by the Constitution, nor prohibited by it to the States, are reserved to the States respectively, or to the people.

Amendment XI
February 7, 1795

The Judicial power of the United States shall not be construed to extend to any suit in law or equity, commenced or prosecuted against one of the United States by Citizens of another State, or by Citizens or Subjects of any Foreign State.

Amendment XII
June 15, 1804

The Electors shall meet in their respective states and vote by ballot for President and Vice-President, one of whom, at least, shall not be an inhabitant of the same state with themselves; they shall name in their ballots the person voted for as President, and in distinct ballots the person voted for as Vice-President, and they shall make distinct lists of all persons voted for as President, and of all persons voted for as Vice-President, and of the number of votes for each, which lists they shall sign and certify, and transmit sealed to the seat of the government of the United States, directed to the President of the Senate;—The President of the Senate shall, in the presence of the Senate and House of Representatives, open all the certificates and the votes shall then be counted;—The person having the greatest number of votes for President, shall be the President, if such number be a majority of the whole number of Electors appointed; and if no person have such majority, then from the persons having the highest numbers not exceeding three on the list of those voted for as President, the House of Representatives shall choose immediately, by ballot, the President. But in choosing the President, the votes shall be taken by states, the representation from each state having one vote; a quorum for this purpose shall consist of a member or members from two-thirds of the states, and a majority of all the states shall be necessary to a choice. And if the House of Representatives shall not choose a President whenever the right of choice shall devolve upon them before the fourth day of March next following, then the Vice-President shall act as President, as in the case of the death or other constitutional disability of the President—The person having the greatest number of votes as Vice-President, shall be the Vice-President, if such number be a majority of the whole number of Electors appointed, and if no person have a majority, then from the two highest numbers on the list, the Senate shall choose the Vice-President; a quorum for the purpose shall consist of two-thirds of the whole number of Senators, and a majority of the whole number shall be necessary to a choice. But no person constitutionally ineligible to the office of President shall be eligible to that of Vice-President of the United States.

Amendment XIII
December 6, 1865

Sec. 1   Neither slavery nor involuntary servitude, except as a punishment for crime whereof the party shall have been duly convicted, shall exist within the United States, or any place subject to their jurisdiction.

Sec. 2   Congress shall have power to enforce this article by appropriate legislation.

Amendment XIV
July 9, 1868

Sec. 1   All persons born or naturalized in the United States and subject to the jurisdiction thereof, are citizens of the United States and of the State wherein they reside. No State shall make or enforce any law which shall abridge the privileges or immunities of citizens of the United States; nor shall any State deprive any person of life, liberty, or property, without due process of law; nor deny to any person within its jurisdiction the equal protection of the laws.

Sec. 2   Representatives shall be apportioned among the several States according to their respective numbers, counting the whole number of persons in each State, excluding Indians not taxed. But when the right to vote at any election for the choice of electors for President and Vice President of the United States, Representatives in Congress, the Executive and Judicial officers of a State, or the members of the Legislature thereof, is denied to any of the male inhabitants of such State, being twenty-one years of age, and citizens of the United States, or in any way abridged, except for participation in rebellion, or other crime, the basis of representation therein shall be reduced in the proportion which the number of such male citizens shall bear to the whole number of male citizens twenty-one years of age in such State.

Sec. 3   No person shall be a Senator or Representative in Congress, or elector of President and Vice President, or hold or any office, civil or military, under the United States, or under any State, who, having previously taken an oath, as a member of Congress, or as an officer of the United States, or as a member of any State legislature, or as an executive or judicial officer of any State, to support the Constitution of the United States, shall have engaged in insurrection or rebellion against the same, or given aid or comfort to the enemies thereof. But Congress may by a vote of two-thirds of each House, remove such disability.

Sec. 4   The validity of the public debt of the United States, authorized by law, including debts incurred for payment of pensions and bounties for services in suppressing insurrection or rebellion, shall not be questioned. But neither the United States nor any State shall assume or pay any debt or obligation incurred in aid of insurrection or rebellion against the United States, or any claim for the loss or emancipation of any slave; but all such debts, obligations and claims shall be held illegal and void.

Sec. 5   The Congress shall have power to enforce, by appropriate legislation, the provisions of this article.

Amendment XV
February 3, 1870

Sec. 1   The right of citizens of the United States to vote shall not be denied or abridged by the United States or by any State on account of race, color, or previous condition of servitude.

Sec. 2   The Congress shall have power to enforce this article by appropriate legislation.

Amendment XVI
February 3, 1913

The Congress shall have power to lay and collect taxes on incomes, from whatever source derived, without apportionment among the several States, and without regard to any census or enumeration.

Amendment XVII
April 8, 1913

The Senate of the United States shall be composed of two Senators from each State, elected by the people thereof, for six years; and each Senator shall have one vote. The electors in each State shall have the qualifications requisite for electors of the most numerous branch of the State legislatures.

When vacancies happen in the representation of any State in the Senate, the executive authority of such State shall issue writs of election to fill such vacancies: *Provided,* That the legislature of any State may empower the executive thereof to make temporary appointments until the people fill the vacancies by election as the legislature may direct.

This amendment shall not be so construed as to affect the election or term of any Senator chosen before it becomes valid as part of the Constitution.

Amendment XVIII
January 16, 1919

Sec. 1   After one year from the ratification of this article the manufacture, sale, or transportation of intoxicating liquors within, the importation thereof into, or the exportation thereof from the United States and all territory subject to the jurisdiction thereof for beverage purposes is hereby prohibited.

Sec. 2   The Congress and the several States shall have concurrent power to enforce this article by appropriate legislation.

Sec. 3   This article shall be inoperative unless it shall have been ratified as an amendment to the Constitution by the legislatures of the several States, as provided in the Constitution, within seven years from the date of the submission hereof to the States by the Congress.

Amendment XIX
August 18, 1920

The right of citizens of the United States to vote shall not be denied or abridged by the United States or by any State on account of sex.

Congress shall have power to enforce this article by appropriate legislation.

Amendment XX
January 23, 1933

SEC. 1 The terms of the President and Vice-President shall end at noon on the 20th day of January, and the terms of Senators and Representatives at noon on the 3d day of January, of the years in which such terms would have ended if this article had not been ratified; and the terms of their successors shall then begin.

SEC. 2 The Congress shall assemble at least once in every year, and such meeting shall begin at noon on the 3d day of January, unless they shall by law appoint a different day.

SEC. 3 If, at the time fixed for the beginning of the term of the President, the President elect shall have died, the Vice President elect shall become President. If a President shall not have been chosen before the time fixed for the beginning of his term, or if the President elect shall have failed to qualify, then the Vice President elect shall act as President until a President shall have qualified; and the Congress may by law provide for the case wherein neither a President elect nor a Vice President elect shall have qualified, declaring who shall then act as President, or the manner in which one who is to act shall be selected, and such person shall act accordingly until a President or Vice President shall have qualified.

SEC. 4 The Congress may by law provide for the case of the death of any of the persons from whom the House of Representatives may choose a President whenever the right of choice shall have devolved upon them, and for the case of the death of any of the persons from whom the Senate may choose a Vice President whenever the right of choice shall have devolved upon them.

SEC. 5 Sections 1 and 2 shall take effect on the 15th day of October following the ratification of this article.

SEC. 6 This article shall be inoperative unless it shall have been ratified as an amendment to the Constitution by the legislatures of three-fourths of the several States within seven years from the date of its submission.

Amendment XXI
December 5, 1933

SEC. 1 The eighteenth article of amendment to the Constitution of the United States is hereby repealed.

SEC. 2 The transportation or importation into any State, Territory or possession of the United States for delivery or use therein of intoxicating liquors, in violation of the laws thereof, is hereby prohibited.

SEC. 3 This article shall be inoperative unless it shall have been ratified as an amendment to the Constitution by conventions in the several States, as provided in the Constitution, within seven years from the date of the submission hereof to the States by the Congress.

Amendment XXII
February 27, 1951

SEC. 1 No person shall be elected to the office of the President more than twice, and no person who has held the office of President, or acted as President for more than two years of a term to which some other person was elected President shall be elected to the office of the President more than once. But this Article shall not apply to any person holding the office of President when this Article was proposed by the Congress, and shall not prevent any person who may be holding the office of President, or acting as President, during the term within which this Article becomes operative from holding the office of President or acting as President during the remainder of such term.

SEC. 2 This Article shall be inoperative unless it shall have been ratified as an amendment to the Constitution by the legislatures of three-fourths of the several States within seven years from the date of its submission to the States by the Congress.

Amendment XXIII
March 29, 1961

SEC. 1 The District constituting the seat of Government of the United States shall appoint in such manner as the Congress may direct:

A number of electors of President and Vice President equal to the whole number of Senators and Representatives in Congress to which the District would be entitled if it were a State, but in no event more than the least populous state; they shall be in addition to those appointed by the States, but they shall be considered, for the purposes of the election of President and Vice President, to be electors appointed by a state; and they shall meet in the District and perform such duties as provided by the twelfth article of amendment.

SEC. 2   The Congress shall have power to enforce this article by appropriate legislation.

Amendment XXIV
January 23, 1964

SEC. 1   The right of citizens of the United States to vote in any primary or other election for President or Vice President, for electors for President or Vice President, or for Senator or Representative in Congress, shall not be denied or abridged by the United States or any State by reason of failure to pay any poll tax or other tax.

SEC. 2   The Congress shall have power to enforce this article by appropriate legislation.

Amendment XXV
February 10, 1967

SEC. 1   In case of the removal of the President from office or of his death or resignation, the Vice President shall become President.

SEC. 2   Whenever there is a vacancy in the office of the Vice President, the President shall nominate a Vice President who shall take office upon confirmation by a majority vote of both Houses of Congress.

SEC. 3   Whenever the President transmits to the President pro tempore of the Senate and the Speaker of the House of Representatives his written declaration that he is unable to discharge the powers and duties of his office, and until he transmits to them a written declaration to the contrary, such powers and duties shall be discharged by the Vice President as Acting President.

SEC. 4   Whenever the Vice President and a majority of either the principal officers of the executive departments, or of such other body as Congress may by law provide, transmit to the President pro tempore of the Senate and the Speaker of the House of Representatives their written declaration that the President is unable to discharge the powers and duties of his office, the Vice President shall immediately assume the powers and duties of the office as Acting President.

Thereafter, when the President transmits to the President pro tempore of the Senate and the Speaker of the House of Representatives his written declaration that no inability exists, he shall resume the powers and duties of his office unless the Vice President and a majority of either the principal officers of the executive department or of such other body as Congress may by law provide, transmit within four days to the President pro tempore of the Senate and the Speaker of the House of Representatives their written declaration that the President is unable to discharge the powers and duties of his office. Thereupon Congress shall decide the issue, assembling within forty-eight hours for that purpose if not in session. If the Congress, within twenty-one days after receipt of the latter written declaration, or, if Congress is not in session, within twenty-one days after Congress is required to assemble, determines by two-thirds vote of both houses that the President is unable to discharge the powers and duties of his office, the Vice President shall continue to discharge the same as Acting President; otherwise, the President shall resume the powers and duties of his office.

Amendment XXVI
July 1, 1971

SEC. 1   The right of citizens of the United States, who are eighteen years of age or older, to vote shall not be denied or abridged by the United States or by any State on account of age.

SEC. 2   The Congress shall have power to enforce this article by appropriate legislation.

Amendment XXVII
May 7, 1992

No law varying the compensation for the services of the Senators and Representatives shall take effect, until an election of Representatives shall have intervened.

THE DECLARATION OF INDEPENDENCE

July 4, 1776

In Congress, July 4, 1776,
THE UNANIMOUS DECLARATION OF THE THIRTEEN
UNITED STATES OF AMERICA,

When in the Course of human events, it becomes necessary for one people to dissolve the political bands which have connected them with another, and to assume among the Powers of the earth, the separate and equal station to which the Laws of Nature and of Nature's God entitle them, a decent respect to the opinions of mankind requires that they should declare the causes which impel them to the separation.

We hold these truths to be self-evident, that all men are created equal, that they are endowed by their Creator with certain unalienable Rights, that among these are Life, Liberty and the pursuit of Happiness. That to secure these rights, Governments are instituted among Men, deriving their just powers from the consent of the governed. That whenever any form of Government becomes destructive of these ends, it is the Right of the People to alter or to abolish it, and to institute new Government, laying its foundation on such principles and organizing its powers in such form, as to them shall seem most likely to effect their Safety and Happiness. Prudence, indeed, will dictate that Government long established should not be changed for light and transient causes; and accordingly all experience hath shown, that mankind are more disposed to suffer, while evils are sufferable, than to right themselves by abolishing the forms to which they are accustomed. But when a long train of abuses and usurpations, pursuing invariably the same Object evinces a design to reduce them under absolute Despotism, it is their right, it is their duty, to throw off such Government, and to provide new Guards for their future security.—Such has been the patient sufferance of these Colonies; and such is now the necessity which constrains them to alter their former Systems of Government. The history of the present King of Great Britain is a history of repeated injuries and usurpations, all having in direct object the establishment of an absolute Tyranny over these States. To prove this, let Facts be submitted to a candid world.

He has refused his Assent to Laws, the most wholesome and necessary for the public good.

He has forbidden his Governors to pass Laws of immediate and pressing importance, unless suspended in their operation till his Assent should be obtained; and when so suspended, he has utterly neglected to attend to them.

He has refused to pass other Laws for the accommodation of large districts of people, unless those people would relinquish the right of Representation in the Legislature, a right inestimable to them and formidable to tyrants only.

He has called together legislative bodies at places unusual, uncomfortable, and distant from the depository of their Public Records, for the sole purpose of fatiguing them into compliance with his measures.

He has dissolved Representative Houses repeatedly, for opposing with manly firmness his invasions on the rights of the people.

He has refused for a long time, after such dissolutions, to cause others to be elected; whereby the Legislative Powers, incapable of Annihilation, have returned to the People at large for their exercise; the State remaining in the mean time exposed to all the dangers of invasion from without, and convulsions within.

He has endeavoured to prevent the population of these States; for that purpose obstructing the Laws of Naturalization of Foreigners; refusing to pass others to encourage their migration hither, and raising the conditions of new Appropriations of Lands.

He has obstructed the Administration of Justice, by refusing his Assent to Laws for establishing Judiciary Powers.

He has made Judges dependent on his Will alone, for the tenure of their offices, and the amount and payment of their salaries.

He has erected a multitude of New Offices, and sent hither swarms of Officers to harass our People, and eat out their substance.

He has kept among us, in times of peace, Standing Armies without the Consent of our legislature.

He has affected to render the Military independent of and superior to the Civil Power.

He has combined with others to subject us to a jurisdiction foreign to our constitution, and unacknowledged by our laws; giving his Assent to their acts of pretended legislation:

For quartering large bodies of armed troops among us:

For protecting them, by a mock Trial, from Punishment for any Murders which they should commit on the Inhabitants of these States:

For cutting off our Trade with all parts of the world:

For imposing taxes on us without our Consent:

For depriving us in many cases, of the benefits of Trial by Jury:

For transporting us beyond Seas to be tried for pretended offences:

For abolishing the free System of English Laws in a neighbouring Province, establishing therein an Arbitrary government, and enlarging its Boundaries so as to render it at once an example and fit instrument for introducing the same absolute rule into these Colonies:

For taking away our Charters, abolishing our most valuable Laws, and altering fundamentally the Forms of our Governments:

For suspending our own Legislature, and declaring themselves invested with Power to legislate for us in all cases whatsoever.

He has abdicated Government here, by declaring us out of his Protection and waging War against us.

He has plundered our seas, ravaged our Coasts, burnt our towns, and destroyed the lives of our people.

He is at this time transporting large armies of foreign mercenaries to compleat the works of death, desolation and tyranny, already begun with circumstances of Cruelty & perfidy scarcely paralleled in the most barbarous ages, and totally unworthy the Head of a civilized nation.

He has constrained our fellow Citizens taken Captive on the high Seas to bear Arms against their Country, to become the executioners of their friends and Brethren, or to fall themselves by their Hands.

He has excited domestic insurrections amongst us, and has endeavoured to bring on the inhabitants of our frontiers, the merciless Indian Savages, whose known rule of warfare, is an undistinguished destruction of all ages, sexes and conditions.

In every stage of these Oppressions We have Petitioned for Redress in the most humble terms: Our repeated Petitions have been answered only by repeated injury. A Prince, whose character is thus marked by every act which may define a Tyrant, is unfit to be the ruler of a free People.

Nor have We been wanting in attention to our Brittish brethren. We have warned them from time to time of attempts by their legislature to extend an unwarrantable jurisdiction over us. We have reminded them of the circumstances of our emigration and settlement here. We have appealed to their native justice and magnanimity, and we have conjured them by the ties of our common kindred to disavow these usurpations, which, would inevitably interrupt our connections and correspondence. They too have been deaf to the voice of justice and of consanguinity. We must, therefore, acquiesce in the necessity, which denounces our Separation, and hold them, as we hold the rest of mankind, Enemies in War, in Peace Friends.

We, therefore, the Representatives of the united States of America, in General Congress, Assembled, appealing to the Supreme Judge of the world for the rectitude of our intentions, do, in the Name, and by Authority of the good People of these Colonies, solemnly publish and declare, That these United Colonies are, and of Right ought to be Free and Independent States; that they are Absolved from all Allegiance to the British Crown, and that all political connection between them and the State of Great Britain, is and ought to be totally dissolved; and that as Free and Independent States, they have full Power to levy War, conclude Peace, contract Alliances, establish Commerce, and to do all other Acts and Things which Independent States may of right do. And for the support of this Declaration, with a firm reliance on the Protection of Divine Providence, we mutually pledge to each other our Lives, our Fortunes and our sacred Honor.

JOHN HANCOCK.

New Hampshire
   JOSIAH BARTLETT,
   WM. WHIPPLE,
   MATTHEW THORNTON.

Massachusetts-Bay
   SAML. ADAMS,
   JOHN ADAMS,
   ROBT. TREAT PAINE,
   ELBRIDGE GERRY.

Rhode Island
   STEP. HOPKINS,
   WILLIAM ELLERY.

Connecticut
   ROGER SHERMAN,
   SAM'EL HUNTINGTON,
   WM. WILLIAMS,
   OLIVER WOLCOTT.

New York
   WM. FLOYD,
   PHIL. LIVINGSTON,
   FRANS. LEWIS,
   LEWIS MORRIS.

Pennsylvania
   ROBT. MORRIS,
   BENJAMIN RUSH,
   BENJA. FRANKLIN,
   JOHN MORTON,
   GEO. CLYMER,
   JAS. SMITH,
   GEO. TAYLOR,
   JAMES WILSON,
   GEO. ROSS.

Delaware
   CAESAR RODNEY,
   GEO. READ,
   THO. M'KEAN.

Georgia
   BUTTON GWINNETT,
   LYMAN HALL,
   GEO. WALTON.

Maryland
   SAMUEL CHASE,
   WM. PACA,
   THOS. STONE,
   CHARLES CARROLL OF CARROLLTON.

Virginia
   GEORGE WYTHE,
   RICHARD HENRY LEE,
   TH. JEFFERSON,
   BENJA. HARRISON,
   THS. NELSON, JR.,
   FRANCIS LIGHTFOOT LEE,
   CARTER BRAXTON.

North Carolina
   WM. HOOPER,
   JOSEPH HEWES,
   JOHN PENN.

South Carolina
   EDWARD RUTLEDGE,
   THOS. HEYWARD, JUNR.,
   THOMAS LYNCH, JUNR.,
   ARTHUR MIDDLETON.

New Jersey
   RICHD. STOCKTON,
   JNO. WITHERSPOON,
   FRAS. HOPKINSON,
   JOHN HART,
   ABRA. CLARK.

Selected Landmark Federal Legislation

This appendix describes some features of important federal laws referred to in the text. The number or numbers at the end of each entry are those of the chapters in which the act is discussed.

Act	Year	Subject	Significance
Judiciary Act	1789	Organization of the federal judiciary	Established first federal district and circuit courts; allowed appeal from state to federal courts; set stage for *Marbury v. Madison.* [8]
Reconstruction Acts	1866–67	Treatment of southern blacks	Gave citizenship rights to blacks in former rebel states; led to Fourteenth Amendment. [4]
Pendleton Civil Service Act	1883	Civil service reform	Created first merit-selected civil service positions; beginning of attack on spoils system. [10]
Interstate Commerce Act	1887	Federal regulation of interstate commerce	Created the first of several federal regulatory commissions (Interstate Commerce Commission) for the purpose of regulating interstate railroads and shipping in order to prevent restraints of trade. [10]
Federal Reserve Act	1913	Federal Reserve System	Established a Board of Governors and a system of banks to control supply of money and credit. [12]

Act	Year	Subject	Significance
Espionage Act	1917	Free speech limitations	Upheld in *Schenck v. United States* in which Oliver Wendell Holmes established "clear and present danger" as the standard for determining if government had the right to limit speech. [9]
Budget and Accounting Act	1921	Budget reform	Gave president responsibility to present a budget to Congress; created Bureau of Budget (now Office of Management and Budget) to help him do this. [7]
Social Security Act	1935	Major federal pension system	Established a pension system administered by the federal government for Americans over age sixty-five and disabled persons. [3]
Hatch Act	1939	Civil service	Barred federal civil servants from partisan political activity. Modified in 1993. [10]
Employment Act	1946	Economic policy	Committed the federal government to "promote maximum employment, production, and purchasing power." [12]
Legislative Reorganization Act	1946	Congressional reform	Reduced number of committees in Congress; established present committee structure, with some additions and changes since. [6]
Regulation of Lobbying Act	1946	Lobbying	Required lobbyists to register and report their spending; largely ineffective because of loopholes. [5]
Civil Rights Act	1964	Racial equality	Outlawed race and sex discrimination in employment and businesses serving the public, such as hotels and restaurants. [2, 7, 8, 9]
Tonkin Gulf Resolution	1964	Use of U.S. forces in Southeast Asia	Approved President Johnson's request to use U.S. forces in Southeast Asia with only two

Act	Year	Subject	Significance
			opposing votes; followed by drastic escalation of U.S. troop commitment in Southeast Asia. [7]
Voting Rights Act	1965	Voting rights for minorities	Nullified various state laws and practices that kept blacks and other minorities from voting; established federal supervision of state and local election laws in some areas. [7]
National Environmental Policy Act	1969	Environmental policy	Proclaimed national policy of protecting the environment; environmental impact statements required on major projects regulated by or using federal funds. [5]
Legislative Reorganization Act	1970	Congressional reform	Began process of making Congress more democratic and more open to public scrutiny; opened committee meetings to the public to a much greater extent; required roll call votes rather than voice votes on some proceedings; in the Senate, took away from the chair the sole authority to call committee meetings. [6]
Postal Reorganization Act	1970	Post office reform and reorganization	Took post office out of the cabinet and made the Postal Service a government corporation that should, if possible, charge patrons the costs of services. [10]
Federal Election Campaign Act	1971	Campaign financing	Established spending limits for candidates and candidates' families and on what candidates could spend on media; replaced in 1974. [4]
Endangered Species Act	1973	Plant and wildlife preservation	Required planning and limited commercial use of land where endangered species are known to exist if such use would risk species extinction. [3]

Act	Year	Subject	Significance
War Powers Resolution	1973	War powers of Congress and the president	Limited president to sixty days without congressional approval when troops are committed to combat; contained a legislative veto, now probably unconstitutional. [6, 7, 11]
Comprehensive Employment and Training Act	1973	Employment and training	Consolidated several different federal training programs under one block grant program; gave states and localities greater flexibility for targeting federal money for job training in their areas. [3]
Budget and Impoundment Control Act	1974	Impoundment and budget reform	Restricted impoundment; required Congress to set up Budget Committees and become more responsible for the budget process; created Congressional Budget Office. [7, 10]
Federal Election Campaign Act	1974	Campaign financing	Provided for public funding of presidential campaigns and set tight restrictions on individual contributions; established Federal Election Commission; modified by *Buckley v. Valeo* and 1976 Federal Election Campaign Act. [4]
Hughes-Ryan Amendment	1974	Intelligence and covert operations	Required covert operations of U.S. intelligence agencies to be reported to eight congressional committees; the number was reduced to two in 1980. [7]
Trade Reform Act	1974	International trade	Created the International Trade Commission, which served as a check on presidential power. [11]
Civil Service Reform Act	1978	Civil service reform	Created Senior Executive Service; provided merit bonuses for good performance; allowed the president to shift personnel among agencies;

Act	Year	Subject	Significance
			mostly failed to achieve its objectives. [10]
Ethics in Government Act	1978	Lobbying	Restricted right of former executive branch officials to lobby ex-colleagues in government; does not apply to former congresspersons. [10]
Balanced Budget and Emergency Deficit Control Act (Gramm-Rudman-Hollings)	1985	Deficit reduction	Mandated severe budget cuts if deficit reduction targets were not met; was amended to extend target dates. [7, 10, 12]
Tax Reform Act	1986	Tax reform	Confirmed Reagonomics by consolidating tax rates, reducing tax categories, and eliminating several loopholes.
Ethics Reform Act	1989	Private financing of trips and gifts to public officials	Restricted honoraria, privately financed domestic travel, and certain gifts to government officials. [5]
Omnibus Budget Reconciliation Act	1990	Deficit reduction	Modified Gramm-Rudman-Hollings, applying discipline but failing to control the deficit. [10]
Civil Rights Act	1991	Hiring practices	Shifted the burden of proof back on the employer to justify legality of employment practices. [8, 10]
Gulf War Resolution	1991	Use of U.S. forces in the Middle East	Approved President Bush's request to use U.S. forces to regain Kuwait, which had been invaded by Iraq; authorized military action under UN auspices and U.S. leadership. [7]
Family and Medical Leave Act	1993	Employment practices	Required businesses with fifty or more employees to allow time off for medical and family matters, including child rearing. [6]
Omnibus Budget Reconciliation Act	1993	Deficit reduction	Combined tax increases and spending cuts to save approximately $500 billion over five years. [10, 12]

Presidents of the United States

Year	Democratic-Republican or Democratic	Federalist, Whig, or Republican
1789		George Washington (F)
1793		George Washington (F)
1797		John Adams (F)
1801	Thomas Jefferson (D-R)	
1805	Thomas Jefferson (D-R)	
1809	James Madison (D-R)	
1813	James Madison (D-R)	
1817	James Monroe (D-R)	
1821	James Monroe (D-R)	
1825	John Q. Adams (D-R)*	
1829	Andrew Jackson (D)	
1833	Andrew Jackson (D)	
1837	Martin Van Buren (D)	
1841		William H. Harrison (W)
(1841)		John Tyler (W)**
1845	James K. Polk (D)	
1849		Zachary Taylor (W)
(1850)		Millard Fillmore (W)**
1853	Franklin Pierce (D)	
1857	James Buchanan (D)	
1861		Abraham Lincoln (R)
1865		Abraham Lincoln (R)
(1865)	Andrew Johnson (D)***	
1869		Ulysses S. Grant (R)
1873		Ulysses S. Grant (R)
1877		Rutherford B. Hayes (R)
1881		James A. Garfield (R)
(1881)		Chester A. Arthur (R)**
1885	Grover Cleveland (D)	

Year	Democratic-Republican or Democratic	Federalist, Whig, or Republican
1889		Benjamin Harrison (R)
1893	Grover Cleveland (D)	
1897		William McKinley (R)
1901		William McKinley (R)
(1901)		Theodore Roosevelt (R)**
1905		Theodore Roosevelt (R)
1909		William H. Taft (R)
1913	Woodrow Wilson (D)	
1917	Woodrow Wilson (D)	
1921		Warren G. Harding (R)
(1923)		Calvin Coolidge (R)**
1925		Calvin Coolidge (R)
1929		Herbert C. Hoover (R)
1933	Franklin D. Roosevelt (D)	
1937	Franklin D. Roosevelt (D)	
1941	Franklin D. Roosevelt (D)	
1945	Franklin D. Roosevelt (D)	
(1945)	Harry S Truman (D)**	
1949	Harry S Truman (D)	
1953		Dwight D. Eisenhower (R)
1957		Dwight D. Eisenhower (R)
1961	John F. Kennedy (D)	
(1963)	Lyndon B. Johnson (D)**	
1965	Lyndon B. Johnson (D)	
1969		Richard M. Nixon (R)
1973		Richard M. Nixon (R)
(1974)		Gerald R. Ford (R)**
1977	Jimmy Carter (D)	
1981		Ronald Reagan (R)
1985		Ronald Reagan (R)
1989		George Bush (R)
1993	Bill Clinton (D)	

* Party distinctions blurred in this election.
** Attained office following death or resignation of previous president.
*** Andrew Johnson, a Democrat, was nominated as vice-president by the Republicans and elected with Lincoln on the National Union ticket. Johnson became president upon Lincoln's death.

Major U.S. Supreme Court Cases

This appendix provides a historical picture of selected constitutional law cases. Some relate to the subject matter of chapters in this textbook. Others are included to illustrate how the Supreme Court applies general principles of law to specific areas. The numbers at the end of an entry are those of the chapters in which the case is discussed.

Case	Year	Decision	Significance
Marbury v. Madison	1803	Section 13 of Judiciary Act of 1789 declared unconstitutional.	Supreme Court's power of judicial review established. [8]
Dartmouth College v. Woodward	1819	Corporate contract obligations affirmed; the sanctity of prior contract obligations affirmed. A contract, once entered into, cannot be broken.	Business growth encouraged.
McCulloch v. Maryland	1819	State tax on national bank struck down.	Broad interpretation of national government's power. [3]
Gibbons v. Ogden	1824	Steamboat monopoly granted by New York struck down as infringing on federal commerce power.	National control of interstate commerce strengthened.
Dred Scott v. Sandford	1857	Overturned legislation prohibiting slavery in some territories.	Contributed to outbreak of Civil War. [8]
Bradwell v. Illinois	1873	Women denied the right to practice law in Illinois.	Traditional gender roles upheld despite Equal Protection Clause of Fourteenth Amendment. [1, 2, 9]
Reynolds v. United States	1879	Federal antipolygamy law upheld.	Freedom of religion limited. [9]

Case	Year	Decision	Significance
Santa Clara County v. Southern Pacific Railroad Co.	1886	Corporations declared "persons" and entitled to Fourteenth Amendment protections.	Increased power of Supreme Court to make law and policy through constitutional interpretation. [8]
Pollock v. Farmers' Loan and Trust Co.	1895	Federal income tax declared unconstitutional.	Sixteenth Amendment reversed this decision. [8]
Plessy v. Ferguson	1896	Segregation in public transportation upheld.	"Separate but equal" doctrine established. [9]
Lochner v. New York	1905	Regulation of working hours declared unconstitutional.	Court supports libertarian economics. [8]
Muller v. Oregon	1908	State regulation of working hours for women upheld.	Acknowledged special protection under the law for women. [9]
Quang Wing v. Kirkendall	1912	Tax exemption for female-owned laundries upheld.	Traditional gender roles upheld again. [9]
Schenck v. United States	1919	Conviction of antidraft agitator upheld.	Free speech can be limited in times of "clear and present danger." [9]
Missouri v. Holland	1920	Migratory bird treaty upheld against state challenge.	National government's power to make treaty with foreign countries upheld.
Adkins v. Children's Hospital	1923	Minimum wages for women workers struck down.	Minimum wage laws unconstitutional. [8]
Gitlow v. New York	1925	Conviction of communist for advocating revolution upheld.	First Amendment freedom of speech made applicable to states. [9]
Powell v. Alabama	1932	Criminal conviction as a result of an unfair trial struck down.	Required that counsel be provided for major state cases. [8]
Schecter Poultry Co. v. United States	1935	Franklin Roosevelt's National Industrial Recovery Act declared unconstitutional.	Impact of New Deal limited. [8]
Brown v. Mississippi	1936	Confessions produced by physical coercion declared inadmissible.	Fifth Amendment protection against self-incrimination made applicable to the states. [9]
United States v. Curtiss Wright Export Corp.	1936	Upheld a joint resolution of Congress that delegated some foreign policy decisions to the president.	Increased presidential powers in foreign policy. [11]
National Labor Relations Board v. Jones and Laughlin Steel Corp.	1937	New Deal labor law upheld.	Court reverses its stand on New Deal.

Case	Year	Decision	Significance
Cantwell v. Connecticut	1940	Jehovah's Witnesses declared to have a constitutional right to distribute religious literature door to door.	First time an action motivated by religion given constitutional protection. [9]
Minersville School District v. Gobitis	1940	Jehovah's Witness children's right not to salute the flag denied.	National unity overrides the religious freedom of a minority. [9]
West Virginia State Board of Education v. Barnette	1943	Overturned *Minersville School District v. Gobitis* by upholding the rights of Jehovah's Witness children not to salute the flag.	Freedom to express one's views, protected by the First Amendment, made applicable to states. [9]
Smith v. Allwright	1944	All-white Texas Democratic party primary declared unconstitutional.	Federal protection of black voting rights in the South established.
Everson v. Board of Education of Ewing Township	1947	State funds for busing of parochial school children upheld.	Establishment clause made applicable to states. [9]
Dennis v. United States	1951	Conviction of Communist party leaders for advocating overthrow of government upheld.	"Clear and present danger" limits on free speech reaffirmed. [9]
Brown v. Board of Education of Topeka	1954	Segregation in schools declared unconstitutional.	"Separate but equal" overturned. [8, 9]
Roth v. United States	1957	Federal anti-obscenity law upheld.	Obscenity can be prohibited if "without redeeming social value."
Yates v. United States	1957	Convictions of Communist party leaders for advocating overthrow of government upheld.	Scope of *Dennis* decision limited. [9]
Hoyt v. Florida	1961	Florida law excluding women with children from jury duty, unless registered, upheld.	Did not require equal rights and responsibilities of political citizenship to women. [9]
Mapp v. Ohio	1961	Evidence found in illegal search declared inadmissible in court.	Exclusionary rule applied to states. [9]
Engel v. Vitale	1962	Prayer in schools declared unconstitutional.	Church-state separation strengthened. [8, 9]
Baker v. Carr	1962	Malapportionment of state legislatures could be considered by federal courts.	Political power of urban areas increased. [8]

Case	Year	Decision	Significance
Gideon v. Wainwright	1963	Indigent defendant granted right to court-appointed attorney.	Right to counsel at public expense established for states. [9]
Reynolds v. Sims	1964	"One person, one vote" reapportionment and redistricting standards affirmed for state elections.	Political power of urban areas increased. [8]
Wesberry v. Sanders	1964	Standard to be used in congressional reapportionment established.	Equality among voters affirmed (one person, one vote) for national elections. [3]
Griswold v. Connecticut	1965	Connecticut law banning the use of birth control devices struck down.	Expanded interpretation of rights protected by the Constitution. [8]
Miranda v. Arizona	1966	Confessions obtained without advising the suspect of rights declared inadmissible in courts.	Right to remain silent applied to states. [9]
Phillips v. Martin Marietta Corp.	1971	Company policy of not hiring women with young children declared in violation of the Civil Rights Act.	Gender equality in the workplace affirmed. [9]
Reed v. Reed	1971	Law favoring men over women as executors struck down.	Gender equality under the law affirmed. [1, 9]
New York Times Co. v. United States	1971	Right of newspapers to publish classified government documents upheld.	Clear and present danger doctrine narrowed. [9]
Swann v. Charlotte-Mecklenburg County Board of Education	1971	Charlotte, North Carolina, schools required to bus students to eliminate school segregation.	Busing to achieve desegregation widely applied. [9]
Furman v. Georgia	1972	Death penalty statutes in Georgia and Texas struck down as a violation of the Eighth Amendment.	Temporarily suspended executions, prompting states to revise their death penalty statutes. [9]
Wisconsin v. Yoder	1972	Right of Amish to remove their children from schools after eighth grade upheld.	Freedom of religion broadened. [9]
Frontiero v. Richardson	1973	Gender-differentiated dependent benefits struck down.	Gender equality expanded. [9]
Miller v. California	1973	Conviction of pornographic bookseller upheld.	Definition of obscenity to be determined by "community standards." [9]

Kammen, Michael. 1986. *A Machine That Would Go of Itself: The Constitution in American Culture.* New York: Alfred A. Knopf.

Karl, Terry Lynn. 1992. "El Salvador's Negotiated Revolution." *Foreign Affairs* 71 (Spring): 147–64.

Karnow, Stanley. 1983. *Vietnam: A History.* New York: Viking Press.

Karsh, Efraim, and Inari Rautsi. 1991. *Saddam Hussein: A Political Biography.* New York: Free Press.

Kaufman, Herbert. 1976. *Are Government Organizations Immortal?* Washington, D.C.: Brookings Institution.

———. 1977. *Red Tape: Its Origins, Uses, and Abuses.* Washington, D.C.: Brookings Institution.

Kaufman, Hugh. 1992. Environmental Protection Agency, Washington, D.C. Interview by Robert E. Elder, 19 October.

———. Undated a. *Brief Chronology of Key Events: WTI Incinerator.* East Liverpool, Ohio.

———. Undated b. *Overview: WTI Incinerator.* East Liverpool, Ohio.

Kaus, Mickey. 1988. "The Government Should Make Welfare Recipients Work." In *Poverty: Opposing Viewpoints,* ed William Dudley, 212–19. St. Paul, Minn.: Greenhaven Press.

Kayden, Xandra, and Eddie Mahe, Jr. 1985. *The Party Goes On.* New York: Basic Books.

Kaza, Gregg. 1991. "Lansing with Wolves: Can Michigan's Engler Pull Off His Taxpayers Revolution?" *Policy Review,* no. 57 (Summer): 74–77.

Kearns, Doris. 1976. *Lyndon Johnson and the American Dream.* New York: Harper and Row.

Keefe, William J., and Morris S. Ogul. 1993. *The American Legislative Process: Congress and the States.* 8th ed. Englewood Cliffs, N.J.: Prentice-Hall.

Kegley, Charles W., and Eugene R. Wittkopf. 1981. *World Politics: Trend and Transformation.* New York: St. Martin's Press.

Kelly, Alfred H., and Winfred A. Harbison. 1963. *The American Constitution: Its Origin and Development.* 3d ed. New York: W. W. Norton.

Kemp, Jack. 1979. *An American Renaissance.* New York: Harper and Row.

Kennan, George F. [X]. 1947. "The Source of Soviet Conduct." *Foreign Affairs* 25 (July): 566–82.

———. 1972. "X plus 25 [interview]." *Foreign Policy,* no. 7 (Summer): 5–21.

———. 1982. *The Nuclear Delusion: Soviet-American Relations in the Atomic Age.* New York: Pantheon Books.

Kennedy, Paul. 1987. *The Rise and Fall of the Great Powers: Economic Change and Military Conflict from 1500 to 2000.* New York: Random House.

Kenyon, Cecelia M., ed. 1966. *The Antifederalists.* Indianapolis: Bobbs-Merrill.

Kerber, Linda K., and Jane De Hart-Mathews, eds. 1987. *Women's America: Refocusing the Past.* 2d ed. New York: Oxford University Press.

Kernell, Samuel. 1986. *Going Public: New Strategies of Presidential Leadership.* Washington, D.C.: Congressional Quarterly Press.

———, **and Samuel L. Popkin.** 1986. *Chief of Staff: Twenty-Five Years of Managing the Presidency.* Berkeley and Los Angeles: University of California.

Kessel, John H. 1984. *Presidential Campaign Politics: Coalition Strategies and Citizen Response.* 2d ed. Homewood, Ill.: Dorsey Press.

Kessler, Richard. 1986. "Marcos and the Americans." *Foreign Policy,* no. 63 (Summer): 40–57.

Ketcham, Ralph., ed. 1986. *The Anti-Federalist Papers and the Constitutional Convention Debates.* New York: New American Library.

Kettl, Donald F. 1986. *Leadership at the Fed.* New Haven, Conn.: Yale University Press.

Keynes, John M. 1935. *General Theory of Employment, Interest, and Money.* New York: Harcourt, Brace and World.

King, Gary, and Lyn Ragsdale. 1988. *The Elusive Executive: Discovering Statistical Patterns in the Presidency.* Washington, D.C.: Congressional Quarterly Press.

King, Mary. 1987. *Freedom Song.* New York: William Morrow.

Kirkpatrick, Jeane. 1979. "Dicatatorships and Double Standards." *Commentary* 68 (November): 34–45.

Kissinger, Henry. 1979. *White House Years.* Boston: Little, Brown.

Klapper, Joseph T. 1960. *The Effects of Mass Communication.* Glencoe, Ill.: Free Press.

Kleppner, Paul. 1982. *Who Voted? The Dynamics of Electoral Turnout, 1870–1980.* New York: Praeger.

Klingberg, Frank L. 1952. "The Historical Alternation of Moods in American Foreign Policy." *World Politics* 4 (January): 239–73.

Koch, Adrienne. 1966. *Madison's "Advice to My Country."* Princeton, N.J.: Princeton University Press.

Koch, Edward III. 1993. "The Mandate Millstone." In *American Intergovernmental Relations: Foundations, Perspectives, and Issues,* 2d ed., ed. Laurence

J. O'Toole, Jr., 297–304. Washington, D.C.: Congressional Quarterly Press.

Kolko, Joyce, and Gabriel Kolko. 1972. *The Limits of Power: The World and United States Foreign Policy, 1945–1954.* New York: Harper and Row.

Kosters, Marvin H. 1992. "A White Collar Recession?" *American Enterprise,* March/April, 20–23.

Kozol, Jonathan. 1991. *Savage Inequalities.* New York: Crown.

Kranz, Harry. 1976. *The Participatory Bureaucracy: Women and Minorities in a More Representative Public Service.* Lexington, Mass.: Lexington Books.

Krasnow, Erwin G., Lawrence D. Longley, and Herbert A. Terry. 1982. *The Politics of Broadcast Regulation.* New York: St. Martin's Press.

Krauss, Melvyn. 1986. *How NATO Weakens the West.* New York: Simon and Schuster.

Krislov, Samuel. 1974. *Representative Bureaucracy.* Englewood Cliffs, N.J.: Prentice-Hall.

Krugman, Paul. 1992. *The Age of Diminished Expectations: U.S. Economic Policy in the 1990s.* Cambridge, Mass.: MIT Press.

Ladd, Everett Carll, Jr. 1978. *Where Have All the Voters Gone?* New York: W. W. Norton.

———, **and G. Donald Ferree.** 1980–81. "Were the Pollsters Really Wrong?" *Public Opinion* (December/January): 13–20.

———, **and Charles D. Hadley.** 1975. *Transformations of the American Party System: Political Coalitions from the New Deal to the 1970s.* 2d ed. New York: W. W. Norton.

Lader, Lawrence. 1979. *Power on the Left: American Radical Movements since 1946.* New York: W. W. Norton.

Lamis, Alexander P. 1984. *The Two-Party South.* New York: Oxford University Press.

Landess, Thomas H., and Richard Quinn. 1985. *Jesse Jackson and the Politics of Race.* Ottawa, Ill.: Jameson Books.

Lang, Gladys Engel, and Kurt Lang. 1983. *The Battle for Public Opinion: The President, the Press, and the Polls during Watergate.* New York: Columbia University Press.

Lansing State Journal.

Lay Commission On Catholic Social Teaching and the U.S. Economy. 1984. *Toward the Future—Catholic Social Thought and the U.S. Economy: A Lay Letter.* New York: Lay Commission.

Lazarus, Edward. 1991. *Black Hills White Justice: The Sioux Nation versus the United States, 1775 to the Present.* New York: HarperCollins.

Leamer, Laurence. 1983. *Make-Believe: The Story of Nancy and Ronald Reagan.* New York: Harper and Row.

Lebergott, Stanley. 1984. *The Americans: An Economic Record.* New York: W. W. Norton.

Lee, Dwight R. 1986. *Taxation and the Deficit Economy: Fiscal Policy and Capital Formation in the United States.* San Francisco: Pacific Research Institute.

Leeson, Susan M., and James C. Foster. 1992. *Constitutional Law: Cases in Context.* New York: St. Martin's Press.

LeFeber, Walter. 1984. "The Burdens of the Past." In *Central America: Anatomy of Conflict,* ed. Robert S. Leiken, 49–67. New York: Pergamon Press.

LeMoyne, James. 1989. "El Salvador's Forgotten War." *Foreign Affairs* 68 (Summer): 105–25.

Lenin, Vladimir I. 1972 [1916]. *Imperialism, the Highest Stage of Capitalism: A Popular Outline.* New York: International.

Lerner, Michael. 1969. "A Bibliographical Note." In *Personality and Politics: Problems of Evidence, Inference, and Conceptualization,* ed. Fred I. Greenstein, 154–84. Chicago: Markham.

Leuchtenburg, William E. 1983. *In the Shadow of FDR: From Harry Truman to Ronald Reagan.* Ithaca, N.Y.: Cornell University Press.

Levin, Murray B. 1971. *Political Hysteria in America.* New York: Basic Books.

Levine, Arthur. 1974. "I Got My Job through CREEP." *Washington Monthly,* November, 35–46.

Levy, Jacques E. 1975. *Cesar Chavez: Autobiography of La Causa.* New York: W. W. Norton.

Levy, Leonard W. 1986. *The Establishment Clause: Religion and the First Amendment.* New York: Macmillan.

———. 1988. *Original Intent and the Framers' Constitution.* New York: Macmillan.

Lewis, Anthony. 1964. *Gideon's Trumpet.* New York: Random House.

Lewis, Gregory B. 1988. "Progress toward Racial and Sexual Equality in the Federal Civil Service?" *Public Administration Review* 48 (May/June): 700–7.

Lewis, Jane. 1986. "Feminism and Welfare." In

What Is Feminism? ed. Juliet Mitchell and Ann Oakley, 85–100. New York: Pantheon Books.

The Libertarian Party Represents You! 1992. Brochure. Washington, D.C.: National Libertarian Committee.

Lichter, S. Robert, Linda S. Lichter, and Stanley Rothman. 1986. *The Media Elite.* Bethesda, Md.: Adler and Adler.

Lienesch, Michael. 1988. *New Order of the Ages.* Princeton, N.J.: Princeton University Press.

Limbaugh, Rush H., III. 1992. *The Way Things Ought to Be.* New York: Pocket Books.

Linsky, Martin. 1986. *Impact: How the Press Affects Federal Policymaking.* New York: W. W. Norton.

Lipset, Seymour M. 1987. ''Blacks and Jews: How Much Bias?'' *Public Opinion* 1 (July/August): 4–5, 57–58.

''Lobbies.'' 1986. In *Current American Government,* ed. Mary Cohen, 116–29. Washington, D.C.: Congressional Quarterly Press.

Locke, John. 1937 [1689]. *A Letter Concerning Toleration.* Ed. Charles L. Sherman. New York: D. Appleton-Century.

———. 1967 [1689]. *Two Treatises of Government.* Ed. Peter Laslett. 2d ed. London: Cambridge University Press.

Lockwood, Charles, and Christopher B. Leinberger. 1988. ''Los Angeles Comes of Age.'' *Atlantic,* January, 31–56.

Louisville Courier-Journal.

Lowenthal, Abraham F., ed. 1991. *Exporting Democracy: The United States and Latin America.* 2 vols. Baltimore: Johns Hopkins University Press.

Lowi, Theodore J. 1969. *The End of Liberalism: Ideology, Policy, and the Crisis of Public Authority.* New York: W. W. Norton.

———. 1979. *The End of Liberalism: The Second Republic of the United States.* 2d ed. New York: W. W. Norton.

Lugar, Richard G. 1992. ''The Republican Course.'' *Foreign Policy,* no. 86 (Spring): 86–98.

Lukas, J. Anthony. 1985. *Common Ground.* New York: Vintage Books.

Lupfer, Michael B., and J. P. Rosenberg. 1983. ''Difference in Adults' Political Orientations as a Function of Age.'' *Journal of Social Psychology* 119 (February): 125–33.

Lustig, R. Jeffrey. 1982. *Corporate Liberalism.* Berkeley and Los Angeles: University of California Press.

Luttwak, Edward N. 1984. *The Pentagon and the Art of War: The Question of Military Reform.* New York: Simon and Schuster.

Lynch, Frederick R. 1991. *Invisible Victims: White Males and the Crisis of Affirmative Action.* New York: Praeger.

MacBride, Roger L. 1976. *A New Dawn for America: The Libertarian Challenge.* Ottawa, Ill.: Green Hill.

Macedo, Stephen. 1986. *The New Right v. the Constitution.* Washington, D.C.: Cato Institute.

Maddox, William S., and Stuart A. Lilie. 1984. *Beyond Liberal and Conservative: Reassessing the Political Spectrum.* Washington, D.C.: Cato Institute.

Magdoff, Harry. 1969. *The Age of Imperialism: The Economics of U.S. Foreign Policy.* New York: Monthly Review.

Main, Jackson Turner. 1961. *The Anti-Federalists: Critics of the Constitution, 1781–1788.* Chapel Hill: University of North Carolina Press.

Maisel, L. Sandy. 1982. *From Obscurity to Oblivion.* Knoxville: University of Tennessee Press.

Malbin, Michael J. 1980. *Unelected Representatives: Congressional Staff and the Future of Representative Government.* New York: Basic Books.

Malia, Martin. 1992. ''Yeltsin and Us.'' *Commentary,* April, 21–28.

Mandelbaum, Michael, and Strobe Talbot. 1987. *Reagan and Gorbachev.* New York: Vintage Books.

Manley, John F., and Kenneth M. Dolbeare, eds. 1987. *The Case against the Constitution.* Armonk, N.Y.: M. E. Sharpe.

Mansbridge, Jane J. 1986. *Why We Lost the ERA.* Chicago: University of Chicago Press.

Marcuse, Herbert. 1969. ''Repressive Tolerance.'' In *A Critique of Pure Tolerance,* ed. Robert Paul Wolff, 81–123. Boston: Beacon Press.

Marx, Karl, and Friedrich Engels. 1967 [1848]. *The Communist Manifesto.* Baltimore: Penguin Books.

Mason, Todd. 1990. *Perot: An Unauthorized Biography.* Homewood, Ill.: Business One Irvin.

Mathews, Donald R. 1960. *U.S. Senators and Their World.* Chapel Hill: University of North Carolina Press.

Mayberry, Richard. 1992. ''Public Servant v. Private Citizen: Finding Hatchways through the

Hatch Act." *Campaigns and Elections*, September, 54–55.

Mayer, William G. 1992. "The Shifting Sands of Public Opinion: Is Liberalism Back?" *Public Interest*, no. 107 (Spring): 3–17.

Mayhew, David R. 1986. *Placing Parties in American Politics: Organization, Electoral Settings and Government Activity in the Twentieth Century*. Princeton, N.J.: Princeton University Press.

McCombs, Maxwell E., and Donald L. Shaw. 1977. *The Emergence of American Political Issues: The Agenda-Setting Function of the Press*. St. Paul, Minn.: West.

McCormick, James M. 1985. *American Foreign Policy and American Values*. Itasca, Ill.: F. E. Peacock.

McDonald, Forrest. 1958. *We the People: The Economic Origins of the Constitution*. Chicago: University of Chicago Press.

———. 1985. *Novus Ordo Seclorum: The Intellectual Origins of the Constitution*. Lawrence: University Press of Kansas.

McElvaine, Robert S. 1984. *The Great Depression: America*. New York: Times Books.

McFarland, Andrew S. 1984. *Common Cause: Lobbying in the Public Interest*. Chatham, N.J.: Chatham House.

McGlen, Nancy E., and Karen O'Connor. 1983. *Women's Rights*. New York: Praeger.

McLellan, David. 1979. *Marxism after Marx: An Introduction*. Boston: Houghton Mifflin.

McNeil, Frank. 1988. *War and Peace in Central America*. New York: Charles Scribner's Sons.

McPherson, Marian. 1993. Staff Specialist for American Bar Association's, Commission on the Status of Women in the Legal Profession, Washington, D.C. Telephone interview by Robert E. Elder, Jr., 16 June.

McQuail, Dennis. 1979. "The Influence and Effects of Mass Media." In *Mass Communication and Society*, ed. James Curran, Michael Gurevitch, Janet Woollacott, et al. 70–94. Beverly Hills, Calif.: Sage Publications.

Mead, Walter B. 1987. *The United States Constitution: Personalities, Principles, and Issues*. Columbia: University of South Carolina Press.

Medcalf, Linda J., and Kenneth M. Dolbeare. 1985. *Neopolitics: American Political Ideas in the 1980s*. New York: Random House.

Meese, Edwin, III. 1986. "The Battle for the Constitution." *Policy Review*, no. 35 (Winter): 32–35.

Mendeloff, John. 1979. *Regulating Safety: An Economic and Political Analysis of Occupational Safety and Health Policy*. Cambridge, Mass.: MIT Press.

Menos, Dennis. 1992. *Arms over Diplomacy: Reflections on the Persian Gulf War*. Westport, Conn.: Praeger.

Michaels, Marguerite. 1992–93. "Retreat from Africa." *Foreign Affairs* 72 (America and the World): 93–108.

Michelman, Kate. 1992. *Statement of Kate Michelman*. National Abortion Rights Action League, Washington, D.C. 6 November.

Mikva, Abner, and Patti Saris. 1983. *The American Congress: The First Branch*. New York: Franklin Watts.

Mill, John Stuart. 1965. *Collected Works of John Stuart Mill*. Ed. John M. Robson. 33 vols. Toronto: University of Toronto Press.

Miller, Jones. 1987. *Democracy Is in the Streets: From Port Huron to the Siege of Chicago*. New York: Simon and Schuster.

Miller, Susan Heilmann. 1978. "Reporters and Congressmen: Living in Symbiosis." *Journalism Monographs* 53 (January): 1–25.

Miller, Thomas A. W. 1989. "Is Deregulation Working?" *Public Opinion* 11 (March/April): 9–11, 59.

Millspaw, Andrea. 1993. American Agricultural Movement, Washington, D.C. Telephone interview by Jack E. Holmes, 17 June.

Milwood, H. Brinton, and Hal G. Rainey. 1983. "Don't Blame the Bureaucracy!" *Journal of Public Policy* 3 (May): 149–50.

Mitchell, Broadus, and Louise Pearson Mitchell. 1975. *A Biography of the Constitution of the United States: Its Origin, Adoption, and Interpretation*. 2d ed. New York: Oxford University Press.

Modern Healthcare.

Moe, Terry. 1985. "The Politicized Presidency." In *The New Direction in American Politics*, ed. John E. Chubb and Paul E. Petterson, 235–71. Washington, D.C.: Brookings Insitution.

Mondale, Walter F. 1989. "Eleven Points for the Next President." In *The Presidency in Transition*, ed. James P. Pfiffner and R. Gordon Hoxie, 464–69. New York: Center for the Study of the Presidency.

Morgan, Edmund S. 1988. *Inventing the People*. New York: W. W. Norton.

Morgan, Richard E. 1984. *Disabling America: The "Rights Industry" in Our Time*. New York: Basic Books.

Morici, Peter. 1992. "Free Trade with Mexico." *Foreign Policy*, no. 87 (Summer): 88–104.

Morlan, Robert L. 1955. *Political Prairie Fire: The Nonpartisan League, 1915–1922.* Minneapolis: University of Minnesota Press.

Morris, Charles R. 1993. "It's Not the Economy, Stupid." *Atlantic*, July, 49–62.

Moser, Charles. 1985. *Combat on Communist Territory.* Chicago: Regnery Gateway.

Mosher, Frederick C. 1968. *Democracy and the Public Service.* New York: Oxford University Press.

Moulds, Elizabeth Fry. 1982. "Women's Crime, Women's Justice." In *Women, Power, and Policy*, ed. Ellen Boneparth, 205–31. New York: Pergamon Press.

Mowry, George Edwin. 1958. *The Era of Theodore Roosevelt, 1900–1912.* New York: Harper and Brothers.

Moynihan, Daniel Patrick. 1986. *Family and Nation.* New York: Harcourt Brace Jovanovich.

Mueller, John E. 1973. *War, Presidents, and Public Opinion.* New York: John Wiley.

———. 1985. *War, Presidents, and Public Opinion.* Reprint. Lanham, Md.: University Press of America.

Muir, William Ker, Jr. 1992. *The Bully Pulpit: The Presidential Leadership of Ronald Reagan.* San Francisco: Institute for Contemporary Studies.

Muravchik, Joshua. 1986. *The Uncertain Crusade: Jimmy Carter and the Dilemmas of Human Rights Policy.* Lanham, Md.: Hamilton Press.

———. 1988. Review of *Covert Cadre: Inside the Institute for Policy Studies.* In *Commentary* 4 (October): 60.

Murray, Charles. 1982. *Safety Nets and the Truly Needy.* Washington, D.C.: Heritage Foundation.

———. 1984. *Losing Ground: American Social Policy, 1950–1980.* New York: Basic Books.

———. 1988. *In Pursuit of Happiness and Good Government.* New York: Simon and Schuster.

Murray, Robert K. 1955. *Red Scare: A Study in National Hysteria, 1919–1920.* Minneapolis: University of Minnesota Press.

Murray, Yxta Maya. 1993. "Employer Liability after Johnson Controls: A No-Fault Solution." *Stanford Law Review* 45 (January): 453–83.

Nachmias, David, and David H. Rosenbloom. 1980. *Bureaucratic Government USA.* New York: St. Martin's Press.

Nalbandian, John. 1989. "The U.S. Supreme Court Consensus on Affirmative Action." *Public Administration Review* 49 (January/February): 38.

Nathan, Richard P. 1975. *The Plot That Failed: Nixon and the Administrative Presidency.* New York: John Wiley and Sons.

———, et al. 1987. *Reagan and the States.* Princeton, N.J.: Princeton University Press.

National Committee for a Free Congress. 1987. *Annual Report.* Washington, D.C.

National Journal.

National Review.

Nelson, Michael, ed. 1988. *The Presidency and the Political System.* 2d ed. Washington, D.C.: Congressional Quarterly Press.

———. 1993. *The Presidency and the Political System.* 3d ed. Washington, D.C.: Congressional Quarterly Press.

Neuhaus, Richard John. 1987. "What the Fundamentalists Want." In *Piety and Politics: Evangelicals and Fundamentalists Confront the World*, ed. Richard John Neuhaus and Michael Cromartie, 12–18. Lanham, Md.: University Press of America.

Neustadt, Richard E. 1980. *Presidential Power: The Politics of Leadership from FDR to Carter.* New York: John Wiley and Sons.

Nevin, David. 1978. *The Mexican War.* Alexandria, Va.: Time-Life Books.

The New Congress: Younger, More Diverse House and Senate Take Aim at Political Gridlock. 1993. Congressional Quarterly Special Report, 16 January. Washington, D.C.: Congressional Quarterly Press.

"The New Congress' Fluidity and Oscillation." 1989. In *Congress Reconsidered*, 4th ed., ed. Lawrence C. Dodd and Bruce I. Oppenheimer, 443–49. Washington, D.C.: Congressional Quarterly.

New Republic.

New York Times.

New York Times Magazine.

Newsweek.

Nice, David C. 1987. *Federalism: The Politics of Intergovernmental Relations.* New York: St. Martin's Press.

Nie, Norman H., Sidney Verba, and John R. Petrocik. 1976. *The Changing American Voter.* Cambridge, Mass.: Harvard University Press.

1992 National Platform of the Libertarian Party. 1991. Washington, D.C.: Libertarian National Committee.

Nisbet, Robert. 1986. *Conservatism: Dream and Reality.* Minneapolis: University of Minnesota Press.

Niskanen, William A. 1980. "Auto Regulation." *Regulation* 4 (November/December): 24–27.

"No-Pass No-Play and Other Vital Issues of the Day Straight from the S.C. Blue-Ribbon Panel of A.D.'s." 1986. *Scholastic Coach* 55 (March) 50–52, 56.

Norris, Pippa. 1987. *Politics and Sexual Equality: The Comparative Position of Women in Western Democracies.* Boulder, Colo.: Lynne Rienner.

North, Liisa. 1985. *Bitter Grounds: Roots of Revolution in El Salvador.* 2d ed. Westport, Conn.: Lawrence Hill.

Northeast-Midwest Congressional Coalition, Northeast-Midwest Senate Coalition, and Northeast-Midwest Institute. 1979. *The State of the Region: Economic Trends in the 1970s in the Northeast and Midwest.* Washington, D.C.: Northeast-Midwest Congressional Coalition.

———. 1988. *The Budget and the Region: A Regional Analysis of the President's Fiscal 1989 Request.* Ed. Deborah Cooney. Washington, D.C.: Northeast-Midwest Congressional Coalition.

Nozick, Robert. 1974. *Anarchy, State, and Utopia.* New York: Basic Books.

Nye, Joseph, Jr. 1990. *Bound to Lead: The Changing Nature of American Power.* New York: Basic Books.

O'Brien, David M. 1986. *Storm Center: The Supreme Court in American Politics.* New York: W. W. Norton.

Office of Management and Budget. *See under* Budget.

Oleszek, Walter J. 1989. *Congressional Procedures and the Policy Process.* 3d ed. Washington, D.C.: Congressional Quarterly Press.

Olson, Mancur. 1982. *The Rise and Decline of Nations: Economic Growth, Stagflation, and Social Rigidities.* New Haven, Conn.: Yale University Press.

103rd Congress First Session Directory. 1993. Washington, D.C.: Hopkins and Sutter.

O'Neill, Timothy J. 1985. *Bakke and the Politics of Equality: Friends and Foes in the Classroom of Litigation.* Hanover, N.H.: Wesleyan University Press, distributed by Harper and Row.

Ornstein, Norman J., and Shirley Elder. 1978. *Interest Groups, Lobbying, and Policymaking.* Washington, D.C.: Congressional Quarterly Press.

O'Toole, Laurence J., ed. 1993. *American Intergovernmental Relations: Foundations, Perspectives, and Issues.* 2d ed. Washington, D.C.: Congressional Quarterly Press.

Padover, Saul K. 1978. *Karl Marx: An Intimate Biography.* New York: New American Library.

Page, Benjamin I., and Robert Y. Shapiro. 1992. *The Rational Public: Fifty Years of Trends in America's Policy Preferences.* Chicago: University of Chicago Press.

———, **and Glenn R. Dempsey.** 1990. "What Moves Public Opinion?" In *Media Power in Politics,* 2d ed., ed. Doris A. Graber, 108–23. Washington, D.C.: Congressional Quarterly Press.

Paletz, David L., and Robert Entman. 1981. *Media Power Politics.* New York: Free Press.

———, **Peggy Reichert, and Barbara McIntyre.** 1971. "How the Media Support Local Governmental Authority." *Public Opinion Quarterly* 35 (Spring): 80–92.

Palmer, Kenneth T. 1984. "The Evolution of Grant Policies." In *The Changing Politics of Federal Grants,* ed. Lawrence D. Brown, James W. Fossett, and Kenneth T. Palmer, 5–53. Washington, D.C.: Brookings Institution.

Palonsky, Stuart B. 1987. "Political Socialization in Elementary Schools." *Elementary School Journal* 87 (May): 493–506.

Pangle, Thomas. L. 1988. *The Spirit of Modern Republicanism: The Moral Vision of American Founders and the Philosophy of Locke.* Chicago: University of Chicago Press.

Parenti, Michael J. 1987. *Democracy for the Few.* 5th ed. New York: St. Martin's Press.

———. 1993. *Inventing Reality: The Politics of the News Media.* New York: St. Martin's Press.

Parks, James. 1993. AFL-CIO Committee on Political Education, Washington, D.C. Telephone interview by Jack E. Holmes, 17 June.

Paschal, Joel Francis. 1951. *Mr. Justice Sutherland: A Man against the State.* Westport, Conn.: Greenwood Press.

Pateman, Carol. 1991. "Feminist Critiques of the Public/Private Dichotomy." In *Philosophical Topics,* ed. Philip Petit, *Contemporary Political Theory,* 116–40. New York: Macmillan.

Patterson, Bradley H. 1988. *The Ring of Power: The White House Staff and Its Expanding Role in Government.* New York: Basic Books.

Patterson, Thomas E. 1990. "Views of Winners and

Losers." In *Media Power in Politics*, 2d ed., ed. Doris A. Graber, 176–83. Washington, D.C.: Congressional Quarterly Press.

Payne, Robert. 1968. *Marx.* New York: Simon and Schuster.

Pearson, Frederic S., and J. Martin Rochester. 1988. *International Relations: The Global Condition in the Late Twentieth Century.* 2d ed. New York: Random House.

Pederson, William, ed. 1989. *The "Barberian" Presidency.* New York: Peter Lang.

Pember, Don R. 1987. *Mass Media in America.* 5th ed. Chicago: Science Research Associates.

Penner, Rudolph G. 1987. "Government Deficits: The Case of the United States." In *Private Saving and Public Debt*, ed. Michael J. Boskin, John S. Flemming, and Stefano Gorini, 105–25. New York: Basil Blackwell.

People and Politics. 1985. 3d ed., ed. Herbert R. Winter, et al. New York: Macmillan.

The People, the Press and Political Campaign '92. 1992. Washington, D.C.: Times Mirror, Center for the People and the Press. 28 October.

The People, the Press and Politics: Post-Election Typology Survey. 1988. Los Angeles: Times Mirror. November.

The People, the Press and Politics: Campaign '92, Voters Say "Thumbs Up" to Campaign, Process and Coverage. 1992. Washington, D.C.: Times Mirror, Center for the People and the Press. 15 November.

People Weekly.

Perot for President Committee. Undated. "A Biography of Ross Perot."

Perspectives on the Reagan Presidency: An Analysis of a Times Mirror Survey Conducted by the Gallup Organization. 1988. Los Angeles: Times Mirror. April.

Pertschuk, Michael, and Wendy Schaetzel. 1989. *The People Rising: The Campaign against the Bork Nomination.* New York: Thunder's Mouth Press.

Peterson, Paul E., Barry G. Rabe, and Kenneth K. Wong. 1986. *When Federalism Works.* Washington, D.C.: Brookings Institution.

Peterson, Theodore. 1956. "The Social Responsibility Theory of the Press." In *Four Theories of the Press*, ed. Fred S. Siebert, Theodore Peterson, and Wilbur Schramm, 7–77. Urbana: University of Illinois Press.

Petracca, Mark P., ed. 1992. *The Politics of Interests: Interest Groups Transformed.* Boulder, Colo.: Westview Press.

Petre, Peter, and H. Norman Schwarzkopf. 1992. *It*

Doesn't Take a Hero: The Autobiography of General H. Norman Schwarzkopf. New York: Bantam.

Petrocik, John R. 1981. *Party Coalitions: Realignment and the Decline of the New Deal Party System.* Chicago: University of Chicago Press.

Pfiffner, James P. 1993. "The President's Chief of Staff: Lessons Learned." *Presidential Studies Quarterly* 23 (Winter): 77–102.

Pfiffner, John M., and Robert V. Presthus. 1967. *Public Administration.* 5th ed. New York: Ronald Press.

Phelps, Edmund S. 1987. "Appraising the American Fiscal Stance." In *Private Saving and Public Debt*, ed. Michael J. Baskin, John S. Flemming, and Stefano Gorini. 95–104. New York: Basil Blackwell.

Phi Delta Kappan.

Pietila, Hikka, and Jeanne Vickers. 1990. *Making Women Matter: The Role of the United Nations.* London: Zed Books.

Pika, Joseph. 1988. "A New Vice-Presidency?" In *The Presidency and the Political System*, 2d ed., ed. Michael Nelson, 463–82. Washington, D.C.: Congressional Quarterly Press.

Pinkston, Elizabeth A. 1984. "The Rise and Fall of Bus Regulation." *Regulation* 8 (September/December): 45–52.

Pious, Richard M. 1979. *The American Presidency.* New York: Basic Books.

Piven, Frances Fox, and Richard A. Cloward. 1971. *Regulating the Poor: The Functions of Public Welfare.* New York: Pantheon Books.

———. 1988. *Why Americans Don't Vote.* New York: Patheon Books.

Plano, Jack C., and Milton Greenberg. 1993. *The American Polticial Dictionary.* 9th ed. Fort Worth: Harcourt Brace Jovanovich.

Players, Politics and Turf of the 103rd Congress. 1993. Congressional Quarterly Special Report, 1 May. Washington, D.C.: Congressional Quarterly Press.

Politics in America. Biannual. Washington, D.C.: Congressional Quarterly Press.

"Politics and the Public: An American Dilemma." 1992. Kevin Coleman. *CRS Review*, June/July, 1–3.

Polk, James K. 1988 [1846]. "Polk's Message on War with Mexico," May 11. In *Documents of American History*, ed. Henry Steele Commager and Milton Cantor, 310–11. Englewood Cliffs, N.J.: Prentice-Hall.

Pollack, Norman. 1962. *The Populist Response to*

Industrial America. Cambridge, Mass.: Harvard University Press.

Pomper, Gerald M. 1989. *The Election of 1988: Reports and Interpretations.* Chatham, N.J.: Chatham House.

Porter, William E. 1981. "The Media Baronies: Fewer, Bigger, More Powerful." In *What's News: The Media in American Society,* ed. Elie Abel, 97–115. San Francisco: Institute for Contemporary Studies.

Posen, Barry R., and Stephen W. Van Evera. 1987. "Reagan Administration Defense Policy: Departure from Containment." In *Eagle Resurgent? The Reagan Era in American Foreign Policy,* ed. Kenneth Oye, Robert Lieber, and Donald Rothchild, 75–114. Boston: Little, Brown.

Posner, Richard A. 1985. *The Federal Courts: Crisis and Reform.* Cambridge, Mass.: Harvard University Press.

Powell, Walter. 1987. "The Blockbuster Decades: The Media as Big Business." In *American Media and Mass Culture: Left Perspectives,* ed. Donald Lazare, 53–63. Berkeley and Los Angeles: University of California Press.

Power in Congress: Who Has It, How They Got It, How They Use It. 1987. Washington, D.C.: Congressional Quarterly Press.

Prados, John. 1986. *Presidents' Secret Wars: CIA and Pentagon Covert Operations since World War II.* New York: William Morrow.

"Presidential Election." 1989. In *The Election of 1988: Reports and Interpretations,* ed. Gerald M. Pomper, 129–52. Chatham, N.J.: Chatham House.

Presidential Elections since 1789. 1975. Ed. Robert E. Diamond. Washington, D.C.: Congressional Quarterly Press.

President's Private Sector Survey on Cost Control: A Report to the President. 1984. [Grace Commission.] Washington, D.C.: Government Printing Office.

Press, Charles, and Kenneth VerBurg. 1988. *American Politicians and Journalists.* Glenview, Ill.: Scott, Foresman.

Prestowitz, Clyde V., Jr. 1988. *Trading Places: How We Allowed Japan to Take the Lead.* New York: Basic Books.

———. 1992. "Beyond Laissez-Faire." *Foreign Policy,* no. 87 (Summer): 67–87.

Price, David E. 1971. "Professionals and Entrepreneurs: Staff Orientation and Policy-Making on Three Senate Committees." *Journal of Politics* 33 (May): 316–36.

———. 1984. *Bringing Back the Parties.* Washington, D.C.: Congressional Quarterly Press.

Pritchett, C. Herman. 1968. *The American Constitution.* 2d ed. New York: McGraw-Hill.

Provine, Doris Marie. 1980. *Case Selection in the United States Supreme Court.* Chicago: University of Chicago Press.

Prucha, Francis Paul. 1984. *The Great Father: The United States Government and the American Indians.* Lincoln: University of Nebraska Press.

Public Interest Profiles, 1992–1993. 1992. Washington, D.C.: Congressional Quarterly Press, Foundation for Public Affairs.

Public Opinion.

Pye, Lucian W. 1990. "Political Science and the Crisis of Authoritarianism." *American Political Science Review* 84 (March): 3–19.

Quaintance, Marilyn Koch. 1983. "The Impact of the Uniform Selection Guidelines on Public Merit Systems." In *Readings in Public Administration,* ed. Felix A. Richardson and Lloyd G. Nigro, 262–71. New York: Harper and Row.

Quandt, William B. 1977. *Decades of Decision: American Policy toward the Arab-Israeli Conflict, 1967–1976.* Berkeley and Los Angeles: University of California Press.

Quint, Howard H. 1953. *The Forging of American Socialism: Origins of the Modern Movement.* New York: Bobbs-Merrill.

Raddatz, Fritz J. 1978. *Karl Marx: A Political Biography.* Boston: Little, Brown.

Rainey, Gene E. 1975. *Patterns of American Foreign Policy.* Boston: Allyn and Bacon.

Rakove, Jack N. 1986. "Mr. Meese, Meet Mr. Madison." *Atlantic,* December, 77–86.

Rauch, Jonathan. 1989. "Is the Deficit Really So Bad?" *Atlantic,* February, 36–42.

Ravenal, Earl C. 1979. *Strategic Disengagement and World Peace: Toward a Noninterventionalist American Foreign Policy.* San Francisco: Cato Institute.

———, **and William R. Van Cleve.** 1985. "U.S. Defense Strategy: A Debate." In *American Defense Annual, 1985–1986,* ed. George E. Hudson and Joseph Kruzel, 19–50. Lexington, Mass.: D.C. Heath.

Reading, Brian. 1992. *Japan: The Coming Collapse.* New York: Harper Business.

Reagan, Ronald. 1990. *An American Life.* New York: Simon and Schuster.

Redman, Eric. 1973. *The Dance of Legislation.* New York: Simon and Schuster.

Reed, Adolph L., Jr. 1986. *The Jesse Jackson Phenomenon: The Crisis of Purpose in Afro-American Politics.* New Haven, Conn.: Yale University Press.

"Refusing to Be Silenced." 1992. A Forum. *Ms.* 2 (January/February): 34–45.

Rehnquist, William H. 1987. *The Supreme Court: How It Was, How It Is.* New York: William Morrow.

Reichley, A. James. 1985. *Religion in American Public Life.* Washington, D.C.: Brookings Institution.

Reid, Jeanne L. 1992. "Making Delinquent Dad Pay His Child Support." *Ms.* 3 (July/August): 86–88.

Reid, T. R. 1980. *Congressional Odyssey: The Saga of a Senate Bill.* San Francisco: W. H. Freeman.

Remini, Robert Vincent. 1981. *Andrew Jackson and the Course of American Freedom, 1822–1832.* New York: Harper and Row.

———. 1984. *Andrew Jackson and the Course of American Democracy, 1833–1845.* New York: Harper and Row.

Renszetti, Claire M., and Daniel J. Curran. 1992. *Women, Men, and Society.* Boston: Allyn and Bacon.

Report of the Congressional Committees Investigating the Iran-Contra Affair. 1988. Abridged. New York: Time Books.

Report to the President. See *President's Private Sector Survey on Cost Control.*

Republican Congressional Campaign Committee Spokesperson. 1989. Washington, D.C. Interview by Robert E. Elder, Jr., 24 May.

Reuss, Henry S. 1970. *Revenue Sharing: Crutch or Catalyst for State and Local Governments?* New York: Praeger.

Richardson, Laurel, and Verta Taylor. 1993. *Feminist Frontiers III.* New York: McGraw-Hill.

Richardson, William D., and Lloyd G. Nigro. 1987. "Administrative Ethics and Founding Thought: Constitutional Correctives, Honor, and Education." *Public Administration Review* 47 (September/October): 367–376.

Ridding, Alan. 1985. *Distant Neighbors: A Portrait of the Mexicans.* New York: Alfred A. Knopf.

Riemer, Neal. 1986. *James Madison; Creating the American Constitution.* Washington, D.C.: Congressional Quarterly Press.

Rieselbach, Leroy N. 1986. *Congressional Reform.* Washington, D.C.: Congressional Quarterly Press.

Riker, William H. 1964. *Federalism: Origin, Operation, Significance.* Boston: Little, Brown.

Rivlin, Alice. 1992a. "Reviving the American Dream." *Brookings Review* 10 (Summer): 5.

———. 1992b. *Reviving the American Dream: The Economy, the States, and the Federal Government.* Washington, D.C.: Brookings Institution.

Robinson, Michael Jay. 1981. "A Statesman Is a Dead Politician." In *What's News: The Media in American Society*, ed. Elie Abel, 159–86. San Francisco: Institute for Contemporary Studies.

Rocky Mountain News (Denver).

Roelofs, Joan. 1982. "Judicial Activism as Social Engineering: A Marxist Interpretation of the Warren Court." In *Supreme Court Activism and Restraint*, ed. Stephen C. Halpern and Charles M. Lamb, 249–66. Lexington, Mass.: Lexington Books.

Rohde, David W., and Harold J. Spaeth. 1976. *Supreme Court Decision-Making.* San Francisco: W. H. Freeman.

Roper Center Surveys at the University of Connecticut, Storrs. 1991. Compilation of 1991 Surveys. Prepared by Marc Maynard at the request of the authors.

Rose, Arnold M. 1986. "Power Is Pluralistic." In *Points of View: Readings in American Government and Politics*, 3d ed., ed. Robert E. DiClerico and Allan S. Hammock, 347–85. New York: Random House.

Rosenstone, Steven J., Roy L. Behr, and Edward H. Lazarus. 1984. *Third Parties in America: Citizen Response to Major Party Failure.* Princeton, N.J.: Princeton University Press.

Roshco, Bernard. 1975. *Newsmaking.* Chicago: University of Chicago Press.

Rossi, Alice S. 1982. *Feminists in Politics: A Panel Analysis of the First National Women's Conference.* New York: Academic Press.

Rossiter, Clinton. 1960. *The American Presidency.* 2d ed. New York: Harcourt, Brace and World.

———. 1966. *1787: The Grand Convention.* New York: Macmillan.

Rostow, Eugene V. 1952. "The Democratic Character of Judicial Review." *Harvard Law Review* 66 (December): 193–224.

Rothenberg, Randall. 1984. *The Neoliberals: Creating the New American Politics.* New York: Simon and Schuster.

Rothfeder, Jeffrey. 1992. *Privacy for Sale: How Computerization Has Made Everyone's Private Life an Open Secret.* New York: Simon and Schuster.

Rothman, Stanley, and S. R. Lichter. 1989. "Media and Business Elites: Two Classes in Conflict?" *Public Interest* 69 (Fall): 117–25.

Rubin, Barry. 1980. *Paved with Good Intentions: The American Experience and Iran.* New York: Oxford University Press.

———. 1984. "Reagan Administration Policymaking and Central America." In *Central America: Anatomy of Conflict.* ed. Robert S. Leiken, 299–318. New York: Pergamon Press.

———. 1987. *Secrets of State: The State Department and the Struggle over U.S. Foreign Policy.* New York: Oxford University Press.

Ruckelshaus, William D. 1989. "Toward a Sustainable World." *Scientific American* 261 (September): 166–74.

Rusher, William. 1988. *The Coming Battle for the Media: Curbing the Power of the Media Elite.* New York: William Morrow.

Russell, William A., Jr. 1989. "The Federal Communications Commission." In *Mandate for Leadership III: Policy Strategies for the 1990s,* ed. Charles L. Heatherly and Burton Yale Pines, 401–7. Washington, D.C.: Heritage Foundation.

Sabato, Larry J. 1984. *PAC Power: Inside the World of Political Action Committees.* New York: W. W. Norton.

———. 1988. *The Party's Just Begun: Shaping Political Parties for America's Future.* Boston: Scott, Foresman.

Sale, Kirkpatrick. 1973. *SDS.* New York: Random House.

Salisbury, Robert J., et al. 1986. "Soaking and Poking among the Movers and the Shakers: Quantitative Ethnography along the K Street Corridor." In *Congress and Pressure Groups: Lobbying in a Modern Democracy.* Report prepared for the Subcommittee on Intergovernmental Relations, 99th Congress, 2d sess. Committee Print, June.

San Francisco Chronicle.

Savage, David G. 1992. *Turning Right: The Making of the Rehnquist Supreme Court.* New York: John Wiley and Sons.

Savas, Emanuel S. 1982. *Privatizing the Public Sector: How to Shrink Government.* Chatham, N.J.: Chatham House.

Schaffer, Diane. 1988. "The Feminization of Pover-

ty Prospects for an International Feminist Agenda." In *Women, Power and Policy: Toward the Year 2000,* 2d ed., ed. Ellen Boneparth and Emily Stoper, 223–46. Elmsford, N.Y.: Pergamon Press.

Schattschneider, E. E. 1942. *Party Government.* New York: Holt, Rinehart and Winston.

Schlafly, Phyllis, ed. 1984. *Child Abuse in the Classroom.* Westchester, Ill.: Crossway Books.

Schlesinger, Arthur M. 1949. *Paths to the Present.* New York: Macmillan.

Schlesinger, Arthur M., Jr. 1946. *The Age of Jackson.* Boston: Little, Brown.

———. 1973. *The Imperial Presidency.* Boston: Houghton Mifflin.

———. 1985. "Leave the Constitution Alone." In *Reforming American Government,* ed. Donald L. Robinson, 50–54. Boulder, Colo.: Westview Press.

———. 1986. *The Cycles of American History.* Boston: Houghton Mifflin.

Schlesinger, Joseph. A. 1965. "Political Party Organization." In *Handbook of Organizations,* ed. James G. March, 764–801. Chicago: Rand McNally.

Schlesinger, Stephen, and Stephen Kinzer. 1983. *Bitter Fruit: The Untold Story of the American Coup in Guatemala.* Garden City, N.Y.: Doubleday.

Schlozman, Kay Lehman, and John T. Tierney. 1986. *Organized Interests and American Democracy.* New York: Harper and Row.

Schneider, Jerrold E. 1979. *Ideological Coalitions in Congress.* Westport, Conn.: Greenwood Press.

Schneider, Stephen A. 1989. "The Changing Climate." *Scientific American* 261 (September): 70–79.

Schneider, William. 1987. "Rambo and Reality; Having It Both Ways." In *Eagle Resurgent? The Reagan Era in American Foreign Policy,* ed. Kenneth Oye, Robert Lieber, and Donald Rothchild, 41–74. Boston: Little, Brown.

Schnorbus, Robert, and William Bergman. 1992. "1992 Outlook: A Question of Confidence." *Chicago Fed Letter,* no. 54, February.

———. 1993. "1993 Outlook: Recovery Amidst Restructuring." *Chicago Fed Letter,* no. 66, February.

Schoenfeld, A. Clay. 1979. "The Press and NEPA: The Case of the Missing Agenda." *Journalism Quarterly* 56 (Autumn): 577–85.

Schroeder, Pat. 1989. *Champion of the Great American Family.* New York: Random House.

Schwab, Larry M. 1991. *The Illusion of a Conservative Reagan Revolution.* New Brunswick, N.J.: Transaction.

Schwartz, Bernard, and Stephan Lesher. 1983. *Inside the Warren Court.* Garden City, N.Y.: Doubleday.

Schwartz, David N. 1983. *NATO's Nuclear Dilemmas.* Washington, D.C.: Brookings Institution.

———. 1984. *Ballistic Missile Defense.* Washington, D.C.: Brookings Institution.

Schwartz, Herman. 1988. *Packing the Courts: The Conservative Campaign to Rewrite the Constitution.* New York: Scribner.

Schwartz, Michael. 1984. *The Persistent Prejudice: Anti-Catholicism in America.* Huntington, Ind.: Our Sunday Visitor.

Schwarz, John E. 1983. *America's Hidden Success: A Reassessment of Twenty Years of Public Policy.* New York: W. W. Norton.

———. 1988. *America's Hidden Success: A Reassessment of Public Policy from Kennedy to Reagan.* New York: W. W. Norton.

Schwieterman, Joseph P. 1985. "Fare Is Fair in Airline Deregulation: The Decline of Price Discrimination." *Regulation* 9 (July/August): 32–38.

Scigliano, Robert. 1971. *The Supreme Court and the Presidency.* New York: Free Press.

Seidman, L. William. 1992. "Lecture #2." In *Focus on the '90's: Economics at Home, Turmoil Abroad,* ed. Mel G. Grinspan, 32–44. Memphis, Tenn.: Rhodes College.

"The Senior Executive Service (SES): Morale and Staffing Problems—A Brief Overview." 1987. James McGrath. *Congressional Research Service Report for Congress.* 19 August.

Sewell, John W., and Christine E. Contee. 1987. "Foreign Aid and Gramm-Rudman." *Foreign Affairs* 65 (Summer): 1015–36.

Shafritz, Jay M., Albert C. Hyde, and David H. Rosenbloom. 1981. *Personnel Management in Government: Politics and Process.* New York: Marcell Dekker.

Shanklin, John. 1962. *Multiple Use of Land and Water Areas.* Washington, D.C.: Outdoor Recreation Resources Review Commission.

Sharpe, Rochelle. 1992. "Capitol Hill's Worst Kept Secret: Sexual Harassment." *Ms.* 4 (January/February): 28–31.

Sherrill, Robert. 1976. *The Last Kennedy.* New York: Dial Press.

Simmons, Robert H., and Eugene P. Dvorin. 1977. *Public Administration: Values, Policy and Change.* Port Washington, N.Y.: Alfred.

Simonton, Dean Keith. 1987. *Why Presidents Succeed: A Political Psychology of Leadership.* New Haven, Conn.: Yale University Press.

Sinclair, Barbara. 1983. *Majority Leadership in the U.S. House.* Baltimore: Johns Hopkins University Press.

Skowronek, Stephen. 1988. "Presidential Leadership in Political Time." In *The Presidency and the Political System,* 2d ed., ed. Michael Nelson, 115–59. Washington, D.C.: Congressional Quarterly Press.

Smallwood, Frank. 1983. *The Other Candidates: Third Parties in Presidential Elections.* Hanover, N.H.: University Press of New England.

Smeal, Ellie. 1992. "Why I Support a New Party." In *American Government 92/93,* ed. Bruce Stinebrickner, 189–90. Gullford, Conn.: Dushkin.

Smith, Adam. 1948. *Adam Smith's Moral and Political Philosophy.* Vol. 5. Ed. Herbert W. Schneider. New York: Hafner.

———. 1981 [1776]. *An Inquiry into the Nature and Causes of the Wealth of Nations.* Vols. 1 and 2. Ed. R. H. Campbell and A. S. Skinner. Indianapolis: Liberty Classics.

Smith, Eric. 1989. *The Unchanging American Voter.* Berkeley and Los Angeles: University of California Press.

Smith, Gene. 1970. *The Shattered Dream: Herbert Hoover and the Great Depression.* New York: William Morrow.

Smith, Hedrick. 1988. *The Power Game: How Washington Works.* New York: Random House.

———, et al. 1980. *Reagan the Man, the President.* New York: Macmillan.

Smith, Steven S., and Christopher J. Deering. 1984. *Committees in Congress.* Washington, D.C.: Congressional Quarterly Press.

Smith, Wayne S. 1987. *The Closest of Enemies.* New York: W. W. Norton.

Smoller, Fredric T. 1990. *The Six O'Clock Presidency.* New York: Praeger.

Sobel, Richard. 1984. "Public Opinion about United States Intervention in El Salvador and Nicaragua." *Public Opinion Quarterly* 53 (Spring): 114–28.

Socialist Workers 1992 Campaign. 1992. Campaign brochure. New York: Socialist Workers 1992 National Campaign Committee.

Sorauf, Frank J. 1984a. *Party Politics in America.* 5th ed. Boston: Little, Brown.

———. 1984b. *What Price PACs?* New York: Twentieth Century Fund.

———. 1988. *Money in American Elections*. Glenview, Ill.: Scott, Foresman.

Sowell, Thomas. 1984. *Civil Rights: Rhetoric or Reality?* New York: William Morrow.

Spiegel, Steven. 1985. *The Other Arab-Israeli Conflict*. Chicago: University of Chicago Press.

State Government News.

Statistical Abstract of the United States. Annual. Washington, D.C.: Government Printing Office.

Stein, Herbert. 1969. *The Fiscal Revolution in America*. Chicago: University of Chicago Press.

Steiner, Gilbert Y. 1985. *Constitutional Inequality: The Political Fortunes of the Equal Rights Amendment*. Washington, D.C.: Brookings Institution.

Steingraber, Fred. 1987. "Competitiveness: Low Key Solutions to a High Profile Problem." *Vital Speeches of the Day*, 1 October, 758–62.

Stetson, Dorothy McBride. 1991. *Women's Rights in the U.S.A.: Policy Debates and Gender Roles*. Pacific Grove, Calif.: Brooks/Cole.

Stevens, Robert Warren. 1976. *Vain Hopes, Grim Realities: The Economic Consequences of the Vietnam War*. New York: New Viewpoints.

Stewart, David O. 1993. "Holding the Center." *ABA Journal* 79 (March): 48.

Stillman, Richard J., II. 1984. *Public Administration: Concepts and Cases*. 3d ed. Boston: Houghton Mifflin.

Stockman, David. 1986. *The Triumph of Politics: How the Reagan Revolution Failed*. New York; Harper and Row.

———. 1992. "Hands Off the Economy." *New York Times*, 27 January, A21.

Stone, Clarence N., and Heywood T. Sanders, eds. 1987. *The Politics of Urban Development*. Lawrence: University Press of Kansas.

Stone, Irving. 1956. *Men to Match My Mountains: The Opening of the Far West, 1840–1900*. New York: Doubleday.

Strategic Survey. Annual. Ed. Sidney Bearman. London: International Institute for Strategic Studies.

Stuadt, Kathleen, and Jane Jaquette. 1988. "Women's Programs, Bureaucratic Resistance and Feminist Organizations." In *Women, Power and Policy: Toward the Year 2000*, 2d ed., ed. Ellen Boneparth and Emily Stoper, 263–81. Elmsford, N.Y.: Pergamon Press.

Stubbing, Richard A., and Richard A. Mendel. 1986. *The Defense Game*. New York: Harper and Row.

Sussman, Barry. 1988. *What Americans Really Think: And Why Our Politicians Pay No Attention*. New York: Pantheon Books.

Sylvia, Ronald D. 1989. *Critical Issues in Public Personnel Policy*. Pacific Grove, Calif.: Brooks/Cole.

Szatmary, David P. 1980. *Shays' Rebellion: The Making of an Agrarian Insurrection*. Amherst: University of Massachusetts Press.

Taking the Stand: The Testimony of Lieutenant Colonel Oliver L. North. 1987. New York: Pocket Books.

Taylor, Samuel Jared. 1992. *Paved with Good Intentions: The Future of Race Relations in Contemporary America*. New York: Carroll and Graf.

Tedford, W. W. 1967. "Causes Which Led to the Movement." In "An Agrarian Development." In *History of the Wheel and Alliance, 1889*, W. Scott Morgan. In *The Populist Mind*, ed. Norman Pollack, 258–70. Indianapolis: Bobbs-Merrill.

Thernstrom, Abigail. 1987. *Whose Votes Count? Affirmative Action and Minority Voting Rights*. Cambridge, Mass.: Harvard University Press.

Thimmesch, Nick. 1985. *A Liberal Media Elite*. Washington, D.C.: American Enterprise Institute for Public Policy Research.

Thomas, William R. 1976. *The Burger Court and Civil Liberties*. Brunswick, Ohio: King's Court.

Thompson, Frank, Norma M. Riccucci, and Carolyn Ban. 1991. "Drug Testing in the Federal Workplace: An Instrumental and Symbolic Assessment." *Public Administration Review* 51 (November/December): 515–25.

Thornton, James. 1993. "Some Things Never Change." *New American* 26 (July): 33–34.

Thurow, Lester C. 1985. *The Zero-Sum Solution*. New York: Simon and Schuster.

Time.

Tivnan, Edward. 1987. *The Lobby: Jewish Political Power and American Foreign Policy*. New York: Simon and Schuster.

Tolchin, Susan, and Martin Tolchin. 1983. *Dismantling America: The Rush to Deregulate*. New York: Oxford University Press.

Traub, James. 1991. "Oklahoma City: Separate and Equal." *Atlantic*, September, 24–37.

Tribe, Laurence H. 1985. *God Save the Honorable Court: How the Choice of Supreme Court Justices Shapes Our History*. New York: New American Library.

————. 1988. *American Constitutional Law*. Mineola, N.Y.: Foundation Press.

Tufte, Edward. 1978. *Political Control of the Economy*. Princeton, N.J.: Princeton University Press.

Tulis, Jeffrey K. 1988. "The Two Constitutional Presidencies." In *The Presidency and the Political System*, 2d ed., ed. Michael Nelson, 85–113. Washington, D.C.: Congressional Quarterly Press.

Tullock, Gordon. 1983. *Economics of Income Redistribution*. Boston: Kluwer-Nijhoff.

————. 1986. *The Economics of Wealth and Poverty*. New York: New York University Press.

Tyson, James. 1981. *Target America: The Influence of Communist Propaganda on U.S. Media*. Chicago: Regnery Gateway.

Understanding the Riots. 1992. Los Angeles: Times Mirror.

United Nations Association of the United States of America. 1987. *Issues before the 41st General Assembly of the United Nations*. Lexington, Mass.: Lexington Books.

United Nations Charter. 1986. *Basic Facts about the United Nations*. New York: United Nations Publications.

The United States Government Manual. Annual. U.S. General Services Administration, Office of the Federal Register. Washington, D.C.: Government Printing Office.

U.S. Advisory Commission on Intergovernmental Relations. 1985. "Fiscal Interdependence among American Government." In *American Intergovernmental Relations: Foundations, Perspectives, and Issues*, ed. Laurence J. O'Toole, Jr., 85–87. Washington, D.C.: Congressional Quarterly Press.

U.S. Bureau of the Census. *See Statistical Abstract.*

U.S. Commission on Civil Rights. 1979. *Toward an Understanding of Bakke*. Washington, D.C.: U.S. Commission on Civil Rights.

U.S. Department of Defense. 1971. *United States–Vietnam Relations, 1945–67*. Washington, D.C.: Government Printing Office for the House Committee on Armed Services.

U.S. News and World Report.

U.S. Office of Management and Budget. *See under Budget.*

USA Today.

USA Today Magazine.

Vail Daily.

Vetterli, Richard. 1982. *Orrin Hatch: Challenging the Washington Establishment*. Chicago: Regnery Gateway.

Vetzner, Steve. 1993. Press secretary for Lane Evans, Washington, D.C. Interview by Jack E. Holmes, 8 June.

Vigilante, Richard. 1984. "Beyond the Burger Court." *Policy Review*, no. 28 (Spring): 20–26.

Viguerie, Richard. 1981. *The New Right: We're Ready to Lead*. Falls Church, Va.: Viguerie.

Vital Statistics on American Politics. Biannual. Ed. Harold W. Stanley and Richard G. Niemi. Washington, D.C.: Congressional Quarterly Press.

Vital Statistics on Congress. Biannual. Ed. Norman Ornstein, Thomas E. Mann, and Michael J. Malbin. Washington, D.C.: Congressional Quarterly Press.

Vogler, David J. 1980. *The Politics of Congress*. 3d ed. Boston: Allyn and Bacon.

————. 1988. *The Politics of Congress*. 5th ed. Boston: Allyn and Bacon.

von Hayek, Friedrich August. 1944. *The Road to Serfdom*. Chicago: University of Chicago Press.

————, ed. 1954. *Capitalism and the Historians*. Chicago: University of Chicago Press.

von Holst, Hermann E. 1980. *John C. Calhoun*. New York: Chelsea House.

von Mises, Ludwig. 1977. *A Critique of Interventionism*. Trans. Hans F. Sennholz. New Rochelle, N.Y.: Arlington House.

Wald, Kenneth D. 1987. *Religion and Politics in the United States*. New York: St. Martin's Press.

Walker, Samuel. 1985. *Sense and Nonsense about Crime: A Policy Guide*. Monterey, Calif.: Brooks/Cole.

Wall Street Journal.

Washington Information Directory. Annual. Washington, D.C.: Congressional Quarterly.

The Washington Lobby. 1987. 5th ed. Washington, D.C.: Congressional Quarterly Press.

Washington Post.

Washington Post National Weekly Edition.

Washington Representatives: Who Does What for Whom in the Nation's Capital. Annual. Washington, D.C.: Columbia Books.

Washington Times.

Watergate: Chronology of a Crisis. 1975. Washington, D.C.: Congressional Quarterly Press.

Watson, Bruce W., et al. 1991. *Military Lessons of the Gulf War.* Novato, Calif.: Presidio Press.

Watson, Thomas E. 1967a [14 April 1893]. "Imperial Tendencies." In *The Populist Mind,* ed. Norman Pollack, 23–26. Indianapolis: Bobbs-Merrill.

———. 1967b [October 1892]. "The Negro Question in the South." In *The Populist Mind,* ed. Norman Pollack, 360–74. Indianapolis: Bobbs-Merrill.

Way, H. Frank, Jr. 1968. "Survey Research on Judicial Decisions: The Prayer and Bible Reading Cases." *Western Political Quarterly* 2 (June): 189–205.

Wayne, Stephen J. 1978. *The Legislative Presidency.* New York: Harper and Row.

———. 1988. *The Road to the White House: The Politics of Presidential Elections.* 3d ed. New York: St. Martin's Press.

———. 1992. *The Road to the White House: The Politics of Presidential Elections.* 4th ed. New York: St. Martin's Press.

Webb, LeVarr. 1980. "The Sagebrush Rebellion: Coming on Strong." *State Legislatures,* April, 18–21, 32.

Weems, John Edward. 1988. *To Conquer a Peace: The War between the United States and Mexico.* College Station, Tex.: Texas A and M University Press.

Weidenbaum, Murray L. 1987. "The Pedagogy of Competition." *Society* 25 (November/December): 46–54.

Weinberger, Caspar. 1990. *Fighting for Peace: Seven Critical Years in the Pentagon.* New York: Warner Books.

Weinstein, Bernard L., and Richard W. Wigley. 1987. *Regional Biases in Federal Funding.* Washington, D.C.: Sunbelt Institute.

Weissberg, Robert. 1985. *Understanding American Government.* Champaign, Ill.: PDQ Printing.

Wellman, Judith. 1991. "The Seneca Falls Women's Rights Convention: A Study of Special Networks." *Journal of Women's History* 3 (Spring): 9–37.

Wells, Robert V. 1982. *Revolutions in Americans' Lives: A Demographic Perspective on the History of Americans, Their Families and Their Society.* Westport, Conn.: Greenwood Press.

Whalen, Charles, and Barbara Whalen. 1985. *The Longest Debate: A Legislative History of the 1964 Civil Rights Act.* Washington, D.C.: Seven Locks Press.

Where the Money Goes. 1991. Congressional Quarterly Special Report, 7 December. Washington, D.C.: Congressional Quarterly Press.

Where to Live and Look for Jobs. 1992. U.S. Bureau of Labor Statistics. Washington, D.C.: Department of Labor.

Whitaker, Robert H. 1982. *The New Right Papers.* New York: St. Martin's Press.

White, Leonard Dupree. 1948. *The Federalists.* New York: Macmillan.

———. 1954. *The Jacksonians, 1829–1861.* New York: Macmillan.

———. 1955. *Introduction to the Study of Public Administration.* 4th ed. New York: Macmillan.

———. 1956. *The Jeffersonians, 1801–1829.* New York: Macmillan.

———. 1958. *The Republican Era, 1869–1901.* New York: Macmillan.

White, Theodore H. 1975. *Breach of Faith: The Fall of Richard Nixon.* New York: Atheneum.

Who's Who of Women in World Politics. 1991. Ed. William C. Dowling. New York: Bowker-Saur.

Wiarda, Howard. 1990. *Foreign Policy without Illusion.* Glenview, Ill.: Scott, Foresman/Little, Brown.

Wicker, Tom. 1968. *JFK and LBJ: The Influence of Personality upon Politics.* New York: William Morrow.

Wiecek, William M. 1987. "The Witch at the Christening: Slavery and the Constitution's Origins." In *The Framing and Ratification of the Constitution,* ed. Leonard W. Levy and Dennis J. Mahoney, 167–84. New York: Macmillan.

Williams, Juan. 1987. *Eyes on the Prize: America's Civil Rights Years, 1954–1965.* New York: Viking Press.

Williams, T. Harry. 1969. *Huey Long.* New York: Alfred A. Knopf.

———. 1981. *Huey Long.* Reprint. New York: Vintage Books.

Wills, Garry. 1987. *Reagan's America: Innocents at Home.* Garden City, N.Y.: Doubleday.

Wilson, Graham K. 1981. *Interest Groups in the United States.* Oxford, England: Clarendon Press.

Wilson, Roger. 1992. "Committed to Equality." *State Government News* 35 (April): 14–15.

Wilson, Woodrow. 1885. *Congressional Government.* Boston: Houghton Mifflin.

Wofford, Harris. 1992. "The Democratic Challenge." *Foreign Policy,* no. 86 (Spring): 99–113.

Wolff, Robert Paul, Barrington Moore, Jr., and Herbert Marcuse. 1965. *A Critique of Pure Tolerance.* Boston: Beacon Press.

Wolfinger, Raymond E., and Steven J. Rosenstone.

1980. *Who Votes?* New Haven, Conn.: Yale University Press.

Woll, Peter. 1977. *American Bureaucracy.* New York: W. W. Norton.

Wolters, Raymond. 1984. *The Burden of Brown: Thirty Years of School Desegregation.* Knoxville: University of Tennessee Press.

Wood, Gordon S. 1969. *The Creation of the American Republic, 1776–1787.* Chapel Hill: University of North Carolina Press for the Institute of Early American History and Culture.

Woodward, Bob, and Scott Armstrong. 1979. *The Brethren: Inside the Supreme Court.* New York: Simon and Schuster.

Woodward, C. Vann. 1938. *Tom Watson: Agrarian Rebel.* New York: Macmillan.

The World Almanac and Book of Facts. Annual. New York: Scripps Howard Company.

World Development Report, 1991: The Challenge of Development. 1991. New York: Oxford University Press for the World Bank.

World Resources 1992–1993. 1992. A report by the World Resources Institute in collaboration with the United Nations Environment Programme and the United Nations Development Programme. Oxford, England: Oxford University Press.

The World's Women 1970–1990: Trends and Statistics. 1991. New York: United Nations.

Wormuth, Francis D., and Edwin B. Firmage. 1986. *To Chain the Dog of War.* Dallas: Southern Methodist University Press.

Wright, Deil S. 1985. "Models of National/State/Local Relations." In *American Intergovernmental Relations: Foundations, Perspectives, and Issues,* ed. Laurence J. O'Toole, Jr., 58–66. Washington, D.C.: Congressional Quarterly Press.

Yarbrough, Tinsley E. 1988. *Mr. Justice Black and His Critics.* Durham: Duke University Press.

Yearbook of American and Canadian Churches. Annual. Nashville, Tenn.: Abingdon Press.

Yeltsin, Boris. 1990. *Against the Grain: An Autobiography.* Trans. Michael Glenny. New York: Summit Books.

Youngdale, James M. 1975. *Populism: A Psycho-Historical Perspective.* Port Washington, N.Y.: Kennikat Press.

Zipp, John F. 1985. "Perceived Representativeness and Voting: An Assessment of the Impact of 'Choices' vs. 'Echoes.'" *American Political Science Review* 79 (March): 50–61.

Zuckert, Michael P. 1987. "A System without Precedent: Federalism in the American Constitution." In *The Framing and Ratification of the Constitution,* ed. Leonard W. Levy and Dennis J. Mahoney, 132–50. New York: Macmillan.

Zwier, Robert. 1982. *Born-Again Politics.* Downers Grove, Ill.: InterVarsity Press.

INDEX